# Introduction to International Political Economy

## Fifth Edition

## David N. Balaam
*University of Puget Sound*

## Bradford Dillman
*University of Puget Sound*

**Longman**

Boston   Columbus   Indianapolis   New York   San Francisco   Upper Saddle River
Amsterdam   Cape Town   Dubai   London   Madrid   Milan   Munich   Paris   Montreal   Toronto
Delhi   Mexico City   São Paulo   Sydney   Hong Kong   Seoul   Singapore   Taipei   Tokyo

Senior Acquisitions Editor: Vikram Mukhija
Editorial Assistant: Toni Magyar
Senior Marketing Manager: Lindsey Prudhomme
Project Coordination, Text Design, and Electronic Page Makeup: Hemalatha/
  Integra Software Services, Ltd.
Production Manager: Fran Russello
Art Director: Nancy Danahy
Manager, Visual Research: Beth Brenzel
Photo Researcher: Rona Tucillo
Manager, Rights and Permissions: Zina Arabia
Printer and Binder: Courier Companies, Inc.

If you purchased this book within United States or Canada you should be aware that it has been imported without the approval of the publisher or the Author.

2 3 4 5 6 7 8 9 10—CRS—13 12 11

**Longman**
is an imprint of

ISBN-13: 978-0-205-00864-3
ISBN-10:     0-205-00864-X

# BRIEF CONTENTS

# CONTENTS

## CHAPTER 10
### The Knowledge and Technology Structure   235

## PART III    States and Markets in the Global Economy

## CHAPTER 11
### The Development Conundrum: Choices Amidst Constraints   265

## CHAPTER 12
### Regionalism: Toward a More Perfect (European) Union   295

## CHAPTER 13

### Moving into Position: The Rising Powers   323

## CHAPTER 14

### The Middle East: The Quest for Development and Democracy   351

# PART IV   Transnational Problems and Dilemmas

## CHAPTER 18
## Food and Hunger: Market Failure and Injustice   463

## CHAPTER 19
## Oil and Energy: Dependency and Resource Curses   489

# PREFACE

Even before we started working on this edition of the text, most of us felt as if a dark cloud had come over the world. Reading the international section of any major newspaper—a growing number of which have since gone bankrupt—it seemed as though the world was on the brink of a global catastrophe of one sort or another. What began as a combined banking and financial crisis in the United States in the fall of 2007 quickly spread into most industrialized and developing nations alike. As of December 2009, despite some claims that economic recovery was under-way, the crisis continued to inflict severe social and even psychological damage on people the world over. Some experts and pundits expect yet another deep global recession—if not a second Great Depression. The November 2009 Copenhagen meeting on climate change produced another tepid agreement that signaled that generating economic growth, and with it carbon dioxide, was as yet a higher prior-ity than addressing major environmental dilemmas, which some conclude may result in another global tragedy—one that may not be reversible.

Many people hoped that the election of Barack Obama as the first African-American president of the United States would bring about an improvement in economic conditions everywhere; thus far, little has seemed to change for the better. The IMF reports that many countries are suffering unemployment rates as high as they have ever been in the last forty years. Several G-8 and G-20 meetings to deal with the battered global economy have produced no consensus as to the nature of the problem or concrete strategies to deal with it. For many, global governance seems to have broken down at the same time that the dominant economic liberal ideology and policies associated with globalization have come under serious intellectual and political challenges. So far nothing has emerged to replace this popular ideology.

The war in Iraq continues, while the U.S.-led campaign against terrorism in Afghanistan has escalated and spread into Pakistan. Ethnic and religious conflicts persist in parts of the Middle East, South and Southeast Asia, and parts of Africa including Somalia, Sudan (especially Darfur), Congo, Kenya, and Ethiopia. Other growing sources of tension include control over weapons of mass destruction and strategic energy resources, poverty and the lack of economic development, grow-ing numbers of political and economic refugees and immigrants, and increasing illicit economic activities.

In the summer of 2008, international oil price hikes contributed to a variety of major problems including yet another world food crisis that saw agricultural commodity and food prices skyrocket. While the U.S. real estate bubble was begin-ning to deflate, the number of seriously hungry and starving people in the world increased by at least 125 million, generating fears of another Malthusian nightmare of overpopulation, war, and global epidemics. For many, the Copenhagen talks in 2009 have generated hope for recovery of the earth's ecology and environment while generating new technologies and policies that support a "green" economic recovery.

How are we to understand this current historical juncture that appears to be on the verge of an abyss and that lacks a clear political, economic, and social order? Can states, international organizations, nongovernmental organizations, and global social movements effectively deal with the effects of hypermobile capital, balance the need to generate economic growth while not overtaxing the environment, and satisfy political and social demands peacefully? These are a few of the many questions we raise in this fifth edition of the text.

However, as has always been our major goal, we seek to provide both students and faculty with the tools necessary to delve deeper into many issues, develop their reflective thinking skills, and understand many of the theoretical and policy dynamics of the global political economy. Rather than profess one set of ideas or explanations, we offer a variety of different perspectives and views so that our readers will be able to form their own opinions about controversial issues. In this edition, however, each chapter concludes with a more critical edge to it than in past editions, which lays the foundation for students to assess and evaluate these issues for themselves.

## NEW TO THIS EDITION

The fifth edition of the text is a major revision of more than 60 percent of the last edition. Most of the chapters contain extensive coverage of the connection of the global financial crisis to IPE theories, structures, and policy issues. Three completely new chapters have been written. Finally, Bradford Dillman is the new co-editor and co-author of the text. Professor Dillman specializes in illicit economies and the Middle East and North Africa (MENA), topics he wrote about in the last edition.

Here's what to look for by way of revision in the text:

- Chapter 1, "What is International Political Economy?" is a revised introductory chapter that shows students how IPE can help them understand the financial crisis. It updates and clarifies many of the concepts and ideas of IPE. Students are also introduced to the concept of globalization, which is now discussed throughout the book. The conclusion of the text in the fourth edition has been revised and appears in the conclusion of Chapter 1 in this edition. Instructors can assign it at any time during the term.
- Chapter 2 revises and extends coverage of economic liberalism to include how and why the current financial crisis has contributed to still more criticism of what has been the most popular IPE perspective since the early 1980s.
- Chapter 4, "Economic Determinism and Exploitation: The Structuralist Perspective," reframes and revises the presentation of Marxist and structuralist ideas and applies them to the global financial crisis.
- Chapter 5, "Alternative Perspectives on International Political Economy" significantly expands and updates the coverage of constructivist and feminist perspectives.
- Chapter 7, "The International Monetary and Finance Structure," includes a substantial revision and update of the changing economic structure, globalization, and the weakening U.S. dollar.
- Chapter 8, "International Debt and Financial Crises," includes detailed coverage of the Asian and current global financial crises.

- Chapter 10 offers significantly revised content and new perspectives on "The Knowledge and Technology Structure."
- Chapter 11, "The Development Conundrum: Choices Amidst Constraints" now includes an outline and discussion of development strategies that correspond to the three IPE perspectives.
- Chapter 13, "Moving into Position: The Rising Powers," is a new chapter on the rising powers of India, China, and the post-communist countries.
- Chapter 18, "Food and Hunger: Market Failure and Injustice," is also a completely revised chapter on food and hunger and the 2008 world food crisis.
- Chapter19, "Oil and Energy: Dependency and Resource Curses," has returned to the text based on reviewer request and focuses on oil in relation to resource scarcity and conflict.
- Chapter 20, "The Environment: Steering Away from Global Disaster," examines the controversy surrounding the issues of global warming and climate change, including the recent talks in Copenhagen.

## FEATURES

While covering many of the "nuts and bolts" of IPE theories and issues, many of the chapters provide students with a historical context in which to understand the subject. More importantly, in contrast to other introductory texts, we challenge students to think critically when it comes to applying these theories to different issues and policy problems. Toward this goal, all chapters highlight more explicit connections between different IPE perspectives and policy issues.

As in previous editions, the book begins with five chapters designed to set out some basic tools for studying IPE. Chapter 1 introduces the fundamental elements of the subject and some recent developments in what has become a very popular field of study. We begin with relatively simple tools and concepts that deal with the nature of IPE—its subject boundaries, the three dominant IPE theories, four global structures, and the levels of analysis. In this edition, Chapter 1 includes a new section that discusses the major themes or "pillars" that connect the theories and subjects covered throughout the book. Thereafter, each chapter conclusion connects its material back to these central ideas. The conclusion of the text in the fourth edition has been revised and appears in the conclusion of Chapter 1 in this edition. Instructors can assign it at any time during the term.

Chapters 2, 3, and 4 explore the three dominant analytical approaches to studying IPE that reflect powerful forces in history and that remain influential today: mercantilism, economic liberalism, and structuralism. Chapter 5 introduces two important alternative perspectives (constructivism and feminism) to help students understand different IPE questions and events. Note that the rational choice material of the last edition is available to instructors and students online at the IPE textbook website at www.upugetsoundintroipe.com.

Part II of the text examines the web of relationships or structures that tie together a variety of international actors including nations and their citizens with international organizations, nongovernmental organizations, and other groups. Chapter 6 focuses on the production and international trade structure. Chapter 7 provides an outline of the international monetary and finance structure and problems, which in Chapter 8 are applied to Third World debt and the current global financial crisis. Chapter 9 focuses on a number of recent developments in the international security structure including shifts from national to individual security concerns and the possibility of a transition from a unipolar to a multipolar balance of power. Chapter 10 examines struggles among international actors over knowledge and technology, with particular attention to intellectual property rights.

In Part III, Chapter 11 examines the problem of development and some of the different strategies that many of the less developed countries have used to "grow" their economies and modernize their political institutions. It also serves as theoretical background for Chapter 12 dealing with the European Union where the experiment in regional integration has resulted in many tensions and transformations of markets, states, and societies. Chapter 13 is a new chapter that focuses on an array of issues associated with some of the postsocialist economies in general but India and China in particular as they try to transform and incorporate a bigger role for markets in their national political economies. Chapter 14 covers the Middle East and North Africa, regions fraught with what seem like insurmountable development and security problems.

Finally, in Part IV, as part of an effort to understand a number of important global problems and issues, Chapter 15 covers illicit activities involving trafficking of people, drugs, and other items. Chapter 16 examines the increasingly dynamic and problematic issue of the movement of people in the international political economy—in this case through tourism and migration. Chapter 17 examines the important role of transnational corporations in the international political economy. Chapters 18, 19, and 20 discuss the interconnections between global food, energy, and environmental problems, again employing many of the same analytical tools developed earlier in the book.

All the chapters end with a list of key terms that are in bold print in the chapter, discussion questions, and suggested readings. The recommended websites have also been transferred to the text website at **www.upugetsoundintroipe.com**, where they can be updated more often. The website will also include a list of recommended videos and documentaries faculty and students can use to gain more detailed background and ideas about different topics.

## SUPPLEMENTS

Longman is pleased to offer several resources to qualified adopters of *Introduction to International Political Economy* and their students that will make teaching and learning from this book even more effective and enjoyable.

### For Instructors

**MyPoliSciKit Video Case Studies.** Featuring video from major news sources and providing reporting and insight on recent world affairs, this DVD series helps instructors integrate current events into their courses by letting them use the clips as lecture launchers or discussion starters.

**Instructor's Manual/Test Bank.** This resource includes learning objectives, lecture outlines, multiple-choice questions, and essay questions for each chapter. Available exclusively at the Instructor Resource Center (IRC), an online hub that allows instructors to quickly download book-specific supplements. Please visit the IRC welcome page at **www.pearsonhighered.com/irc** to register for access.

## For Students

**MySearchLab** Need help with a paper? MySearchLab saves time and improves results by offering start-to-finish guidance on the research/writing process and full-text access to academic journals and periodicals. To learn more, please visit www.mysearchlab.com or contact your Pearson representative. To order MySearchLab with this book, use ISBN 0205798616.

*Longman Atlas of World Issues* (0-321-22465-5). Introduced and selected by Robert J. Art of Brandeis University and excerpted from the acclaimed Penguin Atlas Series, the Longman Atlas of World Issues is designed to help students understand the geography and major issues facing the world today, such as terrorism, debt, and HIV/AIDS. These thematic, full-color maps examine forces shaping politics today at a global level. Explanatory information accompanies each map to help students better grasp the concepts being shown and how they affect our world today. Available at no additional charge when packaged with this book.

*Goode's World Atlas* (0-321-65200-2) First published by Rand McNally in 1923, Goode's World Atlas has set the standard for college reference atlases. It features hundreds of physical, political, and thematic maps as well as graphs, tables, and a pronouncing index. Available at a discount when packaged with this book.

# ACKNOWLEDGMENTS

This textbook is truly a cooperative effort. We would like to thank all of the people at Pearson Education who have been so helpful to us, including our editor Vikram Mukhija and editorial assistant Toni Magyar for their suggestions, and most of all for their patience throughout this process. We would like to thank University of Puget Sound Deans Kris Bartanen and Sarah Moore for funding student research assistance. We would also like to thank and recognize Professors Pierre Ly, Cynthia Howson, and Kristine Kalanges for providing valuable comments and suggestions in this edition of the text. Nazir Olangian, Elizabeth Butt, Kirsten Schlewitz, Georgina Allen, Rahul Madhavan, Ryan Cunningham, Jess Martin, Drew Cameron, and Dave Peters did research and/or provided editorial assistance on various chapters of the text. A number of people in our local communities supported us every day by way of amenities and encouragement: Jill Killen, Elthea Karr, and the gang at Cloud City Coffee in Seattle; Tom Stevens for use of the Rum Shack where Dave and Beau could work in peace; and Paul Rudnick, Ed Jones, Oscar Velasco-Schmitz, Bill Hochberg, John Domer, *sensei* Joe Blenis, Josh Woodfin, and Roberta Melcore, who engaged us in provocative discussions and introspection along the way. And we could not have written this book without the many ideas, critiques, and feedback of our IPE students at the University of Puget Sound.

Finally, Dave would like to thank his sons David Erin and Brendan for their comments and support, and his wife, Kristi Hendrickson, for her editorial assistance, patience, and loving support throughout the project. Brad would like to thank Joanne, Harry, and Noelle for their incredible patience, encouragement, and love.

Our thanks, also, to the reviewers: Olufemi Babarinde, Thunderbird School of Global Management; Jill Crystal, Auburn University; Anthony Gadzey, Auburn University; Julie George, Queens College City University of New York; John Liscano, Napa Valley Community College; Joel Ostrow, Benedictine University; Raju Parakkal, Florida International University; Mark Rupert, Syracuse University; Houman Sadri, University of Central Florida; Mitchell P. Smith, University of Oklahoma; and Stephen Twing, Frostburg State University.

We dedicate this edition of the text to all those people everywhere who have suffered and lost so much because of the global financial crisis. We also dedicate it to Professor Michael J. Carey, formerly of Loyola-Marymount University in Los Angeles, who left this world in the summer of 2009. Dedicated teacher, true friend, author, poet, critic, measured cynic, and ally (he'd like that word) of the University of Puget Sound IPE program, Mike read and critiqued many of the chapters in all editions of this text. More importantly, he stood for the values and ideals we hope this book will contribute to in the development of the lives of students who read it.

DAVID N. BALAAM
AND BRADFORD L. DILLMAN
SEATTLE AND TACOMA, WASHINGTON

# ABOUT THE AUTHORS

Back Row *from left to right:* Monica DeHart, Nick Kontogeorgopoulos, Sunil Kukreja, Dave Balaam
Front Row *from left to right:* Leon Grunberg, Brad Dillman, Ross Singleton, Richard Anderson-Connolly.
Not Pictured: Hendrik Hansen

**Richard Anderson-Connolly** is Professor of Comparative Sociology at the University of Puget Sound and teaches courses in methodology.

**Dave Balaam** is Professor Emeritus of International Political Economy at the University of Puget Sound and teaches courses in international political economy, food and hunger, international organizations, and U.S. foreign policy. His publications include articles on agricultural trade policy and various food and hunger issues.

**Monica DeHart** is Associate Professor of Anthropology at the University of Puget Sound and teaches courses on the cultural politics of global development and transnational migration in and from Latin America. She is the author of *Ethnic Entrepreneurs: Identity and Development Politics in Latin America* (Stanford University Press, 2010).

**Bradford Dillman** is Associate Professor of International Political Economy at the University of Puget Sound and teaches courses in IPE, the Middle East, the illicit global economy, and intellectual property rights. He authored *State and Private Sector in Algeria* (Westview Press, 2000) and numerous articles and book chapters on the Middle East and North Africa.

**Leon Grunberg** is Professor of Comparative Sociology at the University of Puget Sound and teaches courses in social stratification and sociology through literature. His research interests focus on globalization, the changing world of work and organizations, and patterns of cross-national stratification.

**Hendrik Hansen** is Lecturer in Politics and Government at the University of Passau, Germany, where he teaches courses in international political economy and the history of political ideas. His publications include articles and books on the IPE perspectives, the roots of communism and radical Islamism, and the totalitarian character of the GDR regime.

**Nick Kontogeorgopoulos** is Professor of International Political Economy at the University of Puget Sound and teaches courses in international political economy, development, and tourism. His publications focus on ecotourism and wildlife tourism in Southeast Asia.

**Sunil Kukreja** is Professor of Comparative Sociology at the University of Puget Sound, with teaching and research interests in the sociology of development, the political economy of Southeast Asia, and race relations. He is editor-in-chief of the *International Review of Modern Sociology*.

**Ross Singleton** is Professor of Economics at the University of Puget Sound and teaches courses in microeconomics and regulatory and managerial economics. His research interests are in comparative antitrust law and regulatory economics.

# Introduction to International Political Economy

# Perspectives on International Political Economy

The first chapter of the text deals with the fundamental nature of international political economy (IPE) and some analytical issues related to its multidimensional character. Chapters 2 through 4 are the core chapters of the text that explore the history and policies associated with the three dominant IPE perspectives, namely economic liberalism, mercantilism, and structuralism. These theoretical tools are useful in understanding many of the political, economic, and social issues in the global economy of the past as well as the present. Chapter 5 develops two alternative IPE perspectives—constructivism and feminism—that derive, in part, from the three main outlooks under study.

# What is International Political Economy?

What it all comes down to.

Chris Jordan

*When a philosopher has once laid hold of a favorite principle, which perhaps accounts for many natural effects, he extends the same principle over the whole creation, and reduces to it every phenomenon, through by the most violent and absurd reasoning. Our own mind being narrow and contracted, we cannot extend our conception to the variety and extent of nature . . .*

David Hume, "The Sceptic"

# THE DARKNESS ON THE EDGE OF TOWN

What are the chances you will find a good paying job —or any job for that matter—when you graduate from college in the next few years? Have your folks lost their jobs, the family home, or a big chunk of their retirement savings? How are you adjusting to the current financial crisis that started in 2007? Forced to cut spending on clothes, vacation, or dinners out with your friends? Or, maybe things haven't been that bad for you, yet! Whatever your situation, are you confused when you hear the words *hedge fund*, *debt swap*, *CDO*, *subprime mortgage*, *AIG*, *Bear Stearns*, *Goldman Sachs*, *Wall Street vs. Main Street*, *the TARP*, *the G-20*, and *the IMF*? When the names *Milton Friedman*, *John Maynard Keynes*, *Timothy Geitner*, *Larry Summers*, or even *Bernie Madoff* are mentioned, do you know the role of these individuals in the financial crisis?

As we write in the fall of 2009, the world is in the grip of a severe global financial crisis brought on when some of the world's biggest banks and financial institutions went bankrupt. Reading the headlines of any major newspaper—a growing number of which have closed their doors—has left many wondering if the world is on the brink of some sort of global economic catastrophe, if not a second Great Depression. The U.S. banking and financial crisis that began in September of 2007 has spread throughout most developed and developing nations. The effects of the global financial crisis have made many people feel tense, fearful, and depressed.

The financial crisis is alleged to have contributed to

- massive numbers of mortgage defaults and the failure of many major banks and financial institutions all over the world (see Chapter 8).
- high unemployment rates in most countries.
- growing demand for trade protectionist measures in states (see Chapter 6).
- undermining of development gains in poor countries, many of whom are questioning the economic liberal development strategies promoted by the industrialized nations (see Chapter 11).
- intensification of ethnic, religious, and class conflicts in many parts of the Middle East, South and Southeast Asia, and Africa (see Chapter 9).
- conflicts between many states over issues like food and hunger, energy, and environmental protection (see Chapters 18–20).
- severe weakening of the humanitarian efforts of many international organizations (IOs) and nongovernmental organizations (NGOs) (see Chapters 9, 11, 19, and 20).
- acceleration of migration within states and immigration between states (see Chapter 16).
- delaying investment in alternative energy resources (see Chapter 19).

The International Monetary Fund (IMF) reports that the advanced countries are already in a deep recession. In the United States alone, the unemployment rate reached over 10 percent, or 15 million people without a job. Economic growth has also slowed in most industrialized nations but declined rapidly in Brazil, Russia, and a number of countries in Southeast Asia and Latin America. The economy is beginning to recover in China, but many states have lost the capacity to earn income by exporting goods because consumers have less money to spend on purchasing imports, and their countries are raising trade barriers to protect their own producers.

People the world over have lost their homes and welfare benefits because of unemployment and have been forced to move in with family or friends. Many lost their medical insurance or pension funds, or have delayed their retirement. In many countries, the crisis has reduced funds in local government treasuries, resulting in dramatic cuts in local health care, education, police, and social services. These trends have also heightened concerns about terrorism, poverty, inequality, famine, immigration, HIV/AIDS and other diseases, and increased energy and environmental problems. In China and many other developing countries, thousands of industries closed down, driving many workers back to the countryside they had left to escape poverty.

Since the last edition of this text, the events surrounding the latest financial crisis have become even more monumental than the end of the Cold War in 1990 or the 9/11 attacks on the New York Twin Towers and the Pentagon. While the 9/11 attacks certainly caused a good deal of fear around the world, the current crisis has penetrated much deeper into most societies, transforming economies and lives in unexpected ways. Despite the measures adopted by officials to deal with the crisis, many still fear that the current "deep recession" could easily turn into a second Great Depression. As the first Great Depression did in 1929 when the New York stock market crashed, the current financial crisis has undermined people's trust and confidence in national and international political institutions that have promoted capitalism and democracy.

It is no wonder that the current crisis has generated a fierce debate about its primary causes, potential solutions, and the implications it has for the future global political economy. Each of these aspects of the crisis centers on the interrelationship of the state, market, and society in different nations. One of the arguments we make in this edition of the text is that to adequately describe, explain, and understand the current global financial crisis—or any of the other issues covered in the different chapters—we must use an analytical approach that synthesizes methods and insights derived from economics, political science, and sociology as conditioned by an understanding of history and philosophy.

As discussed in more detail below, the IPE method is an attempt to synthesize analytical elements of separate academic disciplines to better explain complex, real-world problems that span physical and intellectual boundaries. While this statement might sound a bit formal and confusing at this point, keep in mind that we do not think you need to be an economics major or a finance expert to understand the basic parameters of the current global financial crisis and what it means for your future. This book is written for students who have almost no background in political science, economics, or sociology, as well as for those who want to review an assortment of topics in preparation for graduate school.

In the next section, as a warm-up to more details about the financial crisis later in the book, we briefly outline and discuss basic developments that set off the crisis. We will then examine the issue of how to study IPE—its three distinct analytical perspectives and a number of methodological issues with which IPE students should become acquainted. All the chapters in the book cover a variety of important theoretical and policy issues that have connections to the financial crisis. In this way we hope to provide students with the tools they need to study these and similar issues now and in the future, so that they might better understand different dimensions of the problems and then make some reasoned judgments about how to solve them.

Later in this chapter, we define and discuss the popular phenomenon of globalization as a way to introduce students to many of the political-economic conditions that led up to the global financial crisis. Many IPE experts have asserted that the economic liberal ideas behind globalization (discussed below) may have contributed to the crisis. Likewise, opinions differ, however, on whether or not the crisis may signal the end of laissez-faire economic liberal ideas and policies associated with globalization, or even the end of capitalism itself.

We then outline the text's 13 major themes and preview the topics covered in the book. Finally, we conclude with a brief discussion of what we feel are some of the most important ideas to take away from the book. Instructors may want to have their students read one or both of the last two sections of this chapter now or come back to either of them later in the class.

## THE MAGIC OF THE MARKET? — OR — POOF, YOU'RE A GONER!

In 2001 the dot-com bust in the United States had captured headlines when a large number of hi-tech firms went broke almost overnight. In late summer of 2008, most people worldwide were caught off guard when another economic bubble burst. This time it was some of the world's most reputable "big" banks and investment institutions who found themselves on the verge of collapse, taking a big chunk out of the value of many people's retirement funds and other investments. Banks such as Morgan Chase, Bank of America, and Wells Fargo soon merged with other banks, while Lehman Brothers, Bear Stearns, Merrill Lynch, and Wachovia fell by the wayside. The global insurance firm American Insurance Group (AIG) was also on the verge of bankruptcy, which threatened to leave most big banks without financial protection. The financial crisis quickly spread into most developed and developing nations, generating what many regard as the worst financial crisis the world has seen since the Great Depression of the 1930s.

Why did so many banks fail so quickly? The answers are many and complicated (and covered in more detail in Chapters 2 and 8). Many people point to the connection between overvalued U.S. homes and bank failure as the main source of the problem. In the 1990s, many mortgage companies and big banks that dominated the New York Stock Exchange adopted a variety of programs to attract new home-buyers into the fast-growing home real estate markets. In an environment of increasingly relaxed banking regulations, some companies created new "exotic" loan products such as ARMs (adjustable rate mortgages), "interest only" mortgages, and loans with "teaser rates" to attract first-time buyers and especially those who otherwise might not have been able to purchase a home (so-called **NINJAs**—people with no income, no jobs, and no assets).

Many critics also charge that the lack of state regulation during a period of a laissez-faire outlook about the state's role in the economy (see Chapter 2) made it easy for loan agents to *intentionally* sign up mortgage customers they knew would have difficulty making their monthly mortgage payments. Lenders were often less interested in the qualifications of the borrower than in "making the deal" to collect lucrative sign-up fees and improve the bank's rating in the eyes of investors. Moreover, many borrowers believed that as the economy continued to grow, the market value on homes would increase and they would be in a better position to borrow against the increased future value of their houses. Later when they "refinanced" their homes at a higher market value, they might also obtain a lower interest rate, which would allow them to pocket the difference between the new value of the home and what they owed on it under the old loan. With their "profit," they could pay off credit cards, take trips, buy more expensive cars, or save for their kids' college education.

These practices led to higher home values, which then fed growing speculation in housing and real estate markets. While the United States spearheaded this movement, it gradually caught on and became a part of many Western and Eastern European economic development policies. Speculation by developers and foreign investors translated into increased demand for U.S., British, Spanish, Irish, Icelandic, Lithuanian, Estonian, and other assests throughout the world.

Things got messy and opaque when banks and lenders packaged risky home loans in bundles and then resold them as **securities** (something whose value is protected against a loss in value) to other banks, **hedge funds**, and foreign financial institutions. Investors throughout the international financial system saw these securities as good investments with the potential for high returns. But these complex financial instruments (often referred to as "innovations") concealed the weakness of many of the underlying mortgages that made up the securities. All the money chasing these securities and other kinds of investments derived from them increased the market value of real estate, which led global investors to believe (mistakenly) that their assets were safe and a "can't lose" bet.

## Whatever Goes Up Must Come Down!

Eventually it became clear that many of the assets owned by investors were overvalued, and as everyone tried to sell, the market was flooded with overvalued "toxic assets," which further drove down home values in a negative feedback loop. By September 2008, most of the big banks had billions of dollars worth of toxic assets in mainly home mortgages on their books. Likewise, many of them were overleveraged—loaning out more money than they had in reserves to cover their loans. As conditions worsened, investors simply voted with their feet, either withdrawing from the market or seeking more secure ventures elsewhere. Meanwhile big banks were no longer willing to loan to one another, or to "main street" banks—those in local neighborhoods—that routinely loan capital to small businesses. Local businesses began downsizing or shutting the door for good. You have probably seen many of these places in your neighborhood.

As the crisis worsened in the United States, it spread elsewhere because big banks had become so interconnected (interdependent) with other banks in the major industrialized nations. Manufacturers and service providers started laying off or firing large numbers of people. As personal incomes dropped, consumers cut spending significantly. Declines in tax revenues meant that local governments had to cut spending on schools and social services. One out of ten homeowners in the United States could not make payments on their homes. Mortgage and bank defaults rose to record levels in England, Ireland, Iceland, Italy, and Eastern Europe. Many banks were stuck with properties they were forced to auction off at huge losses. Under these circumstances, most of the big banks could not borrow enough capital to make loans for new borrowers, which led to the depreciation in their credit ratings.

What had started as a home mortgage crisis in the United States morphed into a *global* financial (credit) crisis where capital became scarce when big banks refused to loan to almost anyone, for any reason. The Bush and the new Obama administrations both believed that if the U.S. government failed to do something, the global financial system would suffer a total meltdown, resulting in a deep, drawn-out recession or depression. With the United States' encouragement, many states did adopt a variety of measures—so-called "stimulus" packages—to restart their economies. These rescue packages fly in the face of many of the ideas associated with the popular economic liberal ideology that has shaped state–market relations since the early 1980s (discussed below and in Chapter 2). They also angered many ordinary folks who felt that the bailouts rewarded the very same financial elites who caused the crisis in the first place.

In the next few chapters (and in Chapter 8) we will encounter more discussion of the current financial crisis. Other factors such as greed, corruption, and even economic liberalism have been put forward as causes of the crisis. Many have questioned the appropriateness of the U.S. "wildcat" version of capitalism—and even capitalism itself. Some critics claim that the principles and policies that produced this shadow of darkness that has beset the world are, paradoxically, the very same principles and policies that policy makers are trying to preserve through economic recovery programs.

## THE WHAT, WHY, AND HOW OF IPE

Our discussion of the financial crisis and its consequences makes clear that today's complex issues can no longer be easily described, analyzed, and understood by using any *single* set of disciplinary methods and concepts. Those who study IPE are, in essence, breaking down the analytical and conceptual boundaries between politics, economics, and sociology to produce a unique explanatory framework. Below are several examples of how traditional academic disciplines might try to explain the world financial crisis by focusing on different actors and interests:

- *International Relations:* How much has the financial crisis detracted from the ability of states to pay for military defense? How has the crisis affected the conditions of war or terrorism in weaker or poor states?
- *International Economics:* How has the crisis impacted foreign investment, international trade, and the values of different currencies?
- *Comparative Politics:* What is the capability of political institutions within different nations to respond to the needs of the unemployed, elderly, or poor?
- *Sociology:* What is the impact of the crisis on consumption trends for different groups such as the wealthy, middle class, labor, or the poor?

■ *Anthropology:* How have different societies in history dealt with crises related to how they allocate scarce resources? And how have these crises impacted their cultures, values, and societal norms?

Scholars from different disciplines who focus on a narrow range of methods and issues enhance intellectual specialization and the analytical efficiency that goes with it. But each discipline offers an *incomplete* explanation of global events. Specialization promotes a sort of scholarly blindness or distorted view that comes from using one set of analytical methods and concepts to explain what most decidely is a complex problem that could benefit from analysis offered by a multidisciplinary perspective.

## What is International Political Economy (IPE)?

When defining IPE, we first make a distinction between the term "international political economy" and the acronym IPE. The former refers to what we study—commonly referred to as a *subject area* or field of inquiry that involves tensions amongst a variety of state, market, and societal actors and institutions. In this text we tend to focus on a variety of either "international" (between or among nation-states) or "transnational" (across the national borders of two or more states) actors and issues. Increasingly today, however, instead of *international political economy* more analysts use the term "global political economy" to explain problems such as AIDS or hunger that have spread over the entire world, and not just a few nations. In this book, we often use these two terms interchangeably.

Second, the acronym IPE connotes a *method of inquiry* that is multidisciplinary. IPE fashions the tools of analysis of its antecedent disciplines so as to be able to more accurately describe and explain the ever-changing relationships between states, markets, and societies across history and in different geographical areas. What are some of the central elements of the antecedent fields of study that contribute to what we refer to as IPE? First, IPE includes a *political* dimension that accounts for the use of power by a variety of actors including individuals, domestic groups, states (acting as single units), international organizations, NGOs, and transnational corporations (TNCs). All these actors make decisions about the distribution of tangible things such as taxes or intangible things such as security. In almost all cases, politics also involves the making of *rules* pertaining to *how* states and societies achieve their goals. Another aspect of politics is the kind of public and private, formal and informal, *institutions* that have the authority to pursue different goals. These institutions vary from country to country and region to region within states, and from group to group in different societies.

Politics also puts a good deal of emphasis on how much *power* actors have to attain a variety of goals, many of which conflict with those of other actors. Many international relations theorists view the international system as exhibiting a potential state of anarchy or war at any time. In Chapter 9 we examine some of the instruments such as military weapons and economic leverage that states often use to help secure themselves in a world where security cannot be guaranteed by any political actor.

Second, IPE involves an *economic* dimension that deals with how scarce resources are distributed among individuals, groups, and nation-states. A variety of public and private institutions routinely allocate resources on a day-to-day basis in local markets where we shop. Today, markets are not just a place where people go to buy or exchange something face-to-face with the product's maker. The market can also be thought of as a *driving force* that shapes human behavior when consumers spend their money or invest in something. These depersonalized transactions are part of what has become a sophisticated global economy that links trading on stock exchanges with other economic activities all over the world. Charles Lindblom also makes an interesting case that the economy is actually nothing more than a system for coordinating social behavior! What people eat, their occupation, and even what they do when not working are all organized around different agricultural, labor, and relaxation markets. In effect, markets often perform a social "coordinating without a coordinator" function.[1]

Third, the work of such notables as Robert Heilbroner, Lester Thurow, and Charles Lindblom helps us realize that IPE does *not* reflect enough the *societal* dimension of different international problems.[2] A growing number of IPE scholars argue that states and markets do not exist in a social vacuum. There are usually many different social groups *within* a state that share an identity, norms, behaviors, and associations based on tribal ties, ethnicity, religion, or gender. Likewise, a variety of transnational groups (referred to as **global civil society**) have interests that cut *across* national boundaries. A host of NGOs have attempted to pressure local, national, and international organizations on issues such as climate change, refugees, migrant workers, and gender-based exploitation. All of these groups are purveyors of ideas that potentially generate tensions between them and other groups but that play a major role in shaping global social, political, and economic behavior.

## How to Study IPE: Contrasting Perspectives and Methodologies

The three dominant perspective of IPE are mercantilism, economic liberalism, and structuralism. Each perspective focuses on the relationships between a variety of political, economic, and social actors and institutions. A strict distinction between these institutions is quite arbitrary and has been imposed by disciplinary tradition, at times making it difficult to appreciate their connections to one another. Each perspective emphasizes different values, actors, and solutions to policy problems but also obscures some important elements highlighted by the other two perspectives.

**Economic liberalism** (particularly "neoliberalism"—see Chapter 2) is most closely associated with the study of markets and the rational behavior of different actors within them. A major concern for all economic liberals is the state's role in the market and other parts of the economy. Later we will explain why there is an increasing gap between **orthodox economic liberals (OELs)**, who champion free markets and free trade, and **heterodox interventionist liberals (HILs)**, who support more state regulation and trade protection to sustain the market. Increasingly, HILs have stressed that markets work best when they are embedded in (connected to) society and when the state intervenes to resolve problems that markets alone cannot handle. In fact, many HILs acknowledge that markets are the *source* of many of these problems.

As we discuss in Chapter 2, many liberal values and ideas are the ideological foundation of globalism and the globalization campaign. They are derived from notable thinkers such as Adam Smith, David Ricardo, John Maynard Keynes, Friedrich Hayek, and Milton Friedman. The so-called laissez-faire principle that the state should leave the economy alone is attributed to Adam Smith in his famous book *The Wealth of Nations*.[3] More recently, liberal ideas have been associated with former President Ronald Reagan and his acolytes, who contended that economic growth is best achieved when the state severely limits its involvement (interference) in the economy.

Under pure market conditions (i.e., the absence of state intervention or social influences), people are assumed to behave rationally (see Chapter 2). That is, they will naturally seek to maximize their gains and limit their losses by producing and selling things. This desire to exchange is a strong motive behind their behavior, along with pressure to generate wealth by competing with others for sales in local and international markets. According to OELs, people *should* strongly value *economic efficiency*, the ability to use and distribute resources effectively and with little waste. Why is efficiency so important? Efficiency requires that society's scarce resources be put to their best use. When an economy is inefficient, scarce resources go unused or could be used in other ways that would be more beneficial to society such as in support of education and health care. This idea has been applied to the new global economy and is one of the basic principles behind globalization.

**Mercantilism** (also called economic nationalism) is most closely associated with political science, and especially the political philosophy of **Realism**, which focuses on state efforts to accumulate wealth and power to protect its society from physical harm or the influence of other states (see Chapters 3 and 9). In theory, the **state** is a legal entity and an autonomous system of institutions that governs a specific geographic territory and population or "**nation**." Since the mid-seventeenth century, the state has been the dominant actor in the international community based on the principle that it has the authority to exercise **sovereignty** (final authority) over its own affairs.

States use two types of power to protect themselves. **Hard power** refers to tangible military and economic assets employed to compel, coerce, influence, fend off, or defeat enemies and other competitors. **Soft power** is comprised of selective tools that reflect and project a country's cultural values, beliefs, and ideals. These instruments include films, cultural exports and exchanges, information, and diplomacy that convince others that the ideas you sponsor are legitimate and are the ones you want them to share and adopt. Soft power can in many ways be more effective than hard power because soft power rests on persuasion and mutual exchange.[4] For example, Nobel Peace Prize recipient Barack Obama orchestrated a resurgence in public support for the United States in the rest of the world through a discourse emphasizing multilateral cooperation.

**Structuralism** is rooted in Marxist analysis but not limited to it (see Chapter 4). It looks at IPE issues mainly in terms of how different class segments of society are shaped by the dominant *economic* structure. It is most closely associated with the methods of analysis employed by many sociologists. Structuralists emphasize that markets have never existed in a social vacuum. Some combination of social, economic, and political forces establishes, regulates, and preserves them, and as we will see in the case of the financial crisis, even the standards used to judge the effectiveness of markets and market systems reflect the dominant values and beliefs of those forces.

## The Benefits of IPE

Each perspective in IPE acts like a lens that focuses on different actors, issues, and developments in the global political economy. Each viewpoint always sheds light on some aspects of a problem particularly well, but casts a shadow on other important aspects. By using a *combination* of the three dominant IPE methods and concepts (outlined in Table 1-1 below), we can move to the "big picture"—the most comprehensive and compelling explanation of global processes and patterns.

Not surprisingly, an analytical problem arises out of an attempt to mix together the three different disciplinary perspectives. Because each discipline has its own set of analytical concepts, core beliefs, values, and methodologies, the analytical boundaries between economics, politics, and sociology make it difficult to establish a *single* explanation to any IPE problem. Does this weaken the utility of IPE? Not at all!

We must recognize that IPE is not a "hard science"; it may never establish a comprehensive theory with easily testable propositions about cause and effect. The world is a messy laboratory. Social science has always reflected this in its explanations of human behavior. IPE today represents an effort to *return* to the kind of analysis done by political theorists and social scientists *before* the study of human social behavior became fragmented into the discrete fields of political science, economics, and sociology. Both Adam Smith and Karl Marx, for example, considered themselves to be political-economists in the broadest sense of the term. One of our goals is to point out ways in which by mixing the elements of different disciplines we are better able to explain different aspects of the global political economy.

One of the ways of doing this is to think of the antecedent disciplines of IPE as tall grain silos standing very near to one another. Since the end of the Cold War in particular, these silos have been leaning into one another and sloshing their grain together. Just as new varieties of plants are produced by splicing parts of them together, the mixing of disciplinary grains has produced a productive and powerful hybrid field of study called IPE.

So what does the new mixture look like? To help answer this question, Susan Strange suggests that we focus on a number of common analytical and conceptual issues that cut across disciplinary boundaries. For her, the starting point for mixing states, markets, and society is to focus on the question of *qui bono?*: Who benefits from complex interactions in the international political economy? In a complementary fashion, we can follow the example of Pietra Rivoli in her book *The Travels of a T-Shirt in the Global Economy* and conduct a "commodity chain" study.[5] Rivoli traces a t-shirt from the time the cotton in it is grown in West Texas, to textile manufacturing in China, to sales in the United States, and then on to Africa, where many donated t-shirts end up as goods sold cheaply in local markets. Her work examines the *process* by which her husband's favorite

**TABLE 1-1**

**Conflicting Political Economic Perspectives about State–Market Relations in Capitalist Societies**

| | Monetarism (Orthodox Economic Liberals) | Keynesian (Heterodox Interventionist Economic Liberals) | Developmental State Model (Mercantilism) | Socialism (Structuralism) | Social Democracy (Structuralism) |
|---|---|---|---|---|---|
| **Main Ideas about Capitalism** | "Laissez-faire"; minimal state intervention and regulation of the economy | The state primes (injects money—liquidity) into the economy to restore confidence in it and to stabilize it | The state plays a proactive role in the economy to guide and protect its major industries | The state controls (is?) the economy. Prices set by state officials. Emphasis on state planning and agenda setting | The government cooperates with businesses to promote economic growth and distribution |
| **Values** | Economic efficiency, technology, open and integrated international markets, globalization | Efficiency mixed with a variety of state political and social objectives | National security, state-managed economy, relative equality | Equality | Equity and relative equality |
| **Thinkers** | Adam Smith, David Ricardo, Friedrich Hayek, Milton Friedman, "the Chicago School" | John Stuart Mills, John Maynard Keynes, Robert Reich, Joseph Stiglitz, Dani Rodrik, Jeff Sachs | Friedrich List, Alexander Hamilton, Ha-Joon Chang | Karl Marx, Vladimir Lenin, Mao Zedong, Fidel Castro | James Galbraith, Robert Kuttner |
| **Policy Tools** | Preferably few. Monetary and fiscal policies necessary at times to help market function well. Free trade | States use monetary and fiscal policies. Promote "fair trade" policies that include some protectionist measures | Protectionist industrial and trade policies oftentimes necessary to make markets work and enhance national wealth and welfare | Monetary, fiscal, and fair trade policies that redistribute income to everyone in society | States use monetary and fiscal policies to redistribute income |
| **Trade Policy Experts** | Doug Irwin, Martin Wolf | Deepak Lal, Jagdish Bhagwati | Ha-Joon Chang | Walden Bello, Benjamin Barber | Amartya Sen |
| **State Examples** | Hong Kong, U.S., Great Britain | Germany, India, Mexico | Japan, South Korea | Former East Germany, China before 1982 | Sweden |

t-shirt is made, transported, marketed, and then resold. In so doing she raises many issues that involve politics (the power of special interest groups to affect production and trade rules), markets (for t-shirts in the United States and all over the world), and different societies (how t-shirt manufacturing has changed the lives of factory workers in China and small African businessmen). Rivoli documents her work with plenty of hard evidence and raises a variety of ethical and human rights questions.

We believe that Strange and Rivoli offer two very good ways for students to start to think about the nature and different dimensions of IPE. It is not sufficient to just examine and explain something from several different angles or perspectives. We must also key in on who benefits or loses from the processes we observe; how actors acquire and use their political power and economic resources; and the relationships between different groups in different societies.

IPE gives students the freedom to select an analytical approach or combination of approaches they feel best suits a particular issue. It is important to note that most of the time the way one explains a problem depends on the questions asked about it, the data available, and the theoretical or ideological outlook of the analyst herself. Benjamin J. Cohen, for example, sheds light on this issue in his discussion of the "transatlantic divide" between the way scholars in the United States and Great Britain tend to view IPE.[6] U.S. universities tend to prefer IPE theories organized around issues of causation. Emphasis is placed on asking questions for which there is "hard" data. The goal is to test theories with statistical techniques and empirical evidence to determine what causes particular "pattern of relations." However, many British schools tend to think of IPE in terms of problems that are not as easy to quantify or for which statistical tests are not very useful. Their methods are rooted more in historical and philosophical understanding and centered on normative issues such as ethics, equity, and social justice.

In conclusion of this section, we can say then that IPE attempts to blend together distinct perspectives to produce a more holistic explanation of something. It is more flexible than most disciplines because it asks the analyst to choose why and how something should be studied and with what tools. Hopefully, with a multidimensional outlook we can conduct better analysis that may result in better and more effective solutions to global problems.

## The Four Levels of Analysis

When it comes to explaining issues, IPE theorists have applied the concept of the **level of analysis** to their research. In his famous book on the causes of war, *Man, the State, and War*,[7] Kenneth Waltz argues that explanations for causes of international conflict are located on different stages of an *analytical scale of increasing complexity*, ranging from individual behavior and choices (the individual level), to factors within states (the state/societal level), to something stemming from the interconnection of states (the interstate level). More recently, many have argued that there is also a fourth global level that account for such factors as globalization (discussed below) that can also be identified as causing specific problems.

The characteristics of the different levels of analysis are as follows:

*The Global Level.* This is the broadest, most comprehensive level of analysis. Explanations focus on how important global factors like changes in technology, commodity prices, and climate, for example, create constraints on and opportunities for *all* governments and societies.

*The Interstate Level.* This level emphasizes how the relative balance of political, military, and economic power *between* states affects the probablity of war, prospects for cooperation, rules related to transnational corporations, or the ways in which governments exercise leverage over their allies and states with mutual interests.

*The State/Societal Level.* Paradoxically, because the focus *narrows* to factors within states, explanations contain *more* description and explantory factors. At this level, we emphasize how lobbying by socio-economic groups, electoral pressures, and culture influence the foreign policies of countries. In addition, we focus on how different types of governments and decision-making processes *within* a state shape the way that the state interacts with others. For example, these factors help explain why some countries are highly protectionist or why democracies almost never go to war against other democracies.

*The Individual Level.* This is the *narrowest* level and yet it contains the *biggest* number of factors that explain why individuals (usually state leaders) choose certain policies or behave in particular ways. This level emphasizes the *psychology* and *choices* made by policy makers. For example, we might speculate that French President Nicolas Sarkozy tends to not go along with G-20 recommendations to deal with the financial crisis because as French presidents are want to do, he is suspicious that Great Britain and Germany will benefit from them at France's expense. Or, in terms of his *personality,* Sarkozy does not like to be upstaged in front of other European leaders.

The four levels of analysis help us *organize* our thoughts about the different causes of, explanations for, and solutions to a particular problem. Like the three IPE perspectives, *each* level pinpoints a distinct but *limited* explanation for why something occurred. For example, global warming can be linked as much to U.S. resistance to the Kyoto Treaty as to the ineluctably rising demand for energy due to a rising global population. Thus, one of the paradoxes of the level of analysis problem is that to get a *bigger and more complex picture* of a problem, one is tempted to look at all the levels for possible answers. However, mixing the levels usually produces no *single* satisfactory answer to a problem. What to do? The level of analysis problem teaches us that in order to arrive at a satisfactory explanation, students and researchers must be very conscientious when it comes to how they frame questions, what data they look at, and what they *expect* to find.

Figure 1-1 highlights the four levels of analysis and their connection to another conceptual organizing device we deal with next.

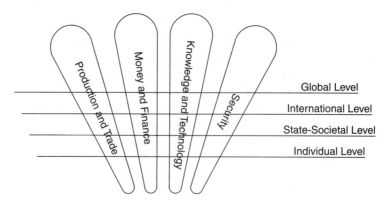

**FIGURE 1-1**

The Levels of Analysis and Four Structures.

## Susan Strange's Four IPE Structures

In the text we will often refer to Susan Strange's four *structures* of production and trade, security, money and finance, and knowledge and technology. For Strange, these "networks," configurations, or "webs" are complex arrangements that function as the *underlying foundations* of the international political economy. Each contains a number of state and nonstate institutions, organizations, and other actors who determine the rules and processes that govern access to trade, finance, knowledge, and security.

The "rules of the game" in each structure take the form of signed conventions, informal and formal agreements, or "bargains." They act as girders and trusses that hold together each of these four major structures. As one might expect, each IPE structure is often filled with tension because different actors are constantly trying to preserve, challenge, or change the rules of the structure to better reflect their own interests, points of view, or values. For example, at times the outlook of actors in production and trade may be more economic liberal oriented whereas at other times more protectionist.

Finally, issues in one structure often impact issues in another, often generating a good deal of tension and even conflict between a wide range of actors. According to Strange, much of the tension in these structures is related to trying to "shape and determine the structures of the global political economy within which other states, their political institutions, their economic enterprises . . . (and) people have to operate."[8] In our discussion of the four structures below, you can see examples of how these structures connect to the levels of analysis discussed above. We have pinpointed in brackets the causal factors and forces at different levels.

The four **IPE structures** are as follows:

> **The Security Structure.** Feeling safe from the threats and actions of other states and nonstate actors is perhaps the most basic human need. At the global level, the security structure is comprised of those persons, states, international organizations, and NGOs that contribute to or provide

safety for all people everywhere. In Chapter 9 we will see why many experts claim that the demise of the Soviet Union and the end of the Cold War [*interstate level changes*] led to an *increase* in the number of small conventional wars *between* states along with insurgencies *within* nations, especially in developing nations. The 9/11 attacks on the New York Trade Center also led to profound changes in the informal rules of the security structure when George W. Bush's administration [*an individual level factor*] decided to shift away from multilateralism and tried to impose its own version of hegemonic-unilateral leadership on the rest of world.

**The Production and Trade Structure.** The issue of who produces what, for whom, and on what terms lies at the heart of the international political economy. Making things and then selling them to other nations [*a global-level process*] earns countries and their industries huge sums of money, which ultimately can quite easily shift the global distribution of wealth and power. As we will see in Chapter 6, in recent decades there have been dramatic changes in international trade rules [*an interstate level factor*] that have resulted in a shift in the manufacturing of consumer goods such as electronics and automobiles away from the United States and Western Europe. Many of the corporations that make these items have moved to newly emerging economies such as South Korea, Mexico, Brazil, China, the Czech Republic, Hungary, Poland, and Vietnam [*a global level process*]. During the 1990s, many of the governments of these emerging economies sought to cooperate with foreign investors to promote the production of a range of goods and services. At the same time, production conditions in many of these countries led to criticism of human rights violations related to sweatshops in many of their assembly facilities [*a state/domestic level factor*]. As emerging economies have earned more income but also had to deal with the effects of the current financial crisis, some have been reluctant to agree to new open market trade policies in the negotiations over new rules of the World Trade Organization (WTO) because of pressure from vested interest groups [*a state/societal level factor*] (see Chapter 6).

**The Finance and Monetary Structure.** With perhaps the most abstract set of linkages between nations, this structure determines who has access to money, when, and on what terms, and thus how certain resources are distributed between nations. In this respect, money is often viewed as a means, not an end in itself. Money generates an obligation between people or states. International money flows [*a global level factor*] pay for trade and serve as the means of financial investment in a factory or a farm in another country. Financial bargains also reflect rules and obligations, as money moves from one nation to another in the form of loans that must be repaid.

Recently, the global financial and monetary structure has been marked by relaxed international regulation of the movement of "hot money" chasing quick profits from one country to another. Many believe that unregulated financial markets were in part responsible for financial crises in the 1990s in Mexico, parts of Asia and Latin America, and Russia, as well as for the current financial crisis (see Chapter 8). Some critics also charge that unregulated capitalism associated with increasing globalization may be partly responsible for breeding both poverty and support for terrorists in some of the depressed areas of the world.

**The Knowledge and Technology Structure.** Knowledge and technology are sources of wealth and power for those who use them effectively. Nations with poor access to industrial technology related to scientific discoveries, medical procedures, or new communications systems, for example, find themselves at a disadvantage relative to others [*an interstate level phenomenon*]. Increasingly in the world today, the bargains made in the security, production and trade, and finance and monetary structures depend on access to knowledge in its several forms.

The connection between technology and terrorism tightens by the day. Newspapers are full of stories about weapons of mass destruction (WMD). New technologies have revolutionized the size of weapons and the effects they have when put to use [*a global level factor*]. Many weapons can easily be transported in a backpack or a briefcase. The ultimate miniature weapon may no longer be an atomic bomb or a chemical mixture, but a few grams of anthrax on a letter.

## PUTTING THE PIECES TOGETHER: GLOBALIZATION, THE FINANCIAL CRISIS, AND STATE–MARKET–SOCIETAL RELATIONS

One of the terms students will encounter throughout the book is **globalization.** In this section, we define this popular concept and use the different IPE perspectives to explain who it benefits, why, and its relationship to a variety of issues including the recent financial crisis. Our discussion of globalization here is important because it has framed the four structures of the international political economy outlined above. Many of the rules and processes related to trade, money, technology, and even security reflect a variety of ideas and policies associated with this popular concept. Globalization has brought about a significant change in the way many experts and officials think about the international political economy. It has both strengthened and weakened the power of many institutions and actors along the way.

The term "globalization" began appearing in the IPE lexicon in 1985 to describe the growing **interdependence** (interconnections) amongst people and states all over the world that resulted from new information and communications technologies and the spread of Western (U.S.) ideas and culture. Globalization also accounted for the increased dependency of a nation's gross domestic product (GDP) on trade and other economic activities outside the state. Even though technically levels of globalization were higher around World War I, beginning in the 1990s the world seemed to be going through another phase of major global transformation that involved more intense connections with other states and their societies. Many

IPE analysts suggested that a shift had occurred from a predominately Cold War, military-oriented world order (1947–1990), where states were preoccupied with territorial security and war, to something more akin to a truly global world order in the 1990s dominated by economic issues. Many academics, journalists, and public officials labeled this nearly 25-year period of history "globalization."

Many people trace the origins of globalization to the early 1980s when U.S. President Ronald Reagan and Great Britain's Prime Minister Margaret Thatcher popularized the ideas and policies associated with economic liberalism and free trade. In the later part of the 1980s and throughout most of the 1990s, many of the newly industrializing states in Southeast Asia grew quickly and steadily. Many of these states had turned their trade policies outward by adopting export-led growth strategies and integrating themselves into what many referred to as the new "global economy." During this period, the United States, Great Britain, and other industrialized nations engaged in a campaign to promote globalization with the explicit and implicit promise that together with capitalism, globalization would increase economic growth while laying the groundwork for democracy the world over.

In the 1990s, many government officials, businesspeople, academics, and media pundits in the industrialized nations remained ethusiastic about the potential economic benefits to be gained by interconnecting people the world over in new, different, and profound ways. Columnist Thomas Friedman, for one, made globalization out to be a siren song (addiction) that could not be denied. Globalization is usually characterized as

- An *economic process* that reflects accelerated and intense interconnections based on new technologies and communications systems and the mobility of trade and capital
- The *integration* of national and regional markets into a single global market
- A *political process* that weakens state authority and replaces it with deregulated market outcomes
- A *cultural process* that reflects a densely growing network of complex cultural interconnections and interdependencies in modern society.

Some analysts further claim that globalization[9]

- Is an *inevitable* occurrence that has produced a new form of capitalism—hypercapitalism
- Is a process for which *nobody is in charge*
- *Benefits* everyone, especially economically, and
- Furthers the spread of *democracy* in the world.

For good or for bad, globalization connected people by reaching around the world farther, faster, deeper, and more cheaply through an array of new communications and information technologies that included the Internet, fiber optics, and a host of other exotic communications devices. Globalization emphasizes increased production and the free flow of huge amounts of capital in search of investment opportunities and new markets around the world. *Speed* was the new and necessary major feature of twenty-first-century communications, commerce, travel, and innovation. Along with economic growth and personal wealth comes the demand for Western (read U.S.) mass consumer products such as electronic goods, music, clothing, and food.

For Friedman and economic liberal state officials, globalization manifested the power of unregulated and integrated markets to trump politics and greatly benefit society. In his popular book *The Lexus and the Olive Tree*,[10] Friedman asserted that globalization often required a "golden straightjacket"—a set of political restrictions or undesirable state policies that must be adopted and implemented if states want to realize globalization's benefits. **Globalism**, which stands for the economic liberal ideas behind globalization, became synonymous with production efficiency, the free flow of currency (capital mobility), free trade, open markets, and individual empowerment. The payoff would be a "triumph of market" that produced economic prosperity and democracy everywhere in the world.

Friedman has gone on to argue that today an even more intense and competitive version of globalization—hyperglobalization—both reflects and fosters yet a new brand or phase of capitalism that drives individuals, states, and TNCs to continually produce new and better products. In his latest book *The World is Flat*,[11] he argues that new technological developments are *in the process of* leveling the relationship of individuals to their states and to one another. Leveling generates new opportunities for individuals to compete with people in their own society and with those in other countries. In short, despite a few shortcomings, globalization is here to stay and should be embraced. Not surprisingly, globalization shaped the development strategies of developing countries (see Chapter 11) and has remained quite popular with elites and large numbers of the masses in the developed nations as well. Many state officials and leaders of international organizations claimed that developing nations would grow out of their debt and prosper if they adopted neoliberal policies and integrated into the global economy. Because of its emphasis on economic growth, globalization was supposed to help create more peaceful relations between states that traded with one another, especially if U.S. hegemony (leadership) promoted it as an attractive option for the world's poor and downtrodden, who might otherwise support rogue states and terrorists. Globalization was also expected to help transform the global society by increasing flows of people across borders that might eventually lead to a better understanding between different groups.

As globalization grew in popularity, so did local resistance (in some parts of the world referred to as *jihad*)[12] to many of its effects. In the 1990s, the antiglobalization movement gained momentum on a global scale. Many NGOs and other public-interest groups pitched their cause in newspaper articles, on their websites, and in journal articles. Much of their focus was directed at, among other things, sweatshop production conditions in many poor countries, damage to the environment, and income distribution issues.[13] Many of these groups formed coalitions with labor, environmental, and peace activists and held massive demonstrations that often turned violent in major cities such as Seattle, Washington, DC, Salzburg, Genoa, and Prague. Protests were aimed at WTO, IMF, and World Bank policies that reflected support for the "Washington Consensus" (see Chapter 8) about the benefits of globalization. Issues surrounding globalization have decisively affected local, regional, and even national elections.[14] Others even argue that antiglobalization might have been a motive behind the 9/11 terrorist attacks on the United States.[15]

For many people living in poorer countries, globalization was merely a shibboleth for a "wildcat" version of capitalism that meant higher standards of living and consumer consumption for a few but an increase in the misery for a vast majority of people. For Ignacio Ramonet and many others, society had become a slave to the market, which operates like clockwork, driven by economic and Social Darwinism, leading to excessive competition and consumption and the necessity of people to adapt to market conditions, at the risk of becoming social misfits and slowing the global economy.[16]

Many HILs, structuralists, mercantilists, and even Thomas Friedman himself became concerned about the extent to which globalization was having a homogenizing effect on cultures the world over when they become consumers of U.S. labels—from Big Macs and iMacs to Mickey Mouse—along with U.S. business practices. When markets trump politics and society, predictably the outcome often is devastating for the masses of poorer people. Friedman acknowledged that globalization alone would not automatically achieve success for everyone. In fact, he suggested that if it increased the rich–poor gap or left too many behind, it would likely generate opposition and be viewed as a destructive force in the world.

By the turn of the twenty-first century, it became clear that most developing nations were not growing out of poverty as expected. Many of the Asian Tigers (Singapore, Hong Kong, Taiwan, and South Korea—see Chapter 11), Southeast Asian economies such as Malaysia, Indonesia, and Thailand, and a few other newly industrializing countries (NICs) did experience tremendous national and per-capita growth. And yet a number of newly emerging economies in Asia and other parts of the world experienced a series of financial crises of their own (see Chapter 8) in the second half of the 1990s. Unfettered (unchained) markets tended to help the well off in these societies, while the gap between rich and poor expanded.

In a tacit admission that globalization was not delivering on its promises, the United Nations (UN) in 2000 established Millennium Development Goals (MDGs) directed at increasing foreign aid for poorer nations, halving global hunger, reducing debt, and fighting diseases like AIDS (see Chapter 11). Nor has globalization produced world peace or even less conflict as economic liberals suggested it would. After 9/11 many became more critical of globalization for its role in intensifying tensions between the western industrialized nations and many Islamic countries in the Middle East, Asia, and Africa. Finally, globalization was often criticized for contributing to poverty, which many linked to increasing numbers of conventional and nonconventional wars in developing regions—especially in "failed states" such as Sudan and Somalia (see Chapter 9).

As explained in Chapters 19 and 20 many HILs, structuralists, and realists became concerned that neoliberal ideas and pro-globalization policies were responsible for many of the global environmental problems that face us today. One aspect of this issue is that everyone on earth supposedly makes short-term rational economic choices that have led to a series of energy and environmental catastrophes that already may not be reversible. Many would like to reform capitalism and redesign globalization such that people would curtail the excessive use of the earth's resources. Many scholars expect major problems in adjusting to a sustainable level of resource use in the industrialized nations—at the same time that China, India, and other developing nations make increasing demands on the resources of "Spaceship Earth."

Finally, the current global financial crisis has generated still more (intense) criticism of globalization and its economic liberal oriented ideas, values, and institutions. As we write in the fall of 2009, a few pundits are claiming that there are signs that "green shoots" are beginning to appear that herald recovery from the recent financial crisis. And yet unemployment numbers still continue to rise in many countries. Others believe that recuperation is not likely for yet another two to three years. Some have suggested that until the financial crisis is adequately dealt with, globalization and globalism will continue to come under severe criticism, not only from anti-globalization protestors but also from a number of economic liberal academics and policy officials who feel that more *managed* globalization would better serve everyone.

## OUTLINE OF THE TEXT'S MAIN THEMES

As students read through the book, they will encounter a variety of theoretical and policy issues. Each chapter ends with a brief discussion of the connection between the chapter topic, the financial crisis, and some of the main themes of the book (discussed below). As we noted at the outset of this chapter, instructors and students can choose to either skip the rest of this chapter and read it later as a conclusion or read it now as an overview of what they can expect by way of topic coverage and many of the major themes of the text.

The main themes highlighted in the text are the following:

- *Globalization:* Efforts to manage its negative externalities and impacts on the environment, resources, and society (discussed throughout the text).
- Tensions between *market fundamentalism and protectionism* and efforts to re-embed the market into society and its cultural institutions (see especially Chapters 2–4).
- Tensions between rising *production* and *distribution* of gains (see especially Chapters 4, 6, 11, and 19).
- Tensions between a state's *domestic needs and its international obligations* (throughout the text).
- Balancing *security and freedom* (see especially Chapter 9).
- How *social groups* influence markets and states (see especially Chapters 5 and 16).
- *Global inequality* between and within countries (see especially Chapter 11).
- How the rise of *China, India,* and other newly industrializing countries is fundamentally reshaping the global economy (see Chapter 13).
- *Development and transformation:* strategies and dilemmas (see especially Chapters 11–14).
- *Regionalism* as a development strategy many countries, such as those in the European Union, use to maintain wealth and power (see Chapters 6 and 11).
- The issue of *hegemony or leadership* over the global political economy (see especially Chapter 9).
- *Global governance,* management, and systemic order provided by a variety of institutions, along with resistance to them (throughout the text).
- The *increasing analytical and policy linkages* of issues to one another (see especially Chapters 18–20).

In Chapters 2–5, we cover each of the three dominant IPE perspectives and two alternative theories: feminism and constructivism. A number of cross-cutting themes of these chapters are related to different outlooks about *globalization* and the financial crisis. The financial crisis in particular has helped to sharpen the debate about what *is* and what *should be* the proper balance among the state, society, and the economy. To many journalists and academics, the dispute pitted the supporters of the laissez-faire version of liberalism, namely, OELs (see Chapter 2), against supporters of the ideas of John Maynard Keynes (HILs), who 75 years ago recommended state interventionist policies to deal with the Great Depression.

Chapter 3 covers many of the ideas of mercantilists, some of whom are critical of globalization and concerned about protecting society from the vagaries of the market. Likewise, in Chapter 4 we will encounter more critical views of economic liberalism and globalization from a (Marxist) structuralist vantage point related to issues of exploitation and equity. At a deeper level, though, these three chapters in particular raise questions not only about such themes as the tensions between *market fundamentals and protectionism* but also about *production and distribution* and *global inequality*. In fact, all the other chapters of the book shed some light on these same themes.

In Chapter 5, we discuss why many have argued that constructivism should be regarded as a fourth dominant IPE perspective. Constructivism reminds us of the power of *ideas* to shape the interests and actions of governments and market actors. Social groups, civil society, and NGOs usually lack substantial material resources, but they still influence the global political economy profoundly by spreading new norms and ideas, framing problems in new ways, and reinterpreting the causes of global processes. Similarly, feminist scholars point out that a full understanding of the four IPE structures—how the rules of trade, finance, security, and knowledge were formed and their consequences—requires much more attention to gender relations and the position of women in society.

Please note that the rational-choice ideas discussed in the previous edition of the text have been moved to the textbook blogsite at www.upugetsoundintroipe.com, along with the figures related to supply and demand and the discussion of economic assumptions and policy tenets.

Chapters 6–8 cover the global production and trade and monetary structures which govern international economic intercourse, foreign exchange convertibility, and the movement of capital throughout the world. These topics all involve tensions related to a state's *domestic needs* (which are often to protect domestic jobs and industries) versus its *international obligations* to honor conventions and treaties that are supposed to sustain open markets. Chapter 6 covers global trade and regional trade groups such as the European Union and the North American Free Trade Area (NAFTA) that can be viewed as attempts to expand free trade on a regional basis without throwing open all domestic markets to the threat of global competition. Bilateral and multilateral agreements continue to be popular because of the potential income trade can generate.

In Chapters 7 and 8, we explain why the global financial structure has become so crisis prone as of late. The rules of the international finance and monetary structure have *discouraged* capital controls and allowed for and even *encouraged* currency and other forms of investment speculation of the type that led to the current financial crisis. In Chapter 8 we explain the connection between the financial crisis and the global balance of payments problem. Many of the newly emerging economies including Saudi Arabia and China have built up huge capital reserves and run big trade surpluses. Some of these funds were invested in U.S. government securities and stock markets, fueling a borrowing binge in the United States before the crisis.

In Chapter 9, we explain why the global security agenda has been expanding in terms of actors who shape its rules and conventions and the issues this global structure has dealt with since the end of the Cold War in 1990. Phone calls, e-mail messages, library and bank records, and numerous other databases are routinely monitored in many countries for suspicious activity that could be connected to terrorist plots. Although many of these measures remain acceptable to the majority of people, many civil society groups have been front and center in condemning limits on *personal freedoms* and threats to privacy. *Globalization, distribution issues, and inequality* have also contributed to tensions within states between ethnic and religious groups. Open markets have contributed to security threats by facilitating the spread of WMDs and small arms and creating more opportunities for black market activities (see Chapter 14). For the sake of *national security*, many business firms that deal in national defense goods such as parts for submarines, missile guidance systems, or nuclear reactors have not been keen on national or international (UN) security regulations that might stifle their sales of more advanced weapons systems.

Chapter 10 focuses on the global knowledge and technology structure and keys in on the controversial issue of intellectual property rights (IPRs). Much of the debate about IPRs centers on rules that give transnational corporations unprecedented control over new technologies and cultural products. Developing nations in particular criticize these rules for interfering with their efforts to preserve biological diversity, educate the poor, and provide affordable health care to all. Individuals and companies throughout the world regularly defy these rules by engaging in piracy, counterfeiting, and patent infringement.

Chapter 11—a pivotal part of the book—focuses on *development and the transformation of society*. Most development studies focus on economic growth and a series of political, economic, and social issues associated with achieving it. We cover three development strategies that match the three dominant IPE perspectives, and one more—Self-Reliance—which has become the most popular model because it combines elements of economic liberalism, mercantilism, and structuralism. For many emerging economies and poorer nations, development involves not just production for the sake of economic growth but also the question of how to achieve a more *equitable distribution of income and nontangible benefits* in different societies such as India, China, and the Middle East. This chapter also examines some of the efforts by states, IOs, and NGOs to solve a host of problems related to Third World poverty and humanitarian relief efforts.

Chapter 12 analyzes conditions in the EU, which has been hit hard by the financial crisis. Many of its members are questioning the old assertion that economic growth can be achieved via political, economic, and social integration. While many like integration, it has become harder to *preserve state rights* while simultaneously *meeting community obligations*. The EU's institutions have struggled to reconcile the interests of new and older members and to find common policies that meet the needs of countries at different levels of development. Yet many point out that the EU has the potential to be the world's largest economy (and even a potential global hegemon).

In Chapter 13, we examine how, growing like gangbusters in the last 15 years, China and India have managed the social disruption that accompanies economic development and how they have flexed their muscles in the international economy. In China, the global financial crisis led to the closure of many state and private industries, laying off of workers, and threats to the export obsession of the communist political elites. Even though the financial crisis generated a good deal of harm to the Chinese economy and society, China's recent stimulus spending has helped it survive the global crisis. Meanwhile, its leaders are grappling with massive pollution, inequality, and society's insistence that companies and elites be more accountable. India's recent success may be due in part to it insulating itself from the global economy and slowly integrating back into it. Many speculate that its relatively *protectionist policies* have helped it weather the recent financial crisis and lead the recovery of the global economy.

Chapter 14 covers the Middle East, which exhibits many of the themes of the text when it comes to *production and distribution, inequality,* the role of *society* in the market, *regional conflict,* and *development.* However, the Middle East is too often portrayed as an exotic part of the world with a disproportionate amount of conflict, age-old tensions, terrorism, and dictatorship. While some parts of the region suffer from these problems, most of the region is deeply integrated into the global economy, playing a critical role in international finance, energy markets, and even environmental problems. With the notable exceptions of Syria and Iran, most of the governments in the Middle East have close military ties with Western countries.

Chapter 15 deals with many of the reasons why states and IOs have great difficulty dealing with a large illicit market where important goods and services, such as drugs, arms, and women to be sexually exploited, are trafficked across national borders. The chapter links illicit activities to the *transformation of social order* and the inability of states to enforce regulations, leaving some parts of the world in near anarchy.

Chapter 16 deals with some of the same themes, especially those related to *transformation of societies.* Migration sometimes occurs with the help of people smugglers, and it also exposes tensions concerning rules that govern the movement of people across borders. Ironically, while developments in the global economy may have contributed to migration, they have also improved opportunities for tourism in many of the very countries migrants have left to seek a better life. The chapter also shows that markets are ever separate from the people who work in them and form the human connections that make it possible for exchanges of goods, services, and labor to occur between countries.

Chapter 17 deals with transnational corporations (TNCs) and their role in the global political economy. They were placed in this part of the book for strategic reasons, as many of the issues covered in the second part of the text deal with how such corporations' investments transfer capital, technology, equipment, goods, and people between nations. Specifically, many TNCs play a role in generating and sustaining growth in least developed countries (LDCs). Much controversy surrounds how much they transform societies and affect the lives, opportunities, and work conditions of hundreds of millions of people. Moreover, TNCs have the power to exacerbate or lessen inequality as they shift wealth and power between countries, which is why states constantly try to impose conditions on their behavior.

The last three chapters of the book deal with the related issues of food and hunger, energy, and the environment (18–20). All three issues involve *production and distribution, market fundamentals versus protection, and domestic needs versus international obligations.* Many experts view all of them as aspects of global security that go beyond national and even regional security to present the world with some of the most serious threats to nature and all of humanity. The financial crisis has made food, energy, and environment problems increasingly harder to separate from one another. Markets alone have proved incapable of mitigating the problems of hunger, environmental unsustainability, and climate change.

## CONCLUSION

### Standing on the precipice

One way to think of recent developments in the international political economy in the past 200 years at least is to see most states and societies engaged in an effort to develop economically. For most people in developed parts of the world, history really only began during the industrial revolution. Since then many states have employed a mixture of mercantilist and economic liberal ideas and policies to achieve tremendous economic development, while much of the world has been unable to attain anything near that objective. What seems clearer to us all the time is that development, as we have conceived it, may not be realized for many societies. Furthermore, it is not something that ends once a nation looks like a modern industrialized country. Instead, development is an ongoing process of perpetual political, economic, and social transformation in all societies, regardless of their economic development status. As discussed below, there are good reasons to shift the definition of development away from quantifying economic growth.

Meanwhile two other major global developments are currently impacting states and societies

in ways unimagined even 30 years ago. The first pertains to major shifts in the distribution of global wealth and power. Most of the security headlines of the early 2000s dealt with terrorism and state efforts to combat it after 9/11. Many experts and state officials have had to come to grips with the idea that the war on terrorism may not be "winnable" in any real sense of the term. For a variety of reasons related to the availability of certain technologies, porous state borders, and increased frustrations related to poverty and underdevelopment, state and personal insecurities may in fact be increasing.

For the major powers, the Cold War seemed to be *passé*, yet the tendency for the U.S., Russia, China, the EU, and even Japan has been to fall back into viewing the global political economy from a familiar realist outlook that emphasizes power and conflict. Interestingly, not only terrorism but also the emergence of India and China as global powers now challenges many state officials to suggest that the global center of the balance of power is shifting even faster than expected as a reflection of many planned and unexpected changes in the world economy.

This shift could very well increase North–South tensions and, as we have seen, has already complicated and weakened global governance when it comes to solving problems such as trade, hunger, energy, and climate change.

India and China, taken together, share about a third of the world's population. Optimists in the North see this as a huge potential market, but pessimists see enormous (often labeled unfair) economic competition that raises the stakes in any North–South negotiations. In the UN Copenhagen climate summit (see Chapter 20) many experts were upset that it did not go far enough to deal with global warming and other related issues. At the core of the negotiations, however, were the intransigent national interests of developed nations, opposed by rising powers such as China, India, and Brazil, that now find themselves positioned between richer and poorer nations. While optimists viewed the Copenhagen accords as acknowledgment of a serious problem, it remains to be seen if efforts to adopt more specific measures to deal with the interconnected issues of earth's limited resources and energy issues can be reconciled with the goal of economic growth that exacerbates these issues.

Finally, a third recent major shift in the global political economy, which has been bubbling up from within states and communities, relates to the benefits and costs associated with globalization. Clearly, the global financial crisis not only generated more skepticism about government bailouts and free markets but also resulted in renewed support for more government intervention to save both individual national economies and the entire international finance system. This development raises another major issue we touch on throughout the book: If globalization and economic liberal values and policies have proved *not* to be politically and economically beneficial to all, how is the *global political economy to be managed or governed* without generating even bigger problems?

Many mercantilists and realists would point out that solutions to such issues are not likely to be separated from the interests of states.

Likewise, many structuralists would question the extent to which reform of globalization is even possible without profoundly changing the neoliberal principles and values that are its foundation. It would seem obvious then that because of the interconnectedness of states, institutions, and societies at all levels, international institutions *must* play some role in solving international problems. Paradoxically, precisely at a time when the global political economy could use more cooperation to solve an assortment of interrelated issues, we suggest that the compulsion of actors to cooperate for the sake of providing **global governance** remains weak. Dealing with the global financial crisis, among other important global issues, is just one such case.

For many experts, the problem comes down to either fixing economic liberalism or finding another perspective that blends some alternative theories together in such a way as to produce something more pragmatic. In the meantime, as we find in cases of migration and refugees, civil society is rapidly changing and making demands for democracy and human rights, which are harder than ever for regimes to suppress. We find that illicit markets reveal the limits of state sovereignty, international cooperation, and even compassion for the most vulnerable people in the world.

We end this chapter with two questions for you to contemplate throughout the text. First, are the political-economic insitutions of states and societies able to deal with the conflicting tendencies of making economic growth and security the highest priorities of states without destroying the earth's capacity to sustain development? Second, is it time for the popular economic liberal perspective to be replaced by something else that can reconcile industrialization and commercial activity with the shared need to provide proper stewardship of the earth and its natural resources?

We hope these two questions are the best ones to ask given where we are today. It would be interesting to know your views on them.

## KEY TERMS

NINJAs  4
securities  5
hedge funds  5
international political
   economy (IPE)  7
global civil society  8
economic liberalism  8
orthodox economic liberals  8
heterodox interventionist
   liberals  8

mercantilism  9
realism  9
state  9
nation  9
sovereignty  9
hard power  9
soft power  9
structuralism  9
the level of analysis  12
IPE structures  14

security structure  14
production and trade structure  15
finance and monetary
   structure  15
knowledge and technology
   structure  16
globalization  16
interdependence  16
globalism  18
global governance  25

## DISCUSSION QUESTIONS

1. Pick a recent news article that focuses on some international or global problem, and give examples of how and where states, markets, and societies interact and at times conflict with one another. How hard is it to determine the analytical boundaries between the state, market, and society in this case?

2. Review the basic elements and features of the IPE approach: the three main theoretical perspectives, the four structures, the levels of analysis, and the types of power. Which ones do you feel you understand well and which ones need more work? Discuss the connection between each of the three theoretical perspectives and your own values related to IPE.

3. Define and outline the major features of globalization. Explain the connection between economic liberal ideas and globalization. Which of the three IPE perspectives (or combination of perspectives) about globalization do you agree with most? Explain why.

4. Based on what you have learned so far in this chapter and from reading newspapers, etc., outline a few things you know about the connection between globalization, the financial crisis, and capitalism. Do you agree with those who suggest that the financial crisis raises serious concerns about the viability of capitalism? Explain.

5. If you read the section on the main themes of the book as a conclusion to the class, discuss any three major themes that come up in two topics of your choice, either in two chapters or throughout the text.

## SUGGESTED READINGS

Thomas L. Friedman. *The Lexus and the Olive Tree: Understanding Globalization.* New York: Farrar, Straus and Girous, 1999.

Robert Gilpin. Especially chap. 1 in *The Political Economy of International Relations.* Princeton, NJ: Princeton University Press, 1987.

William Greider. *One World, Ready or Not: The Manic Logic of Global Capitalism.* New York: Simon & Schuster, 1997.

Pietra Rivoli. *The Travels of a T-Shirt in the Global Economy: An Economist Examines the Markets,* *Power, and Politics of World Trade,* 2nd ed. Hoboken, NJ: John Wiley, 2009.

Joseph Stiglitz. *Globalization and Its Discontents.* New York: W. W. Norton, 2004.

Susan Strange. *States and Markets: An Introduction to International Political Economy.* New York: Basil Blackwell, 1988.

Kenneth N. Waltz. *Man, the State, and War: A Theoretical Analysis.* New York: Columbia University Press, 1959.

# NOTES

1. See Charles Lindblom, "The Market Ascendant" in his *The Market System* (New Haven, CN: Yale University Press, 2001), p. 14.

2. See Robert Heilbroner and Lester Thurow, "Capitalism: Where Do We Come From?" in their *Economics Explained* (New York: Simon & Schuster, 1994).

3. See Adam Smith, *The Wealth of Nations* (London: Methuen & Co. Ltd., 1904).

4. For a detailed discussion of soft power and its utility in the international political economy, see Joseph Nye, *Soft Power: The Means of Success in World Politics* (New York: Public Affairs, 2006).

5. See Pietra Rivoli, *The Travels of a T-Shirt in the Global Economy: An Economist Examines the Markets, Power, and Politics of World Trade*, 2nd ed. (Hoboken, NJ: John Wiley & Sons, 2009).

6. See Benjamin J. Cohen, "The Transatlantic Divide: Why are American and British IPE so Different?" *Review of International Political Economy, 14* (May 2007), pp. 197–219.

7. Kenneth N. Waltz, *Man, the State, and War: A Theoretical Analysis* (New York: Columbia University Press, 1959). Waltz wrote about three "images" rather than three "levels," and both terms are used in discussions of this concept. The recent focus on globalization has generated a good deal of attention on a global level of analysis.

8. See Susan Strange, *States and Markets: An Introduction to International Political Economy* (New York: Basil Blackwell, 1988), pp. 24–25.

9. For a more detailed overview and discussion of globalization and globalism, see Manfred Steger, Globalisms: The Great Ideological Struggle of the Twenty-First Century, 3rd edition, (Lanham, Md: Rowman & Littlefield).

10. See Thomas Friedman, *The Lexus and the Olive Tree: Understanding Globalization* (New York: Farrar, Straus & Giroux, 1999).

11. Thomas Friedman, *The World Is Flat: A Brief History of the Twenty-First Century* (New York: Farrar, Straus & Giroux, 2005).

12. The term is used in this broad manner by Benjamin Barber, *McWorld vs. Jihad* (New York: Ballantine Books, 1995, 2002).

13. See, for example, many of the articles in Robin Broad, ed., *Global Backlash: Citizen Initiatives for a Just World Economy* (Boulder, CO: Rowman & Littlefield, 2002).

14. See, for example, Jorge Castañeda, "Latin America's Turn to the Left," *Foreign Affairs, 85* (May/June 2006), pp. 28–43.

15. It should be noted that many historians point out that if globalization is measured as the connections of an economy to economies outside of itself, globalization was actually greater before, during, and after World War I. Also, a relatively small number of academics and experts do not believe in the existence of globalization at all. Often referred to as "globaloney" types, they do not view the phenomenon as novel; instead, many of them view globalization as merely another marketing tool that capitalists use to sell things. See, for example, Michael Veseth's aptly titled *Globaloney: Unraveling the Myths of Globalization* (New York: Rowman & Littlefield, 2005).

16. See Thomas Friedman and Ignacio Ramonet, "Dueling Globalization: A Debate Between Thomas Friedman and Ignacio Ramonet," *Foreign Policy, 116* (Fall 1999), pp. 110–127.

# "Laissez-Faire": The Economic Liberal Perspective[1]

Someone has to clean up the mess.

Getty Images

Like many other terms in international political economy (IPE), the generic term liberalism suffers from something of a personality disorder. The term means different things in different contexts. In the United States today, for example, a liberal is generally regarded as one who believes in an *active* role for the state in society, such as helping the poor and funding programs to address social problems. Since the mid-1980s, someone who has been thought of more narrowly as an *economic liberal* believes *almost* (but not exactly) the opposite. For economic liberals (also referred to as neoliberals),[2] the state should play a *limited*, if not *constricted*, role in the economy and society. In other words, today's economic liberals have much in common with people who are usually referred to as "conservatives" in the United States, Europe, Canada, and Australia.

This chapter traces the historical rise of **economic liberalism** in eighteenth- and nineteenth-century England and in the United States and Europe in the twentieth century. We outline some of the basic tenets of capitalism, a focal point of liberal thought. Throughout the chapter, we also discuss the views about state–market–society relations of some of the most famous liberal political economists: Adam Smith, David Ricardo, John Maynard Keynes, Friedrich Hayek, Milton Friedman, and recent supporters of globalization.

The chapter ends with an explanation of the popularity of globalization, which helped divide **orthodox economic liberals (OELs)** from **heterodox interventionist liberals (HILs)** (see Chapter 1). Finally, we contrast the views of OELs and HILs on the recent financial crisis, focusing on the extent to which the crisis has weakened the precepts and policies associated with economic liberalism.

The appendix "The Market Model, Market-Based Resource Allocation, Economic Efficiency, Efficiency Versus Equity," which appears in the Instructor's Manual and at http://www.upugetsoundintroipe.com, lays out the characteristics of a formal market model, develops the notion of efficiency, and then contrasts efficiency with equity. Students are encouraged to review the model in some detail to understand the basic assumptions many economists make about the role of the market in a liberal society.

There are four main theses in this chapter. First, economic liberal ideas continue to evolve as a reflection of changes in the economy and the power and influence of actors and institutions. Second, economic liberalism gained renewed popularity due to its association with the laissez-faire Reagan and Thatcher administrations, culminating in the globalization campaign of the 1990s. Third, since then orthodox economic liberalism has increasingly come under attack for its failure to predict or sufficiently deal with such things as the financial crisis and poverty in LDCs. Fourth and finally, we end with the suggestion that although weakened, laissez-faire ideas and policies are likely to remain popular in the United States and many other nations.

## ROOTS OF THE ECONOMIC LIBERAL PERSPECTIVE

The liberal perspective today reveals many insights about political economy that mercantilists miss or do not address. Essentially, the broad term "liberalism" means "liberty under the law."[3] Liberalism focuses on the side of human nature that is competitive in a constructive way and is guided by reason, not emotions. Although liberals believe that people are fundamentally self-interested, they do not see this as a disadvantage because competing interests in society can engage one another constructively. This contrasts with the mercantilist view, which, as we will see in Chapter 3, dwells on the side of human nature that is more aggressive, combative, and suspicious.

Classical economic liberalism is rooted in reactions to important trends in Europe in the seventeenth and eighteenth centuries. François Quesnay (1694–1774) led a group of French philosophers called the Physiocrats or *les Économistes*.

Quesnay condemned government interference in the market, holding that, with few exceptions, it brought harm to society. The Physiocrats' motto was *laissez-faire, laissez-passer,* meaning "let be, let pass," but said in the spirit of telling the state, "Hands off! Leave us alone!" This became the theme of Adam Smith (1723–1790), a Scottish contemporary of Quesnay who is generally regarded as the father of modern economics. Smith and many since him including David Ricardo, Friedrich Hayek, and Milton Friedman display respect, admiration, and almost affection for the market, juxtaposed with different degrees of distaste for the state, or at least for its abusive potential.

In his famous book *The Wealth of Nations,* Smith opposed the mercantilist state of the eighteenth century, established on the principle that the nation is best served when state power is used to create wealth, which produces more power and national security (see Chapter 3). For classical economic liberals, individual freedom in the marketplace represents the best alternative to potentially abusive state power when it comes to the allocation of resources or organizing economic activity. However, for Smith the term "state" meant Britain's Parliament, which represented the interests of the landed gentry, not those of the entrepreneurs and citizens of the growing industrial centers. Not until the 1830s was Parliament reformed enough to redistribute political power more widely. As a Scot without land, who therefore could not vote, Smith had some reason to question the power structure of his time.

Smith also believed in the cooperative, constructive side of human nature. For him, the best interest of all of society is served by (rational) individual choices, which when observed from afar appear as an "invisible hand" that guides the economy and promotes the common good. He wrote:

> He [the typical citizen] generally, indeed, neither intends to promote the public interest, nor knows how much he is promoting it. By preferring the support of domestic to that of foreign industry, he intends only his own security; and by directing that industry in such a manner as its own produce may be of the greatest value, he intends only his own gain, and he is in this, as in many other cases, directed by an invisible hand to promote an end which was no part of his intention.[4]

Smith was writing at a time when the production system known as capitalism was replacing feudalism. He was the first to develop a comprehensive portrait of capitalism in *The Wealth of Nations,* originally published in 1776. What follows is a brief overview of some of the ideals and tenets of capitalism based in large part on Smith's work—or at least the way many economic liberals (both OELs and HILs) today interpret his work.

## The Tenets of Capitalism

The five main elements of capitalism are as follows:

- Markets *coordinate* society's economic activities
- Extensive markets exist for the exchange of land, labor, commodities, and money

- Competition *regulates* economic activity; consumer self-interests motivate economic activity
- Freedom of enterprise
- Private property

The first three tenets address the nature and behavior of markets. In the modern market, products and services are commodified—that is, a market price is established for goods and services as a result of producers setting prices for their goods and buyers paying for them. The political scientist Charles Lindblom makes an elaborate case for how markets *organize* and *coordinate* society today in ways quite different from the past.[5] Whereas before capitalism the economy was organized to serve society, today markets organize most of our lives in ways we are not aware of. Markets not only determine our jobs but also shape our choices about travel, entertainment, and food.

Another feature of capitalism is the existence of markets for land, labor, and money. The economic historian and anthropologist Karl Polanyi wrote extensively about how modern capitalism gradually came about in seventeenth-century Great Britain when land was privatized, people moved off the countryside and into small factories, and capital (money) was generated by trade. Land, labor, and capital were all commodified, which provided the financial foundation and labor for the industrial revolution and the society that today we recognize as capitalist.[6]

When economists say that competition *regulates* economic activity, they are referring to the ways in which markets convert the pursuit of consumer self-interests into an outcome that inevitably benefits all of society. According to Smith, the pursuit of individual self-interest does not lead to civil disorder or even anarchy; rather, *self-interest serves society's interests*. Smith famously said, "It is not from the benevolence of the butcher, the brewer, or the baker that we expect our dinner, but from their regard to their own interest. We address ourselves, not to their humanity but to their self-love, and never talk to them of our necessities but of their advantages."[7]

In a capitalist economy, self-interest drives individuals to make rational choices that best serve their own needs and desires. However, it is competition that *constrains* and *disciplines* self-interest and prevents it from becoming destructive to the interests of others. Under ideal circumstances, producers must compete with others, which forces them to charge reasonable prices and provide quality goods to their customers, or lose their business. Consumers also face competition from other consumers who may be willing to pay more for a product. Even if producers might want to push prices high to satisfy their narrow economic interests, and buyers might want to push prices low for the same reason, the force of competition keeps the pursuit of self-interest from going to the extreme.

Capitalism assumes that price competition also results in the *efficient* allocation of resources among competing uses. When economists say that markets coordinate society's economic activity, they generally mean that no one (especially the state) should be in charge of how resources are allocated. Market coordination entails a decentralized (spread out) resource allocation process guided by the tastes and preferences of individual consumers.

For capitalists, government intervention in the market generally distorts resource reallocation and frustrates the coordination function we have described. Competition also requires firms to be production efficient, in the sense that it pays to adopt cost-saving innovations in the production of goods and to remain on the cutting edge of product and process innovation, the delivery of services, and the management of resources. The leaders of even the most powerful firms such as Microsoft, Ericsson, or Petrobas must keep one step ahead of technologically audacious newcomers if they wish to retain their share of the market.

The last two tenets of capitalism deal with the role of the state in establishing freedom of enterprise and private property. Freedom of enterprise means that individuals are free to start up any new business enterprise without state permission, thereby channeling resources to the production of goods and services that are in high demand while simultaneously intensifying competitive pressures in these industries. When individuals are free to make their own career choices, they naturally prepare for and seek out careers or lines of employment in which they are likely to be most productive. Likewise, as economic circumstances change, labor resources will be rapidly redeployed to growing sectors of the economy as individuals take advantage of new opportunities.

Capitalists are adamant that the owner of a resource is legally entitled to the income that flows from the resource. The income of those who own capital is usually in the form of profits (as opposed to wages). Capital goods—plants, equipment, and tools that workers need—are the important subset of all commodities that are required to produce other commodities. In a capitalist economy, the owners pay for the costs of production—the wages of the workers, the raw materials, and all intermediate goods used in production—and then sell the finished commodities on the market. Whatever is left over, the difference between the revenue and the costs, belongs to the capitalists. This is a legal right of ownership, referred to as capitalist property rights. A capitalist may completely own a business, a local bar, or a high-tech start-up, for example. But many of the largest enterprises are corporations where ownership is distributed in the form of stocks, which can be bought and sold on a stock market.

When property rights are less clear, the incentive to use resources efficiently diminishes. Private property—clear title to land, for example—also encourages the owner to make investments in improving the land and provides the owner the collateral with which to obtain the credit necessary to do so. Consequently, the resource owner makes every effort to ensure that the resource is used efficiently.

Freedom of enterprise allows entrepreneurs to test new ideas in the marketplace. In a dynamic world of changing tastes and preferences, the availability of resources and new technologies foments product and production process innovation. In such an environment, entrepreneurs must rapidly redeploy their resources to changing circumstances when new opportunities arise. Freedom of enterprise also allows firms to increase or reduce their labor force as necessary. Because firms can easily expand and contract, the associated risk of changes is minimized, and competition is consequently enhanced.

What Smith is most known for, then, is the view that ideally a capitalist economy is self-motivating, self-coordinating, and self-regulating. Consumers determine how resources will be allocated; self-interest motivates entrepreneurs to develop and firms and their workers to produce the goods and services consumers desire; the market coordinates economic activity by communicating the ever-changing tastes and preferences of consumers to producers; and competition ensures that the pursuit of self-interest serves social (consumer) interests.

## Smith, the Cynic and Moralist

Yet many historians and philosophers have come to view Smith as a more complex, nuanced philosopher, rather than associating him with only the "invisible hand" of the market, a phrase used only once in *The Wealth of Nations*. In fact, many of the ideas in his other major work, *The Theory of Moral Sentiments,* appear to contradict the more orthodox economic liberal ideas with which he is most often associated. We group Smith's caveats about the tenets of capitalism into three interrelated categories: the role of the state, the motives and behavior of capitalists related to preservation of the market, and a variety of moral issues.

Smith is clear that the state has some necessary and legitimate functions in society, especially with regard to defending the country, policing, building public works, preventing the spread of diseases, enforcing contracts, keeping the market functioning, and helping to achieve individual rights. However, he is also quite adamant in his distrust of businesspeople and capitalists. Another of his famous quotes is that "people of the same trade seldom meet together, even for merriment and diversion, but the conversation ends in a conspiracy against the public, or in some contrivance to raise prices."[8] The pursuit of self-interest by a monopoly producer, for example, often leads to restricted output, higher prices for goods, and a consequent loss of social welfare. Smith also distrusted bankers and noted that employers always sought to keep wages low: "When the regulation . . . is in favor of the workmen, it is always just and equitable; but it is sometimes otherwise when in favor of the masters."[9]

How do businesspeople get these advantages? Smith believed that merchants often had a disproportionate influence over the Parliament and could press their "private interests." These special interests often solicited the power of the state to allow them to disregard competitive pressures and to convince those in power that "what they wanted was identical to the general interest."[10] Manufacturers often easily influenced the legislature such that they acquired the exclusive use of licenses, franchises, tariffs, and quotas. Often their trading companies gained the sole right to sell products, keeping market prices above the natural price.

An example today is in the area of intellectual property rights, where companies like IBM, Samsung, Pfizer, and many others have convinced governments to strongly protect patents, which are legal, temporary monopolies on inventions allowing a manufacturer to prevent others from using the invention without the manufacturer's permission. In 2007 alone, IBM and Samsung together won more than 5,800 patents. Pfizer has a patent on Lipitor, the world's most popular drug, which by the end of 2008 had an astonishing $12 billion in cumulative sales (the drug goes off patent in 2010). Large-scale firms attempt to marshal the necessary resources and the power to control the markets for their new products with patents and copyrights. The risks of introducing new products, given the huge investments and time lags involved, are mitigated if these firms are *guaranteed* captive markets and consumer acceptance. Thus, many successful firms invest heavily in shaping and molding consumer tastes and preferences via expensive, sophisticated, and sometimes subtle marketing campaigns. At the same time, corporations hire major lobbying firms to press the U.S. Congress or English parliament for legislation that would help preserve their competitive advantage over other industries.

A comprehensive understanding of Smith's concerns about the role of the state in the economy and his unease about the integrity of capitalists elicits something more subtle than the dictum of laissez-faire universally associated with him. On the one hand, he *opposed* having the state try to direct investments because it might be counterproductive and unnecessary. And yet he *supported* the state exercising vigilance and enforcing competition policies to preserve competition and help the market work properly. Today we would say that in capitalist economies Smith feared **rent-seeking** (the manipulation of the state to rig the market in such a way as to reward powerful business interests with high prices and high profits). For Smith, absent competition, the invisible hand can no longer make competition work for the benefit of all society. While Smith leaves open the question of more specific issues about the how, when, and why of state regulation (an issue explored in more detail in Chapter 3), it is clear that he viewed the state (the *visible* hand?) as necessary if there was to be competition, lest capitalists themselves or powerful political interests represented by the state, destroyed the market.

Unlike *The Wealth of Nations*, Smith's book *The Theory of Moral Sentiments* has been largely overlooked until recently. His views in it reflect his ambition to proactively structure the market in such a way that commercial activity would produce righteous and prudent people. As the labor force grew in size, he argued that the welfare of "servants, laborers, and workmen of different kinds" should be the prime concern of economic policy. Sounding a bit like Marx (see Chapter 4), Smith argued that "no society can surely be flourishing and happy, of which the far greater part of the members are poor and miserable."[11]

For Smith, the passion to pursue self-interest leads mercantilists to cutthroat competition in which winners create losers. On the other hand, economic liberals also pursue their self-interests, but their passions are *restrained* by competition that prevents anyone from gaining too much power that could lead to coercion. Serving one's own interests in a competitive society means competing to best serve *the interests of others*, to behave honestly, and to gain a reputation for *fairness*. In a world of intense competition, commercial society was a way to channel self-interest into a less morally corrupt society than during feudalism.

# THE TRANSFORMATION OF LIBERAL IDEAS AND POLICIES

Adam Smith's writings were part of a broader intellectual movement that engendered intense economic and political change in society. Classical liberals, in general, at the time are represented by the writings of John Locke (1632–1704) in England and Thomas Jefferson (1743–1826) in the United States. Economic theorists tend to think of laissez-faire in terms of markets. However, this philosophy also implies that citizens need to possess certain negative rights (freedoms *from* state authority, such as freedom from unlawful arrest), positive rights (which include unalienable rights and freedoms *to* take certain actions, such as freedom of speech or freedom of the press), and the right of democratic participation in government, without which positive and negative freedom cannot be guaranteed.[12] These classical liberal political ideas are embedded firmly in the U.S. Declaration of Independence and the Bill of Rights, which were becoming well known about the same time as Adam Smith's notion of consumer freedom.

Economic liberals tend to focus on the domain in which nation-states show their cooperative, peaceful, constructive natures through harmonious competition. As we will see in Chapter 6, international trade is seen as being mutually advantageous, not cutthroat competition for wealth and power. What is true about individuals is also true about states. As Smith wrote, "What is prudence in the conduct of every family can scarce be folly in that of a great kingdom. If a foreign country can supply us with a commodity cheaper than we ourselves can make it, better buy it of them with some part of the produce of our industry, employed in a way in which we have some advantage."[13] Smith generally opposed most state restrictions on free international markets. He condemned the tariffs that mercantilists used to concentrate wealth and power. "Such taxes, when they have grown up to a certain height, are a curse equal to the barrenness of the earth and the inclemency of the heavens."[14] However, Smith *did* support the mercantilist Navigation Acts that protected British industries by requiring their goods be shipped to British colonies in British vessels, an act of mercantilism (see Chapter 3).

David Ricardo (1772–1823) followed Smith in adopting the classical economic liberal view of international affairs. He pursued successful careers in business, economics, and as a Member of Parliament. Ricardo was a particular champion of free trade, which made him part of the minority in Britain's Parliament in his day. He opposed the **Corn Laws** (see the box below "Britain's Corn Laws"), which restricted agricultural trade. About trade, Ricardo was one of the first to explore some of the precepts of a natural (scientific) law about trade. He argued:

> Under a system of perfectly free commerce, each country naturally devotes its capital and labour to such employments as are most beneficial to each. The pursuit of individual advantage is admirably connected with the universal good of the whole. By stimulating industry, by rewarding ingenuity, and by using most efficaciously the peculiar powers bestowed by nature, it distributes labour most effectively and most economically: while, by increasing the general mass of productions, it diffuses general benefit, and binds together, by one common tie of interest and intercourse, the universal society of nations throughout the civilized world.[15]

# BRITAIN'S CORN LAWS

Britain's Parliament enacted the Corn Laws in 1815, soon after the defeat of Napoleon ended 12 long years of war. The Corn Laws were a system of tariffs and regulations that restricted food imports into Great Britain. The battle over the Corn Laws, which lasted from their inception until they were finally repealed in 1846, is a classic IPE case study in the conflict between liberalism and mercantilism, market and state.

Why would Britain seek to limit imports of food from the United States and other countries? The "official" argument was that Britain needed to be self-sufficient in food, and the Corn Laws were a way to ensure that it did not become dependent on uncertain foreign supplies. This sort of argument carried some weight at the time, given Britain's wartime experiences (although Napoleon never attempted to cut off food supplies to Great Britain).

There were other reasons for Parliament's support of the Corn Laws, however. The right to vote in Parliament was not universal, and members were chosen based on rural landholdings, not on the distribution of population. The result was that Parliament represented the largely agricultural interests of the landed estates, which were an important source of both power and wealth in the seventeenth and eighteenth centuries. The growing industrial cities and towns, which were increasingly the engine of wealth in the nineteenth century, were not represented in Parliament to a proportional degree.

Seen in this light, it is clear that the Corn Laws were in the economic interests of the members of Parliament and their allies. They were detrimental, however, to the rising industrial interests in two ways. First, by forcing food prices up, the Corn Laws indirectly forced employers to increase the wages they paid workers. This increased production costs and squeezed profits. Second, by reducing Britain's imports from other countries, the Corn Laws indirectly limited Britain's manufactured exports to these markets. The United States, for example, counted on sales of agricultural goods to Britain to generate the cash to pay for imported manufactured

goods. Without agricultural exports, the United States could not afford as many British imports.

Clearly, the industrialists favored repeal of the Corn Laws, but they lacked the political power to achieve their goal. However, the Parliamentary Reform Act of 1832 revised the system of parliamentary representation but also reduced the power of the landed elites who had previously dominated the government, and increased the power of emerging industrial center representatives. The 1832 Reform Act began the political process that eventually abolished the Corn Laws by weakening their political base of support.

In an act of high political drama, the Corn Laws were repealed in 1846, which changed the course of British trade policy for a generation. Although this act is often seen as the triumph of liberal views over old-fashioned mercantilism, it is perhaps better seen as the victory of the masses over the agricultural oligarchy. Britain's population had grown quickly during the first half of the nineteenth century, and agricultural self-sufficiency was increasingly difficult, even with rising farm productivity. Crop failures in Ireland (the potato famine) in the 1840s left Parliament with little choice: Either repeal the Corn Laws or face famine, death, and food riots.

The repeal of the Corn Laws was accompanied by a boom in the Victorian economy. Cheaper food and bigger export markets fueled a rapid short-term expansion of the British economy. Britain embraced a liberal view of trade for the rest of the century. Given its place in the global political economy as the "workshop of the world," liberal policies were the most effective way to build national wealth and power. Other nations, however, felt exploited or threatened by Britain's power and adopted mercantilist policies in self-defense.

The Corn Laws illustrate the dynamic interaction between state and market. Changes in the wealth-producing structure of the economy (from farm to industry, from country to city) led eventually to a change in the distribution of state power. The transition was not smooth, however, and took a long time—important points to remember as we consider countries that have tried to open their economies and societies today. The case also illustrates that the market can be dominated by particular groups and is not apolitical or asocial, but reflects important social and cultural power.

For Ricardo, free commerce makes nations efficient, and efficiency is a quality that liberals value almost as highly as liberty. Individual success is "admirably connected" with "universal good"—like Smith, no conflict among people or nations is envisioned here. The free international market stimulates industry, encourages innovation, and creates a "general benefit" by raising production. In IPE jargon, economic liberals view the outcomes of state, market, and society relations as a **positive-sum game**, in which everyone can potentially get more by making bargains with others as opposed to not trading with them. Market exchanges of goods and services are mutually advantageous to both parties. Mercantilists, on the other hand, tend to view life as a **zero-sum game**, in which gains by one person or group necessarily come at the expense of others (see Chapter 3).

Sounding more like a social scientist than a philosopher, Ricardo argued that these positive-sum payoffs of trade bind together the nations of the world by a common thread of interest and intercourse. As is often argued by those who support globalization today, free individual actions in the production, finance, and knowledge structures create such strong ties of mutual advantage among nations that the need for a tie of security is irrelevant, or nearly so. Through open markets, the nations of the world are becoming part of a "universal society" united, not separated, by their national interests, weakening or entirely eliminating reasons for war.

## JOHN STUART MILL AND THE EVOLUTION OF THE LIBERAL PERSPECTIVE

Political economy is a dynamic field, and the liberal view has evolved over the years as the nature of state–market–societal interaction has changed to reflect changing cultural values and ideas. A critical person in the intellectual development of liberalism was John Stuart Mill (1806–1873), who inherited the liberalism of Smith and Ricardo. His textbook, *Principles of Political Economy with Some of Their Applications to Social Philosophy* (1848) (published the same year as Marx's *The Communist Manifesto*), helped define liberalism for half a century.

Mill held that liberal ideas behind what had emerged as full-blown capitalism in Europe had been an important *destructive* force in the eighteenth century—even if they were also the intellectual foundation of the revolutions and reforms that weakened central authority and strengthened individual liberty in the United States and Europe. He developed a philosophy of social progress based on "moral and spiritual progress rather than the mere accumulation of wealth."[16] Mill doubted the extent to which the competitive process and economic freedom inherent in capitalism would turn the most powerful human motive—the pursuit of self-interest—into the service of society's welfare. At the time, many people were working in factories but living in much more wretched conditions than those that existed in Smith's and Ricardo's times. Whole families worked six days a week for more than eight hours a day. Many were routinely laid off with little notice.

Mill acknowledged the problems created by the market's inherent inequality of outcomes. He proposed that to achieve social progress, the state *should take* definitive action to supplement the market, correcting for its failures or weaknesses. He advocated *selective* state action in some areas, such as educating children and assisting the poor, when individual initiative might be inadequate in promoting social welfare. In general, Mill supported as much decentralization as was consistent with reasonable efficiency; the slogan was "centralize information, decentralize power." He believed parents had a duty to educate their children, and might be legally compelled to do so, but it was obviously intolerable to make them pay for this education if they were already poor. It was also dangerous for the state to take over education as a centralized activity. Thus, some state action—grants for people to pay for private school and the operation of "model schools," for example—was the suggested remedy.[17]

Mill's views on education and other social issues reflect the evolution of liberalism in his time. The guiding principle was still laissez-faire: When in doubt, state interference was to be avoided. However, within a political economy based on the connection of markets to individuals and society, some limited government actions were desirable. The questions for Mill, as for liberal thinkers since his time, are: when, how, and how far is government's *visible* hand justified as an assistant to or replacement for the invisible hand of the market? How far can the state go before its interference with individual rights and liberties is abusive?

Note: To understand many of the fundamental assumptions and principles in formal economic thought, students and instructors who are not well versed in formal economic theory may refer to the appendix to the chapter, which is located in the Instructor's Manual and on the University of Puget Sound IPE website at http://www.upugetsoundintroipe.com. It develops the concepts of economic efficiency and distinguishes between equity and efficiency.

## JOHN MAYNARD KEYNES AND THE GREAT DEPRESSION

One of the most influential political economists of the twentieth century was John Maynard Keynes (1883–1946)—pronounced "canes," or "keinz" if you are British—who stands out in the evolution of liberalism for developing a subtle and compelling strain of liberalism called the **Keynesian theory** of economics, or sometimes referred to as Keynesianism. Much like Mill who was concerned with the negative impact of markets on society, Keynes's ideas were increasingly popular in the 1930s up through the Great Depression and World War II until the early 1970s. As was the case in the 1930s, in the face of the current financial crisis many experts have become critical of the popular laissez-faire outlook and looked back to ideas of Keynes to explain the crisis and provide a variety of solutions to it.

A civil servant, writer, farmer, lecturer, and Director of the Bank of England, Keynes is known for refuting some of the basic principles of economic liberalism. He believed that the Great Depression was evidence that the invisible hand of the market sometimes errs in catastrophic ways. As early as 1926, he wrote:

Let us clear from the ground the metaphysical or general principles upon which, from time to time, laissez-faire has been founded. It is *not* true that individuals possess a prescriptive "Natural liberty" in their economic activities. There is *no* "compact" conferring perpetual rights on those who Have or on those who Acquire. The world is *not* so governed from above that private and social interest always coincide. ... Nor is it true that self-interest generally *is* enlightened; more often individuals acting separately to promote their own ends are too ignorant or too weak to attain even these. Experience does *not* show that individuals, when they make up a social unit, are always less clear-sighted than when they act separately.[18]

Keynes suggested that the laissez-faire version of classical liberalism can hardly offer an explanation of booms and busts because according to that model, such disruptions should not even occur. Remember that for OELs the market translates the rational and selfish behavior of individual actors (consumers, workers, firms, etc.) into an outcome that is socially optimal. The market is also seen as a self-correcting institution so that deviations from full employment—something that resulted from an outside "shock" to the system—should set in motion changes in prices, including wages and interest rates, that will quickly restore full employment.

In Keynes's view, the cause of recessions and depressions is that individuals tend to make decisions that are particularly unwise when faced with situations in which the future is *uncertain* and there is no effective way to share risks or coordinate otherwise chaotic actions. Keynes emphasizes that it *is* possible for individuals to behave rationally and in their individual self-interest, and yet for the *collective result* to be both irrational and destructive—a clear failure of the invisible hand. The stock market crash of 1929, the Asian crisis of 1997, and the current global financial crisis demonstrate what can happen when investors are spooked and stampede out of the market (see Chapter 8).

In these conditions, people often predict a very bleak future or at least find it difficult to "think rationally" about the future, leading to what Keynes calls a **paradox of thrift**. What is the rational thing to do when one is threatened by unemployment? One rational response to uncertainty about your future income is to spend less and save more, to build up a cushion of funds in case you need them later (just as many people are doing today in the financial crisis). But if everyone spends less, then less is purchased, less is produced, fewer workers are needed, and income declines. Furthermore, the recession and unemployment that everyone feared *will* come to pass is in fact *sustained* by the very actions that individuals took to protect themselves from this eventuality. Keynes also worried about speculation in the international economy and the damage it could do if it was not regulated in some fashion. These conditions, then, make financial markets fragile and prone to economic disaster.

For Keynes, the solution (referred to as **Keynesianism**) is to combine state and market influences in a way that, in the spirit of Adam Smith, still relies on the "invisible hand" but supports a *larger but still limited* sphere of constructive state action. For Keynes, to offset its collective irrationality, society should direct "intelligence through some appropriate organ of action over many of the inner intricacies of private business, yet it would leave private initiative and enterprise unhindered."[19] That appropriate organ is the state. According to Keynes, the problem was to "work out a social organization which shall be as efficient as possible without offending our notions of a satisfactory way of life."[20]

During the Great Depression, many states used a combination of monetary and fiscal policy to sustain wages for labor and to stimulate economic growth. Because businesses were afraid to invest, instead of worrying about inflation, states temporarily ran a deficit so as to encourage production and consumption. In the United States, President Franklin Roosevelt adopted many other Keynesian policy suggestions including public works projects to stimulate employment, unemployment insurance, bank deposit insurance to improve investor confidence in banks, and social security.

Keynes also made clear that the state should use its power to improve the market, but *not* along the aggressive, nationalistic lines of mercantilism. He worried that under the strain of the Great Depression people could easily turn toward an ideology like Fascism or Nazism for solutions to their problems. He found communism and the Soviet regime repressive and their disregard for individual freedom intolerable. In contrast to his archrival Hayek, Keynes argued that a liberal system is one that respects individual freedom, not one that limits it for the sake of security. Much like Adam Smith, he argued that economics is a tool *not* to be divorced from issues related to how it can serve society. Beyond all else, Keynes was a moral humanist who wanted to get beyond the problem of accumulating wealth, which he viewed as "a somewhat disgusting morbidity," to a society where most people could instead spend their leisure time contemplating and living a good life.

## The Keynesian Compromise: Reconciling State and International Interests

Keynes is also noted for the role he played in helping to reconstruct Western Europe after World War II and establishing the new international economic order. At a meeting of the Allied nations at Bretton Woods, New Hampshire, in 1944 two new institutions were created to manage the postwar economy: the IMF and the World Bank. Three years later, the General Agreement on Tariffs and Trade (GATT) was created to manage international trade. Keynes headed the British delegation, and the institutional result, though not his plan, certainly reflected many of his ideas.

One of the problems that arose from the meeting was how to square two objectives the Allies agreed were necessary to restore stability and economic growth to the international economy while helping states recover from the war. On the one hand, Keynes believed that on the domestic front positive government action was both useful and necessary to deal with problems the invisible hand did not solve. At the same time, he himself envisioned a liberal or open international system in which market forces and free-trade policies would play major roles in each state's foreign economic policy objectives. The **Keynesian compromise** was the idea that management of the international economy would be conducted through peaceful cooperation of states represented in the three Bretton Woods institutions based on embedded (entrenched) Keynesian ideas about the international political economy. States would work to *gradually* reduce their state regulatory policies so as to open their national economies as they recovered and became more competitive. The result was that domestic trade protection and capital controls became accepted exceptions to economic liberal polices in international negotiations.

The Keynesian flavor of **embedded liberalism**—strong international markets subject to social and political restraints and regulations reflecting domestic priorities—became the mainstream IPE view in the industrialized world from the 1930s into the 1970s, as many industrialized nations used state power to supplement, strengthen, and stabilize the market economy within the liberal Bretton Woods system of international institutions. In the early days of the Cold War, the international economy opened slowly generating a tremendous amount of economic productivity and growth. The mid-1960s were regarded as a "golden age" of steady economic growth in both the United States and Western Europe. In places such as Great Britain, France, West Germany, Sweden, and other nations, the role of the state was emphasized to a greater degree, creating something akin to a democratic-socialist system. In the United States, state policy became much more activist than in previous decades. The U.S. federal government played a very active role in the economy at home and abroad through such varied areas as space exploration, promoting civil rights, implementing the "Great Society" antipoverty programs, helping the elderly with Medicare medical insurance, and regulating business.

Many political economists argue that this post–World War II system worked well because the United States covered many of the expenses associated with maintaining the global monetary system and providing for the defense that each of the allies would have had to pay for alone. As a result, Japan and Western Europe could spend more for their recovery while benefiting from a system of open trade, sound money, and peace and security that stimulated the growth of markets everywhere. More generally, **hegemonic stability theory** is the idea that international markets work best when a **hegemon** (a single dominant state) accepts the costs associated with keeping them open for the benefit of both itself and its allies by providing them with certain international **public goods** at its own expense.[21]

But as time went on, U.S., West European, and Japanese interests changed, and as they did, hegemony gradually became more expensive for all involved to sustain (or put up with depending on one's perspective). By the late 1960s, states were driven by their domestic agendas to either sustain or increase the protection of their industries and growing economies. Economic growth gradually shifted wealth and power away from the United States and toward Western Europe and Japan, changing the fundamental (cooperative) relationship of the United States to its allies. At the same time, the United States felt strongly that the costs of fighting the war in Vietnam were becoming prohibitive without more allied financial and political support. It became more difficult to keep the international trade, monetary, and financial systems open.

# THE RESURGENCE OF CLASSICAL LIBERALISM

In the late 1960s, President Nixon and others attacked Keynesianism and the cost of President Johnson's Great Society program, seeking to put more emphasis on economic growth instead of stability. As discussed in Chapter 7, in 1973 the United States replaced its fixed exchange rate system with a flexible exchange rate system, which led to increased speculation on currencies and more money circulating in the international economy. That same year OPEC (Organization of the Petroleum Exporting Countries) oil price hikes led to an economic recession in the industrialized nations, but also massive amounts of OPEC's earnings recycled back into Western banks. Meanwhile, many Western European states, Japan, Brazil, Taiwan, and South Korea were competing with the United States for new trade markets. Keynesian policies to deal with the recession generated stagflation—the coexistence of low growth and high inflation, which were not supposed to occur together.

In this environment of low economic growth and increasing competitiveness, Keynes's ideas were gradually replaced by those of the Austrian Friedrich Hayek (1899–1992) and Milton Friedman (1912–2006). Their more orthodox economic liberal policy ideals and values featured "minimally fettered" capitalism—or a *limited* state role in the economy. These increasingly popular ideas laid the intellectual groundwork for what became a distinct variation of liberalism, otherwise known as economic liberalism or **neoliberalism**.

Hayek's most influential work, *The Road to Serfdom*, explored growing state influence that he felt represented a fundamental threat to individual liberty. In his view, the growing role of government to provide greater economic security was nothing more than the first step on a slippery slope to socialism or fascism. He warned against reliance on "national planners" who promised to create economic utopias by supplanting competition with a government-directed system of production, pricing, and redistribution. Drawing on older theories of economic liberalism, Hayek argued that the only way to have security *and* freedom was to limit the role of government and draw security from the opportunity the market provides to free individuals.

Contrasting the "collectivist" ideas of socialism with the virtues of an economy with real freedom, he wrote:

> . . . The virtues which are held less and less in esteem . . . are precisely those on which Anglo-Saxons justly prided themselves and in which they were generally recognized to excel. These virtues were independence and self-reliance, individual initiative and local responsibility, the successful reliance on voluntary activity, noninterference with one's neighbor and tolerance of the different, and a healthy suspicion of power and authority. Almost all the traditions and institutions which . . . have molded the national character and the whole moral climate of England and America are those which the progress of collectivism and its centralistic tendencies are progressively destroying.[22]

Echoing Hayek's foundation, Milton Friedman wrestled with the problem of keeping government from becoming a "Frankenstein that would destroy the very freedom we establish it to protect." According to Friedman, government "is an instrument through which we can exercise our freedom; yet by concentrating power in political hands, it is also a threat to *freedom*."[23] In his book *Capitalism and Freedom*, he consciously returns to the classical liberalism of Adam Smith. Friedman stresses the classical liberal view that the market preserves and protects liberty. A state that takes its citizens' freedom through anything more than absolutely necessary action is no better than one that seizes their freedom guided by mercantilist, socialist, or fascist notions of security. Capitalism, with its free competitive market, naturally diffuses power and so preserves freedom.

## REAGAN, THATCHER, AND THE NEOLIBERALS

In the early 1980s, the classical economic liberal view of IPE reasserted itself even more forcefully through a movement called neoliberalism. Prime Minister Margaret Thatcher of Great Britain and U.S. President Ronald Reagan were the chief practitioners of policies that owed much more to Smith, Hayek, and Friedman than to Mill or Keynes. Thatcher's motto was TINA—"There Is No Alternative" to economic liberal policies.

Neoliberalism emphasizes economic growth over stability. President Reagan promoted "supply-side economics," which is the idea that lower taxes instead of increased spending by government would increase the money supply and generate its own demand, unleashing capital to businesses and consumers. The top income tax rate in the United States was cut in stages from 70 percent in 1980 to 33 percent in 1986.

Other features of **"Reaganomics"** (as it was popularly known then) were *deregulation* of banking, energy, investment, and trade markets (i.e., promoting free trade). Many national telecommunications, airline, and trucking industries were *privatized* (sold off to wealthy individuals or corporations) to allow for greater competition and freedom to set prices. Some public housing in Britain was privatized, and welfare programs in both the U.S. and Great Britain were "rolled back" (shrunk). Many neoliberals argued that the state was too big and not to be trusted. Echoing Smith, they maintained that its interests reflected powerful special interests, whereas the market was a neutral tool that redistributes income to those who are most efficient, innovative, and hard working. Although these policies might lead to greater income inequality, economic growth at the top of society would gradually "trickle down" to benefit labor and society's masses. Finally, the rule of thumb for both popular leaders was that the state was to minimally interfere in all areas of public policy except security, where both advocated a strong anticommunist stance.

As we discussed in Chapter 1, in the mid-1980s the United States began promoting globalization—the extension of economic liberal principles the world over—as a process that would expand economic growth and bring democracy to those nations integrated into this capitalist structure. Emphasizing the role of *unfettered* markets (unchained by the state), globalization promised to enhance production efficiency, spread new technologies and communication systems, and generate jobs in response to increased demand.

An integrated global economy was also expected to benefit millions of people trapped in poverty in developing nations. In the late 1980s, the "Washington Consensus" about the benefits of economic liberal policies and their connection to democracy was promoted in the policies of the GATT, the IMF, and the World Bank. The success of these laissez-faire policies in the United States and Great Britain, combined with the collapse of communism in Eastern Europe in 1990, led some leaders in the faster-growing developing economies in Southeast Asia and Latin America to support more market-friendly policies. Most of the ex-communist regimes of Eastern Europe replaced centralized, inefficient state planning with more market-oriented development strategies.

## THE 1990s AND 2000s: NEOLIBERALISM AND GLOBALIZATION UNDER ATTACK

Many attribute the global economic recovery after 1992 to deregulation and privatization, which became widespread policies in most parts of the world. It became commonplace to read that neoliberalism was practically and theoretically "triumphant." The Clinton administration continued to emphasize neoliberal ideas, negotiating a plethora of free-trade deals such as NAFTA and helping create the WTO (see Chapter 6). Neoliberal-style capitalism and open markets continued to be directly linked to U.S. economic and military interests. Some Central and Eastern Europe states became members of the European Union's (EU) single market. Mexico, India, and China all adopted pro-market "reforms," encouraged foreign investment, and massively boosted trade with the United States.

However, in the mid-1990s neoliberalism encountered increasing criticism, especially by anti-globalization protestors who accused it of causing violations of human rights, damaging the environment, depriving poorer countries of effective representation in international economic organizations, and fostering sweatshops in developing countries. Mass anti-globalization protests in major cities—capped by the "Battle of Seattle" in the spring of 1999—demonstrated that many civil society groups had lost faith in laissez-faire capitalism. Major recessions in Mexico in 1994, Russia in 1996, and throughout much of Southeast and East Asia in 1997 and 1998 led many officials in developing countries to question the merits of weakening regulations and encouraging massive capital flows across borders. And yet overall support for globalization among Western policy makers, business elites, and economists remained strong.

By the mid-2000s, some public officials and intellectual *supporters* of globalization began to address potential problems with rapid, unregulated globalization. A good number of these critics were *not* inherently opposed to economic liberal ideas, but merely wanted today's IPE to be *managed better*. For example, Joseph Stiglitz, the former chief economist of the World Bank and Nobel Prize winner in Economics, has criticized IMF policies for making it difficult for many developing nations to get out of debt and benefit from globalization.[24] Economist Dani Rodrik has pointed out that too much economic integration, free trade, and unfettered capital flows pose a threat to democratic politics. Markets, he argues, have to be "embedded in non-market institutions in order to work well."[25] They will not be viewed as legitimate unless they reflect individual countries' national values, social understandings, and political realities such as voters' unwillingness to accept rampant inequality and limits on sovereignty.

Thomas Friedman, whose influential 2005 book *The World Is Flat* was something of a paean to globalization, also began to address some problems with neoliberalism—especially environmental damage. While acknowledging that open markets and technological change are bringing unprecedented opportunities for the rise of new middle classes in China and India, in his 2008 book *Flat, Hot and Crowded* Friedman deals with the costs due to loss of biodiversity, climate change, and energy shortages. Sounding more like a mercantilist, he suggests that governments need to create incentives for technological innovation leading to widespread renewable energy.[26] In fact, in a chapter called "China for a Day (But Not for Two)," he muses that the United States should have a day of authoritarian government to force the country to adopt good energy policies and energy efficiency standards—and then revert back to democracy and free-market capitalism!

Another scholar who recognizes unsustainable consequences of global neoliberalism is David Colander, an economist at Middlebury College. He argues that in a global economy, the operation of what economists call the "law of one price" means that wages and prices in the world *in the long run* would become more equalized as technology and capital spread more production and outsourcing to other countries. As a result, the United States would gain less and less from trade, wages would inevitably go down, and growth would decline as the United States loses its comparative advantage in most industries. Moreover, Colander believes that trade and outsourcing—which have benefited the majority *in the short run*—will soon cause the United States "to enter into a period of long-run relative structural decline, which will be marked by economic malaise and a continued loss of good jobs."[27]

And even liberal development economists by the mid-2000s were starting to acknowledge the problems that neoliberalism either caused or seemed to be incapable of solving in developing countries. Former World Bank economist William Easterly criticizes Western institutions for promoting policies and doling out foreign aid that utterly failed to help the poorest countries get out of poverty. The UN, the World Bank, the IMF, and others were imposing market-based policies on countries that lacked the social and political institutions like good government, accountable leaders, and uncorrupt courts to actually make markets work properly.[28] Easterly argues that poor countries need to be allowed to develop their own institutions to support a market system, even using protectionism and relying on innovative NGOs.

From a different angle, former World Bank director of research Paul Collier defends globalization for creating huge opportunities for about four billion people in developing countries. Yet at the same time he criticizes it for leaving a billion people stuck in a poverty trap. This bottom billion are stymied by political, economic, and geographical problems that markets alone cannot overcome: civil war, natural resource abundance that undermines democracy, and being landlocked. Instead of more globalization as the way out, Collier advocates some decidedly state interventionist help: military intervention in some failed states to restore order, allowing temporary trade protection, and setting up new international charters to promote norms and standards (through international pressure) that help reformers in the poorest countries.[29]

Thus, by the mid-2000s, a unique confluence of economic liberal scholars and anti-globalization activists pointed to the mounting problems and unintended consequences of neoliberal-inspired globalization. They proposed different solutions but shared the idea that the global economy needed some kind of better regulation and governance. Without always explicitly saying so, they recognized the idea that markets need to be embedded in social and political institutions in order to have legitimacy and to resolve fundamental human problems. In the short run, unfettered global markets failed to help the world's poorest and were destroying the environment. In the long run, through outsourcing and environmental degradation, they might even undermine the prosperity of those developed countries that uncritically worshipped them. It would take the global financial crisis that started in 2007 to convince policy makers that neither more globalization nor incremental, piecemeal reforms to globalization were enough to save economies from the tsunami of contradictions that neoliberalism had created.

## The Financial Crisis: A Stake in the Heart or Just a Scratch?

(Note: This section focuses on the ideological debate between OELs and HILs, and not the specifics of the financial crisis itself. Before reading this section, instructors and students may want to read the more detailed coverage of the crisis in Chapter 8.)

While there had been many grumblings about neoliberal globalization, no single event in recent history has seemingly undermined economic liberalism as much as has the recent financial crisis, which produced the most severe economic collapse since the Great Depression. At one particular moment in time the public could hear the hammer drive the stake further into the gap between laissez-faire and market interventionist supporters when the shaken former Chairman of the Federal Reserve Alan Greenspan gave testimony before the U.S. Congress in October 2008. He admitted that his faith in the self-regulating nature of financial markets had been misplaced—that "those of us who have looked to the self-interest of lending institutions to protect shareholders' equity, myself included, are in a state of shocked disbelief."[30] Greenspan also admitted that he made a "big mistake" and blamed his state of incredulity on a "flaw in the (economic) model" that defines how the world works.

The deep global recession seemed to shake the faith of even some of the most ardent proponents of free market capitalism. Before the crisis, Greenspan himself regularly assured Congress that financial markets and new complex financial instruments (derivatives) were self-regulating, and that rational, profit-maximizing financial actors would take all necessary precautions to ensure that excessive risk-taking and insufficient due diligence (regarding mortgage lending) would not be tolerated (although in 1996 he had famously cautioned about "irrational exuberance" in the stock market).

In retrospect, it appears that many banks and investment firms in capital deficit countries such as the United States and in parts of the European Union were more than willing to *incur excessive economic risk*, and that many institutions, state officials, and individuals egged them on. In fact, in an environment of free-wheeling "wildcat" capitalism, the beauty of high-yielding types of investments was that the original investors *profited* handsomely from the original deals they made, while the *risks* associated with these types of instruments were spread out to new investors and mortgage holders.[31] These schemes actually worked and made purchasing an expensive asset seem reasonable and reinforcing, virtually institutionalizing excessive risk-taking.

Until the financial crisis, many U.S. and British officials felt that the state should have a laissez-faire outlook of limited regulation and essentially let the banks police themselves. Today, many state officials and experts the world over have suggested that they had no recourse but to bail out their banks and other financial institutions. Certainly, Presidents Bush and Obama have believed it; neither felt he could afford the possibility of being wrong because the political and economic stakes were so high. Their drastic measures were not so much to save greedy and unethical bank officials whose improprieties generated huge profits for their institutions, but to stabilize the financial system and correct the policies that threatened to destroy it. For the most part the debate about state regulation of major banks and other financial institutions remains centered on who should do the bailing out and how much money should be spent on it.

So how did this happen? Why did banks take on so much risk? How could the ideas associated with neoliberalism that had proved to be scientifically correct and so popular seem to go down in flames? Or have they? In this section, we examine some of the connections between neoliberal theories, globalization, and the financial crisis.

## An Outdated Economic Theory and Ideology

As noted earlier, Keynes was adamant that markets are prone to failure, with the Great Depression being a prime example of that reality. Since his time, many governments became better at dealing with smaller recessions that were considered a normal part of the business cycle. Using a variety of fiscal and monetary tools, they could tinker with supply and demand to right the economy through choppy waters. Milton Friedman and other monetarists associated with the so-called Chicago School emphasized that the nation's money supply was the key to inflation and that the market is a self-correcting mechanism. A companion theory, the Efficient Market Hypothesis, claimed that "at every moment, *shares price themselves* in the market through attracting the input of all information relevant to their value."[32]

Policies based on these outlooks about the validity of free markets complemented by weak state deregulation seemed to work for some time in the developed countries. Fed Chairman Greenspan criticized excessive state regulation of banks, and together with investors seemed to view recessions in the United States as a thing of the past. Furthermore, he and many banking institutions also seemed to regard investments by other nations in the United States—which helped finance U.S. spending and trade deficits—as evidence of the correctness of an ideology that had spread throughout the international economy.

In the crisis aftermath, the economic liberal news journal *The Economist* uncharacteristically accused the "dismal science" of economics of being "seduced by their models" that are, however, full of holes, especially when it comes to quantifying fundamentals such as preferences, technology, and resources that do not fit the real world. Essentially, these models assume an equilibrium in markets when in fact (as Keynes maintained) many markets exhibit uncertainties (or disequilibrium). The result has been a focus on mathematical and deductive methods that encourage the belief that risk can be carefully managed. While these ideas have sounded simplistic, they have also been confusing—and "policymakers often fall back on highest order principles and broadest presumptions."[33] According to *The Economist*, macroeconomists in academia and within central banks have been too preoccupied with fighting inflation and too cavalier about recurring asset bubbles in markets.

In effect, some argue that free market theorists have underestimated distortions in markets, overestimated markets' ability to self-adjust, and failed to account for the long-term problems resulting from markets' short-term incentives. They have also suggested that the financial crises could shake up the discipline of economics and force it to rethink some of its basic scientific assumptions. However, indications are that it has not very much yet. A recent study of economic curricula points to the entrenchment of rational-choice assumptions and a bias toward teaching the benefits of free markets.[34] Of course, many OEL-oriented faculty defend their discipline and offer alternative interpretations of market theory.[35]

What factors account for the continued popularity and tenacity of laissez-faire ideas outside academia? First, behavioral economist Robert Schiller suggests that "group think" among politicians and officials in the finance and business sectors is part of the reason for the entrenchment of theories that are slow to change. Similarly, economist James Galbraith suggests that laissez-faire is a "doctrine that serves as a legitimizing myth."[36] It outlines the rules and boundaries of the debate; clarifies those opposed to it; and restricts the flow of information and alternative ideas about it. Second, many believe that "letting the market decide" public policy is a correct and simple recommendation based on an "objective" study of the market. Laissez-faire policies have also been much easier to understand as opposed to the "messy" role of politics, social values, and civil society in determining the appropriate distribution of resources both inside and between countries.

Third, free market models have focused on generating economic growth instead of social stability and relative equality of income distribution. Ironically, the *promise* of greater wealth, faster growth, better jobs, and cheaper prices has been easier for the public (i.e., the masses) to buy into than the alternative of higher taxes for more social programs, slower growth for environmental sustainability, and collective sacrifice today to benefit future generations. Fourth, laissez-faire has been heavily supported by the wealthy, whom people tend to admire, who dominate the media, and who provide crucial financing to political parties throughout the industrialized democracies.

Fifth, Simon Johnson, the former Chief Economist for the IMF, has argued that over the years a financial oligarchy has developed in the United States composed of private firms and actors that call the shots in Washington in a way that serves their interests even at the expense of the public. They are an interconnected group of politically powerful people who move back and forth between Wall Street and Washington (and some university offices), "amassing a kind of cultural capital—a belief" that "large financial institutions and free-flowing capital markets were crucial to America's position in the world."[37]

## We Are All Keynesians Now (Again! At Least for a While?)

The financial crisis has brought to the fore a division between economic liberals. In this section, we contrast some of their recent arguments to demonstrate the richness of the debate, the different views about the role of the state and globalization, and the re-emergence of Keynesian thought among HILs. For most HILs, Keynes has been a key figure because he explained uncertainty—exclusive of rational expectations—and justified efforts to manage the economy in such a way as to serve the broader interest of society instead of the wealthy. The crisis has led HILs to assert that states must act to save the financial system and even capitalism itself. Interestingly, some OELs agree. For example, in a recent *Financial Times* piece titled "The Seeds of Its Own Destruction," the predictable OEL Martin Wolf acknowledges that "the era of financial liberalization has ended and that the state can be expected to play a bigger role in rescuing banks and adopting other interventionist measures."[38]

A few of the most often-discussed HIL proposals (discussed in more detail in Chapter 8) are as follows:

- Spend more to grow the economy, without worrying too much about inflation. It is more important to create jobs
- Invest more in new technology for energy and transportation, infrastructure, education, and health care
- Impose tougher regulations on banks related to derivatives, deposit requirements, pay, and bonuses
- Break up big banks to increase competition
- Better manage globalization, but without stopping it

Most HILs agree on the need to increase government spending and expand the powers of existing regulatory institutions at the national and international levels. As Keynes would suggest, the financial system requires a sophisticated and effective regulatory and legal framework that only the state can provide—a state strong enough to enforce those laws but without stifling the profit motive, economic freedom, and individual liberty.

Most HILs are *not* opposed to globalization per se, but would like to see policies and programs that distribute the wealth it produces to the masses in industrialized nations and poorer people in developing nations. They recognize the need to reform institutions like the World Bank, the IMF, and the WTO to get away from a "one-size-fits-all mentality" of how economies should be run and of what rules countries have to follow. Related to this is a new emphasis on creating "policy space" for developing countries (at least in the short run) to be more protectionist, restrict capital flows somewhat, and have more lax rules on intellectual property rights. Presumably, this will allow them to grow faster and buffer them somewhat from global instabilities in currencies, investment flows, and commodity prices. HILs note that China and India have fared much better during the financial crisis precisely because these two have *not* fully adopted neoliberalism.

HILs also believe that the developed countries must actively help developing countries in ways they have not before. They emphasize that developed countries need to drop their remaining protectionist barriers to key LDC exports like textiles and agricultural goods and stop subsidizing their own industries. They need to allow more immigration from poorer countries. It would also be in their interest to forgive excessive debt held by poorer countries and increase foreign aid massively. HILs favor inducing countries to adopt more free market reform and democracy by offering them assistance rather than pressuring them.

Many HILs are open to the possibility of creating a different economy and social system, something that shifts the state–market formula to the left—akin to social democracies in Western Europe (see the "Ordoliberalism" box below). A number of HIL scholars have found that Nordic countries and other nations that have some of the highest openness to the international economy (measured by the ratio of trade to GDP) also have some of the highest public expenditures on social programs (measured by the ratio of spending to GDP). This suggests, contrary to OELs, that high government spending is compatible with being open to and benefiting from global market participation. HILs also tend to accept—and even justify—the maintenance of different models of national capitalism within a broader global free market economy. Coordination between these different national systems of capitalism is more important than harmonizing all of their institutions and policies. In other words, when it comes to designing global institutions and rules, Dani Rodrik stresses the need for maintaining "escape clauses" and "opt-outs" so that individual countries can benefit from globalization in a way that is most consistent with their political realities, cultural needs, and resource constraints.[39]

## ORDOLIBERALISM AND THE SOCIAL MARKET ECONOMY

Economic liberalism had been largely discredited in Europe by the 1920s. Economic liberalism, particularly in Germany's post–World War I Weimar Republic, had come to be associated with economic chaos, political corruption, and the exploitation of the working class.[a] In response to this perception and to Hitler's consequent rise to power, a small group of academics at Freiburg University developed a new conception of liberalism they called *ordoliberalism*. Walter Eucken (1891–1950), Franz Böhm (1895–1977), and Hans Grossman-Doerth (1894–1944) founded this school of thought. Ordoliberals believe that the failings of liberalism resulted from the failure of nineteenth-and twentieth-century *laissez-faire* policy makers to appreciate Adam Smith's insight that the market is embedded in legal and political systems.

Ordoliberal thought reflects the humanist values of classical liberalism, including the protection of human dignity and personal freedom. Ordoliberals espouse the classical liberal notions that private decision making should guide resource allocation, that competition is the source of economic well-being, and that economic and political freedom are inextricable. Like classical liberals, they also believe that individuals must be protected from excessive state power and that political power should be dispersed through democratic processes that maximize participation in public decision making. Ordoliberals also emphasize that individual freedoms must be protected from private power in the form of monopoly control of markets and influence used to create special privileges that rig markets in favor of those dominant firms.

Ordoliberals believe that the market process will support and promote liberal values only if appropriate rules governing the market process (property law, contract law, trade law, competition policy, etc.) are established by the state. *Ordo*, from the Latin, means "order." The rules governing the market process should be "constitutional" rules immune from political manipulation that reflect the shared liberal values of society. With such a framework in place, the market process will reinforce the economic and political freedoms so central to the liberal conception of the good society. With such a framework in place, the efforts of powerful firms to subvert the market process (via price controls, import restrictions, subsidies, restrictive licenses, etc.) will be deemed "unconstitutional." Politicians will be in a strong position to resist the special pleadings of powerful interest groups, and the power of the state in general to influence market outcomes will be severely restricted. A privilege-free economy will be the highly desirable result.

Ordoliberal thought has had a profound influence on economic and political policy in the European Union. Current European competition policy clearly incorporates ordoliberal principles. It severely restricts the behavior of dominant firms—particularly, any practices that might inhibit the entry of small- or medium-sized rivals. By maintaining open markets, European competition authorities hope to foster economic freedom in the form of freedom of entry, thereby enhancing economic opportunity, promoting competition, and diffusing economic and political power. Microsoft's antitrust problems in Europe can be better understood in this light.[b]

Ordoliberalism does have an inherent ethical stance. Market outcomes generated within an appropriate legal and political framework are nondiscriminating, privilege-free outcomes and are likely to be just outcomes.[c] Ordoliberals recognize, however, that some income redistribution will likely be called for, given the limited productivity of some individuals—often due to circumstances beyond their control.

Other German intellectuals, principally Alfred Müller-Armack (1901–1978), accepted key ordoliberal principles but challenged the ordoliberal notion that market outcomes are just outcomes. Müller-Armack argued that supplemental "social" policies are necessary to ensure that market outcomes will indeed be consistent with a "good" society. Further, these supplementary rules might indeed affect specific market outcomes so as to privilege certain segments of society. Müller-Armack is credited with developing the basis of the "social" market economy that characterizes many modern European states.[d]

### References

[a]The discussion of ordoliberalism in this and the following paragraphs is based largely on David J. Gerber, "Constitutionalizing the Economy: German Neo-Liberalism, Competition Policy and the 'New' Europe," *The American Journal of Comparative Law, 42* (1994), pp. 25–88.
[b]"Microsoft on Trial," *The Economist*, April 28, 2006, www.economist.com/agenda/displaystory.cfm?story_id=E1_GRSDSRP.
[c]Victor J. Vanberg, "The Freiburg School: Walter Eucken and Ordoliberalism," Walter Eucken Institute, Freiburg Discussion Papers on Constitutional Economics, November 2004, p. 2.
[d]Ibid.

As HILs have adopted a more nuanced set of assumptions about global state–market relations, OELs have been less accepting of this foray back into Keynesianism. As we write, it appears that the Obama administration has sided more with HILs than OELs by trying to adopt more regulations so that the system cannot "go back to the way it was." Why? It may be that the president fears a backlash in the next election if he does nothing to reform Wall Street. A number of Democratic lawmakers share his more interventionist views. However, many powerful Congress people and members of the financial sector share the outlook of OELs. Alex Berenson goes even deeper to suggest that Americans are by nature "basically conservative people" who distrust the state, but who also have an "appetite for risk."[40] While Europeans might prefer social democracy, an oligarchy of wealthy elites in the United States prefers a wilder version of capitalism.[41] Also distasteful to most Americans are the new crop of populist-socialist societies in Venezuela, Bolivia, Chile, and Ecuador that have made a wider distribution of goods and services to the masses one of their key political objectives.

In light of these factors and others, OELs prefer to keep the main laissez-faire characteristics of the free market, subject to a few, more passive reforms. They propose to

- limit government support for banks, infrastructure projects, and social welfare programs
- decrease regulation of many parts of the economy

- cut taxes of the wealthy and middle class to stimulate economic growth
- foster *more* globalization, which is good for the United States and the world.

When it comes to the financial crisis, many OELs argue that it was the fault of government, not banks. The Federal Reserve created the housing bubble beginning in 2001 by dropping interest rates that decreased the cost of borrowing. This put more money into the hands of homebuyers who could not afford payments in the long run. OELs also argue that the crisis was an exceptional event in the history of capitalism, one that occurs very infrequently—due more to flaws in human nature than flaws in capitalism itself.

Globalization has also proved to be a good thing, given the growth it produced in the industrialized states and the number of people it has lifted out of poverty in developing nations. OELs would like to see the United States push for a resumption of the Doha Round trade negotiations to lower more trade barriers in agriculture, services, and government procurement. They also believe that the United States needs to lower its out-of-control budget deficit, with the goal of reducing its trade deficit and increasing national savings. They fear that big stimulus spending by world governments will generate inflation and more debt future generations will have to pay off (by consuming less). In addition, OELs want governments to rapidly deleverage the commitments they have made to banks and industries, returning bailed out companies and assets to private control.

At this point in time, most experts and policy officials tend to agree that there is no clear set of policies that can solve the financial crisis in the near future. Capitalism and its dominant economic liberal foundation are likely to continue to be intellectually and politically challenged. Despite their problems, nothing has so far emerged to replace them, as many fear that the alternatives are potentially worse. Many of the more successful developing countries such as China, India, and Brazil remain sanguine about the benefits of "free market" capitalism. It remains to be seen if these states can effectively manage and sustain state-market-society relations in ways that benefit their societies.

# CONCLUSION

## Economic Liberalism Today

This chapter has explained how the ideas and values associated with the economic liberal version of liberalism have changed in recent history to reflect major historical, political, economic, and social developments. Political economists Smith, Ricardo, Mill, Keynes, Hayek, Milton, and others have debated the relationship of the state to the economy, and today there is an emerging split between orthodox and heterodox liberals when it comes to this issue.

Although capitalism took centuries to unfold, it has unleashed market forces that both reflect and influence consumers' demand for certain items along with how these items are produced. Capitalism has spread over large parts of the world. Countries on every continent have introduced market-oriented reforms in pursuit of a better life for their citizens. The free-trade paradigm at the heart of globalization profoundly shapes global production and distribution.

During the Great Depression, a split emerged between those HILs who supported a positive role for the state in the economy and those OELs who saw the state's role in the economy and society as decidedly negative. In the 1980s, the chasm widened even more. Globalization and the current financial crisis have led to serious criticisms of neoliberal ideals and neoliberal faith in markets. Many HILs maintain that some state intervention serves the public interest, especially when it protects social groups and countries from the negative effects of the seemingly Darwinian global economy. Despite their differences, both orthodox and heterodox liberal perspectives seek to answer the same two fundamental questions: What values should markets serve, and whose interests should they promote?

In Chapters 3 and 4, we will explain two other IPE perspectives—mercantilism and structuralism—and present some of the many explanations they offer for these same sorts of theoretical issues and practical dilemmas.

## KEY TERMS

economic liberalism   29
heterodox interventionist
    liberals (HILs)   29
orthodox economic liberals
    (OELs)   29
rent-seeking   34
Corn Laws   35

positive-sum game   37
zero-sum game   37
Keynesian theory   38
paradox of thrift   39
Keynesianism   39
Keynesian compromise   40
embedded liberalism   41

hegemonic stability
    theory   41
hegemon   41
public goods   41
neoliberalism   42
Reaganomics   43

## DISCUSSION QUESTIONS

1. Explain Adam Smith's concept of the "invisible hand." What roles do self-interest and competition play in this concept?
2. Now that you have read the chapter, how would you characterize the view of Adam Smith? Is he the economic liberal many people assume he is? Write a five-sentence paragraph summing up his main outlook about political economy.
3. Explain how the Corn Laws debate in nineteenth-century Britain illustrates the conflict between mercantilist and economic liberal views of international trade. Which side of the debate do you favor? Explain.
4. John Stuart Mill and John Maynard Keynes thought that government could play a positive role in correcting problems in the market. Discuss the specific types of "market failures" that Mill and Keynes perceived and the types of government actions they advocated.
5. Ronald Reagan and Margaret Thatcher are often cited for their support of neoliberal ideas and policies. Summarize those ideas and policies and discuss how they differ from those of their economic liberal predecessors. Finally, explain why you think they are still popular today. Or are they?
6. Explain how OELs and HILs are similar and different in terms of values, ideas, and policies. Which do you favor? Explain.
7. Based on what you know about the current financial crisis, do you agree with the suggestion that the crisis has seriously undermined economic liberal ideas and policies? Explain.

## SUGGESTED READINGS

Jagdish Bhagwati. *In Defense of Globalization.* Oxford: Oxford University Press, 2005.

Thomas L. Friedman. *The World Is Flat: A Brief History of the Twenty-First Century.* New York: Farrar, Straus and Girous, 2005.

Robert Skidelsky. *Keynes: The Return of the Master.* New York: Public Affairs, 2009.

Dani Rodrik. *One Economics, Many Recipes: Globalization, Institutions, and Economic Growth.* Princeton, NJ: Princeton University Press, 2007.

Joseph Stiglitz. *Making Globalization Work.* New York: W. W. Norton, 2006.

## NOTES

1. Ross Singleton has been the chief architect of this chapter since the first edition of the text. Richard Anderson-Connolly also worked on this edition of the chapter.

2. In this book we use the term *neoconservatives* or "neocons" to refer to members of the George W. Bush administration (and its supporters) who had a decidedly unilateral outlook about the world and U.S. power and capabilities to manage it (see Chapter 9).

3. Ralf Dahrendorf, "Liberalism," in John Eatwell, Murray Milgate, and Peter Newman, eds., *The Invisible Hand: The New Palgrave* (New York: W. W. Norton, 1989), p. 183.

4. Adam Smith, *The Wealth of Nations* (New York: The Modern Library, 1937), p. 400.

5. See Charles Lindblom, *The Market System* (New Haven, CT: Yale University Press, 2001).

6. Karl Polanyi, *The Great Transformation: The Political and Economic Origins of Our Time* (Boston, MA: Beacon Press, 1944).

7. See Smith, *The Wealth of Nations*, p. 114.

8. Ibid., p. 117.

9. Cited in David Leonhardt, "Theory and Morality in the New Economy," *The New York Times Book Review*, August 23, 2009.

10. See Jerry Mueller, *The Mind and the Market: Capitalism in Western Thought* (New York: Anchor Books, 2002), p. 69.

11. Cited in ibid., p 64.

12. Michael W. Doyle, *The Ways of War and Peace* (New York: W. W. Norton, 1997), p. 207.

13. Smith, *The Wealth of Nations*, p. 401.

14. Ibid., p. 410.

15. David Ricardo, *The Principles of Political Economy and Taxation* (London: Dent, 1973), p. 81.

16. Alan Ryan, "John Stuart Mill," in Eatwell et al., eds., *The Invisible Hand*, p. 201.

17. Ibid., p. 208.

18. John Maynard Keynes, "The End of Laissez-Faire," in *Essays in Persuasion* (New York: W.W. Norton, 1963), p. 312.

19. Ibid., pp. 317–318.

20. Ibid., p. 321.

21. U.S. economist Charles Kindleberger is generally credited as the originator of the hegemonic stability theory. See his *Money and Power: The Economics of International Politics and the Politics of International Economics* (New York: Basic Books, 1970).

22. Friedrich Hayek, *The Road to Serfdom* (Chicago, IL: University of Chicago Press, 1944), pp. 127–128.

23. Milton Friedman, *Capitalism and Freedom* (Chicago, IL: University of Chicago Press, 1962), p. 2. Italics added.

24. See Joseph Stiglitz, *Globalization and Its Discontents* (New York: W. W. Norton, 2002).

25. Dani Rodrik, "Feasible Globalizations," in Michael Weinstein, ed., *Globalization: What's New?* (New York: Columbia University Press, 2005), p. 197.

26. Thomas L. Friedman, *Hot, Flat, and Crowded: Why We Need a Green Revolution—And How It Can Renew America* (New York: Farrar, Straus and Giroux, 2008).

27. David Colander, "The Long Run Consequences of Outsourcing," *Challenge*, 48, 1 (January/February 2005), p. 94.

28. William Easterly, *The White Man's Burden: Why the West's Efforts to Aid the Rest Have Done So Much Ill and So Little Good* (New York: Penguin Press, 2006).

29. Paul Collier, *The Bottom Billion: Why the Poorest Countries Are Failing and What Can Be Done about It* (Oxford: Oxford University Press, 2007).

30. "Greenspan Concedes Error on Regulation," *The New York Times*, B1, October 24, 2008.

31. Robert J. Shiller, *The Subprime Solution: How Today's Global Financial Crisis Happened, and What to Do about It* (Princeton, NJ: Princeton University Press, 2008).

32. See Kevin Phillips, *Bad Money: Reckless Finance, Failed Politics, and the Global Crisis of American Capitalism* (New York: Viking, 2008), p. 74. Emphasis added.

33. See "The Other-Worldly Philosophers," *The Economist*, July 18, 2009, p. 66.

34. See Patricia Cohen, "Ivory Tower Unswayed by Crashing Economy," *New York Times*, March 4, 2009.

35. See Robert Lucas, "In Defense of the Dismal Science," *The Economist*, August 28, 2009.

36. James K. Galbraith, *The Predator State: How the Conservatives Abandoned the Free Market and Why Liberals Should Too* (New York: The Free Press, 2008), p. xi.

37. Simon Johnson, "The Quiet Coup," *The Atlantic*, May 2008.

38. Martin Wolf, "Seeds of Its Own Destruction," *Financial Times*, March 8, 2009.

39. Dani Rodrik, *One Economics, Many Recipes: Globalization, Institutions, and Economic Growth* (Princeton, NJ: Princeton University Press, 2007).

40. See Alex Berenson, "How Free Should a Free Market Be?" *New York Times*, October 5, 2008.

41. See Robert Wade, "The Global Slump: Deeper Causes and Harder Lessons," *Challenge, 52* (September–October 2009), pp. 5–24.

# Wealth and Power: The Mercantilist Perspective

The state in action.

Jacob Silberberg

*Our economic rights are leaking away. . . . If we want to recover these rights . . . we must quickly employ state power to promote industry, use machinery in production, give employment to the workers of the nation. . . .*[1]

Sun Yat-sen, 1920

In Chapter 2, we noted how the financial crisis has generated a shift in outlook by many economic liberal state officials and experts toward the view that the state *must* play a bigger role in regulating banks, speculators, and financial markets in general. Many officials worry that in the highly integrated global economy, the financial crisis threatens their state's national security by undermining their ability to secure themselves physically and psychologically against a variety of political and economic threats. Many state officials are also concerned about their capacity to deal with many of the unacceptable political and social costs of the crisis such as unemployment, the loss of health care, and damage to the environment.

**Mercantilism** is the oldest and psychologically most deeply embedded of the three IPE perspectives. It accounts for one of the basic compulsions of all people and nation-states: to create and sustain wealth and power in order to preserve and protect the nation's security and independence from any number of real and imagined threats. Historically, **classical mercantilism** connoted efforts by states to promote exports and limit imports, thereby generating trade surpluses that would enhance state wealth and power while protecting certain groups within society.

**Realism** is closely related to mercantilism in that it also emphasizes state efforts to achieve security (which are explored in more detail in Chapter 9). While mercantilists usually focus on economic threats to a state, realists emphasize a wider variety of physical threats—and encourage the use of both military and economic instruments to defend the state or deter military attacks on it. Of course, in today's interconnected and globalized international political economy, it gets harder all the time to separate economic from military threats to nation-states. Today, **neomercantilism** accounts for a more complex world marked by intensive interdependence and globalization where states use a wider variety of instruments—especially economic ones—to protect their societies.

In this chapter, we explore many of the political-philosophical ideas associated with classical mercantilism, realism, and neomercantilism. The chapter follows a chronology that covers how and why mercantilist ideas evolved from the sixteenth century until today. We then discuss a number of neomercantilist policies related to the debate about how much the state should or should not interfere in markets in the face of globalization and the recent financial crisis.

We stress five theses in this chapter. First, historically, mercantilism is rooted in the desire for protection by both the individual and the state. Second, the history of mercantilism demonstrates that states have been and will always be compelled to regulate markets, and that there are no beneficial effects of markets without the state's willingness to allow, sustain, and manage them. Third, states that pursue economic liberal objectives that include opening markets and promoting free trade do so when those objectives coincide with state national interests. Fourth, paradoxically, globalization has *not* reduced the compulsion of states to protect themselves as economic liberals suggested it would. Rather, globalization has actually further *entrenched* national insecurities due to the increased tensions and conflicts it generates. Finally, mercantilists usually argue that states are finding it hard to cooperate with one another and with other global actors to solve problems such as the recent financial crisis.

# MERCANTILISM AS HISTORY AND PHILOSOPHY

The history of mercantilism varies a good deal from that of economic liberal history (see Chapter 2). The classical mercantilist period of history is inextricably linked to the rise of the modern nation-state in Europe during the sixteenth through nineteenth centuries. During this period in Western Europe, the idea of state building and intervention in the economy for the sake of making the nation-state secure dominated political-economic thought. A **nation** is a collection of people who, on the basis of ethnic background, language, and history—or some other set of factors—define themselves as members of an extended political community.[2] The **state** is viewed as a legal entity, theoretically free from interference by other nations, which monopolizes the means of physical force in its society and exercises **sovereignty** (final political authority) over the people of a well-defined territory.[3] The political philosophy of mercantilism suggested why and how nation-states could generate the wealth and power needed to protect their societies and evolving economies from external threats.

The economic historian Charles Tilly emphasizes that war was the primary factor that motivated monarchs and other officials to organize their societies and adopt measures that would help secure the nation. Around the fifteenth century, small fiefdoms were compelled to form larger state units in order to be better able to protect themselves against other states.[4] Warrior-kings created bureaucratic agencies that performed a variety of functions related to keeping a budget, using money, and collecting taxes.[5] To control the nobles who often performed these functions in different locales, kings declared themselves the manifestation of state authority (what Louis XIV meant when he said: *le stat c'est moi*—I am the state). Many kings conceded absolute property rights and limits on their power to nobles in return for their support in staffing the king's armies and assessing and collecting taxes. Some historians suggest that these agreements eventually led to the creation of "people parliaments," which were the genesis of modern democracy and constitutionalism when they secured more rights for peasants.

Over the next century, what we commonly recognize as nation-states emerged, albeit in a very uneven fashion. France, for instance, was already a "nation-state" in the fifteenth century, soon to be followed by England, Holland, Spain, and Sweden. (Germany and Italy would not be consolidated into national entities until later in the nineteenth century.) The Cambridge economist Ha-Joon Chang explores some of the many ways that the Tudor monarchs Henry VII and Elizabeth I pursued what today we would call an **industrial policy** (a state-planned strategy to promote certain businesses).[6] These measures include the land enclosure acts (1760–1820), monopoly rights for certain businesses, and industrial espionage. Henry VII used tariffs and export subsidies in support of Britain's effort to capture control of the woolen industry from Holland. He sent royal missions to locate suitable places in England to manufacture woolen goods. For the next 100 years, England employed an import substitution policy (i.e., it allowed no woolen imports in order to promote local production—see Chapter 11) to compete with and intentionally ruin woolen manufacturing in the Low Countries (Belgium and the Netherlands).[7]

The practice of mercantilism gained a full head of steam after the Thirty Years War ended in 1648. While gradually states came to be regarded as sovereign over the people within their territories, political authority became centralized in (national) state officials. Increased demands for security led to more efforts to extract income and resources from towns and cities. While agriculture had constituted the dominant source of income a century earlier, it was no longer enough. Monarchs and state officials increasingly looked to merchants and their trade as a much larger source of income for state treasuries. To promote economic growth, larger state bureaucracies set about connecting local and regional markets, establishing common currencies and weights, keeping records, and promoting infrastructural development. As a consequence, merchants acquired more property rights and rose to a higher social position, while increasing their investment in the economy.

Most accounts of the period suggest that the threat of war and violence marked the history of European states at the time. In the nascent European state system, no state could be counted on to guarantee the security of others, therefore each state could look only to itself and its own wealth and power to protect its domain. These situations often resulted in a **security dilemma** whereby other states were easily threatened by the first state's efforts to increase its war-making capabilities. State officials tended to have a **zero-sum** outlook about state power whereby *absolute gains by one state meant absolute losses by another*. Territorial defense was always considered the state's first priority because prosperity and peace were useless if the nation was not protected from foreign invaders or internal groups who might overthrow the state. But because it was expensive to raise, equip, and maintain armies and navies, wealth also came to be regarded as one of the essential ingredients for acheiving and preserving national security.

To many historians, mercantilism is also synonymous with the first wave of exploration and imperialism from 1648 to the end of the Napoleonic Wars in 1815. The search for gold and silver bullion by a variety of adventurers and conquerors helped fill state coffers. **Colonialism,** the occupation of another territory or state, backed by military power, was another important instrument states used to control trade and generate wealth and power. Colonies served as exclusive markets for the goods of the mother country and as sources of raw materials and cheap labor. The growing merchant class also supported a strong state that would protect its interests, and in return the state sanctioned monopolistic merchant control over certain industries that profited both merchants and the state via commercial trade. Many states employed subsidies to generate exports and promote the development of their colonial empires. The Dutch were quite successful, followed by the British who also created charter companies and supported commerce in urban centers where new technologies were employed to produce items to market and trade.

Economic historians Kenneth Pomeranz and Steven Topik have studied how the colonial powers beginning in the 1400s used these mercantilist policies to move up the global hierarchy.[8] They argue that the dominant powers regularly used violence and occupation to harness advantages for their own traders and government-chartered companies in the global market. Slavery was integral to their strategies of building cheap labor forces to extract raw materials like cotton, sugar, and tobacco from the New World. Britain forced China to open itself to opium exports from India so that Britain could balance its trade deficit with India. European powers competed with each other to control access to raw materials like cocoa, rubber, tea, and coffee, and they deliberately spread production of these commodities to areas under their control and ability to tax. For commercial gain and control of territory, they essentially committed genocide against indigenous peoples in the Americas and the Belgian Congo. In a rebuke of classical liberals who predicted that international commerce would lead to peace and prosperity, they state, "This rosy picture of the healthy effects of the spread of the market economy unfortunately hides the historic foundation of violence upon which it was built and the continuing use of force that persistently underlay it, particularly in the non-European world."[9] In other words, during the historical accumulation and redistribution of wealth, "Bloody hands and the invisible hand often worked in concert; in fact, they were often attached to the same body."[10]

Rather than emphasizing economic growth only through trade and colonialism, Prime Minister Walpole (1721–1742) continued his efforts to promote England's woolen industry as another source of revenue. The British sheep and textile industries increased the profitability of land and generated jobs along with the consumption of taxable goods. To protect British manufacturing, the government raised tariffs on competitive goods and subsidized exports. Competitive imports into Great Britain from its colonies were banned, including cloth from India that was superior to that of the British, which destroyed Irish mills and delayed the emergence of the U.S. textile industry. All of these efforts were directed at enhancing state wealth and power in an increasingly economically competitive and politically hostile environment. Without these state protectionist measures, Great Britain would not have been able to support its growing economic wealth and imperial power.

## The Economic Liberal Challenge to Mercantilism

Between the 1840s and 1870s, economic liberal ideas attributed to Adam Smith and David Ricardo grew in popularity in Great Britain and gradually replaced mercantilism as the cornerstone of its political-economic outlook. Even then many policy makers accepted the idea that markets were self-adjusting and that the role of the state should be *laissez-faire*—to stay out of the market. What accounts for the rise of these economic liberal ideas (see Chapter 2) that challenged mercantilism?

Adam Smith's *The Wealth of Nations* was published in 1776, and it attacked mercantilism for restricting economic competition that led to production inefficiencies. Yet, it wasn't until the end of the Napoleonic Wars in 1815, when Great Britain became the most efficient producer of manufactured goods, that officials began to press for free trade. England finally adopted a free-trade policy in 1840 but did not completely eliminate its trade tariffs until 1860. A variety of accounts suggest that Great Britain adopted a free-trade policy only as more officials and thinkers made the case that free trade was better for Great Britain than mercantilism (see the box: "Britain's Corn Laws" in Chapter 2). Following on the heels of Smith, the famous businessman and Member of Parliament (MP) David Ricardo helped popularize the idea of **comparative advantage**—that even when a country can produce a variety of goods more efficiently than other countries, it should specialize in producing only a select number of items and trade with other countries for the other goods it needs.

Despite his reputation, Smith was not the doctrinaire defender of free enterprise as most of his followers presume. He did champion individual (consumer) liberty and worried that the state could mess up an economy, but he also had a bit of a protectionist side. He supported taxes on luxury carriages, alcohol, sugar, and tobacco. As many historians note, he favored the Navigation Acts that required that only English ships could transport goods between Great Britain and its colonial possessions. Both Smith and Ricardo also viewed free trade as a policy that would help manufacturers market woolen and other British products throughout the world. Ricardo himself accepted exceptions to free trade "within narrow limits" until they were no longer necessary.

Clearly, free trade was *not* an ideological end in itself. The noted economic historian Karl Polanyi argues that there is strong historical evidence that, contrary to the precepts of economic liberalism, economically liberal states *themselves* merely used free-trade policy as another tool to protect and support their own industries, while seeking to gain a competitive advantage over other states.[11] Theories of comparative advantage and free trade would have others specialize in growing and selling wheat to Great Britain, while buying expensive British manufactured goods. Britain also did not oppose the use of trade tariffs to help British companies acquire and sustain technological leads over others, especially in the case of textile manufacturing.[12] Interestingly, in the face of rising European and American competition by the late 1870s, wealthy British financiers and manufacturers joined working class groups in a growing **countermovement** *against* open market policies and in favor of market regulation and trade protection. A mercantilist historical outlook also emphasizes that as universal suffrage (the right to vote) spread in the late nineteenth century, the state came under pressure to provide more benefits to society.

Most historians note that with renewed emphasis on mercantilism after 1870, **economic nationalism** (people's strong sense of identification with and loyalty to their nation-state) became even more entrenched in interstate relations and helped generate a second wave of imperialism at the end of the century. Germany, Japan, and Italy arrived on the scene and began acquiring their own colonies. According to Polanyi, the retreat from economic liberalism in Great Britain significantly weakened the European balance of power system, which would be replaced by a bipolar structure that led to World War I in 1914.

## Meanwhile on the Other Side of the Atlantic: Overlooked Protectionism in U.S. History

In the nineteenth century, emerging powers such as the United States and the German principalities protected themselves from what they perceived as Britain's aggressive economic liberal policies. Two important examples of contributions to mercantilist thought at the time came from the American **Alexander Hamilton** (1755–1804) and the German Friedrich List (1789–1846). In his *Report on the Subject of Manufactures* to the first Congress, Hamilton argued (in opposition to the ideas of Thomas Jefferson) that specialization in agricultural production was not in the best interest of the United States. Specializing in farming would not make the United States either economically or militarily powerful enough to compete with potential enemies, let alone compete with Britain's ability to manufacture a variety of industrial goods and services the new nation needed. In terms that are familiar even today, Hamilton argued for the protection of the United States' **infant industries** and a strong role for the state in promoting its own domestic industries.[13] He also favored export subsidies to make U.S. goods more competitive abroad and to offset subsidies granted by foreign states. Hamilton wrote:

> It is well known . . . that certain nations grant bounties [subsidies] on the exportation of particular commodities, to enable their own workmen to undersell and supplant all competitors in the countries to which those commodities are sent. Hence the undertakers of a new manufacture have to contend not only with the natural disadvantages of a new undertaking, but with the gratuities and remunerations which other governments bestow. To be enabled to contend with success, it is evident that the interference and aid of government are indispensable.[14]

The nineteenth-century German political economist **Friedrich List** was an even more vigorous proponent of mercantilist policies. Exiled from his home—ironically for his radical free-trade views—List came to the United States in 1825 and witnessed firsthand the results of Hamilton's economic nationalist policies. The United States was building itself up and achieving independence and security. In his essay "The Theory of the Powers of Production and the Theory of Values," he argued that "*the power of producing* [is] *infinitely more important than wealth itself*."[15] In other words, it is more important to invest in the future ability to produce more than to consume the fruits of today's prosperity.

For List, the manufacturing of industrial goods along with investment in education and the development of new technology was more important than investment in agriculture alone. The production of a wide variety of goods and services was the most desirable basis for national wealth and power. List wrote that manufacturing and other occupations "develop and bring into action an incomparably greater variety and higher type of mental qualities and abilities than agriculture" and that "manufactures are at once the offspring, and at the same time the supporters and the nurses, of science and the arts."[16]

The writings of Hamilton and List incorporated a spirit of patriotic economic nationalism that was very much a reaction to Great Britain's economic liberal ideas and free-trade policies. List argued that these policies did not equally benefit exporters and importers; because British technology was more advanced and its labor more efficient than European labor, its goods were more attractive to the Europeans than those produced locally. List argued that in a "cosmopolitan" world there could be no free trade until states could compete with one another on an *equal footing*. To the extent that Great Britain opposed mercantilist policies, it was "kicking away the ladder" for other countries, preventing them from climbing the ladder of development with the same policies Great Britain itself had used to achieve its wealth and power. He recommended that until the United States and Europe had "caught up" with Great Britain, they had to protect their "infant" industries as a way to "level the playing field" with the British. He also suggested that Prussian and German city-states would benefit by forming a union (which they did some forty years later), whose combined economic and military might would be able to withstand Britain's power. Ironically, one of the motives of countries that formed the European Economic Community after World War II was to be able to better compete with the United States and Japan.

During the nineteenth century, the U.S. government encouraged people to go west, work hard, and establish property rights. Ideas of Manifest Destiny and economic expansion sanctioned by God left a big impression on the emerging national psyche. During the War of 1812, the U.S. Congress doubled tariffs, which became part of a U.S. economic development plan until World War II. From 1800 to 1848, a series of land treaties, wars, and negotiations expanded the territory of the United States to incorporate the Louisiana Territory, Florida, Oregon, Texas, and the Mexican concession. President Lincoln developed a canal system and raised tariffs to 50 percent, where they remained until World War I. After the Civil War, the Homestead Act of 1862 granted 160 acres to anyone who claimed and farmed it for five years. The army cleared (ethnically cleansed) the west of native Indian tribes. Congress subsidized railroads along with manufacturing, coal, iron, steel, banking, and real estate. While the Army Corps of Engineers helped build the country's infrastructure, a lenient immigration policy encouraged and rewarded mainly white settlers. All of these government-funded developments contributed to economic prosperity and helped the United States arrive on the world scene as a major economic power by the 1880s.[17]

In the area of trade policy, in 1913 Congress reduced trade tariffs, but it raised them back up to 37 percent by 1925 for manufactured goods, helping the United States become the fastest growing country in the world. Other countries were also growing behind tariff walls: Germany, Austria, Sweden, and France. At the onset of the Great Depression, the Smoot–Hawley Tariff Act raised average U.S. tariff rates to a record high of 48 percent. As many nations adopted similar policies to protect and promote their industries, it was inevitable that national interests would clash with "beggar-thy-neighbor" behavior. Many blame the Smoot–Hawley tariffs for contributing to the Great Depression and then World War II. However, according to Ha-Joon Chang, trade tariffs were not a radical departure from history. In the United States and many other countries, markets were never more than partially open, and trade was really not all that free.[18]

## Keynes, the Great Depression, and the Postwar Order

Just as many today blame unregulated market forces, greed, and stupidity for causing the 2007 global financial crisis, many people in 1929 blamed banks and speculators for the stock market crash, which subsequently increased unemployment and poverty in many parts of the world. Many lost faith and confidence in market capitalism, which led to increasing support for Fascism and Nazism. Germany experienced rampant unemployment, which increased economic nationalism and the tendency of officials to see others as evil.[19] Many revolutionary movements emerged in Europe, Latin America, and Asia.

Recall from Chapter 2 that in the 1930s the ideas of John Maynard Keynes gained in popularity because of pressure on the state to respond to more voters and higher expectations, rendering the *laissez-faire* ideology no longer politically acceptable. Keynes offered more positive ideas about how the industrialized nations could restart their economies and deal with the social effects of the depression. Keynes believed that not only do markets sometimes fail but also that recessions and depressions can last a long time. To diffuse the tendency of people to support authoritarian leaders, Keynes argued that states should step in and prime the pump of the national economy to stimulate employment, deal with the negative social effects of the depression, and restore confidence in the capitalist system.

After World War II, Keynes's ideas also substantially shaped the design and role of the three Bretton Woods institutions—the GATT, the IMF, and the World Bank. Economic liberals tend to argue that after the war, under the leadership of the United States and in cooperation with its World War II allies (minus the Soviet Union and China), a new international political-economic order promoted a variety of economic liberal objectives. The GATT brought down trade barriers. (Interestingly, Keynes himself supported Great Britain continuing to use high trade tariffs to help its recovery and the recovery of its former colonies). The IMF helped eliminate currency discrimination. The World Bank helped European nations recover from the war, and later helped LDCs develop. U.S. officials proposed that under the leadership of the United States a *gradual* opening of international markets would also prevent the sort of mercantilist conflicts that had plagued states before World War II.

On the other hand, mercantilists (and their realist cousins) focus on a combination of political-economic objectives that these same institutions served. The economic liberal role of the Bretton Woods institutions could not be separated from the efforts of the United States and its allies to *sustain* capitalism within the pro-Western industrialized nations and to *defend* these capitalist countries by "containing" Soviet and international communism (see Chapter 9). Furthermore, there would be no economic liberal order without military power to back it up. The United States benefited from the use of the U.S. dollar as the world's key currency (see Chapter 7) and from the U.S. hegemonic role as provider of liquidity, finance, aid, and military protection to the Atlantic Alliance. Other collective goods that the United States provided its allies to earn their Cold War support included trade concessions (e.g., reduced import tariffs) and food aid.

Most mercantilists and realists would agree that the United States made a *political bargain* (the visible hand) with its Atlantic partners (plus Japan and later South Korea) whereby the United States let them be somewhat protectionist economically if they did what they could to contain communism. U.S. trade concessions involved sacrifices or costs that took the form of gradual gravitation of some jobs to lower-paid workers in Europe and Japan as they recovered after the war. For many allied policy makers at the time, a big concern was whether opening the international economy too quickly could hurt the recovery of Europe and Japan, making it possible for communism to gain a foothold there. This consideration was yet another reason to allow Europe and Japan to continue using a variety of international trade and domestic protectionist measures and to *gradually* open their markets until they were better able to compete with the United States.

# THE ENTRENCHMENT OF NEOMERCANTILISM

In 1973, the **Organization of Petroleum Exporting Countries (OPEC)** oil cartel changed the face of the international political economy when it suddenly raised the price of oil by four times overnight, embargoed oil shipments to the United States and the Netherlands, and reduced oil shipments to the rest of the world by 25 percent (see Chapter 19). The resulting increase in the price of oil—followed by another price hike in 1979—and the transfer of massive amounts of currency to oil-rich countries were thought to have economically weakened the West and made OPEC a political and an economic power with which to reckon. Most of the major industrialized nations and many developing nations incurred major economic recessions. The dependence of the West on OPEC oil helped push the issue of *economic security* higher on the policy agenda of oil-importing nations everywhere in the world. Control over oil and its production suddenly became as important as solidarity among NATO alliance members (who split over how to manage the oil crisis).

Aside from the issue of oil dependency, at least two other factors produced a significant shift in the international political economic structure in the early 1970s. One was a change in the power structure of the world from bipolarity to multipolarity (see Chapter 9). After the United States withdrew from Vietnam in 1973, the Nixon administration implemented a pentagonal balance of power configuration, in part based on increasing **interdependence** between national markets. At the same time, many of the industrialized economies shifted away from Keynesian ideas about economic stability to more market-led economic growth strategies.

In response to the oil crisis and recession, the United States and many of its allies pushed for more emphasis on free trade and cooperation to open international markets in GATT negotiations and on a bilateral basis. As U.S. debt increased, trade was often looked to as a way to increase exports and generate jobs. States such as Japan and South Korea would take advantage of a more open international economy with bigger markets by adjusting their national growth strategies to focus on export-led growth.

Before World War II, many states had erected high tariff barriers, boycotted other states' exports, or even gone to war in response to other states' mercantilist policies. But by the 1970s, these measures were less politically useful and acceptable because their negative effects on society would be too costly. Increasing (complex) interdependence between the military, economic, and foreign policy interests of many states made it harder to be overtly protectionist or isolationist. In order to protect local producers and defend a variety of national, political, and economic interests, states turned to neomercantilism—a set of more subtle and craftily designed policies that had the effect of reducing their vulnerability to international competition without undermining their overall commitment to freer trade under the GATT. Many of the neomercantilist techniques were not explicitly prohibited by international trade agreements.

States used a variety of neomercantilist policies to generate economic growth, control the business cycle, and eliminate unemployment. These measures included government spending for various programs, regulation of industries, capital controls, and interest rates changes. Also, a variety of state industrial policies included subsidies for research and development, state-owned corporations, and state-distributed banking credits. Some states employed export subsidies to lower the price of goods, making them more attractive to importers. The United States and the European Community routinely subsidized their farmers and used export subsidies to reduce their commodity surpluses and to counter the subsidies of competitors for larger shares of export markets (see Chapter 6). By the 1980s, neomercantilist measures played an increasingly greater role in the arsenal of state measures to defend their societies and protect their interests.

An important example of neomercantilism in the 1970s was the U.S.-led campaign with many of the industrialized states to decrease their dependence on OPEC countries in order to enhance their economic security. The United States sponsored the development of a "strategic petroleum reserve" and promoted development of the North Slope oil fields in Alaska. Other national policies included tax breaks for people who adopted measures to cut home energy use, a 55-mile-per-hour automobile speed limit, daylight savings time, and state funds for the development of alternative energy resources. Congress imposed fuel mileage requirements on automobile manufacturers to push them to design more fuel-efficient cars. Even today, many states continue to wrestle with the issue of dependency on foreign oil by providing incentives to insulate homes, fund public transportation, and support the manufacturing of a variety of vehicles that run on biofuels, natural gas, or electricity.

Another example of neomercantilism in the 1970s was the increasing use of **nontariff barriers (NTBs)** (see Chapter 6) such as complex government regulations pertaining to health and safety standards, licensing and labeling requirements, and domestic content requirements that blocked imported goods or distributed them in favor of certain industries. Similarly, countries imposed **import quotas** that specified the quantity of a particular product that could be imported. The United States and the European Union still use import quotas on many agricultural items such as sugar to help their domestic producers compete with foreign producers. Another way to limit imports was through a Voluntary Export Agreement (VEA)—a negotiated quota or "gentlemen's agreement" between an exporter and an importer whereby the exporter "voluntarily" complies with the importer's "request" to limit exports, for fear that the importer may resort to imposing a more costly form of protection on the exporter's goods.

Japan was particularly successful at using neomercantilist policies to achieve its "economic miracle." By the late 1970s, many development experts concluded that Japan's success in export led-growth was partly due to heavy state involvement in the economy. Japan's state-dominated style of capitalism made use of an industrial policy whereby the government—especially the Ministry of International Trade and Industry (MITI)—cooperated with industry officials and Liberal Democratic Party (LDP) members to carefully guide the development of the economy.[20] Certain industries were selected to receive state and bank subsidies to make them more competitive with U.S. and European firms.

Japan complemented its protectionist trade measures with foreign direct investment and ownership of homeland businesses and industries. Clyde Prestowitz argues that Japan did more than support its most competitive industries; it also intentionally adopted an aggressive strategic trade policy. Because it lacked a natural comparative advantage in the production of certain products, it used a combination of state assistance and industry efforts to *purposefully* create such an advantage in favor of its industries.[21] Japan's success would later be emulated by the successful emerging economies, especially the Asian Tigers (South Korea, Hong Kong, Singapore, and Taiwan) and China.

## Neomercantilism and the Globalization Campaign

As noted in Chapters 1 and 2, the 1980s and 1990s marked a period of greater interdependence and increasing popularity of economic liberal ideas. This set the stage for the launching of the globalization campaign that included in its objectives efforts to integrate states into a global economic capitalist-oriented systemic structure (see Chapter 2). While Reagan and Thatcher focused on market-oriented policies to produce more wealth and chipped away at the role of the state in the domestic economy, they simultaneously used political and military powers to advance their countries' interests in the global economy. All states faced a delicate balancing act of adapting to globalization but also moderating its negative effects on jobs and some national industries.

Globalization accelerated interdependence between states, which meant that there was greater political sensitivity to trade as it became a bigger proportion of GDP and affected more sectors of the economy. The policies that states adopted in response to this sensitivity often provoked disputes with trading partners. As the noted political economist Robert Gilpin argued, it was difficult for states to select the appropriate counter-responses without knowing what those states' intentions were. Gilpin made a useful distinction between **malevolent** and **benign mercantilist** intimidations. The former is a more hostile version of economic warfare and the expansionary economic policies nations employed to intentionally expand their territorial base and/or political and economic influence at the expense of other nations beyond what is regarded as reasonable to protect themselves. In contrast, benign mercantilism is more defensive in nature, as "it attempts to protect the economy against untoward economic and political forces."[22] Of course, the problem is how to discriminate between the two in an environment where the difference seems to be a matter of degree rather than of kind.

Reagan is famous for redirecting the Nixon–Kissinger multipolar system of the distribution of power of the 1970s back into a bipolar order of yesteryear that featured the Soviet Union as the "evil empire." In conjunction with this security goal, the Reagan Doctrine encouraged (some would say coerced) many LDCs to adopt not only the anticommunist cause but also the economic liberal policies of the IMF, the World Bank, and the GATT (see Chapters 6–8). The Reagan administration and many academics expected that as developing nations integrated into the international economy, they would grow faster and become more democratic.

President Reagan also mixed economic liberal and mercantilist objectives at the start of the Uruguay Round of multilateral trade negotiations in 1985. One economic liberal goal of these negotiations was to "level the playing field" by cutting NTBs and other trade restrictions, so that states could compete economically with one another following the same set of rules and policies. In the 1980s and 1990s, Japan's relations with the United States, Europe, and other countries became acrimonious at times because it kept running a huge trade surplus. The

United States and Europe blamed their trade deficits on Japan's aggressive export-led growth strategy and import restrictions. Japan maintained that it sought only to strengthen its own national security through the use of benign neomercantilist industrial policies.

President Reagan often threatened to use Super 301 legislation (see Chapter 6) to *punish* Japan and Brazil for dumping their products on the market or using export subsidies to unfairly compete with the United States. He also threatened NATO allies with trade sanctions if they continued to import natural gas from the Soviet Union. The United States gradually put more pressure on Brazil, Japan, South Korea, and many newly emerging economies to lower their trade barriers and open their markets to more foreign (especially U.S.) investment and competition. As we will see in the chapters to follow, U.S. efforts have not met with much success as most of these countries continue to run huge balance-of-trade surpluses compared to long-term U.S. trade deficits.

In cases like Japan and Europe, the United States often found itself limited in the amount of pressure it could put on its most important allies. At the time—as is the case with China and Saudi Arabia today (see Chapter 7)—the United States was dependent on Japan to buy its exports and invest in U.S. Treasury bonds and securities. And pressuring NATO allies about their dependence on the Soviet Union merely strengthened criticism of U.S. foreign policy in Europe.

The United States and Japan repeatedly confronted one another in a series of trade disputes over items such as automobiles, rice, beef, and semiconductors. The "U.S. Beef and Japanese National Security" box explains how the U.S. government continues to accuse Japan of engaging in malevolent mercantilism designed to weaken the economies of other nations. What one state regards as benign, another might interpret as malevolent behavior, especially when the policies of the first state inflict a good deal of stress and anxiety on the society of the second.

## ▶ U.S. BEEF AND JAPANESE NATIONAL SECURITY

In 2003, the United States discovered its first known case of "mad cow disease" (or bovine spongiform encephalopathy [BSE]), a degenerative, fatal disease that affects the central nervous system of adult cattle. People who eat contaminated beef products from BSE-affected cattle can contract the life-threatening Creutzfeldt-Jacob disease. Japan, one of the largest importers of U.S. beef, placed a ban on U.S. beef beginning in 2003, costing the United States an estimated $1.4 billion annually. During the ban, public officials such as Senator Chuck Hagel (R, Nebraska) insisted that "U.S. beef is the safest and highest-quality in the world."[a] In 2005, the Japanese

reopened their country's border to U.S. beef imports, only to close it again two months later when they detected spinal cords in a shipment of East Coast veal. Asian countries consider backbones to be at risk of mad cow disease because inner organs of the animal are most likely to harbor the disease.

In June 2006, Japan decided to lift the ban on U.S. beef imports, but under the condition that it be allowed to inspect meat-packing plants in the United States. A spokesman for the Texas and Southwestern Cattle Raisers Association remarked, "It's USDA's [the U.S. Department of Agriculture's] job to regulate our processing industry, not Japan's."[b] Another cattlemen's group argued that the United States was setting a precedent by allowing another country to inspect U.S. plants. The Japanese insisted that the beef they import be from cows less than 20 months old, as these would be less likely to have the disease. They also reached an agreement with the United States to conduct surprise inspections of U.S. plants, accompanying U.S. inspectors. In return, Japan agreed that in the event of another case, it would target individual shipments rather than banning all beef imports. Tyson Foods, the world's largest beef-processing company, accepted the terms of Japan's officials to inspect its plants, but other industry officials remained guarded about Japan's "empty promises and continued delays" in reopening the market.

This case of Japan's resistance to beef imports from the United States blurs the line between acceptable and unacceptable forms of protectionism. The core issue for Japan, the European Union, and many other nations is their authority to control the types of goods they allow into their nations, that is, their sovereign right to protect their societies from possibly unhealthy foods and commodities, including genetically modified ones. The loss of beef sales to Japan did not significantly affect the U.S. balance of trade, but the case had great symbolic importance and may set precedents.

The big questions in this case are the rationale for protection and acceptance of the motives behind the policies that banned beef. Scientists and the general public accepted the evidence that mad cow disease is a serious health risk. The U.S. public, the USDA, and many U.S. beef interests accept (even if grudgingly) the Japanese claim that U.S. beef may pose a threat to their society. However, it is harder to claim that the beef import ban was a conscious attempt to redirect trade to local producers or that the Japanese set out to damage or bring down the U.S. beef industry. Japan's insistence on inspections was more easily accepted as they opened their market to U.S. beef exports once again.

### References

[a]Betsy Blaney, "Mixed Response as Japan Decides to Lift Beef Ban," *The Seattle Times,* June 22, 2006.
[b]Ibid.

## Neomercantilism and the Financial Crisis

Since the early 1990s, the neomercantilist and competitive policies of some states raised the stakes for others that had to grapple with lost jobs and broken families, the loss of electoral support for legislators, and ultimately the real or imagined loss of national wealth and power. The benefits of globalization and complex interdependence did not trump societies' vulnerability and sensitivity to competitors. People found it increasingly harder to adjust to globalization's dislocations and the instability of markets. In these situations, state officials were often pressured to respond with countermeasures of their own—to "strike while the iron is hot"—for fear of otherwise sending a message of weakness or disinterest to foreign competitors. Political and economic competition *between* states has not ended; in fact, it has intensified in a more globalized world. In many cases, businesses have felt compelled to go abroad in search of cheaper labor, resources, and more markets. Outsourcing labor has become the economically efficient and rational thing to do.

Many neomercantilists go a step further and argue that globalization tends to *undermine* itself.[23] As more wealth and power are diffused around the world, more states and people have an investment in either protecting themselves from globalization's negative effects or sustaining its positive effects. Both situations require state power and instruments that in effect (re)invigorate states that are in danger of losing their power and authority.[24]

For mercantilists, the recent global financial crisis is a good example of how laissez-faire ideas and globalization have undermined themselves (see Chapters 2 and 8). The crisis has increased tensions, hostilities, and conflicts between states, many of whom blame the United States for almost bringing down the global financial system. This has sparked renewed interest in protectionist and national security-oriented perspectives everywhere in the world. Many experts agree that the financial crisis has already uprooted many political, economic, and social institutions—challenging social values and other cultural idiosyncrasies in ways that may yet generate more tensions and even in some cases war.

The crisis has fueled illegal economies, weakened the dollar, and increased U.S. dependence on China and other emerging economies. Many countries have used it as an excuse to postpone or avoid dealing with potentially catastrophic energy and environmental issues. It has tended to shift order away from U.S. hegemony to a more multilateral system.[25] The United States has even reverted to some blatant forms of protection, as when in 2009 it slapped a 35 percent tariff on tires imported from China.

The financial crisis has also had tremendous implications for the attractiveness of neoliberal and democratic ideas associated with capitalism in many developing nations. It has undermined the idea that the U.S. economy is a model for the world. At the same time, it has convinced some countries that the United States is trying to maintain its wealth and power at the expense of others. The growth of populist movements in Latin America,[26] along with the entrenchment of authoritarian regimes in many parts of the world, cannot be separated from issues of protection from globalization and the associated financial turmoil.

## LDC NEOMERCANTILIST POLICIES

As we will see in other chapters of this book, developing nations—just like developed countries—have been searching for a more pragmatic and subtle mix of policies that accounts for not only the interests of the market but also those of society and the state. They have continued to adopt neomercantilist measures in response to international economic competition and what some officials regard as malevolent threats.

Cambridge University economist Ha-Joon Chang is one expert who explains some of the important reasons why many developing nations like Malaysia, Brazil, and China have continued to adopt neomercantilist trade policies as part of their development campaigns. According to Chang, developing countries have wanted to "catch up" with the richer and more technologically advanced countries (see Chapter 11). However, many have found that if while trying to "climb up the ladder" they accept the same rules as the leading countries, they may never get to the top of the ladder. As we outlined in Chapter 2, many IOs that reflect the interests of the major powers have worked to do away with a variety of protectionist measures. Making a case similar to List's, Chang believes that developing nations need a (temporary) handicap of sorts.

Chang uses an analogy in sports to make the point. When players or conditions for each team are unequal, we often object that the competition is unfair and that there needs to be a "level playing field." Just as we separate athletes by age and weight, it is only fair to allow developing countries to use some tools to compete more "fairly" with developed states that have many economic advantages and who originally made the rules in favor of their interests.

For many developing nations, trade protection not only plays a vital role in generating income but also helps in protecting local producers from foreign competition. And yet, as noted in Chapter 6, developing nations played almost no role in multilateral negotiations after World War II that produced the General Agreement on Tariffs and Trade (GATT). It is important to note that early GATT agreements reflected the interests of the developed nations in trade rules—which included preserving trade protection while only gradually curtailing the use of import tariffs on industrial products. In the early 1990s, a number of developing nations did play a role in converting the GATT into the WTO in the Uruguay Round from 1986 to 1994. However, by then the basic principles and norms of the international trade regime were set and difficult to change.

While most developing countries signed on to the new WTO agreement in 1994 that introduced new liberal norms for agricultural trade subsidies, trade in services, NTBs, and intellectual property rights (IPRs), they did not benefit as much from the final agreement as they had hoped they would. This laid the foundation for their unwillingness later on to reach a new deal in the Doha round (see Chapter 6). They also redoubled efforts to form a number of their own negotiating coalitions to overcome what they feel are unfair trade rules that do not adequately reflect their interests.

Similarly, in the 1990s, the poorer developing countries complained that IMF and World Bank **Structural Adjustment Policies (SAPs)** and open market policies imposed on them felt like malevolent mercantilism. Many mercantilists charged that LDC growth rates actually *declined* over the same period when markets in many developing countries were supposedly opening up.[27] SAPs amounted to nothing more than a "mission creep" (at least for the working class and poor) and the imposition of economic liberal policies on many developing nations. As List might argue today, IMF and World Bank SAPs were merely another example of state power being used to increase U.S., European, and Japanese wealth and power—and not noble, let alone useful, development tools as so often claimed.

The problem of *intentions* behind trade and structural adjustment policies tends to generate conflicts in multilayer trade negotiations such as those in the Doha round. Many LDCs charge that a new agreement would make it difficult for developing countries to protect some of their "infant industries." They also suspect that industrialized countries trying to adopt measures to require high labor or environmental standards in all countries are masking protectionist support for their own inefficient industries. For many LDCs, despite the formal commitment to the international goals of opening up international trade and reducing trade barriers, members of the WTO remain quite protective of their own economic security and national independence.

## NEOMERCANTILIST POLICIES TODAY

The kinds of contemporary neomercantilist policies that states frequently adopt depend on each state's level of development and its relative power in the international system. Poorer countries, as we have noted above, have a particular interest in "catching up" to the industrialized countries, but they must work within ideological and political constraints imposed on them by major powers and neoliberal institutions like the WTO, the World Bank, and the IMF. Advanced industrialized nations face the double challenge of competing with one another in high technology and knowledge-based industries while stemming the loss of blue-collar manufacturing industries to emerging economies with abundant, low-cost labor. As globalization and international agreements have wedded all countries to a complex set of broadly economic liberal principles, states have looked for new forms of benign mercantilist policies and carved out realms where they can still use tried-and-true mercantilist policies like quotas, tariffs, and plain old arm-twisting.

In this section, we survey two common types of neomercantilist policies found today: industrial and infrastructural policies and strategic resources policies. Although we focus on the developed countries' use of these policies, keep in mind that many developing countries resort to them as well. In fact, LDCs often point out that today's advanced industrialized nations used a variety of these policies throughout their *early history*, and thus it is somewhat hypocritical of them to try to stop LDCs from using some of the very same policies today. What many emerging economies want are weak protection of IPRs, a mix of protectionism with some free trade, and time to improve institutions without undue pressure by Western countries to quickly become democratic and get rid of corruption. But the developed countries seem to be saying to emerging economies: "Do as we say, not as we did (and sometimes still do)!"

## Industrial and Infrastructural Policies

Many states limit foreign investments in their country in a variety of subtle and not so subtle ways—often in an attempt to reduce threats to independence or national sovereignty. They can limit the percentage of shares in a domestic company (like an oil company) that foreigners can own or they can ban foreign investments in strategic industries like natural resource extraction, power generation, banking, and media. It is also common to make it difficult for foreigners to buy land or real estate on which to build factories, set up services, or accumulate office space. The intent of these policies is often to give domestically-owned companies an advantage or to prevent foreigners from gaining too much control of a sector of the economy by forcing them to cooperate with local companies.

Chang points out that the United States and European countries had many such restrictions until well into the twentieth century. Similarly, countries like Japan, Korea, and Finland had many formal and informal restrictions on foreign direct investment until well into the 1980s, but they still managed to grow rapidly.[28] For example, post–World War II European countries regulated foreign companies by controlling their access to foreign exchange and requiring them to buy some supplies from local producers. Japan prohibited foreign direct investment (FDI) in vital industries and limited foreign ownership at 50 percent in many industries. Instead of favoring foreign takeovers of local companies, it pressured foreign companies to license technology to local companies so that they could learn to manufacture products themselves. The legacy of these restrictions is very clear today. In 2006, the stock of FDI as a percentage of GDP in Japan was a paltry 2.5 percent, compared to

13.5 percent in the United States, 25 percent in Germany, and 33 percent in France. And Finland had draconian restrictions on FDI until the 1980s: among other things, foreigners could not own more than 20 percent of a company and foreign banks were completely prohibited. Clearly, Japanese, Korean, and Finnish models of economic success owed almost nothing to FDI, a finding that conflicts with economic liberal insistence on unfettered capital inflows.

Robert Wade, in his influential book *Governing the Market*, argues that industrial policies had a decisive role in the East Asian development "miracles," especially Japan, South Korea, and Taiwan.[29] The political elites and heads of bureaucracies in these countries steered domestic investment into sectors of the economy like shipbuilding and hard disc drives that the government considered key to economic transformation. They encouraged high rates of saving and manipulated prices in the economy to support infant industries. They also used a lot of public investment to complement private investment. They allowed the formation of large conglomerates. Moreover, they nudged firms to improve the quality of products and to export a high percentage of their finished products. All of these neomercantilist policies—characteristic of what Wade calls a "**developmental state**"—have been imitated by countries like Brazil, Mexico, and Argentina, but without many of the same positive results.

Other significant government interventions in today's markets that many industrialized nations have adopted are designed to increase a country's competitiveness without being malevolently protectionist. Massive investments in public infrastructure and research are vital to business success, and they are effectively subsidies. When a state builds roads, power plants, and transportation systems, the benefits of its spending usually accrue to domestic workers and capitalists who become more efficient and productive as a result. One could argue that California has been a large, successful agricultural producer and exporter because of massive public investments for many decades in irrigation systems that bring water to the state from hundreds of miles away. Similarly, former investment banker Felix Rohatyn argues in a recent book that massive American *public* investments in infrastructure and education had a key role in making the United States a powerful, innovative (and capitalist) country. These programs, parallels to which can be seen today in other countries, included the following: the Erie Canal, the Transcontinental Railroad, land-grant colleges, the Panama Canal, the GI Bill, and Eisenhower's interstate highway system.[30]

Likewise, public education and investments in higher education give widespread economic benefits to many nations. India and China have invested heavily in education and especially in research and development in health sciences, engineering, and the natural sciences, all of which have huge spillovers for domestic companies. Developed countries have done the same to spur innovation and the development of a "knowledge-based economy" (see Chapter 10).

In addition, government procurement can be a powerful neomercantilist mechanism to spread benefits to local businesses that are denied to foreigners. Most governments want their huge spending on goods and services produced by the private sector to help local companies and labor. One of the best examples is U.S. defense spending that has helped aircraft producers like Boeing (see Chapter 18), who use the spillovers related to defense spending to become more competitive with Airbus in the commercial airliner industry. Australian political economists Linda Weiss and Elizabeth Thurbon emphasize how the U.S. government uses procurement policies to create "national champions"—big, globally-competitive companies like Lockheed, Motorola, IBM, and Microsoft—that relied on long-term government contracting. Even as the United States implements its own "buy national" procurement policies—most recently in the 2009 stimulus bill—it tries to get other countries to open up their public works projects to American companies. Weiss and Thurbon conclude that "although subject to multilateral discipline, government procurement offers a powerful tool for national economic promotion in an era of economic openness."[31]

Finally, Canadian political scientist Patricia Goff reminds us that the purpose of helping one's own companies and industries is not necessarily just to save jobs, boost exports, or hurt foreigners.[32] In fact, the purpose may be much more defensive and noneconomic. She has examined how Canada and the European Union have strongly protected their culture industries—music, television, radio, film, and magazine publishing—from an American onslaught over the last 60 years. They use public ownership of some culture industries (like public television), tax incentives for local private investment in movie production, public loans and grants for culture producers, minimum local content requirements (on TV and radio programming), and ownership rules to preserve and nurture domestic culture producers. They do so not so much to keep foreign cultural products out as to promote their own distinct national identity, cultural diversity, and social cohesion. Preserving "cultural sovereignty" in the face of globalization's homogenizing effects is an eminently political goal, vital for nurturing a democratic citizenry that is well informed about its *own* history and values.

## Strategic Resources Policies

Neomercantilists also believe that interdependencies are not always symmetrical (felt equally) between states. The suppliers of oil and other **strategic resources** or commodities tend to view their capacity and the resulting dependency of others as something positive that improves their power and security. In many cases, the relatively high cost of oil, coupled with supplier threats to cut it off to client states, makes the issue of dependence on any resource or vulnerability to a supplier of that resource synonymous with a national security threat. Ideally, only complete self-sufficiency in raw materials would make a nation-state politically and economically secure. In the real world, however, states are constantly trying to minimize their dependence on others while fostering conditions that make others dependent on them.

Examples of this are common. France deliberately and massively expanded its nuclear power industry after the 1973 oil crisis. China has signed long-term oil supply agreements with countries in Africa and Latin America and invested in exploration as a way of getting "first dibs" on these global commodities instead of buying them in open markets in the future. The U.S. government has built costly strategic stockpiles of oil and tantalum (a key ingredient in cell phones and electronic equipment), along with dozens of other minerals and metals used in electronics and weaponry. Even the Centers for Disease Control and Prevention maintains a Strategic National Stockpile of medicines in case of a national emergency such as a terrorist attack or epidemic.

The motivation for these kinds of benign neomercantilism is in large part derived from the legitimate fear that other countries will use malevolent mercantilist polices to hurt another country. These fears today are not unfounded. Powerful countries and even the UN have imposed economic sanctions on countries such as Serbia, Iran, and Iraq, threatening their security and political stability. Industrial espionage is still widely practiced, whereby one country tries to steal the advanced technology of another. Theft of intellectual property, which can be thought of as strategic knowledge resource, is increasingly widespread in the world, manifested in counterfeiting and patent infringement, which can severely damage a country's companies (see Chapter 10).

Access to and control over strategic resources has always been a top concern of industrialized nations who fear that being "cutoff" from energy, minerals, and metals will cripple their economy and weaken their war-fighting ability. In the past, colonial powers took direct control of many territories with important resources, or they built powerful militaries to guard these sources or prevent rival empires from threatening them. Industrialized democracies today usually try to establish political and military alliances with governments of big resource-producers like Saudi Arabia (oil) and Morocco (phosphates)—despite those countries' undemocratic political regimes. At the same time, they may establish stockpiles of resources or encourage domestic exploration and extraction by offering subsides to national producers or by leasing public lands to them cheaply.

Industrialized nations and rapid industrializers like China also encourage their national companies to diversify suppliers overseas, buy foreign resource-extracting companies, and buy concessions (exploration and production rights) in other countries. Right now, foreign oil companies are scrambling to buy concessions to explore offshore West Africa, where many think vast oil deposits may exist. The United States has deliberately and successfully diversified its oil and gas supplies as a matter of national security. Its top five suppliers of imported oil, in order of significance, are Canada, Saudi Arabia, Mexico, Venezuela, and Nigeria—only one of which (Saudi Arabia) is in the conflict-prone Middle East. Japan has been much less successful in diversifying and reducing energy imports. Although it has increased energy efficiency and invested in nuclear power, 90 percent of all its oil imports are from the Middle East.

There is an ongoing tension in the global political economy as commercial development and national security are increasingly wedded in the minds of policy makers and corporations. As nations such as China and India develop major industrial production economies, the battle for control of scarce energy resources will no doubt become more intense. The United States' actions in responding to the attempt by a Chinese company to buy Unocal Corporation in 2005 (see box) may well have set a new paradigm for international trade that is far more guarded and complicated—and neomercantilist—than the economic liberal globalization of the past three decades.

# CHINA VS. UNOCAL[a]

In April 2005, Chevron Corporation, the largest U.S.-based oil conglomerate, made a $16.5 billion bid comprised of cash and stock offerings to acquire a controlling stake in its smaller domestic rival, Unocal. While financial analysts and key players on all sides considered the offer, another multinational energy giant stepped into the game with an unsolicited counter bid. The Chinese National Offshore Oil Corporation (CNOOC), a firm in which the Chinese government holds a 70 percent stake, leveraged its strong fiscal reserves to make what was at first glance a significantly more compelling proposal: $18.5 billion for Unocal, paid entirely in cash.

For Unocal's shareholders, however, choosing the better option quickly became more complicated than a simple analysis of balance sheets. As word of the CNOOC bid spread, concern arose in the United States over the prospect of a foreign government taking control of critical resource production. The deal quickly became a national security issue. On June 27, 2005, key Republicans and Democrats on Congressional energy committees wrote a letter to President George W. Bush warning that China's "aggressive tactics to lock up energy supplies" threatened domestic interests.[b] More than 40 members of Congress signed a similar letter to the Treasury Department, urging a review of the deal for security reasons, and former CIA Director James Woolsey publicly referred to the CNOOC offer as part of a "conscious long-term effort" to take control of U.S. energy resources.[c] Days later, the House of Representatives overwhelmingly (398 to 15) passed a resolution urging the president to block the deal as a threat to national security.[d]

Shortly after the Congressional resolution passed the House, the Chinese Foreign Ministry issued a harsh statement condemning the United States for erecting barriers in the face of business. The statement demanded that Congress "correct its mistaken ways of politicizing economic and trade issues and stop interfering in normal commercial exchanges between enterprises of the two countries."[e] Despite this tough rhetoric, CNOOC ended up

dropping its bid. The U.S. government never directly blocked the deal as the House resolution was nonbinding and never cleared the Senate. Ultimately, the political barriers created by the controversy discouraged hopes for the efficacy of a CNOOC-operated Unocal. Fiscal advisors from top Wall Street firms came to a consensus that the extra $2 billion in cash was not worth the hassle that CNOOC's bid incited.[f]

Both China and the United States operated under fundamental mercantilist principles in approaching the China/Unocal incident, but neither addressed these reasons directly in public discourse. The United States framed the issue under the guise of realism as a security concern, and China retaliated with classic economic liberal language about interfering in the market. Ultimately, these political factors became part of the economic equation that favored Chevron's offer.

Though Unocal was a small player in the global oil industry—producing less than 200,000 barrels daily worldwide—its most lucrative holdings were based largely in and around Asia, and it claimed to be the largest producer of geothermal energy on that continent. According to its last quarterly Securities and Exchange Commission (SEC) filing as an independent firm, 57 percent of its revenue came from its Asian operations in Thailand, Indonesia, Myanmar, and Bangladesh.[g] China's incentive to control these regional energy resources is clear: for the first time in its history, the budding industrial nation has come to rely on foreign energy imports to meet its growing demand for oil. Acting through its controlling interest in CNOOC, the Chinese government was attempting to secure an oil supply line for its rapidly growing economy—a perfect example of neomercantilism at work.

The United States acted with equally mercantilist motivation in moving to block the deal. As the debate unfolded in the United States, many energy experts remained skeptical of the national security concerns ostensibly behind the controversy. They criticized the logic that the Unocal bid was part of a larger Chinese military supply strategy antagonistic to the United States, pointing out instead that the industrial growth inciting China's oil demand in the first place is dependent largely on the United States as a primary importer of Chinese industrial goods. Indeed, it is this trade situation that provided a much more genuine cause for U.S. concern: By the time CNOOC submitted its bid, the United States already had a $160 billion trade deficit with China.[h] Moving to correct this rapidly expanding trade imbalance and block China from acquiring a strategic commercial asset, congressional leaders were clearly leveraging their political power in the name of national commercial interests.

## References

[a]Ryan Cunningham conducted the research and produced a draft for this topic. Our thanks to him.

[b]Paul Blustein, "Many Oil Experts Unconcerned over China Unocal Bid," *The Washington Post,* July 1, 2005, p. D1.

[c]John Tamney, "Unocal Hysteria," *The National Review,* June 30, 2005.

[d]Peter S. Goodman, "China Tells Congress to Back Off Business," *The Washington Post*, July 5, 2005, p. A1.

[e]Ibid.

[f]"Why China's Unocal Bid Ran Out of Gas," *Business Week Online,* August 4, 2005, www.businessweek.com/bwdaily/dnflush/Aug 2005/nf20058084_5032_db0lb.htm?chan-search (accessed March 19, 2007).

[g]Unocal Corporation Form 10-Q, Filed August 4, 2006, p. 29.

[h]Goodman, "China Tells Congress to Back off Business," p. A1.

## CONCLUSION

Of the three ideological perspectives most often used to explain IPE, mercantilism is the oldest and arguably the most powerful because it is so deeply entrenched in the psyches of state officials and their societies. For many neomercantilists, as it was for classical mercantilists and colonial powers in the nineteenth century, economic liberalism is simply another tool that state officials employ to protect their industries so as to achieve more wealth and power. All nations in the past have employed mercantilist policies and measures, as Great Britain did in the nineteenth century during the height of the popularity of economic liberal ideas about free trade. Likewise, the United States did the same throughout the twentieth century, even when it advocated free trade and globalization.

Mercantilist ideas have evolved over the years and adapted to changing conditions in the international political economy. The nature of mercantilism has changed as the types of security threats have changed, and the tools used to protect society have also changed. Classical mercantilism tended to view threats to a nation's security by foreign armies, foreign firms and their products, and even from foreign influence over international laws and institutions. Both mercantilists and their realist cousins would also note that by their very nature states *can* be expected to use the economy, either legally or illegally, as a means to generate more wealth and power.

Certainly, mercantilist motives and neomercantilist policies are still responsible for a good deal of international conflict. Efforts to maintain and increase state wealth and power have proliferated since World War II, as a result of the growing interdependence of nations and globalization of the international political economy. Managing the international economy remains a complicated task that befuddles politicians and academics alike. Many of these issues demonstrate that despite OELs' efforts to isolate economics and markets from politics and society, mercantilists and HILs do not believe it can be done.

With the onset of deep interdependence between states in the 1970s and the globalization campaign of the 1990s, many state officials and academic experts became increasingly aware of the tightening connection between domestic and foreign policy issues. The end of the Cold War in 1990 also helped blur the line between economic and broader national security concerns for most states. However, as discussed in Chapter 1, since the mid-1980s the popular ideas of economic liberalism and globalization envision a limited role for the state in the economy resulting in less conflict between nation-states. Curiously, some OELs envision the withering away of the nation-state as the global economy integrates into a single economic unit.

As long as states exist, they can be expected to give first priority to their own national security and independence followed by advancing their economic wealth. Today, all states continue to use a variety of protectionist measures to assist some of their manufacturing, agricultural, and service sectors. To a great extent, the *success* of globalization has also helped undermine the openness of the international political economy when it comes to state economic interests as well. As states and national industries have become more dependent on external sources of revenue and markets, public officials have also felt more *vulnerable* to developments in the international political economy, leading to arguments that market forces have weakened state power and authority significantly. Yet, protectionist trade, financial, and monetary policies have periodically proliferated as governments have attempted to reassert themselves and better manage their economies.

If Hamilton and List were still around, they would likely argue that as long as states are the final source of political (sovereign) authority, markets cannot be separated from politics and the role of the state in society. But they would inject more attention to the impact of the market on society and vice versa. Their views tied together the importance of linking a nation-state's interests and goals to a positive role for the state in the economy and sacrifice for future gain.

For mercantilists and realists today, despite the popularity of economic liberal ideas discussed in Chapter 2, the world has not been ready for the market to rule all for very long. Globalization and financial crises have exposed the inadequacy of the market alone to protect states and their societies. Markets are often not self-regulating or self-adjusting, and therefore states should not leave it to markets to make key decisions related to human issues and problems. But things are not that simple, either. State-guided policies often fail to accomplish their objectives and can sometimes cause great damage to a society. Nevertheless, states will probably always face the fact that politics forces them to re-embed society into the market. Voters and citizens want protection from the excesses of the market at the same time that they want competitive markets to work better. As suggested in Chapter 2, HILs would agree with mercantilists that there would be no market without the state, and the invisible hand must serve more than the interests of a select few.

## KEY TERMS

## DISCUSSION QUESTIONS

1. Each of the IPE perspectives has at its center a fundamental value or idea. What is the central idea of mercantilism? Explain how that central idea is illustrated by the mercantilist period of history, mercantilist philosophy, and recent neomercantilist policies.

2. What is the difference between benign mercantilism and malevolent mercantilism in theory? How could you tell the difference between them in practice? Find a newspaper article that demonstrates the tensions between these ideas, and explain how the issue is dealt with by the actors in the article.

3. How much is economic globalization a threat to nation-states? Make a brief list of the positive and negative potential effects of a more integrated global economic system, and explain the basis for your opinion.

4. Compare and contrast some features of the Great Depression with those of the global financial crisis today. If Keynes were alive, what do you suppose he would propose the state do about the current crisis?

## SUGGESTED READINGS

Ha-Joon Chang. *Bad Samaritans: The Myth of Free Trade and the Secret History of Capitalism*. New York: Bloomsbury Press, 2008.

Alexander Hamilton. "Report on Manufactures," in George T. Crane and Abla Amawi, eds., *The Theoretical Evolution of International Political Economy: A Reader*. New York: Oxford University Press, 1991, pp. 37–47.

Friedrich List. *The National System of Political Economy*. New York: Augustus M. Kelley, 1966.

Mark A. Martinez. *The Myth of the Free Market: The Role of the State in a Capitalist Economy*. Sterling, VA: Kumarian Press, 2009.

Felix Rohaytn. *Bold Endeavors: How Our Government Built America and Why It Must Rebuild it Now*. New York: Simon & Schuster, 2009.

## NOTES

1. Sun Yat-sen (1920), cited in Robert Reich, *The Work of Nations* (New York: Knopf, 1991), p. 30.

2. The concepts of *nation* and *nationalism* are the focus of the classic work by Hans Kohn, *The Idea of Nationalism* (New York: Macmillan, 1944) and of Eric J. Hobsbawm's *Nations and Nationalism Since 1780,* 2nd ed. (Cambridge: Cambridge University Press, 1992).

3. The classic definition of the state is Max Weber's, which emphasizes its administrative and legal qualities. See Max Weber, *The Theory of Social and Economic Organization* (New York: The Free Press, 1947), p. 156.

4. See Mark A. Martinez, *The Myth of the Free Market: The Role of the State in a Capitalist Economy* (Sterling, VA: Kumarian Press, 2009), pp. 106–110.

5. The history discussed in this section draws on Ha-Joon Chang's *Bad Samaritans: The Myth of Free Trade and the Secret History of Capitalism* (New York: Bloomsbury Press, 2008), pp. 40–43.

6. Ibid.

7. Ibid., especially Chapter 2.

8. See Kenneth Pomeranz and Steven Topik, *The World That Trade Created: Society, Culture, and the World Economy*, 2nd ed. (Armonk, NY: M.E. Sharpe, 2006).

9. Ibid., p. 141.

10. Ibid., p. 149.

11. See Karl Polanyi, *The Great Transformation: The Political and Economic Origins of Our Time* (Boston, MA: Beacon Press, 1944).

12. See Pietra Rivoli, *The Travels of a T-Shirt in the Global Economy: An Economist Examines the Markets, Power, and Politics of World Trade*, 2nd ed. (Hoboken, NJ: John Wiley, 2009), pp. 207–211.

13. For a detailed account of Hamilton's works, see Henry Cabot Lodge, ed., *The Works of Alexander Hamilton* (Honolulu, HI: University Press of the Pacific, 2005).

14. Alexander Hamilton, "Report on Manufactures," in George T. Crane and Abla Amawi, eds., *The Theoretical Evolution of International Political*

*Economy: A Reader* (New York: Oxford University Press, 1991), p. 42.

15. Friedrich List, *The National System of Political Economy* (New York: Augustus M. Kelley, 1966), p. 144. Italics are ours.

16. Ibid., pp. 199–200.

17. The history in this paragraph is drawn from Martinez, *The Myth of the Free Market*, Chapter 6.

18. See for example, Chang, *Bad Samaritans*.

19. Martinez, *The Myth of the Free Market*, p. 150.

20. See, for example, Chalmers Johnson, "Introduction: The Idea of Industrial Policy," in his *The Industrial Policy Debate* (San Francisco, CA: ICS Press, 1984), pp. 3–26.

21. See, for example, Clyde Prestowitz, *Trading Places: How We Allowed Japan to Take the Lead* (New York: Basic Books, 1988).

22. Robert Gilpin, *The Political Economy of International Relations* (Princeton, NJ: Princeton University Press, 1987), p. 33.

23. See, for example, Tina Rosenberg, "Globalization: The Free Trade Fix," *The New York Times Magazine,* August 18, 2002.

24. See, for example, Linda Weiss, *The Myth of the Powerless State* (Ithaca, NY: Cornell University Press, 1998), and Robert Wade, "Globalization and Its Limits: Reports of the Death of the National Economy Are Greatly Exaggerated," in Suzanne Berger and Ronald Dore (eds.), *National Diversity and Global Capitalism* (Ithaca, NY: Cornell University Press, 1996), pp. 60–88.

25. See Parag Khanna, *The Second World: How Emerging Powers Are Redefining Global Competition in the Twenty-first Century* (New York: Random House, 2008).

26. See, for example, Michael Shifter and Vinay Jawahar, "Latin America's Populist Turn," *Current History, 104* (February 2005), pp. 51–57.

27. See Chang and Robert Wade for analysis of LDC growth rates in the 1980s.

28. See Chang, *Bad Samaritans*, for many examples (especially his Chapter 4 "The Finn and the Elephant").

29. Robert Wade, *Governing the Market: Economic Theory and the Role of Government in East Asian Industrialization,* 2nd paperback ed. (Princeton, NJ: Princeton University Press, 2004).

30. Felix Rohaytn, *Bold Endeavors: How Our Government Built America and Why It Must Rebuild It Now* (New York: Simon & Schuster, 2009).

31. Linda Weiss and Elizabeth Thurbon, "The Business of Buying American: Public Procurement as Trade Strategy in the USA," *Review of International Political Economy, 13*, no. 5 (2006), p. 718.

32. See Patricia Goff, *Limits to Liberalization: Local Culture in a Global Marketplace* (Ithaca, NY: Cornell University Press, 2007).

# Economic Determinism and Exploitation: The Structuralist Perspective[1]

The sinews of the global economy.

Jacob Silberberg

On April 11, 2002, the president of Venezuela, Hugo Chávez, was ousted in a coup d'etat by a faction of the military and police. Chávez, a democratically-elected socialist, was replaced by Pedro Carmona, head of the Venezuelan Chamber of Commerce, a conservative business organization. *The Observer of London* reported that the "coup in Venezuela was tied closely to senior officials" in the United States, but the Bush administration, although admitting to meeting with several opposition leaders in the weeks before the coup, insisted it encouraged a change in leadership through constitutional means only.[2]

Whatever the degree of outside involvement, the overthrow of a leftist Latin-American president opposed by the United States and his replacement with a pro-U.S., pro-business dictator would have been no great surprise to many structuralists. Throughout the twentieth century, the United States was directly or indirectly involved in the overthrow of leftist governments in Nicaragua, Guatemala, Brazil, the Dominican Republic, and Chile by consistently using foreign aid to support right-wing military dictatorships.[3] The U.S. Army School of the Americas, now called the Western Hemisphere Institute for Security Cooperation, trained Latin American military officers and sent them back to their home countries where many were accused of torture and other human rights violations.[4]

But the Chávez coup did not follow the same twentieth-century script. The first Latin-American coup attempt of the twenty-first century failed. In a dramatic reversal, the pro-Chávez faction in the military restored Chávez to the presidency. Something, it seems, had changed in the world, and this change goes to the heart of the structuralist perspective. **Structuralism** has its roots in the ideas of Karl Marx but today encompasses a much broader group of scholars and activists. While most structuralists do not share the commitment to a socialist system as envisioned by some Marxists, they do believe that the current global capitalist system is unfair and exploitative and can be changed into something that distributes rewards in a more just manner. Indeed, the *structure* in "structuralism" is the global capitalist system. The global capitalist economy acts as an underlying system or order that is the driving force in society. It shapes society's economic, political, and social institutions and imposes constraints on what is possible.

Many claim that the sudden demise of socialist economies in the former Soviet Union and Eastern Europe and the more gradual transformation of Chinese communism into something closer to capitalism means that "Marx is dead." They believe we should stop using a structuralist analysis of these conditions and embrace free markets as the best political-economic system. But the presidency of Hugo Chávez in Venezuela and other democratically–elected leftist administrations in Bolivia, Ecuador, and Brazil remind us that some think there is an alternative to free market capitalism. Furthermore, the recent developments related to the global financial crisis highlight not only the failures of free market capitalism but also the political clout of the economic elite, who receive bailouts while ordinary taxpayers struggle. Outside the seats of official power, millions of citizens continue to protest against free-trade organizations or U.S. imperialism. Those who feel excluded from economic progress, who believe that their share of the economic pie is too small, or who reject the legitimacy of the global capitalist elite represent a force that cannot be overlooked.

The structuralist perspective has no single method of analysis or unified set of policy recommendations. Rather it is the site of an active, exciting debate that forces us to ask important questions. What are the historical events that created the capitalist structure? How does the global capitalist system operate? How are resources allocated? Is it fair? What comes next and how do we get there? Moreover, this perspective is, at its roots, a critical one that challenges the existing state of affairs.

The main theses of this chapter are as follows: First, many see in structuralism not only the tools to conduct a scientific analysis of existing capitalist arrangements but also the grounds for a moral critique of the inequality and exploitation that capitalism produces within and between countries. Second, this framework of analysis is the only one that allows us to view IPE "from below," that is, from the perspective of the oppressed classes, the poor, and the developing "Third World" nations. In contrast to mercantilism and liberalism, it gives a voice to the powerless. Third, this perspective raises issues about human freedom and the application of reason in shaping national and global institutions. Finally, structuralism focuses on what is dynamic in IPE. It views capitalism and other modes of production as driven by conflict and crisis and subject to change. What exists now is a system and set of structures that emerged at a particular time and may one day be replaced by a different system of political economy.

After outlining some of the major ideas, concepts, and policies associated with both Marx and Lenin, we explore some of the more recent theories of dependency, the modern world system, and neoimperialism. We also briefly discuss some structuralist arguments about the recent financial crisis and conclude with some structuralists' views about reform of the global political economy.

## FEUDALISM, CAPITALISM, SOCIALISM—MARX'S THEORY OF HISTORY

The first great scholar to pioneer a structural approach to political economy was Karl Marx (1818–1883). Born in Trier, Germany, Marx did his most significant work while living in England, spending hours on research at the British Museum in London. Many of his views reflect the conditions he and his collaborator Friedrich Engels observed in English mills and factories at the height of the Industrial Revolution. Adults and children often labored under dreadful working conditions and lived in abject poverty and squalor. Marx's theory of history, his notion of class conflict, and his critique of capitalism must all be understood in the context of nineteenth-century Europe's cultural, political, and economic climate.

Marx understood history to be a great, dynamic, evolving creature, determined fundamentally by economic and technological forces. Marx believed that through a process called **historical materialism** these forces can be objectively explained and understood just like any other natural law.[5] Historical materialism takes as its starting point the notion that the *forces of production* of society, defined as the sum total of knowledge and technology contained in society, set the parameters for the whole political-economic system. As Marx put it, "The hand mill gives you society with the feudal lord, the steam mill society with the industrial capitalist."[6] At very low levels of technology (primitive forces of production), society would be organized into a hunting-gathering system. At a higher level, we would see an agricultural system using steel ploughs and horses, oxen, or other beasts of burden. This technological advancement (although still considered "primitive" by modern standards) causes a change in the social relations in society, specifically the emergence of feudalism. Instead of hunters and gatherers banding together in small-scale tribes with a relatively equal division of the economic output, feudalism is characterized by a large strata of peasant-farmers and a smaller aristocracy. The key Marxist claim is this: the change in technology *determines* the change in the social system. Thus Marx has been considered a *technological determinist*, at least within his theory of history.

Marx sees the course of history as steadily evolving from one system of political economy (or "mode of production," in Marx's words) to another due to the growing contradiction between the technical forces of production and the social class or property relations in which they develop. In each of these modes of production, there is a **dialectical process** whereby inherently unstable opposing economic forces and counterforces lead to crisis, revolution, and to the next stage of history. Over long periods of human history, the forces of production will continually improve because technology is simply an aspect of human knowledge. Once a discovery is made, whether the smelting of copper and tin into bronze or the development of a faster computer processor, the knowledge tends to be retained and can be used and improved upon by subsequent generations. Human knowledge and technology have a ratchet-like quality—they can go forward a bit at a time but will not go backward.

For Marx, the agents of change are human beings organized into conflicting social classes. Because class relations change more slowly than technological development, social change is impeded, fostering conflict between the classes that in a capitalist society gradually produces a face-off between the bourgeoisie and the proletariat. According to Marx, the **bourgeoisie** are wealthy elites who own the means of production—or what today would be bigger industries, banks, and financial institutions. In British society, the bourgeoisie also made up the members of Parliament and thus controlled the government—or state, as Marx would refer to it. In Marx's day, the **proletariat** were the exploited workers (including their families) in Britain's woolen mills, who received very low wages and often died on the job. Gradually, it was thought, workers would realize their common interests and would organize and press on the bourgeoisie for higher wages and better working conditions.

Marx identified three objective laws that would, at some point, destroy capitalism from within. First, *the law of the falling rate of profit:* Over time as investment causes machines to replace workers, profits must decline and ultimately disappear. Second, *the law of disproportionality* (also called the *problem of underconsumption*)[7] suggests that capitalism, because of its anarchic, unplanned nature, is prone to instability such that workers cannot afford to buy what they make. Like other classical economists, Marx believed in the *labor theory of value*, which argues that the value of a commodity is related to the amount of labor required for its production. Marx tried to demonstrate that workers were paid less than the full value of what they produced. Because workers were abundant (as poorer people moved from the countryside and into cities looking for work), the bourgeoisie were able to pay them less and make more profit for themselves from the sale of the goods the workers produced. And yet, poorer workers could not afford these goods, which turned into an oversupply of products, driving down their owners' profits. This disproportionality between supply and demand leads to wild fluctuations in the history of capitalism, with periodic booms and busts such as the one the world finds itself in now with regard to surplus credit, which we discuss later in the chapter (see also Chapter 8).

Third and finally, *the law of concentration* (or *accumulation of capital*) holds that capitalism tends to create increasing inequality in the distribution of income and wealth. As the bourgeoisie continue to exploit the proletariat and as weaker capitalists are swallowed by stronger, bigger ones, wealth and the ownership of capital become increasingly concentrated in fewer and fewer hands. Marx viewed these as objective, inescapable features of the capitalist mode of production, which he predicted will result in the ultimate collapse of the system.

For Marx, capitalism is more than an unhappy stop on the road to socialism. It is also a *necessary* stage, which builds wealth and raises material living standards. It is the dynamic nature of market capitalism that lies at the heart of political economy. According to Marx, capitalism plays two historic roles. First, it transforms the world and in so doing breaks down feudalism, its historical antecedent. Second, it creates the social and economic foundations for the eventual transition to a "higher" level of social development. Marx argued that when class conflict becomes so severe that it blocks the advance of human development, a social revolution will sweep away the existing legal and political arrangements and replace them with ones more compatible with continued social and technological progress. In this way, history has already evolved through distinct epochs or stages: primitive communism, slavery, feudalism, and capitalism. Marx's *Communist Manifesto,* published in 1848, was a call for a revolution that would usher in a new epoch of history—socialism—which would, after yet another revolution, finally produce pure communism.

As we will see below, neo-Marxists and structuralists still accept the notion of exploitation, although it has been separated from the labor theory of value. Also, most neo-Marxist scholars no longer accept the claim that capitalism will someday destroy itself. Rather, it is generally accepted that Marx's mathematical analysis that produced this prediction was simply erroneous.[8] When socialism was regarded as inevitable it made sense to plan for it, but now that capitalism is recognized as a viable economic system, the entire discussion about socialism has shifted. Socialism may be a possible future, but it would have to be a political choice, not something imposed on society by Marx's deterministic laws of historical epochs. Nonetheless, many other ideas from Marx or from the school of thought he established contribute to an explanation of phenomena we still observe today in the international political economy.

## SOME SPECIFIC CONTRIBUTIONS OF MARX TO STRUCTURALISM

A word of caution is in order concerning the nature of Marxist thought and its relationship to contemporary structuralism. Marx wrote millions of words; in so vast a body of work, he necessarily treated the main themes repeatedly and not always consistently. What Marx "said" or "thought" about any interesting issue is therefore subject to dispute. At the same time, Marxist scholars have interpreted his writings in many ways. Here we explore four ideas that are found in varying degrees within Marx's work and that have been further developed by neo-Marxists, structuralists, and other varieties of radicals up to the present. Some ideas that Marx considered to be of great importance are no longer regarded as useful by most current scholars. And many ideas that he presented have been modified (and hopefully improved) by subsequent scholars, which can be seen as part of the normal development in any field of academic inquiry.

The following four Marxist ideas are central to contemporary structuralist analyses of the international political economy: the definition of class, class conflict and the exploitation of workers, capitalist control over the state, and ideological manipulation.

## The Definition of Class

To understand the Marxist notion of class, we must first define capital. Capital, what Marx called the means of production, refers to the privately owned assets used to produce the commodities in an economy. Car factories are capital, as are all the machines and tools inside them. A computer, when owned by a company, is capital. So are the desks, filing cabinets, cranes, bulldozers, supertankers, and natural resources like land and oil. Almost all production requires both workers and physical assets, and in modern economies production processes can indeed be very capital-intensive.

When we speak of "capital goods" we mean more than simply the existence of such productive assets. Humans have used tools for much longer than capitalism has existed and socialist societies have machines and factories just like capitalist ones. To call an asset capital also means that it is privately owned, that somebody has legal ownership and effective control over that asset. In many cases today that ownership is merely a piece of paper or a computerized account representing stock in a corporation. The property rights in a capitalist society dictate that the owners of capital will receive the profits from the sale of commodities produced by the capital they own and the labor they hire.

Class is determined by the ownership, or lack of ownership, of capital. A minority of people will own a disproportionate share of the productive assets of the society; these constitute the capitalist class, also referred to as the bourgeoisie. In the United States, for example, the wealthiest 1 percent of the population owns 50 percent of all stocks and the top 10 percent owns 86 percent, leaving 14 percent of this financial asset for the remaining 90 percent of society.[9] Real estate, excluding a household's principal residence, has a similarly unequal distribution, while bonds are even more concentrated among the wealthy. The majority of the population will own very little capital and indeed many people will own no productive assets or any shares of stock; these constitute the working class, known as the proletariat. Note that workers may own assets—houses, cars, appliances, and so on—but these are not productive assets but simply possessions. They cannot be mixed with labor to form a commodity that could be profitably sold on a market. Implicitly, if not explicitly, Marxists regard the original distribution of assets as unjust, noting that historically a small number of people confiscated large amounts of land and other resources by means of violence and coercion. Thus, the contemporary consequences of this distribution are criticized for moral reasons.

## Class Conflict and the Exploitation of Workers

For households in the capitalist class, profits are the leading source of income. For example, if the average return in the stock market is 5 percent per year and a capitalist household owned $50 million worth of stock in various corporations, then the income produced by that ownership would be $2.5 million in one year ($50 million times 0.05). This leaves the original $50 million intact and it comes without any requirement that the capitalists actually perform any work.

Workers, on the other hand, have little or no capital and therefore must sell their ability to labor to capitalists if they are to receive an income. In other words, businesses hire workers and pay them a wage or salary. Workers must work to receive an income. For Marxists, this inevitably leads to the exploitation of workers because of their weak bargaining position. In a capitalist economy, there is always a certain level of unemployment; that is, some workers are denied access to capital and thus the ability to produce goods (remember that production requires the combination of physical assets and labor). By restricting access to their productive assets, capitalists, in effect, create an artificial scarcity of capital. At the same time that 5 percent or even 10 percent of the workforce might be unemployed, there is likely sufficient idle machinery that could put everybody to work if put into operation. But it is actually more profitable for businesses to keep some capital out of use in order to maintain a certain amount of unemployment. The presence of unemployed workers functions to keep down the wages of the employed—if one worker does not accept the going rate, then he or she can be easily replaced. Thus, unemployment allows capitalists to dominate workers and serves as the foundation for exploitation.

The exploitation of workers by capitalists is a specific instance of power relations more generally. To say that actor A has power over B (or can dominate B) is to say that A is able to get B to act in ways that promote the interests of A and are contrary to B's.[10] This does not necessarily mean that B has literally no choice but simply that the options are configured to benefit A. When the armed robber tells the hapless victim, "Your money or your life!" the victim could choose the latter. Nonetheless, it is the case that the robber, due to the presence of a gun, has power over the victim because in either scenario the robber will make off with the money. The victim is coerced into making the least bad choice.

Many workers are in a similar situation: Either accept low wages or starve! Capitalism depends on "the existence of workers who in the formal sense voluntarily, but actually under the whip of hunger, offer themselves."[11] Joan Robinson, the famous socialist-leaning post-Keynesian economist, captured the position of workers by remarking that the only thing worse than being exploited under capitalism is not being exploited. In other words, the worst outcome for those in the working class is to be unemployed, and it is the fear of unemployment that forces workers to accept low wages. Workers technically do have a choice, but the game is structured such that the best choice is still a bad choice for them but a good one for the capitalists. In sum, exploitation means that capitalists, because they have greater labor market power, are able to expropriate a share of the economic output that should belong to workers. Essentially, the capitalists force the workers to accept a bad deal because the alternative is even worse.

We should be clear that class conflict does not necessarily mean a state of warfare or even hostility of any sort. In fact, many individuals may not even recognize the conflicting nature of their relationship with the other class. Class conflict usually results in a gain for one side at the expense of the other. The degree to which individuals in different classes act upon this fact is hard to predict. Furthermore, even when the conflict is recognized, it is possible that a compromise between classes can be found. The welfare states of Western Europe may be considered instances of such compromise. In states such as France, Germany, and Sweden, organized labor renounces the goal of a socialist society and offers a relatively harmonious relationship with business in exchange for high wages, adequate unemployment compensation, universal health care, paid vacations, and generous pensions.

Because workers are exploited, they share an objective economic interest in changing the economic system, while capitalists will have an interest in maintaining the status quo. The presence of an "objective" interest does not necessarily mean that workers will actually form a socially and politically active group or movement. Workers (1) may not subjectively recognize their common objective interest, or (2) they may recognize their interest but be unable to organize. The first is an instance of **false consciousness** (discussed in section "Ideological Manipulation"). The second may be the result of class struggle in which an organized capitalist class prevents the successful organization of the working class, for example, into unions, or the result of collective action problems that impede the working class from organizing itself (and these two may be interrelated in complex ways). In Marxist language, workers are often a class *in itself* without becoming a class *for itself*.

The central idea, however, is that the relationship between capitalists and workers is built upon an objective division of the economic output of a society into wages and profits. The actions of individual workers and capitalists will depend on many concrete historical variables, leading to civil war or revolution, to class compromise, or to passivity due to subjective ignorance. But regardless of the way in which the conflict plays itself out, class conflict is a fundamental objective characteristic of capitalist societies.

## Capitalist Control over the State

The state is defined as the organization in a society that governs, by force if necessary, a population within a particular territory. Despite globalization, the modern state is still usually the most powerful organization within any society, typically possessing the strongest tools of repression in the form of military and police forces. Based on its powers, the state also exercises tremendous influence in picking economic winners and losers through taxation, spending, and regulations. Some of its most important regulations involve workplace and labor issues such as setting the minimum wage, writing and enforcing child labor laws, and establishing the ease or difficulty in forming labor unions. While states and their leaders are not omnipotent, they do indeed have the ability to help their friends and punish their enemies. It is therefore reasonable that both capitalists and workers would seek to "capture" the state, to apply the capacities of the state to their particular interests.

In the struggle to control the state, capitalists and workers have very different resources. The capitalist class has greater financial resources, and this often translates easily into influence in the political system. Capitalists are typically able to donate more money to probusiness candidates. The "think-tanks" used by officials to craft policies, such as the Brookings Institution or the Heritage Foundation, are largely funded by corporations or individual members of the capitalist elite. Furthermore, the state depends upon the investments of businesses in order to provide tax revenue and employment for its citizens; a climate that is too antibusiness will cause capital to flee elsewhere or at least reduce investment. Thus, even without direct attempts by capitalists to influence the state, many policies will promote their interests regardless.

Workers, for their part, have greater numbers. To turn this into political power the state must have strong democratic institutions that give workers a substantial role in policy making, and workers must also be sufficiently organized. Capitalists therefore will not always prefer democratic institutions. They certainly want (capitalist) property rights defended along with a reasonably stable investment climate, but these can be found in undemocratic countries. In fact, in the most democratic systems, such as Western European countries that have proportional representation voting, workers' parties (Social Democratic or Socialist Parties) often win majorities or significant pluralities.

Workers may also attempt to influence the political system through strikes and protests. Capitalists may have the power to relocate or reduce investment, but workers are able to withhold their labor, that is, they can strike. Workers will be stronger to the extent that the strike involves many participants (including few who will cross the picket line) and when the workers can survive for a long time without the wages from the employer. Often a strike is the response of a single union to a particular grievance with a firm, but when a large segment of the population is involved in a general strike the entire economy can be halted and governments can be forced to respond to the demands of the working class. For this reason it is no surprise to Marxists that general strikes, or even the more limited secondary or sympathy strikes, have been made illegal in the United States. On the other hand, social action in the form of protests or riots cannot be as easily regulated by the state and may have class objectives. But again the efficacy of these actions depends heavily on the degree of solidarity among its members. If workers do not hang together, then the capitalists will find it easy to divide and conquer.

Structuralists believe that the superior financial resources of capitalists and the difficulties inherent in forming large worker or social movements give capitalists the advantage in most countries today. If this is true, we would expect that policies generally favor capitalists, at least as a class, even if many capitalist firms will be permitted to fail due to competition (although note the power of certain firms or sectors to receive government "bailouts").

Structuralists recognize that the influence of the state does not necessarily end at the border. Like mercantilists, structuralists agree that any state can be regarded as an actor in a global system made of other states. States can form treaties or trade agreements. States can also go to war with each other or be in colonial relationships whereby one state controls or even occupies another. As mercantilists emphasize, the relative military and economic strengths of the states involved will generally determine the winners and losers in any conflict. There is little disagreement between structuralists and mercantilists regarding the importance of the powers that states wield. The difference between the two concerns the motives behind the use of state power. Whereas mercantilists see the state as an actor with its own interests (or perhaps the interest of all its citizens), structuralists believe that a state will act to advance the narrower interests of the class that dominates it—typically the capitalists, as mentioned above. Thus, Marxists see **imperialism** as a natural feature in the global capitalist system, which we discuss later in the chapter.

Finally, in their search for profits, capitalists in the rich states not only exploit domestic workers but workers in other countries as well. The international situation, however, is complicated because capitalists in any country are not only in conflict with their own workers but also have a complex relationship with capitalists in other countries. Capitalist firms do compete with other firms both domestically and internationally, yet they also form alliances with those firms on issues that impact the functioning of the global capitalist system. Thus, depending on the issue, capitalists in New York or London often form alliances with the local capitalist elite in Mexico City or Riyadh in order to keep profits up, workers weak, and wages down.

## Ideological Manipulation

Power derives from the control over hard resources, like capital or the military, and the ability to force others to act in certain ways by structuring the choices of the weaker to the benefit of the stronger (see Chapter 9). Yet, structuralists also accept that power has a softer side, the control over people's hearts and minds. The traditional Marxist term for this is *ideology*.

*Idea* is the root word of *ideology*. An idea is a belief or thought, and an *ideology* is simply a set of beliefs. But in the Marxist tradition, this term takes on particular importance when linked to the notion of class, generating the notions of a capitalist (or bourgeois) ideology and a working-class (or proletarian) ideology. The domain of ideology is another terrain upon which the class struggle is fought. An important goal of capitalist ideology is to give *legitimacy* to the capitalist economic system. To believe that a system is legitimate is to believe that it is appropriate and just. This is quite clear in the realm of state governance.

Most authoritarian regimes are regarded as illegitimate by their own citizens when the people do not believe that those who hold power have a fair and proper claim to it. Under such conditions, many individuals will be motivated to undermine or overthrow the government.[12] Thus, somewhat paradoxically, a dictatorship, which relies upon brute military and police strength, can be seen as the least stable system of government because it requires consistently high levels of surveillance and repression to maintain. A democracy, on the other hand, is generally seen as a legitimate form of governance. When citizens can participate in fair elections, the leaders typically earn the consent of the led, including even those who voted for a different candidate or party. Those with less power believe that it is appropriate that they lack certain powers (although they may not consent to being completely powerless) because those with more power are seen to possess a fair claim to it. While even democratic societies possess arsenals of surveillance and repression, they tend to be less intrusive than those found in authoritarian systems.

The concept of legitimacy applies not only to political institutions but to the economy as well. When capitalism is regarded as legitimate, individuals believe that the system is proper and just, meaning that those with fewer resources will believe that they *should* have fewer resources. Furthermore, a belief by workers in the legitimacy of the capitalism ensures that (1) they will not seek to replace it with something else (e.g., socialism) and (2) they will work harder within the present system, thus increasing the income of the capitalists. When capitalism is regarded as legitimate by the working class, then the capitalists generally do not have to use force in order to protect the wealth they have obtained through the exploitation of workers; workers consent to their own exploitation.

Given the importance of legitimacy, many Marxists argue that the capitalist class will actively seek to create an ideology in society that gives legitimacy to procapitalist institutions (see the box "Antonio Gramsci and Intellectual Hegemony" below). Elements of this ideology, like the belief in free trade (see Chapters 3 and 6), are actively promoted. This marketing of ideas requires resources and, although ideas cannot literally be bought and sold, their production in many ways is similar to the production of ordinary commodities. Noam Chomsky, a linguist at MIT and structuralist theorist, has analyzed the ways by which the consent of the proletariat is "manufactured" by powerful interests in society, including the state and the corporate media.[13] For example, the threat of foreign enemies has been used by those in power to draw attention away from internal, class-based, conflicts. For much of the twentieth century, the Soviet Union served that function but has been replaced more recently by Iraq, the "axis of evil," and (Islamic) terrorism in general. Writing on the Bush administration, Chomsky observed, "Manufactured fear provided enough of a popular base for the invasion of Iraq, instituting the norm of aggressive war at will, and afforded the administration enough of a hold on political power so that it could proceed with a harsh and unpopular domestic agenda."[14] Almost a century earlier, many socialists and communists were greatly disillusioned by World War I, because workers in different countries—who all had a common *objective* interest in fighting the capitalists—accepted the patriotic propaganda of their countries, resulting in the slaughter of workers by other workers.

Just like the competition between the classes for control of the state, Marxists see an unfair fight in the realm of ideology where capitalists use their resources to promote their ideology while workers, who have fewer resources, attempt to promote their own competing set of beliefs. The superior financial resources of the capitalists typically means that the procapitalist messages—the benefits of free trade, the need for low taxes on the rich, the problems with unions, and so on—will be stronger than those favored by workers. Workers, of course, are not powerless and at certain times on certain issues may succeed in persuading the public. But the game is biased in favor of capitalists. It is a great tragedy, according to Marxists, that capitalists not only exploit workers but also take part of this undeserved wealth and use it to manipulate the beliefs of workers so that they are ignorant of, or apathetic about, their own exploitation. The wealth produced at the hands of workers gets transformed into ideas that poison their minds.

From a Marxist perspective, the belief in the legitimacy of capitalism by workers is analogous to the belief in the legitimacy of a dictatorship by its citizens. Is it possible that people could ever be fooled like this? We should recall that the rule by monarchs in the Middle Ages in Europe was at least partially legitimized by an ideology promoted by the Catholic Church asserting a Divine Right to govern: to challenge the rule of the aristocracy was to offend God. Even today, in Thailand it is a serious crime to insult the king.[15]

According to Marxists, belief in the legitimacy of capitalism by workers is *false consciousness*. Workers are often fooled into believing that capitalism will benefit them, which makes it easier for them to continue to be exploited. We could say that Marxists regard capitalism as a dictatorship in which the people have been fooled, while economic liberals would see capitalism as a democracy that has earned its legitimacy because people view it as a fair system. The evaluation seems to depend on whether or not one believes that capitalists, in fact, exploit workers.

For many people, Marxism is equated with socialism or communism. Yet, we can now see that Marx envisioned those systems as epochs of history that would come after capitalism. Marx's four major contributions to IPE (discussed above) can be separated from his theory of history and its prediction regarding the inevitability of socialism and then communism.

## ANTONIO GRAMSCI AND INTELLECTUAL HEGEMONY

One of the most influential structuralists of the twentieth century—and one whose ideas are particularly relevant to the global political economy of the twenty-first—is the Italian Marxist Antonio Gramsci (1891–1937). Gramsci provides a broader account of the nature of class relations.

Gramsci lived in a time of tremendous economic and political tension, where he witnessed the rise of fascism in the 1920s and 1930s and the intense conflicts among nations and between classes. He proposed a philosophy of *praxis*—that we should demonstrate our beliefs through our actions. He edited an intellectual journal, *Ordine Nuovo* (The New Order), and led worker protests in the Italian industrial center of Turin, especially against the manufacturing giant FIAT. His political and intellectual activities drew the attention of Italy's proindustry fascist government, which imprisoned him. In his *Prison Notebooks,* Gramsci attempted to revise Marxist theory to account for changing conditions in the advanced industrial world. He died in prison at the age of 46.

According to Gramsci, the dominant class in society maintains its position in two fundamentally different ways: through coercion and through consent. Coercion is an obvious mechanism, applying economic and political power directly to keep the subordinate class in line. In Gramsci's time, for example, government police and manufacturer-backed thugs employed violence against protesting workers. In contemporary times, one might substitute the images of police at antiglobalization protests such as the 1999 World Trade Organization meetings in Seattle, Washington.

Coercion is a powerful tool, Gramsci said, but ideas are even more powerful because they allow rule over the masses. The dominant class produces and promulgates an ideology or worldview that supports and legitimizes its interests. These popular ideas permeate society through education and the communications media. Once the subordinate class accepts this worldview, whether intentionally or by osmosis, its thoughts and actions are brought into line with the interests of the dominant class. Police are not necessary because the idea of taking actions that oppose the dominant class is not part of society's accepted values and norms. Many contemporary writings, such as Benjamin R. Barber's *Jihad vs. McWorld* (see Suggested Readings), which oppose the increasing control of global media by an elite group of private owners, express a Gramscian-type concern about **intellectual hegemony.**

In Gramsci's view, there are no truly independent intellectuals. Traditional intellectuals, such as professors, like to "put themselves forward as autonomous and independent of the dominant group,"[a] but this self-image is inaccurate, as all intellectuals are products of particular historical events and social relationships. What is needed is for workers to develop, from within their own class, **organic intellectuals** who remain connected to their class while providing organization, leadership, and a vocabulary that challenges the ideology of the dominant class and articulates a different vision of the future. If they can also win over many of the traditional intellectuals, the formulation of a counterhegemonic ideology becomes all the more likely and legitimate. Schools, colleges, newspaper cartoons and editorials, political slogans, songs, and coffee shops will then reverberate with debate and demands for change.

**Reference**

[a]Antonio Gramsci, *Selections from the Prison Notebooks*, Quintin Hoare and Geoffrey Nowell Smith, trans. and eds. (New York: International Publishers, 1971), p. 7.

# LENIN AND INTERNATIONAL CAPITALISM

V. I. Lenin (1870–1924) is best known for his role in the Russian Revolution of 1917 and the founding of the Soviet Union. In many ways he turned Marx on his head, placing politics over economics when he argued that Russia had gone through its capitalist stage of history and was ready for a second, socialist revolution. Lenin is also known for his views on imperialism based on Marx's theories of class struggle, conflict, and exploitation. In his famous book *Imperialism: The Highest Stage of Capitalism* (1917),[16] Lenin explains how, through imperialism, advanced capitalist core states expanded control over and exploited what his contemporaries called "backward" colonial regions of the world, leaving them unevenly developed, with some classes to prosper and others mired in poverty. By the end of the nineteenth century, new colonies were established mainly in Central and Southern Africa, and they became the main sources of cheap labor, scarce resources, and an outlet for industrial investment of the advanced capitalist nations. These colonies produced coffee, tea, sugar, and other food commodities not found in mother countries.

The critical element fueling imperialism, in Lenin's view, was the centralization of market power into the hands of a few "cartels, syndicates and trusts, and merging with them, the capital of a dozen or so banks manipulating thousands of millions."[17] Because capitalism led to monopolies that concentrated capital, it gradually undermined the ability of capitalists to find sufficient markets and investment opportunities in industrial regions of the world. Of course profit-seeking capitalists were unwilling to use their surplus capital to improve the living standards of the proletariat so that they could purchase more goods and services. To prevent capitalism from imploding, Lenin and others argued that imperialism therefore was a necessary outlet for surplus finance and allowed capitalism to survive. Imperialism allowed rich capitalist nations to sustain their profit rates while keeping the poorer nations underdeveloped, deep in debt, and dependent on the rich nations for manufactured goods, jobs, and financial resources.

For Lenin, imperialism also signified the monopoly phase of capitalism or "the transition from capitalism to a higher system," by which he meant that the presence of monopolies and imperialism that followed was yet *another* epoch of history between capitalism and socialism, unaccounted for by Marx.[18] Finally, imperialism helped convert the poorer colonial regions into the new "proletariat" of the world or "international capitalist systems." According to Lenin, "Monopolist capitalist combines—cartels, syndicates, trusts—divide among themselves, first of all, the whole internal market of a country, and impose their control, more or less completely, upon the industry of that country," generating a world market.[19]

It is not surprising that Lenin's theory of imperialism has been very influential, especially among intellectuals in the less developed countries, where his views have shaped policies and attitudes toward international trade and finance generally. Before and especially after World War I, cutthroat competition among capitalist nations contributed to international tensions and conflict. Elites in poorer nations competed for capital and investment, which made them easy targets for production monopolies. In these regions and countries, communist revolutionaries and leaders, like Mao Zedong in China, Ho Chi Minh in Vietnam, and Fidel Castro in Cuba organized anticolonialism and anti-imperialism campaigns and fought "wars of national liberation" against capitalist imperial powers.

Today, most structuralists no longer believe that the falling rate of profit for capitalists will cause the collapse of the capitalist mode of production. However, Leninist arguments about imperialism still remain influential in China, Vietnam, Cuba, Venezuela, and even in some industrialized nations that have active socialist and communist parties. Leaders of these and other countries still view capitalists as profit-seeking imperialists who seek opportunities abroad where democratic political institutions and the working class are weak.

No attempt to consider the IPE of relations between developed and developing countries is complete without considering theories of imperialism. We include Lenin's theory of imperialism under the general heading of "structuralism," as we did Marx's theories, because its analysis is based on the assumption that it is in capitalism's nature for the finance and production structures among nations to be biased in favor of the owners of capital. In theory, the relationship between capital-abundant nations and capital-scarce nations *should be* one of *interdependence*, because each needs the other for maximum growth. But for many structuralists, the result in practice is *dependence*, exploitation, and uneven development.

## IMPERIALISM AND GLOBAL WORLD ORDERS

In this section, we explore some of the more recent structuralist theories of dependency, the modern world system, and modern imperialism (or "neoimperialism") that trace their analytical approaches and policy prescriptions to both Marx and Lenin.

### Dependency Theory

A structuralist perspective that highlights the relationships between what are referred to as core and peripheral countries, while calling attention to the constraints put on countries in the latter group, is called **dependency theory.** A wide range of views can be grouped together under this heading. Their differences, however, are less important to us here than what they have in common, which is the view that the structure of the global political economy essentially enslaves the less developed countries of the South by making them reliant to the point of being vulnerable to the nations of the capitalist core of the North. Theotonio Dos Santos sees three eras of dependence in modern history: colonial dependence (during the eighteenth and nineteenth centuries), financial-industrial dependence (during the nineteenth and early twentieth centuries), and a structure of dependence today based on the postwar multinational corporations.

Andre Gunder Frank has focused a good deal of attention on dependency in Latin America and is noted for his "development of underdevelopment" thesis.[20] He argues that developing nations were never "underdeveloped" in the sense that one might think of them as "backward" or traditional societies. Instead, once great civilizations in their own right, the developing regions of the world *became* underdeveloped as a result of their colonization by the Western industrialized nations. Along with exploitation, imperialism produced underdevelopment. In order to escape this underdevelopment trap, a number of researchers, including Frank, have called for peripheral nations to withdraw from the global political economy. In the 1950s and 1960s, the leadership of many socialist movements in the Third World favored revolutionary tactics and ideological mass movements to change the fundamental dynamics of not only the political and economic order of their society but also the world capitalist system.

Recently, some dependency theorists have recommended a variety of other strategies by which developing nations could industrialize and develop. Raul Prebisch, an Argentinean economist, was instrumental in founding the United Nations Committee on Trade and Development (UNCTAD). The developing nations that have joined this body have made it their goal to monitor and recommend policies that would, in effect, help redistribute power and income between Northern developed and Southern developing countries. Many dependency theorists, however, have been more aggressive about reforming the international economy and have supported the calls for a "new international economic order" (NIEO), which gained momentum shortly after the OPEC oil price hike in 1973. The important point to make here is that dependency theories have served as part of a critique of the relationship of the core to peripheral nations. Whether that relationship can—or even should—be equalized is a matter usually played out in the political arena.

## Modern World System Theory

One fascinating contemporary variant of the structuralist perspective focuses on the way in which the global system has developed since the middle of the fifteenth century. This is the **modern world system** (**MWS**) theory originated by Immanuel Wallerstein and developed by a number of scholars, including Christopher Chase-Dunn. Capitalist in nature, the world system largely determines political and social relations, both within and between nations and other international entities.

For Immanuel Wallerstein, the world economy provides the sole means of organization in the international system. The modern world system exhibits the following characteristics: a single division of labor whereby nation-states are mutually dependent on economic exchange; the sale of products and goods for the sake of profit; and, finally, the division of the world into three functional areas or socioeconomic units which correspond to the roles that nations within these regions play in the international economy.[21] From the MWS perspective, the capitalist **core** states of northwest Europe in the sixteenth century moved beyond agricultural specialization to higher-skilled industries and modes of production by absorbing other regions into the capitalist world economy. Through this process, Eastern Europe became the agricultural **periphery** and exported grains, bullion, wood, cotton, and sugar to the core. Mediterranean Europe and its labor-intensive industries became the **semiperiphery** or intermediary between the core and periphery.

It would be easy to define the core, periphery, and semiperiphery in terms of the types of nations within each group (such as the United States, China, and South Korea, respectively), but the MWS is not based primarily on the nation-state. In this theory, the core represents a geographic region made up of nation-states that play a partial role in the MWS. The force of bourgeois interests actually exists, in varying degrees, in every country. Every nation has elements of core, periphery, and semiperiphery, although not equally. In common with Marx, then, the MWS theory looks at IPE in terms of class relations and patterns of exploitation.

According to Wallerstein, the core states dominate the peripheral states through unequal exchange for the purpose of extracting cheap raw materials instead of, as Lenin argued, merely using the periphery as a market for dumping surplus production. The core interacts with the semiperiphery and periphery through the global structure of capitalism, exploiting these regions and also transforming them. The semiperiphery serves more of a political than an economic role; it is both exploited and exploiter, diffusing opposition of the periphery to the core region.

Interestingly, on some issues Wallerstein attempts to bridge mercantilism (and political realism) with Marxist views about the relationship of politics to economics. For instance, as a mercantilist would, he accepts the notion that the world is politically arranged in an anarchical manner—that is, there is no *single* sovereign political authority to govern interstate relations. However, much like a Marxist-Leninist, he proposes that power politics and social differences are also conditioned by the capitalist structure of the world economy. According to Wallerstein, capitalists within core nation-states use state authority as an instrument to maximize individual profit. Historically, the state served economic interests to the extent that "state machineries of the core states were strengthened to meet the needs of capitalist landowners and their merchant allies."[22] Wallerstein also argues that, once created, state machineries have a certain amount of autonomy.[23] On the other hand, politics is constrained by the economic structure. He asserts, for instance, that strong (core) states dominate weak (peripheral) ones because placement of the nation-state in the world capitalist system affects its ability to influence its global role. As Wallerstein puts it, "The functioning then of a capitalist world economy requires that groups pursue their economic interests within a single world market while seeking to distort this market for their benefit by organizing to exert influence on states, some of which are far more powerful than others but none of which controls the world-market in its entirety."[24]

One problem with Wallerstein's theory is precisely what makes it so attractive: his comprehensive yet almost simple way of characterizing IPE. Many criticize his theory for being too deterministic, both economically and in terms of the constraining effects of the *global* capitalist system. Nation-states, according to Wallerstein, are not free to choose courses of action or policies. Instead, they are relegated to playing economically-determined roles. Finally, Wallerstein is often faulted for viewing capitalism as the end product of current history. In this sense he differs from many structuralists who feel that political-economic systems are still a choice people have and not something structurally determined.

## Neoimperialism, Neocolonialism, and Empire-Building Redux

As we suggest in several chapters throughout this text, the term **neoimperialism** describes a newer, more subtle version of imperialism that structuralists claim the United States and other industrialized nations have been practicing since the end of the Vietnam War in 1975. Neoimperialism differs from classic imperialism in that states no longer need to occupy other countries in order to exploit or control them.

Harry Magdoff (1913–2006), who edited the socialist journal *Monthly Review*, provides a good example of the older, *orthodox* version of Marxist-Leninist ideas related to U.S. imperialism. In his 1969 book *The Age of Imperialism: The Economics of U.S. Foreign Policy*, Magdoff established some of the same themes adopted by dependency and MWS theorists—especially those that focused on capitalism's expansive nature. He argued that the motives behind U.S. efforts to promote the economic liberal policies of the GATT, the IMF, and the World Bank could not be separated from U.S. security interests. During the Cold War, U.S. intervention abroad was not the result of one leader's decision, but the result of underlying structural economic, political, and military forces governing U.S. foreign policy.

Contrary to realists who argued that the United States intervened in Vietnam and other developing nations to "contain communism," the United States was motivated by a breakdown of British hegemony, coupled with the growth of monopoly capitalism—domination of the international economy by large firms that concentrate and centralize production.[25] President Eisenhower had earlier linked maintaining access to the natural resources of Indochina (Vietnam, Laos, Cambodia, and Thailand) to U.S. security interests. But in his farewell address, Ike warned of the growing influence of the military–industrial complex and its tendency to exaggerate the strength of enemies in order to justify military spending.

When the Vietnam War ended in 1975, many believed that the "naked" version of classical imperialism was over. U.S. hegemony declined as U.S. economic growth slowed and the U.S. dollar weakened when the Bretton Woods system formally collapsed in 1971 (see Chapters 7 and 9). The 1973 OPEC oil crisis exposed the United States' and other core countries' dependence on foreign oil. The U.S. public opposed military intervention in developing nations outside the U.S. "sphere of influence" in Europe, Japan, and Latin America.

However, by the late 1970s, a more classic type of imperialism resurfaced in the combined economic and military objectives President Carter established in his Carter Doctrine, proclaiming the United States' willingness to intervene in the Persian Gulf to protect U.S. oil interests. In 1979, the Iranian Revolution overthrew the U.S.-backed Shah of Iran, threatening U.S. control over oil and U.S. influence in the Middle East. Soon after, the U.S. CIA supported efforts of the Mujahedeen in Afghanistan against the Soviet occupation.

In the 1980s, as part of the Reagan Doctrine, the United States renewed its efforts to intervene in developing nations that threatened U.S. economic and security interests. Reagan assisted Saddam Hussein in the Iran–Iraq war and unsuccessfully intervened in Lebanon in 1983 and 1984. To contain communism in the western hemisphere, Reagan backed the *Contras* in Nicaragua. The United States also supported pro-Western authoritarian regimes in Guatemala, El Salvador, and other South American countries. All this time, he (and the presidents that followed him) never let up from seeking to control oil and assist Western oil corporations in the Middle East. One method of maintaining that influence was by giving military and other forms of aid to states like Saudi Arabia.

After the fall of the Soviet Union in 1990 and the Persian Gulf War in 1991, President Bush I ushered in what many structuralists view as a "new age of imperialism." From the perspective of U.S. policy makers, because the Soviet threat was gone, the globalization campaign provided the United States with an opportunity not to intervene as much as it did during the Cold War. Core nations could penetrate peripheral states via trade, investment, and other policies that rendered them dependent on core states. The United States and other industrialized nations promoted globalization as a beneficial package of policies that would help all developing countries grow. The "Washington Consensus" that economic liberal trade and investment best served this purpose became the rationale for policies for the IMF, the World Bank, and the WTO.

Many structuralists viewed these financial institutions as mere "fronts" for a U.S. goal to exploit the periphery, especially in Southeast Asia and Central and Latin America. Throughout the 1990s, President Clinton promoted economic liberal policy objectives with *selective* military intervention abroad. His campaign of "engagement and enlargement" mixed hard and soft power to explicitly draw other countries into the global capitalist economy while expanding the scope of democracy. Based on some of the lessons learned in Vietnam, Clinton was not as overtly interventionist as Reagan. However, U.S. troops continued to be staged in many regions—for short periods of time. The U.S. military hit terrorist targets in Sudan and Afghanistan with cruise missiles launched from U.S. warships. In cases where U.S. interests were not as clear, such as Rwanda, the United States failed to intervene to save hundreds of thousands who died in a campaign of genocide. Clinton's preference for multilateral (relatively equal) relations with the United States's main allies set the tone for joint NATO operations in the Balkans and for intervention in Kosovo in 1998.

As we discussed in Chapter 1, it was during the 1990s that many structuralists became quite critical of the latest phase of global capitalism—often referred to as hypercapitalism—that drives TNCs to produce new products in a supercompetitive global atmosphere in which individuals are made to feel better off but really are not. For many antiglobalization protestors, capitalism and globalization weaken local environmental laws, exploit labor, and are a major cause of poverty. And in many developing nations, they exacerbate class struggle between the world's richest fifth and nearly everyone else.

In the 1990s, the idea of "imperialism" once again appeared in U.S. policy-making circles but not in the *negative* context of military intervention abroad to protect economic interests. A growing number of neoconservatives (aka "neocons") such as Charles Krauthammer and Max Boot deplored the fact that when the Soviet Union fell, the United States missed an opportunity to capitalize on a "unipolar moment" by imposing its (benevolent) will on the rest of the world.[26] After 9/11, many policy officials and academics encouraged the new Bush administration to seize the moment and make maintaining U.S. hegemony—especially against "Islamo-fascism"—a central premise of U.S. foreign policy. Issuing a new Bush Doctrine that brazenly proclaimed that the United States "will not hesitate to act alone" or be restrained by conventions of international law, the Bush II administration invaded Afghanistan and Iraq.[27] In essence, when it came to security, the United States could do what it wanted, whenever it wanted, and with whatever instruments it chose.

Increasingly, a number of experts and academics also encouraged the administration to embrace the idea of *promoting* an American empire.[28] Although the administration never officially adopted the policy of empire-building, many argued that, in effect, many U.S. policies constituted behavior similar to that of the Roman and British empires. These policies included maintaining U.S. military installations and troops around the world and promoting the moralistic idea that the U.S. principles of liberty, equality, and individualism could not be questioned.[29]

Today, many structuralists argue that the Bush II administration's case for U.S. hegemony (and an empire) appeared to be more of the "naked" type of imperialism evident in earlier administrations. Professor of Geography and Anthropology Neil Smith argues that recent efforts to pacify Iraq and the Middle East have been part of a larger war and endgame to control not only oil but the global economic structure.[30] For some Bush administration neocons, the war in Iraq has indeed been a conscious quest for empire, albeit not labeled as such. Once again, globalization and U.S. interests complemented one another.

Contrary to the assurances of economic liberals, these efforts have failed to produce an equitable distribution of wealth; instead, they have led to violence and more inequality. Hegemony is yet another tool of the global bourgeoisie in the capitalist struggle against the proletariat who are confined to the sweatshops of the TNCs. Moreover, many structuralists maintain that Thomas Friedman's golden straitjacket of neoliberal policies do not empower and free people. Instead, these policies are totalitarian in nature, as communist dogma was in the Soviet Union. Globalization is merely part of a new religious-like canon pretending to explain the natural order of society.[31]

# A STRUCTURALIST ANALYSIS OF THE FINANCIAL CRISIS OF 2007

Today, many structuralists focus on a variety of international and domestic factors that resulted in the financial crisis of 2007 (see Chapter 8 for more details of the crisis itself). They would start by pointing to the contradiction between the global *glut* of capital and the growing *debt* in most countries. Much of this capital was earned from export sales by the emerging economies in the 1990s and early 2000s and *not* invested back in the United States, which left it with a major debt problem that, in part, contributed to the global financial crisis. Walden Bello and others argue that the global glut of capital problem is endemic to capitalism in that, as Marx suggested, heavy investment in production leads to overproduction that outruns the capacity of consumers to buy enough goods to keep prices from falling.[32] In other words, the United States should *not* have to rely on investments by other countries to sustain its economic growth. The real issue is the unequal distribution of income within nations that prevents their consumers from purchasing more goods and services.

Thus, many structuralists point to the massive increase in the inequality of income and wealth in the United States that began around 1970.[33] In 1970s, the mean income of the richest 20 percent of Americans was around $103,000.[34] Adjusted for increases due to inflation, this had grown to $168,000 by 2007, a 63 percent increase. Over the same time, the mean income of the poorest 20 percent increased by only $2,000 from $9,500 to $11,500, an increase of only 21 percent. The share of total national income going to the richest 20 percent of Americans grew from 43 percent in 1970 to 50 percent by 2001, while the share going to the poorest 20 percent fell from 4.1 percent to 3.4 percent. Thus, the richest fifth of the population received half the nation's income while an equal number of people, the poorest fifth, share about one-thirtieth. Again adjusting for inflation, the median earnings of a full-time year-round male worker were actually higher in 1972 than in 2007.[35] Over this 35-year period, the richest Americans claimed virtually all of the increase in new income produced by the economy, increasing the power of capitalists over workers and resulting in a higher degree of exploitation of the working class.

As discussed in Chapters 1 and 8, from the 1990s to 2008, large numbers of middle class and poor people could more easily get credit cards and home mortages. From 1989 to 2007, the mean level of mortgage debt for the middle class, defined as those between the 40th and 60th income percentiles, increased from $45,000 to $104,000.[36] This form of debt would not have been as troubling if housing prices kept increasing. But when prices started coming down in 2006, many homeowners owed more on their mortgages than they could get by selling their houses. Credit card debt, on the other hand, is not backed up by any assets and is simply a promise to pay out of future income. Although the amounts are smaller, the mean credit card balances more than doubled, from $2,600 in 1989 to $5,600 in 2007, for those in the middle 20 percent of the income distribution. Overall, the degree of indebtedness grew for the middle class, leading the ratio of total debt to total assets to increase from 20.6 to 24.3 percent between 1998 and 2007.[37]

Initially, debt provides a boost to the economy because those who borrow the money are very likely to spend it on a car, consumer goods, improvement to a house, or a vacation. Of course, the loan plus interest must be repaid. Now borrowers have less income to spend on consumer goods because they have to pay back the (wealthier) lenders. However, economic growth is usually anemic whenever households in the middle class must spend a large portion of their income to service their debt, which transfers a good deal of income to the wealthy instead of purchasing goods and services. This leads to less production and lower employment in other firms, which generates ripple effects that decrease spending and production and increase unemployment in other parts of the economy. Structuralists also argue that when lenders are repaid, they tend to consume a *smaller* share of their higher income. From a structuralist viewpoint then, the U.S. economy has been operating on an unstable foundation of debt and inequality. Any trouble, such as an unexpected drop in housing prices or a setback in some other sector of the economy, could easily trigger a serious recession. While the bailout policies of many governments attempt to improve the balance sheets of banks and other financial institutions, the amount of debt held by the average household will remain at a very high level, generating still more bankruptcies. Many households will find themselves unable to borrow money for a renovation or car purchase that they would have funded through debt in the past. The economy will probably continue to grow but at a relatively slow pace.

On a global level, structuralists connect the current financial crisis to a variety of their concepts and ideas. Since World War II, core nations of the industrial North have promoted the spread of neoliberal policies throughout developing regions of the world through the IMF, the World Bank, the WTO, and TNCs. The whole world has become the frontier for the neoimperial policies whose goals are the search for labor and natural resources, rendering most developing nations more dependent on the North and worse off. This reality frames many of the recent developments associated with the financial crisis in that many TNCs looked to LDCs as export markets and investment opportunities, adding to the glut of dollars in circulation around the world. Interestingly, it has been many of the semiperipheral nations that have employed protectionist measures that helped insulate them from many of the effects of the crisis. And now many of these states have shown signs of leading the recovery from the financial crisis before the core states.

According to most structuralists, the fundamental fix for the economy is no longer violent revolution but fairly substantial government regulation of both the global and national economies in order to transfer wealth from the upper class to those in the middle and working classes. Domestically, many structuralists focus on *strengthening* the capacity and willingness of the state to regulate the shadow banking and financial system. Of the suggestions mentioned in Chapter 8, some have supported the idea of temporarily nationalizing banks and establishing more state institutions to compete with those in the private sector. Many would like to see stricter measures to regulate derivates, executive salaries, and insider trading. If the masses are to regain confidence and trust in the financial system, states must do more to assure their taxpayers that they are *not* bailing out banks with their money while at the same time *rewarding* greedy officials with high salaries and bonuses. Many structuralists are also disappointed that policy makers themselves who espouse economic liberal values have not been more upset by the desire of financial institutions and officials to continue risky lending and investment practices.

Finally, many point to an assortment of "bad behaviors" by bankers, elected officials, and even individual voters as causes of the financial crisis. When it comes to state officials finally discovering people like Bernie Madoff who run Ponzi schemes that bilk their investors out of millions of dollars, Marx would be quick to say, "I told you so." Likewise, he and Gramsci would also not be surprised that state regulators failed to act on tips that Madoff's investment company was a scam because many of them were smitten by the laissez-faire outlook that discourages proactive state regulation of the economy. Nor would they be surprised that serious reform that reflects the interests of the working class has been difficult to pass in many national legislatures because most public officials reflect the interests of the financial elite.

More so than anything else, many structuralists blame the financial crisis on the shortcomings of laissez-faire economic ideas and policies. They would prefer a new ideology that accounts for the negative effects of the winner-take-all, individualist style of hypercapitalism, while justifying a more equitable distribution of income and the preservation of community values. These ideas are reflected in some of the social democracies of Europe.

On the global level, most structuralists support a variety of efforts to eradicate poverty, hunger, debt, and sickness in developing nations. Although IOs do not play a major role in Marxist theory, they have become increasingly important for any number of structuralist-oriented NGOs and activist groups. Many UN agencies have promoted programs that target women's issues, relief efforts for refugees, human rights, and the preservation of indigenous societies. Many structuralists are also behind proposals to increase regulation of TNCs (see Chapter 18).

## CONCLUSION

### Structuralism in Perspective

Some people ask whether studying Marxism or structuralism in the post-communist era is worthwhile. But one does not need to support Soviet-style socialism in order to see the value in Marx's analysis of capitalism as a political economic system. In this chapter, we separated Marx's four main contributions to IPE—the definition of class, class conflict and the exploitation of workers, control of the state, and ideological manipulation—from his theory of history, which predicted the inevitable collapse of capitalism and its replacement with socialism (and ultimately communism). Structuralists, drawing upon core ideas from Marxism, emphasize the class-based nature of the contemporary international political economy. One cannot understand domestic economic policies nor the international political economy without recognizing the conflict over the income derived from the division of the economic output into profits and wages.

Structuralists reject the optimistic liberal interpretation of free trade and deregulated markets, asserting instead that the inequalities in power between capitalists and workers, and the rich and poor countries, produces exploitation, inequality, unemployment, and poverty. The capitalist system tends to reproduce itself such that those who begin with more power and wealth are able to maintain that position at the expense of labor and the poor. Dependency, modern world systems, and theories about imperialism demonstrate that, given states' vastly unequal starting places, it is naïve to believe that free markets operate on a level playing field that will somehow lead to the end of poverty. This is because the state itself is seen as largely responding to the pressure of the capitalist-elite class, a group that is increasingly global in their orientation, seeking profits wherever they can be found, and having almost no loyalty to the citizens of their home countries.

The structuralist version of globalization calls for greater unity among workers from all countries and international trade and investment arrangements that no longer expose vulnerable developing countries to conditions that favor the core. This will require coordinated political action by those with fewer economic resources. Even Marx implied that not all decisions must be seen as beyond our collective control when he stated that "men make their own history, but . . . . they do not make it under circumstances chosen by themselves, but under circumstances directly encountered, given and transmitted from the past."[38] Thus, for many structuralists today, a deep understanding of the economic structure *permits* the exercise of human freedom, understood as the application of human reason to the shaping of our world. Of course, not every change is possible; but some very substantial improvements almost certainly are. The precondition for such action will be the development of a new consciousness—one that sees the free market version of globalization as simply ideological manipulation by those in power with an economic interest in perpetuating the status quo.

Despite the current economic crises and international conflicts, or perhaps because of them, there are many who agree with the structuralist agenda. One interpretation of the election of Hugo Chávez and other leftist leaders, or the massive protests against meetings of the global financial elite, is the claim that many people reject TINA (there is no alternative), the slogan of the neoliberals, and instead prefer the slogan of the World Social Forum: Another World Is Possible!

## KEY TERMS

structuralism  82
historical materialism  83
dialectical process  84
bourgeoisie  84
proletariat  84

false consciousness  88
imperialism  89
intellectual hegemony  92
organic intellectuals  92
dependency theory  94

modern world system (MWS)  95
core  95
periphery  95
semiperiphery  95
neoimperialism  97

## DISCUSSION QUESTIONS

1. Summarize the four main contributions of Marxism to contemporary structuralism.
2. Compare and contrast Marx's and Lenin's views of capitalism. How and why did their views differ? Be specific and give examples from the chapter.
3. Outline the essential characteristics or features of dependency theory, the modern world system approach, and neoimperialism.
4. Outline the key elements of the structuralist explanation of the current financial crisis.
5. If you were to come up with a new ideology to replace the wildcat version of U.S. capitalism, what, if any, structuralist elements would it include? Discuss.

## SUGGESTED READINGS

Jeff Faux. *The Global Class War: How America's Bipartisan Elite Lost Our Future—And What It Will Take to Win It Back.* Hoboken, NJ: John Wiley, 2001.

John Bellamy Foster and Fred Magdoff. *The Great Financial Crisis: Causes and Consequences.* New York: Monthly Review Press, 2009.

Antonio Gramsci. *Selections from the Prison Notebooks,* Quintin Hoare and Geoffrey Nowell Smith, transl. and eds. London: Lawrence and Wishart, 1971.

William Greider. *One World, Ready or Not: The Manic Logic of Global Capitalism.* New York: Simon & Schuster, 1997.

V. I. Lenin. *Imperialism: The Highest Stage of Capitalism.* New York: International Publishers, 1939.

Karl Marx and Friedrich Engels. *The Communist Manifesto: A Modern Edition* (with an introduction by Eric Hobsbawm). New York: Verso, 1998.

Joseph Schumpeter. *Capitalism, Socialism, and Democracy.* New York: Harper & Brothers, 1942.

Immanuel Wallerstein. "The Rise and Future Demise of the World Capitalist System: Concepts for Comparative Analysis," *Comparative Studies in Society and History*, September 1974.

# NOTES

1. Richard Anderson Connolly revised this chapter, previously written by Leon Grunberg.

2. See Ed Vulliamy, "Venezuela Coup Linked to Bush Team: Further Trouble for President Chavez as Force Chief and Three Other Generals Killed in Helicopter Crash," *The (London) Observer*, April 21, 2002, p. 22.

3. Many scholars have documented the history of U.S. involvement in Latin America. See, for example, Michael Grow, *U.S. Presidents and Latin American Interventions: Pursuing Regime Change in the Cold War* (Lawrence, KS: University of Kansas Press, 2008); Alan McPherson, *Intimate Ties, Bitter Struggles: The United States and Latin America Since 1945* (Washington, D.C.: Potomac Books, 2006); and Fred Rosen, ed., *Empire and Dissent: The United States and Latin America* (Durham, NC: Duke University Press, 2008).

4. Visit *School of the Americas Watch* at http://www.soaw.org/article.php?id=230&cat=63.

5. For a discussion of Marx's methodology see Todd G. Buchholz, *New Ideas from Dead Economists* (New York: New American Library, 1989), pp. 113–120.

6. Karl Marx, *The Poverty of Philosophy* (New York: International Publishers, 1963), p. 122.

7. A more analytical definition of disproportionality and its place in Marx's theory can be found in Paul M. Sweezy, *The Theory of Capitalist Development* (New York: Monthly Review Press, 1970), chap. 5.

8. Ian Steedman, *Marx after Sraffa* (New York: Verso, 1977), pp. 170–175.

9. Edward N. Wolff, *Top Heavy: The Increasing Inequality of Wealth in America and What Can Be Done about It* (New York: The New Press, 1996), p. 64.

10. Steven Lukes, *Power: A Radical View* (London: MacMillan Education, 1991), p. 27.

11. Max Weber, *General Economic History* (New Brunswick, NJ: Transaction Books, 1981), p. 277.

12. The uprising of Iranians after the presidential election in June 2009 is a good example of the response by citizens when those in power make an illegitimate claim to it.

13. Edward S. Herman and Noam Chomsky, *Manufacturing Consent* (New York: Pantheon Books, 1988).

14. Noam Chomsky, *Hegemony or Survival: America's Quest for Global Dominance* (New York: Owl Books, 2004), p. 121.

15. A French novelist, Harry Nicolaides, was sentenced to three years in prison (reduced from the original six) for a passage in his work that was deemed unflattering to the crown prince. See "Thailand's Lèse-Majesté Law: The Trouble with Harry," *The Economist*, January 24, 2009, p. 48.

16. V. I. Lenin, *Imperialism: The Highest Stage of Capitalism* (New York: International Publishers, 1993 [1939]).

17. Ibid., p. 88.

18. Ibid., p. 68.

19. Ibid.

20. See Andre Gunder Frank, "The Development of Underdevelopment," *Monthly Review* 18 (1966).

21. Immanuel Wallerstein, "The Rise and Future Demise of the World Capitalist System: Concepts for Comparative Analysis," *Comparative Studies in Society and History*, September 1974, pp. 387–415.

22. Ibid., p. 402.

23. Ibid.

24. Ibid., p. 406.

25. See John Foster Bellamy, *Naked Imperialism: The U.S. Pursuit of Global Dominance* (New York: Monthly Review Press, 2006), especially pp. 107–120.

26. See Charles Krauthhammer, "The Unipolar Era," in Andrew Bacevich, ed., *The Imperial Tense* (Chicago, IL: Ivan R. Dee, 2003).

27. See The National Security Strategy of the United States, The White House, September 17, 2002, www.hytimes.com/2002/09/20/politics/20STEXT_FULL.html

28. See, for example, Deepak Lal, "In Defense of Empires," in Andrew Bacevich, ed., *The Imperial Tense* (Chicago, IL: Ivan R. Dee, 2003).

29. See Chalmers Johnson, *The Sorrows of Empire: Militarism, Secrecy, and the End of the Republic* (New York: Metropolitan Books, 2004).

30. Neil Smith, *The Endgame of Globalization* (New York: Routledge, 2005).

31. This is one of the themes of Duncan K. Foley, *Adam's Fallacy: A Guide to Economic Theology* (Cambridge, MA: Harvard University Press, 2006).

32. See Walden Bello, "A Primer on Wall Street Meltdown," http://monthlyreview.org/mrzine/bello031008p.html.

33. See John Bellamy Foster and Fred Magdoff, "Financial Implosion and Stagnation: Back to the Real Economy," *Monthly Review*, December 2008, pp. 1–29.

34. Carmen DeNavas-Walt, Bernadette D. Proctor, and Jessica C. Smith, *U.S. Census Bureau, Current Population Reports, P60–235, Income, Poverty, and Health Insurance Coverage in the United States: 2007* (Washington D.C.: U.S. Government Printing Office, 2008), Table A3, Selected Measures of Household Income Dispersion: 1967–2007. This report is updated annually and can be downloaded from www.census.gov/prod/www/abs/income.html.

35. Ibid., Table A2.

36. U.S. Federal Reserve, "2007 Survey of Consumer Finances Chartbook," www.federalreserve.gov/PUBS/oss/oss2/2007/scf2007home.html.

37. Brian K. Bucks, Arthur B. Kennickell, Traci L. Mach, and Kevin B. Moore, "Changes in U.S. Family Finances from 2004 to 2007: Evidence from the Survey of Consumer Finances," *Federal Reserve Bulletin*, February 2009, Table 12.

38. Karl Marx, *The 18th Brumaire of Louis Bonaparte* (New York: Mondial, 2005).

# Alternative Perspectives on International Political Economy

Darfur—refugee women enduring.

Jacob Silberberg

The international political economy manifests many boundaries and tensions due to conflicting interests, points of view, or value systems that increasingly come into contact with one another. The mainstream IPE theories of economic nationalism, liberalism, and structuralism frame IPE issues in ways that capture some, but not all, of the most important elements of IPE today. One of the main intellectual projects of contemporary IPE is to expand its domain to include actors, frameworks, and ways of thinking that cannot easily be classified under the three main perspectives. One of the goals of this chapter is to highlight some of the ways in which IPE can be more inclusive—"without fences," as Susan Strange would say—when it comes to honestly confronting a broader range of important issues and theories in today's world without necessarily abandoning IPE's intellectual roots.

This chapter presents two alternatives or complements to the mainstream IPE theories: constructivism and feminist theory. Each of these critiques asks us to think of IPE in a different and generally broader way. IPE in the next few decades, however it develops, will necessarily reflect and condition each of these views.

We begin with constructivism, a new, vibrant theory that focuses on the beliefs, ideas, and norms that shape the views of officials, states, and international organizations in the global system. More than other alternative theories, constructivism focuses on society and culture and posits that policies change when people's values and fundamental beliefs change. It identifies an important role for global civil society in shaping the identity and interests of actors that wield enormous economic, military, and political power.

Feminist theory is concerned with the status of women and the role they play in relation to a variety of IPE issues, especially human rights and development. Along with constructivism, feminist theory focuses on the connections between gender and wealth, power, and authority. It identifies issues that are often ignored, such as the importance of family security, reproduction, and gendered beliefs in today's world. In the last twenty years in particular, a host of international organizations (IOs) and nongovernmental organizations (NGOs) have taken up the cause of promoting women's rights and improving conditions for women in all countries, but especially in developing nations. In many cases, IOs and NGOs have made end runs around states to accomplish these objectives.

Note that a discussion of the rational choice approach that appeared in this chapter in the previous edition has been moved to the Instructor's Manual. It applies what was originally an economic methodology to a variety of issues and problems in the social sciences. Students are encouraged to review the "rat choice" approach to understand the way individuals and the aggregate units that represent them, such as states and other actors, make decisions.

Before we begin, a word of caution is in order. Both of the IPE critiques described here are complex and controversial. As in the case of the three dominant IPE perspectives, many different viewpoints or variations exist within each critique. Thus, it is either bold or foolhardy to try to concisely and simply sum up either of these schools of thought. The analysis presented here, however, *is* concise and therefore intentionally incomplete, and also therefore necessarily superficial. This chapter was not written for experts of these theories as much as it was written for IPE students. Our aim is to acquaint students with a variety of other analytical tools and perspectives that may lead them to a deeper understanding of some of the issues surrounding IPE.

# CONSTRUCTIVISM

Many students find the constructivist perspective exciting because it focuses on issues and actors that are often overlooked in typical studies that are labeled "the IPE" of something or other. **Constructivism** is a relatively new perspective in IPE and international relations, and it focuses on the role of ideas, norms, and discourse in shaping outcomes. Constructivists reject the realist assertion that by simply observing the distribution of military forces and economic capabilities in the material world we can explain how states will interact. Institutions like the state, the market, or IOs are constructed in a social context that gives them meaning, purpose, and patterns of behavior. How power is used, what goals states have, and how countries interact depend on the ideas that actors have about those things. As actors interact with each other, they create meanings about their own identity and purpose, and those meanings can change. In this section, we explore the ideas of constructivists and provide many examples of the tools they use to interpret important global issues. We look at constructivists' understanding of war and peace issues, the actors they assert are important shapers of the world, and some of the analytical tools they use.

## Views of Conflict and Cooperation

Constructivism makes different fundamental assumptions than realism and economic liberalism about the structure of the IPE and its ability to condition state or individual behavior. Whereas realists (see Chapters 3 and 9) argue that the balance of power conditions states' behavior, constructivists suggest that conflict or cooperation between two or more actors is a product of those actors' different values, beliefs, and interests. One of realism's central assumptions is that a potentially anarchic "self-help" world forces all actors to make security their first priority, lest they be killed or overtaken by other states. Questions of identity and interest formation are considered to be analytically irrelevant. Social factors such as beliefs and values do not have causal power because they will always be overwhelmed by the structural realities of a self-help world.[1]

Likewise, economic liberals share the realist assumption of an anarchic world but hold that well-designed institutions can create the possibility for countries to share positive-sum gains. Like the realists, economic liberals have a rational view of the world, in which institutions such as capitalism or conditions such as interdependence order the international political economy. Social factors have little direct effect on these institutional structures or processes.

On the other hand, constructivist Alexander Wendt argues that "structure has no existence or causal power apart from processes. Self-help and power politics are institutions, not essential features of anarchy. Anarchy is what states make of it."[2] In other words, the existence of potential anarchy alone is not sufficient to produce a self-help world. A combination of social processes associated with different actors' assorted identities and subjective interests causes them to view anarchy in terms of a world of potential chaos and disorder. For Wendt, we do live in a self-help world, only because over time we have come to "believe" that self-help is a consequence of anarchy. The international system is quite orderly; most of the time, states act in accordance with formal and informal rules and norms.[3] The fact that some states are now regarded as "rogue states" is testimony to the idea that they are "deviant" in some fashion (see Chapter 9) because they have not behaved in a way acceptable to the community of nations.

Drawing more on the individual and state/societal levels of analysis (see Chapter 1), constructivists contend that states are not only political actors, they are also social actors to the extent that they adhere to norms (rules of behavior) and institutional constructs that reflect society's values and beliefs. Why do some people or states cooperate more than others? Is it because they are threatened by a more powerful state? Perhaps! More often than not, though, states cooperate because they are predisposed to work with other states. Their societies value cooperation and prefer cooperative tactics to more violent means of solving common problems. A good example of this is the states in the United Nations that tend to have reputations for "neutrality," or that act assertively to promote diplomatic or peaceful settlements of disputes, or that volunteer troops for UN peacekeeping missions—Canada, Norway, Sweden, Denmark, Belgium, and the Netherlands, to name only a few. Many of these states are also the first to sign on to arms control treaties or human rights conventions because of strong personal and public views in their nations about the nature of international relations and foreign policy.

Constructivists have found that sometimes seemingly implacable rivals cooperate with one another because they come to have a shared understanding that they are part of a "**security community**"—a group of people that is integrated with a sense of a shared moral purpose and a certain level of mutual trust. Israeli political scientist Emanuel Adler has looked at how the Organization for Security and Co-operation in Europe (OSCE), set up in the mid-1970s as a process by which the Cold War sides could cooperate on security matters in Europe, eventually became a transmission belt for liberal ideas about the importance of freedom of the press, arms control, and protection of human rights.[4] The process of interaction the OSCE has set up between states, NGOs, and experts inexorably spread a new, shared idea among participants that how a country treats its citizens within its own borders is a legitimate concern of other states and that that treatment would be governed by shared principles emerging through diplomacy and discussion.

This idea conflicted with traditional notions of state sovereignty and opened up the way for cooperation on security issues and resulted in constraining states in the Warsaw Pact, perhaps even supporting their prodemocracy movements. Since the collapse of the Berlin Wall, the OSCE has played a vital role in convincing European states—especially in Eastern Europe—to adopt new commitments to government transparency, free elections, and protection of minority rights. Constructivists argue that the OSCE shapes state behavior by defining what a "normal" European country comes to believe are its obligations to other states and its own citizens, irrespective of the country's particular foreign policy goals, historical rivalries, or military and economic power. As more states formally commit themselves to these obligations and discuss them, it becomes harder to accept the alternative of violating them—not so much because of the "costs" of doing so but because of the shock it would pose to a country's own identity.

In addition to explaining international conditions that do not simply reflect the material distribution of power, constructivists also observe how states behave in ways that do not seem to reflect a cost–benefit calculation or some other kind of rational self-interest. States sometimes constrain themselves even when they might gain more by shirking international rules and using military force. For example, powerful states often respect the sovereignty of other weaker states even when it would be much more expedient to "teach them a lesson." In the face of egregious piracy by Somalis in the Indian Ocean and the Gulf of Aden, no major military has launched raids on well-known pirate lairs along Somalia's coast. Even on the high seas, the navies of powerful countries have respected international rules about search and seizure of suspected Somali pirate boats, even when it would be easier to just "shoot and ask questions later."

Also, militarily powerful states have been extremely reluctant to accept or enforce changes in the borders of existing states, even when it would be in their interest to do so. Only grudgingly and after many years did NATO members who were policing Kosovo since 1999 accept its independence from Serbia. In places like Somalia and Iraq, where it is obvious that the borders are probably never going back to what they were before civil war started, the United States and the EU refuse to recognize the independence of pro-Western autonomous regions like Somaliland and Iraqi Kurdistan. The norms of sovereignty and border fixedness are so strong that powerful states will forego the opportunity to "solve" major headaches by violating those norms.

When it comes to WMD like nuclear and chemical weapons, constructivists help us understand why powerful states have not used them since World War II, even though these states possess them and could trounce many adversaries by using them. International relations scholar Nina Tannenwald has analyzed the **"nuclear taboo"**—the strongly held norm among the permanent members of the Security Council that first use of nuclear weapons is unthinkable.[5] Even nondemocracies or states like Israel and Pakistan, which face implacable enemies in their regions, have apparently internalized the norm that the use of nuclear weapons would be morally unacceptable. Tannenwald argues that the acceptance of the taboo—generated by a grassroots antinuclear weapons movement around the world—is what constrains states more than the fact of deterrence or an enemy's ability to retaliate. Similarly, international relations theorist Richard Price looks at how use of chemical weapons has become almost unthinkable. The stigmatization of their use is at odds with their obvious utility. Price explains how nonuse springs from a country's understanding of itself: "Abiding by or violating social norms is an important way by which we gauge 'who we are'—to be a certain kind of people means we just do not do certain things."[6]

## Actors That Spread New Norms and "Socialize" States

Constructivists have made an important contribution to IPE by explaining how a variety of non-state actors influence the behavior of states and markets. These scholars assert that economic liberals and realists have overlooked and underestimated social forces that generate and spread values, norms, and ideas that change the way the world works. We will focus on three "actors" that feature prominently in constructivist literature: transnational advocacy networks, epistemic communities, and IOs. As they interact with these actors, states learn ideas and are socialized to behave in new ways.

Constructivists often focus on transformation of an idea or set of beliefs about something. Examples abound, such as the increasing importance of human rights, a variety of environmental issues (see Chapter 20), and the importance of debt relief (see Chapters 8 and 11). In these and other instances, constructivists see an important role for non-state actors like NGOs and social movements in shaping and propagating new norms that states eventually accept, internalize, and craft their policies upon.

Political scientists Margaret Keck and Kathryn Sikkink, for example, have written about **transnational advocacy networks** (TANs), defined as "those actors working internationally on an issue, who are bound together by shared values, a common discourse, and dense exchanges of information and services."[7] These interconnected groups include NGOs, trade unions, the media, religious organizations, and social movements that spread information and ideas internationally, frame new issues, and try to get states to accept new norms and interests, often about "rights" claims. TANs' influence comes more from their ideas than their often meager economic resources. They act as "norm entrepreneurs," using testimonies, symbolism, and name-and-shame campaigns to create a shared belief among political elites and social actors that, for example, human rights protection is an obligation, that torture is never acceptable, that debt relief for poor countries is "the right thing," or that human trafficking is a new form of slavery. According to Keck and Sikkink, TANs spread their ideas by rapidly communicating information, telling stories that make "sense" to audiences far away from a problem, and holding states accountable for the principles that they have already endorsed in their own laws and international treaties.

The International Campaign to Ban Landmines is an example of the role of TANs in using issue framing and information politics to initiate global change. As discussed in the box "Landmines," the Treaty to Ban Landmines was signed and ratified faster than almost any other treaty in history. Among the factors that led to its quick ratification were the efforts of treaty supporters to change the beliefs of people everywhere, along with the views of the security establishments of different states, regarding the need for landmines. World public opinion was swayed dramatically by information and photos about the effects of landmines, which often meant the loss of a leg or arm by civilian noncombatants, especially in developing nations. People's values and beliefs were also challenged by the background studies of many NGOs that were easily communicated via the Internet and by rock stars and famous dignitaries such as Princess Diana of England.

You can probably find many other examples of TANs—and you may even be a member of a TAN without knowing it. For example, Greenpeace, the Natural Resources Defense Council, university students, and a number of affiliated groups led a grassroots campaign beginning in 2004 to convince Kimberley-Clark, the world's largest tissue manufacturer, to stop using pulp from old-growth forests in its Kleenex, Scott paper towels, and Cottonelle toilet paper. In 2009, the company finally agreed with this TAN to switch to a new sourcing policy based on recycled fibers and to support sustainable forest management. In another recent case, an international coalition has been leading a campaign to stop torture—and particularly the repeated playing of ear-splittingly loud music—to break down suspected terrorists detained in places like Guantanamo Bay and other U.S. detention centers around the world. The unlikely TANish coalition against "music torture" includes musical groups like R.E.M. and Pearl Jam, major British music industry organizations, and Reprieve (an international human rights NGO that fights the death penalty).

Another group of non-state actors who diffuse ideas in the global political economy are "**epistemic communities**," defined as "professionals with recognized expertise and competence in a particular domain and authoritative claim to policy-relevant knowledge within that domain or issue area."[8] These are global networks of experts—often scientists—who have detailed knowledge about complex issues and who share common understandings of the truth about these issues, based on the standards of their profession. Although these epistemic communities are not politically motivated actors, political elites rely upon them for advice, technical explanations, and policy options. Thus, these experts can have a very profound role in "educating" power holders about what problems exist, how important they are, and even what can be done about them. The epistemic communities have "power" through the ideas and values they collectively transmit to policy makers and IOs.

Constructivists have studied many examples of how epistemic communities' knowledge and ideas matter. Peter Haas has shown how atmospheric scientists around the world studying the ozone layer gathered and disseminated the consensus scientific evidence about the effects of chlorofluorocarbons (CFCs) on ozone depletion. In coordination with colleagues in the UN Environmental Programme and the U.S. Environmental Protection Agency, they generated knowledge that provided an impetus to international negotiations on the Montreal Protocol to ban CFCs. Similarly, Haas points out that many international regimes to regulate global environmental problems such as climate change and acid rain have come about through a process of "**social learning**," in which epistemic communities taught policy elites and international institutions the expert scientific consensus on environmental issues. In other words, epistemic communities provided political negotiators "usable knowledge"—defined as knowledge having credibility, legitimacy, and saliency—that persuaded them to adopt sustainability treaties even though the negotiators may have been politically reluctant to do so initially.[9]

There are many other epistemic communities in the world, ranging from arms-control experts to development experts. Economists are also a community that disseminates fundamental ideas about economics to policy makers. Networks of economists spread the ideas of John Maynard Keynes in the 1930s and 1940s, laying the foundation for trade and financial policies adopted at Bretton Woods after World War II (see the next section). Similarly, Latin American economists (sometimes called the "Chicago Boys") trained in the United States had an important role in shaping the policies of neoliberalism in their home countries in the 1980s. By understanding the ideas these economists were socialized to believe in during graduate school in the United States, political scientist Anil Hira shows how these economists formed "knowledge networks" that enabled and rationalized the adoption of structural adjustment policies in Chile and other Latin American countries.[10]

In addition to TANs and epistemic communities, international organizations are also norm entrepreneurs: They "teach" states the interests they should have, the norms they should adhere to, and the policies they should adopt. In other words, IOs have a role in shaping what a state *is* (its identity), *wants* (its interests), and *does* (its policies). Constructivists stress that IOs often perform these things through discourse and social interactions with political elites and civil society in a country, not necessarily through military force, sanctions, conditionality, or material rewards.

Several examples of IOs that have been studied carefully by constructivists include the International Committee of the Red Cross (ICRC), the World Bank, and the United Nations. Martha Finnemore finds that individuals in the ICRC over many years convinced states that they should abide by humanitarian limits during war.[11] These norms about how to behave during war have become internalized in a number of states that observe these norms even though they would gain some by flouting them. The World Bank and the UN have tried to spread norms of poverty alleviation and the Millennium Development Goals that most developed countries have accepted as obligations (see Chapter 11).

Although the general public often perceives the UN as weak and ineffectual, it has had a very important role in spreading norms of gender equality and women's empowerment throughout the world. Its panoply of conferences, commissions, and protocols have not changed gender policies overnight, but they have set the stage for states to engage in a dialogue about women's rights when they otherwise might not. And they have convinced states to write periodic reports about gender policies and to subject themselves to periodic supervision of their policies toward women. As the belief has spread that a respectable, "modern" member of the international community must accept the goal of greater gender equality and women's empowerment, recalcitrant states find it ever more costly and isolating to resist the gender mainstreaming discourse.

While constructivists agree with realists and economic liberals that states, in pursuit of their own self-interests, create some of the norms and values enshrined in the charters of IOs, they point out that these same states often find themselves constrained by these same norms and values. Martha Finnemore points out that a "unipole" like the United States spreads and institutionalizes liberal values in an effort to legitimize its own behavior and goals and to reinforce its soft power.[12] It was very successful in doing so through the Bretton Woods institutions. However, the United States weakens its soft power when it violates the very principles it has convinced its own people and other countries it stands for. For example, the United States was viewed as hypocritical for proclaiming its values of humanitarianism but breaking them by enforcing sanctions on Iraq from 1991 to 2003 that caused enormous suffering and death of civilians. While proclaiming the importance of international law, the Clinton administration launched military action against Serbia in 1999 without the formal sanction of the UN Security Council (repeated again in 2003 against Iraq). And while professing to promote democracy throughout the world, the Bush administration tried to undermine Hamas after it won a majority of Palestinian legislative seats in free elections in 2005. States are haunted by their own principles and are usually less likely to violate them when they lose legitimacy from doing so. Constructivists believe that states often hold other states accountable by withholding legitimacy or crying "hypocrisy" when those states ignore what they say they stand for.

## Tools and Concepts of Analysis

The four basic assumptions of constructivism applied to IPE are that:

1. Ideas, values, norms, and identities of individuals, groups, and states are socially constructed.
2. Ideas and values are social forces that are as important as military or economic factors.

3. Conflict and cooperation are products of values and beliefs.
4. Change can be explained by examining changes in the values and beliefs of actors over time.

Constructivists have developed a number of concepts to describe processes that involve the power of ideas. They also have a number of analytical tools to trace how ideas and norms are important to explaining outcomes in the global political economy. In this section, we look at several of these concepts and tools: framing, problematization, discourse analysis, and the life cycle of ideas.

**Framing** is the ability to define what the essence of a global problem is: What is causing it, who is involved, what are its consequences, and therefore the approach to mitigating or resolving it. All actors try to frame through language, reports, propaganda, and storytelling. Frames are always political constructs or lenses that focus on a particular story that may or may not be the "right way" to analyze a complex problem. Frames make us see a problem in a certain way as opposed to another, and therefore greatly influence how we understand how we should behave toward the problem. By exploring framing and framers, constructivists help explain who influences the global agenda and how our approach to problems changes over time.

For example, by framing deforestation and the loss of biodiversity as tied to the historic disempowerment of indigenous peoples and corruption in poor countries, we overlook an alternative understanding that global environmental destruction is rooted in consumption patterns in rich industrialized countries. The frame that we adopt will radically change the way we interpret our own behavior and what we must do to deal with the problem. Similarly, by framing the mounting U.S. military failure in Afghanistan as rooted in the inability to control warlords' profits from heroin trade that fund the Taliban, the U.S. government downgrades an alternative story that failure is the inevitable result of widespread resistance to foreign occupation and NATO forces' "crimes" against innocent civilians.

"Blood diamonds" has been pitched as a new frame to understand conflicts in Africa. TANs convinced some states that civil wars in places like Sierra Leone and Congo are tied to struggles over access to natural resources like diamonds and other minerals. Combatants fight not only to control the sources of these resources but also to gain money from them to buy weapons, destabilize governments, and terrorize civilians. We are led to believe that conflict can be reduced by cutting off combatants' ability to profit from diamonds by denying them access to international markets. The Kimberley Process is one such approach to conflict reduction arising from this framing (see Chapter 16). Critics argue that although this framing may have gotten countries and companies to "do something" about Africa, it obscured the more important reasons for conflict rooted in colonial history, ethnic rivalries, and bad governance.

**Problematization** is an important domestic and international process by which states and TANs construct a problem that requires some kind of coordinated, international response. Constructivists argue that problems exist because we talk them into existence. Of all the problems in the world, ask yourself, what are the ones on your radar screen? How do you know what you should care about in the world or be worried about in the world? Which are the problems your country cares about and which it does not? What we care about as people or states is a reflection of our social environment, our culture, and the beliefs we share with others in our society. The problems we care about are also "constructed" by political elites, powerful lobbying organizations, and social groups. The problems form lenses or filtering devices for you; rarely do you choose them yourself.

Constructivists trace the process by which "problems" become defined as problems. It is our perception of the problem that determines what countermeasures we will adopt. Today, much of the international community defines the following as problems: global warming, drug trafficking, Islamic terrorism, offshore tax havens, and North Korean missiles. These "problems" are not just "out there"; they become what we make them to be. For example, German political scientist Rainer Hülsse finds that the OECD countries talked the money-laundering problem into existence in recent years, even though it was never a big issue before and had always existed.[13] Similarly, Peter Andreas and Ethan Nadelmann note that until the twentieth century, drug trafficking and drug use were not considered crimes that required a global prohibition regime.

Similarly, constructivists suggest that states have choices in terms of who they identify with and against. Enemies have to be defined into existence as problems. There are no laws that will tell us who our enemies and friends are: We make them through a discursive, deliberative process informed by our culture, history, prejudices, and beliefs. Why has Iran been problematized as a pariah in the world in the last three decades? Haggai Ram argues, for example, that Israel has constructed an anti-Iran phobia, viewing Iran as posing an existential threat, in part because of completely unrelated anxieties in Israel over ethnic and religious changes within its own society.[14] In a similar way, countries create enemies by projecting their own fears on others like Iran and by attributing the characteristics of monsters, devils, madmen, and new Hitlers to leaders of some countries.

**Discourse analysis** is a particularly powerful tool for understanding where important concepts and terms come from and how they shape state policies, sometimes in very undesirable ways. Some constructivists trace changes in language and rhetoric in the speeches and works of important officials or actors on the state or international level. This is part of understanding the role of ideas in foreign policy. Officials talk their state's interests into existence, sometimes by adopting a discourse that resonates with an important lobbying group or sector of public opinion. Foreign policy can be seen as a social construct springing from a country's culture. We look at three examples of foreign policy issues that constructivists have interpreted through discourse analysis: Islamic terrorism, torture, and the clash of civilizations.

International politics professor Richard Jackson shows us that the way in which academics and states talk about problems creates meaning and limits the range of possibilities for actions. Through discourse analysis, he claims, we can understand the "ways in which the discourse functions as a 'symbolic technology,' wielded by particular elites and institutions, to: structure... the accepted knowledge, commonsense and legitimate policy responses to the events and actors being described; exclude and de-legitimize alternative knowledge and practice; naturalize a particular political and social order; and construct and maintain a hegemonic regime of truth."[15] He finds that an academic and political discourse has developed about "Islamic terrorism" that draws upon and reinforces historical stereotypes about Muslims, obscures understanding of the workings of Islamist movements, and paints a threat to Western civilization as so great that only counterterrorism or eradication are seen as appropriate responses to the Enemy.

Richard Jackson has also used discourse analysis to explain how political elites in the United States repeatedly used a "highly-charged set of labels, narratives and representations" in such a way that "the torture of terrorist suspects became thinkable to military personnel and the wider public."[16] In other words, official public discourse created the conditions for a "torture-sustaining reality" in the United States by using language that dehumanized suspected terrorists and made the public—despite minority opposition—willing to accept the necessity to abuse them. Without assessing the power of this discourse, it is hard to explain how the United States could adopt a set of practices so at odds with its moral values.

Similarly, constructivists have analyzed how political scientist Samuel Huntington's concept of the *clash of civilizations* became a popular way in the 1990s to explain the roots of global conflicts. The more this clash of civilizations rhetoric was used to describe relations between countries, the more it became a sort of self-fulfilling prophecy that constructed conflict itself. In effect, the clash exists because we believe it exists and we act on that belief. The clash discourse has become accepted as the truth—a causal explanation—even in the face of overwhelming social scientific studies that find no significant link between religious beliefs and terrorism and that point out the difficulty in even ascribing a common set of values to huge groups of people like the "Islamic world" or the "West."

The final constructivist method we describe is tracing the **life cycle of ideas.** The aim is to determine where ideas and norms originate, how they spread, the other ideas they come in conflict with, and how they become "naturalized," that is, accepted by states and IOs as the self-evident justification of policies. This may require going back in history to look at individuals or movements that promoted what at the time seemed like radical or even naïve ideas. Or it may mean studying the spread of ideas through negotiations over an international treaty or internal deliberations of a big organization like the World Bank. Of the many ideas floating out there in the world about what the nature of problems are and what states should do about them, only a few come to shape state interests and identities. Constructivists show us how those ideas become institutionalized and very resistant to change, especially when widely accepted in IOs, treaties, and the discourse of states. Sometimes it takes a traumatic event or crisis—a war, a depression, the collapse of the Berlin Wall, or massive, sustained street demonstrations—to shake organizations out of their routine thinking and accept alternative ways of viewing the world and defining their role within it.

For example, international relations theorist Charlotte Epstein has traced the life cycle of ideas about preservation of the environment and natural resources. These ideas originated with American Romantic authors and environmental organizations like the Sierra Club in nineteenth-century America.[17] As these ideas were transmitted to the global level they became focused on protection of endangered species, and industrialized states cooperated to preserve highly symbolic individual species like whales. Northern states and NGOs like Greenpeace "socialized" biodiverse Southern states and ex-colonies to believe that taking a "green turn" toward species preservation was what a "good" member of the international community should do. This way of looking at protection of individual organisms has, to some extent, crowded out a different—and more sustainable—way of thinking about environmentalism that is focused on preservation of *entire ecosystems*.

Others have traced how dominant economic ideas have changed over time within academic communities, states, and IOs. John Maynard Keynes's ideas spread rapidly after World War II and became the underpinning of the Bretton Woods institutions (see Chapter 2). But a new neoliberal discourse rose to challenge these ideas in the 1970s and 1980s, spread by American economists who constructed a different worldview about development, protectionism, and the role of the state in an economy. Individuals within the IMF in particular spread the notion that capital account liberalization, that is, unrestricted flows of capital across borders, was an inevitable force in the global economy and a necessary policy for every state that wanted to develop rapidly. As with many of the ideas of the Washington Consensus, the liberalization ideas lost some of their intellectual hold on governments only in the face of shocks such as the Asian financial crisis and development failures in Africa and Latin America.

Similarly, in the 1990s the World Bank began to change some of its neoliberal views (and thus policies) of development in the face of sustained efforts by TANs, which slowly convinced it through shaming and lobbying to believe that promoting environmental and social norms like sustainable development, poverty alleviation, and gender equality were part of its mission—indeed even critical to its own identity and purpose as an organization.[18] Even the first four chapters of this textbook have looked at the life cycle of many academic ideas—and particularly how the 2007 global financial crisis has given birth to new ideas about global financial markets.

Depending on the topics students study and the questions they ask, constructivism can provide enlightenment about some dimensions of an issue that are not captured in other perspectives. That alone makes it worth knowing something about.

## ▶ LANDMINES[a]

The case of antipersonnel landmines (APLs) directly connects the issue of personal security to the growing role of NGOs in the new global security structure. Landmines have a long history of use in conventional wars and low-intensity conflict settings. APLs were particularly popular during the 1970s and 1980s, when insurgent groups took advantage of their low price and simple use. They are hockey-puck-size containers buried in the ground that explode when someone steps on them or drives over them, and they cost approximately $3 each to make.

After the Cold War, APLs were considered by many to be unreasonable weapons because they "do not distinguish between civilians and combatants; indeed, they probably kill more children than soldiers."[b] This new realization of the detriment of APLs motivated a worldwide effort in the early 1990s to eliminate them completely. With worldwide support of the issue, including publicity from such celebrities as Princess Diana and Linda McCartney, the International Campaign to Ban Landmines (ICBL) gained rapid popularity after its founding in 1992. Current estimates put the number of remaining APLs at around seventy million,[c] most of them in developing countries such as Angola, Afghanistan, Cambodia, and Mozambique, which injure an estimated 25,000 people (a third of them children) every year.

The ICBL is an umbrella organization pulling together a number of NGOs into an antilandmine advocacy campaign cosponsored by the Vietnam Veterans of America Foundation and Medico International.[d] Beginning with six core organizations, the ICBL has since expanded to include about 1,400 groups. In a very short time, the ICBL produced a comprehensive treaty that completely bans the use of landmines. Created under the auspices of the UN, the treaty calls on signatories to "never under any circumstances" "use," "develop, produce, otherwise acquire, stockpile, retain or transfer to anyone" antipersonnel mines. Each party also undertakes the duty "to destroy or ensure destruction of all anti-personnel mines." In Canada in December 1997, some 122 nations signed the treaty, officially named the Convention on the Prohibition of the Use, Stockpiling, Production and Transfer of Anti-Personnel Mines and on Their Destruction, but known more commonly as the Ottawa Treaty. As of September 1998, some 40 nations had ratified the treaty, bringing it into international law in March 1999.

An interesting feature of the campaign itself was the method the NGOs used to further their cause. The ICRC commissioned an analysis of the military utility of APLs by a retired British combat engineer, who found them to be unnecessary and not as useful as has often been assumed. A number of NGOs also conducted extensive education campaigns to inform the public and state officials of the horrible effects of APLs, all the while lobbying, and also, in some cases, shaming state and military officials who resisted their discontinuation.

The Clinton administration claimed to support the treaty, but the United States did not sign it, for reasons related to the use of APLs as a defense mechanism in South Korea near the Demilitarized Zone (DMZ). As of the end of 2008, Russia, China, India, and the United States had not become signatories to the treaty. China has been a major supplier of cheap landmines, especially to African nations.[e] Thus far the ICBL is credited with the destruction of over two million antipersonnel mines and has been awarded the Nobel Peace Prize for its efforts. Its work is done primarily through advocacy networking and NGOs. The Hazardous-Life Support Organization (HALO Trust), a British de-mining organization, has been at the forefront of this effort since the beginning.

Most urgent for the international community to address in the war against APLs is increased cooperation of states and other IOs to help move the process along, particularly their willingness to share information and allow de-mining forces into their countries. In Afghanistan alone, HALO estimates there are still about 640,000 landmines, and although progress is slow, there is a foreseeable end to the blind violence.

### References

[a]Many thanks to our students Meredith Ginn and Lauren Whaley, who helped research this issue.

[b]Warren Christopher, "Hidden Killers: U.S. Policy on Anti-Personnel Landmines," *U.S. Department of State Dispatch* 6 (February 6, 1995), p. 71.

[c]www.minesawareness.org.

[d]For an excellent discussion of the politics of the ICBL see Richard Price, "Reversing the Gun Sights: Transnational Civil Society Targets Land Mines," *International Organization* 52 (Summer 1998), pp. 613–644.

[e]www.minesawareness.org.

## FEMINIST CONTRIBUTIONS TO IPE

**Feminism** has contributed to IPE scholarship in a variety of ways, and its influence can be seen throughout the discipline. Feminists began to make significant inroads in the social sciences during the 1970s, when IPE first developed as a discipline and the need for more interdisciplinary approaches became apparent. Feminists argue that every area of IPE—from the structure of state power to the allocation of political and economic resources—is impacted by gendered processes. Feminist theories and constructivist theories are often complementary because both perspectives challenge the positivist idea that concepts in IPE are unbiased or "value-free." This section explains what feminism is, why it is important, and what are some areas of consensus and debate. Although almost all feminists agree that women and men are equally valuable and that gender "matters," they disagree on many other issues. Not surprisingly, feminists who subscribe to economic liberal, mercantilist, or structuralist perspectives often advocate different policies and approach research in different ways.

## Women Matter; Gender Matters

Gendered analysis takes into account not just sex (biological males and females) but *gender* as the *socially constructed norms* that determine what is masculine or feminine. *Women* matter simply because women are intrinsically valuable as human beings. *Gender* matters to IPE scholars because to understand many issues in IPE we need to understand the way our values and assumptions about gender affect institutions. Seems pretty simple, right? But it took a long time to convince mainstream scholars and policy makers of those two points. In the examples below, we will look at how some policies have ignored women, with unfortunate consequences. Furthermore, feminists argue that efforts to "add women" to existing frameworks have often failed to adequately explain the role of gendered social norms and to produce gender-equitable outcomes.

Believing that men and women are *equally* valuable is the defining feature of feminism. This means that if a policy hurts women, feminists would argue that the policy is bad—even if it does not hurt men or children. For example, overexploitation of forest resources is a problem that concerns many governments and international aid donors like the World Bank. One effective policy response is for international actors (like donors and environmental NGOs) to work with governments and include local communities in Joint Forestry Management (JFM). Communities promise to protect the forest from illegal timber harvesting, grazing, and even fire, in exchange for non-timber resources. This is a sustainable, participatory policy, so it should be great for everybody, right? The problem in some cases such as India, Andrea Cornwall points out, is that women, who are not well represented on village committees that take up JFM, are still responsible for cooking, which means they still need wood.[19] In this case, criminalizing deforestation without providing women an alternative fuel for cooking food just means that women have to break the law and sneak into the forest at night to gather wood in order to fulfill their *gendered obligations as women* (providing food). Good for the community, but not so good for women.

Policies like JFM have different impacts on men and women. In fact, gender is so important that we might say *most* major policies—from food stamps to timber tariffs—affect men and women differently. During the first debates in 2009 over President Obama's stimulus package, feminists pointed out that promoting jobs in construction (as was advocated by many) meant job creation primarily for men. If women matter as much as men, some said, then stimulus money should also be directed toward sectors where there is greater representation of women in the labor force, such as health and education. The same question applies to international trade policy. Bilateral trade agreements may benefit men in the most powerful industries more than women in less important sectors of the economy. For example, NGOs like Action Aid and Women in Development Europe (WIDE) have criticized Europe's negotiations with India over a free-trade agreement because it privileges large corporations and ignores potential effects on women and other vulnerable groups.[20] How will this kind of agreement affect small farmers and informal sector traders who cannot compete with large producers? Does it matter that women tend more to be in the former groups than the latter?

A nonfeminist might argue that large industry and infrastructure investments are important types of spending, and women will benefit from more jobs and an improved economy even if most new jobs go to men. Historically, when gender experts have not been included in policy design, gender has been ignored. Often, this has a negative impact on women, but it also frequently works to the detriment of the policy's overall objectives as well. In the case of JFM, failure to consider gender-differentiated outcomes failed to protect women, but in doing so, it also failed to find a solution to women's overexploitation of forest resources. That is one reason why gender matters.

So, feminists have convinced IPE scholars as well as policy makers that women matter and therefore, gender-differentiated policy impacts matter. But gender matters for another reason. The roles assigned to men and women, our gendered resources and obligations, the things we buy, where we work, how much money we make, and our room for maneuver in making decisions—these gender-influenced things shape markets and affect the distribution of power and resources in society. To understand how gender affects policies and other issues in IPE, we contrast some feminist ideas regarding economic liberal, mercantilist, and structuralist perspectives. Keep in mind that most people do not fit neatly into one IPE perspective, but support policies or viewpoints that are influenced by multiple schools of thought.

## Liberal Feminisms

Even within liberal traditions, there are many debates among feminists. Classical liberal feminists (sometimes called libertarian feminists) are most concerned with individual freedoms, freedom from coercion, and "self-ownership" for men and women. Politically, they are concerned primarily with *de jure* inequality, meaning laws that proactively discriminate against women by barring their right to vote, to enter contracts, to transfer property in a free market, to use contraception, and to be protected by the state when their inalienable rights are threatened. Laws that condone marital rape, domestic violence, or men's control over women's property are all examples of discriminatory practices.

In defining freedom in terms of individual rights and seeking to limit the coercive power of the state, liberal feminists often do not support laws that promote women specifically, including those that would regulate equal pay with men or guarantee access to public office. Some liberal feminists argue that "just" laws will not necessarily lead to actual equality. This means they support only laws that protect individuals from direct coercion (e.g., threats against one's body or property). Justice, from this perspective, requires only that the state apply just means, not that the resulting society be equitable.

Other liberal feminists tend to support individual rights and free markets, but argue that men hold a disproportionate share of power in society. Because this *institutionalized patriarchy* is not confined to the state, liberal feminists advocate for both legal and social change. For example, they advocated that state universities in the United States be required to provide equal athletic opportunities to both men and women (known as Title IX rules). They also lobbied for the Violence against Women Act (VAWA), in response to the systematic difficulty in effectively prosecuting perpetrators of rape, domestic violence, and other gender-based crimes. These laws attempted to compensate for existing social discrimination rather than to curb inherently discriminatory laws. Until the 1980s, liberal feminist advocacy and research tended to pay only limited attention to the gendered implications of macroeconomic policies that IOs like the World Bank and the IMF began to impose on poor countries.[21]

Since then, liberal (and other) feminists have studied the many effects of global markets and development projects on women. Structural Adjustment Programs (SAPs), instituted in many developing countries during the 1980s and 1990s, have been criticized for (among other things) reducing governments' investment in health, education, and other social services so as to disproportionately hurt women and children. Similarly, development programs and government aid have been found to disproportionately benefit men, who have greater access to capital, land, salaried jobs, pensions, and political networks. Many women spend a disproportionate amount of time doing unremunerated labor such as housework, subsistence farming, fuel gathering, and caring for children, the sick, and the elderly. In the case of the JFM example, liberal feminists criticized the original projects because they were not designed to have gender equitable impacts by taking these particular roles of women into account.

In addition, Pietra Rivoli argues that the advent of free trade and globalization has been a great benefit to women in many poorer countries.[22] As textile and apparel production has moved to countries like China, it has created relatively high-paying jobs in urban areas for hundreds of thousands of young women who otherwise would be stuck in rural poverty. Despite the sweatshop-type conditions and poor labor practices in many of these clothing factories, women employed in them have gained higher incomes, economic autonomy, and even social liberation. Women's economic empowerment comes from China's industrialization and openness to global markets and investment. Over time, as the "bottom" of society rises, women may even gain more employee, union, and political rights.

Finally, liberal feminists (like many other feminists mentioned below) stress that the level of political rights that women enjoy in a country, along with their overall treatment, have important impacts on a country's overall economic health. Countries with stronger women's rights, lower fertility rates, better education for girls, and more women in government tend to have higher economic growth rates and more prosperous societies.

## Feminist Critiques of Mercantilist Perspectives

Feminist scholars have played an influential role in questioning the assumptions and approaches of IPE scholars in the mercantilist and realist traditions. They have sought to redefine our understanding of international power and national security. Traditionally, the study of IPE has privileged macrolevel structures: the actions of nation-states, peace and war, international diplomacy, and global security, to name a few. By focusing research questions on states rather than cities, TNCs rather than small producers or grassroots organizations, and countries rather than households, IPE scholars make implicit assumptions that macrolevel institutions are masculine. Certainly, women's influence in society has been most visible in smaller arenas. In this way, by privileging the state, IPE scholars have (perhaps unwittingly) rendered women's contributions all but invisible.

Some feminist scholars have had considerable influence simply by approaching research from different levels of analysis, often by beginning at the household or community level. They learned that because men and women have different gendered obligations, they also play very different roles in global processes and are impacted differently by them. More importantly, ignoring certain levels of analysis can lead to false assumptions. For example, feminists point out that economists previously assumed that households pool resources: Whatever money (or asset) comes in is shared by the family members. In fact, there is often conflict or negotiation between individuals about access to household resources, and that conflict is very often gendered.

Similarly, feminist scholars point out that state-centric IPE scholars have overlooked the informal and non-wage-based economy in which many women work. This sector is a critical underpinning of the market system as a whole and of the ability of a state to compete in the global economy. Many sectors of national economies have become "feminized," including caregiving, domestic services, education, and sexual services, where women face low wages, marginalization, and exploitation. Other service industries including telephone customer service, administration, and health care are dominated by women. Some of these services can be provided to Europe or the United States electronically from India at much lower labor costs.

Feminist scholars have redefined the concept of security, showing the ways in which international relations are gendered and making women's often invisible roles more apparent. At the same time, feminist activists have promoted women's ability to participate in spheres of international diplomacy and military security. Traditional theories of international relations and national security have tended to ignore gender as an analytical tool. Many feminists argue that this is not just because women are excluded from positions of power, but because women's roles are considered unimportant.

For example, in an intriguing recent study, a team of political scientists, a psychologist, and a geographer have found a significant correlation between the security of women and the security of states.[23] States that have high levels of physical security for women (measured by the prevalence of various forms of violence against women) tend to be more peaceful and have better relations with their neighbors. Conversely, states with high level of violence against women tend to be involved in more civil wars and violent conflicts with other states. Similar studies have found that states with higher levels of gender equality tend to be involved in fewer violent interstate disputes and conflicts. All of this research suggests that the status of women in societies has an important impact on interstate relations.

In her influential book *Bananas, Beaches and Bases*, Cynthia Enloe shows how diplomats and soldiers depend on the often unpaid and devalued work that women do. By studying the role of diplomats' wives or the way military bases depend on cooks, laundresses, nurses, and sex workers, she shows how private and personal relationships influence the international political arena. International policy makers, she argues, "have tried to hide and deny their reliance on women as feminized workers, as respectable and loyal wives, as 'civilizing influences,' as sex objects, as obedient daughters, as unpaid farmers, as coffee-serving campaigners, as consumers and tourists."[24] It would be easy to argue that these practical functions of everyday military operations or lawmaking do not directly influence larger processes like the laws or military campaigns themselves. But the practical dynamics of political negotiations and military engagements can have a tremendous influence on their outcomes.

Feminist security theory shows how the invisibility of gender in theories of war has masked important dynamics, including the myth that wars are fought to protect society's most vulnerable sections. For example, women form the bulk of refugees and civilian deaths in war, and mass rape has been an important form of gender violence. But rape as a weapon of war is not just another part of violence, and it is not only about women. When soldiers are allowed to rape, their leaders are using rape to *construct a particular masculinity*. In Darfur (and elsewhere), rape has been used to humiliate populations, to destroy families, and to drive people out of villages in order to access land. The importance of femininity and protecting women in people's ideas of family makes gender violence an effective tool for achieving a strategic military objective. In this way, gender is crucial for understanding questions of international security.

## Structuralist Feminism

Marxist feminists challenge the idea that capitalism benefits women in almost any instance. Many see gender not as the key factor in exploitation but as a source of oppression that is facilitated by the capitalist system. Evelyn Reed, a prominent Marxist feminist, wrote in 1970: "It is the capitalist system—the ultimate stage in the development of class society—which is the fundamental source of the degradation and oppression of women."[25]

Other structuralist or radical feminists—often influenced by Marx—argue that patriarchy is part of a system of exploitation that requires a complete overhaul (though not necessarily a violent one). They may or may not believe that the best way to end exploitation is to end capitalism, but many would agree with Reed that there is a link between the power mechanisms that determine international relations and those that determine race, class, and gender relations. Women and people of color make up a disproportionate number of the poor in most countries, and structuralists argue that this is a result of systematic exploitation within and between countries.

Where liberal feminists criticize neoliberal economic policies when they hurt women, structuralist feminists see those policies as emblematic of a greater problem. Meanwhile, they criticize development initiatives like microfinance because these loans actively promote women's involvement in capitalist competition, often aggravating inequality between women by failing to benefit the most vulnerable. By highlighting the need to consider sources of inequality other than gender, the influence of structuralism challenged feminists to move beyond domestic policy and household relations toward more systemic and globally relevant arguments.

State-centric IPE scholars have overlooked how globalization has direct, specific effects on women. Many newly industrializing countries have encouraged foreign direct investment in export-oriented manufacturing facilities that employ a large number of women. Melissa Wright has studied how these factories in northern Mexico (called **maquiladoras**) and southern China treat women as "disposable," paying them low wages in dead-end jobs. Even though these women are important to global capital accumulation, a mythical discourse portrays them as "industrial waste" that can be easily "discarded and replaced" when they have lost the "physical and mental faculties" for which they were hired: dexterity, patience, and sacrifice.[26] Wright and others point out that many women resist this marginalization and disposability.

Women also tend to be disproportionately hurt by the restructuring of the global economy and adjustments to crises within it. Cuts in social services and public goods cause male and female unemployment, but have tended to force more women into poverty, double shifts, and informal activities like prostitution, which damage their physical and mental health.

Feminist scholars have made significant contributions to—and criticisms of— the way IPE is studied. Cynthia Enloe may have summed up best the importance of having a "feminist curiosity": "One cannot explain why the international system works the way it does without taking women's lives seriously. 'Experts' may be knowledgeable about banking interest rates, about the oil industry, about HIV/AIDS; nevertheless, if those experts fail to think seriously about women's lives, they are certain to produce deeply flawed understanding—explanation—of today's international political economy."[27]

## SMUGGLING IN SENEGAL: GENDER AND TRADE POLICY

Senegal is one of the highly-indebted poor countries (HIPCs) in West Africa that has adopted a variety of economic liberalization measures advocated by the World Bank and the IMF. One exception is its sugar industry (actually one company, CSS), which has enough political power that the government protects it from international competition by setting sugar import tariffs so high as to effectively ban imports. The Gambia, the small country surrounded by Senegal, has much lower tariffs, and its government is only too happy to have traders buy its cheaper sugar imported from Denmark and Brazil. Here, we have a recipe for smuggling.

In West Africa, market women are very important because trade is one of the few occupations available to women and because villages need access to basic supplies (like sugar). Given Senegal's international trade policy and women's gendered role as traders, women have become the majority of sugar smugglers. Sugar manufactured in Denmark and Brazil is packed, transported, and shipped (mostly by men) to The Gambia where (mostly male) customs officers charge applicable tariffs or determine a combination of tariff and a bribe. The sugar is bought and stored by high-volume wholesalers, and it is eventually picked up by drivers and regional wholesalers, all of whom are men. Finally, it makes its way to rural markets where male and female traders buy 50-kg sacks.

A story will illustrate what happens from Senegal.[a] Fatou Cisse is a mid-level trader in a border town that hosts a market once a week. She makes about $100 during a good month. She pays a neighbor (a 20-year old man) to take her by horse-cart three times a week to The Gambia, where she buys a 50-kg sack of sugar on credit from her regular supplier, a male immigrant from Mauritania. Her driver knows the bumpy terrain well and tries to get back to the village using paths that are not easily reached by customs officers' cars. They are not in luck. A male ex-trader from a nearby village who knows their schedule works with the customs officers as a secret informant. An officer soon finds Fatou and they begin to negotiate. She apologizes for breaking the law, but explains that she is having a very difficult time and desperately needs money for her family. He agrees to seize only half of her sugar (25 kg). According to Senegalese social norms, a good man (reflecting gender) and a good customs officer (reflecting authority figures) must be flexible and generous occasionally. Upon return to the customs bureau, the officer, the informant, and the bureau chief each take 10 percent of the seized sugar (2.5 kg) and report a seizure of 12.5 kg that will be picked up by government officials and resold at auction. Having paid $28 for her sugar, Fatou will sell what she has left at her weekly village market for $17.50. Luckily, she has just enough leftover from the previous week to pay her supplier and try again.

Stories like this one illustrate both the complexity and the gendered nature of the globalization of production. Governments make international trade policies they hope will benefit their economies. For Senegal, this means some protectionism in response to powerful sugar lobbies—negotiations that are dominated by men. Because men and women have different obligations and opportunities, the roles they play are gendered and they will find different niches available to them. In the case of the sugar trade, both men and women make choices and establish norms that will allow them to benefit from the niche created by the trade policy. Although laws are broken, everyone in the story makes a profit, including the governments involved. On the other hand, the opportunities available to women are very different from those available to men.

If you were an IPE scholar hoping to study the impacts of Senegalese sugar policies, you might choose to study only the negotiations between governments and industry officials, but your conclusions would be much more limited than if you considered the role of gender and investigated multiple levels of analysis.

---

[a]A composite account from a survey of women smugglers in Cynthia Howson, "Trafficking in Daily Necessities: Women Cross-Border Traders in Senegal," unpublished PhD dissertation, School of Oriental and African Studies (London), 2009.

## CONCLUSION

Ideas are very powerful and *should* be taken seriously. The constructivist and feminist theories both challenge us to think about IPE in new and different ways. As John Maynard Keynes noted famously in the closing pages of his *General Theory*,

> the ideas of economists and political philosophers, both when they are right and when they are wrong, are more powerful than is commonly understood. Indeed the world is ruled by little else. Practical men, who believe themselves to be quite exempt from any intellectual influences, are usually the slaves of some defunct economist. Madmen in authority, who hear voices in the air, are distilling their frenzy from some academic scribbler of a few years back.[28]

The alternative perspectives discussed in this chapter provide us tools to better understand many global issues. They direct our focus to actors and forces that have been overlooked in the liberal, mercantilist, and structuralist perspectives. In so doing, they suggest that states and markets are not the only shapers of the world; other actors like individuals, women, and social movements profoundly influence global policies and struggles. They also remind us that the study of IPE cannot be divorced from moral and ethical questions. Unless we grapple with the different ways that individuals perceive the world, we will find it hard to explain what motivates their behavior.

## KEY TERMS

constructivism 107
security community 109
nuclear taboo 110
transnational advocacy networks
    (TANs) 111

epistemic communities 111
social learning 112
framing 114
problematization 114
discourse analysis 115

life cycle of ideas 116
feminism 118
maquiladoras 124

## DISCUSSION QUESTIONS

1. Do you think constructivism should get more attention as a social science theory? Why? Why not?
2. How might structuralist feminists respond to companies that outsource labor to sweatshops in poor countries?
3. Why do feminists argue that debates about national security need to consider gender? Do you agree?

4. What criticisms can be made of constructivism? Do constructivists underestimate the importance of material power in affecting global issues?
5. What tools do we have to measure that beliefs or norms actually influence an actor's outlook and actions?

## SUGGESTED READINGS

Barbara Ehrenreich and Arlie Russell Hochschild. *Global Woman: Nannies, Maids, and Sex Workers in the New Economy.* New York: Henry Holt, 2002.

Cynthia Enloe. *Globalization and Militarism: Feminists Make the Link.* Lanham, MD: Rowman and Littlefield, 2007.

Garnet. "Bibliography—Gender in International Political Economy." http://www.garnet-eu.org/fileadmin/documents/news/Bib-GIPE-all_incl_3rd_update-hs-2-2009.pdf

Gender Action. http://www.genderaction.org/

Margaret Keck and Kathryn Sikkink. *Activist without Borders: Norms and Identity in World Politics.* New York: Columbia University Press, 1998.

Nina Tannenwald. *The Nuclear Taboo: The United States and the Non-Use of Nuclear Weapons since 1945.* Cambridge: Cambridge University Press, 2007.

Alexander Wendt. "Anarchy Is What States Make of It: The Social Construction of Power Politics," *International Organization,* 46 (Spring 1992), pp. 391–425.

WIDE. Globalising Gender Equality and Social Justice. http://www.wide-network.org/

## NOTES

1. See Kenneth N. Waltz, *Theory of International Politics* (Reading, MA: Addison-Wesley, 1979).
2. See Alexander Wendt, "Anarchy Is What States Make of It: The Social Construction of Power Politics," *International Organization,* 46 (Spring 1992), pp. 391–425.

3. Steve Smith, Alexander Wendt, and Thomas Biersteker, *Social Theory in International Politics* (Cambridge: Cambridge University Press, 1999).
4. Emanuel Adler, *Communitarian International Relations: The Epistemic Foundations of International Relations* (London: Routledge, 2005).

5. Nina Tannenwald, *The Nuclear Taboo: The United States and the Non-Use of Nuclear Weapons since 1945* (Cambridge: Cambridge University Press, 2007).

6. Richard Price, *The Chemical Weapons Taboo* (Ithaca, NY: Cornell University Press, 1997).

7. Margaret Keck and Kathryn Sikkink, *Activist without Borders: Norms and Identity in World Politics* (New York: Columbia University Press, 1998).

8. Peter Haas, "Introduction: Epistemic Communities and International Policy Coordination," *International Organization, 46,* no. 1 (Winter 1992), p. 4.

9. Peter Haas, "When Does Power Listen to Truth? A Constructivist Approach to the Policy Process," *Journal of European Public Policy,* 11 (August 2004), pp. 569–592.

10. Anil Hira, *Ideas and Economic Policy in Latin America* (Westport, CT: Greenwood, 1998).

11. Martha Finnemore, *National Interests in International Society* (Ithaca, NY: Cornell University Press, 1996).

12. Martha Finnemore, "Legitimacy, Hypocrisy, and the Social Structure of Unipolarity: Why Being a Unipole Isn't All It's Cracked Up to Be," *World Politics, 61,* no.1 (January 2009), pp. 58–85.

13. Rainer Hülsse, "Creating Demand for Global Governance: The Making of a Global Money-Laundering Problem," *Global Society,* 21 (April 2007), pp. 155–178.

14. Haggai Ram, *Iranophobia: The Logic of an Israeli Obsession* (Stanford: Stanford University Press, 2009).

15. Richard Jackson, "Constructing Enemies: 'Islamic Terrorism' in Political and Academic Discourse," *Government and Opposition, 42,* no. 3 (2007), p. 397.

16. Richard Jackson, "Language, Policy, and the Construction of a Torture Culture in the War on Terrorism," *Review of International Studies, 33* (2007), p. 354.

17. Charlotte Epstein, "The Making of Global Environmental Norms: Endangered Species Protection," *Global Environmental Politics,* 6, no. 2 (May 2006), pp. 32–54.

18. Susan Park, "Norm Diffusion within International Organizations: A Case Study of the World Bank," *Journal of International Relations and Development,* 8 (2005), pp. 111–141.

19. Andrea Cornwall, "Whose Voices? Whose Choices? Reflections on Gender and Participatory Development," *World Development, 31,* no. 8 (2006), pp. 1325–1342.

20. WIDE, "The EU-India Free Trade Agreement negotiations: Gender and Social Justice Concerns. A Memo for MEPs," (2009). Available at www.boell-india.org/downloads/MEP_Memo_final__892009.pdf.

21. Gita Sen, "Gender, Markets and States: A Selective Review and Research Agenda," *World Development,* 24, no. 5 (1996), p. 823.

22. Pietra Rivoli, *The Travels of a T-Shirt in the Global Economy: An Economist Examines the Markets, Power, and Politics of World Trade,* 2nd ed. (Hoboken, NJ: John Wiley & Sons, 2009).

23. Valerie Hudson et al., "The Heart of the Matter: The Security of Women and the Security of States," *International Security, 33,* no. 3 (Winter 2008/2009), pp. 7–45.

24. Cynthia Enloe, *Bananas, Beaches and Bases: Making Feminist Sense of International Politics* (Berkeley, CA: University of California Press, 2000), p. 17.

25. Evelyn Reed, "Women: Caste, Class or Oppressed Sex," *International Socialist Review, 31,* no. 3 (1970), p. 40.

26. Melissa Wright, *Disposable Women and Other Myths of Global Capitalism* (London: Routledge, 2006), p. 2.

27. Cynthia Enloe, *Globalization and Militarism: Feminists Make the Link* (Lanham, MD: Rowman and Littlefield, 2007), p. 18.

28. John Maynard Keynes, *The General Theory of Employment, Interest, and Money* (New York: Harcourt Brace Jovanovich, 1964), p. 383.

# Structures of International Political Economy

The first five chapters of this book have provided an intellectual foundation on which to build a sophisticated understanding of the international political economy. In those chapters, we addressed many of the fundamental assumptions about three principal IPE perspectives that are most often used to analyze and interpret IPE problems such as the recent global financial crisis, and two alternative IPE perspectives. The next five chapters examine the "structures" that tie together nation-states and other actors and that link national and global markets in the global political economy. As we suggested in Chapter 1, Professor Susan Strange, a leading IPE thinker, has proposed that the main elements and arrangements of the international political economy can be organized into four core structures: production and trade, money and finance, security, and knowledge and technology.

Each of the four network structures consists of a set of relationships and distinct rules (if not tacit understandings) between and among different political, economic, and social actors in each of these areas. We propose to study how the structures connect the people of the world and condition the behavior of states, markets, and society. In examining the characteristics of these four structures, Strange encourages us to ask the simple question, *Cui bono?* ("Who benefits?"). This question forces us to go beyond description to analysis and eventually evaluation—to identify not only the structure and how it works but also what benefits it provides to those who founded it or to those who manage it today, what sources of power were used to create it, and how it has been managed. Strange also encourages us to ask questions about the relationship of one structure to another. An interesting thing about IPE is that states, markets, and society are involved in a number of simultaneous relationships, often on different terms with different partners. A good example is the way many officials promote trade (an element of the production structure) as an "engine to growth" in development strategies, and at the same time often attempt to use it as a tool of foreign policy to punish another nation (an element of the security structure) by withholding trade from that nation.

In Chapter 6, we explain how production and trade are related to who gains as a result of this production, and what terms or conditions prevail in the exchange of goods and services. Because production and trade are closely connected to income, development, currency exchange rates, finance, technology, and security, they are some of the most controversial issues in IPE.

Our study of the finance and monetary structure is covered in two separate chapters. Chapter 7 examines in some detail the history, vocabulary, and basic concepts everyone needs to know about finance and the workings of various international monetary systems. Chapter 8 is a discussion of recent events surrounding several international financial crises including the global financial crisis that began in 2007. We focus on the causes, effects, and some of the measures put forth by the IMF to address them. The rest of Chapter 8 examines the ongoing "debt crisis" involving many of the poorest developing nations. The chapter ends with a discussion of the increasing role of NGOs in managing global debt.

In Chapter 9, we examine the relationships and rules of behavior that affect the safety and security of states, groups, and individuals within the global political economy. Some parts of the security structure are easy to recognize, such as the role of the major powers in affecting war and peace. Other aspects, such as the role of terrorists, are less visible or certain, but, as the events of September 11, 2001 demonstrated, of equally critical importance.

States, markets, and society are also linked by a set of relationships involving knowledge, ideas, and technology. In Chapter 10, we explore who has access to knowledge and technology, and on what terms. Knowledge and technology represent the ability "to make and do things" that dramatically affect the balance of power between actors in the finance, production, and security spheres. One particular issue is intellectual property rights (IPRs), which profoundly affect who derives benefits from legal claims of ownership of a number of products.

Finally, in contrast to previous editions of the text, in this edition we address each chapter's relationship to the current global financial crisis. Much like 9/11, this crisis has profoundly impacted these and other issues covered later in the text.

# The Production and Trade Structure

Trade connects markets, states, and cultures.

Jacob Silberberg

*In the absence of a world government, cross border trade is always subject to rules that must be politically negotiated among nations that are sovereign in their own realm but not outside their borders.*[1]

Robert Kuttner

Trade is *always* political, economist and columnist Robert Kuttner tells us. Just ask Chinese tire manufacturers who are upset that U.S. President Obama in 2009 imposed high tariffs on imports of Chinese tires into the United States. In fact, many IPE theorists believe that no topic is more quintessentially IPE than trade. If anything, Kuttner's words understate the issue: Trade has become one of the most debated topics in IPE. Not only does it continue to be very important for national officials, but the number of political actors and institutions outside the nation-state that shape international trade and manage the international production and trade structure has increased significantly since the end of the Cold War in the late 1980s.

The international production and trade structure is composed of the set of relationships between and among states, IOs, international businesses, and NGOs that together influence and manage international rules and norms related to what is produced, where, by whom, how, for whom, and at what price. Together with the international financial, technological, and security structures, trade links nation-states and other actors, furthering their interdependence and mutual benefits but also generating tensions between them.

This chapter surveys a variety of developments and changes that have occurred primarily in the post–World War II **production and trade structure.** Some experts argue that recent changes in production methods and products are greater than those that occurred leading up to the Industrial Revolution. Concurrently, in conjunction with the popularity of economic liberal ideas and policies many trade experts and officials in the Northern industrialized nations (the North) have sought ways to liberalize (open) the international trade system—that is, to reduce the level of protectionist barriers that limit or distort trade. The United States and its allies created the General Agreement on Tariffs and Trade (GATT) in 1947 to promote liberal trade values and objectives commensurate with U.S. political and military objectives. In an effort to further liberalize world trade, in 1995 the World Trade Organization (WTO) replaced the GATT.

The chapter concludes with a survey of other important trade issues, namely: the growing number of regional trade blocs, North–South trade relations and their effects on human rights and the environment, and the use of trade as an instrument of foreign policy. These issues make trade one of the most complex and politically contentious areas in the international political economy.

This chapter presents four major theses. First, controversies about production and international trade stem from the compulsion of nation-states (rich and poor alike) and businesses to capture the benefits of production and trade while limiting their negative effects on producers and society. Second, there is an impasse in current international trade negotiations, where many developing nations have resisted efforts to promote more free trade and have adopted protectionist measures. Third, we maintain that recent criticisms of neoliberalism and globalization, coupled with the current global financial crisis, have exacerbated the resistance of many emerging economies to further liberalization of trade. Fourth and finally, the public and state officials in many of the industrialized nations are increasingly resisting some aspects of free trade and globalization.

## GLOBAL PRODUCTION

Because of its direct connection to trade, international production is of increasing significance to IPE students. A recurring theme in Thomas Friedman's work is the transformation in the production process associated with globalization. In an earlier work, *The Lexus and the Olive Tree,* Friedman focused on how people the world over, but mainly in the developed industrialized nations, are using sophisticated technology and communication systems in the form of multifunctional, "postindustrial" age products and services.[2] The Internet connects people all over the world in ways previously unthought of—both for good and for bad. New lines of cars and clothing are routinely mass-produced. After the Industrial Revolution, innovation and production have changed radically, occurring in quantum leaps and at an exponential rate. The production process has also shifted from one based largely on assembly lines to the use of robots and computers to make a wide variety of high-valued merchandise.

While all this has been happening, the production process has also become much more fragmented, resulting in vertical **specialization** and **outsourcing.** For example, in the case of Boeing commercial jets, many production plants do not make their own component parts, but assemble them after the components are produced somewhere else. In his latest work, *The World Is Flat,* Friedman focuses on the continuing transformation of the production process whereby, in just a few years, production processes have not only spread rapidly throughout much of the world (most recently to India and China) but have advanced to the point of empowering individuals to collaborate and compete globally. As anyone who has waited on the phone while speaking to a company "representative" in India can appreciate, the lever that enables individuals to go global so seamlessly is a wireless, satellite network that makes it easier to outsource production and services.

According to Friedman, "Every new product—from software to widgets—goes through a cycle that begins with basic research, then applied research, incubation, development, testing, manufacturing, support, and finally continuation engineering in order to add improvements."[3] Friedman's "flat world" is one of giant video screens, call centers, and the outsourcing of tax returns and flight reservations to places like India where workers are anxious to become part of the global economy and to affect it in some unique way. The transformation and globalization of the production process is not unique to the manufacturing of goods and the development of services; it has also occurred in agriculture and food production, other basic commodities such as cotton for textiles, and in sophisticated private and national security systems.

The World Bank reports that in 2008 the world's GDP totaled $60.5 trillion, with the high-income countries producing $43.2 trillion or 71 percent of the total (up from $34.5 trillion but down from 78 percent of the total in 2005). Middle- and low-income countries produced $17.4 trillion or 29 percent of the total, while low-income countries by themselves produced only $500 billion (down from $1.3 trillion in 2005) or just 0.8 percent of the world's total output (down significantly from 4 percent in 2005).[4] Undoubtedly, the recent global financial crisis has contributed to this reversal in economic growth in the poorer countries.

One way to think about production is in terms of foreign direct investment (FDI) connected to where production takes place. FDI consists mostly of private

| TABLE 6-1 | | | | | |
|---|---|---|---|---|---|
| **Net Inflows of Foreign Direct Investment (in billions of US dollars)** | | | | | |
| Region/Classification | 1980 | 1990 | 2000 | 2004 | 2008 |
| East Asia (including China) | 1 | 9 | 116 | 106 | 186 |
| India | 0.08 | 0.2 | 4 | 6 | 42 |
| Central and South America | 7 | 8 | 88 | 64 | 121 |
| European Union | 21 | 97 | 680 | 223 | 503 |
| United States | 17 | 48 | 314 | 136 | 316 |
| Middle East and North Africa | — | 2 | 7 | 27 | 114 |
| Sub-Saharan Africa | 0.3 | 1.7 | 7 | 17 | 66 |
| Developed Countries | 47 | 172 | 1,118 | 414 | 962 |
| Least Developed Countries | 0.5 | 0.6 | 4 | 13 | 33 |
| World | 54 | 207 | 1,381 | 735 | 1,697 |

*Source:* UNCTAD, FDI/TNC database at www.unctad.org/fdistatistics, March 2010. Data is in current U.S. dollars and current exchange rates.

investments in factories, mines, and land, as well as foreign investments in stocks of local enterprises. As indicated in Table 6-1, between 1980 and 2008, the value of global FDI inflows increased from $54 billion to $1.7 trillion. Today most flows of FDI (57 percent) remain concentrated among the developed nations, although investment continues to spread out to every continent, especially amongst the emerging economies. Within the developed regions, most FDI has flowed to the United States and the EU, which at least until 1990 attracted 70 percent of all incoming FDI. Beginning in the 1990s, the share of total world FDI for developing nations like China, Hong Kong, Singapore, Brazil, Mexico, and some transition economies of Eastern Europe jumped significantly as investors deposited their capital in those countries. Until the mid-2000s, very little FDI flowed to India, the Middle East, and sub-Saharan Africa. But by 2008, India's booming economy enticed investors, as did the oil-rich Middle East. Africa has seen a bigger inflow in recent years, partly due to Chinese interest in commodities in the continent. However, the least developed, poorest countries of the world have since 1980 been unable to attract any significant amount of FDI, undermining their future prospects for economic development.

According to Eric Thun, these patterns of investment have contributed to the mobility of capital and to the tendency of industries to leave the industrialized nations in search of new markets, cheap labor, or other production advantages in developing parts of the world (see Chapter 17). Clearly, until the recent financial crisis, official development aid was falling off while private FDI increased. As expected, many mercantilists and structuralists note that these trends have important consequences for the distribution of the world's wealth and power through international trade as well as for labor conditions, the environment, and many other issues in developing nations that we will discuss in later chapters.

## INTERNATIONAL TRADE

International trade occurs when goods and services cross national boundaries in exchange for money or the goods and services of another nation. Although most of the goods and services produced locally are consumed in confined markets, international trade has grown dramatically as a reflection of increased demand for goods and services that do not exist or cannot be produced locally. Increased international trade also reflects the growing internationalization of production. During the period from 1960 to 2006, for example, world trade in goods and services increased from a total of $62 billion to more than $23 trillion (both figures in constant 2000 dollars).[5]

Trade, then, ties countries together, generating significant economic, political, and social interdependence. For most states, trade is an easy way of generating income and jobs. For many developing nations, it is often a critical component of development plans. Thus, in a highly integrated international political economy, states are compelled to regulate trade in order to maximize its benefits and limit its costs to their economies. In so doing, states reserve the right to adopt a variety of policies to achieve these goals, which generates a good deal of tension between nations. And yet one state's trade policies can easily impose costly socio-economic adjustment problems on another state. Without a set of international rules and procedures, domestic-oriented trade policies could easily undermine the entire production and trade structure.

The production and trade structure pulls national leaders, IO and NGO officials, and the public in three directions at once. It is possible to support the principles of all three IPE perspectives of production and trade at the same time. On the whole economic liberals tend to emphasize that the rational thing for states to do is to agree on a common set of international rules and regulations that will maximize the gains from trade, in a competitive, interdependent international political economy. Likewise, without these rules, many states and groups they represent are likely to incur substantial economic losses. Mercantilists and structuralists agree that there are economic gains to be made from trade, but a variety of other issues related to how trade contributes to national wealth and power and how it benefits some groups more than others makes trade a much more complex and controversial topic.

What follows is a brief overview of trade history and a discussion of how the three perspectives view trade.

## THE THREE PERSPECTIVES ON INTERNATIONAL TRADE

From the sixteenth through the eighteenth centuries, there were no international trade rules as we know them today. Early European states aggressively sought to generate trade surpluses as a source of wealth for local producers, for royalty, and later for the bureaucratic state. To help local industries get off the ground, imports of intermediate goods were discouraged if they meant people would purchase imports instead of buying locally-produced goods. For mercantilists, trade was one instrument that states tried to use to enhance their wealth, power, and prestige in relation to other states.

## Economic Liberals

Many economic liberal ideas about trade are rooted in the late-eighteenth-century views of Adam Smith and David Ricardo, who were reacting to what they viewed as mercantilist abuses at the time. They proposed a distinctly liberal theory of trade that dominated British policy for more than a hundred years and is still influential today. Smith, of course, generally advocated laissez-faire policies (see Chapter 2). Ricardo went one step further; his work on the **law of comparative advantage** demonstrated that free trade increased efficiency and had the potential to make everyone better off. It mattered little who produced the goods, where, how, or under what circumstances, as long as individuals were free to buy and sell them on open markets.

The law of comparative advantage suggests that when people and nations produce goods and services, they give up something else they could have produced, but that would have been more expensive to make than the goods they actually created. This is what economists call opportunity cost. The law of comparative advantage invites us to compare the cost of producing an item ourselves with the availability and costs of buying it from others, and to make a logical and efficient choice between the two. In Ricardo's day, as we saw in Chapter 2, the law of comparative advantage specified that Great Britain should import food grains rather than produce them at home, because the cost of imports was comparatively less than the cost of local production.

For many economic liberals in the late 1800s, the world was supposedly becoming a global workshop where everyone could benefit from trade, guided by the "invisible hand" of the market. As we will see later in this chapter (and in Chapters 7 and 8), these ideas remain quite influential today and are the basis of **free trade**. Lightly regulated trade is also an integral part of other policies associated with the **Washington Consensus** promoted by the United States and other members of the **World Trade Organization (WTO)**. A large (but far from universal) consensus exists that the benefits of a liberal, open international trade system far outweigh its negative effects.[6]

## Mercantilists

As we outlined in Chapter 3, Alexander Hamilton and Friedrich List challenged what became accepted economic liberal doctrine about trade. From their mercantilist perspective, liberalism and free-trade policies were merely a rationale for England to maintain its dominant advantage over its trading partners on the Continent and in the New World. For Hamilton, supporting U.S. infant industries and achieving national independence and security required the use of protectionist trade measures. Likewise, List argued that in a climate of rising economic nationalism, protectionist trade policies such as import tariffs and export subsidies were necessary if Europe's infant industries were to compete on an equal footing with England's more efficient enterprises.[7] More importantly, List also maintained that in order for free trade to work for all, it must be preceded by greater equality between states, or at least a willingness on their part to share the benefits and costs associated with it.

Many neomercantilists today challenge the assumption that comparative advantage unconditionally benefits both or all of the parties engaged in trade. People employed in different industries or sectors of any economy can be expected to resist being laid off or moving into other occupations as comparative advantages quite easily shift around to different nations. In many cases, states can intentionally *create* comparative advantages almost overnight in the production of new goods and services simply by adopting **strategic trade policies** that invest heavily in those projects. New technology, skills, and other resources such as cheap labor can easily help one state's new industries gain a comparative (competitive) advantage over the industries of another state. This has been the case for auto, steel, and textile producers,[8] along with farmers, who almost continually seek trade protection for their commodities and products.

Another political reality that does not easily square with free trade is that in democratic nations with representative legislatures it is the state's *duty to protect* society and its businesses from the negative effects of trade. When many domestic groups and industries appeal to the state for protection, they are likely to receive help because legislators are threatened when these constituents face layoffs or competition from cheaper imports. In many cases, protection is a built-in feature of many democratic systems. Those who benefit from a small savings on the price of an imported article of clothing or new car, for instance, usually do not register their support for free trade as loudly as workers displaced by those policies and who seek protection.

Trade protection is also associated with a fear of becoming too dependent on other nations for certain goods, especially food and items related to defense. In some cases such as rice and energy imports, Japan has worried that too much dependency on another state can lead to either its economic or political exploitation. Such was the intention of the United States when it exported soybeans to Japan in the early 1970s and then cut off those exports when U.S. mothers complained of high meat prices and used soy as a replacement for meat.

Finally, some neomercantilists are concerned that the protectionist trade policies of a regional trade alliance such as North American Free Trade Agreement (NAFTA) or the EU (discussed below), which are designed to help local industries, might either intentionally or unintentionally disrupt another country. Often, this disruption is followed by an assortment of defensive or retaliatory neomercantilist policies meant to counter the original measures or in essence "even the score" with another state.

## ▶ THE VOCABULARY OF INTERNATIONAL TRADE POLICY

Some of the more important protectionist measures include the following:

- *Tariffs:* Taxes placed on imported goods to raise the price of those goods, making them less attractive to consumers. These are used to raise government revenue (particularly in developing nations) or, more commonly, as a means to protect domestic industry from foreign competition.

- *Import quotas:* Limits on the quantity of an item imported into a nation. By limiting the quantity of imports, the quota tends to drive up the price of a good at the same time it restricts competition.

- *Export quotas:* Measures that restrict the quantity of an item a nation can export, with the effect of limiting the number of goods imported by another country. Examples include Voluntary Export Restraints (VERs) and Voluntary Restraint Agreements (VRAs). For example, the Multifibre Agreement (MFA) established an international set of rules for textile export quotas for both developed and developing countries.
- *Export subsidies:* Measures that effectively reduce the price of an exported product, making it more attractive to potential foreign buyers.
- *Currency devaluations:* The effect of making a nation's currency worth less makes exports to other countries cheaper and imports from abroad more expensive. Currency depreciation thus tends to achieve the effects, temporarily at least, of both a tariff (raising import prices) and an export subsidy (lowering the costs of exports). However, currency changes affect the prices of all traded goods, whereas tariffs and subsidies generally apply to one good at a time (see Chapter 7).
- *Nontariff barriers (NTBs):* Other ways of limiting imports, including government health and safety standards, domestic content legislation, licensing requirements, and labeling requirements. Such measures make it difficult to market imported goods and significantly raise the price of imported goods.

- *Strategic trade practices:* Efforts on the part of the state to *create* comparative advantages in trade by methods such as subsidizing research and development of a product or providing subsidies to help an industry increase production to the point at which it can move up the "learning curve" to achieve greater production efficiency than foreign competitors. Strategic trade practices are often associated with *state industrial policies,* that is, intervention in the economy to promote specific patterns of industrial development.
- *Dumping:* The practice of selling an item for less abroad than at home. Dumping is generally regarded as an unfair trade practice when used to drive out competitors from an export market with the goal of generating monopoly power.
- *Countervailing trade practices:* State defensive measures taken to counter the advantage gained by another state when it adopts protectionist measures. Such practices include antidumping measures and the imposition of countervailing tariffs or quotas.
- *Safeguards:* Other defensive measures, used when, after tariffs are reduced, a product is imported in quantities that threaten serious injury to domestic producers of like or directly competitive products.

As many mercantilists see it, economic liberal theories about trade cannot account adequately for the real political world in which states manipulate production and trade for a host of social, political, and economic reasons. Because there is no guarantee of security in the international security structure, there is no guarantee that, even when states say they subscribe to free trade, they will not engage in protectionism of one form or another. Therefore, the rational thing for states to do is to be prepared to act in their own interest by protecting themselves.

## Structuralists

Structuralists label the early mercantilist period as one of classical imperialism. The drive to colonize underdeveloped regions of the world by the major European powers originated in their own economies. Mercantilist policies that emphasized exports became necessary when industrial capitalist societies experienced economic depression. Manufacturers overproduced industrial products, and financiers had a surplus of capital to invest abroad. Colonies served at least two purposes: They were a place to dump these goods and a place where investment could be made in industries that profited from cheap labor and access to plentiful (i.e., inexpensive) quantities of natural resources and mineral deposits. Trade helped colonial mother countries dominate and subjugate the people and economies of the colonial territories.

Lenin and other Marxist theorists argued that national trade policies benefited most the dominant class in society—the bourgeoisie (see Chapter 4). During the early colonial period, developing regions of the world remained on the periphery of the international trade system and provided their mother countries with primary goods and mineral resources along with markets for manufactured products. In the period of modern imperialism toward the end of the nineteenth century, capitalist countries used trade to spread capitalism into underdeveloped regions of the world. Lenin was attempting to account for the necessity of states with excess finance to take colonies in order to postpone revolution in their capitalist econom-ics. The "soft" power of finance as much as the "hard" power of colonial military conquest helped to generate empires of dependency and exploitation.

Structuralists argue that industrializing core nations converted these resources and minerals into finished and semifinished products, many of which were sold to other major powers and back to their colonies. To this day, trade plays a key role in helping the imperialist industrialized nations subjugate the masses of people in the developing regions of the world. Although particular sectors (enclaves) of core economies have developed, political and economic conditions for the masses of people within peripheral nations and regions *have become underdeveloped* since contact with the industrialized nations through trade.[9]

Immanuel Wallerstein stresses the linkage between capitalist core countries and periphery and semiperiphery regions of the world.[10] Today, patterns of international trade are determined largely by an international division of labor between core, semi-peripheral, and peripheral states that drives capitalism to expand globally. The integration of global markets and free-trade policies associ-ated with globalization are an extension of the same economic motives of imperial powers of the nineteenth and twentieth centuries.

In sum, all three IPE perspectives on trade also contain a variety of different ideo-logical outlooks. Today, a majority of academics and policy officials still favor an eco-nomic liberal international trade system within an order that is supposed to be *gradually* liberalizing or opening up. And yet, as we will see, in cases such as the recent global financial crisis, most nations tend to behave in a mercantilist fashion and adopt protectionist measures when their national interests are threatened. And as we will see in the next section, more than ever before, developing and industrialized nations are concerned that trade may be more exploitative than mutually advantageous.

## GATT AND THE LIBERAL POSTWAR TRADE STRUCTURE

Until after World War II trade rules largely reflected the interests of the dominant states, especially Great Britain. Despite a few decades in which economic liberal ideas prevailed, protectionism was the order of the day. Trade rules were enforced at the point of a gun—or cannon, as in the case of the United States forcing Japan to open its doors to U.S. trade in the 1860s.

The post–World War II structure of much of the capitalist world's political economy was established in 1944 at the Bretton Woods conference in Bretton Woods, New Hampshire. There, Allied leaders, led by the United States and Great Britain, created a new economic order based on economic liberal ideas (see Chapter 2) they hoped would prevent many of the interwar economic conflicts and problems that had led to World War II. By the turn of the twentieth century, protectionist trade policies had been on the rise as the major powers raced to stimulate industrial growth. During the Great Depression of the 1930s, protectionism spiraled upward while international trade decreased significantly, by an estimated 54 percent between 1929 and 1933, strangled in part by the Smoot–Hawley tariffs in the United States and onerous trade barriers enacted elsewhere. According to some historians, the trade situation and the depressed international economy helped generate the bleak economic conditions to which ultranationalist leaders such as Mussolini and Hitler reacted. It is important to note that, in contrast to the common assumption that the United States has always supported free trade, it was not until 1934 that it officially adopted a free-trade policy, until then routinely protecting most of its traded items.

In conjunction with this effort the United States promoted the establishment of an International Trade Organization (ITO) that was to oversee new liberal trade rules that would gradually reduce tariffs, subsidies, and other protectionist measures, offsetting domestic protectionist and mercantilist tendencies. The ITO never got off the ground because a coalition of protectionist interests in the U.S. Congress forced the United States to withdraw from the agreement, effectively killing it. President Harry Truman advanced a temporary alternative structure for multilateral trade negotiations under the **General Agreement on Tariffs and Trade (GATT)**. In 1948, the GATT became the primary organization responsible for the liberalization of international trade[11] through a series of multilateral negotiations, called *rounds,* at which the world's main trading nations would each agree to reduce their own protectionist barriers in return for freer access to each other's markets.

Two basic principles of the GATT were **reciprocity** and **nondiscrimination.** Trade concessions were reciprocal—that is, all member nations agreed to lower their trade barriers together. This principle was conceived as a way to discourage or prevent nations from enacting unilateral trade barriers. The loss in protection of domestic industry was to be offset by freer access to foreign markets. Designed to prevent bilateral trade wars, the principles of nondiscrimination and the **Most Favored Nation (MFN)** trading status required that imports from all countries be treated the same, whereby imports from one nation could not be given preference over those from another. Theoretically, the GATT's membership was open to any nation, but until the 1980s most communist countries refused to join it, viewing it as a tool of Western imperialism.

Reciprocity and nondiscrimination would prove to be potent during the early years of GATT negotiations in a series of trading rounds, as members began slowly to peel away the protectionist barriers they had erected in the 1930s, which allowed international trade to expand dramatically. In many cases, however, it was not possible to divorce politics from trade, even under GATT rules. Some nations were not always willing to grant reciprocity to their trading partners automatically, but granted it selectively to those they favored politically or wanted to assist, while for any number of reasons withholding it from other states. Later in the chapter, we will discuss the case of the United States using trade as a strategic instrument by withholding MFN status from China to achieve a variety of U.S. foreign policy objectives.

Keep in mind that the GATT was not a set of rules that could be enforced by the organization but depended on the members to fulfill multilateral trade obligations with one another. Policy decisions were made on the basis of consensus, and thus implementation of polices often reflected a combination of political and economic interests. Written into the GATT were a series of exceptions from generalized trade rules for certain goods and services, including tariffs and quotas on textiles and agricultural products along with regional trade agreements (RTAs), discussed below. At first, these exemptions allowed many of the war-ravaged nations to resolve balance-of-payments shortages. In the case of agriculture they also reflected food shortages in Europe and the need for financial assistance to farmers and other groups.

## Mercantilism on the Rebound

During the 1960s and early 1970s, the pace at which the Western industrialized economies had grown after the war began to slow appreciably. The OPEC oil crisis began in 1973 and soon resulted in economic recession in many of the Western industrialized nations. Throughout this period international trade continued to grow, but not at the rate at which it had earlier. Under increasing pressure to stimulate economic growth, many nations reduced their tariff barriers. At the same time, however, they devised new and more sophisticated ways of protecting their exports and otherwise limiting imports. By the time the Tokyo round of the GATT (1973–1979) got underway, the level of tariffs on industrial products had decreased to an average of 9 percent. The Tokyo GATT round tried to deal with a growing number of **nontariff barriers (NTBs)** that many believed were stifling world trade. Rules or codes covered a range of discriminatory trade practices, including the use of export subsidies, countervailing duties, dumping, government purchasing practices, government-imposed product standards, and custom valuation and licensing requirements on importers. Some new rules were also devised that covered trade with developing nations.

Many liberal trade theorists at the time argued that the Tokyo round did not go far enough, especially in dealing with the growing problem of NTBs or with enforcing GATT rules. In the 1970s and 1980s, the industrialized nations were encountering a number of old and also new kinds of trade problems. Trade among the industrialized nations quadrupled from 1963 to 1973, but increased only two and one-half times in the next decade. Meanwhile, trade accounted for increasingly higher percentages of GDP in the industrialized nations in the 1980s: around 20 percent for the United States, 20 percent for Japan, and an average of 50 percent for members of the EU. To put it mildly, trade policy continued to be a serious source of tension and disagreement among the industrialized nations, reflecting their increasing dependence on trade to help generate and maintain economic growth.

Japan, the quintessential mercantilist nation during this period, benefited from the liberal international trade system while erecting domestic trade and other protectionist policies. By the 1970s, Japan's export-led growth trade strategy began to bear fruit. Its Ministry of International Trade and Industry (MITI) helped pick corporate winners that it and other government officials felt would prosper in the international economy from state assistance. Most of these industries were high-employment, high-technology firms whose future looked bright. Working closely with their national firms, the Japanese and the NICs began assisting their firms in ways that would put them in a strong competitive position.

The term *strategic trade policy* became synonymous with state efforts to stimulate exports or block foreign access to domestic markets and included "the use of threats, promises, and other bargaining techniques in order to alter the trading regime in ways that improve the market position and increase the profits of national corporations."[12] In the United States, for instance, the Omnibus Trade and Competitiveness Act of 1988 produced **Super 301**, which required trade officials to list "priority" countries that unfairly threatened U.S. exports. Aside from export subsidies and the use of a variety of import-limiting measures, proactive strategic trade policy measures included extended support for "infant industries" complemented by import protection and export promotion measures. Some states went out of their way to form joint ventures with firms in the research and development of new technologies and products. An example was U.S. government assistance to the Microsoft Corporation in an effort to crack down on Chinese computer software pirates.[13]

With the acceptance of some amount of trade protection, a more liberal (open) GATT system seemed compromised. Free trade was slowly replaced as the central principle by the notion of **fair trade** or a "level playing field," where states sought to enact policies to counteract some policies of their trading partners. Trade policy moved from the multilateral arena of GATT to a series of bilateral discussions, as between the United States and Japan and between the United States and the EU. Under conditions of increasing protectionism but also in an effort to benefit more from trade, it was the United States during the Reagan administration that first sought to reassert the liberal vision of free trade. Thus was born the Uruguay round of the GATT.

## The Uruguay Round

The eighth GATT round—the Uruguay round—began in 1986 in Punta del Este, Uruguay, and was completed on December 15, 1993. The Reagan administration had a hand in commencing the multilateral trade talks, not only for the sake of promoting free trade but also to open markets for U.S. goods to help defray the cost of a recession in the United States at the time. As realist-mercantilists point out, however, the administration's goals at the time included economic liberal policies to counter the influence of the "evil empire" (Soviet Union) in developing nations.

Generally speaking, economic liberals tend to view this round as a success because of the effect it had on the volume and value of international trade. Many import quotas were eliminated, and export subsidies were brought under control. FDI surged alongside growth in trade, further connecting national economies into an interdependent international trade network.

The Uruguay round established new rules and regulations related to limiting protectionist measures such as "dumping" (selling goods at below fair market prices) and the use of state subsidies. The round went beyond previous trade rounds and established 15 working groups that covered such items as market access for textiles and agricultural goods; **trade-related aspects of intellectual property rights (TRIPs)** that include such items as copyrights, patents, and trademarks; **trade-related investment measures (TRIMs)**; and the complicated issue of trade in services. TRIMs and service issues reflected recognition that as the nature of production changed and spread to different parts of the world, it affected both the amount and kind of international trade.

For the first time GATT trade negotiations dealt in a comprehensive manner with the contentious issue of agriculture. All of the major producers and importers of agricultural products routinely employ subsidies and other measures that, according to economic liberal critics, distort agricultural trade. Agricultural issues had been intentionally absent from previous GATT rounds because they were politically too contentious and would have prevented progress in areas where agreements were possible. This time trade officials made the issue of agricultural assistance and reform one of the main objectives of the Uruguay round.[14] The United States and the Cairns Group (composed of Australia and 17 other pro–free-trade countries) led a politically radical effort to phase out all agricultural subsidies. After resistance by some U.S. farm groups and government officials, the United States agreed to *gradually* eliminate its domestic farm programs and agricultural trade support measures. EU efforts to significantly reduce their agricultural subsidies were complicated by the EU's Common Agricultural Policy (CAP)—a community-wide farm program that reflected the combined interests of its 15 member states, with France most critical of efforts to decrease agricultural support. Bringing the EU's farm program in line with GATT reform proposals would be a politically difficult and complicated process that took almost five years to complete.

Many U.S. exporters expected a new multilateral agreement to produce 20,000 jobs for every $1 billion increase in exports and access to overseas markets for U.S. semiconductors, computers, and a variety of U.S. agricultural commodities.[15] However, agricultural trade remained one of the major sticking points of the negotiations, shutting down the entire negotiations on several occasions. Eventually, at the eleventh hour in November 1993, an agreement on agriculture was reached that opened the way for agreement on all other issues.

In order to arrive at a consensus the new agreement reflected numerous "deals" or compromises between nations or blocs of nations. Under the new agreement, all countries were to reduce their use of agricultural export subsidies and domestic assistance *gradually* over a period of years. The new rules allowed states to convert nontariff import barriers into tariff equivalents, which were then to be reduced in stages. However, because of the strength of farm lobbies and the importance of agricultural exports in many of these countries, the method for calculating tariff equivalents in most cases actually set new tariff levels *higher* than they had been, effectively nullifying efforts to reduce farm support.

It is important to note that the Uruguay round did produce some 60 or so agreements on a host of other issues, including safeguards, TRIPs, rules of origin, technical barriers to trade, and textiles and clothing. The Uruguay round also became famous for creating the WTO and for institutionalizing what would become a set of global trade rules and regulations. GATT rules and a number of procedures became a legal element of the WTO. Trade officials claimed that progress was made toward liberalizing agricultural trade in the Uruguay round, but in reality, protectionism remained a key feature of agricultural trade. Many delegates intended that problems remaining in agriculture, establishing a services code, and developing nation concerns about how TRIPs gave advantages to developed states would be dealt with more directly in the next round of trade negotiations.

## The WTO

The final agreement of the Uruguay round launched the new World Trade Organization, comprised of 146 members at the time.[16] Headquartered in Geneva, Switzerland, it accounts for over 90 percent of world trade. Its primary job is to implement the latest GATT agreement and to act as a forum for negotiating new trade deals, to help resolve trade disputes, to review national trade policies, and to help developing nations deal with trade policy issues through technical assistance and training programs. Theoretically, WTO decisions are still to be made by a consensus of the members. The WTO's decision-making structure includes a secretariat (administrative body), a ministerial conference that meets at least once every two years, and a general council composed of ambassadors and delegation heads that meets several times a year in Geneva.

The WTO has a **Dispute Settlement Panel (DSP)** that rules on trade disputes, giving the WTO an enforcement mechanism, something the GATT did not have. An impartial panel of experts oversees cases submitted to it for resolution, and members can appeal their findings. The DSP can impose trade sanctions on member states that violate trade agreements. Several cases have gained significant press attention, including a judgment against the EU's attempt to limit imports of hormone-fed U.S. beef into the EU. Likewise, the WTO ruled against the EU's banana import program, which tried to curtail imports of bananas produced by U.S. companies in the Caribbean. Still another case was the transatlantic conflict over the production and use of genetically modified foods and organisms (GMOs) (discussed in Chapter 18).

For the most part, since the founding of the WTO, trade disputes have become more complex and politicized. Some nations have even threatened to withdraw from the IO when DSP decisions go against them. In some cases state officials are accused of "losing state sovereignty" to the WTO when they lose a dispute. So far, however, most states have either accepted the panel's findings or arrived at a satisfactory resolution, because so much is at stake economically or politically or because they feel compelled to participate in the rule-making exercise rather than be left out of it.

## The Doha "Development Round"

The next round of multilateral trade negotiations was to begin in 1999, but the WTO's ministerial talks in Seattle ended in deadlock, with riots in the streets and antiglobalization protestors blocking delegates from entering the negotiations. The "Battle of Seattle" became a rallying cry for many antiglobalization NGOs concerned about the violations of human rights in sweatshops, the large tracts of land farmed by agribusinesses in developing countries, the effects of large capitalist enterprises on the local environment, the lack of transparency in decision-making processes of the WTO, and a host of ethical issues.[17] Critics of all ideological persuasions, including President Bill Clinton, questioned the WTO's ability to deal with these popular issues as well as with institutional issues such as the connection between trade and such topics as investment, competition policy, and WTO decision making.

After the events of 9/11 many trade officials pushed to restart multilateral trade talks. At the 2001 ministerial meeting (far away from protestors), the next multilateral trade round began in Doha, Qatar. From the beginning many developing countries complained openly that agreements reached at the Uruguay round had not resulted in significant gains for them. As expected, they also argued that before new trade agreements could be reached, including those unresolved in the Uruguay round, the developed nations would have to make a concerted effort to include developing nations in the negotiation process. In recognition of this goal the Doha round was nicknamed the "Development Round" to reflect the growing importance of developing nations in the international trade system.

At Cancun, Mexico in November 2003, ministerial talks broke down once again. U.S. Special Trade Representative Robert Zoellick blamed developing nations and NGOs (especially those associated with the antiglobalization campaign) for resisting efforts to reach a new agreement. Many developing countries blamed the WTO for failing to fulfill promises it had made in the Uruguay Round. Some countries claimed to be suffering more poverty, along with environmental, social, and economic damage, after implementing the WTO's new rules. Outside the talks many developing countries were resisting efforts by the United States, the EU, Japan, and others to implement the "Washington consensus" or one-size-fits-all strategy of economic development that included trade liberalization. The Group of 20 (G20) (not to be confused with the financial G20), headed by Brazil, India, South Africa, and China, focused on cutting the farm subsidies of the rich countries. As a bloc, they dismissed 105 changes in WTO rules that would provide more access to their markets by the developed states.[18]

To restart the talks the United States offered to cut subsidies if others did the same. Meanwhile, the 2002 U.S. farm bill passed by Congress had *increased* U.S. farm and agribusiness support by $70 billion, making the U.S. commitment to trade liberalization seem hollow. The result, many critics point out, has been more overproduction and a distortion of world commodity prices, leading to the dumping of excess commodities onto world markets. This displaces local production in developing countries' markets and depresses prices local farmers receive. Even

President George W. Bush recognized that continued subsidies of farm commodities in the United States and the EU hurt poorer farmers in developing nations.[19]

Late in 2005 India, China, Brazil, and the rest of what became the G20 pushed the United States and the EU to cut domestic agricultural support significantly. The United States and the EU complained about each other's support for agricultural subsidies. At the Group of 8 (G8) meeting in the summer of 2006 in St. Petersburg, Russia, the major powers made yet another effort to come to an agreement that would end the Doha round talks. Only days later, however, the Doha round reached yet another impasse when once again agriculture was the major sticking point, blocking agreements on all other trade-related issues.

Other issues on the Doha agenda included TRIPs, which many developing countries argued limited their access to generic medicines by protecting patents held mainly by U.S. companies (see the box "Patent Rights vs. Patient Rights" in Chapter 10). The United States retorted that allowing developing nations to produce cheaper generic drugs with what are called compulsory licenses would hurt (the profits of) major drug manufacturers. The WTO failed to reach consensus on specific measures regarding "cultural products" (such as movies), insurance companies, security firms, banking across national borders, and protectionist "local content" legislation. Another stumbling block has been special and differential treatment (S&DT) rules that define market access to individual developing countries with a *unique* approach in terms of trade policy.

Without an agreement on agriculture and some of the other contentious issues, many OELs and trade officials fear that the Doha round will never be successfully concluded, possibly leading to the demise of the WTO altogether. Some believe that the inclusion of the developing nations in the WTO has created an agenda that has become too large to find consensual positions. Still another result could be "Doha lite"—a watered-down compromise that does not require nations to give up too much.

Finally, some HILs and mercantilists express the view that without an assertive hegemon, the globalization of trade has made it too difficult for states to reconcile economic liberal objectives with domestic pressures to limit the dislocating effects of trade. President Obama has not actively sought to make the United States a global hegemon, let alone push other states into signing off on Doha.

# REGIONAL TRADE BLOCS

Some mercantilist and economic liberal critics of the Doha round suggest that, instead of multilateral talks, the United States and other states ought to pursue bilateral and regional trade agreements. In fact, the United States has already agreed to more than 300 bilateral agreements with other countries, with more on the way. It also belongs to a number of **regional trade agreements (RTAs)** such as NAFTA and Asia-Pacific Economic Cooperation (APEC) (see below), where it is easier for the United States to dictate terms and not face pressures from some pro–free-trade businesses to complete the Doha round, which in most cases has a bigger payoff than an RTA. RTAs also have less bureaucracy and more room to account for the idiosyncrasies of partner states or to reconcile conflicting interests on a geographically regional level.

Regional trade blocs are defined as a formal intergovernmental collaboration between two or more states in a geographic area.[20] They promote a mix of economic liberal and mercantilist trade policies, reducing barriers within the trade bloc while retaining trade barriers with nonmember nations. RTAs number well over 300 and have grown prodigiously since the end of the Cold War. They are estimated to have controlled 43 percent of world trade in 2000. The most well-known regional trade blocs are the EU and the NAFTA. Others include the Central American Free Trade Association (CAFTA), Mercosur, the Association of Southeast Asian Nations (ASEAN), the Economic Community of West African States (ECWAS), and the Asia-Pacific Economic Cooperation (APEC). APEC is an **intraregional trade bloc** that attempts to integrate 18 Pacific and Asian nations into a nonbinding arrangement that would gradually remove trade barriers among members by 2020. As a promoter of the agreement, the United States hopes to further liberalize trade among the members while accelerating economic growth in the Asia-Pacific region. The EU, NAFTA, and ASEAN accounted for 60 percent of all global trade (imports and exports) of merchandise and commercial services in 2008. The EU alone accounted for 39 percent of global trade, compared to NAFTA's 15 percent, ASEAN's 6 percent, and Mercorsur's 1.6 percent. [21]

Why so many RTAs? Are they good for trade? Technically, RTAs violate the GATT and WTO principle of nondiscrimination, but they are nonetheless legal entities. Article XXIV of the GATT and Article V of the General Agreement in Trade and Services (GATS) exempt them, as long as they make an effort to liberalize trade within the bloc. In some cases, RTAs generate more efficient production within the bloc, either while infant industries are maturing or in response to more competition from outside industries. In other cases they attract FDI when local regulations and investment rules are streamlined and simplified. For many economic liberals, regional trade blocs are stepping-stones toward the possibility of a global free-trade zone as they gradually spread and deepen economic integration.

Not all economic liberals support RTAs. The noted supporter of globalization Jagdish Bhagwati is concerned that bilateral and regional agreements are likely to generate a "spaghetti bowl effect" of multiple tariffs and preferences, making it harder to eventually reduce trade protection measures significantly.[22] Other economic liberals believe that RTAs undermine the WTO process and the ultimate goal of *world* free trade, because protectionist measures tend to beget more trade protectionism. A good example is the decision by the Obama administration to impose tariffs on Chinese tires. What many construe as a move to support the American Federation of Labor and Congress of Industrial Organizations (AFL-CIO) labor union to "help preserve American manufacturing" generated a retaliatory threat from China to impose tariffs on U.S. chickens and car parts.[23]

Thus, mercantilists tend to focus on the political rationale behind RTAs as well as the way in which they serve a variety of political and economic objectives. For some nations they can be bargaining tools used to prevent TNCs from playing one state off against another. Another classic case, for example, was one of the arguments President Clinton made in support of U.S. efforts to help organize NAFTA— that the United States should be able to penetrate and secure Mexican markets before the Japanese did.[24] If the United States did not quickly bring Mexico into its trade orbit in 1993, Japanese investments in Mexico would negate U.S. influence over Mexico's future trade policies. As discussed in Chapter 3, these sorts of cases will always exist as long as states are the dominate actor in the international political economy and trade is one of many tools in their arsenal of instruments to generate wealth, power, and security.

## North–South Trade Issues

Tensions between the Northern industrialized and Southern developing nations over trade issues are not new. However, WTO G20 resistance to some of the measures of the Doha round that resulted in a deadlock does reflect the increasing importance and influence of Southern developing nations in the international production and trade structure.

In 1973, when the OPEC nations dramatically raised the price of oil for the first time, a coalition of developing nations in the UN called the Group of 77 (G77) demanded an entirely new international economic order (NIEO).[25] Based on complaints about the terms of trade favoring the developed states, part of the G77's demands included major changes in trade policies that permitted more access of their primary commodities into the heavily protected markets of the Northern industrialized regions of the world. The G77 also demanded a TNC "Code of Conduct" to assure developing nations control over their own resources along with a stronger voice in GATT decision making.

Consistent with the political environment at the time, these demands produced no fundamental change in GATT, IMF, or World Bank policies. The United States and other states responded that, rather than trying to change system rules and procedures, developing nations should become more integrated into the international economy. Because trade is an "engine to growth" and an essential element of development, developing nations would benefit from efficiencies gained from trade if they brought down their tariff barriers on their commodities and products and opened their economies to FDI.

In the 1980s, these same economic liberal ideas became the basis of Northern nation solutions to the debt crisis that emerged early in the decade, when many developing countries borrowed heavily from Western banks and some international finance agencies (see Chapter 8). Again, instead of changing the fundamentals of the international production and trade and monetary structures, the Northern industrialized nations recommended what was essentially the same set of policies they had suggested a decade earlier when it came to trade, this time packaged as the "Washington Consensus." Developing nations should grow their way out of debt by liberalizing their trade policies and opening up their economies to FDI. Many of these economic liberal ideas also served as justification for **structural adjustment policies (SAPs)**—conditions the IMF and the World Bank required developing nations to adhere to when they borrowed money from these institutions to overcome their long-term debt or short-term financial crises (see Chapter 8).

In the 1990s, these same economic liberal ideas about trade also served as an ideological justification for the globalization campaign, and they are still quite popular today. The WTO and the World Bank support the views of many trade experts who argue that countries that have experienced strong export growth have lower levels of import protection than countries with declining exports.[26] They contend that much of the economic growth that has occurred in many developing nations since the 1970s is due, for the most part, to an emphasis on manufactured goods for export (see Table 6-2).

Today, many economic liberals continue to support the objectives of the Doha trade round, especially trade policies that ensure the success of developing countries. The WTO continues to suggest that if developing nations remain committed to the new trade rules, they will attract new foreign and domestic investors. Likewise, the Uruguay round included special provisions that allowed developing nations longer time periods for implementing commitments and provisions requiring WTO members to safeguard the interests of developing nations.

## Structuralist and Neomercantilist Versions of Trade and Globalization

Many structuralists are critical of these ideas about trade and their effects on North–South relations. Some mercantilists do support economic liberal ideas and globalization to the extent that they serve state interests—usually those of the major powers. For others, though, the numbers quoted to demonstrate the gains from trade do not reflect a clear understanding of the consequences of economic liberal trade policies. In the 1960s, 1970s, and even into the 1980s, many structuralists would have recommended that developing countries do as China and insulate themselves from the inherently exploitative capitalist international trade system. At the end of the Cold War, however, many hard-core Marxist structuralists seemed to accept the necessity of trade but continued to criticize the international trade system and shifted their attention to reforming it.

Today, many structuralists argue that the WTO has perpetuated the exploitative relationship of the North to the South. Northern trade and development policies have resulted in economic growth for many states but not for the greater number of people within the poorer ones. Robert Hunter Wade, for example, has carefully calculated that while trade has raised per capita incomes in many states, especially China and India, it has also generated significant inequality between and especially within the developing nations.[27]

Other numbers for developing nations do not look good either. Trade has accounted for as much as 75 percent of the foreign exchange earnings of many developing nations. Many developing nations quadrupled their percentage share of world merchandise exports, from 7 percent in 1973 to 29.7 percent in 2004 (see Table 6-2).[28] However, the vast majority of developing nations still account for only about one-fifth of the world's trade in manufactured goods. Some 40 percent of those exports came from emerging economies (especially the Asian Tigers) in the last quarter-century. During this same period, the share of developing nation trade in agricultural and mining products and fuel declined. Many states in Africa and Latin America suffer chronic trade deficits and have large international debt (see Chapter 8).

The recent financial crisis has only worsened this tendency as a result of weaker global commodity, fuel, and mineral prices, which have contributed to increased LDC deficits and increased dependency on external financing of their

**TABLE 6-2**

**World Merchandise Exports by Region**

| Region/Country | Value (Billions of $) 2008 | Global Share (%) 1995 | 2000 | 2004 | 2008 |
|---|---|---|---|---|---|
| World | 15,717 | 100.0 | 100.0 | 100.0 | 100.0 |
| North America | 2,043 | 17.1 | 19.5 | 12.9 | 13.0 |
| United States | 1,289 | 11.7 | 12.5 | 9.2 | 8.2 |
| South and Central America | 597 | 3.0 | 3.1 | 3.1 | 3.8 |
| Brazil | 204 | 0.9 | 0.9 | 1.1 | 1.3 |
| Europe | 6,444 | 46.5 | 42.0 | 45.2 | 41.0 |
| European Union (27) | 5,611 | — | 38.9 | 41.7 | 35.7 |
| Commonwealth of Independent States (CIS) | 707 | 2.2 | 2.3 | 3.0 | 4.5 |
| Russian Federation | — | 1.6 | 1.7 | 2.1 | — |
| Africa | 550 | 2.2 | 2.3 | 2.6 | 3.5 |
| South Africa | 78 | 0.6 | 0.5 | 0.5 | 0.5 |
| Middle East | 1,022 | 3.0 | 4.3 | 4.4 | 6.5 |
| Asia | 4,354 | 26.0 | 26.4 | 26.8 | 27.7 |
| China | 1,430 | 3.0 | 4.0 | 6.7 | 9.1 |
| Japan | 786 | 8.8 | 7.6 | 6.4 | 5.0 |
| Six East Asian traders | 1,414 | 10.3 | 10.4 | 9.7 | 9.0 |

*Note:* The Six East Asian traders are Hong Kong, Malaysia, Singapore, South Korea, Taiwan, and Thailand.

*Source:* World Trade Organization, *International Trade Statistics 2009.*

debt. Likewise, demands for trade protection have increased in most developing nations as they have in developed states. As Table 6-3 indicates, poor developing countries are much more dependent on trade than wealthy developed countries. By 2008, trade as a percentage of GDP in heavily indebted countries, especially in Africa, had reached more than 70 percent, compared to approximately 50 percent in high income countries. Countries that are highly trade-reliant are more likely to be affected by volatility in prices of exports and imports due to protectionist measures and changes in global demand.

Aside from these numbers, some structuralists and mercantilists focus more on the effects that trade has on specific societies instead of on general trends that provide distorted pictures of consequences. As we discuss in more detail in Chapter 18, Walden Bello and others claim that new trade rules for agriculture have hurt small rice farmers in Malaysia and rice and corn farmers in the Philippines. Trade liberalization and globalization have served the interests of the U.S. agricultural "dumping lobby" and a "small elite of Asian agro-exporters."[29] Many experts argue that the effects of NAFTA on Mexican small farmers have been devastating: Between 1993 and 2002 two million were driven off the land. According to economic liberals, this consequence flows naturally from the shift from an agricultural to a manufacturing-based economy. Yet, the problem for

**TABLE 6-3**

**Trade as a Percent of Gross Domestic Product by Region**

| Region/Classification | 1980 | 1990 | 2000 | 2004 | 2008 |
|---|---|---|---|---|---|
| East Asia and the Pacific | 34 | 47 | 67 | 82 | 64 |
| Latin America and Caribbean | 28 | 32 | 41 | 46 | 47 |
| Europe and Central Asia | — | 44 | 67 | 69 | 68 |
| South Asia | 21 | 20 | 30 | 39 | 52 |
| Middle East and North Africa | 60 | 57 | 52 | 64 | 79 |
| Sub-Saharan Africa | 63 | 52 | 63 | 64 | 77 |
| High Income | 40 | 38 | 48 | 50 | — |
| Highly Indebted Poor Countries | 56 | 47 | 59 | 67 | 71 |
| World | 39 | 38 | 49 | 52 | — |

*Note:* Trade is exports and imports of goods and services.

*Source:* World Bank, *World Development Indicators* database, February 2010.

many structuralists is that the outcome is usually not what society would choose for itself but what is imposed on it by the Northern states.

Some mercantilists note that countries such as the United States have favored free trade when it benefits them but not when it might benefit producers in developing nations at the expense of U.S. producers. As pointed out earlier in the chapter, the developed states have an extensive history using protectionist trade measures to promote their own economic growth at the expense of other states. After World War II, the United States and its allies used the GATT and the WTO, along with other trade and finance organizations, to lower tariff barriers and thereby expose the infant industries of developing nations to competition with the more mature industries of the industrialized nations.

Yet, even a supporter of managed globalization such as Dani Rodrik points out that many of the world's faster growing economies, such as China, Vietnam, and Malaysia, insulated themselves from the international economy during the recent Asian crisis and now in response to the global financial crisis (see Chapter 8). According to Rodrik, in the past, high-tariff countries grew *faster* than those without tariffs.[30] Now the developed states want to "kick away the ladder" (take away protection) from under the developing nations.[31] Rodrik and Chang would support Bello's argument that protection serves a variety of "socially worthy objectives such as promoting food security for society's low income people, protecting small farmers and biodiversity, guaranteeing food security, and promoting rural social development."[32]

## Economic Liberal and NGO Critics of Globalization

Two other recent developments have influenced North–South relations. The first routinely makes headlines. In the 1990s, a growing number of NGOs, many with structuralist views and closely connected to the antiglobalization movement, have focused attention on the connection between trade and issues such as the environment, global labor conditions, drugs, and even terrorism. NGOs such as Oxfam, Global Trade Watch, and Global Exchange attempted to acquire first-hand information about the effects of Northern trade policies on developing nations and publicized it in speeches, newspapers, journals, and on their websites.[33] Production and trade affect the environment in ways that states and businesses never anticipated, as the demand for more energy resources increasingly makes the true cost of trade incalculable. To some extent, constructivist theorists (see Chapter 5) posit that these civil groups are responsible for changing the way the general population of developed countries thinks about globalization and "free trade."

Polls in the United States indicate that support for free trade has gradually decreased without a consensus about its benefit to the U.S. economy.[34] Two factors have contributed to this shift. First, a large number of jobs in industrialized states have been outsourced to countries such as China. Even though a good case can be made that outsourcing generates more jobs globally than it takes away, the plight of a middle-aged, hard-working U.S. citizen losing her job to a poorly paid Chinese worker is politically hard to swallow. Second, the global financial crisis has seen many states question trade liberalization and globalization in the face of the impact this disaster has had on their societies. Even economic liberals have begun to question the appropriateness of liberal trade for developing nations. In his new book *Making Globalization Work*, Joseph Stiglitz, a former chief economist of the World Bank, argues that states should cooperate to protect the legitimate interests of those hurt by globalization.[35]

NGOs have played a role in monitoring the effects of TNCs on various societies, casting light on many of the ethical and judicial dimensions of outsourcing and job displacement. In some cases, NGOs have been a source of information for WTO dispute hearings. A growing number of NGOs and university students have developed alternative trade strategies. One such effort is the "fair trade" movement that seeks to give workers in developing countries higher prices for certified goods such as coffee, chocolate, handicrafts, quinoa, and timber.[36]

## TRADE AS A FOREIGN POLICY TOOL

Finally, as alluded to above, many state officials over the years have attempted to use trade as an instrument to achieve political, social, and economic objectives. In the 1980s, the Reagan administration applied trade restrictions on nations it felt were either supporters of communist revolutionary movements (for example, Vietnam, Cambodia, and Nicaragua), sponsors of terrorism (Libya, Iran, Cuba, Syria, and the People's Democratic Republic of Yemen), or states such as South Africa that practiced *apartheid* (racial segregation).

After the first Persian Gulf War, the UN sponsored sanctions against Iraq to punish it for invading Kuwait and to compel it to stop producing weapons of mass destruction (WMD). While the use of sanctions as a tool of foreign policy has lost some popularity, the UN Security Council imposed them in the fall of 2006 against North Korea for its failure to stop producing and testing nuclear and other WMDs. These sanctions included inspections of goods coming into and out of North Korea by boat, plane, or train.

By the mid-1990s many states came to view trade sanctions as morally repugnant because of the pain they inflict on ordinary people. Many critics of trade sanctions point out that they usually do not effect any real change in a targeted state's policies.[37] Businesses and governments often can get around trade sanctions because goods produced in one country are hard to distinguish from those produced in another. It is also difficult to determine how the target state will react and adjust to an embargo or boycott. In cases such as Nicaragua in the 1980s, Iraq in the 1990s, North Korea in 2006, and most recently Iran, economic sanctions have helped generate popular support for authoritarian leaders who resist the sanctions-imposing, "imperial aggressors."

These cases demonstrate that there is more to the use of sanctions than simply using trade to punish or reward a state. When it comes to which trade sanctions to use in a given situation, tensions often reflect conflicting interests of different domestic businesses and foreign policy officials. However, many states are reluctant to use trade and other sanctions because they do not always work and often have unintended side effects. For the most part, trade remains a tool many states use to help discipline or send a distinct message to another state.

# CONCLUSION

## The International Production and Trade Structure in Repose

Many economic liberal objectives associated with the production and international trade structure have been achieved since World War II, resulting in a dramatic shift in production both within developed states and into less developed regions of the world. Until recently, this helped increase the volume and value of international trade. However, a number of countertrends coexist within this liberal trade order, demonstrating that its values are not shared by many developing nations and NGOs.

Through a series of multilateral negotiation rounds, the industrialized nations have pushed for the liberalization of international trade in manufactured goods and some services associated with information and communication systems. Many trade experts still contend that economic liberal trade rules that are part of the U.S.-backed globalization campaign will further integrate the global economy and help developing nations grow. And yet, in the Doha round many developing nations have resisted these policies.

From the perspective of many trade experts of all ideological stripes, what was supposed to have been a "sweetheart" deal for developing countries has become an issue of political sensitivity for the Northern industrialized states, who are reluctant to decrease protection for agriculture, textiles, and government procurement. Negotiations have been drawn out over a variety of other issues including information products, pharmaceuticals, TRIPs, and services.

Difficulties in multilateral negotiations also reflect tensions between the North and the South. The WTO's economic liberal trade regulations reflect predominantly the interests of the Northern industrialized nations. Developing countries now have increasing influence in multilateral negotiations, based on their importance to developed states as markets and sources of labor for TNCs. Antiglobalization groups and NGOs have challenged the assumed benefits of free trade and other policies associated with globalization.

One reaction by some of the more developed states to these developments has been to shift attention away from the multilateral trading system and the WTO toward more bilateral and regional trade agreements. RTAs simultaneously embrace both the principle of free trade and the practical need for protectionism, making them acceptable to both mercantilists and economic liberals. In a changed international security environment since 2001, trade has sometimes been an effective tool to achieve any number of political and economic goals.

As we will see in the next two chapters, the money and finance structure has been in dynamic flux recently, especially since the global financial crisis erupted in 2008 (see Chapters 7 and 8). For now, the production and trade structure appears to almost be in a recline position, waiting for recovery from the latest financial crisis and for new developing country coalitions to find their position in an entirely new global order. Thus, for us, the WTO members' current mixture of economic liberal, mercantilist, and sometime structuralist trade practices is best described as a **managed trade system.**

Unless the production and trade structure undergoes major reform, it may paradoxically be undermined by economic forces and policies that will only generate *more* demand for protection in the developed and developing nations. In many cases the state is relatively too weak to prevent private interests from playing the role of gatekeepers between domestic and international interests. At the same time, many states are as yet strong enough in the face of international calamities to fend off many of the forces that would weaken their power. Some fear that, much like the 1930s, trade protection will increase in the face of the global financial crisis. We anticipate that for now, the straightjacket of globalization, as Thomas Friedman likes to refer to it,[38] may be weakening the likelihood that states can be pulled into a truly integrated global production and trade network. If anything, more walls seemed to have gone up rather than come down over trade issues in the last 15 years.

# KEY TERMS

production and trade
    structure   131
specialization   132
outsourcing   132
law of comparative
    advantage   135
free trade   135
Washington Consensus   135
World Trade Organization
    (WTO)   135
strategic trade policies   136

General Agreement on Tariffs and
    Trade (GATT)   139
reciprocity   139
nondiscrimination   139
Most Favored Nation
    (MFN)   139
nontariff barriers (NTBs)   140
Super 301   141
fair trade   141
trade-related intellectual property
    rights (TRIPs)   142

trade-related investment measures
    (TRIMs)   142
Dispute Settlement Panel
    (DSP)   143
regional trade agreements
    (RTAs)   145
intraregional trade bloc   146
Structural Adjustment
    Policies   147
managed trade system   153

# DISCUSSION QUESTIONS

1. Discuss and explain the roles of production and trade in the international production and trade structure. Why is trade so controversial?
2. Outline the basic ways that mercantilists, economic liberals, and structuralists view trade. (Think about the tension between the politics and economics of trade.)

3. Outline and discuss some of the basic features of the GATT and WTO and issues related to the Uruguay and Doha rounds. Are you hopeful the Doha round WTO will be able to continue? Why? Why not?
4. Outline the basic features of RTAs. Do you see them as being primarily liberal or mercantilist in

nature? Explain. Of what consequence is it that officials view them as primarily one or the other?

5. Which of the three IPE approaches best accounts for the relationship of the Northern industrialized nations to the Southern developing nations when it comes to trade? Explain and discuss.

6. How have the United States and other nations used trade as a tool to achieve foreign policy objectives? Be specific and give examples. Research some other examples.

## SUGGESTED READINGS

Jorge G. Castaneda. "NAFTA at 10: A Plus or a Minus?" *Current History* (February 2004), pp. 51–55.

Ha-Joon Chang. "The Dangers of Reducing Industrial Tariffs," *Challenge, 48* (November–December 2005), pp. 50–63.

Brian Hocking and Steven McGuire, eds. *Trade Politics: International, Domestic and Regional Perspectives,* 2nd ed., London: Routledge, 2004.

Douglas A. Irwin. *Free Trade Under Fire*, 2nd ed., Princeton, NJ: Princeton University Press, 2005.

Joseph Stiglitz. *Making Globalization Work.* New York: W. W. Norton, 2006.

## NOTES

1. Robert Kuttner, *The End of Laissez Faire* (New York: Knopf, 1991).

2. Thomas Friedman, *The Lexus and the Olive Tree: Understanding Globalization* (New York: Anchor Books, 1999).

3. Thomas Friedman, *The World Is Flat* (New York: Farrar, Straus & Giroux, 2005), pp. 3–47.

4. From the World Bank's World Development Indicators database, http://siteresources.world bank.org/DATASTATISTICS/Resources/GDP.pdf

5. See World Bank, *World Development Indicators*, February 2010.

6. A good summary of this argument is given by Douglas A. Irwin, *Free Trade Under Fire* (Princeton, NJ: Princeton University Press, 2005).

7. See Friedrich List, "Political and Cosmopolitical Economy," in *The National System of Political Economy* (New York: Augustus M. Kelley, Reprints of Economic Classics, 1966).

8. See, for example, Pietra Rivoli, *The Travels of a T-Shirt in the Global Economy*, 2nd ed. (Hoboken, NJ: John Wiley, 2009).

9. Andre Gunder Frank, *Latin America: Underdevelopment or Revolution* (New York: Monthly Review Press, 1970).

10. Immanuel Wallerstein, "The Rise and Demise of the World Capitalist System: Concepts for Comparative Analysis," *Comparative Studies in Society and History, 17* (September 1974), pp. 387–415.

11. Technically, the GATT was not an international organization but rather a "gentlemen's agreement" whereby member parties (nation-states) contracted trade agreements with one another.

12. Robert Gilpin, *The Political Economy of International Relations* (Princeton, NJ: Princeton University Press, 1987), p. 215.

13. "U.S. Aids Microsoft in War on Software Piracy by Chinese," *Tacoma News Tribune,* November 22, 1994, p. E5.

14. For a more detailed discussion of agriculture's role in the Uruguay round, see David N. Balaam, "Agricultural Trade Policy," in Brian Hocking and Steven McGuire, eds., *Trade Politics: International, Domestic, and Regional Perspectives* (London: Routledge, 1999), pp. 52–66.

15. "U.S. GATT Flap Reverberates Around the World," *The Christian Science Monitor,* November 23, 1994, p. 1.

16. For a more detailed discussion of the Doha round of the WTO, see Aileen Kwa and Fatoumato Jawara, *Behind the Scenes of the WTO* (New York: Zed Books, 2004).

17. See, for example, Janet Thomas, *The Battle in Seattle; The Story Behind and Beyond the WTO Demonstrations* (New York: Fulcrum, 2003).

18. Lori Wallach, "Trade Secrets," *Foreign Policy, 140* (January/February 2004), pp. 70–71.

19. See www.presidentialrhetoric.com/speeches/09.14.05 .html for President Bush's speech to the United Nations.

20. For a detailed discussion of regionalism and Free Trade Agreements, see John Ravenhill, "Regionalism," in John Ravenhill, ed., *Global Political Economy,* 2nd ed. (Oxford: Oxford University Press, 2008), pp. 172–209.

21. Calculated from World Trade Organization, *International Trade Statistics 2009*, pp. 179–180, http://www.wto.org/english/res_e/statis_e/its2009_e/ its2009_e.pdf

22. Jagdish Bhagwati, *In Defense of Globalization* (Oxford: Oxford University Press, 2004).

23. See Keith Bradsher, "China Move to Beat Back A Tire Tariff," *The New York Times*, September, 14, 2009.

24. See John Dillin, "Will Treaty Give U.S. Global Edge?" *The Christian Science Monitor*, November 17, 1993.

25. For a detailed discussion of the NIEO, see Jagdish Bhagwati, ed., *The New International Economic Order: The North South Debate* (Cambridge, MA: MIT Press, 1977).

26. See, for example, Irwin, *Free Trade Under Fire*, especially chap. 2.

27. Robert Hunter Wade, "The Rising Inequality of World Income Distribution," *Finance and Development*, 38 (December 2001), pp. 37–39.

28. See World Trade Organization, *World Trade Development, 2009*, Table 1.1, p. 5.

29. See Walden Bello, "Rethinking Asia: The WTO's Big Losers," *Far Eastern Economic Review,* June 24, 1999, p. 77.

30. Dani Rodrik, "Goodbye Washington Consensus, Hello Washington Confusion?" *Journal of Economic Literature, XLIV* (December 2006), pp. 973–987.

31. See Ha-Joon Chang, *Kicking Away the Ladder: Development Strategy in Historical Perspective* (London: Anthem, 2002).

32. See Bello, "Rethinking Asia," p. 78.

33. See, for example, the Oxfam International website, www.maketradefair.com.

34. See, for example, "Analysis: The Complicated Politics of Free Trade, Unrestricted Trade Makes for Strange Bedfellows," The Pew Research Center for the People and the Press, January 4, 2007.

35. Joseph E. Stiglitz, *Making Globalization Work* (New York: W. W. Norton, 2006).

36. See, for example, Christopher Bacon, "Confronting the Coffee Crisis: Can Fair Trade, Organic, and Specialty Coffees Reduce Small-Scale Farmer Vulnerability in Northern Nicaragua?" *World Development, 33* (2005), pp. 497–511.

37. For a detailed discussion of this argument see Richard Haas, "Sanctioning Madness," *Foreign Affairs, 76* (November/December 1997), pp. 74–85.

38. See Friedman, *The Lexus and the Olive Tree.*

# The International Monetary and Finance Structure[1]

Life in the fast lane.

Jacob Silberberg

Since the 1990s the globalization of the international political economy has enhanced the speed and extended the reach of cross-border flows of capital. Like the other three international structures, oftentimes the monetary and finance structure is embroiled with tensions that render it difficult to manage effectively. As one expert notes, "In all modern societies, control over the issuing and management of money and credit has been a key source of power, and the subject of intense political struggles."[2]

With globalization and deregulation of the global economy since the 1980s have come increased currency exchange and transnational financial flows that influence employment, trade, and foreign direct investment, but also state programs and its security. One of the themes that stands out in this chapter is that, although economic liberal ideas called for states to deregulate their economies and cooperate with other states and IOs to open the global economy, some negative effects of globalization—including the recent global financial crisis—have compelled many states to re-regulate their societies and the monetary and finance structure.

We make six interconnected arguments in this chapter. First, after World War II the United States and its allies constructed a fairly tightly controlled international monetary and finance system that complemented their mutual goals of containing communism and gradually deregulating currency and finance markets. These measures manifested a situation where the United States could pursue "hegemony on the cheap," work toward the stabilization of Western capitalist economies, and contain communism. Second, as some of the security and economic interests of the Western alliance changed and diverged, exchange rates and capital controls were gradually allowed to reflected market conditions. The 1970s and 1980s, however, were marked by OPEC oil price hikes, increasing interdependence among states, and later globalization, along with many efforts to open up international currency and finance markets. At the same time, many states made efforts to control direct economic growth in ways that gradually weakened the international monetary and finance structure.

Third, since the end of the Cold War and pursuant to its continued hegemonic role in the international political economy, the United States has continued to run huge deficits in the current account of its balance of payments. Recently emerging economies such as China and Saudi Arabia have been investing their surplus capital into the United States and other current account deficit nations, which has enabled the United States to cover its balance-of-payments deficits. Fourth, the current financial crisis jeopardizes this U.S. strategy and continues to weaken the U.S. dollar and U.S. leadership of the current monetary and finance structure.

Fifth, the financial crisis has also severely weakened efforts by IOs, others states, and many nongovernmental organizations (NGOs) to resolve problems in debtor countries as well as help the developing nations overcome poverty. Sixth and finally, the global monetary and finance structure remains vulnerable to fluctuating market conditions, which should lead to increased state cooperation to deal with a number of problems, that if not resolved, could result in a global financial meltdown.

This chapter describes a number of fundamental elements of the international monetary and finance structure, including its institutions and who manages them, who determines its rules, how and why these rules change, and who benefits from its operation. This topic has its own specialized vocabulary. Once a student understands and appreciates the role of the basic pieces of this puzzle, it is easier to grasp other important ideas related to international political economy.

We begin the chapter by explaining the role of exchange rates in the international political economy and then move on to discuss three distinct international monetary and finance systems that have existed since the nineteenth century. We have found this history to be especially useful to students because it makes the entire topic easier to understand. In each period, we inquire into the major actors, the interplay of market forces and social interests that shape policies, and what accounts for shifts from one system to another. Inter-spliced between the first and second historical periods we explain the role of the IMF and why its primary functions have shifted over time. We also explain the balance-of-payment problem and its connection to management functions of the IMF.

The chapter moves to a discussion of the role of the U.S. dollar in the international political economy today. Some experts are concerned that confidence in the world's strongest currency has deteriorated, in part due to the financial crisis. The chapter concludes with an assessment of the management of the monetary and finance structure. This discussion is also a conduit to Chapter 8, in which we analyze in more detail short- and long-term international debt and two financial crises, including the recent global financial crisis. As is our practice throughout the book, we use parts of the three major IPE perspectives to help us understand some of the more controversial aspects of this structure.

## A PRIMER ON FOREIGN EXCHANGE

**Foreign or currency exchange** affects the value of *everything* a nation buys or sells on international markets. It also impinges on the cost of credit and debt, and the value of foreign currencies held in national and private banks. A special vocabulary is used when discussing currency or foreign exchange. Just as people in different nations speak different languages (requiring translation to understand one another), they also do business in different currencies, requiring the exchange of money from one denomination to another. Travelers and investors are often exposed to currency exchanges when they decide how much of their national currency it will cost to buy or invest in another country. Travelers can go to a local bank, exchange kiosk, or automated teller machine (ATM); slip in their debit card; and withdraw the needed amount of local currency. The machine (representing the banks that sponsor them) automatically calculates an exchange rate. Table 7-1 is an example of foreign exchange rates at particular points in time for the amount of local currency in your possession.

No wonder exchange rates are more important to banks and investors than to travelers: Each day they are buying and selling millions of dollars, British pound sterling, yen, euros, and other currencies. A change in the value of one currency (contrast 2006 with 2009 in Table 7-1) can mean huge gains or losses depending on how much market prices for currencies have changed in the recent past or might change in the future. What concerns states the most are short- and long-terms shifts in the values of certain currencies to one another (discussed in more detail below).

Before moving on let's look at how **currency exchange rates** work. While most people no longer pay much attention to the math behind these transactions, it is important to learn more about the connection between foreign exchange and the money in your own bank at home. Until the advent of ATMs, most travelers quickly became accustomed to exchange-rate math used to convert one currency into

## TABLE 7-1

### Foreign Exchange Rates for Selected Countries, Various Dates

| Country | Currency | August 2006 Currency Rate Per US$[a] | November 20, 2009, Currency Rate Per US$[b] |
|---|---|---|---|
| Argentina | Peso | NA | 3.8173 |
| Great Britain | Pound | .53 | .67 |
| EU | Euro | .78 | .67 |
| Sweden | Krona | 7.1890 | 6.9648 |
| Japan | Yen | 115.9200 | 88.9650 |
| Mexico | Mexican Peso | 10.8730 | 13.0908 |
| Canada | Canadian Dollar | 1.1182 | 1.0708 |
| China | Renminbi | 7.9897 | 6.8258[c] |
| South Korea | Won | 960.95 | 1,159.15 |
| Russia | Rouble | 26.8337[d] | 29.0020 |
| India | Indian Rupee | 46.45 | 46.6050 |
| South Africa | Rand | 6.9503 | 7.5994 |
| Malaysia | Ringgit | 3.6730 | 3.3855 |
| Indonesia | Rupiah | 9,100[d] | 9,485.00 |
| Israel | Shekel | 4.371[d] | 3.8100 |
| Brazil | Real | 2.1553 | 1.735[c] |

[a]Federal Reserve Statistical Release.
[b]*Financial Times.*
[c]UBC Sauder School of Business PACIFIC Exchange Rate Service.
[d]IMF.

another and back again. If the exchange rate was around $1.50 per British pound sterling, as it often was in the 1990s, it follows that a £10 theater ticket in the West End of London really cost $15 in U.S. currency (£10 at $1.50 per £ = $15). In the same way, that ¥1,000 caffé latte at the airport in Tokyo really cost $10—if the yen–dollar exchange rate was ¥100 per US$ (¥1,000 ÷ ¥100 per $ = $10). Before long, tourists found themselves able to perform complex mental gymnastics to convert from one money, especially the longer they visited another country.

Yet another important feature of foreign exchange is related to how hard or soft certain currencies are. **Hard currency** is money issued by large countries with reliable and predictably stable political economies. This legal tender is traded widely and has recognized value associated with the wealth and power of many industrialized developed nations, including the United States, Canada, Japan, Great Britain, Switzerland, and the Eurozone (European countries that use the Euro—see Chapter 12). A hard-currency country can generally exchange its own currency directly for other hard currencies, and therefore for foreign goods and services—giving it a distinct advantage. Therefore, a hard currency like the U.S. dollar (USD), the euro or the yen is easily accepted for international payments.

**Soft currency** is not as widely accepted, usually limited to its home country or region. Its value may be too uncertain or the volume of possible transactions insufficient based on an absence of trade with other countries or conditions that raise suspicions about the stability of its political economy. Many less developed countries (LDCs) have soft currencies, as their economies are relatively small and less stable than those of other countries. A soft-currency country must usually acquire hard currency (through exports or by borrowing) in order to purchase goods or services from other nations. Another problem with a soft currency is that international lenders are generally unwilling to accept payment in soft currencies. These countries need to earn hard currency to pay their debts, which tend to be denominated in hard currency. Because only hard currencies get much international use, we focus on hard currencies in this chapter.

An important point to remember is that the exchange rate is just a way of converting the value of one country's unit of measurement into another's. It does not really matter what units are used. What *does* matter is the *acceptability* of the measurement to the actors (banks, tourists, investors, and state officials in different countries) involved in a transaction at any given time, and how much values *change* over time. Shifts in exchange rates can vary over different periods of time, depending on a variety of circumstances that impact the demand for one currency or another. Any number of political and economic forces affect exchange rates. These include the following:

- currency appreciation and depreciation
- currency-rate manipulation
- whether one's currency is fixed to the value of another currency
- interest rates and inflation
- speculation.

When a currency's exchange price rises—that is, when it becomes more valuable relative to other currencies—we say that it **appreciates**. When its exchange price falls and it becomes less valuable relative to other currencies, we say it **depreciates**. For example, the USD *depreciated* relative to the European euro (EUR) between 2002 and 2003. A USD cost EUR 1.05 in June 2002, but only EUR 0.88 in July 2003. The fact that the USD *depreciated* relative to the EUR also means that the EUR *appreciated* against the USD. Or simply put, in terms of the USD, the EUR increased in price from about 95 cents to $1.13 during this period. In the case of trade, changes in the exchange rates tend to alter the competitive balance between nations, making one country's goods a better value than another.

Changes in currency values have profound political and social consequences. As currency values change, there are always winners and losers. As we saw in Chapter 6, for example, as a nation's currency appreciates, companies that export goods and services will be hurt as their products become less competitive internationally. However, importers in the same country (consumers of foreign goods and services and companies using foreign inputs in their production processes) will benefit as those imports become cheaper.

Often exchange rates are set by the market forces of supply and demand. Later in the chapter, however, we will see that there is also considerable temptation for nations to purposefully manipulate currency values so as to achieve a desirable outcome for that state. At times, states (secretly) intervene in currency markets, buying up their own currency or selling it in an attempt to alter its exchange value. A **central bank** will buy (demand) and sell (supply) enough of its own currency to alter the exchange rate. At other times when the demand for the country's currency declines, a central bank will use its foreign reserves to buy (demand) its own currency, pushing up the value of its currency again.

Regardless of market conditions, for many states an *undervalued currency* that discourages imports and increases exports can be politically and economically good for some domestic industries. This shifts production and international trade in that state's favor. The dark side of currency depreciation is that when goods such as food or oil must be imported, they will cost more if the currency is undervalued. Undervaluation can also reduce living standards and retard economic growth, as well as cause inflation. As we will see in the case of China (see the box "The Tangled Web of China's Currency Manipulation"), the nation appears to have benefited more than lost from keeping its currency undervalued.

Sometimes LDCs *overvalue* their currency to gain access to cheaper imported goods such as technology, arms, manufactured goods, food, and oil. This may benefit the wealthy and shift the terms of trade in their favor. Although their own exported goods would become less competitive abroad, these LDCs could at least enjoy some imported items at lower cost.

In practice, it is hard for LDCs to reap the benefits of overvaluation in any meaningful way because their currencies are usually soft and not used much in international business and finance. This does not stop them from trying, depending on political circumstances. In many cases, this invariably winds up choking domestic production and leaving the LDCs dependent on foreign sellers and lenders for help. Agriculture seems to be especially sensitive to this problem. In some cases, developing countries with overvalued currencies have unintentionally destroyed their agricultural sectors and become dependent on artificially cheap foodstuffs.

In the 1990s until the end of the decade, the value of the USD steadily climbed relative to the value of the currencies of many developing nations. While this helped the exports of the emerging nations, their consumers paid higher prices for many technological imports and value-added products. To stabilize the relationship between the USD and other currencies many countries decided to peg (fix) their currency to the dollar. China pegged the yuan at 8.28 per USD. Because the United States and the EU are major importers of Chinese goods, if the USD depreciated relative to the euro and most other world currencies, so did the yuan. While the weaker currencies gained some stability in their relationship to the USD, developments in the U.S. economy were easily transferred into the developing nations, depriving them of some flexibility in currency exchange rates.

Two other important issues are inflation and interest rates. *All else being equal*, a nation's currency tends to *depreciate* when that nation experiences a *higher inflation* rate than other countries. Inflation—a rise in overall prices—means that currency has less real purchasing power within its home country. This makes the currency less attractive to foreign buyers, and it tends to depreciate on foreign exchange markets to reflect its reduced real value at home.

Likewise, interest rates and investment returns in general influence the value and desirability of the investments that a particular currency can purchase. If *interest rates decline* in the United States, for example, as they did in the 1990s and throughout the 2000s, then the demand for dollars to purchase U.S. government bonds and other interest-earning investments decreases, pushing the dollar's exchange rate to a lower value. In the same way, higher interest rates lead to an increased demand for the dollar, as dollar-denominated investments become more attractive to foreigners.

Finally, one of the major currency and finance issues that concerned Keynes a great deal (see Chapter 2) was **speculation,** that is, betting that the value of a currency or market price for a certain item or service will go up and earn the owner a profit when it is sold. A currency generally rises and falls in value according to the value of goods, services, and investments that it can buy in its home market. If those who invest in currencies (speculators) believe (based on their understanding of the foreign exchange market model and anticipated changes in the various determinants of demand and supply) that a currency like the peso will appreciate in the future, they will want to buy pesos now to capitalize on the exchange rate fluctuations.

However, the increase in demand for pesos can easily raise their price as a direct result of investors speculating—predicting the value of the peso will rise because the Mexican economy is steadily growing or that it has discovered a new oil field in Baja California. This sort of speculation, which occurred in U.S. real estate most recently after 2001, can drive up the value of an item, generating a big gap (bubble) between the normal market value of the item and a new value that reflects what Alan Greenspan labeled "irrational exuberance." Most real estate agents would say that actually the higher market value is the real price, to the extent that someone is willing to buy the item at that price.

Yet, as we will see in the cases of the Asian and now the current global financial crises (see Chapter 8), bubbles can form when **hot money** (foreign investment in stocks and bonds not regulated by the state) moves quickly into a country, and bubbles can burst when investors rapidly pull their money out in anticipation that market prices will fall. While bubbles in the past caused hardship for many people, the severity of the current global financial crisis has caused many to question whether states and the IMF should not do more to regulate global capital movements.

## THREE FOREIGN EXCHANGE RATE SYSTEMS

Since the nineteenth century, there have been three structures and sets of rules related to foreign exchange rates.[3] The first was the **gold standard,** a tightly integrated international order that existed until the end of World War I. The second was the Bretton Woods fixed-exchange-rate system created by the United States and its allies before the end of World War II and managed by the IMF. The current system is the "flexible" or floating exchange-rate regime. As we explore some of the basic features of these systems, we will also highlight capital mobility across national borders, an issue directly related to currency exchange.

## The Classic Gold Standard: Phase I

We tend to think of the related issues of interdependence, integration, and globalization as post–Cold War phenomena, but from the end of the nineteenth century until the end of World War I, the world was supposedly even more interconnected than it is today. Cross-border flows of money increased in response to, among other things, interest rates and inflation in other countries. The leading European powers also invested heavily in their colonies. The currencies of these nations were part of a *fixed exchange-rate* system that linked currency values to the price of gold, thus the "gold standard." Similar to the EU today, some countries in specific geographic regions created "monetary unions" in which their currencies would circulate.[4]

Under the prevailing liberal economic theory of the time, the system was a *self-regulating* international monetary order. Different currency values were pegged to the price of gold. If a country experienced a balance-of-payments deficit—that is, it spent more money for trade, investments, and other items than it earned—corrections occurred almost *automatically* via wage and price adjustments. A country's gold would be sold to earn money to pay for its deficit. This resulted in tighter monetary conditions that curtailed the printing of money, raised interest rates, and cut government spending in response to a deficit. In turn, higher interest rates were supposed to attract short-term capital that would help finance the deficit. Domestic monetary and fiscal policy was "geared to the external goal of maintaining the convertibility of the national currency into gold."[5] Before World War I Great Britain's pound sterling was the world's strongest currency. And as the world's largest creditor, Great Britain loaned money to other countries to encourage trade when economic growth slowed.

The gold standard had a stabilizing, equilibrating, and confidence-building effect on the system. But by the end of the war the gold standard had died, though it was temporarily resurrected again in the early 1930s during the Great Depression. After World War I Britain became a debtor nation and the U.S. dollar took the place of the pound sterling as the world's strongest and most trusted currency. According to many hegemonic stability theorists, the gold standard folded because the United States acted more in its own interest and failed to meet the international responsibility commensurate with its economic and military power.

Another argument is that while elites were committed to economic liberal values, public policy often reflected the growing influence of labor unions, the poor, and foreign investors who often controlled monetary policy in the colonies. The extension of the electoral franchise produced more government intervention, pressuring governments to avoid the automatic policy adjustments the gold standard required in order to meet domestic needs. Some states preferred to depreciate their currencies to generate trade rather than slow the growth of their economies or cut state spending. In a move to further insulate their economies, many of them adopted capital controls (limits on how much money could move in and out of the country). Even John Maynard Keynes supported these measures, saying, "Let finance be primarily national."[6]

An important point is that many states gradually found that the "embedded" economic liberal ideas of a self-regulating economy did not work. The structuralist economic historian and anthropologist Karl Polanyi wrote that, by the end of World War I, 100 years of relative political and economic stability ended when economic liberal ideas no longer seemed appropriate given world events and conditions.[7] As the European and U.S. economies became more industrialized and interdependent (even more so than today), they had been willing to cooperate with one another in order to live under the rules of a fixed exchange-rate system. However, the negative effects of capitalism led to increased demands for more and different types of protection in various states. Many societies sought relief from a brand of capitalism that periodically failed as evidenced during the Great Depression.

## The Bretton Woods System: The Qualified Gold Standard and Fixed Exchange Rates: Phase II

During the Great Depression the international monetary and finance structure was in a shambles. "Beggar thy neighbor" trade policies that put national interests ahead of international interests resulted in some of the highest trade tariffs in history. The nonconvertibility of currency was also blamed for increasing hostility among the European powers that ultimately resulted in World War II.

In July 1944 the United States and its allies met in Bretton Woods, New Hampshire, to devise a plan for European recovery and create a new postwar international monetary and trade system that would encourage growth and development. In an atmosphere of cooperation, most of the 55 participating countries wanted to overcome the high unemployment conditions of the Great Depression and the malevolent *competitive currency devaluations* of the 1930s. Keynes, Great Britain's representative, believed that unless states took coordinated action to benefit each other, their individual efforts to gain at the expense of their competitors would eventually hurt them all.

At Bretton Woods the Great Powers created the International Monetary Fund (IMF), the World Bank, and what would later become the General Agreement on Tariffs and Trade (GATT) (see Chapter 6). Many argue that these institutions were empty shells that represented only the values and policy preferences of the major powers, especially the United States.[8] The World Bank was to be concerned with economic recovery immediately after the war and then development issues. The IMF's primary role was to facilitate a stable and orderly international monetary system and investment policies. It is still the IMF's role to facilitate international trade, stabilize exchange rates, and help members with balance-of-payments difficulties on a short-term basis. However, today the IMF also attempts to prevent and resolve currency and financial crises that have recently occurred in developing countries (see Chapter 8).

Two distinct IPE perspectives give primary responsibility for the institutional design and mission of the IMF to different players. From the economic liberal perspective (see Chapter 2), John Maynard Keynes was instrumental in convincing the Allied powers to construct a new international economic order based on liberal ideas proposed at the time. Note though that the "Keynesian compromise" allowed individual nation-states to *continue* regulating domestic economic activities within their own geographic borders. In the international arena, in order to avoid another Great Depression, the IMF would collectively manage financial policies with the goal of eventually freeing up financial markets and trade. Global financial crises and collapse were to be avoided by isolating each nation's financial system and then regulating it in consideration of international conditions and developments.

At the conference Keynes himself worked on setting up the World Bank. He was committed to creating an institution that could provide generous aid to both the victors and the vanquished nations after World War II. He especially wanted to prevent a repeat of the brutal and ultimately destructive terms the winners imposed on the losers at the end of World War I. He was adamant that creditors should help debtors make adjustments in their economies. Meanwhile, U.S. Treasury official Harry Dexter White's plan for the bank was to put nearly *all* of the adjustment pressure on debtor countries, without any symmetric obligation for creditors to make sacrifices.

In the case of the IMF, White's suggestions reflected the best interests of the United States, which emerged from World War II as the world's biggest creditor nation, and with no plans to give up that role. The U.S. Congress would not have approved a treaty that forced the United States to sacrifice just because Britain or another debtor country could not pay its bills. (In fact, the United States was adamant that Great Britain honor its wartime debts once the war was over.) The IMF, then, was designed to provide *temporary* assistance to all debtor countries while they adjusted their economic structures to the emerging international economy. The burden of adjustment ultimately fell on the debtors, not on both debtors and creditors, as Keynes had intended.

Immediately after the war, many realists viewed the United States as an *emerging but reluctant* major power, unwilling to assume the hegemonic role that Great Britain had played in the nineteenth century. The United States, which had the most votes on policy decisions (based on holding 31 percent of the IMF reserves at the time), used the IMF as an indirect way to promote an orderly liberal financial system that would lead to nondiscrimination in the conversion of currencies, confidence in a new order, and eventually more liquidity. These goals complemented U.S. liberal values, beliefs, and policy preferences at little cost to the United States.

For both mercantilists and realists, the IMF's institutional structure and monetary rules also reflected the interests of the Great Powers (as they were called at the time). Under pressure from the United States, the IMF adopted a modified version of the former gold standard's *fixed-exchange-rate system* that was more open to market forces, but not divorced from politics. At the center of this modified gold standard was a fixed-exchange-rate mechanism that fixed the rate of an ounce of gold at $35. The values of other national currencies would fluctuate against the dollar as supply and demand for those currencies changed. Additionally, governments agreed to intervene in foreign exchange markets to keep the value of currencies within 1 percent above or below par value (the fixed exchange rate).

As supply and demand conditions for other currencies changed, the trading bands established by the IMF defined limits within which exchange rates could fluctuate. (Note: see Figure 7-6 on the IPE web page at www.upugetsoundintroipe. com for a representation of this arrangement). If the value of any currency increased above or fell below the band limits, central banks behind those currencies were required to step in and buy up excess dollars or sell their own currency until the currency value moved back into the trading bands limits, reestablishing a supply–demand equilibrium (par value). As in the earlier system, central banks could also buy and sell gold to help settle their accounts, which the United States often did. What officials liked about this system was that its *quasi-self-adjusting mechanism* allowed for diverse levels of growth in different national economies.

Confidence in the system relied on the fact that dollars could be converted into gold at a set price. At the end of World War II, the United States started with the largest amount of gold backing its currency. This arrangement politically and economically stabilized the monetary system, which desperately needed the members' confidence and a source of liquidity if recovery in Europe was to be realized. Once the Cold War began in 1947, the United States consciously accepted its hegemonic role of providing the collective good of security for its allies. This arrangement boosted Western European and Japanese recovery from the war and preserved an environment for trade and foreign investment in Western Europe. These policies also helped tie together the allies into a liberal-capitalist, U.S.-dominated monetary and finance system that complemented U.S. efforts to *divide* the West from the Soviet-dominated Eastern Bloc. Capital movements into and out of the communist nations were severely limited.

In this monetary arrangement, the U.S. dollar became the hegemonic currency, or **top currency,** one in great demand often used in international trade and financial transactions. This position afforded the United States many privileges when it came to using the dollar as a tool of foreign policy, but also imposed on it many management responsibilities. The United States benefited both economically and politically from this arrangement because, as part of the postwar recovery process, dollars were in great demand in most of Western Europe and in other parts of the world. When it came to trade and investments, other states often had to convert their currencies into U.S. dollars, which saved the United States a good deal of money on foreign exchange transactions and helped maintain the strength of the U.S. dollar against other currencies. The dollar was also the **reserve currency** that, because its international market value was fixed to gold, was held in central banks as a store of value.

## THE IMF AND THE BALANCE OF PAYMENTS

At Bretton Woods the IMF was set up to create stable and responsive international financial relations, just as central banks seek to create a favorable financial climate within the borders of each country. As of July 2009, it had a membership of 184 countries, a staff of 2,716 from 165 countries, and reserves of $317 billion. As of November 2009, the IMF had made loans of $28 billion to 74 countries. The IMF director heads a board made up of 25 members from different countries who meet twice a year. Although members try to reach consensus, major policy decisions are decided on a weighted voting basis. The weight of a state's vote is related to how much it contributes to the IMF's reserves. Currently the United States has the most votes, with 17.8 percent. Japan is a distant second at 6 percent, with Great Britain and France both at 5 percent.

> **TABLE 7-2**
>
> ### Elements of Balance-of-Payments Accounts
>
> | | Current Account | Capital and Financial Account |
> |---|---|---|
> | Current account surplus examples: Japan, China | Foreign receipts for exports, receipts of investment income (interest and profit), and unilateral transfers are greater than equivalent foreign payments. | Increase in domestic ownership of foreign assets: "creditor" nation. Technically termed a capital and financial account deficit to balance the current account surplus |
> | Current account deficit examples: United States, Mexico | Foreign payments for imports, payments of investment income (interest and profit), and unilateral transfers are greater than equivalent receipts. | Increase in foreign ownership of domestic assets: "debtor" nation. Technically termed a capital and financial account surplus to balance the current account deficit. |

The **balance of payments** registers an accounting of all the international monetary transactions between the residents of one nation and those of other nations in a given year. It reflects what a nation produces, consumes, and buys with its money. Much like a personal check register (see Table 7-2 above), the *current account* records "deposits" or money inflows. For each nation, these deposits are derived from sales of currently produced goods and services, receipts of profits and interest from foreign investments, and unilateral transfers of money or income from other nations. This includes foreign aid a nation receives, private aid flows, and money migrants send home to friends and families. According to the IMF, these receipts *should equal* money outflows related to the purchase of goods and services from other countries, payments of profits and interest to foreign investors, and unilateral transfers to other nations.

When a state has a *current account surplus*, its receipts or earnings are greater than its "withdrawals" or expenditures, so that on net these international transactions have increased national income. However, when a nation has a *current account deficit*, outflows or withdrawals are greater than inflows or deposits in a particular year, and the net effect of these international transactions is to reduce the national income of the deficit country.

What is commonly referred to as the *balance of trade* is usually defined and analyzed separately from other items in the current account. It registers a nation's payments and receipts for the exchange of goods and services only (receipts for exports minus payments for imports). Therefore, the balance of trade only *partially* reflects a nation's current account and so provides only a glimpse of the changes in a nation's financial position. The trade balance is important because of its direct effect on employment, as a large number of jobs in most economies rely on trade.

The other IMF account—the *capital and financial account*—includes money borrowed or acquired as interest payment on an investment. These are longer-term economic transactions related to foreign investments, borrowing and lending, and sales and purchases of assets such as stocks and real estate. The capital account is an indicator of the effect of international transactions on changes in a nation's holdings of assets or wealth with respect to other countries. If there is an overage (surplus) or net inflow of money to the capital and financial account, foreigners are net purchasers of a country's assets. If there is a net outflow (deficit) of funds, the country has increased its net ownership of foreign assets.

The technical language of the balance of payments is quite confusing. It is common practice to say that a nation has a "balance-of-payments deficit." However, normally, a surplus in one account must be offset by a deficit in another—establishing an accounting balance of 0. What people usually mean by a balance-of-payments deficit or surplus is shorthand for a *current account deficit or surplus*, with payments for goods, services, and transfers exceeding the corresponding receipts.

When determining whether a nation is going into debt, state officials tend to regard the current account as being more important than the capital account. A nation with a current account deficit must either borrow funds from abroad or sell assets to foreign buyers to pay its international bills and achieve an overall payments balance. A current account deficit also requires a capital account surplus. Likewise, a current account surplus generates excess funds to purchase foreign assets. There are many political consequences of any nation's balance-of-payments status. If a state has a large foreign debt, for instance, it will need to increase output at home to generate more exports and/or decrease consumption of imports.

Economically, politically, and socially, these are not easy choices for states and their societies to make. Increasing output, for instance, might mean asking workers to accept lower wages, giving tax incentives to business firms, or removing regulatory roadblocks to more efficient production. Decreasing consumption might also involve raising consumer taxes, reducing government subsidies, cutting government programs, or increasing interest rates to discourage consumption, attract savings, and encourage foreign investment in the home economy. In these circumstances, it is easy to see why currency devaluation is so attractive to states, as it can quickly generate more exports by making goods less expensive. As we noted earlier, however, such a move is also likely to invite retaliatory "defensive" moves by other states, negating the economic gains of the first state and generating tension between states, as was the case during the interwar years.

Mexico and the United States, for example, tend to have current account deficits. The current global financial crisis highlights the extent to which the United States pays out more for imports, investment income to foreigners, and unilateral transfers for wars in Iraq and Afghanistan than it receives from exports, investment income, and international transfers. To pay such bills, Mexico and the United States are usually pressed to raise funds on the capital and financial account by increasing their foreign debt or attracting investment funds from abroad, which the United States has been doing as of late (see also Chapter 8).

Table 7-3 includes the current account surplus of different states along with the amounts of **sovereign wealth funds** (**SWFs**) of various economies. As we discuss later in the chapter, SWFs are income states generate from international transactions (especially oil exports) that can be used to purchase foreign assets or to pay off foreign debts incurred in the past. To finance its growing debt the United States has looked primarily to countries like China, Japan, Germany, Saudi Arabia, and other exporters with huge capital reserves earned from trade, to purchase U.S. Treasuries, property, and industries.

### TABLE 7-3
**Current Account Balances and Sovereign Wealth Funds**

| Current Account Balance[a] | | Sovereign Wealth Funds[b] | | |
|---|---|---|---|---|
| G20 Major Economies | $Bil. | Country | Total $Bil. | No. of Funds |
| China | +364.4 Q2 | China | 787.4 | 4 |
| Germany | +158.0 Jul | UAE | 676.5 | 7 |
| Saudi Arabia | +134.0 2008 | Norway | 445.0 | 1 |
| Japan | +114.0 Jul | Saudi Arabia | 436.3 | 2 |
| Russia | +55.3 Q2 | Singapore | 369.5 | 2 |
| Republic of Korea | +34.3 Aug | Kuwait | 202.8 | 1 |
| Argentina | +10.4 Q2 | Russia | 178.5 | 1 |
| Indonesia | +4.4 Q2 | Hong Kong | 139.7 | 1 |
| Mexico | −14.0 Q2 | Libya | 65.0 | 1 |
| South Africa | −15.8 Q2 | Qatar | 65.0 | 1 |
| Turkey | −16.2 Jul | Australia | 49.3 | 1 |
| Brazil | −17.6 Aug | Algeria | 47.0 | 1 |
| Canada | −19.1 Q2 | US | 42.0 | 3 |
| India | −26.6 Q2 | Kazakhstan | 38.0 | 1 |
| Australia | −29.0 Q2 | Ireland | 30.6 | 1 |
| United Kingdom | −50.6 Q2 | Brunei | 30.0 | 1 |
| France | −54.0 Jul | Malaysia | 28.1 | 2 |
| Italy | −59.8 Jul | France | 28.0 | 1 |
| EU | −137.2 Jul | South Korea | 27.0 | 1 |
| US | −542.3 Q2 | Chile | 21.8 | 1 |

[a] *The Economist*, 392(8651), September 29, 2009, pp. 121–122.
[b] Sovereign Wealth Fund Institute, November 30, 2009.

Ideally, the IMF would like to see an equilibrium in a state's balance of payments. Theoretically, nations should spend only as much as they take in. Yet, in order for businesses to expand and the economy to grow, banks lend out more than they have on deposit to back their loans. So the international economy needs a source of liquidity (assets that can be converted to cash) for new investments and production that comes when a country runs a balance-of-payments deficit, which the United States did for all but two years under the Bretton Woods monetary and finance system. A country that performs this collective good for the rest of the system is usually a hegemon, and in these circumstances it is often referred to as a "locomotive." When the hegemon's economy heats up, it helps generate growth that benefits other members of the system. On the other hand, if the United States cut its deficit by buying fewer automobiles, then Japan would probably produce fewer autos and Saudi Arabia would probably produce less petroleum. In essence, one state's falling deficit would be another's decreased surplus. Likewise, our political and economic tensions become their tensions. And as we noted in Chapter 2, the economic and political roles and responsibilities of hegemons are difficult to separate from political costs and benefits.

## The Bargain Comes Unstuck

On the whole, hegemony and the provision of collective goods to U.S. allies after World War II came cheaply to the United States. During these heyday years of the Bretton Woods system from 1956–1964, the rules of the monetary and finance structure gave the United States many benefits and advantages when it came to monetary and security relations between the United States and Western Europe. The United States could spend freely for a variety of domestic programs such as the Great Society and, at the same time, fund the Vietnam War, by merely printing more money. The costs of those programs could not weaken the dollar against the value of gold, because under the rules at that time, the value of the dollar was fixed—or could not depreciate in value against gold. However, the artificially over-valued dollar also resulted in less demand for U.S. exports, which benefited Japan and Western Europe. Given that the United States was relatively less dependent on trade than Western Europe and Japan, the loss of business for the United States was a politically acceptable exchange for successfully achieving other political and economic objectives.

Because the United States was free to continue spending and running a deficit in its balance of payments, it effectively exported inflation (an oversupply of dollars) through the monetary system to its allies. As part of the arrangement Western European banks were committed to buying up surplus dollars to bring the value of their currencies back inside the trading bands (relative to par value). However, the more the United States invested in Europe and spent for the Vietnam War, the more others complained of the United States' privilege, undermining political relations between the allies. Increasingly the United States came under pressure to cut back on government spending or to sell its gold in order to repurchase surplus dollars. At one point, French President Charles DeGaulle complained that France was underwriting the Vietnam War by holding weak dollars in its banks instead of con-verting them to gold, which would have nearly emptied the U.S. gold reserve.

Furthermore, the Western European economies had recovered sufficiently that they no longer needed or wanted as many U.S. dollars. In the words of Benjamin Cohen, the result was that the "political bargain" made between the United States and its allies after World War II, whereby the United States managed the monetary and finance structure to the benefit of all, had become unstuck.[9] In effect, the fixed-exchange-rate system was restricting the economic growth of U.S. allies and limiting the choices of state officials in politically unacceptable ways. The *success* of the fixed-exchange-rate system was also undermining the value of the U.S. dollar, weakening many of the monetary structure's institutions and rules, and weakening U.S. leader-ship of the structure as well. The structure had become too rigid, making it difficult for states to grow at their own pace and to promote their own interests and values.

To prevent a recession at home, in August 1971 President Richard Nixon *unilaterally* (without consulting other states) decided to make dollars nonconvert-ible to gold. The United States devalued the dollar, and, to help correct its deficit in the balance of payments, it imposed a 10 percent surcharge on all Japanese imports coming into the United States. Some scholars have suggested that the United States purposefully abandoned its role as a benevolent hegemon for the sake of its own interests. Both the United States and Western Europe accused one another of not sacrificing enough to preserve the fixed-exchange-rate system. From the U.S.

perspective, Western Europe should have purchased more goods from the United States to help correct the balance-of-trade and balance-of-payments problems. On the other hand, the Europeans argued that trade was not the primary problem; instead, the United States needed to reform its own economy by cutting spending, which meant getting out of Vietnam and/or reducing domestic spending—two things that were politically unacceptable to the administration at the time.

## The Float- or Flexible-Exchange-Rate System: Phase III and the Changing Economic Structure

In 1973 a new system emerged that is commonly referred to as the float- or **flexible-exchange-rate system**, or **managed float** system. The major powers authorized the IMF to further widen the trading bands so that changes in currency values could more easily be determined by market forces. Some states independently floated their currencies, while many of the countries that joined the European Economic Community (EEC) promoted regional coordination of their policies. Many states still had to deal with balance-of-payments issues, but the framework of collective management was meant to be less constraining on their economies and societies.

Several other developments contributed to the end of the fixed-exchange-rate monetary system. In the early stages of the Bretton Woods system, investment funds could *not* move easily among countries to take advantage of possible higher returns on interest or investments. **Capital controls** and fixed-exchange rates were manipulated to allow states to respond to domestic political forces without causing exchange-rate instability. Policy makers intentionally limited the movement of finance and capital between countries for fear that financial crises like those in the 1920s and 1930s could easily spread from one country to many others. Widespread currency convertibility (achieved by 1958), the large numbers of U.S. dollars pumped into the international economy via U.S. current account deficits, and the expansion of U.S. transnational corporation investments in Western Europe all led to pressure on state officials to bring down capital controls and to allow money to move more freely in the international economy.

By the late 1960s many officials and businesses were looking outward for new markets and investments, leading to increased private capital flows in the form of direct TNC investments, portfolio investments (such as purchases of foreign stocks by international mutual funds), commercial bank lending, and nonbank lending. Flexible-exchange rates complemented the relaxation of capital controls, which added yet another source of global liquidity to complement lending by states and loans by the IMF, the World Bank, and regional banks.

The adoption of and structure of the flexible-exchange-rate system reflected several other influential political and economic developments including: the growing influence of the Japanese and West European economies, the rise of the Organization of the Petroleum Exporting Countries (OPEC), and the shift toward a multipolar security structure (see Chapter 9). By the early 1970s Japan's rising living standards and high rates of economic growth turned Japan into a major player in international monetary and finance issues. Robert Gilpin and other realists make a strong case for the connection between the diffusion of international economic growth and wealth at the time and the emergence of a new multipolar security structure.[10] The flexible-exchange-rate system helped entrench a multipolar international security structure that would be cooperatively managed by the United States, the EU, Japan, and (later) China.

The rise of OPEC and tremendous shifts in the pattern of international financial flows after oil price increases in 1973–1974 and 1978–1979 transformed the system into a *global* financial network. Almost overnight, billions of dollars moved through previously nonexistent financial channels as OPEC states demanded dollars as payment for oil. This increased the demand for U.S. dollars in the international economy, which helped maintain the dollar's status as the top currency. Many of the OPEC "petrodollars" deposited in Western banks were recycled in the form of loans to developing countries that were viewed as good investment risks because of the increasing demand for consumer goods and natural resources (especially oil). However, between 1973 and 1979, the debt of developing nations increased from $100 billion to $600 billion, generating a debt crisis that will be discussed in more detail in Chapter 8.[11]

In the early 1980s trade imbalances in the developed countries contributed to stagflation, or slow economic growth accompanied by rising prices—two phenomena that do not usually occur together. As the oil crises subsided, the U.S. dollar weakened in value. U.S. officials focused on fighting domestic inflation by raising interest rates to tighten the money supply, which slowed down the economy and contributed to an international recession. At this time a change in political-economic philosophy occurred in Great Britain and the United States. The prevailing Keynesian orthodoxy was swept aside in favor of a return to the classical liberal ideas of Adam Smith and Milton Friedman discussed in Chapter 2.

The governments of British Prime Minister Margaret Thatcher and U.S. President Ronald Reagan privatized national industries, deregulated financial and currency exchange markets, cut taxes at home, and liberalized trade policy. Theoretically, these measures were supposed to produce increased savings and investments that would stimulate economic growth. In 1983, economic recovery did begin, especially in the United States, stimulated by higher rates of consumption, a less restrictive monetary policy, and attention to fighting inflation—all policies that mainly benefited wealthier people. However, many experts suggest that a drop in world oil prices—more than anything else—stimulated economic growth in the industrialized nations.

Despite the laissez-faire rhetoric, Reagan's defense budget was the biggest since World War II, aimed at renewing the West's effort to contain the Soviet Union and communist expansion. These expenditures and a strong dollar led to increased prices for U.S. exports and lower import prices, which resulted in record U.S. trade deficits, especially with Japan. In order to shrink the U.S. trade deficit, rather than cutting back on government spending or raising taxes, the Reagan and first Bush administrations pressured Japan and other states to adopt adjustment measures that included revaluing the yen. Many mercantilist-oriented trade officials also accused Japan, Brazil, and South Korea of not playing fair when they refused to lower their import barriers or reduce their export subsidies (see Chapter 6).

Paradoxically, much like the case of China today, this situation also *benefited* the United States to the extent that high U.S. interest rates attracted foreign investments in U.S. businesses and real estate. The Reagan version of "hegemony on the cheap" helped correct the U.S. current account deficit and sustain the value of the U.S. dollar. More importantly, a strong dollar helped sustain U.S. hegemonic power and the Reagan administration's struggle against the "evil empire" of the Soviet Union. As was the case in the past, many U.S. allies did not agree with this outlook and pursued monetary and finance policies contrary to those of the United States.

By 1985 the United States had become the world's largest debtor nation, with a balance-of-payments deficit of some $5 trillion.[12] Many countries and U.S. exporters complained that the dollar was overvalued. Rapid capital flows were now contributing to volatile exchange rates, which interfered with FDI and international trade. As it had done 20 years earlier, the United States resisted making hard choices about currency adjustments that could threaten its economic recovery or lead to cutbacks in defense spending. Instead, in 1985 the United States pressed the other G5 states (Great Britain, West Germany, France, and Japan) to meet in New York, where they agreed to *intervene* (contrary to the Reagan administration's preferred policy of nonintervention) in currency markets to *collectively manage* exchange rates. The **Plaza Accord** committed the G5 to work together to "realign" the dollar so that it would depreciate in value against other currencies, thereby raising interest rates in the other economies.

## The Roaring Nineties: Globalization and the Weakening Dollar

As the Reagan administration's neoliberal ideas became even more popular, they continued to influence developments in the international finance and monetary structure in the 1990s and early 2000s. Economic liberal policies and development strategies served as the basis of the "Washington Consensus" and globalization campaign (see Chapter 3). By the end of the Cold War in 1990, many of the controls on capital flows had been removed. Private capital flows came to dwarf official flows. In 1997, for example, net private capital flows amounted to $285 billion, compared to net official flows of only $40 billion. This capital bolstered newly emerging economies in Southeast and East Asia that emphasized export sales, limited imports, promoted savings, and postponed consumer gratification.

In the 1980s and 1990s, revolutionary advances in electronics, computing, and satellite communications enhanced the integration of national economies and further globalized the monetary and finance structure. Increased public and private finance also helped generate tremendous increases in the volume and value of international trade.

In the early 1990s the dollar continued to lose value, depreciating an average of 15 percent against the currencies of major U.S. trade partners. The U.S. Federal Reserve Board decreased interest rates to improve exports and expand growth. By the mid-1990s the U.S. economy had recovered: inflation fell, consumer spent more, and foreign investors increased demand for dollar-denominated assets. The newly created European Central Bank (ECB) maintained price stability for its members and helped insulate European currencies from the U.S. dollar.

These policy changes and efforts to make exchange rates serve state interests caused contradictions. The **Mundell Trilemma** accounts for this muddled situation where typically states desire three things at once: (1) the ability to respond to domestic political forces (often referred to as monetary autonomy), (2) international capital mobility (necessary for efficient international finance), and (3) stable exchange rates (desirable for smooth international trade and investment). The problem is that only any *two* of these goals are possible at the same time as the third option always cancels out the effectiveness of the other two.

For example, the United States and Japan have traditionally had levels of international trade that are relatively small compared with the domestic economy. It is more important for them to have a free hand in domestic economic policy and to have access to international capital markets for financing, instead of stable exchange rates. But Argentina and Hong Kong, both more dependent on the international economy, pegged their currencies to the USD, which made their exchange rates more stable but limited their ability to respond to domestic economic and political problems. As the Mundell Trilemma demonstrates, states could not find a desirable outcome just by deregulating their monetary and financial institutions.

## THE GLOBAL FINANCIAL CRISIS: THE U.S. DOLLAR GOES WOBBLY

In the late 1990s and early 2000s, criticisms of both globalization and wildcat capitalism intensified. The IMF and the World Bank were both criticized for their handling of the Asian and Argentine financial crises. After the dotcom technology bust in 2001 a real estate bubble emerged in the United States and spread into the UK, Ireland, Spain, Australia, and New Zealand, among many other countries. As the bubble grew the United States continued to run huge deficits in the balance of payments and relied on countries like China, Japan, Germany, and Saudi Arabia to invest in the United States to help it overcome its growing debt. As we saw earlier in Table 7-3, SWF and reserve surplus countries often invested in U.S. businesses and bought enormous amounts of U.S. stocks, Treasury bonds, and other securities, which helped the United States correct its balance-of-payments deficits. This situation is the basis of suggestions by economic liberals that therefore these other countries, and not just the United States, had a hand in bringing about the conditions that hurt their economies during the financial crisis.

In Chapter 8 we discuss in more detail the question of whether other states will continue to invest in U.S. assets because of the financial crisis. For our purposes here, the financial crisis has raised a number of issues related to a weakening in the value of the dollar relative to other currencies. For example, even before the crisis many officials and experts felt confident that the euro would eventually overtake the hegemonic role of the U.S. dollar in the global political economy, given the size of the EU market and population. When the euro was officially rolled out in 2002 it was valued at almost one-for-one against the U.S. dollar. By 2007, the dollar had dropped in value to roughly $1.80 to the euro. In the early 2000s, OPEC resisted using weaker dollars in its transactions because it would have to sell more oil to make the same amount of money. In 2007, some OPEC members—especially Venezuela and Iran—pushed for oil to be priced in euros denominated against a basket (average price) of currencies. Only Saudi Arabia's intervention on behalf of the United States prevented this.

Since the crisis started some wonder if the Keynesian recovery strategy of increasing government spending by printing more dollars will lead to excessive inflation, more debt, or even a run on the dollar (i.e., other countries will lose confidence in it and not want to use it). More importantly, some experts and officials are concerned about some of the implications of a weak dollar and its role as the top reserve currency in the global political economy, along with the United States's leadership role in managing the global money and finance structure.

There are a variety of reasons experts give to explain a weak U.S. dollar, especially since the early 2000s: among them are the U.S. balance-of-payments deficits, U.S. trade deficits, overconsumption, and excessive military spending. Between 2003 and 2007, the U.S. current account deficit doubled in size as Americans spent more for imports, invested heavily in businesses the world over, and spent huge sums of money on the Iraq War and the war on terrorism.

When it comes to trade, the United States has never made exports a major priority given its large domestic market, its insatiable high demand for imports and desire to live beyond its means, and generally weak demand for U.S. products in other countries. Trade is usually a concern of multinational corporations that operate abroad or during recessions when unemployment goes up, as it did in the early 1980s or since the financial crisis started. It is no wonder then that the high levels of U.S. domestic spending on entitlement programs, health care, education, and subsidies for industries have been easier to pay for in conjunction with the high demand in the United States for external sources of finance. Interestingly, the economic liberal Fred Bergsten sounds more like a realist when he suggests that it is risky and unsustainable for Americans to count on foreign investors to finance future domestic budgets.[13]

As noted above and in Chapter 6, at times the United States has been involved in many trade disputes. Foreign exchange and monetary policies often play a role in disputes between the United States and other countries. A recent and classic example of this type of situation has been the accusations U.S. officials have made that China has purposefully kept down the value of its currency in order to increase its exports, at the expense of the United States and other nations (see box "The Tangled Web of China's Currency Manipulation"). From 1994 to July 2005, China pegged its currency—the yuan (officially called the renminbi)—to the U.S. dollar at a fixed rate of 8.28 to 1. The People's Bank of China (China's equivalent of the U.S. Federal Reserve) "artificially" maintained this exchange rate by using yuan to buy up U.S. dollars that entered the Chinese market in the form of investment expenditures and export earnings. More yuan in the economy resulted in cheaper Chinese exports, at the expense of the United States and other nations.

Under pressure from these states China let the value of the yuan gradually appreciate to 6.83 to 1 USD. But when the global financial crisis came to a head in 2008, Chinese officials once again fixed the value of the yuan to the dollar to help in their economic recovery. Once again many foreign officials accused China of "not playing fair" by holding down the value of the yuan against the dollar—this time by about 40 percent. To counter what they believe is a classic case of mercantilist competitive devaluation outlawed by the IMF, some U.S. congressmen

# THE TANGLED WEB OF CHINA'S CURRENCY MANIPULATION[a]

In April 2010 the Obama administration was trying to walk a fine line between looking and acting tough, and giving in to the Chinese over the currency manipulation issue.[b] There are many reasons why both the Obama administration and the IMF are not in a hurry to push China harder on the issue. In sum, many experts and policy officials worry that to do so would be quite risky for both the United States and China.

First, China has hinted that it may dump U.S. Treasury bills that it has in its central bank's $2.4 trillion reserve. This is a nightmare scenario that could put further downward pressure on the U.S. dollar (leading to its demise as the top currency—discussed below), depreciate the value of China's holdings in the United States, and further disrupt global financial markets. The immediate impact of such a move would be that the United States would not be able to finance its balance-of-payments deficit and debts. Even if China chose not to dump the dollar, it still could retaliate with other measures of its own such as import tariffs and quotas on imported goods. Second, given U.S. dependency on Chinese imports, driving up the price of Chinese goods *could* trigger rapid inflation in the United States.[c] This might then pressure the Fed into increasing interest rates, which could also slow the recovery of the U.S. economy.

Third, some argue that critics tend to overstate China's responsibility for the trade deficit with the United States and that a big revaluation of the yuan would do little to shrink the U.S.–China trade deficit. Point in fact: the appreciation of the yuan after 2005 did not help close the U.S.–China trade gap that much.

Fourth, and more importantly, U.S. pressure on China at this time could also weaken efforts by the Obama administration to enlist China's help in dealing with North Korea and Iran, terrorism, the environment, and other pressing foreign policy issues.

Finally, some experts note that China's central bank wants to let the yuan gradually appreciate against the dollar anyway, but its Commerce Ministry (which represents the interests of exporters and manufacturers, and increasingly public opinion) would rather the value of the yuan remain where it is. In effect, China's policies resemble those of the United States to the extent that they reflect powerful domestic corporate interests and public opinion that cannot easily be changed by threats or intimidations. Interestingly Mike Whitney also makes the case that in fact many U.S. corporations do *not* want the value of the yuan to appreciate given their investments in export-dependent Chinese corporations.[d]

Whether or not China is guilty of currency manipulation is not as important as the issue of who benefits—*cui bono?*—from the currency situation. The United States and China have a highly interdependent relationship, which means that this issue is likely to be resolved at high diplomatic levels. Because the issue is as inherently political as it is economic, the outcome will not be decided solely on the basis of what is rational, nor is one side likely to prevail over all the issues in this case.

## References

[a]Our thanks to Josh Anderson for helping research and draft the first version of this material in the last edition of the text. Dave Balaam and Brad Dillman revised it for this edition.

[b]See Sewell Chan, "U.S. Will Delay Report on Chinese Currency, While Urging an End to Intervention," *The New York Times*, April 4, 2010.

[c]The relationship between the U.S. budget deficit and U.S. consumption, as well as the danger posed by America's large trade deficit, is explored in: Menzie D. Chinn, "Getting Serious about the Twin Deficits," *Council on Foreign Relations*, September 2005.

[d]See Mike Whitney, "China's Flawed Economic Model," April 6, 2010, at www.counterpunch.org/whitney04062010.html

threatened to introduce a bill imposing a tariff on all Chinese goods unless China stopped manipulating its currency. They also want the IMF and the U.S. Treasury to brand China a "currency manipulator," which would entitle those hurt by China's actions to initiate remedial countermeasures.

## Peak Dollars?

Despite the financial crisis, the dollar has not crashed. For now, many investors continue to bring needed capital into the United States. Yet another factor that worries officials and some experts is continued security costs that now include the war in Afghanistan, which require additional capital flows from abroad. This argument has been made many times in the past by structuralists concerned about "economic overextension" or "overstretch" that often accompany imperial policies (see Chapter 4). Rather than deterring investors, however, during the financial crisis many investors continued to see the U.S. economy as a good hedge. The realist Gabor Steingart of Germany's *Der Spiegel* magazine, for example, argues that many countries continue to see investing in the United States as safe because "one can almost completely rule out the possibility of political unrest in the United States . . . ."[14] Many states and individuals view U.S. "T-Bills" as a stable bet, given that the U.S. government is quite unlikely to default on its debt. U.S. Treasuries also pay interest and are highly liquid—meaning they can be easily turned into cash—which ensures that, as reserves, they are flexible in composition and do not decrease in value over time. To repeat, one of the privileges of being a global hegemon and holding the world's reserve currency is that the U.S. Treasury can repay international debt by creating more national currency and national debt.

However Steingart also notes that as the U.S. stimulus package requires more borrowing and debt, it can also puts downward pressure on the dollar. He likens the U.S. economy to an "economic giant on steroids," dependent on investment shots from countries with surplus capital. At the same time as excessive public expenditures, a *weakening* of U.S. military capabilities could also lead to a tipping point that undermines public support for investment in the United States. A *sudden fear* could also spark a herd instinct, where investors try to dump the U.S. dollar before other investors do. As Steingart so aptly puts it, "As long as the trusting outnumber the mistrustful, all is well . . . . The problems begin on the day this relationship begins to shift."[15]

Despite the possibility, a weak dollar is *not* a significant problem yet. Paul Krugman and others suggest that now that the fear of a global catastrophe has subsided, a weaker dollar is good for U.S. exports and helps close the trade deficit. For the time being many believe that it is likely to remain the world's currency anchor. According to the IMF, at the end of 2007, 64 percent of official foreign exchange holdings were in dollars—a relatively modest decline from 71 percent in 1999. Paradoxically, foreign investors might only hurt themselves if the U.S. dollar quickly depreciated as a result of their lack of confidence in it. A dollar crisis could then easily bring about another domestic economic crisis, which, like the current global crisis, could quickly spread to other countries.

## If Not the Dollar, Then What?

In October of 2009, China, France, Japan, Russia, and some Persian Gulf countries reportedly discussed moving away from the dollar and replacing it with a basket of currencies and gold. Political economist Barry Eichengreen points out that many states have been considering this and other alternatives.[16] Some of the most popular recommendations are as follows:

- The dollar remains the reserve currency.
- The euro or Chinese yuan replaces the dollar.
- A supranational currency such as Special Drawing Rights (SDRs) replaces the dollar.
- A reserve system with a basket of currencies emerges.

For Eichengreen, the GDP of euro countries is comparable to that of the United States. But a number of Eurozone members, including Greece, Italy, Ireland, Portugal, and Spain, are experiencing serious financial problems. While the euro may become a bigger reserve currency in the EU, it still is unlikely to become a globally hegemonic currency. So far neither the EU nor any other group of states wants the responsibilities associated with system management.

In China, 60 percent of official reserves are stuck in U.S. dollars. China's central bank governor has recommended that SDRs replace the dollar as the reserve currency. Currently, the Chinese yuan is not convertible everywhere; instead, it is used for cross-border trade and purchasing goods from China. This deters other countries from using the yuan for foreign exchange, trade, and bank payments. To change this, China would have to open its markets, commercialize and supervise its banks, and alter its growth strategy away from bank lending and a pegged currency. Although China is in no hurry to do this, the financial crisis did cause it to spend more for recovery and employment rather than investing in foreign banks and projects, which worries many U.S. officials and bankers all over the world.

A UN commission headed by Joseph Stiglitz recommended that SDRs play the role of a supranational reserve currency. This would help eliminate the privilege of countries like the United States who borrow large amounts of capital and whose domestic policies can impose adjustment problems on other states. The problem for now, however, is that SDRs are not accepted as foreign exchange. They cannot be bought and sold, and they are not liquid enough for states, corporations, and banks. To use them would require high costs and market restructuring. The IMF could help build a market for them, but it must be empowered by states to do so. It would have to issue additional SDRs during period of shortages.

For most realists and HILs, these recommendations to shift away from a hegemonic U.S. dollar parallel a shift away from the unipolar-unilateral outlook of the George W. Bush administration toward a more cooperative, multipolar, and multilateral security structure (see Chapter 9). For the time being, many state officials of the major powers and the emerging nations remain caught in a paradoxical "dollar trap" whereby they have a vested interest in preserving the system as is, but with an eye toward what *might* lie ahead.

# STRUCTURAL MANAGEMENT AND ALTERNATIVE RESERVE CURRENCIES

The scenarios just described would seem to compel rational states to cooperate more than they have with one another to establish and empower institutions to manage and safeguard the financial structure against unexpected events. As we discuss in Chapter 8, states have not been willing to relinquish to IOs much of their authority to regulate the monetary and finance structure. Much like in Jean Jacque Rousseau's analogy of the **stag hunt,** now each actor must decide whether to act in his own interest or cooperate to save the group.[17]

For now, management of the global monetary and finance structure remains ambiguous and weak. The IMF and the World Bank increasingly play less important roles in regulating currency exchange and lending funds. The IMF's role was weakened significantly due to its handling of the Asian crisis when it resisted recommendations from Japan and West European partners. During the recent financial crisis the IMF has resisted seriously evaluating the United States, its main benefactor. For now it is likely that the IMF will have a new role helping nations recover from the crisis, including a number of developed nations such as Greece, Ireland, and Iceland.

Since the 1970s the G8 (United States, UK, Germany, France, Japan, Italy, and Canada—and later Russia) have managed difficult negotiations between finance ministers and central bank presidents. There are other lesser-known IOs that also cooperate on international financial and banking issues. The Basil Committee on Bank Supervision includes 27 member states that coordinate to ensure standards for capital adequacy and supervise banking practices. The International Organization of Securities Commissions (IOSCO) sets standards on securities. It has two delegates from Canada, but none from China or India.[18] The Bank of International Settlements (BIS) is an invitation-only group comprised of the central banks of important countries and others the members choose to include.

The global financial crisis has since spurred the finance G20 (not the same as the WTO's G20), representing more emerging economies who increasingly want to play a bigger role in negotiations on monetary and finance structure rules and processes. Brazil, Russia, India, and China (the BRICs) have gained attention for their intransigence in some negotiations, but also for their hesitation to support stricter economic liberal policies and development strategies. Likewise, a number of the more successful Southeast Asian economies such as Indonesia, Malaysia, Thailand, and the Philippines stand in support of tamer versions of capitalism and a wider variety of emerging countries' (and even poor nations') interests in international negotiations related to FDI and currency exchange. Not unexpectedly, in the three G20 meetings held thus far, very little agreement has been reached on cooperative arrangements to solve the crisis.

# CONCLUSION

In the United States and Western Europe, post–World War II monetary and finance policies were heavily influenced by fresh memories of the Great Depression. By isolating each nation's financial system and then regulating it, policy makers wanted to avoid another global financial crisis and collapse. Under the Bretton Woods system (1947–1971), investment funds could not move easily among countries to take advantage of higher returns. To stabilize and generate confidence in the system, the value of the U.S. dollar was fixed to gold, and exchange-rate fluctuations were limited to narrow foreign exchange trading margins. As the Western economies recovered, the structure and rules of the international financial system restricted states that wanted to realize more economic growth. The Bretton Woods fixed-exchange-rate system gave way to a flexible-exchange-rate system and less control over exchange rates and capital transfers.

The 1970s marked both an era of increasing interdependence and two international recessions related to high oil prices. In the 1980s, neoliberal policies and the onset of the globalization campaign spurred deregulation of finance, currency exchanges, and trade. After the Cold War ended, laissez-faire domestic policies and globalization grew in popularity, resulting in record amounts of global capital transfers. Many emerging economies including Brazil and China acquired huge amounts of capital from exports sales to developed nations. By the mid-1990s, globalization and wildcat versions of capitalism were also gradually undermining the global monetary and finance structure, along with the U.S.'s leadership position. Currency and financial crises in Asia and now in the United States (see Chapter 8) have raised serious challenges to a structure that allowed U.S. hegemonic privileges to continue. The United States continues to borrow from (or be dependent on) surplus capital states to finance its deficit and high levels of domestic consumption, which recently contributed to a real estate bubble and near collapse of the global financial system in 2008.

Once again U.S. hegemonic responsibilities have become very expensive, both financially and politically. Because currency fluctuations and capital mobility can dramatically affect domestic employment and investment, the United States continues to look to other states to finance its deficits, which, paradoxically, could further undermine the stability of the global monetary and finance structure. Despite the popularity of economic liberal ideas, states still feel compelled as

ever to intervene in foreign exchange and finance markets to achieve their own national objectives.

While there is evidence that the financial crisis has weakened the U.S. dollar, at this time it would be hard to imagine another currency as strong or trusted as the U.S. dollar, given its relative strength since World War II. Cooperation still exists between the United States and states that benefit from U.S.-dominated international policies. Consequently, the monetary and finance structure reflects a situation where in terms of the Keynesian compromise, domestic considerations still weigh more heavily than international interests. Today's global political economy is much more integrated than it was 20 years ago. Interdependence and globalization have redistributed wealth and political power. However, this has made it exceptionally difficult to manage the finance and monetary structure in ways that reflect the interests of all but the stronger and more developed states of the global political economy.

Increasingly, some emerging and other states are no longer willing to cede management control of the monetary and finance control to the United States, nor should they be expected to given their economic position in the global economy. This has made management of this structure both cumbersome and difficult. For that reason alone, in a more multipolar and multilateral system, it is possible the global financial crisis might yet compel states to cooperate to produce a new order that satisfies their interests, lest the unpredictable hand of history makes those choices for them.

In the next chapter, we use many elements of the monetary and finance structure covered in this chapter to explain debt crises, investment bubbles, and speculative attacks on currencies. Much controversy surrounds IMF and World Bank's efforts to solve a series of problems related to both financial crises and long-term debt. We will then examine the recent U.S. financial crisis, caused by many of the same conditions that precipitated earlier crises. We conclude with a brief overview of some popular proposals to solve debt and financial problems.

# KEY TERMS

foreign exchange rates   158
Currency exchange rates   158
hard currency   159
soft currency   160
appreciation   160
depreciation   160
central bank   161
speculatio   162

hot money   162
gold standard   162
fixed exchange rate system   163
top currency   166
reserve currency   166
balance of payments   167
sovereign wealth funds
   (SWFs)   168

flexible exchange rate
   system   171
managed float   171
Capital Controls   171
Plaza Accord   173
Mundell Trilemma   173
stag hunt   179

# DISCUSSION QUESTIONS

1. Outline the political, economic, institutional, and procedural features of the gold standard, the fixed-exchange-rate, and the flexible-exchange-rate systems. What are some of the political and economic advantages and disadvantages of each system?

2. Outline the institutional features of the IMF and its role in settling current account deficits.

3. If the U.S. dollar depreciates dramatically relative to the Chinese Yuan, what effect would this likely have on consumers and businesses in each country? When is a falling dollar good or bad for the United States? Explain.

4. How have globalization and economic liberal ideas shaped developments in the monetary and finance structure? Cite specific examples from the chapter and in news articles.

5. The United States has recently experienced huge current account deficits that have made it dependent on investments from other states. What specific political and economic factors contributed to this condition? Who has the United States relied on the most to invest in the United States? Are these states rational to do this? What impact does this situation have on the value of the U.S. dollar? If you were an investor, would you be investing in the United States? Why or why not?

# SUGGESTED READINGS

C. Fred Bergsten. "The Dollar and the Deficits: How Washington Can Prevent the Next Crisis" *Foreign Affairs 88* (November/December 2009).

Benjamin J. Cohen. *The Geography of Money.* Ithaca, NY: Cornell University Press, 1998.

Barry Eichengreen. *Globalizing Capital: A History of the International Monetary System.* Princeton, NJ: Princeton University Press, 1996.

Barry Eichengreen. "The Dollar Dilemma: The World's Top Currency Faces Competition" *Foreign Affairs 88* (September/October 2009), pp. 53–68.

Robert Wade. "The First-World Debt Crisis of 2007–2010 in Global Perspective," *Challenge 51* (July/August 2008), pp. 23–54.

# NOTES

1. Ross Singleton has been the primary author of earlier editions of this chapter and consulted with the editors on this edition.

2. Eric Helleiner, "The Evolution of the International Monetary and Financial System," in John Ravenhill, ed., *Global Political Economy* (Oxford: Oxford University Press, 2005), p. 152.

3. For a more detailed discussion of the history of the monetary and finance structure see Helleiner, "The Evolution of the International Monetary and Financial System," pp. 151–175.

4. Two examples of these unions were the Latin American Union, which in 1865 included France, Switzerland, Belgium, and Italy; and the Scandinavian

Union, which in 1873 included Sweden, Denmark, and later Norway. See Helleiner, ibid., p. 153.

5. Ibid., p. 155.

6. Cited in ibid., p. 156.

7. See Karl Polanyi, *The Great Transformation: The Political and Economic Origins of Our Time* (Boston, MA: Beacon Press, 1944).

8. See, for example, Oswaldo De Rivero, *The Myth of Development: The Non-viable Economies of the 21st Century* (New York: Zed Books, 2001), pp. 54–61.

9. See Benjamin J. Cohen, "The Revolution in Atlantic Relations: The Bargain Comes Unstuck," in Wolfram Hanrieder, ed., *The United States and Western Europe: Political, Economic, and Strategic Perspectives* (Cambridge, MA: Winthrop, 1974).

10. See Robert Gilpin, *The Challenge of Global Capitalism* (Princeton, NJ: Princeton University Press, 2000), p. 6.

11. Reported in Thomas Lairson and David Skidmore, *International Political Economy: The Struggle for Power and Wealth*, 3rd ed. (Belmont, CA: Wadsworth, 2003), p. 104.

12. Gilpin, *The Challenge of Global Capitalism*, p. 6.

13. C. Fred Bergsten, "The Dollar and Its Deficits," *Foreign Affairs*, 88, November/December 2009.

14. See Gabor Steingart, "Playing with Fire," Spiegel Online, www.spiegel.de/international/0,1518,druck-440054,00.html.

15. See Gabor Steingart, *The War for Wealth: The True Story of Globalization, or Why The Flat World Is Broken* (Emmeryville, CA: McGraw Hill, 2008), p. 87.

16. See Barry Eichengreen, "The Dollar Dilemma: The World's Top Currency Faces Competition," *Foreign Affairs*, 88 (September/October 2009), pp. 53–68.

17. For a discussion of the stag hunt see Kenneth Waltz, *Man, the State, and War: A Theoretical Analysis* (New York: Columbia University Press, 1959).

18. See Robert Wade, "The First-World Debt Crisis of 2007–2010 in Global Perspective," *Challenge 51* (July/August 2008), pp. 23–54.

# International Debt and Financial Crises

The Haves and Have-nots.

Georgina Allen

As we saw in Chapter 7, financial markets and monetary issues have transcended national borders to become the form and substance of the global financial structure. The *globalization* of finance has been the single most important feature of this structure. The movement of money and finance goes on 24 hours a day. Until the recent financial crisis of 2007, an estimated $8 trillion of foreign exchange was traded *per day* in global markets. These foreign exchange and investment markets represent the largest financial flows in the world, dwarfing even the vast economy of the United States. We also saw in Chapter 7 how volatile the global financial system is, in terms of both capital mobility and currency exchange rates. One complicated issue is debt, which was previously viewed as a problem of developing nations. The recent global financial crisis demonstrated the vulnerability of all nations to some combination of the debt–finance predicament.

Drawing on some of the themes introduced in Chapter 7, in this chapter we examine three interrelated debt–finance issues that some claim to be of crisis proportions. The first part of the chapter covers the IMF and World Bank roles in overcoming debt problems in the early 1980s, when outright default on Mexico and Brazil's debt seemed imminent. Second, in an era of unfettered capital and currency exchange markets during the 1990s, the IMF worked in conjunction with the World Bank to combat a different series of financial debt problems, including the Asian crisis in 1997 created by financial investment bubbles and currency speculation. We then discuss the recent financial crisis, triggered by a real estate mortgage bubble in the United States, which burst and then spread into many other economies.

The third part of the chapter deals with long-term issues related to perpetual poverty in the world's poorest countries. Recently, a number of international organizations (IOs), and relief agencies, together with vast numbers of nongovernmental organizations (NGOs), have launched a campaign to do more than wait for the heavily indebted poor countries (HIPCs) to work themselves into the global economy and out of debt. Debt relief, or cancellation of the debt altogether, is one of the major goals of this international movement.

The theses of this chapter are as follows: First, the events of the past 30 years indicate that, contrary to first impressions, many parts of the global financial and monetary structure are quite fragile, subject to debt and currency crises, financial bubbles, and speculative attacks. Second, although states are still reluctant to give up control over the global financial system, a system of more effective global governance is needed to promote greater stability, account for inadequacies in this structure, and weigh the impact of these markets on the world's poorest people.

## THE DEBT CRISIS OF THE 1980s

By most accounts, the first LDC debt "crisis" began in 1982, when Mexico announced that it would default on its bank debt, generating fear that other countries with substantial debt, such as Brazil, would follow Mexico's lead.[1] This crisis was a consequence, in part, of the early stages of the globalization of finance in the 1970s. As financial flows became more global in scope, powered by market deregulation and technological change, financial centers in the industrial North increasingly sought new investments possibilities and higher returns. As noted in Chapter 7, many banks were flush with recycled OPEC petrodollars that were reinvested into the industrialized nations and their banks. These banks and other financial institutions turned their attention to LDCs in the South, which were receiving less financial assistance from Official Development Assistance (ODA) sources.

Northern finance ministers and state policy makers encouraged LDCs to borrow some of this money, especially because inflation rates were running ahead of interest rates on loans—creating negative *real* rates, which traditionally favor borrowers.[2]

Liberal theory states these loans should have resulted in economic growth and higher returns for both borrower and lender. Many LDCs had resources (including oil), the prices for which in a scarce market were unusually high. The low-cost labor and favorable LDC economic development policies also favored new investment opportunities (see Chapter 11). In practice, however, the uncoordinated actions of the market generated a "debt trap"[3] for both debtor states and their creditors. In retrospect, too much was loaned to too many.

International banks continued to make additional loans to states with growing debt both to provide more resources for economic development and to sustain interest payments on earlier loans. However, the debt continued to grow exponentially, generating a major burden on LDCs and risking the solvency of the financial institutions involved. With so much debt outstanding, the banks were in as much trouble as the debtor nations—a typical Keynesian concern. Debtor nations owed more than they could reasonably repay, yet they continued to borrow more in order to meet their short-run obligations. IMF debt management policies included austerity measures (cutbacks in state spending), debt rescheduling with commercial banks, and new public and private lending. In essence, debtor states only refinanced their loans and stretched out the time period for repayment of the loans. Most states restrained imports and promoted exports to generate income. Eventually, economic growth in these countries slowed and the situation grew worse. Only Korea and Turkey recovered; others went deeper into the red.

U.S. Treasury Secretary James Baker initiated a plan—the Baker Plan—to implement market-oriented structural changes to debtor economies combined with $20 billion in new loans, provided by commercial banks over three years. These efforts continued to focus on enabling debtor nations to "grow" their way out of the debt. However, the plan did not work. As countries tried to expand their exports all at once, commodity and oil prices collapsed, leaving many nations (especially African countries) worse off than before the loans. This problem was exacerbated by a recession that slowed down economic activity throughout the industrialized North, shrinking the market for LDC exports. In some cases, loan money was used in unprofitable projects or was siphoned off by corrupt leaders.[4] Political tensions in many countries prevented them from pursuing structural reforms. Most countries could barely afford to service their debt. Finally, new sources of credit from banks and the World Bank were ill-timed and slow in coming.

By the late 1980s, many debtor states faced "donor fatigue," whereby social and political tensions related to policies adopted to relieve the debt grew and dissatisfaction with international debt management festered. A number of Latin American states unilaterally suspended all or part of their debt-service payments. In response to these and other signs of opposition, other industrialized nations put pressure on the United States to come up with other measures to relieve the debt. Opposed by the Reagan administration at first, *debt swaps* were employed in some cases. Some amount of debt could be swapped with a bank in exchange for land or valuable properties in debtor countries.

Debt relief would obviously have helped debtor nations, by reducing their international obligations, and it might also have helped creditor banks, by clearing their books of bad loans and reducing the risks they faced from default. However, the banks found themselves unable to grant debt relief in this manner, because they were caught in a situation referred to as the "prisoner's dilemma," where each wanted others to forgive the debt but were unwilling to do so themselves, for fear that those who granted relief would bear a cost that would not be shared by those who paid nothing to solve the problem. It was not surprising then, that given the high stakes and the intensely competitive nature of international finance, no one state or bank was willing to forgive LDC debts, and the vicious cycle of debt for these nations continued.

On the other hand, cooperation can be encouraged by a hegemon, whose share of the resulting gains is so great that it is willing to bear the costs of organizing a cooperative effort. The United States played the role of hegemon in the international debt crisis of the 1980s, when it pressured the IMF to adopt certain policies to help LDCs overcome their debt.

In 1989 President George H.W. Bush initiated another program—the Brady Plan—whereby old debt was exchanged for bonds that could be exchanged for new bank loans. Negotiations for these bonds were carried on between the banks and each debtor state. In hegemonic fashion, the United States offered to refinance Mexico's external debt, provided all lenders accepted specific measures of debt relief, including interest-rate cuts, payment rescheduling, and some measure of forgiveness. Private banks exchanged their Mexican debt for a lesser amount of U.S. government securities—Brady Bonds—backed by Mexican obligations. Mexico would pay the United States, which paid the creditors. Under this scheme, Mexico benefited from some debt relief, the banks reduced the risk of default, and the U.S. government avoided increasing international financial instability.

Many banks went along with these and similar schemes because they feared financial disaster if debtor countries defaulted. External debt was still a serious burden for many LDCs in 1991. Brazil's total debt was 36.9 percent of its national income, for example, and the annual interest burden amounted to over 17 percent of its export earnings. Although Brazil and Mexico had the largest debts, Argentina, Nigeria, Chile, and Nicaragua faced the greatest debt burdens relative to the size and strength of their economies. To honor such huge debt and interest burdens would have required harsh mercantilist policies restricting imports and expanding exports, generating problems in the industrialized nations that rely on LDCs to import some of their manufactured goods. The discipline and sacrifice necessary for LDCs to service their debt often generated much social and political unrest, including strikes and riots.

## Debt Crises and a New Role for the IMF

During the mid-1980s, the United States pushed the IMF to work closely with the World Bank on solving LDC debt problems. During this period the *Washington Consensus* (see Chapter 11) gradually emerged as the best strategy for developing nations. According to the neoliberal ideas of the Reagan administration, debt would be overcome as economies opened up and integrated into the growing global economy.

The role of the IMF then shifted away from helping member states deal with balance-of-payments problems into the "lender of last resort" in the international economy, an institution that could help nations overcome their debt burden. World Bank and IMF loans were made subject to **structural adjustment policies (SAPs)**, a series of conditions or actions to which the borrowing government must agree before receiving a loan. If these conditions were violated, IMF or World Bank assistance could be withdrawn.

IMF **conditionality** is controversial to the extent that the terms reflect the neoliberal ideas behind the Washington Consensus and not the individual needs of the borrowing nation. A typical IMF debt plan involves a number of politically unpopular SAPs designed to restore economic balance. Some of such polices include *currency devaluation* to generate trade export; policies that encourage *price stability* to control inflation and encourage savings; *fiscal austerity* to cut state spending and subsidies while privatizing national industries; *tariff liberalization* to encourage imports; *higher interest rates* to attract investment in the short run; and *sound social programs* in reaction to higher import prices, reduced subsidies and programs, and higher taxes.

The logic of the IMF's policies was to reduce the current account deficit (see Chapter 7) by increasing exports and reducing imports and simultaneously help finance the capital account by stemming capital flight and limiting new borrowing needs. In the long run, these policies were also intended to encourage economic growth, creating a situation in which the nation can repay its old debts and be less dependent on credit in the future. In the short run, the debtor-nation government was expected to enact policies that at first lowered living standards and imposed hardship, especially on the poor, in some cases leading to violence and civil unrest. Although in theory the IMF and the debtor-nation government worked together, in practice their relationship was often conflictual, with the IMF responsible for international financial stability while debtor-nation governments dealt with domestic forces opposed to SAPs. The more authoritarian the state, the more likely it would be able to enforce these measures.

By the mid-1990s, amidst volatile international economic conditions, both the IMF and the World Bank found themselves responding to another source of debt. A series of financial crises developed from what economists refer to as a balance-of-payments crisis; these cases included the manic behavior of foreign direct investors and speculators in parts of Asia, among other places (discussed below). Foreign investors flooded these countries with huge amounts of funds, generating an investment bubble that collapsed. The crisis added pressure to currency values in Thailand, leading to a severe devaluation in the baht and other currencies. This resulted in many countries accumulating large international debts that were difficult to repay to the IMF.

## A Balance-of-Payments Financial Crisis

What do economists mean by a balance-of-payments crisis? As noted above, in some cases states borrowed too much money to use for development projects or pay for imports. Just as a student borrows too much from the bank when using his or her credit card, so states often "borrow" from other states in ways that leave them without enough assets to cover their debts.

This type of debt stems from many of the transactions states (and banks within them) conduct every day. Businesses need capital to invest in other countries' industries and to trade with them. As part of these transactions, markets for currencies can easily make investments worth more or less. One prime example is when the cost of oil goes up, the value of the U.S. dollar may decline against other currencies because it often cannot buy as much oil as it did previously. These currency transactions and investments make up large parts of the balance of payments.

For example, if the United States is running a balance-of-payments deficit, it is dependent on other states to offset that deficit with investments in the United States or to sell them more U.S. goods and services. The *lack* of foreign investment often leads to a current account deficit—or financial debt. For the time being, the United States might be unable to borrow under favorable terms, thus disrupting international trade because needed imports may be too expensive to obtain.

These conditions can result in **capital flight,** when investors transfer their bank accounts out of the country to "safe harbor" nations. In turn, this creates an extreme shortage of funds in the debtor nation's banks, which sends national interest rates shooting up. It also puts pressure on states to defend the value of their currency by providing stronger currencies to those who cash out of the local currency on their way out of the country. If they cannot, officials may have no choice but to devalue the currency, which can easily destabilize their economy and society.

Debt problems related to a balance-of-payments crisis brought on by speculation and capital flight can disrupt and distort trade and international financial relationships. A crisis in one nation, along with that nation's attempts to deal with its problems, could spawn additional crises elsewhere, as it did during the Great Depression of the 1930s. Although the current financial crisis is, fundamentally, an economic problem, it also shifts into a political problem, because it usually falls on the state and its political leadership to propose and implement the frequently harsh policies necessary to bring international payments back into balance.

## THE ASIAN FINANCIAL CRISIS

Less than two years after a Mexican peso crisis in 1995, the Asian financial crisis struck, threatening the financial stability of the entire globe. Its effects still linger in East and Southeast Asia.[5] The Asian financial crisis demonstrates how easily crises occur, even in states with otherwise sound economic policies. It raises questions about the trade-offs surrounding speculative attacks in a more integrated global monetary and finance structure.

The crisis started on July 2, 1997, when Thailand's currency, the baht, suddenly collapsed in value. What was referred to as a **currency crisis** was initially reported only on the back pages of the financial sections of world newspapers. It started a chain reaction of economic, political, and social effects, together referred to as the *Asian financial crisis* because it spread to Indonesia, Malaysia, Taiwan, Hong Kong, South Korea, and elsewhere in the region.

The Thai government had guaranteed that the exchange rate between the Thai baht and the U.S. dollar would be *fixed* at a rate of 25 baht per dollar. The

Thai government did this to help Thailand's economy grow by encouraging trade with and investment from the United States and other countries. This could occur because interest rates were *lower* in the United States than they were in Thailand. The government's pledge of a stable currency value encouraged Thai finance companies to borrow U.S. dollars on global markets, convert them to Thai baht at the fixed exchange rate, and then lend them out at a higher interest rate in Thailand to expand businesses, purchase property, and even speculate on Thai stocks. Thai banks borrowed a lot of dollars and other hard currencies, which both created profit and stimulated investment. Consequently, a business bubble began to inflate in Thailand and other countries in the region.

Problems developed when Thai banks were found to have many bad loans on their books—loans that were unlikely to be repaid on time and perhaps could never be repaid at all. Some of these bad loans were blamed on **crony capitalism,** where some Thai finance companies received favorable treatment from the government in return for financial considerations, sometimes given under the guise of loans. When the bad loans were revealed, international investors, concerned about both the health of the Thai banks and the government's ability to honor its exchange-rate pledge, began to pull their funds out of Thailand.

Foreign investors who withdrew their funds wanted to convert them back into dollars. This meant that for every 25 baht withdrawn, the Thai government had to give one U.S. dollar in return. As the flow of funds out of Thailand increased, the Thai government's supply of dollar reserves was drawn down. Conjecture began that the government would not be able to keep its promise—what would it do when it ran out of dollars?

This speculation soon turned into a kind of self-fulfilling prophecy. Because people worried that the Thai government could not keep its exchange-rate promise, many began pulling their funds out of Thailand. When everyone did this at once, it was impossible for the Thai government to pay everyone their dollars at once. These conditions then were perfect for a **speculative attack,** which is essentially a confrontation between a central bank, which pledges to maintain its country's exchange rate at a certain level, and international currency speculators, who are willing to wager that the central bank is not fully committed to its exchange-rate goal.

To provide a bit more detail to what we discussed in Chapter 7 about speculation, currency speculators can attack the currency by borrowing huge amounts of it and then selling it on the currency market. The central bank can keep its pledge by using its currency reserves to buy up the currency the speculators are selling. If the central bank keeps its pledge, speculators stand to lose very little because they can buy back the currency to repay their loans at about the same rate at which they sold it. If, however, the central bank is not willing to intervene to keep its currency stable, or if it runs low on the reserves it needs to do this, then the currency value will depreciate in international markets. Speculators will be able to buy back their currency at a lower price and have great profits left even after they have paid back their loans.

Typically, central banks have billions of U.S. dollars of reserves and access to considerably more funds through agreements with other countries' banks. How, then, is it possible to "break the bank" with such apparent ease? It is because global financial markets, when focused on a single country or industry, have even greater resources. The Hungarian-American hedge fund investor George Soros pocketed $1 billion in profits in 1992 by betting that the Bank of England would not maintain the pound's value relative to European currencies. A **hedge fund** is an investment instrument that attempts to make a profit from the fact that an asset such as a stock or bond might be trading at different prices in different places. The hedge fund bets that the prices will converge and earns a profit if they do. Because such pricing anomalies are typically very small, a hedge fund must be able to mobilize vast sums of money—hundreds of millions or even billions of dollars—with each dollar invested earning a small but quick return. Small profits multiplied by vast amounts equals tidy profits.

Hedge funds can be controversial when speculation zeroes in on a currency that appears to be trading at a higher price than is justified by political-economic conditions. Then the hedge fund's vast potential is used in a speculative attack and considerable damage is done. Speculative currency attacks were responsible for the collapse of the Indonesian rupiah and the Malaysian ringgit in 1997–1998, as well as the British pound and the Italian lira during 1992–1993. Exchange rates can be expected to display a variety of patterns over time, including stability, cycles, booms, and crashes. As long as investment capital is freely mobile between countries, currency crises caused by speculative attacks and investment bubbles are likely to occur.

On July 2, 1997, the Thai government was forced to abandon its pledge of a 25-baht-per-dollar exchange rate. The baht's value collapsed, falling from 25 baht per dollar to about 30 baht per dollar in a matter of days. Seeing the crisis in Thailand, investors "sold Asia," pulling their investment funds out of other countries in the region. The Asian currency crisis continued through the summer and into the fall. When the dust settled, the new exchange rate was about 50 baht per dollar, with similar collapses in other Asian countries. This had a number of serious effects. For Thai citizens, the most direct effect was that foreign goods were suddenly more expensive. A $10 bottle of a U.S.-made prescription drug that used to cost 250 baht was now priced at about 500 baht. This created adverse effects both for Thai people who needed imported goods and for the U.S. firms and workers that made these items. U.S. citizens benefited when a 100-baht sack of Thai jasmine rice, which used to cost $4.00, was now just $2.00. Of course this put pressure on U.S. rice farmers to match the lower Thai prices.

However, the biggest effects were in the financial sectors, where even Thai businessmen who had made good business decisions—perhaps they had lent the money efficiently and would get repaid in full and on time (in baht)—could not possibly repay their U.S.-dollar loan because it required twice as many baht as expected. Many went bankrupt, affecting their families and communities around them. Many people in Southeast Asia had acted rationally and worked hard but found themselves bankrupt—deep in debt, their life savings wiped out, and with few prospects for short-term recovery. The losses in Thailand were enough to lower the per-capita income average of the entire country by about 25 percent in one year. For many, the Asian crisis was an economic collapse similar to the Great Depression.

# THE GLOBAL FINANCIAL CRISIS OF 2007

The current global financial crisis is not a unique event but the latest in a long line of financial crises. By September 2008, the U.S. real estate-mortgage problem had resulted in a full-blown crisis that quickly became a global financial debacle, essentially freezing the circulation of credit within and between states. By the summer of 2009, some of the world's largest financial institutions had either gone bankrupt, been nationalized, or been rescued by the government. Simultaneously, the financial turmoil produced a deep global economic recession with dizzying job losses, record home foreclosures, and a substantial increase in poverty. Public confidence in governments' handling of economic affairs faltered, so much so that ruling parties and coalition governments were ousted in Iceland, Latvia, and Japan.

Why did this happen—especially in advanced, industrialized countries whose economic institutions were supposed to be some of the most efficient and well regulated in the world? Heated debates on the causes of the crisis have occurred in the halls of officialdom, in the news media, and in academia. Some often-mentioned causes include:

- A global economic imbalance rooted in a U.S. balance-of-payments problem.
- A U.S. regulatory regime that led to excessive debt and imprudent lending practices of banks, mortgage companies, and other financial institutions.
- A myopic ideology that promoted globalization and the "magic of the market" without accounting for market failure and the impact of deregulation on financial institutions.
- The irrational, unethical, and even illegal behavior of some individuals and companies.
- Weak global governance.

What follows is a chronological discussion of the causes of the crisis and the key actors in it.

## The Run-up to the U.S. Financial Crisis

In the history of capitalism, recessions were almost a cyclic occurrence and regarded as one of the side effects of capitalism. As noted in Chapters 2 and 3, from the 1930s to the 1960s, public officials in the United States and Europe viewed their economies through a Keynesian lens. In pursuit of socioeconomic and political stability, many states intervened in their economies by using fiscal policy to control inflation, minimize recession, sustain wages for labor, and stimulate economic growth. In the late 1960s, Keynesianism was criticized for encouraging excessive government spending and for emphasizing stability instead of economic growth. Keynes's ideas were gradually replaced by Milton Friedman's more orthodox economic liberal (OEL) ideas, which featured "minimally fettered" capitalism—or a *limited* state role in the economy (see Chapter 2).

As discussed in Chapter 7, in 1973 the United States adopted a more economic liberal outlook and replaced the fixed-exchange-rate system with a flexible-exchange-rate system. This led to increased speculation on currencies and more money circulating in the international economy. That same year OPEC oil price hikes produced an economic recession in the industrialized nations, while massive amounts of OPEC's earnings recycled back into Western banks. Meanwhile, many states in Western Europe and Japan competed with the United States for new trade and investment markets.

As noted earlier, in the early 1980s, U.S. President Reagan and British Prime Minister Thatcher promoted neoliberal ideas and policies designed to unleash new investments and economic growth by reducing taxes and *deregulating* banks, financial institutions, and other market actors. They insisted that markets—not states—could best redistribute income to those who are most efficient, innovative, and hardworking. By the time the Cold War ended in 1990, economic liberal ideas were well entrenched in the ruling elites of the United States and other parts of the world. Former Soviet states and developing nations were encouraged to not only adopt democracy but open markets, privatize, and deregulate their economies.

The Democratic Clinton administration continued promoting economic liberal policies. In the late 1990s, stock prices skyrocketed and the development of new technologies and communication systems enhanced market activity. Investors poured money into dot-com companies, and growth rates were robust in China, India, and many postcommunist countries. By the end of the 1990s, many nations were competing to attract huge amounts of unregulated "hot money." As discussed above, these funds destabilized the Mexican economy in 1994 and helped produce the collapse of many Asian economies in 1997.

In 1999, the U.S. Congress repealed the depression-era Glass–Steagall Act, thereby allowing mergers between commercial and investment banks. This laissez-faire measure led to increased risk-taking in both the domestic and international financial systems. But the dot-com investment bubble burst in 2000 and 2001, taking with it $7 trillion in assets as technology stocks tanked. Even so, the new Bush administration and the Federal Reserve under Alan Greenspan remained adamant about the need to continue deregulation and reduce the state's role in the economy. They continued to believe that markets were efficient, self-regulating, and good at assessing financial risks and setting prices—beliefs that Nobel Prize–winning economist Paul Krugman suggests in retrospect were "dangerously simplistic, naïve, and ahistorical."[6]

The number of structural problems in the U.S. economy mounted, many playing a role in the onset of the financial crisis in 2007. First, the United States was running a huge trade deficit with China, Japan, and other exporters who had been financing this deficit by buying enormous amounts of U.S. stocks, Treasury bills, and other securities. In effect, the trade-surplus countries were loaning money to Americans who had an insatiable appetite for cheap imported goods and risk-taking when it came to speculation. Toward the late 1990s, interest rates were allowed to stay low, which made it easy for Americans to borrow money and spend more, even though their average incomes stagnated after 1999. The United States gradually built up an unsustainable level of personal and public debt.

Second, the Federal Reserve lowered interest rates following the dot-com bubble burst, making it easier to buy a house on credit. Investors looked to real estate for good, low-risk rates of return, driving up housing prices and the profits associated with issuing mortgages or holding pools of mortgages as securities. Lax lending standards and abundant credit kept driving up prices and amounts lent.

Other lenders gave loans with low initial repayments to low-income borrowers without requiring proof of income or any money down. Many banks added to the risk of these investments by keeping "ghost assets" off their balance sheets, hiding their growing debt from new potential investors. In particular, **subprime mortgage loans** (loans made to risky borrowers with weak credit scores who were often allowed to make interest-only repayments early in the loan cycle) are believed to have caused many buyers to make irrational decisions often based on incomplete (hidden) information.

With an expectation of making huge profits, banks and other financial institutions (like hedge funds, private equity firms, and insurance companies) kept borrowing more money to make riskier loans and investments. Deregulation allowed making the "big deal" to overshadow careful risk assessment. Big investment banks like Goldman Sachs, Merrill Lynch, Lehman Brothers, Bear Stearns, and Morgan Stanley became highly *leveraged*—that is, the ratio of loans they made over the amount of funds they kept in reserve grew to unprecedented levels. Based on mathematical models associated with derivatives (see "Coding the Money Tree" box below), they packaged and bought mortgage-backed securities and other investments, whose true underlying value was nearly impossible to measure.

## ▶ CODING THE MONEY TREE[a]

Derivatives, with such lax regulations, were one of the tools that contributed to the financial crisis. The models upon which derivatives are based are *mathematically* accurate. Created to spread default risk over a broad-enough range of assets so as to make them safer to invest in, the model failed to account for human greed. While a proverbial "money tree" was created on paper, derivatives were used by banks that cared more about their own profits than the security of their clients' investments.

Derivatives were first concocted in multiple financial mathematics research departments. Michael Osinski was the first to create a program that streamlined their production. Looking back on his work, Osinski remarks, "I have been called the devil by strangers and 'the Facilitator' by friends. It's not uncommon for people, when I tell them what I used to do, to ask if I feel guilty. I do . . ."[b] At first, paper traders could offer a highly liquid investment with both an almost negligible default risk and an enormously high return; what wasn't to love about them? Soon everyone wanted them. Investment banks

needed a way to accelerate the creation of their assets. Coupled with the deregulation of derivative trading, these instruments shifted from complex sources of short-term gain to dangerous, volatile, mispriced financial weapons. With an overwhelming demand for these assets in the 1990s and the first decade of the 2000s, investment bankers faced very few consequences from losing a single client. With disposable clients, banks and traders started to roll the dice even more, diversifying into even riskier investment sectors like real estate.

The repeal of the Glass–Steagall Act in 1999 and the granting of AAA ratings by credit agencies made it easier for commercial banks to continue shifting to the goal of short-term profit maximization rather than promoting long-term assets and stable growth. When the banks expanded into the subprime housing markets, deciding when, and if, the loans would go under became a difficult task. Yet as Osinski comments again, "Throw some epsilons and thetas on a paper, hoist a few Ph.D.'s behind your name, and now you're an expert in divining the future." This mantra took much of the worry out of derivatives and allowed Osinski's program to facilitate the destruction of Wall Street.

Can tools like his program exist without being misused? According to Keynes and others, regulation is called for when the rational choices of individuals result in collective failure. In this particular instance, it was best for individuals, banks, and investment firms to pursue short-term profits. Yet, many of these institutions seemed to forget that market prices can easily drop. Many firms had invested in derivatives, and this destabilized not only the U.S. and other economies, but in this case the global economy.

In the last decade, the political climate called almost solely for deregulation of financial markets. As a result, regulators have been dissuaded from doing more to limit derivatives. Many national governments are now at a crossroads. In the wake of this tragedy of human greed, the media constantly tried to point fingers, first at banks and financial mathematicians for developing these tools, at traders for misusing them, and finally at economists for promoting the ideology that markets are self-correcting.

However, the issue is more complex. Banks cannot be faulted for misusing tools that regulators, public officials, and dealers themselves viewed as too complex to regulate. Arnold Kling, once a senior economist at Freddie Mac, commented that of all the traders he knows, only a small handful actually understand derivatives, himself not among them.

Officials are left with many concerns: How much state intervention and regulation is needed to prevent private interests from damaging society? What do we do when things are too complex to regulate? How do we punish individuals or firms who try to privatize their profits and socialize their losses? Will the political climate let us diverge from this trend of fast-and-loose American capitalism? This is the new frontier of economic policy, capturing and measuring the human element in order to correct for perverse incentives. It can only be hoped that regulation can keep up with the drive of the individual to benefit when society loses.

### References

[a]Jerome Anton researched and drafted the material for this box.
[b]Michael Osinski, "My Manhattan Project: How I Helped Build the Bomb That Blew Up Wall Street," *New York Magazine*, March 29, 2009.

## The Bubble Bursts

During the Bush administration, a number of experts, including Nouriel Roubini at New York University and Robert Schiller at Yale University, warned national public officials about a growing real estate bubble, but their forebodings attracted little attention until the subprime mortgage market started to crumble in 2006. By early 2007, a slew of large mortgage companies with significant portfolios of subprime loans—worth $13 trillion or 20 percent of U.S. home lending—filed for bankruptcy. In July 2007, it became clear that the subprime market was in free fall when Bear Stearns announced that two of its hedge funds specializing in subprime mortgage debt had lost almost all of their value. Home and mortgage markets in other countries, including the United Kingdom and Japan, began reflecting the same trend occurring in the United States.

By August 2007, a worldwide credit crunch grew amongst banks and hedge funds that held a vast amount of mortgage-backed securities. Both Fed Chairman Ben Bernanke and Treasury Secretary Hank Paulson finally expressed alarm about a growing housing bubble. Troubles at many financial companies around the world unfolded and mounted through the end of the year. The French investment bank PHB Paribas suspended three investment funds that invested heavily in subprime loans. In September the British central bank gave emergency financial support to mortgage lender Northern Rock, which was eventually nationalized in 2008. Merrill Lynch, Citigroup, and other large financial institutions reported billions of dollars of losses on subprime mortgage investments.

Governments responded to these bank failures in an ad hoc manner, mostly by pumping capital into their banking systems to ensure they had enough liquidity. By the end of 2007, the U.S. Federal Reserve and the European Central Bank had injected several hundred billion dollars into the money supply for banks to borrow at a low rate. They also lowered interest rates to encourage more borrowing. At the same time, some **sovereign wealth funds** (**SWFs**—or pools of government money earned from trade and investment transactions that states can use to invest for profit) from the Middle East and Asia provided capital in markets by buying at least $69 billion worth of shares in financial companies in 2007. In fact, some in the United States feared that governments that owned SWFs might use their investments for purposes contrary to U.S. national interests (see China vs. Unocal box in Chapter 3).

In the first half of 2008, financial turmoil continued to spread throughout the global economy. The U.S. stock market suffered big losses and remained volatile. The Federal Reserve helped JPMorgan Chase acquire Bear Stearns, Wall Street's fifth largest and most highly leveraged bank, for $2 a share in a fire sale. In March the FBI arrested 406 buyers and sellers in the mortgage industry on charges of bank fraud. Throughout the world banking system losses were tied to U.S. mortgage securities and other risky investments.

In the summer of 2008 many analysts recognized that eventually banks would not be able to cover their "toxic securities," making them increasingly riskier investments. Growing corporate and consumer debt added to concern about a possible financial crisis. The real estate bubble began to tear in July 2008 after panicky investors started unloading their stocks in the state-created Fannie Mae and Freddie Mac loan agencies, which together owned or guaranteed $6 trillion of the $12 trillion mortgage market in the United States. Congress hastily passed a "rescue plan" to try to assure investors that the loan agencies would remain solvent. But investors were rapidly losing confidence and began disinvesting in the U.S. real estate and stock markets. Speculators left real estate and focused on hot commodities like oil, gold, rice, and wheat, raising fears of higher inflation and negative growth. Oil prices reached $147 a barrel in July 2008, causing increased concerns about the ripple effects of high energy costs on consumers and businesses.

In September, a series of cascading financial crises caused stock markets to plunge and global credit markets to freeze up, almost overnight. Like the Asian crises in 1997, many investors previously willing to take a risk now panicked, causing many stocks and retirement funds to lose a large percentage of their value. On September 7, the U.S. government announced that it would bail out (nationalize) Fannie Mae and Freddie Mac. Within a week, Bank of America took over the giant investment bank Merrill Lynch. But the U.S. government refused to rescue another big investment bank, Lehman Brothers, which collapsed and filed for bankruptcy. This worried other banks that the U.S. government might not be willing to bail out its big banks after all.

Before long, the U.S. Fed did rescue the American International Group (AIG), one of world's largest bank insurers, paying $85 billion and becoming an 80 percent owner of the company. AIG had been heavily involved in issuing **credit default swaps (CDSs)**. CDSs are insurance contracts that made it possible for investors to bet on the possibility that companies would default on repaying their loans. As subprime defaults and bankruptcies rose, AIG did not have the money to pay claims on CDSs, which were worth over $45 trillion. The Fed's aid to AIG—which became a nearly $150 billion bailout package—was a hedge against the possibility that failure of AIG would cause the entire global banking and financial system to collapse.

Near the end of September, the Federal Deposit Insurance Corporation (FDIC) seized Washington Mutual after depositors made a run on the bank, and the FDIC sold WAMU's assets to JPMorgan Chase. Washington Mutual was the sixth largest commercial bank in the country. It was the largest bank failure in U.S. history. When big banks began to fall, the herd effect took over and investors scrambled to disinvest in U.S. mortgages and other securities. *Torchlusspanik* (the German term for "shut-gate") began in earnest as the U.S. stock market tumbled to record lows.

The mortgage crisis quickly generated a **contagion** effect as a broader global financial crisis spread all over the world. Big banks on Wall Street and elsewhere were reluctant to lend to one another, let alone to smaller banks on "Main Street" who financed local businesses and home sales. When smaller businesses could not find capital to borrow, job losses were followed by drastic cuts in state and local budgets. This generated a downward spiral in home values, increased consumer debt as more people used credit cards to substitute for their loss of pay, and caused people to hoard what cash they had left.

## We Are All Keynesians Now

As the fear of not only a recession but a second Great Depression mounted, many journalists, academics, and public officials—including the widely admired former Fed Chairman Alan Greenspan—began to sound more like Keynesian HILs than Milton Friedman OELs (see Chapter 2). After an intense debate in the media and among administration officials, a temporary coalition of officials and academic experts agreed that the U.S. Federal Reserve (along with central banks in other nations) would be the last resort for funds to help prime the economy by putting more money into circulation.

On September 9, 2008, after a variety of closed-door meetings between U.S. officials and many heads of big banks, Treasury Secretary Henry (Hank) Paulson unveiled a controversial $700 billion emergency rescue package to buy up bad assets in banks in the hope of keeping credit moving. Many OELs preferred to let the market run its course, culling a number of big banks and letting the strongest ones survive. It should be noted that some OELs did fear that failure to save the big banks could lead to a global financial catastrophe. Large banks in the United States and a few other countries were "too big to fail," meaning these banks were under the impression that no matter what they did, their governments would always stand behind them.

U.S. Fed Chairman Ben Bernanke suggested that the financial crisis was caused by Japan, the emerging economies of Asia (especially China), Russia,

Saudi Arabia, and a few others. *Financial Times* columnist Martin Wolf argued that the financial crisis was *not* the fault of state policies and individual behavior, but would have worked itself out *if* state officials in emerging economies had pursued neoliberal policies to help solve the U.S. debt problem. Rationally speaking, these emerging economies should have invested in more U.S. Treasury bonds and securities, which (as noted in Chapter 7) would have made money available for the United States to "borrow" and fund its debt.

But most HIL and mercantilist-oriented officials supported a quick injection of new national bank monies in the hope that this would unfreeze the U.S. and global monetary and financial systems. On October 3, 2008, President Bush signed the Emergency Economic Stabilization Act to create the **Troubled Assets Relief Program (TARP)** to help banks and restore confidence in both the U.S. and global financial systems. Soon U.S. officials announced the injection of $250 billion of the $700 billion TARP money into the U.S. banking system, thus gaining an equity stake in some banks. In exchange for restrictions on executive compensation, nine big banks accepted these public (taxpayer) funds. Yet as the crisis went on, some banks continued to pay their executives generous "bonus" packages, generating political controversy over using state (taxpayer) funds to reward executives who had had a hand in the banks' failure.

## Contagion Takes Over

By October, the crisis was spreading through Europe. Central bank officials and finance ministers of the United States, England, Canada, China, Sweden, Switzerland, and the EU met in Washington D.C. to prevent the crisis from worsening. Most agreed to further cut interest rates to stimulate the world economy. Meanwhile, the U.S. Dow Jones Industrial Average dropped 22 percent—its worst week ever—with stocks worth $8.4 trillion less compared to the market high in 2007.

In mid-November, a handpicked group representing the world's largest economies—the new Group of 20 (not to be confused with the WTO's G20) met in Washington D.C., but failed to agree on detailed proposals to "reform" international financial institutions. Including emerging economies in negotiations signaled that solving the financial crisis had to involve more than the current G7 members. Many officials focused on encouraging emerging economies like China and Saudi Arabia to invest in real estate and home mortgages in the United States and other industrialized nations. In effect, globalization would work in reverse, helping rescue the developed nations while making them more dependent on the developing nations.

With big banks not recovering fast enough, Secretary Paulson unexpectedly abandoned his plan to buy toxic assets under the TARP program and turned to recapitalizing financial companies. He gave out $33.6 billion to 21 banks in a second round of disbursements from the TARP, hoping banks would use more of the money to lend to one another. On November 25, several days after the U.S. government rescued Citigroup with $20 billion following a 60 percent plunge in its stock value, the U.S. Federal Reserve announced that it would inject another $800 billion into the economy. The hope was that new money would encourage banks to make more home loans, student loans, auto loans, and small business loans.

By December 2008 the global economy was clearly in a recession as reverberations from the financial crisis continued to rock both Wall Street and Main Street. Central banks slashed interest rates to their lowest levels to try to restart the credit flow. Stock markets in Europe and the United States closed the year having suffered declines of approximately 40 percent in their indexes. In January, companies in the United States and Europe announced huge layoffs of workers, and the IMF estimated that the global economic growth in 2009 would be the worst since World War II.

## Riding Out the Storm

From 2000 to 2007 the average income of those lower on the socioeconomic totem pole had actually decreased slightly. In 2008 the middle class' 401 retirement funds lost $2 trillion. Unemployment was rising rapidly in early 2009. Barack Obama, the U.S. president-elect, supported many of the measures adopted by the Bush administration to deal with the crisis, but also pledged to do more for middle-class and working families who seemed to get less out of the Bush administration's bank-rescue package than the wealthy.

The new U.S. president and many other global leaders all faced a difficult political juggling act between those who strongly supported new forms of regulation for banks, hedge funds, insurers, and other financial institutions and those who wanted to return to the "old system." The president's selection of Timothy Geitner as Treasury secretary and Larry Summers as director of the National Economic Council in the White House raised doubts about the president's commitment to reform monetary and financial policy. Both advisors have close ties with Wall Street and were seen as strongly pro–free market economic liberals. In February, Congress passed the American Recovery and Reinvestment Act, a $787 economic stimulus plan—sort of a mini New Deal—with massive spending on infrastructure to boost job creation and consumer spending. This alarmed many OELs (and some HILs) who saw it as a massive, wasteful government intervention in the market. Many neo-Keynesian economists like Joseph Stiglitz and Paul Krugman urged massive government spending to boost demand, but more OEL-oriented economists warned that too much government spending and regulating would fuel inflation and cause crippling, long-term budget deficits.

Since late 2008 almost every other member of the G20 implemented a large government-spending program. Instead of nationalizing banks, the U.S. Treasury Department announced a new $900 billion public–private partnership to raise capital to buy toxic assets from banks through an auction process. In April the United States and other G20 countries pledged $1.1 trillion to deal with the financial crisis, including $750 billion in additional funding for the IMF.

By the end of summer 2009 it *seemed* that the worst of the crisis was over: "Green shoots" of economic growth were palpable and credit markets were increasing lending to consumers and businesses. Spending on new energy programs, education, and infrastructure boosted demand in the U.S. economy. Global stock markets rallied in March 2009, with many indices rising in value by approximately 25 percent by the end of the summer. China, France, and Germany recorded higher-than-expected GDP growth. Housing prices in the United States and the United Kingdom stabilized.

Despite these few encouraging signs, many officials and economists warned that the recovery was fragile and reversible. Many structural problems remained and new ones loomed ahead—especially excessive government debt. Unemployment continued to increase in 2009, reaching 10.2 percent in the United States in the fall. Home foreclosures mounted, damping prospects for "real" recovery if the workforce could not make their rent or mortgage payments. Yet, as the Institute for Policy Studies reports, the top 20 firms in the United States awarded $3.2 billion to their top five executives in 2008, helping to insulate them from the effects of the financial crisis.[7] With the exception of convicted swindler Bernie Madoff, it seemed that most of the Wall Street insiders and CEOs who had committed illegal acts or engaged in unethical business practices would not be held accountable by their governments. In 2009, billionaire investor Madoff was convicted of running a Ponzi scheme that divested his customers of an excess of $50 billion. State regulators failed to act on many tips that his investment company was a scam, assuming because he was so successful (in the eyes of his investors), he must be clean.

In their rush to help banks and financial institutions return to "normalcy," officials in Europe, the United States, and many emerging economies have delayed or watered down proposals to reform and reregulate their financial systems. New risky investment packages related to insurance policies have already emerged on Wall Street.[8] And yet, neither the Congress nor the Obama administration is comfortable imposing tighter limits on executive pay and bonuses or revamping lending practices and regulator behavior, likely for a multitude of reasons. The banking lobby has spent tens of millions of dollars to oppose regulation. Regulatory agencies resist efforts to change their responsibilities. Many regulators and legislative officials do not understand the exotic instruments they are charged with overseeing and often remain committed to *limiting* regulation. Beyond limiting executive pay and consumer protection issues, the public also remains unfocused, with two wars, education, and healthcare issues competing for their attention.

By late September's meeting in Pittsburgh, the new G20 governments had still not agreed to reforms for credit-rating agencies, capital adequacy requirements for banks, new regulations of derivatives and hedge funds, or limits on executive compensation. Many poorer countries in the world—with the notable exception of China and some of the emerging economies (see Chapter 13)—are likely to struggle with the effects of the financial crisis longer than the wealthier countries. In many countries, the crisis has already reversed years of hard-won gains in employment and poverty reduction. In June 2009 the Food and Agriculture Organization (FAO) estimated that the global economic crisis would bring the number of people living in poverty to over one billion—a record level.

The IMF provided huge loan packages to countries such as the Ukraine, Hungary, Pakistan, and Romania. Even Iceland needed bailing out—the first time in over 30 years that a Western European country turned to the IMF for help. Reductions in global economic activity have lowered the price of oil and commodities such as rubber, beef, coffee, and rice, cutting export revenues of some

countries. At the same time, many countries are adopting more protectionist policies that threaten the growth of global trade and incomes of Southern exporters.
In July 2009, the IMF estimated that world trade would fall 12 percent compared
to 2008. Big labor exporters like Mexico, Bangladesh, and the Philippines are also
suffering from a reduction of remittances from migrant workers.

## LONG-TERM DEBT AND THE HIPCs

Much international attention is now focused on a third type of debt problem: the
hardships of 40 of the world's **heavily indebted poor countries (HIPCs)**.
Primarily in Africa, many of these states face high incidences of poverty and
HIV/AIDS (see Chapter 11). Many have also endured long-term debt resulting
from a variety of sources over the years, including money borrowed from the
World Bank, the IMF, and some international banks. Table 8-1 highlights the
value of debt as a percentage of gross national income (GNI) for the 10 poorest
HIPC states. Some of these states complain about **odious debt,** or obligations
incurred by a former corrupt regime that left a new government owing billions to
outside agencies. Iraq's Saddam Hussein, Ethiopia's Mengistu Haile Mariam,
and Chile's Augusto Pinochet allegedly fit in this category.[9] Debt-relief mechanisms of the global finance and monetary structure were not designed for the
poorest states and so have not been very effective.

Since the late 1990s, the UN, many NGOs, IMF and World Bank officials, a
variety of development experts, rock stars, and other celebrities have campaigned

| **TABLE 8-1** | | | |
|---|---|---|---|
| **External Debt and GNI of the Poorest Countries** | | | |
| Country | External Debt as Percent of GNI (2008) | GNI (2008, Billions of $) | GNI per Capita (2008) |
| Congo, Dem. Rep. | 118 | 10 | 290 |
| Liberia | 515 | 0.7 | 300 |
| Guinea-Bissau | 274 | 0.4 | 530 |
| Eritrea | 59 | 1.6 | 630 |
| Niger | 18 | 5 | 680 |
| Central African Republic | 49 | 2 | 730 |
| Sierra Leone | 20 | 2 | 750 |
| Togo | 56 | 3 | 820 |
| Malawi | 23 | 4 | 830 |
| Ethiopia | 11 | 27 | 870 |

*Note:* Countries shown are the world's 10 poorest, ranked by gross national income (GNI) per capita measured in purchasing power parity.

*Sources:* World Bank, *Global Development Finance Online* and *World Development Indicators Online*
(accessed March 30, 2010).

to rectify this problem. In 1996, after pressure from popular movements in both the North and South, creditors launched the **HIPC Initiative** under the direction of the World Bank. The goal was debt cancellation of the world's poorest countries, but by 1999 only four countries had received debt relief, and the rise in interest payments owed on the debt wiped out any gains.

In 1999, during massive demonstrations at the G7 meeting in Cologne, Germany, supporters of Jubilee 2000 targeted the inadequacy of neoliberal development policies and, in particular, IMF and World Bank practices. Jubilee 2000 is an effort by a coalition of development-oriented NGOs, churches, and labor groups to pressure the industrialized nations into canceling the debt of 20 countries by 2000. Its rationale for debt cancellation is framed in terms of fairness and global justice, a message intended to cut across disparate political, economic, and social boundaries. At the G7 meeting, state leaders pledged to write off $100 billion of poor-country debts.

In 2000, the UN, the IMF, and the World Bank[10] made debt relief an important goal and an instrument of the UN's Millennium Development Goals (MDGs). At the June 2005 G8 meeting (including Russia) in Gleneagles, Scotland, members agreed to fund 100 percent debt relief for 18 of the world's poorest countries (14 of which are in Africa). By the end of the year, 28 countries had been granted debt relief of $56 billion.[11] The World Bank estimates that by the end of 2008 the debt of 35 poor countries in the HIPC Initiative had been cut by more than 50 percent.

Obtaining debt relief grew easier as World Bank policy shifted from support for neoliberal "one size fits all" policies to more of a grab-bag approach to development[12] (see Chapter 11). Yet some countries that could use relief, such as Indonesia, did not qualify as being poor enough, while others, such as Moldova, were not eligible because they were in the former Soviet bloc of nations. Still, a 2009 UN report on the impact of the global financial crisis suggests that the international community was "making notable progress on reducing the external debt burden of developing countries."[13] Table 8-2 highlights the total debt for select

---

**◣ TABLE 8-2**

**Total External Debt of Developing Countries (in billions of dollars)**

| Country | 2000 | 2004 | 2008 |
| --- | --- | --- | --- |
| Russian Federation | 160 | 197 | 402 |
| Turkey | 117 | 160 | 277 |
| Brazil | 242 | 219 | 256 |
| India | 100 | 123 | 231 |
| Mexico | 151 | 171 | 204 |
| Argentina | 141 | 162 | 128 |
| South Africa | 25 | 27 | 42 |
| All Developing Countries | 2,153 | 2,607 | 3,719 |

*Note:* Developing countries include those countries the World Bank categorizes as low-, lower-middle-, and upper-middle-income economies. Figures are in current US dollars.

*Source:* World Bank, *Global Development Indicators Online* (accessed March 30, 2010).

developing countries. In addition, it shows that by 2008 total debt for all developing countries had reached $3.7 trillion.

However, after the crisis hit, many developing nations lost markets for their goods in developed countries or faced new resistance to importing goods. As external financing conditions tightened up, balance-of-payments issues became more frequent. Some currencies have depreciated, creating even more loss of capital and resulting in cutbacks in social welfare programs related to health care, education, and poverty relief. As aid from developed states significantly declined, many developing countries are looking for ways to reschedule or roll over their outstanding debt.

Thirty-five of the forty HIPC nations qualified for this assistance. But many of the G20 states have not been able to meet their obligations in regard to debt-relief measures. The financial crisis threatens to not only impose major economic and social costs on poorer states but make it exceedingly unlikely for them to achieve the MDGs by 2015.

## CRISIS, CHOICE, AND CHANGE

In their famous comparative politics reader *Crisis, Choice, and Change*, Gabriel Almond et al. examined how different societies handle occasional crises.[14] A crisis conditions their political, economic, and social institutions, and some handle their crises better than others. Often these crises impacted nations in unexpected ways. A prime example is U.S. Commodore Perry demanding Japan open its markets to U.S. goods. Later Japanese leaders decided to set off in a new direction, which profoundly changed Japan's political, economic, and social institutions. Japan eventually became one of the world's major economic powers of the twentieth century. For Japan, remaining where they were was not a possibility.

In the last edition of this text, we hinted at the possibility of a global financial crisis, and it has come to pass. Today the world faces a situation that many believe could easily turn into a global catastrophe. Unemployment continues to rise, wiping out economic gains of the past eight years, increasing poverty, and reducing spending for education, health, and other social services for those most desperate. Without radical change to some of the main elements of the monetary and finance structure, it is likely the financial system will be even more prone to crisis.[15]

### Corrections and Courses

Both OELs and HILs generally favor increased international trade and investment opportunities, which have been made available by flexible exchange rates and capital mobility. Market-oriented policies reflect pressure from domestic businesses and TNCs that seek to profit from opportunities to conduct banking and other services in countries that deregulate capital transactions. As more capital becomes available both within nations and worldwide, new factories, processing facilities, and stores are established. More income generates new technologies and communications networks, reinforcing integration and globalization.

**The Global Glut**   In the early 1980s, Japanese investments helped the United States recover from the recession of the late 1970s, but in the current crisis, investments did not arrive to help offset the deficit. Many OELs and some HILs point to the global glut of capital that emerging economies did not (rationally speaking) spend on U.S. bonds and securities as a factor in the current financial crisis. They believe emerging economies with excess capital should stop holding huge foreign currency reserves that protect them from having to turn to the IMF for support. Countries like China, Japan, and Saudi Arabia should increase spending and consumption at home, save less, and adjust their domestic economies to the global economy.[16] China in particular must appreciate its currency to make its goods more expensive, which would help the United States and others earn more for their products (see China Currency Dispute box, Chapter 7).

For many HILs and mercantilists, this misaligned balance of payments demonstrates that markets do not automatically self-correct, as states quite rationally chose not to invest their funds in risky and questionable U.S. businesses. Thus, HILs and mercantilists suggest that relying on others to underwrite the mounting debt of the United States is not sustainable in the long run, even if it is reasonable to expect countries like China to allow their currencies to appreciate and encourage more domestic consumption. The opinion of some mercantilists stems from a reaction to malevolent nations like Japan and China, who purposefully manipulate their currency values in order to sustain massive trade surpluses—and then loan the surpluses back to the United States, making another crisis near certain. Ironically, many analysts point out that by acquiring more capital and saving more, the Asian emerging economies, especially China, may in fact be leading the global recovery from the current crisis.

**Regulation of the Domestic Economy**   Domestic regulation, or lack thereof, contributed to both the Asian and U.S. crises. Whether or not regulation was relaxed was not as important as who benefited. In both the mercantilist states of Asia and the laissez-faire–oriented United States, banks and other financial institutions were encouraged to borrow (heavily in many cases) and run up substantial debt.

Most OELs argue that the state must share the blame for these crises because they intervened too much in the market. They blame Asian mercantilist states for industrial policies that picked winners and losers, and, although export-oriented, restricted imports and investments. The Federal Reserve (with the support of two U.S. presidents) dropped interest rates, making loans more easily available for the middle class. This injection of more credit into the economy made it easier for lending agencies to become more reckless. Rather than intervening in the market, states should limit spending on bailout packages, allow banks to fail, refrain from regulating finance, and decrease taxes, especially for higher-income groups.

Most HILs support using a stimulus package to help the economy recover. Paul Krugman argues that a fiscal stimulus gives "more bang for the buck" to the economy than cutting taxes.[17] As Keynes would suggest (see Chapter 2), recovery of the economy outweighs the political and social costs associated with failing to overcome the crisis. Krugman also notes that historically, the level of debt relative to GDP is low,[18] and it is unlikely inflation will be a big problem in the future provided the economy grows enough to overcome the debt. HILs want reform on the margins of what they believe is basically a good capitalist system gone bad. They wish to strengthen regulation by *increasing competition* as a "disciplining force" over banks and their executives. To counter rent-seeking, no banks should be allowed to grow "**too big to fail.**" Banks that fail should be allowed to fail, and bigger banks should be broken into smaller banks to limit their risk taking. Banks should be required to maintain bigger capital reserves to back their loans, and savings and investment banks should once again be separated. The pay and bonuses of bank officials should be capped and linked to the economic success of the bank. Finally, governments should create more effective programs to help consumers deal with their mortgages and credit cards.

In addition to the reforms suggested by HILs, structuralists believe more effort should be made to control state regulators with connections to or interest in banks or lobbying firms they are supposed to regulate. As the crisis worsened, bank mergers and acquisitions increased, leaving only four or five major banks in the United States. This concerns structuralists who fear a further concentration of capital.

**An Outdated Economic Theory and Ideology**   As discussed in Chapter 2, even the economic liberal-oriented journal the *Economist* attributes the financial crisis to a variety of theoretical issues that led banks and policy makers to be too casual about asset bubbles. Many HILs have proposed various ideas to rectify this problem, all hinging on the fact that economic theory must also include a human element. Economists should investigate human behavior, including human psychology, rather than limiting their focus to a rational-choice methodology. In addition to academic theorizing, they should do more empirical work and test their methods in the real world.

Keynesian HILs believe that globalization can be made to work as long as debt and development issues are considered. Groundbreaking works by Joseph Stiglitz, Dani Rodrik, Jeffrey Sachs, and others reflect this view. But in the finance structure, where the free market ideology is so popular, developing countries must protect themselves to a greater extent, at least until they can compete on a more equal footing with the industrialized states. Like mercantilists, many HILs note that China and India did *not* integrate into the international economy as much as others and yet achieved high rates of economic growth by "cherry-picking" the policies that work best for them (see Chapter 13).

Some mercantilist-realists worry that the Mexican, Asian, Argentinian, and global crises have not made economic liberal ideas and the U.S. version of capitalism and democracy more popular in those societies. These crises and antiglobalization sentiments played a large role in the electoral success of populist-socialist leaders in Venezuela, Bolivia, Brazil, Chile, and Nicaragua. They also have contributed to violent reactions to the reemergence of the left in these and other Mesoamerican societies (Mexico, Guatemala, and El Salvador). Many state leaders are concerned that continued poverty and debt for so many of the world's poor generates conditions that foster terrorism. These and other concerns leave state officials with tough decisions about how much they want to push neoliberal objectives when the cost may be increased threats to their economic and political security. To that end, structuralists often support investigation of the connection of regulators to those regulated while keeping in mind the interests of the poorer classes.

**Men (and Women) Behaving Badly**   All political-economic systems exhibit illicit activity to some extent (see Chapter 15). And yet the recent financial crisis has caused almost immeasurable harm to society, severely corrupting and damaging the states, institutions, and individuals who comprise them. OELs believe the problem is essentially one of corruption. States should regulate only what is clearly illegal, while businesses should voluntarily set higher standards. People can vote with their feet, such as not signing on with a bank and choosing a competitor instead.

For most HILs, these solutions are insufficient, overlooking the fact that banks are self-serving and interested in circulating money based on free market ideals, not acting in society's or an individual's best interest. Some critics view greed and corruption as the addicting adrenalin of the finance industry.[19] If confidence and trust are to be restored in the financial system, the common good cannot be left to markets and economists to decide. HILs want regulatory agencies to be tougher on criminal behavior, by improving and implementing surveillance and information-gathering techniques to catch violators and enforcing longer jail sentences for those violators.

**Global Governance**   Lack of management at the global level almost certainly did not *cause* the crisis but rather *contributed* to it, as there is no authority above the nation-state that could prevent it. Many suggestions have been made about how different nations, public financial institutions, and businesses should respond.

Many OELs (and some mercantilist-realists) prefer *less* global governance and promote the *laissez-faire* policies of the globalization campaign. Globalization rapidly integrates semicapitalist, noncapitalist, and precapitalist areas into the global market economy and is one of the best ways to overcome the financial crisis.[20] OELs prefer laissez-faire–oriented development policies whenever possible (see Chapter 11). They oppose trade restrictions and favor finishing the Doha round (see Chapter 6). OEL experts and officials also discourage states from using capital controls that prevent or limit TNC investment in developing nations.

Concerning the Asian crisis, it was not clear whether IMF-mandated SAPs that pressured states to reduce tariffs, cut government programs, and raise interest rates actually made the situation any better. The IMF acted to protect the interests of the rich and powerful rather than the poor and weak.[21] In both Asia and the United States, large speculative flows and investments in deregulated currency generated big profits for banks, businesses, and wealthy people. In both cases, these crises helped *destabilize* the economy and led to the loss of income, higher unemployment, and rising social tensions.

Despite all this, most HILs are *not* inherently opposed to laissez-faire ideas and globalization but are adamant about dealing with their negative effects. Many would agree with Jagdish Bhagwati that although globalization has clear negative effects on some states and subgroups, most states and businesses cannot, and should not, miss the opportunities afforded by the liberalization of the finance structure.[22] Rather, regional groups should promote cooperation on finance, debt-relief, and bank and investment regulation. Regional institutions such as the EU, the G7-8, and new G20 should encourage capable states to employ their own stimulus packages to help their economies recover, and the IMF should be strengthened to help more desperate states borrow capital to restart their economies.

Yet most experts agree that at the global level, states, IOs, and NGOs have not been able to produce effective and coherent results when dealing with the issues of both debt and financial crises. The IMF continues to receive new pledges of funds from G20 states to help developing nations, but these are rarely fulfilled as nations implement domestic measures to deal with the global financial crisis.

Developing nations often share the structuralist perspective that the financial crisis pushed 100 million people back into poverty.[23] For most structuralists, IMF and World Bank reform is virtually meaningless, because the two agencies represent the interests of the rich, who are not seriously interested in redistributing the world's wealth and power. Most antiglobalization literature focuses on the extent to which capital mobility contributes to debt, hunger, environmental problems, and a host of other issues.[24]

HILs believe the middle class and the poor should be helped by all proposals to mitigate the crisis. More IMF and World Bank funds should be made available to LDCs, and more information should be provided to investors in order to encourage better decisions and prevent another global financial bubble.[25] Developed states should reduce their import tariffs to help developing countries to increase their exports, and the WTO should allow for more trade protection for developing nations. States should find ways to cooperate with the IMF, the World Bank, and the WTO as well as the G7, G20, and regional organizations in order to resolve major balance-of-payments and currency problems. They should also work together to implement welfare programs and other measures to overcome poverty and inequality. Finally, states should continue to pursue the UN's Millennium Goals (see Chapter 11).

If the job of the IMF is to facilitate a stable and orderly international financial system, then it is hard to conclude that in recent years it has been successful (although matters might have been worse without the IMF). As the world moves from monetary crisis to monetary crisis, the IMF is often blamed for making problems worse. Yet in most cases, it was not the weakness of the IMF, the World Bank, or the WTO but rather the inability of member states to square domestic interests with global obligations.

States and financial IOs must determine how to minimize risk taking and speculative bubbles. The classical solution, which Walter Bagehot presented over a hundred years ago, is to designate an international lender of last resort, to lend when no one else will and hold open the "shutting gate" of *torchlusspanik* to stop the panic.[26] Previously this was the role of the IMF, but this responsibility has decreased since the early 2000s, in part because its invisible director of the board—the United States—has focused more on domestic economic recovery than on pursuing a hegemonic role in systemic recovery. It is clear that the IMF is not and cannot be the global lender of last resort. While one issue is the availability of funds, at the same time there is still a good deal of support for preserving speculation and a certain amount of risk. And yet due to the high degree of international interdependence and integration of capital markets, either the global governance structure must expand to match market forces—a bigger IMF with more resources and more power over more actors—or risk the catastrophic collapse of markets as occurred in the 1930s.

# CONCLUSION

All three IPE perspectives agree that the global financial crises of the 1990s and first decade of the 2000s demonstrate that weaknesses in the management of the global financial system are an increasing threat to the entire monetary and finance structure. Today's highly integrated international political economy requires a stable finance system that is able to adapt effectively to changing structural conditions. The popular laissez-faire ideas associated with economic liberal policies and globalization have yet to account enough for the impact of global market failure and deregulation of financial institutions on global society. Corruption and greed have also led to abuse of the minimal rules and regulations that exist.

The current global crisis presents a variety of problems to overcome if system management is to be rendered more effective and fair—a quality espoused by both HILs and structuralists. Aside from lack of U.S. support for a bigger and broader role for the IMF, there are many indications that the IMF lacks the resources and institutional commitment to perform this task effectively. Shifts in exchange rates invite political manipulation and can easily change the terms of international trade and investment between nations. It is also difficult to overcome a realist, state-first attitude. Therefore, financial regulations reflect mainly domestic objectives, not international or global ones, and are therefore uneven, incomplete, and difficult to enforce.

Until the financial crisis, developing nations were making slow progress in influencing the global finance structure. With the emergence of the G20, change that will reflect the ongoing redistribution in global wealth and power is likely. Even so, given the problems the members of the G20 and other states have had dealing with the financial crisis alone, it will not be easy to build a global consensus for reform of the IMF and the World Bank.

It will be interesting to see if the industrialized North, which seems primarily concerned with system confidence and stability, can reconcile its interests with those in the South, who are concerned about fairness, equity, and social justice. Meanwhile, the European nations that adopted the euro (see Chapter 12) have reduced their exposure to global financial risk, but have not spurred momentum for global regulations. Many Southeast and East Asian nations are in the same position. For the time being it is difficult to see who would take the lead in creating a new international financial system or how the interests of so many different groups can be reconciled.

This is just the most recent in a long line of debt and financial crises, but the recent global crisis reveals the necessity of generating new ideas about regulation to move beyond laissez-faire. Loaners are obligated to help debtors. Likewise, it is in the interest of those with SWFs to help preserve systemic stability, but not finance the high rates of U.S. consumption, which cause environmental damage, increase U.S. debt, and sustain risky behavior. If Keynes were here, he might see this as an opportunity to practice politics as the art of the possible. Undoubtedly, he would suggest that we ask who we believe the economy ought to serve: the rich and powerful or the poor and weak?

# KEY TERMS

structural adjustment policies
  (SAPs)   187
conditionality   187
capital flight   188
currency crisis   188
crony capitalism   189
speculative attack   189

hedge fund   190
subprime mortgage loans   193
sovereign wealth funds   195
credit default swaps   196
contagion   196
Troubled Asset Relief Program
  (TARP)   197

heavily indebted poorest
  countries (HIPCs)   200
odius debt   200
HIPC Initiative   201
too big to fail   204

## DISCUSSION QUESTIONS

1. Compare and contrast the three different types of debt problems that were discussed in this chapter in terms of (a) the source of the debt, (b) the major actors in each situation and their interests, and (c) how the situation was resolved, if it was.

2. Why so much fuss over speculation? Why do you suppose Keynes would be concerned about it today? Use Chapter 7 to help answer this question.

3. Explain the connection between debt that results from borrowing money and the debt associated with a deficit in the balance of payments. Use examples from the readings.

4. Which of the main causes of the financial crisis offered in this chapter do you think best explain it? Justify your answer.

5. Explain the role of the IMF in helping to solve these balance-of-payments crises. Do you feel the IMF could do more? Why? Why not?

6. If you were to write up a brief outline of how to solve the crisis, what measures would you emphasize? Explain.

## SUGGESTED READINGS

Clive Dilnot. "The Triumph of Greed," *New Statesman*, December 4, 2008.

Barry Eichengreen. *Globalizing Capital: A History of the International Monetary System*. Princeton, NJ: Princeton University Press, 1996.

Dani Rodrik. "Goodbye Washington Consensus, Hello Washington Confusion?" *Journal of Economic Literature*, XLIV (December 2006), pp. 973–987.

Jeffrey Sachs. *The End of Poverty: Economic Possibilities for Our Time*. New York: Penguin, 2006.

Robert Wade. "The First-World Debt Crisis of 2007–2010 in Global Perspective," *Challenge*, July–August 2008, pp. 23–54.

## NOTES

1. For a good overview of the 1980s debt crisis see Benjamin J. Cohen, *In Whose Interest?* (New Haven, CT: Yale University Press, 1986); especially chap. 8, "Latin Debt Storm."

2. Negative real interest rates exist when inflation rates exceed the interest rate over the term of a loan. This benefits the borrower, because loan repayments have less purchasing power (lower real value) than the amount borrowed.

3. Susan George, *A Fate Worse Than Debt: The World Financial Crisis and the Poor* (Berkeley, CA: Grove Press, 1988).

4. See Carole Collins, Zie Gariyo, and Tony Burdon, "Jubilee 2000: Citizen Action across the North–South Divide," in Michael Edwards and John Gaventa, eds., *Global Citizen Action* (Boulder, CO: Lynne Rienner, 2001).

5. See, for example, David Vines, Pierre-Richard Angenor, and Marcus Miller, *Asian Financial Crisis: Causes, Contagion, and Consequences* (Cambridge: Cambridge University Press, 2004).

6. Paul Krugman, "How Did Economists Get It So Wrong?" *New York Times*, September 3, 2009.

7. See Diane Stafford, "Executives at Financial Firms Who Received Bailout Funds Get Big Salaries, Report Says," *The Kansas City Star*, September 1, 2009.

8. Under the plan banks would buy "life settlements" or life insurance policies that elderly or ill people would sell for cash—maybe $400,000 for a $1 million policy. These plans would be securitized and packaged into bonds and then resold to investors, who would receive payouts when the insured died. See Jenny Anderson, "New Exotic Investments Emerging on Wall Street," *New York Times*, September 6, 2009.

9. Joseph Stiglitz, *Making Globalization Work* (New York: W. W. Norton, 2006), pp. 228–229.

10. Both the IMF and World Bank websites discuss in some detail the efforts both agencies are making to further what has become a very popular movement in many parts of the world.

11. Stiglitz, *Making Globalization Work*, pp. 226–228.

12. See Dani Rodrik, "Goodbye Washington Consensus, Hello Washington Confusion?" *Journal of Economic Literature*, XLIV (December 2006), pp. 973–987.

13. See the United Nations, "Strengthening the Global Partnership for Development in a Time of Crisis," MDB Gap Task Force Report (New York: United Nations, 2009).

14. See Gabriel Almond et al., *Crisis, Choice and Change: Historical Studies of Political Development* (Boston, MA: Little Brown, 1973).

15. For a good overview of the causes of the global crisis and numerous corrective measures see Robert Wade, "The Global Slump: Deeper Causes and Harder Lessons," *Challenge*, (September–October 2009), pp. 5–24.

16. For a sophisticated discussion of this argument see Martin Wolf, *Fixing Global Finance* (Baltimore, MD: Johns-Hopkins University Press, 2008).

17. See Paul Krugman, "Bang for the Buck (Wonkish)," *The New York Times*, January 13, 2009.

18. See Paul Krugman, "Till Debt Does Its Part," *New York Times*, August 28, 2009, and Krugman's "Bad Faith Economics," *New York Times*, January 26, 2009.

19. See Clive Dilnot, "The Triumph of Greed," *New Statesman*, December 4, 2008.

20. For a detailed discussion of this argument see David Held and Anthony McGrew, *Globalization/Antiglobalization; Beyond the Great Divide* (Malden, MA: Polity Press, 2007).

21. Jeffrey D. Sachs, "How to Run the International Monetary Fund," *Foreign Policy*, July/August 2004.

22. See, for example, Jagdish Bhagwati, *In Defense of Globalization* (New York: Oxford University Press, 2004).

23. See Robert Zoellick, "A Stimulus Package for the World," *The New York Times*, January 23, 2009.

24. See, for example, Oswaldo De Rivero, *The Myth of Development: The Non-viable Economies of the 21st Century* (New York: Zed Books, 2001).

25. Stiglitz, *Making Globalization Work*, see Chapter 8, especially pp. 208–209.

26. Walter Bagehot, *Lombard Street: A Description of the Money Market* (Philadelphia, PA: Orion Editions, 1991), p. 8.

# The Global Security Structure

Italian peacekeepers with locals in Lebanon.

with courtesy of the Italian Army General Staff

The security structure may be the most important structure in the international political economy because trade, finance, and technology networks need a stable and secure foundation on which to operate. The global security structure connects major players such as nation-states, international organizations (IOs), nongovernmental organizations (NGOs), international businesses, and subnational groups. They are connected by way of formal treaties, conventions, and other arrangements, rules, and informal norms meant to protect people from violent and nonviolent threats.

During the **Cold War** (1947–1990), security issues were understood primarily in terms of national defense, which is one of the reasons why realism (see Chapter 3) has tended to dominate security debates.[1] Many experts viewed the period as quite stable because of the interaction between only two superpowers—the United States and the Soviet Union. The collapse of the Soviet Union in 1990 was *the* watershed event that broke the foundation of the Cold War security structure, ironically resulting in a good deal of violence in the world. In the following decade, civil war, ethnic and religious conflicts, and genocide occurred, especially in the Balkans, the Middle East, and parts of Africa.

Although the 1990s was the decade of *globalization* when security issues were less pressing for Europe and the United States, many officials were rudely awakened by the September 11, 2001 attacks on the U.S. World Trade Center. The U.S.-led invasions of Afghanistan and Iraq once again thrust international security issues into the headlines. Many officials and experts believed that terrorism had replaced nuclear war as the greatest threat to global peace.

In the past 20 years, a broader range of nontraditional security issues has emerged that involve not only states but specific groups of people and individuals in different societies. In addition, new security problems have grown out of poverty and underdevelopment, famine, scarcity of energy resources, and environmental damage. Many of these issues have implications for the trade, finance, and knowledge structures (see Chapters 6, 7, 8, and 10), resulting in a dynamic security structure that is very difficult to manage.

In this chapter we raise three fundamental questions. First, what accounts for the recent shift to a more unstable and violent international security structure? Second, how do the rules of this structure reflect the interests of various actors? Third, what are some of the implications of these developments for managing this critical structure? The three IPE perspectives and different levels of analysis help us answer these questions.

This chapter presents five major theses. First, *geopolitics*—which emphasizes protecting national borders—is as important today as it was at the beginning of globalization. Second, while conventional and strategic (nuclear) weapons were a grave concern during the Cold War, today there appears to be a very low threat of *total war* between the major military powers, due in part to globalization replacing national security as the primary preoccupation of the wealthier states. However, at the same time, the political and economic interests of the major powers in developing regions often result in many conflicts. Third, paradoxically, as globalization has generated economic growth and spread capitalism, it has also engendered a growing number of security problems. Globalization intensifies physical and psychological threats to individuals via human rights violations, the spread of diseases, and environmental damage—particularly in the poorer regions of the world.

Fourth, globalization and the recent global financial crisis have weakened the economic and political power of the United States and other major actors. The heavily-indebted United States has found it difficult to pursue "hegemony on the cheap." Finally, states have begun to share management of the global security structure with IOs, NGOs, international businesses, and even subnational groups. The result is a world security order with a much broader post–Cold War agenda marked by many informal rules and unregulated practices that make management of the new global security structure harder all the time.

## ACTORS, INTERESTS, AND ROLES

According to realists (see Chapter 3), a hierarchy of nation-states reflects the distribution of power in the global political economy. At the top are the United States—the world's remaining superpower—and several other major economic and military powers. Until recently, Great Britain, France, Germany, Japan, and Russia have thought about security issues primarily in terms of "great power" wars in which vast armies draw on their states's resources and engage one another in conventional, or possibly even nuclear, warfare.[2] IOs such as UN agencies and the North Atlantic Treaty Organization (NATO) are state-sponsored institutions that increasingly play a bigger role in the global security structure, although they draw most of their authority from the major powers.

On the next level down in the hierarchy are the relatively weaker powers of Western Europe, Asia, Latin America, and Africa. Notable among them are a growing number of newly emerging economies such as China, Brazil, Indonesia, and India. All of these countries focus on traditional security interests that require being prepared to fight wars while protecting their national borders and the population within them. Strongly influenced by realist ideas, most military officials consider the nation-state the source of sovereign (final) authority in determining the nation's interests and objectives.

At the bottom of the hierarchy of power are the majority of poorer developing nations and weak states that often lack the hard- and soft-power resources to deal with internal and external security problems, epidemic diseases, and environmental problems (see Chapter 20). UN peacekeeping forces and NGOs such as Amnesty International are also quite active and play major roles at this level. In almost all the poorer states, poverty exacerbates tensions between different ethnic and religious communities, resulting in human rights violations and in some cases genocide. Some examples include: the conflict between the Tutsis and the Hutus in Rwanda; tensions between Shiites, Sunnis, and Kurds in Iraq; and Muslim–Hindu animosity in India and Pakistan.

## STATES AT THE TOP OR ON THE RISE

Many realists assume that in a *potentially* anarchical international system, in which absolute security cannot be guaranteed, security must be the primary objective of the state. Likewise, many realists are committed to the idea that peace results when power is relatively balanced or distributed between two or more nations. In contrast to economic liberalism, realism views the economy as simply another tool in the state's arsenal to achieve any number of national objectives (see Chapter 3). Even when states pursue economic liberal objectives, they do so ultimately for their own benefit. The most powerful states are often concerned with the distribution of wealth and power in the global security structure. Depending on their wealth, power, and historical circumstances, they may prefer a unipolar, bipolar, or multipolar **balance of power**. Each balance of power usually complements a distinct style of behavior such as "unilateralism" or "multilateralism" on the part of the major powers.

For example, tensions and hostility between the United States and the Soviet Union during the Cold War framed most of the important security issues of the day. In the late 1940s and 1950s, the United States and the Soviet Union mirrored each other in ways that helped entrench a bipolar security arrangement under which the two superpowers organized political, military, and economic alliances in opposition to each other. Other sources of conflict between the two superpowers were based mainly on ideology (democracy versus communism) and geopolitical struggles over territory. Developing nations were prized as members or potential members of each superpower's political and ideological sphere of influence.

Ironically, many security experts viewed the Cold War as a relatively stable period because there were only two dominant powers. Because nuclear weapons are so destructive, they proved to be of little or no utility when it came to fighting frontier wars in places such as Asia, Africa, South America, and the Caribbean. Instead, the battle was joined in proxy wars like those in Vietnam (1960s and 1970s) and in Afghanistan (1980s). Ultimately, the defeats of the United States in Vietnam and of the Soviet Union in Afghanistan weakened the security order by demonstrating that small, weak nations could defeat large, strong nations—or at least weaken their resolve. After the Vietnam War ended, the United States and the Soviet Union reached a détente (relaxation of tension) and cooperated to reduce their nuclear weapons arsenals. The recovery of Western Europe and Japan after World War II and the rapid growth of countries such as South Korea helped redistribute income, making the distribution of power appear to be increasingly multipolar.

In the 1980s, the Reagan administration sought to reimpose a bipolar framework on the international security structure centered on the Soviet Union as the "evil empire." The United States modernized its nuclear arsenal, abandoned arms control talks with the Soviet Union, deployed new short- and medium-range nuclear weapons in Western Europe, and intervened in a number of states in support of efforts to overthrow what it claimed were procommunist regimes. Reagan complemented these efforts with support for neoliberal economic policies designed to promote economic development, capitalism, and democracy in developing nations.

After the collapse of the Soviet Union in 1990, the Clinton administration viewed the international distribution of power as multipolar, best served by a **multilateral approach** that emphasized cooperation with allies and use of more nonmilitary instruments to deal with opponents. As noted in previous chapters, Clinton also promoted economic liberal policies and the globalization campaign in a number of IOs such as the IMF, the World Bank, and the new World Trade Organization (WTO). A few academics and policy officials at the time believed that with the Soviet Union out of the way, the United States should have capitalized on the opportunity to act unilaterally as a liberal (benevolent) hegemonic global power that would promote capitalism and democracy everywhere.[3]

## Bush and the Iraq War

The attacks on the World Trade Center on September 11, 2001, provided the opportunity for the second Bush administration to test this controversial idea. In 2002 the United States and Great Britain invaded Afghanistan to destroy al-Qaeda, the terrorist organization headed by Osama bin Laden, and overthrow the Taliban, the Islamic fundamentalist government that sheltered al-Qaeda. Soon thereafter, the Bush administration invaded Iraq to overthrow President Saddam Hussein.

A number of factors account for the administration's adoption of a unilateralist outlook. First, many U.S. officials, especially the "**neoconservatives**," felt strongly that the 9/11 attacks necessitated that the U.S. fight terrorism proactively.[4] In its 2002 National Security Strategy, the Bush administration asserted that so-called **rogue states**—those that did not adhere to the norms of the international system—could not be allowed to develop or use nuclear weapons or use other **weapons of mass destruction (WMD)** like biological and chemical weapons. These rogue states included Iran, Iraq, and North Korea—three countries President Bush labeled the "axis of evil"—along with Syria and Cuba. The security strategy allowed for the possibility of preemptive strikes against governments or rogue regimes suspected of fomenting terrorism. The administration's goals included promoting democracy in some authoritarian, developing countries. Finally, the administration disdained many IOs (especially the United Nations), seeing them as ineffective and sometimes at odds with U.S. interests.

Second, in the lead-up to the Iraq War, the United States and its Atlantic partners were divided on the Security Council and in NATO. U.S. Secretary of Defense Donald Rumsfeld called France and Germany "old Europe" and implied that these states were weak for not supporting a potential invasion, whereas a "new Europe" comprised of many ex–Soviet-bloc nations would join a coalition with the United States to pressure Iraq and fight terrorism. Although the UN Security Council in November 2002 warned Iraq of "serious consequences" if it did not fully cooperate with UN inspectors seeking to verify that it had eliminated its WMD, the United States was frustrated in March 2003 in its efforts to get the Security Council to formally authorize use of force against Iraq for not complying with the November resolution. Hence, adopting a unilateralist policy, the United States, backed only by Great Britain, invaded Iraq on March 19, 2003, and removed Saddam Hussein from power. No WMDs were found.

By 2006 the Iraq War had become a quagmire, if not a fiasco, according to Thomas Ricks in his book *Fiasco: The Military Adventure in Iraq*. Unexpectedly, strong resistance from a number of insurgent groups including ex-Baathists, foreign fighters, and Sunni and Shia militias foiled U.S. efforts to pacify and rebuild a democratic Iraq. Many insurgents justified their struggle as an effort to liberate Iraq from what they viewed as an imperial power trying to maintain a footprint in the Middle East. These forces were a powerful example of how much the rules of the security game had shifted in the post–Cold War era.[5]

According to a number of experts, the major reasons for the U.S. predicament in Iraq included failure to identify the nature of the threat, failure to adopt an appropriate strategy to "win the war," poor tactics, and lack of a coherent nation-building plan for Iraq. Also, terrorism is a tactic usually employed to achieve political ends and not something that can easily be countered by fighting a broad war against it in a country like Iraq. Although before the war started U.S. Defense Secretary Donald Rumsfeld was in the process of reconfiguring the U.S. force structure to fit the types of war the United States would face in developing regions of the world in the new century, the U.S. military was ill-suited to fighting a prolonged guerrilla war in urban areas. Moreover, the United States relied heavily on civilian contractors to fill in for the lack of U.S. troops, which turned out to be costly and wasteful (see "Privatizing the War in Iraq" box below).

## ◤ PRIVATIZING THE WAR IN IRAQ[a]

Since the early 1990s, the United States has increasingly relied on private military contractors (PMCs) to perform military operations. PMCs were used in the Gulf War in 1991, the Balkans conflict throughout the 1990s, and in Kosovo in 1999.[b] They often provide training, supplemental armed services support, bodyguard personnel, and engineering and building services.

The use of PMCs has become particularly pronounced and markedly different since 9/11, as the United States fights two wars. In the Gulf War, the ratio of active-duty soldiers to private contractors was fifty-to-one, whereas at the beginning of the Iraq invasion the ratio was almost one-to-one. In wars fought against Iraq and Afghanistan, the United States has relied primarily on three security firms—Xe (formerly Blackwater Worldwide), DynCorp International, and Triple Canopy. Additionally, while conventional contractors have staffed nonviolent reconstruction jobs in Iraq, PMCs have adopted new roles: providing "security details for senior civilian officials, non-military site security, and non-military convoy security."[c]

PMCs have a troubling record of violent confrontations with civilians. Perhaps the most well-documented shooting occurred on September 16, 2007, when Blackwater guards opened fire, allegedly without provocation, in Nisoor Square, killing 17 Iraqi civilians.

Not a single PMC was formally prosecuted until the end of 2008. This legal immunity was largely due to Order 17, which the U.S.-led Coalition Provisional Authority unilaterally declared at the beginning of the Iraq War. Order 17 held contractors immune from Iraqi law. The Iraqi government eventually negotiated the elimination of PMC immunity from Iraqi law, and in January 2009 Iraq refused to give Blackwater a license to operate in the country. This only resulted in a transfer of contracts (and former Blackwater employees) to other American PMCs, as the U.S. State Department awarded Blackwater's former contract to Triple Canopy, another American security firm. Blackwater then changed the company's name to Xe (pronounced "zee") in an effort to rebrand the company and reduce negative connotations in Iraq and abroad that Blackwater represented "American violence and impunity."[d]

Some argue that outsourcing military operations to legally unaccountable "mercenaries" may be easily justified as a necessary strategic tool. Military privatization may carry the promise of increased efficiency, while better coordinating both public and private interests through the encouragement of mutually beneficial exchanges. Yet structuralists see privatization of security as contributing to imperial overstretch (cost overruns), perpetuation of wars, and actual threats to peace and security.

**References**

[a]Nikki Brokmeyer authored the material in this box. Our thanks to her.

[b]See Jeremy Scahill, *Blackwater: The Rise of the World's Most Powerful Mercenary Army* (New York: Nation Books, 2007), p. xvi.

[c]David Isenberg, "A Government in Search of Cover: Private Military Companies in Iraq," in *From Mercenaries to Market: The Rise and Regulation of Private Military Companies*, eds., Simon Chesterman and Chia Lehnardt (New York: Oxford University Press, 2007), p. 84.

[d]Rod Nordland, "Ex-Blackwater Workers May Return to Iraq Jobs," *New York Times*, April 3, 2009, 1.

Overall, some realists such as former National Security advisors Brent Scowcroft and Zbigniew Brzezinski took issue with many of the specifics of the Bush administration's unilateral outlook. Some argued that a policy of preemption without imminent military threats would conflict with international norms and the interests of close U.S. allies. Effectively controlling rogue states might even necessitate that the United States take over their governments, eventually producing a costly and ruinous empire. By 2006, the U.S. unilateralist strategy had generated disappointment, suspicion, and animosity between the United States and some of its allies.[6] The U.S. attempt to be the world's policeman contributed to a reputation for arrogance and uncooperative behavior with other states. Some old and new allies refused to lend political and financial assistance, troops, and diplomatic support to the United States in Iraq and Afghanistan. Fundamentally, many realists doubted the extent to which the benefits of unilateralism outweigh multilateralism. And most importantly, the U.S. public was unwilling to bear all the economic and political costs of being the world's hegemon without assistance from allies.

Other critics like *Washington Post* war correspondent Thomas Ricks argue that the United States did not devise an overall joint military–political strategy to win over the "hearts and minds" of the Iraqi people.[7] Instead of trying to defeat guerilla forces, such a strategy would use counterinsurgency special forces and promote civilian acceptance of the United States and its partners. Successfully winning hearts and minds in the Iraq War requires attention to religious differences between the West and Iraq, as well as within Iraq itself. For example, early in the occupation the United States alienated some religious leaders in Iraq like Ali Hussein al-Sistani who have more political influence and authority than many secular leaders. There were also intense debates during the drafting of the new Iraqi Constitution in 2005 about provisions pertaining to religious freedom. Most Iraqis agreed that group rights to religious liberty should be protected, but many did not think that those rights should be extended to individuals to convert from Islam or abandon their faith, both of which are prohibited under certain schools of Islamic thought. These and other controversies have led some scholars and officials to suggest that democracy will work in countries like Iraq and Afghanistan only if it incorporates many Islamic principles. Clearly, multiple aspects of global security—from the sources of security threats to post-conflict rebuilding—require knowledge of and sensitivity to world religions and religious differences.[8]

U.S. prestige diminished nearly everywhere in the world as a result of tactics adopted in Iraq and in the war against terrorism. Often young Iraqi males were rounded up and interrogated in prisons such as Abu Ghraib, where some were tortured. The Bush administration argued that it was not required to treat al-Qaeda and Taliban combatants according to Geneva Convention rules because these prisoners were terrorists, not soldiers. The United States was also accused of rendering suspected terrorists to Egypt, Eastern Europe, and elsewhere outside the United States, where laws against torture are ignored. Even the Obama administration has been accused of detaining insurgents in Afghanistan in a "black jail" run by U.S. Special Operations Forces. At this and another site in Iraq, detainees have allegedly been tortured and denied access to the Red Cross.[9]

These challenges in Iraq and Afghanistan were exacerbated by other unilateral security policies undertaken by the United States under President Bush. For example, the Bush administration unilaterally withdrew support for the Kyoto Treaty (see Chapter 20) and the International Criminal Court, and hesitated to support new efforts to enforce the Biological Weapons Treaty of 1972. Much to Russia's consternation, the Bush administration unilaterally withdrew from the long-standing 1972 **Antiballistic Missile (ABM) Treaty**, which outlawed the development of a space-based missile defense system. Many critics noted that even if an ABM could knock down an incoming missile, terrorists or rogue states were not likely to use such a weapon to attack the United States or its allies. To counter a possible ballistic (long-range) missile attack on the United States or its allies by a rogue nation, the United States—against the advice of many of its allies and Russia—proposed deploying a new version of the **National Missile Defense (NMD)** program. New defensive ABMs would, it was hoped, destroy incoming ballistic missiles before they hit their targets—a feat that required new technology, research, and lots of money.

## Critiques of Bush Administration Security Policies

Many structuralists and realists joined late-night comedians in making cannon fodder of President Bush's security policies. Their criticisms focused on four major issues:

- The Empire thesis
- The new crusade against Islam
- The military–industrial complex
- The relationship of globalization to security.

As we discussed in Chapter 4, the Bush administration never officially adopted a policy of empire-building, but numerous critics charged the administration with pursuing Roman- or British-style empires.[10] In his book *Colossus*, the noted British historian Niall Ferguson wrote eloquently of the need for the United States to pick up the mantle of Great Britain at the end of the nineteenth century and bring order to the world. However, a number of structuralists argue that the Bush Doctrine and invasion of Iraq were motivated by the goal of saving Iraq's oil and maintaining a deeper "footprint" in the Middle East to influence developments related to oil and other economic and security interests elsewhere in the region. For example, when Baghdad was "liberated," protection of the oil ministry took precedence over stopping looting or preserving artifacts in the Iraq Museum.[11]

In *The Sorrows of Empire*, Chalmers Johnson argues that the United States already has an empire, as manifested in the over 700 military installations and numerous troops it maintains all over the world.[12] He and others reject the idea that the Iraq War was to support liberty and democracy, or even to secure the United States from terrorism. For Johnson, the source of U.S. imperial behavior is a "military–industrial complex" that needs to sell military arms and sustain massive U.S. defense spending.

During the Cold War many structuralists focused on how and why U.S. arms manufacturers and their supporters in Congress profited from war. The Defense Department and Congress combine with these arms manufacturers to form their own political subsystem (or iron triangle). Congress supports military installations at home and abroad because of the income it provides for folks in their district. Strong business interests within the United States and other major powers lobby for higher levels of defense spending, both in the name of national security and to promote the economic interests of the firms that supply weapons and defense systems. Some of the U.S. companies often involved in these transactions include Vector Microwave Research, Electronic Warfare Associates, Science Applications International, Loral, McDonnell Douglas (now part of Boeing), and GM Hughes Electronics. Many of these companies utilize former U.S. defense officials to help them sell and acquire new technologies.

Many structuralists have examined how private arms manufacturers and arms-importing countries orchestrate a "feeding frenzy" over weapons and technology, often reinforcing tensions or negative views of an enemy to justify sales.[13] The United States is the leading arms exporter in the world. In 2008 it sold $38 billion in weapons overseas, cornering two-thirds of global sales and accounting for more than 70 percent of all arms sales to developing countries. Russia, Britain, and Israel also have significant public–private ties in their defense industries designed to bolster exports and encourage domestic spillovers.

As in the case of great empires of the past, the Bush administration exhibited a strong sense of moral crusading and assurance that the United States was "chosen by God" to lead the rest of the world. The administration's views generated a Manichean outlook that is usually associated with empire. Islamic neo-fascism replaced communism as the current enemy of the United States.[14] U.S. military and political interests overtly coincided with the spread of global capitalism, supporting the investments of the United States and other major powers.

## Globalization, the Financial Crisis, and Global Security

As realist-mercantilists note (see Chapter 3), wealth and power always complement one another. In the 1990s many academic experts like Michael Ignatieff accepted the claim that globalization helped strengthen the United States—and especially its hegemonic role in the world. And yet by the time the Bush administration left office in early 2009, a growing number of realist critics and many HILs and structuralists were suggesting that the United States was actually losing much of its power, like an engine dripping oil.

During the Reagan, Bush I, Clinton, and Bush II administrations, the neoliberal policies of the IMF, the WTO, and the World Bank often served as strategic instruments that complemented various U.S. economic and political objectives. Commitment to open borders, free trade, floating exchange rates, and the magic of the "invisible hand" in the market—all packaged in the globalization campaign—helped grow the economies of many LDCs by way of trade and foreign investment. Most successful were the Southeast Asian economies, whose mercantilist development policies (see Chapter 11) at the time were viewed as acceptable to the United States, given the trade and investment opportunities they provided for U.S. businesses.

Yet, integrated financial markets and neoliberal policies also contributed to two interrelated political and economic issues. First, reductions in foreign aid and the use of sanctions often engendered hostility toward the United States and its allies because of the impact they both had on the poor in targeted countries. Likewise, TNC exploitation of workers contributed to more inequality along with much violence and instability in many poorer nations (discussed below). A second problem was the debt the United States continued to accumulate against the rest of the world, especially countries that were doing well and eager to finance that debt by investing in U.S. businesses. By the early 1990s, the United States had become increasingly dependent upon an economic liberal international order to finance its foreign policy and security objectives.

The United States' financial arrangement with its investors benefited from a relatively open and minimally regulated global economic structure that complemented U.S. security objectives and hegemony over the emerging global security structure. The United States could continue to pursue "hegemony on the cheap" as it had done since World War II. However, poverty, corruption, and violence in poorer countries could not be overcome until economic development trickled down into these societies.

As the Bush administration kept spending and increasing U.S. debt, China and others financed much of that debt (see Chapter 7), which, in effect, allowed the United States to finance its efforts to overthrow the Afghani and Iraqi regimes. When the global financial crisis of 2008 finally erupted, it was not the global market that touched off this catastrophe, but developments inside the U.S. economy itself (see Chapter 8). Many realists and structuralists maintain that like Reagan, George W. Bush cajoled others to go along with the United States. In so doing, however, the Bush administration inevitably overstretched the U.S. economy, contributing to a loss in confidence about the United States's willingness to pay off its debts and control its imperial ambitions. Perhaps it is not a coincidence that Bush left office just as the effects of the global financial crisis were realized.

## The Obama Administration and Multilateralism

The Obama administration shifted its outlook toward multilateralism based on its understanding that the global security structure now manifests a multipolar distribution of wealth and power. Its judgment also reflected the belief that both the U.S. public and officials of the other major powers had rejected unilateralism and pursuit of empire. At the end of 2009, Obama's multilateral outlook and security agenda included:

- working more positively *with* all U.S. allies and potential partners, especially given the administration's decision to continue the war in Afghanistan
- renewing efforts (especially with Russia) to decrease the number of strategic nuclear weapons and other WMDs
- continuing the war against terrorism, but at reduced cost and without making enemies out of Middle Eastern and heavily-populated Muslim states such as Pakistan or Indonesia
- renewing talks with Cuba, Iran, and other "rogue" states like Venezuela
- supporting efforts to halt the global proliferation of WMDs
- dealing with Iran and North Korea's efforts to (re)build their nuclear-processing facilities
- promoting international efforts to deal with climate change and global warming.

In early December 2009, President Obama announced that the United States intended to send another 30,000 troops to Afghanistan to add to its 71,000 troops already there, to "finish the job" started under the Bush administration. The primary objective is to take out the Taliban insurgents in Afghanistan, but especially al-Qaeda, some of whom are in Pakistan. The administration also wants to help stabilize Pakistan for fear that al-Qaeda could gain access to some of Pakistan's nuclear weapons. Obama also called for NATO members to contribute 5,000–10,000 more troops to the 38,000 NATO troops already there. For the first time in recent military history, the U.S. and NATO military plan is to shift to a "hearts and minds" strategy that incorporates a number of other counterinsurgency tactics.

As expected, many policy officials and experts have raised a variety of questions about this Afghanistan decision. Will it result in another quagmire like Iraq, or even Vietnam? Who is the real enemy in this case—the Taliban or al-Qaeda? Will Pakistan collapse in civil conflict? Can the United States afford the war without a new "war tax"? What impact will costs for the war have on the economic stimulus, health care, and a number of social programs?

Many U.S. and European officials remain deeply divided over this and other security issues. France has already signaled that for now it will not offer any more soldiers. Germany prefers a political solution and will wait to take a decision. However, NATO chief Anders Fogh Rasmussen in Brussels said that NATO would provide at least 5,000 troops. For many NATO countries, the financial crisis has made it difficult to spend more for the war in Afghanistan.

Many HILs, realist-neomercantilists, and structuralists argue that the wars in Iraq and Afghanistan are no longer worth their financial costs. Some contend that the "total war" version of conflict that has resulted in the deaths of thousands of soldiers and civilians has become morally and ethically unacceptable and is a violation of international law.

The Obama administration is also purposefully shifting away from an emphasis on hard power to a combination of hard and soft power. Many experts have argued that hard-power instruments such as nuclear weapons are costly and can make the United States "musclebound."[15] Terrorists and suicide bombers, for example, can threaten and strike even in highly militarized places such as occupied Iraq and Israel's West Bank settlements. Hard power gains territory and destroys military hardware, but soft power affects people more intimately and is a surer long-run road to security.

Joseph Nye believes that the United States—with its broad range of interests, leadership responsibilities, and international economic interdependence—should give more attention to soft-power instruments such as improved information and communication systems, the benefits of globalization, and multilateral cooperation. Soft-power instruments perform a variety of functions that also enable hard-power instruments to work more effectively. A big element of multilateralism is diplomacy. One of Obama's goals is to improve the United States' image as being more cooperative and understanding. His trips to Berlin and other countries (especially in Africa) have attracted huge crowds of supporters, along with the curious. And his Nobel Peace Prize Award for "trying hard" to produce world peace may increase U.S. soft power.

However, it is unclear whether the United States can postpone applying the stick to either Iran or North Korea for their resistance to complying with the International Atomic Energy Agency (IAEA) when it comes to inspections of their nuclear facilities. Most experts agree that the use of economic sanctions has not worked, especially in the case of Iran, where growing resistance to President Ahmadinejad's leadership threatens Iran's domestic stability and the stability of other states in the region.

Then there is the question of Russia's effort to reestablish itself as a global power. Until the global financial crisis Russia was profiting from high oil prices, which helped its economy grow. Many issues remain to be dealt with including corruption, state control of energy resources, and how democratic the state can be given its authoritarian past (see Chapter 13). Russia's willingness to cooperate with other states has swung like a pendulum, making its role in the global security structure quite unpredictable.

China's role in the security structure has also preoccupied many state leaders. Some realist-oriented U.S. officials fear that communist China is bent on confronting the United States on the battlefield in the near future. They key in on reports of China's buildup of nuclear weapons and efforts to become more than a regional hegemon. Other officials have stayed faithful to the economic liberal and realist argument that continued development of trade and other forms of economic relations with the Chinese will diffuse China's need to increase its military power and lead to more emphasis on ways to strengthen mutual political interests (see Chapter 13). In this case, globalization serves those who support this argument. However, some fear that with the financial crisis China may have the upper hand and recycle foreign reserves into its own economy instead of investing abroad, thwarting U.S. economic recovery and leaving the United States in a weak global position.

Finally, former Deputy Secretary of the U.S. Treasury Roger Altman suggests that the global financial crisis is undermining U.S. credibility all over the world. Eurozone countries are resorting to protection, exhibiting signs of both more regulation and deglobalization. Altman suggests that emerging economies will continue to play a bigger role in the global economy and security structure all the time. China has been investing heavily in both oil and food production in Africa and other places. For realists, these sorts of moves leave the door open for China to increase its power and global influence, while weakening U.S. power and leadership.[16]

Some HILs and realists worry that these developments could result in the United States and other major powers becoming more isolationist and less willing to play proactive roles in the global political economy. For now, if history is right, it will be difficult to manage a multilateral security structure. Multilateralists must confront the difficult problem of determining how many and which powers can or should make up the multipolar system. Will the European Union take on more military responsibilities? Perhaps it is time for Brazil and India to also play bigger roles in major power decisions. Although some of these states may see themselves as potential great powers, others, such as Japan and Germany, do not desire the associated responsibilities. History also suggests that security system management is not a given but a role states must actively attend to. Regular NATO meetings have not resulted in agreement on an assortment of issues (discussed below) and are likely to result in more disagreement given the Obama administration's pressure on NATO to provide additional troops in Afghanistan.

# INTERNATIONAL ORGANIZATIONS

Because security is so sacrosanct to nation-states, they have been reluctant to give IOs much authority to solve many of the life-and-death issues surrounding national security. On the other hand, the United States and other major powers have been willing to authorize IOs, NGOs, international businesses, and even subnational actors to deal with an assortment of subsidiary security issues, many of them generated by globalization. Consider, for instance, UN treaties, NATO and UN Peacekeeping, and the International Criminal Court (ICC) as examples of some of the ways in which IOs manage a wide variety of security issues. Do their approaches reflect a different understanding of the global security structure, or do they merely reflect the views of the major powers? Do they exert independent influence, or are they only as strong or effective as states allow them to be? Finally, who decides if or when IO-sponsored treaties or protocols are to be followed?

## The United Nations

Until the early 1970s, the lack of UN security treaties and conventions reflected U.S. and Soviet emphasis on expanding their arsenals and deterring one another from initiating an attack. As U.S. and Soviet relations improved toward the end of the Vietnam War, both superpowers looked to the UN to help establish a number of conventions, treaties, and protocols related especially to problems of nuclear weapons proliferation and control over the arms race. Many developing countries had purchased conventional weapons from one of the two superpowers or major powers, or were trying to build nuclear power plants of their own, ostensibly to generate domestic energy.

Not only are major powers active in the UN, but so are the lesspowerful (minor) states that cannot successfully address most of their security issues by themselves. Countries such as Italy, Spain, the Netherlands, and Belgium, along with middle-income, developing nations such as Brazil, Indonesia, Malaysia, Poland, Hungary, and the Czech Republic, often join alliances with major powers and IOs. As in the case of India and Pakistan, many of these states have some hard-power capabilities, but most cannot protect themselves with these instruments alone. They tend to look more positively than the United States does at international and regional organizations to generate norms, rules, or international standards that will defend and protect them.

The UN first played a decisively important but indirect role in promoting peace and security by serving as a forum for negotiations that resulted in several treaties covering different security issues. The **Treaty on the Nonproliferation of Nuclear Weapons (NPT)** of 1968 obligated states with nuclear weapons not to transfer them to other states, and nonnuclear states not to receive nuclear weapons or devices from any other state. The NPT also created the IAEA, based in Vienna, to inspect nuclear power facilities in member states and to guard against secret military diversions. Today the NPT has been signed by 188 parties. Its supporters argue that it has been quite successful in limiting the spread of nuclear weapons to developing nations. Japan and Germany, and also Brazil, Argentina, and several ex–Soviet-bloc countries, have chosen not to develop their nuclear weapons capabilities.

Some realist critics are quick to point out that without major or superpower support and willingness to enforce all these treaties, they demonstrate only the good intentions of states. A number of nuclear states, including India, Pakistan, and Israel, have not signed the NPT. North Korea withdrew from the treaty in 1993 and resorted to bargaining (some would call it extortion) with the leaders of the major powers for financial assistance in exchange for cooperation on inspections of its nuclear facilities. More recently, North Korea and Iran have pushed ahead with their nuclear development programs, signaling their desire to join the club of states with nuclear weapons. Critics also charge that rogue states and terrorists could acquire these weapons via the expanding sources of suppliers willing to market them.

Another major treaty area is the **Biological and Toxic Weapons Convention (BTWC)**, which was easily endorsed by more than 100 nations at the time of its inception in 1972. The signers included the United States and the Soviet Union, both of whom recognized the lethality of biological weapons and feared that they might be used during a war. The BTWC restricts research on biological weapons to defensive measures, but makes no provisions for inspection because biological weapons are easy to hide. The UN Special Committee (UNSCOM) was charged by the UN Security Council in 1991 with inspecting Iraqi facilities for evidence of anthrax and other biological materials. Iran, Syria, Russia, and at least 16 other countries have been suspected of either producing biological weapons or conducting research in this area.

Other UN-sponsored treaties include the **Comprehensive Test Ban Treaty (CTBT)**, signed in 1996, which outlaws the testing of nuclear weapons under any conditions but does not take effect until all 44 states that are capable of building a crude nuclear weapon have signed and ratified the treaty. The United States, France, China, India, and Pakistan have been slow to come to terms over the CTBT either because they have been developing a new generation of ballistic missiles or have wanted to test weapons in order to catch up with the other nuclear powers. In 1999, the U.S. Senate voted against ratifying the CTBT, a move supported by the new Bush administration. Supporters of the treaty charge that it is basically a moot point, given that many weapons do not need to be tested or can be tested under laboratory conditions.

The **Chemical Weapons Convention (CWC)** of 1992 went into effect in 1997, when some 157 countries pledged to eliminate all chemical weapons by the year 2007 and never to develop, produce, stockpile, or use chemical weapons. Critics of the treaty are suspicious that nations such as Russia, Israel, Egypt, Syria, Libya, North Korea, and, until recently, Iraq have not signed the treaty and may try to develop chemical weapons as a relatively cheap way of countering U.S. conventional and nuclear superiority. Finally, since 1987, countries capable of producing long-range missiles have worked on a convention to prohibit the export of missiles and related technology—the **Missile Technology Control Regime (MTCR)**. Iran, Israel, Saudi Arabia, Pakistan, India, and North Korea have been developing short- and medium-range ballistic missiles. China—which has sold missiles to Pakistan and India—has also come under pressure to adhere to this agreement.

Finally, one of the ways in which developments in the technology and production structures influence security issues at this level is through arms sales. Many security experts are concerned about the extent to which many states, including some rogue states, can easily acquire weapons through commercial and noncommercial channels. The bulk of the arms trade is in conventional weapons.

A number of conditions make it difficult to implement agreements to limit the proliferation of weapons. As many realists and structuralists note, the objective of nonproliferation often conflicts with the economic liberal objective of states to market missiles and other technologies that can be used to produce weapons. Some recipient developing nations may resent attempts to limit their ability to acquire such weapons. Similarly, sellers are reluctant to place sanctions on violators because it is hard to condition the buyer's behavior via these sales or because sellers fear that buyers will purchase from other producers.

Supporters of weapons conventions argue that since the late 1960s the majority of second-tier states, acting through the UN, have been engaged in assertive efforts to create new rules and conventions related to the production, deployment, and sale of conventional weapons and, more recently, WMD and their component parts. These efforts increase awareness about programs and their transparency, thereby enhancing political and security conditions. Supporters also argue that these agreements help generate new norms and promote cooperation.

## NATO Peacekeeping

Since the mid-1990s NATO has handled some regional peacekeeping efforts. In 1999 Poland, Hungary, and the Czech Republic formally joined NATO, bringing the number of members to nineteen. In 1994 NATO also enrolled twenty-five small Eastern

European and Balkan states in its Partnership for Peace (PfP) program, with the intention of increasing confidence and reinforcing stability throughout Europe. These twenty-seven PfP members routinely deal with such common regional problems as peacekeeping, arms control, civil emergencies, and mine action. Today, NATO has a total of twenty-six members, seven of whom had been in the PfP program.

Since the end of the Cold War, many critics have questioned NATO's utility and cost in a changing security atmosphere. Some unilateralists have renewed the attack on NATO, charging that it is simply too expensive in view of the more subdued East–West environment that currently exists. They maintain that the United States should decouple itself from the costs and political burdens associated with defending—and extending nuclear deterrence over—a bigger Europe. Some also question NATO's willingness to act as a coherent unit under military duress and its resolve to protect newer (Eastern European) members.

NATO's role in Kosovo (a small semiautonomous region of Serbia) in the late 1990s gave it new life when it became the basis of cooperative security actions among the United States, Great Britain, and some of the other major powers. NATO authorized air strikes on Serbian military targets in October 1998, when Serbian forces refused to withdraw from Kosovo. In the face of "ethnic cleansing" and other atrocities, an estimated 750,000 refugees sought asylum in Macedonia and Albania. After peace talks between Kosovo Albanians and Serbs failed in late March 1999, NATO began bombing Serbian targets in Kosovo, and later targets in Serbia itself, until early June, when Serbia finally agreed to withdraw its troops from Kosovo.

In the early stages of this conflict, NATO was criticized for not having a clear military strategy and clear political objectives. Public opinion seemed to support NATO's bombing strategy in response to alleged atrocities, but allied national leaders were reluctant to send ground forces into Kosovo proper. Clearly, no one nation or small group of nations could manage this and the earlier Balkan conflicts, nor were the United States and Europe willing to let the UN play a role greater than sanctioning the actions and policies of the major powers.

Questions linger about NATO's role as many issues remain to be settled, including who pays for it and how much. Other issues NATO must be able to deal with include nationalism and ethnic and religious rivalry in member states such as Turkey or nations on NATO's eastern borders that are in line to become members. It remains to be seen whether NATO can deal adequately with drugs, terrorism, weapons proliferation, and immigration issues, just to name a few other pressing security threats its members face.[17] Finally, once again the United States is pressing NATO countries to provide more troops into the Afghanistan theater. As has been NATO's tendency, its members are likely to disagree with one another about not only their economic, troop level, and equipment obligations but also the viability of the objectives in Afghanistan.

## UN Peacekeeping

UN peacekeeping is an integral part of the global security structure that involves the periodic use of member-state troops to help settle disputes and resolve conflicts. In many cases, it serves a critical management function where states cannot be effective or choose not to participate. For nearly the last 20 years peacekeeping has involved not only military operations but also efforts to deal with a variety of other political, social, and cultural conflicts.

Early in the Cold War, when the Security Council was deadlocked about when to use force, the UN created peacekeeping forces as a mechanism for dealing with aggression and conflict in situations that would *not* directly involve the superpowers or other permanent members of the Security Council. UN peacekeepers were to serve as a neutral force between warring states, policing cease-fires, enforcing borders, and maintaining order when states requested their presence. There have been some 63 peacekeeping operations (**PKOs**) over the life of the UN. Many of the early PKOs were made up of specially trained soldiers from perceived "neutral" countries such as Canada, Ireland, and Sweden. Since the end of the Cold War the biggest contributors of forces to UN PKOs have been developing countries such as India, Pakistan, Bangladesh, Nepal, and Nigeria.

After the Cold War ended, the senior President Bush proposed that in a "New World Order" the UN would play a bigger role managing security issues, and that the United States would no longer be the world's policeman. In 1992, UN Secretary-General Boutros Boutros-Ghali tried to break new ground by suggesting that UN peacekeeping forces should play a more assertive and proactive role in "peacemaking" to deal with nationalistic, ethnic, and religious conflicts. He suggested that UN peacekeeping missions needed to include soldiers from the United States, Great Britain, France, Russia, and more developing countries, who would be authorized to defend themselves when fired on. Including big-power troops in these PKOs would help pressure combatants into cooperating with the UN.

Secretary-General Boutros Boutros-Ghali also went so far as to recommend that an "on call" force of 100,000 blue-helmeted troops and support equipment be made available to him to quickly dispatch to world hot spots when needed. More important, he wrote that "while respect for the fundamental sovereignty and integrity of the state remains central, it is undeniable that the centuries-old doctrine of absolute and exclusive sovereignty no longer stands, and was in fact never so absolute as it was conceived to be in theory."[18]

Apart from sanctioning NATO's efforts, the UN played only minor roles in conflicts in Rwanda, Kosovo, East Timor, and, most recently, in Iraq. It has also played only a minor role in Darfur, where once again the major powers are reluctant to label the situation one of genocide. Under Secretary-General Boutros Boutros-Ghali in the late 1980s and early 1990s, the UN increased its operations in poorer states including Angola, Liberia, Rwanda, Haiti, Tajikistan, Georgia, Bosnia, Croatia (two operations), Macedonia, Iraq/Kuwait, Somalia, and Cambodia, to name only a few of the more well-known efforts at proactive peacemaking. In a few cases (such as Cambodia), these missions were deemed successful; in most, they were not well received.

Increasingly, critics question the UN's ability to produce peace in a civil-war environment.[19] UN operations in Somalia, Bosnia, and Rwanda, in particular, generated criticism that the UN often arrives too late to make a difference in many of these internal conflicts.[20] Furthermore, the cost of operations often exceeded estimates, while member states used the UN to substitute for their more expensive campaigns. Because of the complex conditions and factors that generated these regional conflicts, UN peacekeepers could not easily find political, let alone military, solutions to them, all of which contributed to a diminishment of the UN's reputation.

Since the late 1990s, PKOs (seven of them in Africa alone) have been limited to focusing on multidimensional problems where military, civilian police, and other civilian personnel work alongside local governments and groups. NGOs help provide emergency relief, demobilize former fighters, clear mines, organize and conduct elections, and promote sustainable development practices. One of the peacekeeping challenges in places like Kosovo, Lebanon, Iraq, and Darfur is that conflicts are more frequently between religious groups. Soldiers and peacekeepers must contend with a wide variety of nontraditional security issues. For example, how can they ensure that women are not concealing weapons under *niqabs* without violating cultural norms of decency? Also, rival groups habitually target each other for violence during religious holidays or pilgrimages; preventing those attacks requires specific knowledge of holy sites, religious calendars, and religious practices. Should a cessation in hostilities be achieved, it can only be sustained if those responsible for keeping the peace understand and respect local customs.

## ▶ A PEACEKEEPER'S NOTES

Bruno Angelo Porcellana is in the Italian army and served in Albania and Kosovo in the late 1990s. Recently he served twice as a blue-helmeted UN peacekeeper in Lebanon with the United Nations Interim Force in Lebanon (UNIFIL), a military mission directed by the undersecretary of the UN in charge of Peacekeeping Operations (PKOs). Dave Balaam interviewed him in 2009 about a number of issues surrounding peacekeeping today, especially from the perspective of a soldier from a smaller European country. Sabrina Tatta of the University of Washington translated Bruno's written responses to Dave.

DB: Do you see peacekeeping as a viable instrument to solve conflict?

BP: Based on what has been written over the years, peacekeeping is certainly an instrument the United Nations has to deal with unresolved conflict. It allows for a cooling off period in tense situations. Certainly, there have been cases of failure, one above all in Somalia in 1992 when UN personnel left the African nation without securing peace and with many personnel losses. But one must not forget the excellent

job soldiers primarily from Italy, France, Spain, and even China, along with others have done under the authority of the UN carrying out this mission in the south of Lebanon after the last Israel-Lebanon War in 2006.

DB: What problems in promoting peace have you encountered the most?

BP: In the case of Somalia in 1992 the presence of a peacekeeping force was important but not a determining factor given that there was no will on the part of the local parties that the situation be resolved. The absence of a Somali state is still notable today when ships along African coasts are attacked by pirates who have bases in the ex-Italian colony.

DB: In your day-to-day work, what things are most problematic?

BP: Well, working in the international environment and dealing with local people is not easy if you don't have a good language background. The peacekeepers involved in the international environment have good language skills, especially in English and French. Relations with local people are helped by using a translator because most of the locals do not speak any international language. We do not have any problems with money because a soldier's allowance is quite good. The morale of the soldiers here in Lebanon is also quite good. We have been training to manage possible conflict and have the security threat skills needed to get the job done.

DB: What about member-state politics, funding, training, and implementation issues?

BP: Obviously the politics of the United Nations related to PKOs reflects the politics of states in the UN. Given that the Security Council is the "keeper" of international peace and order—according to the UN Charter—any state that participates in the UN in a temporary capacity or who holds a seat within the UN can appeal to other nations should it become necessary to send troops to nations involved in situations that require military intervention.

DB: Why do you think smaller countries like Italy and Spain are willing to support PKOs when the major powers are not? What do smaller countries get out of their contribution?

BP: Belonging to the UN, in addition to being an honor, is something negotiated through annual contributions UN member nations are called upon to make for PKOs. Somalia in 1992, Bosnia and Kosovo in the 1990s,

West Timor in 1999, and the UNIFIL mission in the south of Lebanon today are good examples. Certainly, the question might imply bad intentions on the part of the bigger UN powers like the United States, China, Russia, the UK, and France (who constitute the permanent members of the UN Security Council) to not support putting troops on the ground, but that is not so. For all of these missions, whether they be UN, NATO, or any of other regional security organization, it is normal for their logistical problems to reflect the political climate of the moment and the particular way internal business is carried out by the various nations from whom intervention is sought.

In fact, the United States participated in operations in Somalia in 1992, when Kofi Annan was the vice secretary general and chief of the DPKO. Today, even a small contingency of Chinese deminers is involved in the UNIFIL mission in Lebanon shoulder to shoulder with Italian and Spanish colleagues. In the past, France was present in Africa in the UNAMIR mission in Rwanda in 1994. In other missions, be they UN or not, based on the resolution of the UN Security Council that justified intervention in Kosovo in 1999, Americans worked side by side with Russians, the French, the British, and so on.

This need to account for the ways in which religion impacts security is not limited to military actions or peacekeeping missions. It also affects how various groups understand the very foundations of legal and political order. Global contestation about law is especially visible in the human rights arena, where there are fundamental tensions between the West and predominantly Muslim or other non-Western states (which often defend very different philosophical and cultural traditions). This matters not just theoretically, but practically as well: Judges behind the bench and juries in the box of institutions like the International Criminal Court are ever more diverse.

The UN has often been criticized for its ineffectiveness when it comes to dealing with terrorism. Centered in one particular location or scattered throughout the world, terrorist organizations are not usually controlled by any particular state. So-called state-sponsored terrorists are often financed or supported by governments seeking to affect the behavior of another nation. Iran, North Korea, Sudan, and Syria, among others, have earned reputations as state sponsors of terrorism. Religious terrorists make up one-fourth of all terrorist groups, often mixing religious opposition with ideological justifications such as the right to self-determination. A mix of religion and politics is behind Lebanon's Hezbollah, Palestine's Hamas, and al-Qaeda's transnational operations.[21]

Recently, many states, IOs, and NGOs have recommitted themselves to dealing with terrorism in a cooperative manner, largely because the weapons that are available to terrorists are so lethal, sophisticated, and easy to acquire. UN bodies have passed a series of resolutions to deny financial support and safe havens for terrorists, share information with others states about terrorists, and encourage states to become party to terrorism conventions and protocols. The UN's Counter-Terrorism Committee (*CTC*) was created to monitor implementation of these resolutions but has encountered problems related to defining terrorism, sovereignty, and the interests of arms manufacturers and bankers with investments in weapons manufacturing and trade.

Finally, the IAEA has increased its role by inspecting nuclear facilities in Iraq and most recently in Iran. The International Atomic Energy Agency is underfunded and understaffed— 650 inspectors must cover 900 facilities in some 91 countries.[22] According to many nonproliferation experts, the industrialized states especially should cooperate with IOs in their inspection efforts. They should also recommit themselves to develop poorer economies via more aid, better terms of trade, and direct investment in these states.

## Human Rights and the ICC

The connection between security and human rights issues has become stronger in the new global security structure and IPE studies. Many UN members who cherish their right to self-defense have also gradually felt more willing, even compelled, to transfer some authority to the UN to manage a variety of human rights violations, especially "war crimes" and "crimes against humanity." This movement dates back to the Nazi war crimes trials in Nuremburg, Germany after World War II. In the 1990s, the UN established two truly international war crimes tribunals to deal with atrocities in the Balkans and Rwanda and later added a tribunal that focused on atrocities in Sierra Leone, reflecting some amount of agreement about the conduct of nations and even individuals in war. Located in The Hague, the Netherlands, Kenya, and Sierra Leone, these tribunals have lacked both funding and the authority to arrest suspects.

However, a number of indictments for war crimes have been handed down against various soldiers and citizens. Serbian president Slobodan Milosevic was indicted for crimes against humanity and other war crimes in Kosovo, and died in prison in 2005. The former prime minister of Rwanda, Jean Kambanda, was sentenced to life in prison for genocide in that country in 1994. In 2006, the Special Court for Sierra Leone began a lengthy trial of former Liberian president Charles Taylor, who was accused of war crimes and crimes against humanity in Sierra Leone from 1996 to 2002.[23]

By 2000, 138 nations had signed a treaty to create a permanent **International Criminal Court (ICC)** to hear cases on genocide, war crimes, and crimes against humanity from anywhere in the world after July 1, 2002. The Clinton administration signed the treaty, but the second Bush administration opposed it on the grounds that U.S. officials could be accused of war crimes for any act of war. Great Britain, France, and Germany are helping to finance and contribute staff to the new court. As of 2009, the U.S. Republican-controlled senate had refused to ratify the treaty, even though some 111 nations had either ratified or acceded to it.

Realist critics point out that the new tribunals lack the authority to compel compliance with international laws and conventions that deal with the conduct of war, given that they have no real power to punish nations or groups within them for violating these laws. Establishment of the tribunals, on the other hand, signifies that the issues of conduct during war, and also justice, have moved up on the agenda of states and shifted some authority beyond nation-states to IOs that deal with a relatively new security issue—the rights and treatment of individuals.

In conclusion, IOs such as NATO and UN PKOs have had larger but not always successful roles in dealing with a number of security issues beyond protecting borders. The ICC is another organization that helps manage the security structure by establishing new rules, norms, and expectations in cases of genocide and human rights violations. Even if some of these organizations are still dependent for their authority on the major powers, they have gradually acquired more clout—albeit in reflection of big-power interests.

## POOR AND FAILED STATES COME UNDONE

As we noted earlier, what sets the weak powers apart from major powers or minor powers is their poverty and inability to deal with many internal and external threats to their security. Most of these states suffer routine occurrences of violence—for example, Afghanistan, Pakistan, East Timor, the Philippines, a number of countries in the Balkans after 1990, Palestine, Iraq, Somalia, Sudan, Sierra Leone, Nigeria, and the Congo. Weak states often depend on UN peacekeeping forces and NGOs such as the Red Cross and Red Crescent, Amnesty International, and World Vision to help them mitigate security problems.

Many studies over the years attribute violence to the lack of development, which is a hotly debated issue (see Chapter 11). Some Western development experts believe that trade, foreign investment, and the development of new technologies and communication systems can reduce conflict by generating economic growth in developing economies. Conversely, they assert that security problems either prevent or delay economic development by wasting resources. Other studies focus on how the pursuit of economic liberal policies in poorer countries contributes to ethnic tensions and violence and weakens the chances for democracy.[24] Others focus on the damaging effects of economic growth on the environment, triggering a downward cycle of more tension and conflict as groups struggle over dwindling arable land or other vital resources like water.

As discussed earlier, in an effort to stimulate trade and generate income, many major powers and TNCs that produce conventional weapons and sophisticated technologies have been eager to sell these systems to some of the poorest developing nations. As Table 9-1 suggests, the developed states account for roughly 92 percent of total arms exports (the United States alone accounted for over 50 percent of the market in the late 1990s). By the mid-1990s developing nations—especially in the

**TABLE 9-1**

**Largest Importers and Exporters of Arms in Millions of US$ at Constant 1990 Prices**

| Importers | | Exporters | |
|---|---|---|---|
| Country | 2008 Total | Country | 2008 Total |
| South Korea | 1,898 | U.S. | 6,159 |
| India | 1,847 | Russia | 5,953 |
| Algeria | 1,590 | Germany | 2,837 |
| China | 1,241 | France | 1,585 |
| Pakistan | 1,094 | UK | 1,075 |
| Singapore | 1,014 | Spain | 623 |
| U.S. | 904 | Netherlands | 554 |
| Turkey | 723 | Italy | 484 |
| Poland | 611 | China | 428 |
| UAE | 671 | Israel | 410 |

*Note:* Data in this table are measured in Trend Indicator Values (TIVs).

*Source:* SIPRI Arms Transfer Database, accessed December 7, 2009 at http://www.sipri.org/databases/armstransfers

Middle East and East Asia—accounted for nearly 80 percent of all arms imports. These weapons are not the only source of conflict and tension, but in places such as Sierra Leone, Liberia, and parts of the Middle East, they generate fear in neighboring states and often result in more intense warfare and higher numbers of both civilian and military deaths.

States on the bottom rung of the development ladder often have large slums around their core cities. Even nations like Brazil that are climbing the ladder, with modern cities such as Rio de Janeiro, suffer significant urban violence. Many terrorism experts contend that failed states like Afghanistan are hotbeds for both subnational groups and transnational terrorist groups such as al-Qaeda, which look there to find support for their cause and safe havens. A champion of economic liberal ideas, Thomas Friedman, suggests that many potential terrorists can be found among the unemployed, young men in many Middle Eastern countries who find consolation in religious-ideological struggles.[25]

Many structuralists (see Chapter 4) continue to maintain that the past and present search by developed nations and TNCs for oil and other resources along with markets and wealth in developing regions have led to exploitation, poverty, imperialism, and repressive forms of neocolonialism.[26] The effects of economic liberal policies and the globalization campaign on developing states have on balance had a disastrous effect on their chances for development. The Asian financial crisis that began in the summer of 1997 (see Chapter 8) sparked an effort to reform what had until then been some rather successful economies in Southeast Asia. The IMF imposed stringent fiscal and monetary constraints on Thailand, Indonesia, South Korea, and the Philippines. One outcome of these measures was large demonstrations and rioting in many cities. In some cases, ethnic and minority groups such as the Chinese, who had done well before the crisis started, became targets of disgruntled people.[27]

One of the clearest trends in poorer states is the growing importance of NGOs. The Red Cross and Red Crescent, Amnesty International, Greenpeace, Doctors Without Borders, and Worldvision are motivated by a variety of humanitarian, ideological, and practical concerns and are gaining greater influence in the global security structure. A good example of the impact of NGOs on the security structure is the International Campaign to Ban Land Mines (see the box "Landmines," in Chapter 5). The issue highlights the extent to which public outcries over threats to personal security have chipped away at the sanctity of state control over national security.

Finally, one factor that accounts for some of the success of NGOs has been the powerful images of war and human rights violations that are easily recorded and communicated via satellite around the world, helping to personalize these issues. The **CNN effect**—round-the-clock coverage by the BBC, CNN, and many other global networks—has often helped put a compelling human face on problems such as AIDS, hunger, and genocide and made them more difficult for states to ignore.[28]

# CONCLUSION

## At the Crossroads

For many realists, what was especially good about the Cold War bipolar balance of power between the United States and the Soviet Union was its much more defined structural arrangement, which conditioned and limited the behavior of many states and actors. Since the end of the Cold War, the United States has been the world's only hegemon. For it and many of the other major powers in the global security structure, traditional issues of territorial integrity and balance of power have been some of the most important concerns.

The current global security structure has also become less orderly and more flexible. Its rules and norms are not as clear as they were in the Cold War bipolar structure. In the mid-1980s globalization brought with it a shift in emphasis to open markets and competitive economic growth. The Clinton administration pursued a multilateral approach to complement its own support for free markets. The United States and other major powers also hoped that economic liberal policies would result in democracy and peace in developing nations.

By the mid-1990s, it was clear that globalization was helping make sophisticated conventional weapons and improvements in nuclear, biological, and chemical weapons more available to a wide variety of unwanted public and private customers. While these weapons have seemed to constrain the major powers from fighting one another, the proliferation of all types of weapons has also contributed to instability in developing regions of the world.

After 9/11 the Bush administration adopted unilateralism and attempted to reorder the security structure with the United States as global hegemon. Before it left office, the war in Iraq had become a quagmire. In keeping with some of the developments in the other three structures, globalization and neoliberal policies have fostered a shift in the distribution of wealth and power in the global security structure, and the United States may no longer be able to get hegemony on the cheap. The rising costs of unilateralism coupled with the current financial crisis have left other countries like China and Russia suspicious of U.S. intentions and capabilities. China may or may not continue to finance the United States's debt, depending on its own political and economic interests. The Obama administration has once again shifted to multilateralism in an effort to coax others to share the burden of fighting terrorists in Afghanistan (and Pakistan).

Realists tend not to be too surprised by many of these developments. For them the essence of the international security structure does not fundamentally change. One persistent theme has been that major powers have had a hard time insulating themselves from a growing list of global security issues. However, the question remains: How will the security structure be managed—collectively or by one or even by no major powers? Because security is so sacrosanct to nation-states, they will be reluctant to give IOs too much authority to solve many of the life-and-death issues surrounding national (state) security. Regardless of whether or not the United States remains a global hegemon, the current security structure can no longer be managed by one power. To protect against a growing number of global threats, the United States and the other major and emerging powers will need to cooperate and share security management functions with IOs, regional organizations, and NGOs.

## KEY TERMS

Cold War   211
balance of power   213
multilateral approach   213
neoconservatives   214
rogue states   214
weapons of mass destruction (WMD)   214
Antiballistic Missile (ABM) Treaty   217
National Missile Defense (NMD)   217

Treaty on the Nonproliferation of Nuclear Weapons (NPT)   223
Biological Toxic Weapons Convention (BTWC)   223
Comprehensive Test Ban Treaty (CTBT)   223
Chemical Weapons Convention (CWC)   224
Missile Technology Control Regime (MTCR)   224

Peacekeeping Operations (PKOs)   226
International Criminal Court (ICC)   229
CNN effect   232

## DISCUSSION QUESTIONS

1. Discuss some of the main structural features of the new global security structure.
2. Discuss several ways in which economic developments in the last 20 years have contributed to a weakening of U.S. power.
3. Would you prefer to see the Obama administration pursue a multilateral strategy or unilateral strategy to manage the global security structure? Note the benefits and drawbacks of each approach.
4. Outline some of the security threats and issues that international organizations deal with. Discuss why IOs do not have more success in these sorts of issues and what it would take for them to be more successful.
5. Choose a security threat of your own and assess the IOs dealing with that issue.
6. Choose a security threat in the developing nations and examine:
   a. The primary political, economic, and social causes of the conflict
   b. The extent of other state and IO involvement in the issue
   c. Some possible solutions to the problem.

## SUGGESTED READINGS

Michael Barnett. *Eyewitness to Genocide: The United Nations and Rwanda.* Ithaca, NY: Cornell University Press, 2000.

David Calleo. *Follies of Power: America's Unipolar Fantasy.* New York: Cambridge University Press, 2009.

Amy Chua. *World on Fire: How Exporting Free Market Democracy Breeds Ethnic Hatred and Global Instability.* New York: Anchor Books, 2003.

Chalmers Johnson. *The Sorrows of Empire: Militarism, Secrecy, and the End of the Republic.* New York: Metropolitan Books, 2004.

Brigette Nacos. *Terrorism and Counterterrorism: Understanding Threats and Responses in the Post-9/11 World.* New York: Pearson Longman, 2006.

Joseph Nye. *The Paradox of American Power: Why the World's Only Superpower Can't Go It Alone.* New York: Oxford University Press, 2002.

Thomas E. Ricks. *Fiasco: The American Military Adventure in Iraq.* New York: Penguin, 2006.

# NOTES

1. The classic study outlining the principles of realism is Hans Morgenthau, *Politics Among Nations: The Search for Power and Peace*, 3rd ed. (New York: Knopf, 1960).
2. See John Mearsheimer, *The Tragedy of Great Powers* (New York: W. W. Norton, 2001).
3. See Robert Kagan, "The Benevolent Empire," *Foreign Policy, 111* (Summer 1998), pp. 24–49.
4. For a discussion of neoconservatives, see Francis Fukuyama, *America at the Crossroads: Democracy, Power, and the Neconservative Legacy* (New Haven, CT: Yale University Press, 2006).
5. For a thoughtful, concise analysis of the Iraq War see James DeFronzo, *The Iraq War: Origins and Consequences* (Boulder, CO: Westview Press, 2009).
6. See, for example, Josef Joffe, *Überpower: The Imperial Temptation of America* (New York: W. W. Norton, 2006).
7. See Thomas E. Ricks. *Fiasco: The American Military Adventure in Iraq* (New York: Penguin, 2006).
8 For an analysis of the importance to U.S. foreign policy of understanding religion and Islamic political movements in the Muslim world, see Juan Cole, *Engaging the Muslim World* (New York: Palgrave Macmillan, 2009).
9. See Alissa Ruben, "Afghans Detail U.S. Detention in 'Black Jail,' " *The New York Times*, November 29, 2009.
10. Some important books about empire-building are: Clyde Prestowitz, *Rogue Nation: American Unilateralism and the Failure of Good Intentions* (New York: Basic Books, 2003); and Michael Mann, *Incoherent Empire* (London: Verso, 2003).
11. See Neil Smith, *The Endgame of Globalization* (New York: Routledge, 2005), p. 182.
12. See Chalmers Johnson, *The Sorrows of Empire: Militarism, Secrecy, and the End of the Republic* (New York: Routledge 2005),p.182.
13. See, for example, William Hartung and Michelle Ciarocca, "The Military-Industrial-Think Tank Complex," *Multinational Monitor,* January/February 2003.
14. Neil Smith, *The Endgame of Globalization* (New York: Routledge, 2005).
15. See Joseph Nye, *The Paradox of American Power: Why the World's Only Superpower Can't Go It Alone* (New York: Oxford University Press, 2002).
16. See Roger C. Altman, "The Great Crash, 2008: A Geopolitical Setback for the West," *Foreign Affairs, 88* (January/February 2009).
17. This issue is discussed at some length in Moisés Naím, "The Five Wars of Globalization," *Foreign Policy, 134* (January/February 2003), pp. 29–39.
18. See Boutros Boutros-Ghali, "Empowering the United Nations," *Foreign Affairs, 71* (Winter 1992/1993), pp. 98–99.
19. See David Rieff, "The Illusions of Peacekeeping," *World Policy Journal, 11* (Fall 1994), pp. 1–18.
20. An excellent read on the UN's role in Rwanda is Michael Barnett, *Eyewitness to Genocide: The United Nations and Rwanda* (Ithaca, NY: Cornell University Press, 2000).
21. For a more detailed overview of terrorism in general, see Brigitte Nacos, *Terrorism and Counterterrorism: Understanding Threats and Responses in the Post-9/11 World*, 3rd ed. (New York: Pearson Longman, 2009).
22. Charles Ferguson, "Tackling the Risks of Nuclear Terrorism," *The Seattle Times*, April 26, 2006.
23. Detailed summaries and analysis of the ongoing trial can be found at www.charlestaylortrial.org.
24. See Amy Chua, *World on Fire: How Exporting Free Market Democracy Breeds Ethnic Hatred and Global Instability* (New York: Anchor Books, 2003).
25. Thomas Friedman, "The Global Economy and U.S. Foreign Policy," public address at the University of Puget Sound, Tacoma, WA, September 17, 2002.
26. For a good overview of this argument see Oswaldo De Rivero, *The Myth of Development: The Non-Viable Economies of the 21st Century* (New York: Zed Books, 2001).
27. This is one of the themes of Amy Chua, *World on Fire: How Exporting Free Market Democracy Breeds Ethnic Hatred and Global Instability* (New York: Anchor Books, 2003).
28. See, for example, Norman Solomon, "Mass Media: Aiding and Abetting Militarism," in Carl Boggs, ed., *The Masters of War* (New York: Routledge, 2003).

# The Knowledge and Technology Structure[1]

Pinning our hopes on technology.

Corbis DWF 15-1562

Have you ever illegally downloaded a song or a movie? If so, you're in good company. Since its founding in 2003, Swedish-based The Pirate Bay has attracted millions of surfers looking for copyrighted material for free. Using BitTorrent technology, the site made it simple to find and share digitized files with almost anyone in the world. By 2008, it was listed as one of the 100 most popular sites in the world, with an average of 25 million users per month. It became the bête noire of Hollywood studios and global entertainment companies who repeatedly sued it. In April 2009, a Swedish court found several of the brash young Swedish men running the site guilty of copyright violation and ordered them to pay damages and go to jail. Although at the time of this writing Pirate Bay was still running, it claimed to have switched to a new technology to connect file sharers in a decentralized, trackerless manner. In the furor following the court case, the Swedish Pirate Party, a new political party that advocates limiting copyrights to five years, encouraging file sharing, and getting rid of patents, won 7 percent of the national vote in Sweden to gain a seat in the European Parliament.

The Pirate Bay saga is one of many examples of high-stakes global struggles over knowledge and technology. Individuals around the world seek access to knowledge and knowledge-based products at a low price, and sometimes they are willing to defy laws to get what they believe is their due. Companies that produce knowledge-based goods want to profit from their investments and use technology to keep up with their competitors. States have an interest in nurturing a knowledgeable population and ensuring that they foster innovation in order to secure themselves and maintain a comparative advantage in various industries. Knowledge is the site of political, economic, and social battles that are shaping the future of competition, freedom, and security in ever-changing ways.

In this chapter we examine the **international knowledge structure**—a set of rules, practices, institutions, and bargains that determines who owns and can make use of knowledge and technology, where, how, and on what terms. This structure is rapidly growing and evolving, which adds an exciting dynamic element to it. It profoundly affects the other structures we have examined: trade and production, finance, and security. Knowledge helps determine which countries produce what goods and services, the kind and amount of capital inflows they attract, and their ability to protect themselves from enemies and provide for the basic needs of their citizens.

In the first section, we define the knowledge structure, the actors in it, and some of the issues at stake. Next, we analyze how state and companies work within the knowledge structure to generate innovation and technological advancement. In a related fashion, we also look at the political struggles between states to generate and benefit from highly educated, skilled workers. In the second half of the chapter, the focus turns to **Intellectual Property Rights (IPRs)**, one of the most important new battlefields in the knowledge structure. After defining IPRs—especially patents, copyrights, and trademarks—and the rules protecting them internationally, we analyze the ways in which developed states use them to promote their economic and political interests. We also survey how developing countries are contesting the rules to better serve their efforts to catch up to the world's economic powers. Finally, we contrast the different theoretical perspectives about the benefits and drawbacks, and fairness and inequity, in the system that controls IPRs. As will be clear, the knowledge structure is subject to enormous economic strains and political resistance, creating the likelihood that the winners and losers in it will constantly reshape its contours.

It is said that "knowledge is power." Individuals, businesses, and nations that control access to knowledge in the form of scientific understanding, technological innovation, and knowledge-intensive products and services can often enjoy a clear competitive advantage in the world market, allowing them to dominate political and economic processes. Throughout the chapter we show how these processes play out. In so doing, we posit that there are four important trends in the knowledge structure that have become apparent over the last 20 years. These trends will affect your life and your country's destiny in profound, unsettling, and potentially liberating ways.

First, liberals and mercantilists agree that knowledge and technology have become increasingly important determinants of wealth and power. Economic success and military might are less dependent on control of land or natural resources and much more based on human capital and technological prowess in such areas as engineering, information and communication systems, and basic scientific research.

Second, the pace of technological change has quickened. Companies that cannot invest in research, innovate, and adapt to rapid change will fall behind. Sources of profits in the global economy are shifting away from producers to those who control the knowledge of *how* to produce; who finance, design, and market new products; and who control the *distribution* of knowledge-intensive goods and services.

Third, knowledge is increasingly dispersed but interconnected and therefore harder for any one country to control or monopolize. Countries that maintain openness to global flows of people, goods, and investment—as advocated by economic liberals—will likely benefit from these characteristics of knowledge. However, mercantilists are probably right that governments play a critical role in shaping how well their country will benefit from interconnected knowledge by using subsidies, selective protectionism, and limited monopolies on intellectual property.

Finally, there is a growing tension globally between owners of IPRs and individuals who believe that many forms of knowledge should be "free" or in the public domain. International intellectual property rules that ignore social demands for low-cost or free music, software, movies, news, and medicines will be virtually impossible to enforce. Intellectual property (IP) holders who want more rights and stricter controls face a monumental battle with IP users who want unlimited access, freedom of use, and a redistribution of social benefits from technology.

## THE INTERNATIONAL KNOWLEDGE STRUCTURE: ACTORS AND RULES

The international knowledge structure is a web of rules and practices that determine how knowledge is generated, commercialized, and controlled. *Knowledge* is an umbrella term we apply to many different things, including ideas, technology, information, and intellectual property. Ideas are ethereal, different from traded goods, money, or security. They can be exchanged between people by means of language, education, and cultural practices. Technology is a specific kind of knowledge about how to create and use material objects. It is knowledge of the process or method by which to produce goods and services or to solve problems and to apply science for useful commercial purposes. Information can be thought of as data, news, or entertainment that people consume and recombine to serve economic, cultural, or political purposes. And intellectual property consists of inventions, artistic works, and words and symbols that governments have granted monopoly rights to for limited periods. All of these forms of knowledge have value or can be used to make valuable goods and services.

As you can imagine, there are many rules—whether explicit or implicit—that govern the flows of knowledge around the world. The rules create rights, privileges, incentives, prohibitions, guarantees, and penalties for countries, businesses, and consumers. They determine who can get what advantages and on what terms from knowledge. Many of these rules are created by powerful countries and alliances of business interests that seek to convince the rest of the world of the legitimacy and benefits of these controls. At the same time, many social forces resist these rules through political action, lobbying, negotiation, and even criminality.

One of the sets of rules we look at is national laws and regulations. These include laws about granting of patents or copyrights, educational access, or freedom of information. Rules also come in the form of bilateral and multilateral treaties that determine what obligations a state has toward the intellectual property of other countries. There are also many international agreements on the transfer of technology, technology standards for globally traded products, and cooperation on the use of knowledge to solve global health and environmental problems. A third set of rules and patterns concern business practices. These can include the ways that companies engage in research and development, share information, and profit from their knowledge. The final set of rules is what can be called shared norms or understandings about the appropriate use of knowledge and the moral rights and obligations of producers and consumers of knowledge. These norms change over time and vary significantly across countries and socioeconomic groups.

While there are many actors that shape and are affected by the international knowledge structure, we will focus on four levels of actors: individuals, companies, states, and international organizations. Individuals navigate the knowledge structure mostly as consumers of knowledge. They seek to educate themselves, access entertainment products, and use technology to engage in political action or better their lives. They tend to view knowledge as a basic human right, and they often resist or try to circumvent rules that other actors place in the way of their access. Companies bring individuals together to produce and commercialize knowledge. As profit-making entities, they are keen to control the knowledge they produce, and they constantly need technology to innovate and compete successfully in the global market. States generally want to foster technological development and preserve knowledge-based advantages over other states. Whether they can do so depends on their ability to reconcile the competing demands of individuals and companies and to get other countries to comply with certain rules. Finally, at the global level IOs enforce rules about knowledge, help countries access knowledge, and teach countries how to cooperate with others. Also, many NGOs are trying to change the knowledge structure to better serve the interests of the poor, the exploited, and the vulnerable.

What makes the international knowledge structure especially important today is the extent to which it interacts with the other IPE structures and thus conditions all IPE relationships. The role of knowledge and technology in the security structure was noted in Chapter 9. For example, the strategy of nuclear deterrence was chosen by the United States in the early postwar years in part because technology made nuclear weapons appear to be less costly than conventional weapons.

The high costs of the arms race, which was also a technology race, contributed to the pressures that brought the Cold War to an end in the late 1980s.

Knowledge and technology have had huge effects on the international financial structures discussed in Chapters 7 and 8. Advances in information and communication technology (ICT) have resulted in a borderless, lightly regulated global financial system using complex financial instruments such as derivatives.

Knowledge also conditions the international production structure, which we defined in Chapter 6 as the set of relationships that determine what is produced, where, how, for whom, and on what terms. Advances in technology and knowledge regulation mean that new goods and services are being produced in new places, in new ways, and distributed in new ways to consumers all over the world. For example, innovations in transportation technology like containerization made it possible to shift many manufacturing processes to Asia with worldwide distribution.

Consider some of the consequences of rapid technological change in the production structure. Firms in today's competitive world market find themselves on an innovation treadmill. Success requires constant development of new products and process technologies. The ability to protect technological innovations from immediate imitation is therefore critical. Without patent, trademark, and copyright protection, firms would find it difficult to recoup investment in new technologies. Nations also struggle to become or remain competitive in the new world economy. Clearly, winning or even holding their own in this game will require nations to develop or have access to the newest and best technology.

# THE IPE OF INNOVATION AND TECHNOLOGY ADVANCEMENT

In this section, we examine the conditions under which countries generate technological change and innovation, and how they struggle to turn that knowledge into comparative advantage in the global economy. First, we will examine the ways in which today's developed countries have tried to foster and control **research and development (R&D)**. We will find a surprisingly large role of the state in coordination with market actors. Second, we will look at how developing countries have tried to close the knowledge gap with wealthier countries by gaining a bigger share of global production and accelerating technology transfer. Third, we will examine the mercantilist struggles by the United States and the European Union to attract and retain the world's most highly educated and skilled workers, whose knowledge and creativity are vital for future competitiveness in high-tech manufacturing, services, and research.

A key historical and theoretical question for political economists is this: What have been the appropriate roles for governments and market actors in fostering innovation and accumulation of knowledge? Economic liberals believe that regardless of a country's level of development, private companies should be the primary drivers of innovation through R&D investment protected by IPRs. Mercantilists point out the vital importance of governments in creating the institutions and policies that make an economy able to generate, commercialize, and control new knowledge.

Structuralists contend that states and markets appropriate the knowledge of workers and indigenous people, distributing the fruits of innovation unfairly and inequitably.

As we have seen in discussions about the current financial crisis, trade policy, and the environment, a growing number of political economists such as Joseph Stiglitz, Ha-Joon Chang, and Dani Rodrik believe that states need flexibility to craft policies in sync with their level of development and particular national needs. With regard to knowledge governance, they argue that one size does not fit all in the area of technology policies. In analysis of contemporary and historical practices of developed countries and newly industrializing countries, it has become clear that successful innovation requires extensive coordination between states and markets. How these different actors coordinate, what the relative balance of their contributions is, and how they redistribute resources will profoundly determine a nation's trajectory. Some states try to substitute for the private sector in research and development, some partner with it in a variety of ways, and some simply clear away obstacles in the way of potential private innovators.

Many states view knowledge as a double-edged sword. They want to nurture those who turn technological innovations into products and services exchanged in our international system. They also want to spread knowledge around the world by educating foreigners in their universities and encouraging investments overseas and outsourcing by their TNCs. But at the same time many nations are selfish about their knowledge and technology, intent on staying one step ahead of rivals in innovative fields and in military technologies. They sometimes find it difficult to balance the interests of producers and consumers of knowledge.

## Government Innovation Policies in Developed Countries

Technologically advanced countries are playing a game of global "keep-up," not "catch-up." They want to stay competitive in knowledge-based industries and nurture **"creative industries,"** where value added per worker is high and positive spillovers into other sectors of the economy are great. Some of these signature industries include design, arts and entertainment, biotechnology, health-care technology, and defense. Innovation is premised on political openness, vast educational opportunities, labor mobility, and other characteristics that only a limited number of countries can quickly turn to their advantage.

These nations recognize that technological growth has historically been a key determinant of economic growth. For example, in the nineteenth century the U.S. government founded land-grant colleges throughout the country to spur innovation in agriculture, industry, and engineering. More recently, for example, "advances in knowledge" accounted for an estimated 68 percent of the increase in U.S. labor productivity and 28 percent of the growth in U.S. income between 1929 and 1982. While technological innovation is largely the product of investment in research and development by individual firms, governments have tried to nurture this by subsidizing basic science research at universities and providing incentives to private manufacturers to turn research into profitable products.

Some of the specific ways in which states foster innovation and knowledge-intensive industries are public spending and subsidies, regulation, controls on technology exports, and IPR enforcement (discussed later in this chapter). Building or financing a technology infrastructure is something many states have done historically, often in times of national emergency or interstate rivalry. Massive U.S. investment in the Manhattan Project during World War II gave the country superiority in nuclear technology. As part of its political rivalry with the Soviet Union during the Cold War, the Apollo Project boosted American leadership in space technology. U.S. military spending has played a vital role in the development of satellite technology and the Internet. From 1990 to 2003, the U.S. Department of Energy and the National Institutes of Health funded the Human Genome Project, which had major benefits for commercial innovation in molecular medicine and the life sciences industries.

Governments often identify new R&D needs and provide resources for huge leaps forward beyond the scope of individual firms in areas such as energy innovation, medical research, and fusion. This can be done by direct funding to universities, government research labs, and private companies. Sociologist Henry Etzkowitz stresses the importance of this funding and the cooperation it induces to produce a "triple helix"—a university–industry–government relationship that accelerates innovation.[2] For example, the Bayh-Dole Act of 1980 gave U.S. universities and federal labs the right to gain patents on inventions funded with public money and sell or license those IPRs to private companies. Examples of government-assisted innovation include Gatorade (developed at the University of Florida and now licensed to Quaker Oats), Google online searching (hatched at Stanford University), and storm-tracking radar (developed at MIT).

In a related fashion, many governments have programs to provide "venture capital" to small private firms with promising new technology. In 1958, the U.S. government created an agency within the Department of Defense called the U.S. Defense Advanced Research Projects Agency (DARPA) to fund research by industries and universities into technology of use to the military. Technological spin-offs that its sponsored research helped develop include the Internet, virtual memory, computer networking, integrated circuit design, and voice-to-text software.

In the United States, the federal government after World War II funded about two-thirds of all R&D, but in recent decades this has declined to one-third as private industry has bolstered investment. In the OECD countries, about 70 percent of R&D is now funded by businesses. In 2003 the United States led in overall combined government–private R&D, accounting for 36 percent of global R&D spending, compared to 25 percent by the EU15, and 14 percent by Japan (adjusted for PPP).[3] In 2006 the United States accounted for 42 percent of total R&D spending in the OECD. In 1990, it gave the most generous tax incentives for R&D, but many other countries in the OECD are now more generously supporting R&D via tax incentives. R&D has become more internationalized since the 1990s. Transnational corporations are beginning to shift some of it to countries like China and India, because of their large markets and large pools of skilled but low-cost researchers.

Scholars Jakob Edler and Luke Georghiou argue that public procurement has been an important means by which governments generate demand for innovative products by being a direct purchaser ("lead user") of them.[4] Or governments create incentives like tax rebates for consumers and businesses to purchase innovative products, thus encouraging faster commercialization of them by private producers. One example of this is so-called "green procurement," where consumers get long-term loans or rebates from the government to install energy-saving appliances, install solar panels on their homes (in California at least), or get "cash-for-clunkers" for trading up for cleaner, gas-saving cars.

Besides funding R&D, some governments help private sector actors cooperate with one another and create uniform standards. Sometimes this involves forcing companies to share their patents with others. The United States did this during World War I to spur the aircraft industry and afterward among radio manufacturers. Governments can also help private companies identify and establish common standards so that commercialization of technology quickens. Such was the case with standards for MPEG-2 technology, HDTV, and wireless communication.

Like the United States, the EU has taken an aggressive approach to building a knowledge-based, competitive economy. As laid out in its 2000 Lisbon Strategy, the EU seeks to increase research spending—mostly by the private sector—to equal at least 3 percent of EU GDP by 2010. The EU27 realize that they have an "innovation performance deficit" compared with other OECD countries. Their 2008 Global Innovation Scoreboard, a comparison of national innovation performance around the world, showed that in 2005 the top 10 scorers were Sweden, Switzerland, Finland, Israel, Japan, the United States, Denmark, Korea, Canada, and Germany—only four of which are EU members.

In addition to fostering innovation, developed states seek to prevent the diffusion of some forms of advanced technology to other countries. During the Cold War, the United States worked hard to deny the Soviet Union access to American technology that could have military use. The United States still has many export controls on weapons systems (and information related to them), nuclear technology and materials, and dual-use technologies that could help enemies or economic competitors like China. The control system is based on licenses and approvals for certain lists of exports, but it also requires multilateral cooperation among allies.

The United States also has "deemed export controls" that limit the transfer of export-controlled items or protected technical information to foreigners working or studying in the United States. Universities or private contractors with this kind of information have to obtain licenses to allow foreigners to access this information, particularly if the institutions get federal funding. But as the global economy changes, it is a lot harder for any country to control the spread of information. The technology behind military items is often the same as behind dynamic and competitive civilian commercial technology. Export controls hamper the ability of U.S.-based firms to compete globally and conduct joint research with firms in some other countries.

## Closing the Knowledge and Technology Gap

Many processes of innovation and technological change occur without any specific state role; they result from the individual decisions of millions of companies or as a result of processes inherent in global capitalism. For example, high-tech (knowledge) industries have been termed **Schumpeterian industries**—after Joseph Schumpeter (1883–1950). Schumpeter believed that only firms with some degree of monopoly power would likely have the *incentive* (a large payback resulting from a long imitation lag) and the *ability* (in the form of monopoly profits) to invest in risky, expensive, and long-term R&D projects. Consequently, many key industries were likely to be monopolistically structured. However, over time, technologically audacious newcomers would displace once-dominant firms. "Gales of creative destruction" would destroy established monopolies and create new dominant firms.

Because of economies of large scale (including network economies), competition in many industries today is not for market share but for the market itself—competition becomes a "winner take all" or at least a "winner take most" proposition. This reality has obvious political-economic implications, particularly from a mercantilist perspective, in which the location of that dominant firm is of paramount concern. In order to foster the development of national champions that dominate Schumpeterian industries, mercantilist-minded policy makers will put in place industrial policies that marshal the resources and power of the state to this end. Even liberal-minded policy makers will recognize the importance of creating conditions within their countries that will promote the development of entrepreneurs capable of competing in Schumpeterian industries—conditions described in Michael Porter's best seller *The Competitive Advantage of Nations.*[5] The ability to acquire, create, and control technology has become central to international competition in the twenty-first century and has provided many developing countries with a new avenue into the world economy.

Political economist Raymond Vernon has discussed another way in which markets diffuse technology around the world. He observed that some of the products that the United States once produced and even exported were eventually produced abroad and became imports. This product life cycle (from export to import) is in part based on the interaction of product and process innovation. The United States—with its individualistic, liberal IPE perspective—has for years been especially strong in **product innovation,** or the development of new or better products. U.S. firms invent new products, develop them for the home market, and eventually export some of their production to other countries with similar needs.

Other nations such as Japan have shown success in **process innovation**—the development of more efficient, lower-cost production techniques. As process innovation is applied, production is shifted abroad from U.S. factories. The new producer may be an especially innovative firm in Japan, or it could be a low-cost producer in a newly industrialized country (NIC) or a less developed country (LDC), especially if innovation has standardized the product and simplified its construction. The cycle is completed when the United States then ends up importing at low cost the item it once exported.

The cycle that Vernon described has rapidly accelerated in the last 20 years to produce what we refer to as the globalization of production, and while it is substantially a market-driven process, governments in developing economies now have a much more direct role in making it happen and managing its effects. The United States, the European Union, and Japan are quickly learning that they will no longer easily dominate the product cycle because many product and process innovators are mushrooming in places like China and India. Through partnerships between government and business, investment in education, and acquisition of technology from foreign sources, the Asian "Tigers" now compete head-to-head for world market share in high-value-added goods with U.S. and European firms.

Political economists such as Gary Gereffi analyze more complex, contemporary forms of the product cycle called **global value chains,** which account for "the full range of activities that firms and workers do to bring a product from its conception to its end use and beyond."[6] Many different firms in different countries are linked in a set of relationships (or a division of labor) that leads to the delivery of goods and services. The high-value functions that Western firms engage in along the chain have been finance, basic research, design, product branding, and marketing, while the low-value functions performed in developing countries are low-wage manufacturing, subcontracting, and raw material extraction and processing. LDCs want to move up the value chain to more profitable activities, but to do so they need to close the technology gap with developed countries by ensuring a rapid diffusion of knowhow in their societies.

Taiwan and Korea have followed Japan's example for how to move up the value chain to capture more profit. They created national champions through deliberate industrial policy and strategic trade policies, among other things (see Chapters 6 and 11). Their companies started out by manufacturing or assembling parts and components for global corporations. Then their companies began to engage more in product design and upgraded their manufacturing technology. Finally, they became leaders in some industries, accumulating patents and copyrights and manufacturing their own brands. At this stage, their companies are global players in their own right like Taiwan's Acer and Korea's Samsung, LG, and Hyundai.

China and, to a lesser extent, India are following the Japanese and Korean model of creating national champions through deliberate industrial policy and transfer of technology. China is encouraging much more R&D within national companies and buying overseas high-tech assets like IBM's PC division, called Lenovo since 2004. The Chinese, Indians, and others in Asia are determined to attract cutting-edge research. Singapore is becoming a biomedical research center. China is rapidly becoming a leading manufacturer of solar panels. High-tech and medium-tech manufacturing exports represent a significant share of exports for China and Brazil (as in Japan, Germany, Ireland, and the United States). Overseas research labs are popping up in China and India. And multinationals are also outsourcing high-skill tasks to these countries like software development, engineering services, and drug testing.

## Struggles over Education and Skilled Workers

Innovative societies require more than just spending on R&D and good institutions; they need well-educated and skilled professionals who can create innovative businesses and generate valuable intellectual property. The United States has had the best of both worlds since World War II: a strong educational system and the ability to attract highly skilled workers. It is trying to hold on to this edge, while other OECD countries are trying to attract more foreign skilled workers. Developing countries like India and China are producing more highly trained workers and trying to keep them from choosing to emigrate permanently (see Chapter 16). Struggles over knowledge embodied in people involve higher education policies and visa policies.

Labor mobility within a country is a critical contributor to an innovative society, particularly the ability of well-trained individuals to move from one company to another and to set up new businesses. Economists have found a lot of innovation in regional high-tech clusters like Silicon Valley and North Carolina's Research Triangle with high labor mobility. Similarly, innovation is spurred by in-migration from other countries, that is, international labor mobility.

The United States has harnessed foreign knowledge by attracting able students to its institutions of higher education. In 2008–2009 there were 671,000 foreign students in American universities, a record high number.[7] Almost 40 percent of these students came from the top three sending countries: India, China, and South Korea. Almost half of all students were studying business, engineering, and physical and life sciences. Foreign students make up a vital percentage of all students in graduate programs in the United States. More than half of engineering PhD degrees awarded each year go to foreign nationals. In 2006, 45 percent of PhD graduates in physical, computer, and life sciences were foreign-born.

The U.S. economy benefits tremendously from harnessing the skills of these graduates who remain in the United States and enter the labor force, often with permanent residency. In a testament to their importance, INTEL chief Andrew Grove said once that the government should staple a Green Card to the diploma of every foreign student graduating in the United States! According to Vivek Wadhwa, "During the closing decades of the 20th century, roughly 80 percent of the Chinese and Indians who earned U.S. PhDs in science, technology, engineering, and mathematics (STEM) fields have stayed in the United States and provided a critical boost to the nation's economy."[8] He found that 25 percent of engineering and technology companies founded between 1995 and 2005 in the United States had at least one key foreign-born founder.[9] The vast majority of these companies, many founded by Indians, were in software and innovation/manufacturing-related services. In Silicon Valley specifically, half of all start-up companies in engineering and technology between 1995 and 2005 were founded by immigrants.

Other indicators demonstrate the importance of U.S. ethnic scientific communities to innovation and commercialization of products in high-tech and professional fields. Foreign nationals in the United States have received a large number of U.S. patents. Census data show that in the United States 30 percent of computer software developers are foreign nationals.[10] One-third of foreign-born engineers and architects in the workforce came from just five Asian countries. Twenty percent of engineers and architects and 15 percent of nurses in the United States are foreign-born. And more than 400,000 Europeans with science and technology degrees work in the United States, attracted by better salaries, more funding, and better opportunities for advancement than in the EU.[11]

A changing global economy, however, means that the United States has to compete more than ever for the best foreign students and skilled workers. China and India churn out many more undergraduate and graduate students than the United States in engineering and IT and computer science. From only 3.4 million university students in 1998, by 2008 China had 21.5 million.[12] U.S. industries complain that the U.S. government does not issue enough H-1B work visas for highly talented foreigners.

Many foreign students are returning home after studying or working in the United States, mitigating a lot of the previous brain drain. Their return is a very important mechanism of technology transfer. Many are working in new research labs in their home countries set up by the likes of IBM, GE, and Cisco. TNCs in OECD countries have been increasing their R&D expenditures abroad (see Chapter 17).

The return home of foreign students says as much about the relative decline of the United States as it does about the rise of India and China. In 2008, Wadhwa used *LinkedIn* to survey almost 1,200 high-skilled young professional Indians and Chinese who had returned to their home countries after working or studying in the United States. The vast majority of those surveyed indicated that opportunities for professional advancement were better at home and that they could find a better quality of life and better "family values" in their native country than in the United States.[13] This indicates the rising standard of living for the upper classes in these rising powers (see Chapter 13). Clearly the "land of opportunity" has a lot of new competition.

## THE IPE OF INTELLECTUAL PROPERTY RIGHTS

In addition to R&D and technology, IPRs are a key component of the knowledge structure today. Intellectual property rights are the rights to control use of intellectual property—an invention or a creative work such as a novel or poem. Patents, copyrights, trademarks, and other systems of IPRs are the mechanisms normally used to govern access to new ideas. There are also other forms of IPRs that many states have assigned to such things as geographic indications, industrial designs, trade secrets, databases, and the publicity rights of celebrities.

IPRs are government-granted rights, often for a limited amount of time, to control the use of an invention, a creative output, or the name of a product or company. The kinds of things many states deem worthy of granting rights to has varied significantly over the last 200 years, as has the strength and length of protection. These rights have always been the product of political and economic struggles within and between countries. Control of these rights in ideas and the products that are associated with them has important effects on innovation, profits, access to knowledge, and the distribution of wealth.

Historically different countries have had many different rules and standards regarding IPRs, and often they did not respect the IPRs of other countries. In a global economy, however, IPRs have become a more critical issue both for those nations that own patents, copyrights, and so on and for those nations that seek to use them to produce goods and services. There are a number of ways in which countries coordinate their IPR policies, such as through the **Trade-Related Aspects of Intellectual Property Rights (TRIPs)** agreement of the WTO, which requires countries to provide some minimum level of IPR protection and enforcement. However, global actors will have to grapple with the many differences in national regulations of IP. Many officials struggle over when and under what conditions these rights can be overridden to protect the general public and the poor.

We begin by explaining some of the main forms of intellectual property—patents, copyrights, and trademarks. It is important to remember that individual states define specific forms of IP in different ways that reflect historical differences in their laws, legal traditions, and political evolution.

**Patents** are issued by a government and confer the exclusive right to make, use, or sell an invention for a period usually of 20 years (counted from date of filing). Governments give these rights in order to encourage scientific research and innovation. Without these rights, many companies would be unable to capture all of the benefits of their R&D expenditures. While the criteria for gaining a patent vary from one country to another, usually the invention must be new, useful (have some kind of industrial application), and be nonobvious to someone who is skilled in the field. In exchange for the temporary monopoly on the use of the invention, an inventor must disclose the details of it in writing to the public. Companies can amass considerable revenues from creating new patent-protected products. Companies can also license the use of their patents to others or sell the patents.

Patent rights are not unlimited. Countries place limits on what is patentable. For example, the EU members do not offer patents for computer programs, methods for treatment of the human body, or inventions whose commercial exploitation conflict with morality or violate public policy. Governments reserve the right to override patents in some circumstances such as when patent holders abuse their market power by acting like a monopoly or cartel. Governments can issue a compulsory license, which allows a firm to use someone's patent without their permission in exchange for a specified payment to the patent owner. And governments will sometimes override patents in times of national emergency such as war.

**Copyrights** protect the *expression* of an idea, not the idea itself. Copyright protection is provided to authors of original works, including literary, artistic, and scientific works. This includes books, movies, television programs, music, magazines, photographs—and even software and databases in a growing number of countries. Copyrights generally allow the owner to prevent the unauthorized reproduction, distribution (including rental), and sale of original work. The WTO TRIPs agreement requires members to offer copyright protection that lasts at least the life of the author plus 50 years. In the United States and Europe, protection lasts for the life of the author plus 70 years—and in the United States corporate works (works for hire) are protected for 95 years. Lengths of copyright protection have grown longer in the last 100 years while the value of trade in copyrighted products has mushroomed. There is a growing debate about whether so many creative works should be kept out of the public domain for so long. In the United States, the major copyright industries—movies, music, book publishing, and software—contribute to about 6.4 percent of overall GDP—more than $890 billion.[14]

Like patents, copyrights are necessary to encourage innovation. Without this protection, rapid reproduction by rivals would diminish the return on investments in new creative works. Governments provide a number of exceptions to copyrights in the public interest; in other words, we can make use of copyrighted material in certain circumstances without asking permission from or paying the copyright holder. For example, it is considered "fair use" in many countries to reproduce or use a portion of a work for criticism, parody, news reporting, or teaching. Similarly, in most countries it is legal to reproduce or record a book, song, or TV program for personal, noncommercial use. After all, that's what a photocopier, a digital video disc (DVD) burner, and TiVo are mostly used for! And once we purchase a physical copy of a copyrighted item, we are free to sell it or rent it to whomever we want.

**Trademarks** are signs or symbols (including logos and names) registered by a manufacturer or merchant to identify goods and services. Protection is usually granted for 10 years and is renewable. A trademark gives a company the right to prevent others from using the symbol, name, expression, slogan, or even product shape. Examples of trademarks include the Nike swoosh, the brand name Kleenex, and MGM's lion's roar. In most countries, one cannot get a trademark for a term denoting kind, quality, value, or origin like "excellent," "extra," "cheap," or "Norwegian."

Trademarks are essential for the efficient functioning of the market. They help prevent unfair competition from imitators and consumer confusion about the true source or maker of a product. They help consumers select products of high quality and reliability and they motivate producers to maintain quality standards. Producers who do so know they will be rewarded with repeat purchases by consumers who have come to trust their trademark. Without adequate trademark protection, then, consumers will necessarily spend more hours attempting to discern quality differences, and producers will be discouraged from investing in the production of quality goods and services. Trademarks also convey information about a buyer and his or her social status.

Governments also assign IPRs to other kinds of things as well. Trade secrets are any information used in a business that has economic value and that the business actively tries to keep secret, such as the formula for Coke, Colonel Sanders' Secret Recipe, and lists of customers. **Geographical indications** identify a good as coming from a specific locale with some characteristic attributable to that locale. Examples are French cognac, champagne, and scotch. **Publicity rights** are the names, images, or identifying characteristics of famous persons. In some countries, celebrities can ban unauthorized depictions of themselves (with exceptions for activities like news reporting). These rights can be inherited or sold to third parties who want to use them for marketing. For example, Albert Einstein's publicity rights are owned by the Hebrew University in Israel, which has licensed the use of his name and image to Disney (for the Baby Einstein products), Nestlé (for a Japanese coffee), and Zambezi Ink (for an ad campaign for Nike's Zoom Kobe III sneakers).

## The Politics of IPRs in Developed Countries

The United States, the EU, and Japan have largely shaped the global rules governing IPRs. They have defined the nature and scope of IPRs, signed international agreements, and set up multilateral institutions to enshrine the rules in international relations. These countries seek to enforce these rules and expand them, using political power, international diplomacy, and threats. Much of the support for and resistance to strong IPRs is coming from powerful business, scholarly, and consumer groups of these countries.

The United States has taken the lead in promoting the protection of IPRs, under pressure to do so in the last 25 years from U.S. businesses. The Intellectual Property Committee, an ad hoc coalition of 12 major U.S. corporations representing the entire spectrum of industries, was established in 1986 and contended that there was a link between the protection of IPRs and U.S. international competitiveness. Without adequate protection of IPRs, U.S. firms would find it difficult to profit from product and process innovation. Foreign firms that infringe on IPRs have lower development costs because they are merely copying original technological innovations. Consequently, these infringing firms can underprice the U.S. firms that incurred the original development costs. The companies also painted a picture of an epidemic of piracy of entertainment media, and they estimated the overall losses to U.S. business from foreign infringement of IPRs in the tens of billions of dollars every year.

As political scientists Susan Sell and Aseem Prakash have documented, this movement was spearheaded by a network of individuals and companies mostly in the software, video, music, agricultural chemicals, and pharmaceutical industries to better protect American IP. They also developed alliances with similar companies in Europe to create powerful international lobbying efforts. They were very successful in framing IPRs as rights—not government-granted privileges—and in spreading a discourse about the dangers of "piracy" to free markets.[15]

Their most important goal was to create a set of enforceable international minimum standards for IPRs. In the 1980s there were already in existence multilateral agreements to protect IPRs including the Berne Convention, concluded in 1886 to define copyright protection, and the Paris Convention, signed by the United States in 1887, which ostensibly provides protection for patents, trademarks, and industrial designs. In 1967, the World Intellectual Property Organization (WIPO), a UN agency, was created to monitor adherence to these conventions. But the business networks and U.S. and European governments were dissatisfied with these agreements because they had low standards, did not have enforcement mechanisms, and did not include many developing countries.

During the Uruguay round of trade negotiations from 1986 to 1994, the United States and other developed nations insisted on the establishment of a new treaty on TRIPs, which WTO members would be obliged to accept, along with the new GATS and the revised GATT. TRIPs requires countries to provide a minimum level of intellectual property protection and adhere to the Berne and Paris Conventions. Special concessions were also negotiated for developing countries that need time to amend IPR laws in order to conform to the minimum standards.

TRIPs was a coup for major IP producers in developed countries, because it tied IP protection to participation in the liberalized international trade system. Many developing countries did not particularly like the agreement and had little role in crafting it, but accepted it as a price to pay for gaining other trade benefits within the WTO. TRIPs expanded the kinds of IP protected to include geographical indications (GIs), plant varieties, and trade secrets. Developed countries especially liked TRIPs because it had a mechanism for binding dispute resolution and required countries to enforce IPRs.

Not surprisingly, the developed nations have also supported the efforts spearheaded by the United States to enhance the international protection of IPRs beyond just the TRIPs standards. The WIPO has been a key forum outside the WTO where developed nations have sought to further cooperation. WIPO administers its own convention and some 24 international agreements on IPRs. It has an

Arbitration and Mediation Centre (WIPO Center) that can resolve disputes between private parties over domain names and cybersquatting. In 1996, WIPO produced two treaties that harmonize the protection of IPRs on the Internet and thereby promote international electronic commerce. In 2000 WIPO also adopted a Patent Law Treaty to harmonize patent application procedures across countries.

Under U.S. trade law, the government can impose unilateral retaliatory trade sanctions against countries that fail to protect IPRs adequately. Special Section 301 of the 1988 Omnibus Trade and Competition Act, generally called **Super 301**, requires the United States Trade Representative (USTR) to retaliate against countries that "deny adequate and effective protection of intellectual property rights" or "deny fair and equitable market access to United States persons that rely upon intellectual property protection." Super 301 requires the USTR to create a list every year of "priority foreign countries" that have failed to protect IPRs adequately. After investigating the policies of the offending country, the USTR may institute immediate trade sanctions or may choose to negotiate a bilateral agreement. The USTR also creates a "watch list" and a "priority watch list" for countries that have shortcomings in the protection of IPRs. The 2008 Special 301 Report includes an assessment of the effectiveness of intellectual property protections in 78 countries. Of those countries, 46 were placed on the priority watch list, the watch list, or were singled-out for special monitoring. Concerns regarding IPR protections in China and Russia received special attention in the report (see box "China: Coming of Age?")

## CHINA: COMING OF AGE?

China's rapid rise as an industrial power has transformed the international production and knowledge structures.[a] China has become the world's center for counterfeiting and piracy. The routine infringement of patents, trademarks, and copyrights by Chinese firms continues to be a major source of conflict between China and the United States. The most recent report by the USTR regarding Special 301 provisions highlights growing U.S. concerns over continuing piracy and counterfeiting in China.[b] By placing China on its "priority watch list," the United States is attempting to bring unilateral pressure on China to increase its enforcement of IPRs. The United States is also engaged in ongoing bilateral negotiations with China regarding IPRs and is working through WTO processes to bring multilateral pressure on China in this regard.[c]

Though China has recently tightened its enforcement of intellectual property laws, the effect on piracy and counterfeiting has been negligible. Chinese officials have been unwilling to this point to seriously crack down on factories that produce illegal copies because those plants are often major employers in towns and cities across China. Although some Chinese courts have awarded monetary damages to foreign firms that have been victimized by piracy, the IIPA calculates the losses to U.S. firms from illegal copying of music and business software in China at $3.5 billion in 2008.[d] Chinese piracy that limits the flow of U.S. exports to China also exacerbates the U.S. trade deficit with China.

As China further develops its own capacity to produce and export products and services incorporating new technologies, its interest in promoting the protection of IPRs should naturally increase. In April 2006, the Chinese government promulgated a new order requiring all computers sold in China to come with legitimate preloaded operating-system software. Shortly thereafter, Lenovo, the Chinese computer maker that recently bought IBM's PC business, announced a deal to purchase $1.2 billion of Microsoft's Windows software. Lenovo's chairman Yang Yuanqing noted that to help the growing number of Chinese technology companies compete around the world, China must implement measures to better protect intellectual property at home, thus providing the incentive to innovate.[e]

### References

[a]See "How China Runs the World Economy," *The Economist*, July 30, 2005, for a detailed account of China's growing economic influence.

[b]www.ustr.gov/sites/default/files/Full%20Version%20of%20the%202009%20SPECIAL%20301%20REPORT.pdf

[c]"U.S. Perfecting WTO Case against China IPR Violations—Commerce Undersecretary," *Forbes.com*, July 26, 2006, www.forbes.com/markets/feeds/afx/2006/07/26/afx2904774.html

[d]See www.iipa.com/rbc/2009/2009SPEC301PRC.pdf

[e]"Chinese PC Giant Takes on Big Role in Piracy Fight," *The Seattle Times*, April 18, 2006, p. C1.

With the stick of unilateral trade sanctions firmly in hand, the United States has successfully negotiated bilateral and regional agreements with many countries to improve the protection of IPRs. It has also signed free-trade agreements with about two dozen countries including Chile, Peru, Colombia, Korea, Singapore, and Morocco that require these countries to provide even more IP protection than the minimum provided by TRIPs. In 2004 the USTR signed the Dominican Republic-Central America-United States Free Trade Agreement (CAFTA-DR), a trade pact incorporating strong IPR protections with the Dominican Republic, Costa Rica, El Salvador, Guatemala, Honduras, and Nicaragua.

There has also been a concerted effort among developed nations to reach agreements to "harmonize" IPR laws across national boundaries. Separate from the WIPO or WTO, a voluntary agreement called the Anti-Counterfeiting Trade Agreement (ACTA) is being negotiated to create new enforcement standards for IP and to increase law enforcement cooperation across countries. Actions like these are part of what Susan Sell has described as an ongoing campaign by powerful political actors and business groups to ratchet up global IPR enforcement and tie counterfeiting and piracy to security issues, border control, lost business revenues, and lost taxes.[16]

Although developed countries are cooperating in important ways, conflict between and among them over IPRs still exists to a significant degree, given the centrality of knowledge and technology to competitive advantage. For example, the EU and the United States have divergent policies concerning database protection. The EU since 1996 has provided much stronger IPRs than the United States to producers of databases, who can prevent unauthorized "extraction" and "re-utilization" from the database for fifteen years. If the database is substantially updated, its holder can get another fifteen years of protection. Japan and the EU also provide protections for fashion designs (of clothing, bags, and accessories) for three and ten years, respectively, but the United States does not give rights to designers to allow them to prevent copies of their designs.

GIs have emerged as a new bone of contention between the Old World and the New World. The TRIPs agreement defines GIs as "indications which identify a good as originating in the territory of a Member, or a region or locality in that territory, where a given quality, reputation or other characteristic of the good is essentially attributable to its geographical origin." Examples include Champagne, Roquefort, Scotch, Vidalia onions, Florida oranges, Idaho potatoes, and Napa Valley wine. The GIs establish a relationship between a place of origin and the characteristics of a product, which are sometimes tied to the climate or the land. They are a collective monopoly given to producers in a specifically defined area. Often producers in the region can only use the GI if they are in the region and agree to a way of producing or using specified ingredients. One of the main justifications for them is that they prevent the public from being misled about the origin or quality of a product.

Since negotiations began on the TRIPs agreement, the European countries have insisted on strong GI protections, especially for wines and spirits. Europe has the largest number of historically well-known GIs. It has sought to use the GIs as a form of protection against competition from low-cost agricultural producers in the United States, Australia, and the New World who want to imitate the original products. If GIs are restricted to producers in a given region, that prevents other producers in the world from labeling their product as the same thing. In the face of resistance from the United States and Australia, the EU is even trying to "**claw back**" to GI protection the names of several dozen meats, cheeses, and alcoholic goods that are considered generic words, including Parmesan cheese, feta cheese, and chablis. Within the WTO, the EU has negotiated hard for an international register of GIs and an extension of the strong GI protection currently applying to wines and spirits to include other products like food.

In recent years, many countries outside of Europe have begun to warm to the idea of promoting their own GIs, through national laws and bilateral treaties. GIs like Basmati rice, tequila, Darjeeling tea, and Washington State apples can be used to protect important national products from competition, but also to create niche markets for artisanal products. As the size of global markets has increased, so has the potential market value of GIs. GIs can potentially encourage innovation in new artisanal markets, promote local industries, and encourage sustainable production and growing practices. Some see them as a way of resisting standardized, global brands that hurt small companies. GIs can protect and promote "authenticity," "heritage," and diversity of products.[17] Law scholar Madhavi Sunder calls GIs the "poor people's IPRs," because they can be used to promote and give more value to the collective contributions of farmers and craftspeople.[18] It seems likely that more and more countries will use GIs for a variety of purposes, including protectionism, export promotion, promoting small companies, and satisfying consumer demand for high-quality products.

## North–South Conflicts over Intellectual Property Rights

Developing nations have increasingly opposed the IPR norms and policies that developed countries promote. This resistance initially emerged in reaction to TRIPs but has spread to a much wider set of institutions and issues. One part of the opposition is to the minimum standards for protection of IP in TRIPs. LDCs want more flexibility to craft their *own* IP standards consistent with their level of development. They have forcefully demanded recognition of their right to make use of already-existing flexibilities in the TRIPs agreement like compulsory licensing of essential drugs. They have also sought to redefine some of the guiding principles of IP law to include promotion of human rights, public health, education, and cultural autonomy. Finally, some developing countries are seeking to extend IPRs to forms of knowledge that they can potentially obtain enormous benefits from, including biodiversity and traditional knowledge.

Developing countries have enunciated an alternative understanding of the goal of IPRs as promotion of development. In other words, they, along with many development agencies and NGOs, assert that provisions of TRIPs that hamper development should be resisted and that new development-enhancing policies should be incorporated into IP laws. These objectives are being pursued through the Development Agenda in WIPO. For the poorest countries, the WTO has granted an extended period of transition for implementation of the TRIPs requirements until at least 2016. But LDCs have not been happy with the WTO forum and have launched an alternative in the WIPO. In 2004, Argentina and Brazil spearheaded a Development Agenda for WIPO that was formally adopted by the WIPO General Assembly in 2007. The Agenda is a set of forty-five recommendations under which the WIPO is supposed to stress technology transfer to developing countries, recognize that IP rules should account for different levels of development, and recognize that IPRs should not just focus on economic growth but serve a variety of social and cultural goals.

There are no guarantees that developing countries will benefit from strengthening their systems of IPR protection. However, for those countries attempting to follow export-oriented development strategies, the risk of trade retaliation and the need to attract FDI provide strong incentives to comply with developed-country demands for stronger IPR protection. Developed countries have responded to some of the LDCs' foot-dragging in IP law implementation and enforcement through bilateral and multilateral efforts. At the bilateral level, they have pressured individual countries to do better by threatening trade penalties. The newest front is through negotiations over the ACTA, which were launched by OECD countries in 2007 outside of the WTO and the UN. This would be a type of freestanding agreement between countries with similar interests. It would be a set of voluntary standards of enforcement that developed countries will adopt to ratchet up the fight against counterfeit goods and copyright infringing actors, especially through border controls and actions by customs agencies.

## Debates over Patented Medicines

One of the most successful efforts to challenge the TRIPs agreement has been in the area of compulsory licensing, parallel imports, and access to medicines. Many poorer countries after 1994 felt that TRIPs unfairly limited their ability to issue compulsory licenses for the manufacture of lifesaving medicines that were under patent. A **compulsory license** is a license a state grants to a local party such as a private company or government body, with or without the consent of the right holder, to produce and sell a good under patent. **Parallel imports,** which are permitted under some circumstances by TRIPs, are imports of patented goods without the permission of the patent holder, who might be trying to sell the good at different prices in different countries. Compulsory licensing is allowable under the TRIPs if a government first negotiates with the patent holder or, in the case of a national emergency, without consulting the patent holder. TRIPs requires WTO members to offer patents on pharmaceutical products, not just processes for making drugs.

By the late 1990s, developing countries started to complain that the flexibilities under TRIPs to issue compulsory licenses were not easy to exercise. In the face of an HIV/AIDS epidemic, South Africa's government voted in 1998 to permit parallel imports of cheap generic antiretroviral drugs from India and to allow compulsory licensing of patented antiretrovirals in South Africa (see the box "Patent Rights versus Patient Rights").

## PATENT RIGHTS VS. PATIENT RIGHTS

In 1998, about one in five adults living in South Africa was infected with HIV/AIDS. Unfortunately, the patent-protected antiretroviral drug "cocktail" that held the disease in check cost about $15,000 per patient per year in the United States. Consequently, only the richest South Africans could afford the treatment. Government subsidization of the drugs, at these prices, would have overwhelmed the budget. Generic versions of the drug "cocktail" produced in India cost only $200. Because India did not issue patents on pharmaceuticals, this allowed the development of a competitive generic drug industry. South Africa, on the other hand, has long had very strong patent laws.

Faced with this tragic public health crisis, the government of South Africa voted in 1998 to permit "parallel imports" and "compulsory licensing" of these drugs. The U.S.-led pharmaceutical industry responded to South Africa's new law by instigating a lawsuit. Thirty-nine pharmaceutical companies were party to this suit, which attempted to block South Africa's action. Activists around the world, incensed by this legal action, rallied against the lawsuit with the slogan, "Patient Rights over Patent Rights." When the lawsuit finally reached the courtroom in March 2001, the pharmaceutical companies withdrew the suit under mounting public pressure in an effort to avoid a public relations debacle.[a]

Developing countries then successfully pressured WTO officials at their ministerial meetings in Doha in November 2001 to affirm their right to parallel imports and to issue compulsory licenses, especially in the face of national emergencies or conditions of national urgency like widespread HIV, malaria, tuberculosis, and other epidemics. This interpretation of the TRIPs agreement was a breakthrough for the poorest countries, many of whom were also given an extension on the requirement to offer patents on drugs until 2016. However, the Doha Declaration still did not resolve many disputes over IPRs and the right to health. Many countries do not have companies with sufficient technological capacity to produce generics under compulsory licenses for their own domestic market. And generics produced in other countries under compulsory licenses must be produced primarily for the domestic market.

Developing countries insisted that they should be able to import generic versions of patented medicines from countries such as India and Brazil and as an alternative to issuing a compulsory license locally without violating trade laws. After much hemming and hawing by the United States, the EU, and Big Pharma, WTO members in 2003 agreed to this waiver, and most members by December 2009 had formally accepted it as a change to the TRIPs agreement. Since 2005, many countries have permitted compulsory licenses for export. Brazil has been very active in using the threat of compulsory licenses to get price reductions from patent holders. Thailand, however, was put on the U.S. Section 301 Priority Watch list as punishment for issuing compulsory licenses in 2006 and 2007 for several anti-AIDS and anticancer medications and the heart drug Plavix.

**References**

[a]The description of these events in this and the following paragraph was drawn from Amy Kapczynski, "Strict International Patent Laws Hurt Developing Countries," *YaleGlobal*, December 16, 2002, yaleglobal.yale.edu/display.article?id=562

A new global coalition called the Access to Medicines campaign led by NGOs and developing countries emerged to reframe the discussion of IPRs in light of the HIV crisis. They sought to discredit big pharmaceutical companies for focusing on monopoly patents rather than saving lives. They pointed out that in national emergencies a country should be able to override the rights of some patent holders. At the same time the United States was resisting the campaign's efforts, hypocritically the U.S. Congress threatened to issue a compulsory license for Cipro production in 2001 during the anthrax scare. Bayer—the patent holder of this antibiotic—responded by agreeing to radically reduce prices and expand production.

Pharmaceutical companies have also responded to the AIDS crisis in more sophisticated ways, pledging hundreds of millions of dollars for HIV/AIDS assistance in developing countries, most of it in cash. Major manufacturers of antiretrovirals have drastically reduced the price per dose they charge poor countries for patented HIV/AIDS drugs through a variety of mechanisms like discounting, tiered pricing, and voluntary licensing programs. Private companies have also partnered with NGOs and governments in multilateral initiatives such as the Global Fund to Fight AIDS, Tuberculosis, and Malaria (to increase funding and access for healthcare) and the Global Alliance for Vaccines and Immunization (to increase research on "neglected" diseases and delivery of vaccines at affordable prices that still protect the IPRs of pharmaceutical companies). It is hoped that a combination of more generics, more compulsory licensing, more voluntary cooperation by Big Pharma, more foreign funding, and more flexibility in IPR laws can make essential medicines more accessible throughout the world.

## Struggles over Traditional Knowledge

Another IPR struggle between South and North is over **traditional knowledge (TK),** which is the accumulated knowledge and practices of indigenous or local communities as they relate to such things as plants, plant uses, agriculture, land use, folklore, and spiritual matters. Indigenous peoples and local communities around the world over many generations have developed deep understandings of their physical environments and the plants they use for food and medicine. They have preserved and developed a wide variety of plant diversity through harvesting and breeding practices. In fact, many of the major food crops in North American and Europe originally came from these local communities.

Colonial powers historically and Northern companies today often appropriated TK for their own selfish purposes. As Madhavi Sunder notes: "The poor's knowledge is often considered simply the discovered bounty of nature—age-old knowledge that, remarkably, has remained static over millennia, and thus 'raw material' waiting to be turned into 'intellectual property' by entrepreneurs, largely from the Global North."[19] The economic value of TK is potentially very high. Billions of dollars worth of prescription drugs sold every year are derived from tropical plants whose medicinal properties were learned from indigenous peoples. Countries like Brazil, India, the Philippines, and Indonesia have begun insisting that those who want to take seed samples, do genetic modification of local plants, or find local plants with chemicals that can be used in medicine must get permission (prior informed consent), acknowledge the source of subsequently patented materials, and share benefits with the local communities whose traditional knowledge they initially relied upon. Developed countries have resisted the protection of TK, partly because TK conflicts with historic notions of what is intellectual property and promises to redistribute some of the gains from global innovation to poorer countries.

Just as developing countries seek to valorize their control over biodiversity and medicinal plant uses, many countries are also trying to protect TK from appropriation and misuse by nonindigenous groups. This is a novel effort to give new cultural rights to indigenous peoples. Through the WIPO and in individual countries like Canada there are campaigns to give indigenous peoples copyrights over their own folklore and artwork—including stories or sacred texts passed down over generations. Maoris in New Zealand and Native Americans have fought to prevent symbols associated with their people from being used as trademarks by private businesses. Similarly, some indigenous communities are seeking to establish their own trademarks over collective symbols and to apply design protections for handicrafts and carpets. India is rapidly trying to create a digital library of local, traditional knowledge so that it cannot be privatized by nonIndians.

## Perspectives on Intellectual Property Rights

In light of the struggles over IPRs we have discussed so far, we conclude by contrasting some key theoretical arguments about IPRs and their effects on the global knowledge structure. While economic liberals tend to agree that IPRs help some markets function more efficiently, they are aware that IPRs are essentially government-granted, temporary monopolies that can sometimes undermine competition. While mercantilists recognize the need for the long arm of the state in IPRs, they note that whether a particular state will find it in its interest to strongly protect or routinely violate IPRs depends on its level of development and technological capacity. Structuralists tend to see IPRs as a means for powerful countries and capitalist enterprises to extract rent from and exploit the less powerful, but they recognize some new forms of IPRs as actually empowering and protecting weak social actors. After surveying some of the mainstream views of the three perspectives, we will examine several other categories of views on intellectual property—constructivist, balancing, and abolitionist—that reflect some more nuanced understandings about the effects of IPRs on democracy, culture, innovation, and the distribution of economic benefits.

In the economic liberal view, property rights are fundamental to the functioning of a market system. Property rights create a powerful incentive to use resources efficiently. Property rights establish a direct link between effort and reward. Knowledge is potentially expensive to make, but it is hard to exclude people from accessing it or copying it cheaply. The knowledge one firm uses can also be used by other firms. This potentially leads to market failure, because there will be free riders—users of knowledge who do not pay for it. Consequently, unless firms can legally deny the use of newly created knowledge to other firms, rapid imitation will eliminate the profits from innovation necessary to recoup the original investment in R&D that created the new knowledge.

When a government provides the creators of knowledge a legal, but temporary, monopoly, they can exclude people from accessing their knowledge without paying for it. Creators are remunerated for their effort (a reward) by gaining adequate returns on their investment in generating intellectual property. IPRs, therefore, provide incentives for creativity and innovation. As a result, consumers worldwide supposedly get a wider variety of new products at reasonable prices. Trademarks and IPR enforcement also help provide consumers higher quality and safer products than would otherwise be the case. And countries that protect intellectual property tend to attract more FDI and benefit from more technology transfer.

Mercantilists see the process of technological innovation in a much different light. Nations must develop and then closely guard their own technology, and technology controlled by other nations is supposed to be acquired. The protection of IPRs for domestic firms is clearly appropriate in order to foster domestic technological innovation. Equal protection for technology owned by foreign firms, however, is not always in the national interest. Rather, government policy in this area often facilitates the acquisition of foreign-owned technology at the lowest cost possible. Increased international protection of IPRs is, then, not necessarily in the interest of every state. Protecting intellectual property of national firms in domestic and foreign markets is appropriate, but reciprocal protection for foreign firms in domestic markets should be resisted.

An additional insight provided by mercantilists considers imbalances in stages of national development. List and Hamilton, early mercantilists (see Chapter 2), argued that free trade benefits the most developed manufacturing nation(s) at the expense of less developed nations. Similarly, international conventions that protect IPRs will benefit those nations with the most advanced technological capabilities at the expense of less technologically developed nations. In this regard, mercantilist and structuralist thought is similar.

Peter Yu points out that when it comes to technological laggards they need to fight for more "policy space" in IPRs, that is, the ability to craft their own IP laws based on their own "conditions, capabilities, interests and priorities."[20] From a mercantilist perspective, many countries can make the best use of their limited resources by stealing IP: Their businesses will save on R&D and absorb technology faster; their citizens will get much cheaper products; and the government will not have to spend money on a bureaucracy to protect the IPRs of foreigners. The Chinese seem to have taken this lesson to heart, just as in previous generations the Japanese, Koreans, and Americans did.

Structuralists contend that developed nations use IPRs to monopolize Third World markets and to extract and repatriate excessive profits from Third World countries. IPRs are simply an excuse for neocolonialism, whereby the North expropriates from the South in exchange relations. The capitalists that hold IPRs behave like international monopolists and cartels. They are not really interested in competition or innovation, both of which they will sacrifice on the altar of rent-seeking and litigation. As Carolyn Deere notes, 90 percent of global cross-border royalties on IP and technology licensing fees go to just 10 developed countries.[21]

Christian Zeller claims that capitalists want to appropriate, control, and commodify intellectual creativity everywhere that it exists.[22] Economic elites always seek to create private property rights from "socially-produced knowledge." Capitalists dispossess "researchers, skilled workers, and also rural communities" of the "knowledge and information which they generate in collective work," transferring the rents to "venture capital, investment funds and license companies."[23] In this structuralist vision, the real creators of knowledge—farmers, indigenous peoples, scholars, and hardworking employees—never really reap the fruits of their creativity.

## Alternative Perspectives on Intellectual Property Rights

Beyond these three perspectives, there are other complex and overlapping points of view on IPRs from the constructivists, "balancers," and "abolitionists." Constructivists help us explain how we talk about IP and frame the stakes involved. As we discovered in Chapter 5, constructivists see our social world as constructed: What we value and the interests we have are defined by our shared discourse about them. We have constructed a discourse that something called "intellectual property" is like real "property" and that there are "rights" we should ascribe to that property. While today it may seem natural to see most creative ideas and knowledge-based products as having rights attached to them, historically that was not the case.

Constructivists trace over time how we define IPRs and talk about them; by so doing we better understand whose interests in society are being served by this discourse. Since the 1980s, powerful economic lobbies have defined IP as an international trade issue. They frame IP as something that belongs to creative and innovative people who work hard, invest, and seek a just reward for their efforts. Creators are pitted against forces described as "pirates" and "counterfeiters" who unjustly take what is not theirs and hurt honest people and companies.

Constructivists also explain that other social forces are trying to offer an alternative set of ideas about IP and how knowledge is created and circulated in the world. For example, according to legal scholar James Boyle, postmodernists offer us another construction of reality: "All creation is re-creation, that there is no such thing as originality, merely endless imitation."[24] In this discourse, no one truly owns their creative output because it is built on the ideas of many people and companies who preceded them. As Newton said, "If I have seen further it is only by standing on the shoulders of giants." If creation is cumulative and informed by everyone around us and before us, then it is hard to argue that we should own what we make from shared knowledge.

A different perspective on IPRs comes from "balancers," who want to strike an appropriate balance between individual rights, communal rights, and national rights. At the individual level, balancers want to make sure that individuals can be creative, spontaneous, and free while still respecting the legitimate economic rights and privacy rights of others. James Boyle, for example, stresses that a large "public domain" and many "fair use" guarantees encourage creative activity in a society. Similarly, Kembrew MacLeod asserts that artistic creativity has always relied upon borrowing, sampling, ripping, and imitating. Therefore, to criminalize these actions when they occur without "permission" is to impede artistic creation itself.[25]

Balancers want to prevent IPR holders from stifling competition, misusing monopoly rights, or excessively suing individuals or companies for alleged infringement. Boyle also points out that many copyright industries tried in the past to resist new technologies—including the Xerox machine, the VCR, cassette tapes, and TiVo—because it threatened their business model. Balancers argue that societies should limit the length and scope of IPRs. They want broad fair use allowances, particularly for educational or noncommercial purposes. They abhor the "permission society," where individuals constantly have to ask copyright holders for permission to access almost every cultural product. Instead, balancers like David Bollier assert that societies need to preserve a large knowledge commons or public domain from which everyone can draw freely to be creative and productive. He touts the collective generation of valuable content by sharing and peer production through networks where oppressive copyright laws are unenforceable.[26] This resistance to existing IP laws comes from society and manifests itself in many forms including the Creative Commons movement, the Open Source movement, mashups, blogs, and social networking.

The last main perspective is that of the "abolitionists," who want to see the elimination or radical reduction of IPRs. Economists Michele Boldrin and David Levine argue that IPRs distort markets, undermine competition, and reduce innovation.[27] They find that in the absence of IPRs, competitive markets still reward innovators who produce goods and services at reasonable prices for consumers. Many economists have found little evidence that IPRs spur more competition, and in many sectors of the global economy such as the fashion industry, database services, software development, and agriculture, there have been significant innovations and thriving markets even in the absence of IPR protections.

## CONCLUSION

The issues surrounding the development and control of knowledge and technology clearly play a central role in IPE. Whether viewed from a liberal, mercantilist, or structuralist perspective, knowledge and technology form an increasingly critical basis of wealth and power. In this era of global competition, individuals, firms, and nations understand that knowledge and technology confer competitive advantage. That the protection of IPRs has risen to the status of a major foreign policy concern for the United States and many other countries is not surprising. The knowledge structure, like the production structure, the finance structure, and the security structure, clearly constrains the options and conditions the behavior of individuals, firms, and nations, and therefore affects the wealth and power they enjoy. The knowledge structure has high stakes as it sets parameters for which companies and economies will turn innovation into economic benefits such as higher productivity, market share, and increased exports. It also helps determine the distribution of benefits from innovation such as better goods and services, lower prices, competition, and productive capacity.

The debates and struggles over IPRs will continue for many years. There is greater recognition by some economic liberals that too many IPRs can have negative consequences for competition, innovation, and a vibrant public domain. As Madhavi Sunder argues, intellectual property is tied to a lot of rights that we care about, like health, education, cultural survival, and human rights in general.[28] People insist on being able to digitally manipulate material, share files, and network unimpeded with masses of people around the world, instantaneously. This genie is not going back into the bottle, and governments will have a nearly impossible task putting it back in the bottle through rigid enforcement of IPRs. Countries too are insisting that IP holders should not be allowed to place roadblocks or speed bumps in the way of their development.

Key questions concerning the knowledge structure include the following: How will the forces of globalization affect the creation, control, and dissemination of knowledge? Will stricter enforcement of IPRs enhance or hinder development among the poorest nations of the world? Will piracy and counterfeiting undermine the incentive to innovate in much of the world? Will the dominance of the United States in science and technology continue, or will it be severely eroded by developments in China and India and other emerging economies? Will competition among nations for new technologies lead to a new era of economic nationalism? The answers to these questions will have profound effects on the lives of present and future generations.

## KEY TERMS

international knowledge structure 236
Intellectual Property Rights (IPRs) 236
research and development (R&D) 239
creative industries 240
Schumpeterian industries 242

product innovation 243
process innovation 243
global value chains 244
Trade-Related Intellectual Property Rights (TRIPs) 246
patents 247
copyrights 247
trademarks 248

geographical indications (GIs) 248
publicity rights 248
Super 301 250
claw back 252
compulsory license 253
parallel imports 254
traditional knowledge 255

## DISCUSSION QUESTIONS

1. What are intellectual property rights, and why are they important in today's global markets?
2. Compare and contrast the mercantilist, liberal, and structuralist views of IPRs.
3. Describe the nature of the TRIPs provisions. Provide arguments both for and against stronger IPR protections in poor countries.
4. Provide two examples of piracy and/or counterfeiting. What countries have been identified as major sources of pirated or counterfeited products? What do you believe are the best ways for developed countries to deal with violations of IPRs?
5. What are some of the most important ways that countries can nurture an innovative and technologically advanced society?

## SUGGESTED READINGS

William Baumol, Robert Litan, and Carl Schramm. *Good Capitalism, Bad Capitalism, and the Economics of Growth and Prosperity*. New Haven, CT: Yale University Press, 2007.

Michele Boldrin and David Levine. *Against Intellectual Monopoly*. Cambridge: Cambridge University Press, 2008.

*Creative Economy Report 2008*. UNCTAD, 2008. At: http://www.unctad.org/en/docs/ditc20082cer_en.pdf

Carolyn Deere. *The Implementation Game: The TRIPS Agreement and the Global Politics of* *Intellectual Property Reform in Developing Countries*. Oxford: Oxford University Press, 2008.

*Intellectual Property Rights: Implications for Development*. UNCTAD-ICTSD, 2003. At http://www.iprsonline.org/unctadictsd/policyDpaper.htm

Susan Sell. *Private Power, Public Law: The Globalization of Intellectual Property Rights*. Cambridge: Cambridge University Press, 2003.

Madhavi Sunder. "IP3," *Stanford Law Review 59*, no. 2 (November 2006), pp. 257–332.

## NOTES

1. Ross Singleton was the primary author of this chapter in the first four editions of this text. Bradford Dillman revised the chapter for this edition.

2. Henry Etzkowitz, *Triple Helix: A New Model of Innovation* (Stockholm: SNS Press, 2005).

3. Steven Ezell, "Benchmarking Foreign Innovation," *Science Progress*, January 12, 2009.

4. Jakob Edler and Luke Georghiou, "Public Procurement and Innovation—Resurrecting the Demand Side," *Research Policy, 36* (2007), pp. 949–963.

5. Michael Porter, *Competitive Advantage of Nations* (New York: The Free Press, 1990).

6. For more background on GVCs see http://www.globalvaluechains.org/concepts.html

7. For detailed information on foreign students in the United States see http://opendoors.iienetwork.org/

8. Vivek Wadhwa, "A Reverse Brain Drain," *Issues in Science and Technology*, Spring 2009, pp. 45–46.

9. Vivek Wadhwa et al., "Where the Engineers Are," *Issues in Science and Technology*, Spring 2007, p. 82.

10. "Immigration and Jobs: Where U.S. Workers Come From," *The New York Times*, April 7, 2009, http://www.nytimes.com/interactive/2009/04/07/us/20090407-immigration-occupation.html

11. Jeff Chu, "How to Plug Europe's Brain Drain," *Time Europe*, January 11, 2004, http://www.time.com/time/europe/html/040119/brain/story.html

12. Ian Johnson, "China Faces a Grad Glut after Boom at Colleges," *Wall Street Journal*, April 28, 2009, p. A1.

13. Vivek Wadhwa, "America's Immigrant Brain Drain," *BusinessWeek*, March 5, 2009.

14. Stephen Siwek, *Copyright Industries in the U.S. Economy: The 2003–2007 Report* (International Intellectual Property Alliance, 2009), http://www.iipa.com/pdf/IIPASiwekReport2003-07.pdf

15. Susan Sell and Aseem Prakash, "Using Ideas Strategically: The Contest between Business and NGO Networks in Intellectual Property Rights," *International Studies Quarterly, 48* (2004), p. 157.

16. Susan Sell, "The Global IP Upward Ratchet, Anti-Counterfeiting and Piracy Enforcement Efforts: The State of Play," June 2008, http://www.twnside.org.sg/title2/intellectual_property/development.research/SusanSellfinalversion.pdf

17. Kal Raustiala and Stephen Munzer, "The Global Struggle over Geographic Indications," *The European Journal of International Law, 18*, no. 2 (2007), pp. 337–365.

18. Madhavi Sunder, "IP3," *Stanford Law Review, 59*, no. 2 (November 2006), p. 301.

19. Madhavi Sunder, "IP: Social and Cultural Theory—A Reply to the Question 'Why Culture?'" March 13, 2009, http://uchicagolaw.typepad.com/faculty/2009/03/ip-social-and-cultural-theory-a-reply-to-the-question-why-culture-madhavi-sunder.html. See also Madhavi Sunder, "The Invention of Traditional Knowledge," *Law and Contemporary Problems, 70* (2007), pp. 97–124

20. Peter K. Yu, "Intellectual Property Rulemaking in the Global Capitalist Economy," 2008, http://www.peteryu.com/andersen.pdf

21. Carolyn Deere, *The Implementation Game: The TRIPS Agreement and the Global Politics of Intellectual Property Reform in Developing Countries* (Oxford: Oxford University Press, 2008), p. 10.

22. Christian Zeller, "From the Gene to the Globe: Extracting Rents Based on Intellectual Property Monopolies," *Review of International Political Economy, 15*, no. 1 (February 2008), p. 91.

23. Ibid., p. 110.

24. James Boyle, *The Public Domain: Enclosing the Commons of the Mind* (New Haven, CT: Yale University Press, 2008), p. 154.

25. Kembrew MacLeod, *Freedom of Expression®: Resistance and Repression in the Age of Intellectual Property* (Minneapolis, MN: University of Minnesota Press, 2007).

26. David Bollier, *Viral Spiral* (New York: The New Press, 2008).

27. Michele Boldrin and David Levine, *Against Intellectual Monopoly* (Cambridge: Cambridge University Press, 2008).

28. Madhavi Sunder. "IP3," *Stanford Law Review 59,* no. 2 (November 2006), pp. 257–332.

# States and Markets in the Global Economy

Part III presents four case studies of international political economy (IPE) analysis: the developing countries, the European Union (EU), the "rising powers" such as China and India, and the Middle-Eastern and North African states. Although these studies are informative about four important sets of nations, they are intended to have broader application. Each study poses particular questions or explores particular themes that apply around the globe. Students are challenged to master the specific applications and at the same time appreciate the more general themes that derive from them.

In this edition of the text we discuss the development conundrum in Chapter 11, as the chapters that follow connect to the issue of development in one way or another. The new edition of this chapter covers three different development strategies. Another idea we want to raise in the three chapters that follow Chapter 11 is that development is not a finite process but one that carries on even in "developed" countries. This aspect of the development process is highlighted in the chapter on the EU in particular.

Chapter 12 examines regionalism, one of the most important political and economic trends in contemporary IPE, with specific emphasis on the European Union. The survey of EU history examines what many regard as an experiment in integration that has reached a point unlike any others in history. Beginning as six nations after World War II, the EU is now composed of 27 nations, some of whom were former members of Warsaw Pact countries dominated by the Soviet Union during the Cold War. Sixteen nations in the EU now have a common currency that has been gaining in strength since it was introduced in 2001. A number of other policy issues such as immigration, interstate travel, communication, and defense, among many more, are issues that EU institutions deal with every day.

Chapter 13 analyzes postcommunist countries, China, and India as they have moved to more market-oriented and, in the cases of parts of the former Warsaw Pact, more democratic systems of political economy. How have the countries managed the transition to participation in globalized markets? How do economic reforms affect political decisions? We will also examine the development contradictions and social problems that face these rising powers, including Russia. We contrast different views on how these countries are challenging the power of the United States and other developed countries.

Finally, in Chapter 14 we explore many of the patterns of political, social, and economic relations in several Middle Eastern and North African states. Although these states exhibit some common institutions, religions, and cultural traits, they differ from one another in ways that are usually not communicated in press and television news accounts. Thus, this chapter goes a long way toward dispelling some of the many myths about this region. We show how the region is integrated into the global economy despite a legacy of conflicts.

# The Development Conundrum: Choices Amidst Constraints[1]

Finding new directions in development.

Corbis 42-21865494

The overwhelming majority of the world's population still has not experienced the economic prosperity and affluence enjoyed by the majority of people in developed countries. An obvious question is this: Given the great amount of wealth produced in the world each year, why have so many developing nations remained impoverished, "underdeveloped," or "undeveloped"? This chapter examines various political-economic dilemmas associated with the controversial issue of development that most of the less developed countries (LDCs) have struggled with since the mid-twentieth century. Development promised less poverty, an improved standard of living, longer life, and greater status. But the path to development often has a cruel side, raising concerns about the costs and paths associated with this dream.

Aside from the trade-offs involved in pursuing development, LDCs have found themselves in the center of intense debates in IPE about the essential prerequisites to get to the promised land. Can economic liberalism and the virtues of globalization propel the poor to a higher standard of living? Or will the lure of the market and globalization be yet another mirage, raising expectations of an impending prosperity only to disappoint?

To better appreciate the development riddle confronting the poorer nations, this chapter provides a systematic examination of the central issues. First, we describe the common attributes of developing nations. We then outline the period we call "Independence and Underdevelopment" that spans the 1950s and 1960s: The time when many LDCs emerged from colonialism into a world of growing international markets, transnational corporations, and the Cold War. Three options presented themselves to LDCs: accept this reality of the international system, try to change it, or drop out of it. Discussions of LDC development strategies were influenced by the assumptions and policies associated with economic liberals, mercantilists, and structuralists. The self-reliance strategy, introduced in this chapter, pragmatically mixes elements of the other three perspectives. The heart of the chapter focuses on these development strategies, including their flaws. The final section of the chapter on the Millenium Development Goals (MDGs) discusses UN targets to be achieved in overcoming a plethora of development barriers and problems. We also outline some of the critical ideas of the development expert Jeff Sachs, who has actively sought an alternative development model and strategies not based solely on economic liberal ideas and policies.

## WHAT ARE DEVELOPING NATIONS?

The countries included in the South, the LDCs, the developing countries, or the emerging economies are societies with diverse histories, cultures, economies, and political systems. The characteristics that they do share, however, are important:

- high instances of poverty; earnings less than $2 per day
- income inequality and lack of a middle class
- lack of education
- inadequate health care
- hunger
- high instances of infant mortality
- lack of infrastructure
- weak governments
- dependency on foreign aid and humanitarian assistance.

What they often have in common is devastating and persistent economic poverty, and hence the imperative to confront a host of development issues. While incomes have risen and material living standards have improved in the North over the past 500 years, living standards have changed very little for a large cross-section of people in the South. Millions continue to live perilously close to the edge and are constantly at the mercy of natural and humanmade threats. One measure of the material living standards of a country is income available per person per day to spend on food, shelter, health care, education, and so forth. In industrialized countries, this figure is relatively high. Per capita income in the United States, for example, is about $100 per person per day on average. An income of $100 per day can provide a comfortable and healthy lifestyle by global standards. By comparison, many in the South have a per capita income of $2 per day or less, and hundreds of millions live on less than $1 per day.

Table 11-1 shows the incidence of severe poverty in the global South. The first three columns show the proportion of population living on less than US $1.25 of income per day in 1990, 1999, and 2005. A $1.25 a day is a critical point in discussing real poverty. Less than this amount means inadequate diet, high infant mortality, and shortened life span. About half of the people in the South experienced material living standards equivalent to less than $1.25 per day, with the deepest poverty in sub-Saharan Africa and South Asia. The good news is that deep poverty has declined in several regions. The bad news is that the overall figures are still high. Many readers of this book are able to feed their pets better than many LDC parents are able to feed their children.

The next three columns in Table 11-1 shows the population percentage with income less than the equivalent of $2 per day in 1990, 1999, and 2005. The difference between existing on $1.25 per day and $2 per day is significant. With $1.25 or less, a person struggles to survive. Two dollars, considering the conditions of poverty we are discussing here, buys a little more than bare subsistence and therefore offers the possibility of better health and human dignity. Of course, two dollars a day is so small an amount to most in industrialized countries that it may seem an inadequately modest goal, yet it is not realized for hundreds of millions of people around the world. Note that, according to this indicator, the incidence of

## TABLE 11-1

### The Incidence of Extreme Poverty, 1990, 1999, and 2005

| Regions | Population (%) Living on $1.25 Per Day or Less | | | Population (%) Living on $2 Per Day or Less | | |
|---|---|---|---|---|---|---|
| | 1990 | 1999 | 2005 | 1990 | 1999 | 2005 |
| East Asia and Pacific | 56.0 | 35.5 | 18.0 | 80.0 | 61.5 | 39.6 |
| Europe and Central Asia | 3.9 | 5.6 | 4.1 | 10.6 | 15.0 | 9.3 |
| Latin America and the Caribbean | 10.0 | 10.5 | 7.9 | 20.4 | 15.0 | 9.3 |
| Middle East and North Africa | 4.3 | 4.2 | 3.6 | 19.7 | 18.9 | 16.9 |
| South Asia | 51.7 | 44.1 | 40.4 | 82.7 | 77.3 | 73.9 |
| Sub-Saharan Asia | 57.8 | 58.2 | 51.2 | 76.1 | 77.6 | 72.9 |
| Total | 42.3 | 33.7 | 25.7 | 63.7 | 57.1 | 47.3 |

*Source:* Martin Ravallion and Shaohua Chen, "The Developing World Is Poorer than We Thought, but No Less Successful in the Fight against Poverty," World Bank 2008. The final incidence figures are updated with POVCAL as of September, 2008.

poverty is much more geographically widespread, with high poverty rates not just in South Asia and sub-Saharan Africa but in East Asia, Latin America, and even Eastern Europe.

Much is made of the gap between North and South and whether global inequality has increased, decreased, or remained about the same over the last half century. Inequality, both between nations and within nations, is an important issue, and there are endless debates over how the global pie ought to be divided and why the division is so uneven today. There is no debate, however, about the need to improve the material and human living standards of much of the world's population. Escaping poverty is the desirable face of economic development, yet there are many costs that must be borne in economic, social, political, cultural, and environmental terms to achieve this goal.

## Independence and Underdevelopment

As the colonial empires gradually disintegrated during the mid-twentieth century, new nation-states emerged into an international order shaped by the Cold War between the United States with its industrial democracy allies (the so-called "First World") and the Soviet Union and its allies (the "Second World"). For these newly formed nations in Asia, Latin America, and Africa—often referred to as the Third World or less developed countries (LDCs)—economic development was practically a universal goal.

In the 1960s, the Martinique-born psychiatrist Frantz Fanon's book, *The Wretched of the Earth*,[2] emerged as a seminal treatise on the struggle of societies to overcome the shackles of colonialism. In this controversial and widely read book, Fanon presents an intricate analysis of the struggle against colonial repression with a discourse on imperialism and nationalism. Many students and scholars regarded Fanon's writing as a powerful and passionate call for the people throughout the Third World to struggle against and even to violently oppose the oppression of Western domination. For our purposes, it is worth noting that Fanon also critiqued the elite of newly independent countries who, as a social class, appeared corrupt and unlikely to genuinely pursue nationwide development.

Fanon's work highlighted concerns about Third World cultural liberation where, among other things, the language of the colonizer, which the colonized societies had been compelled to adopt, would remain as a powerful remnant and enduring influence. It was against this mixed cultural and political backdrop that new Third World countries confronted the pressing questions and concerns about development.

Newly independent LDCs often viewed former colonial powers with disdain and suspicion. Many felt that the exploitation they had endured was surely responsible for the economic "backwardness" of their new nation-state. Development—characterized by a growing and prosperous economy—was crucial in order to establish a national identity and ensure political stability. But many LDCs approached development with mixed emotions. The promises of development were an end to poverty and the start of true independence, which were powerfully attractive to LDCs. On the other hand, development meant exploitation, manipulation, and continued subjugation. This paradox repelled LDCs at the same time as it attracted them. This discord is manifested in the three major forces that shaped the development conundrum for LDCs.

Many LDCs approached development both as a response to the exploitative colonial conditions and as a resistance to cultural domination by the West.[3] These sentiments advocated caution before adopting a Western outlook on economic development. This view remained influential and unified developing countries in the 1970s against the West (see below). The second force to shape development for many LDCs was the Cold War. Proximity to the United States or to its allies or historical connections to former mother countries often shaped the political and economic development strategies LDCs chose. The political significance of pursuing a Western market-oriented development strategy would signal a tacit association with the West in the Cold War. In many cases, association with such Western institutions offered real opportunities for pursuing a partnership with the industrialized nations and for economic development. Likewise, most LDCs supporting the Eastern bloc of nations preferred non-Western development strategies.

Third, and paradoxically, the economic success of the developed countries provided a strong rationale for some LDCs to follow in their footsteps, or at least to adopt market-oriented prescriptions for economic development. The emergence of new international institutions like the IMF, the World Bank, and the GATT, whose role was to coordinate international trade, expanded the significance of the market in the world economy. To many, these institutions were largely controlled by the developed countries.

## Is Development Possible?

Recognizing that, individually, LDCs were unable to exert much influence on the international system and its institutions, a number of them early on attempted to promote a collective identity. The 1955 Afro-Asian Bandung (Indonesia) Conference is regarded as the first major step by LDCs to forge a common identity and is the genesis of what came to be viewed as a Southern perspective. Led by Jawaharlal Nehru of India, Josip Broz Tito of Yugoslavia, Sukarno of Indonesia, and Gamal Abdel Nasser of Egypt, heads of state from the developing countries formed the Nonaligned Movement (NAM) in 1961. This movement had a threefold purpose. First, it was to be the LDCs' political arm for advocating political independence for remaining European colonies (especially in Africa). Second, it was to be their vehicle for positioning themselves outside the sphere of the Cold War scenario. Lastly, it was to promote the interests of the LDCs as a whole.

One of the main priorities of the nations of the "South" was the issue of neo-colonialism, or the continued economic domination of LDCs by the industrialized countries. A number of leaders and intellectuals argued that, while the colonial era was largely over, former colonies were trapped in a capitalist economic system dominated by institutions and mechanisms that favored the developed countries.[4] For instance, multinational corporations and their subsidiaries owned and substantially controlled economic resources in LDCs. The wealth and influence of multinationals, often backed by their home-based governments, permitted the industrialized nations to control international markets for many commodities from LDCs.

Consider the Western oil companies, for example. For much of the twentieth century, seven major oil companies controlled the exploration, processing, and supply of oil in a number of oil-rich regions. These "Seven Sisters," as they were known, often worked to divide the market share, regulate supply, and preserve their control over resources in developing countries. These companies were supported by their respective home governments. In addition, the major oil companies negotiated terms (involving some royalties for the host country) that ensured the companies' control of oil exploration and distribution in the international market.[5]

Advocates of the neocolonial argument claimed that complementing the domination of multinational corporations was a restrictive system of trade, financial, and technology transfer that made LDCs economically vulnerable and weakened their development prospects. In Chapter 6, we discussed the LDC claim that the international terms of trade limited them to be producers of raw materials and primary goods. LDCs were disadvantaged by the lead the industrialized nations had in the production of value-added products and their extensive use of protectionist trade measures. Technological innovations and the associated gains in productivity largely occurred in the developed countries, and LDCs found themselves lagging and unable to compete in the areas of new product development and production. Tight legal controls, copyrights, and licensing often curbed LDCs' access to such technology. The financial power of multinationals, coupled with the developed countries' control of the international financial system, also meant that they could manipulate the LDCs' access to funds for economic development.

Having failed to influence the international system through their collective action, some LDCs began to doubt that development was even possible within the existing international structure. Raul Prebisch provided an important voice in this discussion.[6] He argued that the development dilemma in Latin America was inextricably linked to factors *outside* the region. Prebisch was especially critical of the international division of labor and the free-trade system. He and others argued that the international trade system reinforced the LDCs' role as producers of primary products and raw materials, while the developed countries continued to prosper as producers of industrial products. This international division of labor reinforced the dependence of the LDCs on the developed nations as outlets for primary products. Further, production specialization perpetuated LDC dependence on the developed countries for capital and technology.

Dependence was considered significant, as it resulted in underdevelopment in LDCs. Early dependency theorists made a distinction between *under*development and *un*development. The latter was characterized by lack of development, the former by the outcome of a process that *further* undermined LDC economies, while simultaneously contributing to the prosperity of the industrialized world. On the other hand, Andre Gunder Frank argued that underdevelopment in LDCs was a *by-product* of the development process in industrialized regions.[7] Osvaldo Sunkel and Pedro Paz argued that "both underdevelopment and development are aspects of the same phenomenon, both are historically simultaneous, both are linked functionally and therefore interact and condition each other mutually."[8]

This basic thesis represented the embryo of the critique of dependency theorists during the 1960s and 1970s. For Frank, underdevelopment originated in the European colonial order prior to the twentieth century. Through political domination, the colonial powers successfully extracted raw materials and resources necessary for their own development, while impoverishing their colonies. Although decolonization removed the political dominance of the European powers, the basic economic linkage and division of labor between the two remained largely intact, resulting in neocolonialism. Frank also argued that the international capitalist order was organized along the lines of a metropolis-satellite system, in which the metropolis state exploited and controlled the satellite by extracting economic surplus and wealth from the latter.

Many dependency theorists at the time suggested that several mechanisms reproduce this relationship and worsen the underdevelopment process in LDCs. First, through multinational companies (MNCs), profits generated in LDCs are transferred out of those nations. Investments in technology and other innovations are often outdated or inappropriate and do not enhance the competitive edge of LDCs. The extensive resources of MNCs also enable them to circumvent restrictive and regulatory measures in LDCs. Another mechanism is the unequal exchange relationship. The LDCs' "comparative advantage" in primary products and raw material is vulnerable to international market prices, which are generally well below those of manufactured goods that LDCs must import from the developed countries. This creates a net outflow of revenue from LDCs to the developed countries.

Some dependency theorists find the international financial and foreign aid system to be exploitative. They claim that foreign banks are less interested in the development of a country than they are in acquiring lucrative terms for loans to LDCs. This creates a long-term financial dependence for the indebted country and generous interest receipts for foreign banks. These theorists are also skeptical of foreign aid, arguing that the political and economic strings attached to such assistance often reinforce a dominant–subordinate relationship between the developed and less developed nations.[9]

## UNCTAD and the NIEO: LDCs Organize to Change the System

Frustrated by their meager success, many LDCs turned to their membership within international organizations to cooperate and change the IPE structures. In 1964, the **United Nations Conference on Trade and Development (UNCTAD)** was established, spearheaded by the seventy-seven LDCs that became known as the Group of 77 (G-77). UNCTAD meets roughly every four years. The G-77 sought to make UNCTAD a mechanism for dialogue and negotiation between the LDCs and the developed countries on trade, finance, and other development issues. For the most part, the developed countries resisted UNCTAD initiatives. Nevertheless, through UNCTAD, LDCs were gradually able to secure some concessions and preferential treatment—a Generalized System of Preferences (GSP)—on tariffs for their exports to developed nations.

OPEC helped bring attention to LDCs' concerns in 1973 when the cartel, made up of oil-producing developing countries, embargoed oil shipments to some of the industrialized nations (see Chapter 19).[10] A 400 percent increase in the price of oil jolted the developed economies and temporarily altered the global balance of political and economic power. Following World War II, the industrialized countries had experienced considerable economic growth, aided by cheap and abundant energy. However, OPEC's price hikes dampened economic growth and spurred inflation in the developed countries. LDCs gained considerable political leverage during that time. The developed countries—being highly dependent on oil-exporting countries for their energy—could no longer ignore the considerable impact oil-producing countries from the South had on the economic well-being of the industrialized world.

With OPEC's support, LDCs made an historic attempt at the UN General Assembly in 1974 to establish a **New International Economic Order (NIEO)**. This program was designed to accelerate the pace of development among LDCs and equalize the economic balance between the LDCs and the industrialized nations. Unlike previous efforts, the NIEO was seen by LDCs not as an attempt to fine-tune the existing international economic order but as an effort to elevate the issue of economic development to the top of the international agenda, making institutional structures more conducive to LDC development concerns. The NIEO called for the following actions:

- creating an Integrated Program for Commodities (IPC) to stockpile and control the price of commodities during periods of oversupply and scarcity
- developing a debt-relief program
- increasing official development assistance from the rich, developed nations to the less developed ones
- changing the decision-making process in major international institutions such as the United Nations, the IMF, and the World Bank to give more voice to Southern nations and to reduce developed nations' control of these institutions
- increasing the economic sovereignty of LDCs by ensuring LDCs' greater control over their natural resources, increasing access to Western technology, and regulating multinationals
- creating preferential trade policies to stabilize prices for commodities from LDCs and ensuring these countries greater access to markets of the developed countries.

The general opposition of the industrialized countries to the NIEO initiatives made its implementation difficult. Many industrialized nations also saw demands for a NIEO as a political threat prompted by some radical LDCs to undermine the predominantly market-oriented international economic system and to redistribute global wealth and power

Efforts by LDCs in the 1970s to change the system failed. LDCs were left with the choice of promoting autonomous local development without the global market or accepting global markets—and the possibility of dependent underdevelopment. Many LDCs would approach development cautiously and experiment with a variety of strategies to deal with the development conundrum.

## The Market Unleashed

In the 1980s, the conservative Reagan administration emerged as a strong advocate for free trade, exerting its influence on the IMF, the World Bank, and the GATT to bring LDCs into closer alignment with policies consistent with the free-market ideology and U.S. foreign policy objectives. This period saw the introduction of the

Structural Adjustment Policies (SAPs), which contained stringent conditions that LDCs had to adopt to ensure continued IMF assistance in addressing their short-term economic and financial woes. Officials required LDCs to carry out a number of measures that included the following:

- devalue their currencies
- raise interest rates
- privatize national industries
- cut social welfare programs
- adopt free-trade policies.

By the 1990s, the fall of the Soviet Union and the collapse of communism gave even more momentum to the "Washington Consensus" and the liberal market ideology of the West. Globalization—driven in large measure through international trade, finance, and technological interconnectedness—affirmed and validated a U.S.-led chorus touting the virtues of economic growth and prosperity through greater emphasis on privatization and free trade. Indeed, it was during the early 1990s that India, China, and the Southeast "Asian Tigers" began to achieve tremendous economic growth and emerge as economic successes in their own right. Yet, as we discuss below, there is considerable debate on how these countries attained so much economic growth during this period. Clearly free-market policies played only a small role in their development strategies.

# HOW TO DEVELOP? THE FOUR IPE DEVELOPMENT STRATEGIES

Determining the appropriate strategies for developing countries remains a debated and hotly contested issue in IPE literature. In Table 11-2, we sum up the major elements of the three most popular development strategies. Notice that these three strategies correspond to the three dominant IPE perspectives and are labeled as such. The fourth strategy of self-reliance is not a theoretical model of development per se, but rather the result of many pragmatic failures attributed to the other three. Self-reliance is a unique effort to combine elements of the other three strategies so as to account for the advantages and disadvantages of each state when it comes to achieving development.

## The Economic Liberal Perspective

The economic liberal perspective on development requires that LDCs become intimately integrated into the global market economy. Historically, trade has been seen as critical to this integration process. By emphasizing and relying on their comparative trading advantages, LDCs are able to capitalize on the benefits of international trade and build a robust economy. From the liberal perspective, FDI and MNCs are a major source for capital, jobs, export revenues, and technology in LDCs. There is global competition for FDI, and governments around the world are constantly trying to attract foreign investment. Trade enables poorer economies to export their natural resources and (mainly) agricultural commodities, while affording access to

### TABLE 11-2

## The Classic IPE Development Strategies + 1

|  | Economic Liberalism | Structuralism | Mercantilism | Self-Reliance |
|---|---|---|---|---|
| Strategy Goals | Grow the economy; support manufacturing and industry over agriculture | Eradicate poverty and promote equitable income distribution | Grow the economy to promote wealth and welfare of the state | Grow the economy, but not at the expense of the masses |
| Policy Tools | Promote trade as the "engine to growth;" promote industrial development: the state must be stronger at first to promote change | State-led development, industrial, and wealth and welfare policies; import substitution | State promotes industrial policies that target healthy industries; import substitution and export-led growth | No formal strategy but use a variety of state industrial policies along with trade policies that incorporate open markets when and where possible |
| Side Effects | Masses must postpone gratification; democracy comes later | Slow economic growth | State policies often regarded as protectionist and offensive to other states; state investments reflect special interests | Hard to plan; officials must be wise to figure out what tools work best and when |
| Examples | United States, England, Japan, Asian Tigers, Hong Kong | Cuba, China until 1978, Tanzania, Poland, Hungary, and the Czech Republic until 1990, and today Venezuela. | Japan, South Korea, Malaysia, and Indonesia | Most emerging economies today: China, India, Brazil, Indonesia |

manufactured goods from abroad. As these economies grow from export earnings, gradually they will be able to acquire more foreign technology and knowledge to promote new investments in industrial and manufacturing enterprises. According to this perspective, as "latecomers," LDCs can use the market to develop and industrialize, while learning from the pitfalls and policy mistakes of the now developed nations. Such hindsight translates into less waste of resources and more efficiency, while accelerating the development process for LDCs.

Foreign aid from wealthier nations and IOs, and FDI into developing economies are critical to strengthening the poorer nations' ability to trade and build their economic infrastructure. Some critics have argued that as developing countries compete for FDI, they essentially undercut each other by trying to provide foreign investors with the most lucrative terms in the form of very cheap labor and lax regulation. This generates a "race to the bottom" for wages and conditions that workers in these developing nations have to endure to keep the MNCs and investors from taking their operations to more "investor-friendly" locations in other nations. The common images of lowly-paid and highly-exploited sweatshop factory workers in poor countries producing textiles, leather goods, and footwear are a vivid illustration of this criticism of MNCs and FDI.[11]

One critical feature of the economic liberal model is that a major obstacle to economic development in LDCs stems from the anemic capital, productivity, and technological base in these societies. Other obstacles to development often include shaky infrastructure, weak educational systems, and/or traditional cultural value systems that hinder development. Following this line of reasoning, the neoliberal perspective largely deemphasizes the importance of IPE structural conditions in mitigating the relative lack of development in LDCs. Instead, it focuses on internal conditions in LDCs that stifle economic development.

Other variants of this perspective also emphasize the social aspects of development. Some liberal economists, for example, promote education, training, and skill-development as important ingredients to achieving development. Such an emphasis adds dimension to the aforementioned economic liberal perspective, which for years was primarily focused on emphasizing economic growth. At the end of the chapter we discuss the work of Jeff Sachs, who has tried to combine more social factors into the development process.

Marx, who wrote about sweatshop abuses in Great Britain in the 1850s (see Chapter 4), might not be surprised to know that they still exist in the twenty-first century. For many LDCs, sweatshop industries are the most difficult element of the development conundrum. These countries need jobs, investments, technology, and export earnings, but MNCs often bring dangerous and abusive working conditions. However, the race-to-the-bottom scenario is not the whole story of MNC investment, as Theodore H. Moran has explained. Most MNC investment is North–North in direction, moving from one advanced industrialized country to another, not North–South as is commonly assumed. (Most MNCs invest in industries that pay much more than sweatshop-level wages. Even so, it must be said that these investments do go into low-wage and low-skill industries such as textiles, clothing, leathers, and footwear that are susceptible to sweatshop organization. Frequently the foreign MNCs do not operate sweatshops but rather contract with local suppliers who do, often absolving themselves of responsibility for sweatshop conditions.)

It is worth noting that from the Cold War period until the late 1990s, the **economic liberal outlook** was the most popular development strategy for developing countries. It incorporates Western development strategies and assumes that the relationship of rich to poor countries is beneficial, despite a few shortcomings related to international economics such as terms of trade that do not always favor developing nations (see Chapter 6).

Part of the appeal of this development outlook lies in the interpretation that the United States and other industrialized nations went through a series of "stages of growth," which subsequently became benchmarks by which policy makers understood the development conundrum in LDCs. Part of the assumption was that, like the Western industrial nations, LDCs will also develop through the workings of an open market system and undergo similar "stages of growth." One of the most influential liberal economic theories of development was the work of W. W. Rostow,[12] who served as an advisor to President Kennedy. According to Rostow, LDCs must undergo a series of changes in their socioeconomic system in order to develop. This "evolutionary" change is represented by a series of "stages of (economic) growth" that each society passes through on its way to development. Traditional society experiences low levels of economic productivity due to lack of technological development and a traditional social system of fatalistic values, where individuals are constrained by rigid social goals. Increases in education and literacy, entrepreneurship, and investments in raw material and infrastructure expand the level of commercial activity. The seeds of economic growth are planted, and even if new ideas create a good deal of disharmony, the society is bringing about changes that are compatible with the process of development.

In the critical "take-off" stage, the pace of change accelerates. New industries increase rapidly as the entrepreneurial spirit becomes more dominant. The emergence of a capitalist class accelerates the change by initiating new economic activity, industrialization, and the adoption of new production processes. Conversely, the influence of traditional social values and goals diminishes. Existing economic activities such as extraction of raw materials and agriculture are also modernized. Later stages of development are characterized by the use of advanced technology and an increase in savings and investment (approximately 15–20 percent of GNP), which sustains the drive to economic maturity. Countries with a higher level of savings and investments are, according to Rostow, more likely to grow and develop at a faster rate than those with lower savings. The final stage of mass consumption and self-sustained growth follows when the major sectors of the economy are able to meet the consumer demands for goods and services for a large cross-section of the population, which helps sustain the high level of economic activity.

Rostow's theory of development was largely based on the historical trajectory of Western nations. He perceived the stages of development as universal, arguing that in the long run, the North can model the development process for the South. The historical development and diffusion of technology will inevitably lead to changes that are necessary in the early stages of the economic development process in LDCs.

Proponents of this development model implicitly assume that through this approach, developing countries will transform their economic, political, and social systems and become modern and industrialized nations like England or the United States. Thus modeled on the experience of industrialized nations, development is equated with economic growth and increased GNP and per capital income. It is also assumed that LDCs can and will be able to apply the same process as did the United States and England, and that as their economies grow and a viable middle class emerges, other changes in such societies—such as demands for greater democracy—will follow.

This development strategy prioritizes open markets and free trade and hence places a premium on the need for LDCs to adopt export-oriented growth policies, based on their natural comparative advantages. Trade exports would serve as the "engine to growth," with the state guiding the economy toward efficient allocation of resources.

While MNC investments and FDI facilitate vital economic activity within a developing country, foreign aid helps meet its important infrastructure and strategic needs. As the processes and linkages associated with globalization have become more intense, there has been renewed emphasis among proponents of the economic liberal model on stressing the virtues of greater international interdependence between the developing and developed nations.

Even proponents of this strategy concede that in the initial stages of development, only a small proportion of the population (an elite) will likely reap the benefits of free trade and engagement in the international economy. But there is a conviction that the economic benefits will trickle down to a wider cross-section of society as the economy matures. While the goal of containing poverty may not be a central and immediate priority of this approach, there is an expectation that over time, the trickle-down effect will ease the economic deprivation associated with poverty.

Economic liberal ideas have received considerable attention, related in part to the economic growth achieved by many states, including Japan, the Asian Tigers (Taiwan, South Korea, Taiwan, and Hong Kong), but also the Philippines, Malaysia, Thailand, Indonesia, China, and more recently, Ireland and even Estonia—all of whom adopted some variant of outward-looking export-oriented policies. Yet, as we discuss below, there remains some controversy about whether these countries adopted an approach squarely consistent with the economic liberal model. In recent years, both the antiglobalization campaign and the global financial crisis have generated a series of grave doubts and concerns about why economic liberal ideas achieved their success, and the extent to which the model can and should be transplanted on to poorer developing nations in Asia, Latin America, and especially Africa.

## The Structuralist Perspective

Moran discusses various strategies for trying to improve working conditions in LDCs, such as adopting global labor standards and trying to integrate sweatshop concerns into WTO agreements. He argues that a passive strategy that counts on sweatshop earnings to "trickle down" and eventually create more growth is wrongheaded. The growth does not happen, and there is always even cheaper labor somewhere else. Instead, Moran proposes a "buildup" strategy that uses resources created in part by MNCs to improve worker skills and to attract progressively higher-skill industries and jobs. The buildup strategy must be broad-based, not just aimed at attracting MNC funds. He cites experiences in the Philippines, Costa Rica, and the Dominican Republic as evidence that these government programs can help LDCs to move beyond sweatshops.

The Marxist and early structuralist critiques of the development problem begin with the assertion that the relationship of core to peripheral countries is one of domination of the North over the South, and dependency of the latter on the former. According to this critique, the Western industrial model is inappropriate for LDCs as the developed nations' "neo-imperial" connections to the South via trade, aid, and FDI often result in dual economies. While one consists of wealthy elites, who are well connected to transnational elites in the North, the other is that of the masses, whose fortunes and futures remain bleak and who are rooted in local customs and values. For the ardent Marxist-structuralists, the liberal trickle-down market model ultimately benefits only elites and core nations and does not produce wider societal development.

The Marxist-structuralist model was closely associated with pro-Soviet communist models during the Cold War. While many of the former Soviet-bloc countries did prioritize industrialization, their LDC counterparts (such as North Korea, Cuba, and Vietnam) sought similar benefits by focusing on self-sufficiency and isolation from the capitalist international economy. Radicals promoted revolution and severing of the relationship between core and periphery. LDCs cannot and should not attempt to catch up to the West but instead should work to overcome external dependencies and bring the poor into the economy. LDCs should focus on closing the economy (autarchy to international trade), reject international aid (which furthers dependency), and nationalize local TNC industries. Instead of producing for export, LDCs should implement import-substitution policies (e.g., tariffs on imports and subsidies for local industries), which would protect local producers and limit expensive imports. Furthermore, rather than waiting for the benefits of free trade to trickle down, the state should undertake aggressive measures to eradicate poverty by implementing a more equitable distribution of income and providing strong support for basic health and welfare programs.

Between the 1960s and 1980s, several countries in Latin America opted for more inward-looking strategies generally termed **import-substituting industrialization (ISI).** The import-substitution strategy is guided by a structuralist interpretation of development, and hence views capitalist market forces as a threat to LDCs. Since LDCs are seen as vulnerable to exploitation by a the core while falling behind in their development, structuralists viewed the ISI strategy as a way for countries in the periphery to achieve development while minimizing the risk and adverse effects of dependency ties with the core.

The experience among the major Latin American economies was quite different. During the 1950s, Latin American scholars were increasingly skeptical of the "comparative advantage" road to development, and the dependency critique became an influential framework for development in that region. This critique fostered opposition to dependence on foreign capital and trade, resulting in restrictive trade policies and stringent regulation and control of foreign investment. The inward-looking and nationalistic *import-substitution* approach was implemented to reduce dependence on foreign capital, technology, and markets and to promote "home-grown" industries.

Many were convinced that specializing in primary commodity products was an inherent disadvantage for developing countries in the region. The adverse terms of trade made manufactured imports a major foreign-exchange drain. To change this situation, countries with a relatively fragile industrial base, such as Brazil and Mexico, must undertake significant steps to build a viable manufacturing sector. Given the large internal consumer market in these countries, a shift from importing manufactured consumer products to producing them locally would translate into new jobs across the economy, improve the adverse balance of payment situation, and promote economic development.

The import-substitution path is a series of stages during which countries moved from being exporters of primary commodities to developing an indigenous industrial base. The first stage of the import-substitution strategy was similar to that followed by the East Asian NICs. By the 1950s, Brazil and Mexico were well into the process of promoting local manufacture of consumer goods (such as processed foods, textiles, and footwear) and curtailing foreign imports with protectionist measures. However, significant differences affected the import-substitution strategies in the East Asian and Latin American cases. Historically, the resource- and agriculture-rich Latin American economies have been more dependent on primary exports than their East Asian counterparts like Taiwan and South Korea.[13] Diversifying from this deeply-entrenched primary-product economy was difficult.

Furthermore, protectionist policies were used heavily in countries like Brazil to displace the foreign share of its consumer market, while in East Asia the focus of these measures was to enhance the international competitiveness of locally produced goods. Hence, by the late 1960s, as South Korea was promoting its exports while maintaining some barriers, Brazil and Mexico were moving into the next stage of intensifying their import-substitution strategy. Ironically, instead of reducing their dependence on foreign capital, the countries had to borrow from abroad to finance the deepening of their import substitution. This second stage of import substitution involved expanding the manufacture of labor-intensive consumer goods along with diversifying into capital-intensive goods as well.[14] In this stage, the role of the government and state-owned enterprises expanded. This increasing presence of the state was associated with increased concentration of production in the hands of a few firms (often state owned) that were not as productive as privately owned enterprises.[15]

However, the performance of these economies was not as strong as that of the export-oriented East Asian NICs. Brazil and Mexico had largely managed this growth by depending heavily on the domestic consumer market instead of the international market. In order to sustain growth, production reflected the consumption patterns of those with purchasing power. This further aggravated income inequality as the gap between the "haves" and the "have-nots" increased. By contrast, the income inequality gap among the East Asian NICs narrowed.[16]

Today many structuralists are not so hostile or pessimistic about the LDCs' economic linkages to industrialized nations. Since the fall of the Soviet Union, many structuralists are open to the idea that export-oriented growth and an aggressive trade posture can reap important benefits for a developing nation. Indeed, China and India, which for decades had been inward-focused, have become more receptive to certain mercantilist and market policies. Other structuralists emphasize greater collective efforts among LDCs to gain leverage in international trade agreements and financial institutions to promote better terms of trade, secure meaningful economic aid, and appropriate investment in LDCs.

## The Mercantilist Perspective

Like the economic liberals, the mercantilists consider international trade as essential but also strategic to national development. However, some mercantilists are not enthusiastic about the laissez-faire and limited-government doctrine typically associated with the liberal perspective. States have a critical role to play in coordinating a trade strategy that would be conducive to promoting economic development. Several developing countries in East Asia adopted strategies that, while quite diverse, are generally termed **export-oriented growth.** This mercantilist-oriented strategy relies on strong state policies to mediate the fears of dependency and exploitation associated with the free-market prescription of the economic liberal perspective. The export-oriented approach is based on a combination of mercantilist and liberal prescriptions for economic growth and development. It calls for the state to strongly emphasize its comparative advantages in selected sectors of the economy and to promote exports from these sectors. However, instead of depending on a noninterventionist state and free-trade policies, the East Asian NICs aggressively pursued specific national and international policies that changed the basic structure and functioning of their economies. While there are specific differences among the East Asian NICs, there are certain common trends as well.

First, the export-oriented policies of East Asian NICs involved changing the fundamental composition of their production. Prior to the 1960s, like other developing countries, South Korea and Taiwan began promoting manufacturing with a particular emphasis on labor-intensive consumer goods. To accomplish this, the respective governments set up mercantilist-style restrictions to protect "infant" consumer manufacturing industries from foreign competition. These policies had the added benefit of increasing employment, which also helped stabilize the political situation. The governments provided strong financial backing and incentives to promote manufacturing, which will be discussed later. In this initial push to generate a viable manufacturing sector, these countries did not use the strategy pursued by Japan in the earlier part of the twentieth century and later after World War II.

By the late 1960s, South Korea and Taiwan began the next phase of restructuring. These countries increased their international market share by promoting the export of domestically manufactured durable goods. State intervention again played a strategic role in launching this export-promotion effort. Selective barriers on imported goods remained in place, although raw material imports necessary for manufacturing were encouraged; and selected domestic manufacturing industries were targeted with fiscal incentives to stimulate the level of exports. They devalued the national currencies, making exports from these East Asian countries more competitive in the international marketplace and imports less attractive to domestic consumers.[17] Therefore, the NICs purposefully *created* comparative advantages for their manufactured products through these protectionist measures.

During the 1970s, South Korea's manufacturing sector expanded into heavy (technologically intensive) industries including steel, petrochemicals, and automobiles. By 1980, these efforts in restructuring the economy were bearing fruit. Manufacturing's share of GDP in South Korea climbed from 14 percent in 1960 to 30 percent by 1980, and has remained stable since. Agriculture's share decreased from 37 percent to 15 percent over the same period and in 1995 dropped to 7 percent of GDP. In Taiwan, manufacturing's share of GDP increased from 26 percent (1960) to 40 percent (1993), after hovering at a high of about 47 percent in the mid-1980s. Correspondingly, agriculture's share of GDP declined from 29 percent to only 3.5 percent by 1993.[18]

A second major component of this export-led growth strategy involved promoting a high level of savings and investment (including intense efforts in research and development). A combination of factors contributed to this process. In South Korea, an increase in household savings was a major source of savings, largely stimulated by raising interest rates on bank deposits. The government also helped establish private banks and financial institutions, which began to overshadow traditional and informal money markets widely used by small private customers. This policy allowed the government to increase its oversight of financial stability and savings in the economy.[19] The growth of financial institutions in Singapore and Hong Kong was also crucial to the capital formation process in these countries. Interestingly, the former developed an approach in which the government maintained tight control over financial institutions, while the latter leaned in the opposite direction of minimal regulation of the financial sector.[20]

The influx of foreign capital and aid in East Asia also impacted the capital formation processes. Cold War tensions and the Korean War both influenced the flow of Western aid into South Korea and Taiwan. South Korea's dependence on foreign aid was especially crucial following the Korean War in the 1950s. According to one estimate, approximately 70 percent of South Korea's domestic capital formation came from foreign aid during the 1950s.[21] Taiwan's domestic capital formation also depended heavily on foreign capital during the same period—about 40 percent was externally financed. Recall that this was when South Korea and Taiwan underwent structural transformation in production, by using protective measures to insulate their newly emerging light-manufacturing industries from foreign competition.

Education and human resource development are recurrent themes of development, so it is no surprise that the successes of the East Asian NICs have generated more attention to these issues. The combined impact of investment strategies in education and job training resulted in a quality labor force. This resulted in economic efficiency, industrial flexibility, and greater equality. State initiatives promoting literacy and job training led to the growth of a literate and skilled workforce, which was essential to the success of the industrial and investment policies and has promoted growth in productivity.

As we have seen, the state was instrumental in setting and shaping development policies in these countries. South Korea presents a typical case: Following a coup in 1961, the military established the Economic Planning Board, which, among other things, acquired powers to control the nation's investment strategy. With the guidance of the military government, which dictated economic policy, the board became a coordinating body among the various governmental agencies. This centralization of power corresponded with the weakening of political parties and electoral politics in South Korea. Another significant trend was the systematic weakening of labor unions, which allowed the government greater control over enforcing its economic agenda.

It should be noted that the East Asian Tigers didn't simply "roll back the state" and let free competition reign as advocated by the liberal development strategy. Instead they employed export-oriented growth policies to maximize the benefits of modernization and industrialization. To take advantage of opportunities presented by international markets, they relied on strong state policies to limit domestic economic and political disruption. The export-oriented growth strategy was willing to risk dependency to gain benefits for the state.

## Self-Reliance

From the above, it should be clear that the first three development models reflect different ideological outlooks, historical circumstances, and recommendations of different policies and instruments for states to use to promote development.

The self-reliance strategy reflects the conclusion reached by many development experts and officials that there is no one "magic bullet" approach for development. For any state to rigorously follow any of the standard models is an attempt to fit a square peg in a round hole. In the box "Development: A Customized Approach," we have summarized a recent debate between two students of development, a well-known journalist and a university professor, as an example of the different ideas and attitudes that both agree must go into any set of strategies about development.

## ▶ DEVELOPMENT: A CUSTOMIZED APPROACH

Martin Wolf, the chief economics commentator at the *Financial Times*, reviewed Cambridge University economics professor Ha-Joon Chang's controversial book *Bad Samaritans* (Bloomsbury Press, 2008). Professor Chang argues that neoliberals have hurt developing nations by opposing their ability to regulate inward direct investments and obsessing about the need for privatization. Many neoliberals also exaggerated corruption, the lack of democracy, and an assortment of cultural issues that presumably act as barriers to change. Meanwhile, neoliberals are famous for pointing out that countries like China reversed course from the use of protectionist industrial and trade policies and promoted (free) trade policies in an attempt to open markets in the global economy for their exports. These policies capitalized on China's comparative advantage in the export of manufactured goods and facilitated the country's success. Finally, neoliberals argue that, on the whole, import substitution is not good because it creates small-scale, uncompetitive, rent-seeking monopolies.

In critiquing Chang's book, Wolf asks why South Korea developed as fast as it did, while India has taken much longer. His answer is that while protecting its "infant industries" South Korea *rejected* import substitution and adopted a series of *outward-oriented trade policies* that opened it up to the international economy. Until recently, India remained sealed off from international competition, was more inward

looking, and more directed at protecting local industries. However, Wolf goes on to suggest that each state has different circumstances and advantages that can help it develop. He admits that Hong Kong, China, South Korea, Ireland, Singapore, Taiwan, Japan, and Finland were *not* all free traders by any means. Some relied more heavily on FDI than others. But all used the international economy to their advantage and were more outward than inward looking.

In Chang's response to Wolf, he clarifies that he is not suggesting that free-trade policies are not good, but that they must be used in conjunction with a variety of protectionist policies (including import substitution) to "create the space in which their producers can build up their productive capabilities before they can compete with better producers from abroad."[a] This is what the Japanese did with their car industries for almost forty years, and South Korea did with steel, shipbuilding, autos, and electronics. Economic liberalism doesn't always work. Many poorer countries suffered low growth practicing free trade. For example, while per capital income in Latin America grew at 3.1 percent during the "bad old days" of protectionism of the 1960s and 1970s, growth in the "good old days" of neoliberalism, from 1980 to 2004, slowed to 0.5 percent.

In essence, Chang and Wolf both agree that developing nations want to rapidly grow their economies, and that for most of the poorer countries, industrialization offers the best chance to earn capital and develop technologies and management capabilities. They also agree that, despite their subtle differences about the benefits of different strategies, there is no "magic bullet" to make any one strategy or combination of strategies work. Free trade and economic liberal ideas alone are not the solution to the problem. South Korea and Taiwan might be exceptions to the rule. What is paramount is recognizing the specific challenges involved in each case and adopting the right balance and combination of options appropriate to the situation.

### Reference

[a]See Ha-Joon Chang, "Response by Ha-Joon Chang," *Financial Times,* August 3, 2007.

The self-reliance strategy moves the debate away from compartmentalized strategies based on the three distinct schools of thought toward a search for what works on a case-by-case basis. This model stresses the importance of taking into consideration the unique circumstances, economic challenges, and resources of each country, when considering the combinations of strategies that may be appropriate. Self-reliance allows for the possibility of different outcomes, including one that does not have as its primary objective the narrow and limited goal of achieving economic growth. In most cases, however, it would be hard for officials to reject that goal or to balance it with a variety of social and cultural welfare objectives.

The increasing number of problems poorer states face regarding energy, the environment, culture, history, political realities, and financial issues will affect their ability to choose different courses of action. Which strategy will be adopted should be decided not on the basis of theory alone, but rather on the assessment of the complex domestic and international factors a particular LDC confronts. As such, while some combination of trade and social policies may have worked for South Korea or Taiwan, it is not necessarily true that these would apply in Gambia or Gabon. Similarly, while some strong state-guided industries may not have worked in Vietnam, one cannot rule out that under different circumstances and another country, a similar approach might not be relevant or effective.

## LESSONS OF THE EAST ASIAN MIRACLE AND FINANCIAL CRISIS

What were the lessons learned from the debate between import-substituting industrialization and export-oriented growth? The answer to this question depends on whom you ask and when. By the early 1990s, the evidence seemed to favor an export-oriented strategy based on the dynamic growth experience of the East Asian Tigers and the "Little Dragons" (Thailand, Indonesia, the Philippines, and Malaysia) in the region. In *Looking at the Sun*, James Fallows argued that the East Asian mercantilist-based system of state-led export-oriented economic growth had proved superior to both the ISI strategy and liberal laissez-faire policies.[22] The East Asian results were very strong in creating income and growth.

The results in Latin America were not as good. It had proved impossible to avoid entanglement in international trade and finance. The strategy of borrowing abroad to build domestic industry created huge foreign debt and devastating debt crises in Latin America. The heavy controls adopted to avoid dependency created opportunities for corruption and special-interest manipulation. Latin America experienced less growth and possibly greater inequality. The scorecard seemed clearly to favor East Asia and export-oriented growth over import-substituting industrialization.

In 1993, the World Bank released a study titled *The East Asian Miracle: Economic Growth and Public Policy*, which sought to assess the lessons learned from the debate between import-substituting industrialization and export-oriented growth.[23] The report argued that the "East Asian Miracle"—high growth without great inequality—was due to two basic factors. The first was that the East Asian countries were successful at "getting the fundamentals right." This is development jargon for avoiding the tremendous economic distortions that the Latin American countries were forced to introduce as they sought inward development. Compared with the Latin American countries, the East Asian countries had avoided inefficient wage, price, and exchange-rate distortions at the cost of reduced economic efficiency and flexibility overall. The East Asian countries also promoted high rates of saving (so that investment was possible without large foreign debts), high levels of education and training, and stable macroeconomic policies. In short, their economic strategies avoided certain fatal policy mistakes.

Second, some of the state policies were effective in increasing growth, especially "export-push" policies. According to the World Bank, the contest between state-led import-substituting industrialization and state-led export-oriented growth showed that the key to success was not so much what the government did but what it *avoided* doing. If the state avoids making a number of critical mistakes, development has a pretty good chance.

Many people who read the report concluded that its recommendation was that LDCs avoid *both* types of state-led growth strategies and adopt instead the neoliberal Washington Consensus of free trade, free capital markets, and limited government intervention. This conclusion was highly contested, especially by East Asian leaders and scholars who believed that their state leadership policies were the key to their success. Many observers noted that the World Bank report blamed all failures on the state and credited all successes to natural market forces. They pointed out that many of the positive factors in Asian economic development, such as high savings rates, strong education systems, and relative income inequality, were *dictated by state actions*, not due to the absence of them. In other words, for many, the economic development experienced by East Asian societies was very much the result of carefully crafted mercantilist policies.

The Asian financial crisis that began in 1997 called the World Bank's judgment into question and reopened the debate on development strategies. While some argued that the crisis was caused or exacerbated by unwise state involvement in the economy (often called *crony capitalism*), others argued that it was because of rapid adoption of Washington Consensus policies, especially free capital markets. The Washington Consensus advocated opening developing economies to global financial markets as soon as possible, which was often before necessary domestic institutions and regulations were in place. This "premature globalization" made the Asian economies unusually susceptible to financial crises.

This was an important issue to resolve. Do laissez-faire policies produce rapid growth, as the 1993 report had suggested? Or do they open up an economy to instability and crises, as the 1997 Asian financial crisis seemed to indicate? In 2001, the World Bank released another study called *Rethinking the East Asian Miracle* that addressed these critical questions.[24] Reading this report, one appreciates that both miracles and crises are complicated phenomena that cannot and should not be oversimplified. The Asian financial crisis was created by a combination of market imperfections and what states did (business–government relations that sometimes encouraged financial abuse) and did not do (the lack of effective regulation and more comprehensive social safety nets).

In addition, some scholars contend that the liberal argument that the developed economies achieved success through the methods they preach to the LDCs is a myth. Instead, Ha-Joon Chang writes,

> Almost all of today's rich countries used tariff protection and subsidies to develop their industries. Interestingly, Britain and the USA, the two countries that are supposed to have reached the summit of the world economy through their free-market, free-trade policy, are actually the ones that had most aggressively used protection and subsidies.[25]

In other words, what has worked historically—and also recently, as shown by the experience of several East Asian NICs—are development strategies that acknowledge and effectively incorporate the role of the state in the development process. The key to development in LDCs is not open markets, more government, or less government. Rather, they need good government, which is more complicated. Smaller government (and supposedly a more unregulated market) is not necessarily better government if it sacrifices societal goals and institutions and does not advance development objectives. Similarly, grand state strategies alone are not the key to ensuring successful development. The devil is in the details.

## DEVELOPMENT AND GLOBALIZATION

As LDCs entered the twenty-first century, global changes made economic development seem more attainable but riskier and more complex. We often sum up these changes in a single word: **globalization**. Globalization is not one thing; it is many things. For LDCs, confronting globalization has meant confronting a complicated array of problems and opportunities. The development dilemma is no longer a simple matter of choosing a grand development strategy such as import-substituting industrialization, but rather analyzing how to deal with both the policy choices and critical details that together form the two faces of development today.

## Global Competition and Interdependence

The 1990s began the era of intense global economic interdependence. In the last 40 years, much of the world's population had not been able, or chose not, to participate in global markets. This decade brought three major changes:

- Economic liberalization in China, begun in the 1980s, accelerated as Hong Kong was returned from British rule in 1997 and China was granted membership in the WTO in 2001.
- The collapse of the communist government of the Soviet Union and its Eastern European satellite nations turned them all into "emerging market" economies.
- A series of government reforms in India turned its strategy from inward-looking state development to outward-looking market development (See Chapter 13).

These changes, and numerous smaller ones, meant that more than half of the world's population was, at least theoretically, suddenly part of a global market. Such global competition for products, resources, investment, and markets created problems and opportunities both for LDCs and for the advanced industrial countries.

As we saw in Chapters 7 and 8, by late 2007 the global economy started to experience a notable slowdown. Triggered largely by the financial crisis in the United States, global economic interdependence meant that economies were adversely affected throughout the world. By 2009, the recession in the United States and several other major economies had trickled down to many LDCs that depend on exports to earn foreign exchange.

## Trade and Finance Policies

As the option of completely autonomous development gradually faded from the scene, it was replaced by the notion that development needed to take advantage of global resources and market opportunities. More and more of the resources for development came from financial markets, not from transfers of aid. To repay their debts, with interest, nations had to export and earn enough. LDCs had to export to grow—but on what terms?

A consensus emerged among LDCs that the rules of international trade and financial organizations were unfavorable to the interests of LDCs. For example, as long as LDCs remained buyers of manufactured goods, richer countries favored liberalization of trade in manufactured goods. But things changed, LDC leaders noted, once countries like China and Mexico became major *exporters* of manufactured goods. LDCs began to demand more access to rich-country markets, both for manufactured goods and agricultural exports. LDCs were frustrated that their attempts to develop critical agricultural resources were often undermined by, ironically enough, the existence of heavily *state-subsidized* agriculture policies in the United States and the EU.

The LDC demands were brought to the Seattle WTO meetings of 1999 and then more forcefully to the Doha meetings of 2001. LDCs realized that they needed the global markets, so they could not just walk away, but they also needed rules more favorable to their development interests, which were often not compatible with the subsidized agriculture policies in developed nations.

The Washington Consensus formula for economic development included both free trade and free capital mobility. The case for free trade is a strong one, according to economists, even though it is politically controversial. The case for free capital mobility is less strong, from an economic theory standpoint, but paradoxically it received great political support.

To promote "free capital mobility" is to allow free movement of investment funds into and out of a country. These investment funds come in many forms; some are long-term and stable, others are short-term and volatile. Some go to purchase productive assets and some to make portfolio investments in company stocks, while others are simply speculative. Free capital mobility means allowing potentially dangerous forms of investment along with relatively safe forms, because it is hard to control one without discouraging the other. The risk is that short-term speculative funds—what Keynes called "hot money"—rush in and out, creating a boom, a crisis, and the need for IMF assistance. With capital came financial instability, speculation, and the possibility of a devastating collapse. For LDCs, the returns increased, but so did the risk.

## The Informal Economy and the Mystery of Capital

Microcredit gives many of the poor a chance to participate in the market economy, often through what is termed the **informal economy**. The informal economy is the part of the economic system that operates outside of direct government control or regulation. It is often an important part of the LDC economy and a source of opportunity for grassroots entrepreneurship.

However, in many countries, government regulations and legal issues make it difficult for people to get started in the informal economy, to take full advantage of its opportunities, and to leverage their success. In his book *The Mystery of Capital*, Hernando de Soto argues that capital is the key to unlocking grassroots economic growth potential—an idea that the supporters of microcredit agree with.[26] De Soto continues, however, by stating that in many LDCs the poor often have access to capital in the form of land or property that they use but do not own. A small farmer, for example, might live on and till unused land on an absentee landlord's vast estate. Or a city street vendor might slowly build up a structure on a public sidewalk.

The problem, he says, is that because their use is informal and sometimes illegal, they do not have any *property rights* in their capital. They cannot make full use of it, since it can be easily taken away, and it may be costly and difficult to gain formal legal title. And, of course, it is impossible to use this capital to secure credit to expand a business or to build a permanent house. The poor have capital, perhaps as much as $9.3 *trillion* worth, but they cannot make use of it in the same way that people in developed nations can. If capitalism is to work for the poor, de Soto argues, then the poor need to become capitalists, and that requires that they have rights to the capital they already use.

## Microcredit Versus Macrocredit

One of the most interesting features of the globalization era has been the realization that economic development, if it is to succeed, must proceed at all levels at once. That is, LDCs cannot hope to grow if the focus is *only* on policies of the World Bank and the IMF, or *only* on state development strategies. Both types of initiatives must move forward, and even more must happen; development must get down to the grassroots. One of the great errors of grand development strategies was the notion that development financed by "macrocredit" would trickle down from international capitalist institutions or a planning agency to the villages and city streets. The idea of microcredit renewed interest in the possibility that development could grow from the grassroots up.

**Microcredit** is one of the beneficiaries of this "trickle-up" approach.[27] The idea of microfinance is to provide credit to people to start their own small businesses, lifting themselves from poverty through their own initiative. When they repay the loan, others can have a chance, too. The most famous example of microcredit is **Grameen Bank,** which was founded in Bangladesh by Professor Muhammad Yunus in 1976. By August 2002, the bank had made loans involving over a half million households and had received cumulative loan repayments of more than $3 billion. The loans are very small, often just $20 or $50, but the potential impact is large.

The reason that microcredit institutions are successful involves an economic problem called **asymmetric information.** The problem is, who can be trusted to repay a loan, even a small one? If you know whom to trust, you can lend money at low interest rates. But if you cannot tell who is trustworthy (or creditworthy), then you have to charge everyone a high interest rate to cover expected losses. High interest rates, however, discourage trustworthy individuals from borrowing money, thus diminishing the possibility of them starting or expanding a business. The problem of finding out who is trustworthy, and the cost of monitoring borrowers to be sure they act responsibly, limits grassroots development.

In industrialized countries, lenders and borrowers find ways around the problem of asymmetric information; there are even firms that specialize in providing credit ratings for individuals and businesses. However, the costs are too high in LDCs to provide the same services, especially when the loan amounts are small. So credit, a key to economic development, is unavailable or too expensive for the poor, who need it the most.

Microcredit institutions solve this problem by lending money to small groups of people, usually women. Given that each member of the group is individually responsible for repaying the group's loan, it is in each member's interest to work only with productive and trustworthy colleagues who share the same objective. The information problem—whom can you trust?—is thus shifted from the lender to the members of each group. By moving the burden of knowing who is creditworthy from the bank to the borrowing group, microcredit institutions unlock the possibility of credit-financed grassroots economic development.

How can such small loans create much economic development? People who are used to living in societies where credit is readily available may find it difficult to appreciate how even a little credit can benefit people in very poor, credit-scarce parts of the world. A small group of women can use a loan to purchase fabric or other raw materials that are then processed and sold in local or regional markets. Without funds for the raw materials, the market value of their labor cannot be realized. The small incomes that are thus generated can change both the economic status of the households and the social status of the women.

Yet there are concerns associated with microcredit. Although microcredit institutions often begin with an agenda for socioeconomic change, critics argue that the need to be financially sustainable—to earn higher interest rates and achieve higher loan repayment rates—sometimes alters these priorities. The concern is that the pressure to be economically sustainable may cause them to avoid loans to the poorest of the poor, who are often the people who most need access to credit. There is also a concern that microcredit institutions, if successful, may introduce capitalist practices and values into indigenous societies.

## Development in the New Millennium

Despite years of debates about competing models and strategies, the persistence of poverty remained critical and endemic in many parts of the world. Rock stars like Bono have aggressively campaigned about the need for the international community to make a more meaningful commitment to address the dire conditions of many of the poorest nations. The spotlight on poverty, child malnourishment, and disease, especially in sub-Saharan Africa, served as a glaring reminder that while much about the global development landscape had changed over the years, the poor in many parts of the world are still far from being able to meet most basic needs.

Consider the problem of access to health care. Contagious diseases such as malaria, smallpox, and tuberculosis have been virtually eliminated in advanced industrial countries, because of action by scientists and public health officials. Vast numbers of people in LDCs are not so lucky. Because of the high cost of research and the low incomes of potential buyers, medical research focuses less on diseases of the tropics, which remain a serious problem. Even where drugs are available and medical treatments are well known, the costs of a public-health program are exorbitant. Even governments that are not corrupt may struggle to make public health a high priority.

But the costs of ignoring public health issues are high, too, as the AIDS epidemic in sub-Saharan Africa shows. The UNAIDS/WHO task force estimated that at the end of 2001 there were 28.5 million people living with AIDS in sub-Saharan Africa, but that fewer than 30,000 of these were receiving full drug treatment. Over 11 million children had been orphaned by AIDS. About 9 percent of the adult population was infected, and the problem was getting worse. AIDS remains such a severe problem in sub-Saharan Africa because of many complex reasons. Lack of money for prevention, treatment, and education is part of the problem. Other elements include the attitudes of some government officials, who deny the existence of the problem, and cultural, social, and sexual practices that allow the disease to spread. Solving such devastating problems requires citizens to look abroad for assistance and also reflect on their own practices.

It became increasingly clear that concerted efforts had to be taken to address the desperate condition of impoverished countries. In 2005, the UN announced the

Millennium Development Goals to refocus the international community's commitment to addressing dire economic and human conditions in the world's poorest nations. The Millennium Development project was framed around pursuing the following eight broadly defined goals:[28]

1. To eradicate poverty and extreme hunger by half
2. To achieve universal primary education
3. To advance gender equality and empower women
4. To reduce child mortality by two-thirds by 2015
5. To reduce by two-thirds the maternal mortality ratio
6. To reduce the spread of HIV/AIDS and malaria by half by 2015
7. To secure environmental sustainability
8. To develop a partnership for development that includes an open, rule-based, predictable, and nondiscriminatory trading and financial system.

The secretary-general recruited the renowned development economist Jeffrey Sachs to advise the United Nations. Sachs, having advised multiple governments coping with economic reforms in countries around the world, has been a strong advocate for greater commitments from industrial nations toward achieving the aforementioned goals. He argues that wealthier nations and leading international institutions like the World Bank and the IMF have been partial toward privatization while overlooking the importance of poverty reduction and financial assistance to the poorer countries. He writes:

> Increased foreign financial assistance was deemed not to be needed. Indeed, foreign aid per person in the poor countries plummeted during the 1980s and 1990s. Aid per person in sub-Saharan Africa, for example, expressed in constant 2002 dollars, fell from $32 per African in 1980 to just $22 per African in 2001, during a period in which Africa's pandemic diseases ran rampant, and needs for increased public spending were stark .... Many African countries have heard an earful from the World Bank ... about privatizing their health services, or at least charging user fees for health and education. Yet most of the high-income-country shareholders of the World Bank have health systems that guarantee universal access, and all have education systems that ensure access to public education.[29]

Sachs, as an HIL critical of the market-oriented model of development, believes that the industrialized states can and should provide more aid to the poorest nations. Table 11-3 indicates that net Official Development Assistance (ODA) by major donors has increased. One motive for this increase is to assist those states helping combat the war on terrorism. To those concerned that aid would go to corrupt officials or make matters worse for LDCs, Sachs and the UN both state that LDCs themselves ought to be working toward making government more effective and responsive to the needs of the poor.[30] However, neither Sachs nor the UN are depending on good government alone to solve development problems when issues such as disease prevention, agricultural production, and increasing infrastructure in poor countries are just as important. Sachs is also a vocal proponent for the cancellation of the foreign debts of many desperately poor

TABLE 11-3

**Net Official Development Assistance Disbursements (in billions of dollars)**

| Donor | 1988–1989 Average | 1993–1994 Average | 2000 | 2002 | 2004 |
|---|---|---|---|---|---|
| United States | 8.9 | 10.0 | 10.0 | 13.3 | 19.7 |
| Japan | 9.0 | 12.2 | 13.5 | 9.3 | 8.9 |
| United Kingdom | 2.6 | 3.0 | 4.5 | 4.9 | 7.9 |
| France | 5.6 | 8.2 | 4.1 | 5.5 | 8.5 |
| Germany | 4.8 | 6.9 | 5.0 | 5.3 | 7.5 |
| Canada | 2.3 | 2.3 | 1.7 | 2.0 | 2.6 |
| Italy | 3.4 | 2.9 | 1.4 | 2.3 | 2.5 |

*Source:* Organisation for Economic Co-operation and Development, *Statistical Annex of the 2005 Development Co-operation Report.*

countries, even suggesting that if the wealthier nations opt not to cancel them, the highly indebted poor nations should refuse to service the exorbitant loans they now carry—estimated to be over $200 billion.[31]

A critical part to understanding Sachs' advocacy of the MDGs is to appreciate his critique of past strategies—like the conditional structural adjustment programs—pursued by the IMF. In his book *The End of Poverty*, Sachs argues against conventional economic logic and the "Washington Consensus," asserting that the "main IMF prescription has been budgetary belt tightening for patients much too poor to own belts. IMF-led austerity has frequently let to riots, coups, and the collapse of public services."[32] In lieu of the failed "one size fits all" approach typical of the liberal Washington Consensus perspective, experts need to emulate a "clinical" approach to development practiced in medicine. Not unlike individuals, economies are "complex systems" and hence "differential diagnosis" is essential to differentiate between ailments or illnesses even when some common symptoms may be present between two or more cases. Carrying out "differential diagnosis" is critical to being able to diagnose economic problems—and hence the appropriate case-specific treatment that may be necessary. For Sachs, "clinical economics"[33] can be the method to pursuing the broader eight-point goals articulated in the Millennium Development project.

Many of Sachs' views about development are currently supported by both the IMF and the World Bank.[34] The latter has always been more focused on development issues than the former, and it has gradually shifted its focus to targeting the poor directly as opposed to banking on "top–down" industrial development and market-oriented programs.

# CONCLUSION

This chapter has demonstrated that since World War II economic development has remained an objective of many different states, IOs, and, recently, NGOs. A variety of different strategies have resulted in some successes, especially for the NICs of East and Southeast Asia, modeled on a subtle combination of policies. However, the search for a single solution to the development problems of many developing countries has given way to a growing realization that currently there is no one full-proof strategy for all developing nations, nor might there ever be one. Some of the factors that have helped nations successfully develop include their geopolitical position, their colonial past or history, their position in the international economy (what each produces and trades), and a myriad of domestic factors.

In the case of the world's poorest nations, especially those in sub-Saharan Africa, nothing has worked when it comes to development. In many cases, these nations have encountered numerous problems associated with inappropriate demands made on them by the major powers, the WTO, the IMF, the World Bank, and even the UN. In addition, a myriad of factors within their own societies act as major barriers to change, including geographic location, access to water, government corruption, and ethnic and religious differences among social groups.

The AIDS epidemic and acute poverty in Africa remind us that the goal of development is not just having a higher income; it is also about having a better life, with rights and opportunities. Perhaps we should remain optimistic after all. Many states, IOs, and NGOs are heavily invested in trying to promote reform, if not meaningful change, in developing countries, employing a variety of techniques and methods. Indeed, some economic progress has been made in a number of states, and certainly lessons have been learned. However, development remains a complicated and frustrating challenge. The development conundrum still remains a pressing reality.

## KEY TERMS

United Nations Conference on Trade and Development (UNCTAD)   271
New International Economic Order (NIEO)   272

economic liberal outlook   275
import-substituting industrialization (ISI)   278
export-oriented growth   280
globalization   285

informal economy   287
microcredit   288
Grameen Bank   288
asymmetric information   288

## DISCUSSION QUESTIONS

1. How serious is the problem of global poverty today? Explain citing data from this chapter.
2. What four forces have shaped the development process for LDCs? How do these forces create tensions within LDCs and between LDCs and industrial nations? Explain.
3. Briefly trace how the issues regarding economic development have changed since the early post-colonial days of the 1950s and 1960s. In particular, discuss the tensions between the UNCTAD and the NIEO, between import-substitution industrialization and export-oriented growth, and between the advocates of the Asian Miracle and those who favor the Washington Consensus.
4. The chapter's author argues that developing countries need good government more than they need less government or more government. What are the characteristics of good government with respect to economic development? Explain. (Hint: Consider some of the factors discussed in the last section of this chapter).

## SUGGESTED READINGS

Ha-Joon Chang. *Kicking Away the Ladder—Development Strategy in Historical Perspective*. London: Anthem Press, 2002.

Ha-Joon Chang. *Bad Samaritans: The Myth of Free Trade and the Secret History of Capitalism*. London: Bloomsbury Press, 2008.

Hernando de Soto. *The Mystery of Capital: Why Capitalism Triumphs in the West and Fails Everywhere Else.* New York: Basic Books, 2000.

Stephen A. Marglin. "Development as Poison: Rethinking the Western Model of Unity," *Harvard International Review, 25* (Spring 2003).

Theodore H. Moran. *Beyond Sweatshops: Foreign Direct Investment and Globalization in Developing Countries.* Washington, DC: Brookings, 2002.

Oxfam. *Paying the Price: Why Rich Countries Must Invest Now in a War on Poverty.* Oxford: Oxford International, 2005.

*The Economist.* "Recasting the Case for Aid," January 22, 2005.

Tina Rosenberg. "That Taint of the Greased Palm," *New York Times Magazine*, August 10, 2003, pp. 28–33.

Jeffrey D. Sachs. *The End of Poverty: Economic Possibilities for Our Time.* New York: Penguin Press, 2005.

Joseph E. Stiglitz. *Making Globalization Work.* New York: W. W. Norton, 2006.

Muhammad Yunus. *Banker to the Poor: Micro-Lending and the Battle Against World Poverty.* New York: Public Affairs, 1999.

# NOTES

1. Sunil Kukreja has authored this chapter since the first edition of the text.
2. See Frantz Fanon, *The Wretched of the Earth* (New York: Grove/Atlantic, 1961).
3. See Daniel Chirot, *Social Change in the Twentieth Century* (New York: Harcourt Brace, 1977), p. 173.
4. One of the leading voices of the anti-neocolonial movement was the former president of Ghana, Kwame Nkrumah, who articulated this thesis in his book *Neo-colonialism: The Last Stage of Imperialism* (London: Nelson, 1965).
5. See Joan Edelman Spero, *The Politics of International Economic Relations* (New York: St. Martin's Press, 1981), pp. 246–247.
6. Raul Prebisch, *The Economic Development of Latin America and Its Principal Problems* (New York: United Nations, 1950).
7. Andre Gunder Frank, *Capitalism and Underdevelopment in Latin America* (New York: Monthly Review Press, 1967).
8. Osvaldo Sunkel and Pedro Paz, *El subdesarrollo latinoamericano y la teoría del desarrollo* (Mexico: Siglo Veintiuno de Espana 1970), p. 6, as quoted in J. Samuel Valenzuela and Arturo Valenzuela, "Modernization and Dependency," *Comparative Politics, 10* (1978), pp. 543–557.
9. For a good discussion of this position see Teresa Hayter, *Aid as Imperialism* (Middlesex, England: Penguin, 1971).
10. OPEC was formed in 1960, and its members include Iran, Iraq, Algeria, Nigeria, Gabon, Libya, Kuwait, Qatar, Saudi Arabia, United Arab Emirates, Ecuador, and Venezuela.
11. For a good video that examines this issue, see "Free Trade Slaves," 1999.
12. Walt R. Rostow, *The Stages of Economic Growth: A Non-Communist Manifesto* (London: Cambridge University Press, 1960).
13. See Jorge Ospina Sardi, "Trade Policy in Latin America," in Naya Miguel Urrutia, Shelley Mark, and Alfredo Fuentes eds., *Lessons in Development* (San Francisco, CA: International Center for International Growth, 1989), p. 289.
14. Stephan Haggard, *Pathways from the Periphery: The Politics of Growth in the Newly Industrializing Countries* (Ithaca, NY: Cornell University Press, 1990), p. 26.
15. Youngil Lim, "Comparing Brazil and Korea," in Naya et al., eds., *Lessons in Development*, pp. 102–103.
16. Nigel Harris, *The End of the Third World* (New York: Meredith Press, 1986), pp. 90–91.
17. For example, see Wontack Hong, *Trade, Distortions, and Employment Growth in Korea* (Seoul: Korea Development Institute, 1979).
18. Seiji Naya et al., *Lessons in Development* (San Francisco p. 287; World Bank, *World Development Report 1997* (New York: Oxford University Press, 1997); Carl J. Dahlman and Ousa Sananikone, "Taiwan, China: Policies and Institutions for Rapid Growth," in Danny M. Leipziger, ed., *Lessons From East Asia* (Ann Arbor, MI: University of Michigan Press, 1997), p. 85.

19. William E. James, Seiji Naya, and Gerald M. Meier, *Asian Development: Economic Success and Policy Lessons* (Madison, WI: University of Wisconsin Press, 1989), pp. 69–74.

20. Ibid., p. 81.

21. Haggard, *Pathways from the Periphery*, p. 196.

22. James Fallows, *Looking at the Sun: The Rise of the New East Asian Political and Economic System* (New York: Vintage, 1995).

23. The World Bank, *The East Asian Miracle: Economic Growth and Public Policy* (New York: Oxford University Press, 1993).

24. The World Bank, *Rethinking the East Asian Miracle* (New York: Oxford University Press, 2001).

25. *Ha-Joon Chang,* "Kicking Away the Ladder: How the Economic and Intellectual Histories of Capitalism Have Been Re-Written to Justify Neo-Liberal Capitalism", http://www.paecon.net/PAEtexts/Chang1.htm. See also, *Bad Samaritans: The Myth of Free Trade and the Secret History of Capitalism* (London: Bloomsbury Press, 2008).

26. Hernando de Soto, *The Mystery of Capital: Why Capitalism Triumphs in the West and Fails Everywhere Else* (New York: Basis Books, 2000).

27. See Muhammad Yunus, *Banker to the Poor: Micro-lending and the Battle Against World Poverty* (New York: Public Affairs, 1999).

28. United Nations, http://www.un.org/millennium goals/.

29. Jeffrey D. Sachs, *The End of Poverty: Economic Possibilities for Our Time* (New York: Penguin Press, 2005), p. 82.

30. See Jeffrey D. Sachs, "Institutions Matter, but Not for Everything," *Finance and Development*, June 2003.

31. See Oxfam International, *Paying the Price: Why Rich Countries Must Invest Now in a War on Poverty* (Oxford: Oxfam International, 2005).

32. See Sachs, *The End of Poverty*, Chapter 4, pp. 74–89.

33. Ibid, p. 74.

34. See the World Bank, *Economic Growth in the 1990s: Learning from a Decade of Reform* (Washington, DC: The World Bank, 2005).

# Regionalism: Toward a More Perfect (European) Union[1]

The fall of the Berlin Wall—a defining moment in the international political economy.

AP 89111101356

This chapter examines the political economy of regionalism, which is one of the most powerful dynamics of this era in world history. Increasingly, nations are driven to unite their economies for greater efficiency and growth. Integrated markets do not necessarily mean integrated states, however. The fundamental tension between economics and politics is revealed in high relief in the process of integration. This chapter examines the international political economy of regionalism by looking at its most important example, the integration of Europe.

The **European Union (EU)** formally began life in 1957 as the **European Economic Community (EEC)**, often called the **Common Market.** Its predecessor was the **European Coal and Steel Community (ECSC),** which had been established in 1952. In 1967 the EEC and the ECSC merged (together with EURATOM, the European Atomic Energy Community) to form the **European Community (EC),** often just called "the Community." In 1993 the name was changed again, to *European Union,* in order to emphasize that integration was spreading from the economic sphere to the political and social spheres of European life.

The EU is the product of more than 50 years of political and economic activity aimed at creating a prosperous and cooperative environment for Europe. It is, on one hand, arguably the largest and richest unified market in the world—a postwar success story. It is, on the other hand, arguably a rather weak political alliance, because nation-states retain sovereignty over most fiscal, social, and security policies. The fundamental question that the EU seeks to answer today is whether it is possible to combine economic regional integration with a substantial level of political integration. How much integration do the Europeans need in order to face new global challenges like globalization, competition from India and China, the financial crisis, and new security threats? Can the EU remain a world economic power without also becoming a global political power? These questions remain unanswered even after the ratification of the **Treaty of Lisbon** in November 2009 (discussed later in the chapter).

Regionalism is a distinctive feature of IPE in the twenty-first century, and that this is so comes, perhaps, as a bit of a surprise. We are living in an era when the international political economy seems to be pulled in two directions at once. On one hand, security concerns and the financial crisis make the state as important now as it has ever been from a political standpoint. The need to look after "homeland security" in all its forms and the ability to decisively pursue national interests are strong forces drawing our attention toward the importance of the nation-state. At the same time, however, the forces of economic globalization are blurring the distinction between home and abroad. From an economic standpoint, the world is defined by markets, not state boundaries, and many of those markets—especially financial markets—are global.

This chapter seeks to understand twenty-first-century regionalism through an examination of the most important case of regionalism in the twentieth century, the EU. The EU can be thought of as the world's largest science experiment, testing the hypothesis that nations with a long history of conflict can solve the puzzle of peace and prosperity more successfully as a group than as separate autonomous nation-states. Whether or not the EU has solved the puzzle—and the potential lessons the experiment provides for other nation-states—is the question this chapter explores.

## THE ECONOMICS AND POLITICS OF REGIONALISM

**Regionalism** in IPE refers to the process by which groups of nation-states, usually in the same geographic region, agree to cooperate and share responsibility to achieve common goals. Regional groups are "clubs" formed by nation-states to accomplish objectives that require coordinated or collective action. For example, there are regional environmental agreements, regional economic development programs, regional scientific and health regimes, and regional security arrange-ments. Regionalism is a logical response to problems that are too big for one state to solve by itself or problems caused by the actions of one country having effects in another, as with issues such as flood control, fisheries management, or pollution abatement. There is even a movement, sometimes dubbed the *new regionalism*, that looks for cooperative solutions to common problems at a more grassroots level than the nation-state, through regional initiatives by local governments, nongovernmental organizations, and activists in different countries.

Regionalism is not a new thing; it has always existed in the international polit-ical economy. What is new is the strength of regionalism as an organizing force, due largely to the increasing importance of economic integration and the rise of regional **trade blocs** such as the EU, the North American Free Trade Area (NAFTA), and similar groups around the world (see Chapter 6). Economic integration—making one large market out of several smaller ones—is the shared goal of these regional groups (see Figure 12-1).

## Economic Integration

**Economic integration** is the process by which a group of nation-states agrees to ignore their national boundaries for some economic purposes, creating a larger and more tightly connected system of markets. Nations can commit to several dif-ferent degrees of economic integration. A **free-trade area (FTA)** involves a rela-tively small degree of integration in which nations agree to eliminate tariff barriers to trade in goods and services they produce themselves. Each nation, however, retains the right to set its own tariff barriers with respect to products from outside the FTA. The **North American Free Trade Agreement (NAFTA)** is an example of an FTA between the United States, Canada, and Mexico. The fact that some goods are tariff-free in FTA transactions but other goods are still subject to differential trade barriers complicates intra-FTA trade and therefore limits the effective degree of integration.

The next level of economic integration is called a **customs union** ("customs" is another word for tariff). In a customs union, a group of nations agrees both to tariff-free trade within their collective borders and to a common set of external trade barriers. If NAFTA were to evolve into a customs union, for example, the United States, Canada, and Mexico would need to agree to a unified set of tariff barriers that would apply to products from other countries. The Treaty of Rome, which created the original European Economic Community, was based on the idea of a customs union.

The movement to a customs union is an important step in terms of economic integration because of the greater degree of political cooperation that is required. The nations involved give up some degree of sovereignty or national political autonomy because they can no longer set their own trade barriers without consult-ing their economic partners. What they gain is a far greater degree of economic integration. Products flow more easily within a customs union, with no need for border inspections or customs fees because of the unified trade structure. In prac-tice, of course, the elimination of trade barriers is not as complete as theory sug-gests, because member nations retain the right to impose some nontariff trade

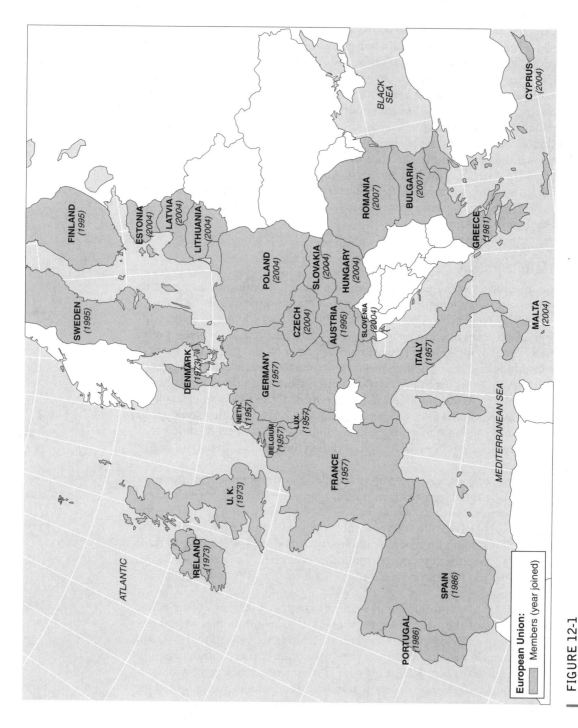

FIGURE 12-1

The European Union, Including Dates of Entry

**European Union:**
Members (year joined)

barriers, such as health and safety standards. Still, a customs union is an effective means of increasing market size and stimulating growth and efficiency.

An **economic union** is the final stage of economic integration. In an economic union, nontariff barriers are eliminated along with tariff barriers, creating an even more fully integrated market. The degree of integration in an economic union goes further than this, however. Member nations in an economic union agree to four "freedoms" of movement: of goods, services, people, and capital. These four freedoms represent significant limitations on national sovereignty, but they can also have significant effects on economic activity. With few exceptions, the EU is such an economic union.

The free movement of goods is more complicated than it may seem, for it goes beyond the elimination of tariff barriers. Free movement of goods requires a variety of governmental health, safety, and other standards and regulations to be "harmonized" so that, at least in theory, a product can be sold anywhere in the economic union (aside from obvious technical barriers that can prevent sale, such as differences in electrical systems among nations, or the differences between left-hand-drive and right-hand-drive automobiles). The EU applies what it calls the "principle of mutual recognition" when there is no common (European) standard: the standard for goods of one country has to be accepted in any other country without objections.

Free movement of services is also more complex than it may seem. Services such as banking and finance are traditionally subject to heavy regulation that varies considerably among nations. Free movement of people requires a unified immigration policy, because a person who is free to enter and work in one member of the economic union can, in theory, live and work anywhere in the union. Finally, free movement of capital means that individual nations give up much of their ability to regulate investment inflows and outflows. Many nations have traditionally imposed capital controls to encourage domestic investment, promote financial stability, or reduce foreign exchange variations. These controls are not eliminated in an economic union, but they must be "harmonized" (or mutually recognized) so that national regulations are similar enough that they do not become a barrier to economic activity. Thus, a common administrative organization (like the European Commission) is inevitable if one wants to realize an economic union. Through economic integration, some level of political integration becomes necessary.

## Effects of Economic Integration

For economic liberals economic integration is appealing because it is a way for nations to achieve greater *efficiency* in their use of scarce resources and higher rates of economic *growth*. In the lingo of economics, integration produces **static efficiency** gains and **dynamic efficiency** gains.

Economic integration promotes greater static efficiency for two main reasons. First, with completely free trade within the area, each member nation is able to specialize in producing the goods and services in which it is most efficient. Protective barriers that preserve inefficient industries and promote redundancy are eliminated. Economists believe that these gains from efficient specialization are significant. Second, the creation of a larger, integrated market promotes efficiency in certain industries in which large-scale production or long production runs are possible. These gains from *economies of scale* make products cheaper and more competitive.

The more important economic benefit of integration occurs in the long run, as dynamic efficiency promotes economic growth. The logic is that a larger and more competitive market is likely to be more innovative. As internal trade barriers are removed, previously protected firms are forced to compete with one another. Firms become more efficient and "nimble."

If economic integration is successful, economic growth rates tend to increase, which raises living standards. Even a small rise in growth can be significant. If, for example, economic integration causes the long-term rate of economic growth to rise by one or two percentage points, the long-run effect will be that at the end of a single generation, the living standard could be double what would have occurred without integration! Thus, economic integration need produce only a little extra growth to have a considerable long-term effect on people's lives.

However, regional trade blocs became controversial in the 1990s because of the **trade diversion effect** of a free-trade area, customs union, or economic union. By dropping internal trade barriers, members create more trade between and among member nations. Some of that trade is indeed "created" by the new opportunities that are provided by barrier-free trade, with no losses elsewhere. However, some of the trade is in fact diverted from other countries. For example, when Mexico joined the North American Free Trade Association (NAFTA), its exports to the United States increased (trade creation), but exports from some other developing countries to the United States fell (trade diversion). Being a member of NAFTA gave Mexico an edge over producers of some products in non-NAFTA countries, which were still subject to U.S. tariffs. This created inefficiency and economic loss for non-NAFTA countries that lacked any way to seek compensation for their losses.

## Political Regionalism

The fundamental political problem posed by regionalism is the loss of sovereignty that occurs when nations form regional blocs. These pluralistic organizations necessarily place constraints on the actions of sovereign nation-states. At some point, each member state risks being forced to ignore national interests—political, economic, social, or cultural—as a consequence of maintaining its regional obligations. This tension between national interests and international obligations is fundamental to multinational institutions and poses a severe dilemma for states, which tend to value security and autonomy above all else.

Given the importance of this political issue, the extent of regional integration we observe in the world today should surprise us more than it does. Why would a nation sacrifice its sovereignty and risk the "democracy deficit" to join a regional organization, especially an economic one? Several arguments stand out:

- As global markets have become more important, the nation-state has been caught in a dilemma. States are too limited (by their territorial definition) to manage many economic forces and to regulate transnational corporations. Political deadlock also prevents the emergence of effective global regulatory institutions (discussed in Chapter 17 with respect to transnational corporations and foreign direct investment, and in Chapter 6 in relation to the World Trade Organization). Regionalism presents an effective middle ground. Regional blocs such as the EU and NAFTA have the potential to provide a foundation of political governance to match expanding market forces.

■ Although deadlock seems to characterize many global negotiations, agreement on at least some regional issues may be easier to reach. Regional groups have a limited number of members, so it is sometimes easier for them to reach agreement than it is for much larger global organizations such as the World Trade Organization. And exceptions to various rules or laws are more common in regional negotiations than they are in global regimes. In short, regional political discussions have greater flexibility and, although this is not a guarantee that compromise can be reached on every issue, this does perhaps speed agreement on those points about which compromise is possible.

■ Another school of thought holds that regionalism is appealing because it represents a way of controlling domestic special-interest groups. A nation might choose to join a regional group in part to break the hold of special interests on domestic policies. Suppose, for example, that the interests of heavy industry prevent adoption of environmental laws in a country. If the responsibility for environmental regulation is shifted to the regional level, it is possible that environmental voices will have more influence, especially if other countries in the regional bloc have strong "green" parties.

■ There is also the realist view that regionalism can actually be sovereignty-enhancing and that some individual nations may gain political power, especially in relations with other nations, by being members of a powerful alliance. This is the argument that Belgium, for example, is a more potent political presence as a leading nation of the EU than if it were simply a small but autonomous European nation making its own way in international politics. It is argued that smaller countries are far more powerful as members of a larger group than they would be as separate, unaffiliated individual nations.

# EUROPE AND THE MIRROR OF REGIONALISM

Regionalism is a complicated balancing act. There are many advantages in terms of politics and economics, but many potential problems as well. What explains regionalism's rapid advance as a force in IPE? One explanation is that, because regionalism is so complex, it can be attractive to many different political and economic actors for many different reasons. A coalition in favor of regionalism can be formed even if the members of that coalition support it for very different reasons. Some may seek the benefits of larger markets, for example, whereas others wish to control domestic interest groups or advance a regional security agenda. Because regionalism is relatively vague, it can be seen to serve many purposes at once. Politics, it is said, makes strange bedfellows—a remark that may apply especially to regional politics.

If we look at the origins of regionalism in post–World War II Europe, for example, we find that the image of a united Europe was like the Mirror of Erised in J. K. Rowling's book *Harry Potter and the Sorcerer's Stone*. In the book, the Mirror of Erised does not reflect reality; rather, it shows each viewer's greatest hopes and fears. Reading the history books, this seems to be what people saw when they looked at European regionalism in the early postwar period (1945–1957):

- The United States supported postwar European regionalism because it saw in the mirror of regionalism the image of a strong anticommunist ally. Its **Marshall Plan** provided European nations with nearly $12 billion in aid (equivalent to more than $90 billion today) for the reconstruction of infrastructure and industries on the condition that these nations cooperate in their use. The motivation for the Marshall Plan was both humanitarian and strategic: Suffering masses in Europe needed to be helped both for their own sake and to prevent the spread of procommunist sentiment.

- Many Europeans—especially the French—supported regionalism in part because they wanted to see a solution to "the German problem"—a way to live with this mighty nation without being dominated by it. The new strategy was to accept Germany's political and economic power, but to embed it in supranational institutions.

- Germany, on the other hand, was seeking to become reintegrated into the international community after the moral disaster of National Socialism (Nazism). Therefore, it perceived the transfer of sovereignty to supranational institutions as a mean of creating trust in the German effort to overcome nationalism. In addition, West Germany suffered greatly from the Cold War because the "Iron Curtain" divided its territory and threatened its existence. The "West-integration" was therefore the main purpose of Chancellor Konrad Adenauer's foreign policy in the 1950s.

- Inspired by the philosophy of Immanuel Kant (1724–1804), some saw a European federation of democratic republics so experienced at settling their disagreements peacefully that it could be the basis for perpetual peace (in stark contrast to the experiences of the two World Wars). The mirror of regionalism showed them a Europe finally at peace with itself.

- British Prime Minister Winston Churchill saw a "United States of Europe" that could balance U.S. influence (and possibly prevent U.S. dominance) in the postwar era. Churchill's mirror revealed his own fears of U.S. dominance and his hope for a European balance to U.S. power.

- French President Charles DeGaulle, on the other hand, envisioned a "Europe of States" in which the structure of regionalism would enhance the sovereignty and status of all its members—especially France, of course. DeGaulle's mirror focused on Europe, whereas Churchill's kept glancing at the United States.

Considering the diversity of fears and hopes, one might wonder how the Europeans were able to achieve close cooperation. Realists stress that what finally brought them together was the need to find a political solution after the catastrophe of World War II, which was perceived largely as the result of excessive nationalism. The Cold War and economic interests also acted as accelerators. The advantages of free trade among partners of a similar level of economic and technological strength were certainly important incentives for regionalism. However, the main motive was political: the promotion of security, peace, and political freedom—in opposition to the totalitarian security structure established by the Soviet Union in Eastern Europe.

For the founding nations of the European Economic Community (France, West Germany, Italy, Belgium, the Netherlands, and Luxembourg), economic integration was, therefore, a means to achieve closer political integration. Cooperating to solve problems that were too big for one state was a way to solve the major problem of peaceful coexistence among sovereign states. This is obvious from the preamble of the **Treaty of Rome** (the document that established the EEC in 1958), in which the signatory states express their determination "to lay the foundations of an ever closer union among peoples of Europe." This is also evident from the institutional design of the EEC, which included not only the European Commission as the main executive body ("guardian of the treaties") but also a Common Assembly of national deputies, named from 1962 on the European Parliament (directly elected since 1979 for a five-year term), and a European Court of Justice. These institutions were constructed with the hidden agenda of a future growth of functions; the expectation was that sooner or later the economic cooperation would "spill over" and lead to strong political cooperation.

## The First Steps of European Regionalism: Coal and Steel and the Community

Many Europeans have helped design European regionalism, but it was Jean Monnet, a French political economist, who provided the key to moving from imagination to reality. Monnet believed that political divisions and disagreements could be overcome, in some cases, by the uniting force of economics. The promise of economic benefits could at least at times cause nations to set aside political disagreements and cooperate.

Although Monnet dreamed of a United States of Europe, he proposed a much narrower alliance along functional economic lines: a zone of free trade uniting the heavy-industry regions that spanned the French–German border. This plan for the ECSC was implemented by Robert Schuman, a French statesman, in 1950. The ECSC was the critical test case for economic and political cooperation between France and Germany. It was, by all accounts, a great success and thereby provided a model for further efforts toward integration in Western Europe. (For an overview of the chronological development of European integration, see Table 12-1 below.)

A fuller measure of economic integration was achieved in 1957 when the Treaty of Rome created the European Economic Community, a customs union that brought together the markets of Italy, France, Belgium, Luxembourg, the Netherlands, and West Germany. This union of "the Six" was a great success because these nations were natural trading partners that could benefit from the postwar global economic boom and the static and dynamic benefits of economic integration.

Great Britain participated in the negotiations for the Treaty of Rome but decided in the end to stand apart from the EEC. There were many reasons for this decision, which was eventually reversed at some cost to Britain. The British were

## TABLE 12-1

### Chronology of the European Communities/European Union

| Year | Month | Event |
|------|-------|-------|
| 1948 | May | A Congress in The Hague by leading supporters of European federalism urges the establishment of an economic and political union. |
| 1950 | May | French foreign minister Robert Schumann proposes placing French and German coal and steel production under a common authority. |
| | October | French Prime Minister René Pleven proposes creation of a European Defence Community (EDC). |
| 1951 | April | The treaty establishing the European Coal and Steel Community (ECSC) is signed by the Benelux states (Belgium, the Netherlands, and Luxembourg) France, Germany, and Italy, and goes into effect in July 1952. |
| 1952 | May | The European Defence Community (EDC) treaty is signed in Paris by the six member states of the ECSC; the treaty is rejected in August 1954 by the French National Assembly. |
| 1957 | March | The Treaty of Rome, establishing the European Economic Community (EEC) and the European Atomic Energy Community (EURATOM), is signed by the six member states of the ECSC; it goes into effect in January 1958. |
| 1960 | January | Agreement to establish a European Free Trade Association (EFTA) is signed by Austria, Denmark, Norway, Portugal, Sweden, Switzerland, and the United Kingdom. The EFTA goes into effect in May 1960. |
| 1963 | January | French President Charles de Gaulle announces his veto against membership of the United Kingdom in the EEC. |
| 1965 | April | The Merger Treaty that establishes a single Council and a single Commission for the European Communities (EC) is signed; it goes into effect in July 1967. |
| | July | Until January 1966, France (led by President de Gaulle) boycotts the European institutions to protest various proposed supranational developments. |
| 1968 | July | Customs Union completed: All internal customs duties and quotas are removed, and a common external tariff is established. |
| 1973 | January | Accession of Denmark, Ireland, and the United Kingdom to the EC. |
| 1974 | December | At a summit meeting in Paris, the heads of state and government of the EC agree to institutionalize their meetings (as the European Council) and to meet at least twice a year. The summit also decides that from 1979 on, the European Parliament will be directly elected. |
| 1981 | January | Accession of Greece to the EC. |
| 1984 | January | Establishment of a free-trade area between the EC and the EFTA. |
| 1985 | December | The European Council agrees on the Single European Act (SEA), which goes into effect in July 1987. |
| 1986 | January | Accession of Spain and Portugal to the EC. |
| 1989 | September–December | Collapse of communist regimes in Central and Eastern Europe. |
| 1990 | October | Reunification of Germany: East Germany becomes part of Germany and the EC. |
| 1992 | March | The European Council signs the Treaty on European Union (EU) in Maastricht, establishing the EU and (as a part of it) the European Monetary Union. |

**TABLE 12-1**  *(Continued)*

**Chronology of the European Communities/European Union**

| Year | Month | Event |
|------|-------|-------|
| 1995 | January | Accession of Austria, Finland, and Sweden to the EU. |
|      | March | Schengen Agreement (which abolishes all border controls) implemented by seven EU member states: Germany, France, the Benelux states, Spain, and Portugal. |
| 1997 | June | The European Council agrees on the Treaty of Amsterdam, which strengthens the institutions of the EU. |
| 1999 | January | The euro goes into effect with 11 of the 15 EU members participating. |
| 2000 | December | The European Council agrees on the Treaty of Nice, which fails to prepare the EU for enlargement. |
| 2002 | January | Euro coins and banknotes enter circulation and replace the national currencies. |
|      | June | The Treaty on the ECSC expires after 50 years. |
| 2004 | May | Accession of 10 new members to the EU: Cyprus, the Czech Republic, Estonia, Hungary, Latvia, Lithuania, Malta, Poland, Slovakia, and Slovenia. |
|      | October | The European Council signs the treaty establishing a Constitution for Europe. |
| 2005 | May | The treaty establishing a Constitution for Europe is rejected in referenda in France (54.5 percent "no") and the Netherlands (61.6 percent "no"). |
| 2007 | January | Accession of Bulgaria and Romania to the EU. |
|      | December | The European Council signs the Treaty of Lisbon ("reform treaty"). |
| 2008 | June | The Treaty of Lisbon is rejected in a referendum in Ireland (53.4 percent "no"). |
| 2009 | June | European Parliament election takes place. |
|      | October | Second referendum on the Treaty of Lisbon in Ireland (67.1 percent "yes"). |
|      | December | The Treaty of Lisbon, ratified by the parliaments or people of the 27 member states, goes into effect. |

*Sources:* Neill Nugent, *The Government and Politics of the European Union* (Durham, NC: Duke University Press, 2006); website of the European Union, http://europa.eu.

concerned, first of all, about the loss of political and economic autonomy that necessarily accompanies economic integration. British politicians (and probably most British citizens) were hesitant to cede decision-making power to others or to share it with the French and the Germans. Britain was forced to weigh the trade-off among self-determination, domestic democracy, and economic growth, which presented a constant tension in economic integration. Britain was also unwilling to give up either its "imperial preferences"—preferential trading relations with the Commonwealth nations—or its "special relationship" with the United States that it so highly valued. Britain balked, therefore, at its first opportunity to enter the EEC, but it dared not to be isolated from free trade in Europe. It therefore organized a weaker alliance of trading nations called the **European Free Trade Area (EFTA)**. However, the EFTA never became the engine of economic growth that the EEC promised to be. Today, only Iceland, Liechtenstein, Norway, and Switzerland remain as members of the EFTA.

Despite its remarkable success in gaining political cooperation among nations that had engaged in two world wars, the EEC should not be viewed through rose-tinted glasses. Trade among member nations took a long time to become entirely free. After 1957, nontariff barriers to trade abounded, and it took decades until national standards and regulations were harmonized or mutually recognized. It was also necessary to create an elaborate and expensive system of agricultural subsidies across the EEC to defuse political opposition from powerful farm groups. The **Common Agricultural Policy (CAP)** provided for a complex pattern of payments to farmers in all EEC nations, although not equally to each (see box "The Common Agricultural Policy"). A unified system of farm payments was an improvement over the pattern of destructive competition in subsidies that might otherwise have resulted.

## THE COMMON AGRICULTURAL POLICY

The Common Agricultural Policy is one of the most controversial and divisive elements of economic and political integration in Europe. The CAP is an EU-wide system of agricultural subsidies, financed through taxes imposed by EU member nations. The CAP has been far and away the largest item of expenditure of the EU and has been a point of contention both within the EU and in its relations with other nations.

The origins of the CAP reach back to the very beginnings of postwar European regionalism. As soon as the guns of World War II had cooled, European governments met to discuss the "farm problem," which was really two problems in one. The first problem was food security—the need to guarantee adequate supplies of agricultural foodstuffs. The second problem was farm incomes, which suffered tremendously from the Great Depression, World War II, and postwar economic conditions. All the nations agreed that something needed to be done, but they disagreed about the right collective policy. As a result, each state enacted its own plan to stimulate production and to support farm incomes.

The signing of the Treaty of Rome was a golden opportunity for the original six EEC members to establish a common farm policy. They agreed on a system of price supports, which guaranteed farmers high prices, and protective barriers against foreign agricultural produce. High prices encouraged farmers to produce more and more, which addressed the food

security concern. And the combination of high prices plus trade barriers guaranteed farmers higher incomes.

Over the years, however, the CAP's guarantees encouraged European farmers to expand production to a vast degree, creating "mountains" of surplus dairy products and "lakes" of surplus wine and olive oil, for example. These mountains and lakes owed their existence entirely to the CAP, because without it, prices would decline and surplus production would be eliminated.

By the 1990s the CAP was under fire from all sides, criticized in particular on three counts:

- First, the CAP was no longer affordable—it had become very expensive, costing more than 40 billion euro in 2001, or almost half of the total EU budget. And these costs would only increase as EU membership expanded.
- Second, the EU's policy harmed poor farmers in other countries, especially LDCs. Farm trade barriers limited LDC access to EU markets, of course, but the subsidized surpluses were the real problem. What happened to the EU's surplus farm goods? In many cases they were sold off or "dumped" on foreign markets, driving down farm prices there and in some cases driving indigenous farmers out of business.
- Finally, the CAP was blamed in part for the breakdown of global trade talks, which were stalled by disagreement between the United States

and the EU over subsides. As long as the EU kept its CAP, it was unlikely that the United States would reduce subsidies either, and the stalemate would continue, much to the displeasure of taxpayers in these countries and poor farmers in the developing world.

Reforming CAP was difficult, especially in the face of resistance from farmers. For example, France received the most subsidies of any CAP nation, about 9 billion euro, and French farmers were vocal, visible, and politically powerful. Not until June 2003 were EU agriculture ministers able to agree on a plan to reform the CAP. The plan does not do away with farm subsidies—that would be politically explosive—but it reconfigures the payments in several useful ways. The most important change is that quantity-based subsidies are replaced, in most instances, with fixed payments to farmers. Farmers keep their subsidies but lose the incentive to overproduce. Moreover, the fixed payments require EU farmers to make progress on issues such as environmental sustainability and food safety (a particular concern since the spread of "mad cow" disease).

## Suggested Readings

"CAP Reform—A Long-Term Perspective for Sustainable Agriculture," *EUROPA*, website of the European Union, http://ec.europa.eu/agriculture/publi/reports/reformimpact/rep_en.pdf.

"From Bad to Worse, Down to the Farm," *The Economist*, March 3, 2001, p. 45.

"Let Them Eat Foie Gras," *The Economist*, June 21, 2003, pp. 45–46.

# THE BICYCLE THEORY: BROADER, DEEPER, EVER CLOSER

In 1967, the EEC, the ECSC, and EURATOM (an organization for European cooperation in the use of nuclear energy) merged and became the European Community (EC). The change in name signaled the intention to move beyond purely economic issues, although economic concerns continued to dominate EC discussions.

This move to expand the political agenda reflected the prevailing wisdom in Europe that is sometimes summed up as the **bicycle theory** of European regionalism. A bicycle is stable so long as it keeps moving, but once it stops, its stability disappears and it tends to fall over. In the same way, according to Walter Hallstein, first president of the **European Commission**, European unity could be sustained only if European nations constantly strived for an "ever closer union."

The EC broadened its geographic vision in several stages. Figure 12-1 and Table 12-1 trace the expansion of European regionalism to the current 27 members of the EU. Great Britain (the United Kingdom) finally entered the EC on January 1, 1973, along with Ireland and Denmark. Britain took the plunge only after two controversial referenda and a series of painful negotiations. Britain's status as a European nation was determined, but its ambivalence about its relationship to Europe remained.

Greece entered the EC in 1981, followed by Spain and Portugal in 1986. In all three cases, EC membership was in part a reward for the triumph of democratic institutions over authoritarian governments. Free trade and closer economic ties were intended to solidify democracy and protect it from potential communist influences.

The broader market was not in all respects a better market, however. The entry of the poorer nations of Ireland, Greece, Spain, and Portugal (at the time they were called "the poor four") magnified a variety of tensions within the EC. Lower living standards limited the extent of their trade with richer member states. Lower wage structures threatened some jobs in EC industries. Finally, the addition of four largely agricultural nations to EC institutions, including the CAP, put severe fiscal strains on the other nations. The broader market was surely in the long-run interest of the EC, but it imposed great stress on cooperative relationships in the short run.

These economic and political stresses reached a peak in the mid-1980s. Higher and higher EC program costs, imposing a disproportionate burden on Great Britain in particular, precipitated a split in the EC. Jacques Delors, the newly appointed president of the European Commission, traveled from capital to capital seeking ways to reunite the governments and peoples of the EC in some common enterprise. What could restore a measure of unity and cooperation and keep the bicycle moving forward? A common defense and foreign policy? A common monetary system? In the end, Delors concluded that international trade, which Monnet had used to bring the EC together in the first place, was the force most likely to reenergize Europe. In 1985, therefore, Delors issued a "white paper" proposing the creation of a single integrated market by 1992. The **Single European Act (SEA)**, which came into effect in 1987, formalized this grand experiment in market deepening—and kept the bicycle upright.

The goals of Europe in 1992 might be characterized as "four freedoms": free movement of goods, services, capital, and people. Each of these freedoms is much harder to achieve in practice than to imagine in theory. Free movement of goods, for example, requires much more than the absence of tariff and quota barriers; there are hundreds of nontariff barriers to the free production and sale of goods that must be addressed. Health, safety, and technical standards, each of which plays a constructive role, can all discourage imports from other countries (by raising the cost of selling) and encourage the purchase of domestically produced goods. These standards must be leveled (or *harmonized*, in the jargon of the trade) to allow, to the maximum possible extent, a good that can be sold anywhere in the group to be sold everywhere. In many industries, this was reached—as mentioned above—by the mutual recognition of standards.

Services represent an increasing proportion of world trade. Achieving free movement of services, such as financial and insurance services, is a tricky task, given the complex systems of financial regulations that each nation has in place. Free movement of money or capital requires the dismantling of capital controls and investment regulations, which affect flows of funds into and out of a nation. Finally, free movement of people requires agreement on many points, most especially the adoption of a common immigration policy. Once a person has entered one EU nation, he or she is free to enter any other.

However, the SEA went beyond improvement of economic freedom in the EC. It also strengthened the political integration and prepared in many respects the big step forward that was made in the early 1990s with the Treaty of Maastricht. One of the major changes of the SEA was to change the requirement of a unanimous vote to approve most legislative decisions concerning the single market. The "unanimity vote" had made decisions on European legislation very difficult to make, because it essentially gave a veto to every single member of the Council of the European Community (the meeting of the national ministers of the member states). The SEA introduced a qualified majority rule, meaning that a decision was taken if a majority of sixty-two of eighty-seven votes was in favor of a proposal (= 71.26 percent; the 87 votes were given to the twelve member states in relation to their size). In addition to its practical advantages, the qualified majority vote had great symbolic value. It meant that, at least with respect to single-market legislation, the European institutions were gaining in importance; that is, from then on it was possible to take decisions against the will of some opposing members. In addition to establishing the qualified majority vote, the SEA gave more power to the pan-European institutions: the European Commission, the European Parliament (EP), and the European Court of Justice (ECJ).

Delors's single-market initiative posed a real challenge to the EC member states: It required each nation to sacrifice its interests on hundreds of small issues, many of which had important domestic political effects, before the four freedoms could be achieved.

National sovereignty and economic growth were often in conflict. Germany, for example, desired to see its own high environmental standards applied to all EC vehicles. Environmentalism is an important social value in Germany, and the Green Party is a potent political force on some issues. These environmental regulations are costly, however, and were opposed on economic grounds by poorer countries such as Greece and Portugal. To a certain extent, at least, the four freedoms for the EC as a whole actually required sacrifice of some domestic freedoms, such as the right to self-determination of environmental and safety standards.

The years 1989 and 1990 brought about an unexpected turn to European politics. With the fall of the Berlin Wall and the collapse of socialist regimes in Central and Eastern Europe, the Western European countries faced a double challenge: German reunification (the formerly socialist German Democratic Republic joined the Federal Republic of Germany on October 3, 1990); and applications for membership from most of the Central and Eastern European countries. The **Treaty of Maastricht,** which established the EU in 1992, was mainly a result of negotiations during the process of German reunification. Both Great Britain's Prime Minister Margaret Thatcher and France's President François Mitterand were reluctant to accept a unified Germany, which brought back memories of German domination in Europe. In this situation, two ambitious plans were proposed by France and Germany. France proposed monetary union—a single currency. This would provide economic gains to offset the costs of eastward enlargement. The German problem would be solved because Germany would be chained to the rest of the EU by a strong link—money—and it would have to give up the most powerful symbol of its economic strength, the Deutsche Mark. The second plan, proposed by Germany and France together, was to move further in European regionalism by promoting political integration. France supported the idea of the European Union in order to gain more control over Germany—and was ready to accept in exchange that it would itself have to give up sovereignty. Germany, on the other hand, was ready to give up national sovereignty in exchange for trust in its reunification.

The conference of Maastricht in December 1991 realized both plans. The heads of state and government of the twelve member states decided to establish a monetary union at the latest on January 1, 1999, and to replace the national currencies with one common currency: the euro (however, the name of the currency was chosen only in December 1995). Two decisions were made in Maastricht to strengthen the new currency. First, the European Central Bank (ECB) was to be independent in its monetary policies from other European institutions and from national governments, and it was committed only to the objective of price stability. Second, only those countries that were fulfilling the so-called convergence criteria—a low inflation rate, low interest rates, and low government debt—were meant to join the "Eurozone." A third decision to strengthen the euro was taken by the European Council in 1997 by agreeing on the "Stability and Growth Pact," which forces the members of the Eurozone, after joining the euro, to respect a certain discipline in government spending. Since then, a high government debt—which risks causing inflation in the whole Eurozone—can be penalized by the European Council.

Although the criteria for nations to be part of the single currency were thought to be very strict, in fact twelve of the fifteen countries in the EU in 1998 were set to enter into monetary union. Denmark, Great Britain, and Sweden elected to remain outside the Eurozone. The ECB took control of the Eurozone's monetary policy on January 1, 1999, and three years later the new banknotes and coins were introduced.

The second plan that was realized in Maastricht was to finally make the step from an economic community to a political union—a step that had already been prepared by the SEA in 1986. The union brings together three areas of cooperation into one legal and institutional structure:

- The **Single Market,** which was started with the EEC treaty in 1957 and accomplished by the SEA in 1986.
- Cooperation in "Foreign and Security Policy," which began in 1970 but remains very difficult even today. Although all members realize that the EU would have more weight in world politics if it spoke with one voice, the national interests of the bigger members are often highly diverging. This can be seen quite well in the differences among the European states regarding the war in Iraq: Some countries, including Great Britain, Italy, and Poland, joined the United States in invading Iraq, whereas France and Germany opposed the invasion.
- Cooperation in "Justice and Home Affairs," which started in the 1970s. One of the important steps toward cooperation in these areas was the *Schengen Agreement* (named after the town in Luxembourg in which the agreement was reached in 1985), which opened the borders between most of the European countries and defined new forms of police cooperation (both realized from 1995 on). As of 2006, this agreement had been signed by Germany, France, Belgium, the Netherlands, Luxembourg, Austria, Italy, Spain, Portugal, Greece, Denmark, Finland, and Sweden. Great Britain and Ireland have not joined the agreement; Iceland and Norway joined it without being members of the EU.

Political decision making differs considerably in these three areas, which are called the "**three pillars**" of the EU. In the Single Market (Pillar 1), the EU institutions work like a national political system with the EU Commission as a government and both the Council of the EU and the European Parliament as legislative bodies that cooperate in the legislative process like the two chambers of a parliament. In Foreign Policy (Pillar 2) and Justice and Home Affairs (Pillar 3) the Council of the EU is the main political institution, and decisions must be unanimous (not taken with qualified majority voting), so that each national government has a veto position. This is why Pillar 1 is called "supranational" and Pillars 2 and 3 are called "intergovernmental": Pillar 1 works like a government beyond the nation-state, whereas Pillars 2 and 3 work like an international organization in which national governments coordinate their policies.

The process of "deepening" the European way of regionalism was followed by "broadening": the big enlargements of 2004 (from fifteen to twenty-five members) and 2007 (with Bulgaria and Romania, to twenty-seven members). It became clear that the institutional design of 1957 based on six members would hardly work for twenty-seven. However, attempts at major reforms of the EU have failed. In 2002, the EU established the European Convention and tasked it with drafting a constitution for Europe. For 18 months, 105 deputies of the EU member states (including the states that would join in 2004 and 2007) discussed the institutional future of the EU. In 2004 the president of the convention, former French President Valéry Giscard d'Estaing, presented the result: the draft of a constitution that reflected a compromise between the need to streamline the decision-making processes, the desire for more political integration, and the fear of giving up too much sovereignty to the EU. In summer 2005, the draft failed in the referenda in France and in the Netherlands; in both countries, a large majority—about 54.5 percent in France and 61.6 percent in the Netherlands—rejected the constitution.

After a period of "reflection" meant to give time to search for new ways of achieving the necessary reforms, officials in June 2007 decided to draft a new Treaty that would realize large parts of the Constitutional Treaty without using the symbolism of a constitution. The Treaty of Lisbon (signed in Lisbon in December 2007 and ratified in November 2009) came into effect in December 2009. The most important changes stipulated by the treaty are:

- Instead of rotating the presidency every six months, the EU will have a President elected for two and a half years (with the possibility of reelection for one term). This change is meant to bring more continuity and more efficiency to EU politics and to improve the external representation of the EU.
- The creation of a new position called the High Representative of the Union for Foreign Affairs and Security Policy to try to resolve frequent disagreements among Europeans on foreign policy. The High Representative— together with the new President of the European Council—should improve the coordination of the EU members in foreign policy and give a face to the EU in the world. These two offices are sort of a response to Henry Kissinger's famous question in the 1970s: "Who do I call when I want to call Europe?"
- The European Parliament will have equal standing with the Council of the EU in most social, economic, and environmental policies (Pillar 1). The purpose is to establish in these policy areas a bicameral system in European legislation,

with the EP and the Council acting as two legislative chambers and the Commission working like a government. This strengthening of the EP is meant to respond to the democratic deficit.

■ After November 2014, qualified majority voting will apply a double majority rule: Decisions will need to be approved by 55 percent of the member states representing at least 65 percent of the EU's population. Most economic and social decisions will be made by qualified majority voting.

## THE DEVELOPMENT OF POLITICAL INSTITUTIONS

European regionalism is always political, even if its appearance is economic. As we have stated before, the purpose of economic integration in the 1950s was to move further toward political integration, and this was the reason for designing an impressive set of political institutions to make policy, to settle disputes, and to provide leadership for Europe. The most important political institutions of the EU today are the European Council, the Council of the EU (also called the Council of Ministers), the presidencies of the Councils, the European Commission, the European Parliament, and the European Court of Justice. Each of these institutions plays a specific role, first in setting the delicate balance between national interests of member nations and second in balancing power and interests on the European level. All of these institutions are characterized by a mix of intergovernmental and supranational qualities, combining the representation of national interests with promotion of a European perspective.

The **European Council** is the meeting of the heads of state and government of all member states. The functions of the European Council can be described as strategic decision making. Most importantly, it negotiates the treaties that are shaping European integration and decides the EU's budget and strategic issues such as enlargement of the EU. The European Council meets at least twice every six months.

The **President of the European Council** is elected for two and a half years and has no national office. His task is to chair European Council meetings and to represent the EU in external relations. In the field of Foreign and Security Policy he gets the support of the European "foreign minister," called the High Representative of the Union for Foreign Affairs and Security Policy.

The **Council of the EU (or Council of Ministers)** is the main lawmaking body of the EU, composed of a single representative from each member nation. It is subdivided into nine "formations" in which the respective ministers of national governments gather.[2] The main functions of the Council are to decide European legislation and to make policy decisions, but some of these functions require cooperation with the Commission and the Parliament. The Council's most important areas of decision-making powers are foreign policy, fiscal policies, and economic policies aimed at maintaining a strong euro and promoting economic growth. Both the European Council and the Council of Ministers are characterized by a strong desire for consensus. To prepare the decisions of the Council of Ministers, each member state of the EU has a number of Permanent Representatives in Brussels (the "capital" of the EU), who meet on a regular basis. In contrast to the ministers, who represent their national governments in the Council and often take a firm national point of view, the Permanent Representatives live in Brussels in a "European environment," which shapes their approach to European politics. This helps in finding solutions for policy or legislative issues below the ministerial level and in preparing the agenda for the ministers in such a way as to ease negotiations.

The **European Commission** acts as the EU's executive cabinet. The membership of the Commission (called the "College of Commissioners") includes 27 commissioners (one for every member state) and the president of the European Commission. Each commissioner—who is appointed for a five-year term—has a specific "portfolio" of responsibilities, such as competition policy, trade, or agriculture, making her or his responsibilities equivalent to those of a cabinet minister or department secretary in a nation-state. Decisions are taken *de jure*, by absolute majority (with a strong tendency to achieve a *de facto* consensus). The main functions of the Commission are to design policy programs, legislative proposals, and budgetary proposals. A second important function of the Commission is to monitor implementation of EU laws by national governments. A third important task is to represent European interests in international organizations such as the World Trade Organization.

The **European Parliament (EP)** has taken on over the years many of the functions of traditional parliaments. Since 1979, it has been elected in direct elections by European citizens for five-year terms. However, because of a general lack of awareness of the role and functions of the EP, election campaigns are often dominated by national issues and not by European politics. Also, election turnouts are significantly lower than in national elections. For example, in the last election in 2009, the turnout was only 43 percent. This has often been attributed to the fact that the EP is not perceived as being representative of a European people, because European citizens do not feel that they are one people in the way that Americans do. The EP, which had 736 deputies in 2009, is organized along political party lines and not according to national citizenship. Socialists from all EU nations act together, for example, as do conservatives and other party groups. The EP's main political functions are, first, to participate in drafting policy programs and European legislation; second, to cooperate with the Council of Ministers in European legislation; third, to vote on the EU budget, which is negotiated by the Council; and fourth, to approve and control the European Commission.

The **European Court of Justice (ECJ)** is composed of twenty-seven judges and eight advocates-general who are appointed to six-year terms. The Court of Justice adjudicates legal conflicts between EU institutions and between the EU and member states. Its decisions usually emphasize the priority of European law over national legislation, and the court is therefore an important promoter of European integration.

Among other institutions of the EU, the most important in the IPE context is the **European Central Bank (ECB)**, which is responsible for monetary policy and price stability in the Eurozone. It also conducts foreign exchange operations, manages the foreign reserves of the member states, and promotes the smooth operation of payment systems in the Eurozone.

These EU institutions provide a comprehensive, if somewhat unwieldy, organization for setting policies and making decisions that affect the entire EU. In the early days of the EU, this political superstructure had more form than substance—its political powers were relatively limited and symbolic. As political and economic integration progressed, however, these political institutions have grown in importance. In a way, the broader and deeper EU has "grown into" its political clothing in the decades since the Treaty of Rome.

The broadening and deepening of the EU over the past twenty-five years has created real political problems that daily test the strength of the EU's political institutions. Deepening necessarily forced each member state to cede some economic and political powers to EU institutions, as more and more policies and regulations became EU-wide, not national, in scope. This has led over time to a very complex relationship between European and national legislation, which is confusing even for specialists. Broadening has also posed political problems, because any increase in the size of the Union necessarily reduces the clout of existing members, who find their votes reduced in relative importance. These threats to nation-state sovereignty pose threats to EU unity. For example, in 1994 Spain briefly threatened to try to block negotiations to admit Sweden to the EU because Spanish leaders feared their nation would lose political power and economic benefits from EU widening. The most important issue created by the enlargement is that the EU has so far not been able to adjust its institutions to the large number of twenty-seven members.

## The Economic and Monetary Union

On January 1, 1999, eleven of the fifteen members of the EU gave up their national currencies (and the ability to influence their individual values) and entered into a monetary union with a single currency, the euro. The eleven countries are Germany, France, Italy, Spain, Portugal, Belgium, Luxembourg, the Netherlands, Austria, Finland, and Ireland. Greece joined in 2001, Slovenia in 2007, Cyprus and Malta in 2008, and Slovakia in 2009. Sweden, Denmark, and the United Kingdom have elected to retain their national currencies, at least for the time being, and are not part of the "Eurozone." The remaining EU countries have applied for membership in the Eurozone but are not yet ready to meet the economic criteria. The euro is so far a success story: 10 years after being introduced, it is the second most commonly held reserve currency in the world. In 2008 about 26 percent of the currency reserves in the world were held in euros, compared with 17 percent in 1999.[3]

The stated goal of monetary union was to give the EU's bicycle the ultimate economic push—a huge single market with a single currency to drive it. It would be easy to conclude that the euro is all about economics, efficiency, and growth, but in fact the most important aspects of the euro are political. For example, its name was chosen because it means nothing in any European language. For a time the name "ecu" (for European Currency Unit) was considered, but this was rejected as "too French," because a coin called the *ecu* once circulated in medieval France. Scenes on euro currency appear to be classic European images, but none of them is authentic. Putting any *real* European scene on the currency would cause political disagreements, so every euro image is created by artists to look European without representing any specific, national monument. Even the euro symbol means nothing, for fear that anything else would cause political divisions.

Ironically, although the euro itself is politically neutral, its implications are politically explosive. In order to qualify for entry into the Eurozone, for example, each nation had to meet a number of economic stability targets, such as low inflation, low interest rates, and low government debt. To achieve these goals has been a great domestic political challenge, because governments sometimes have to make unpopular decisions to either raise taxes or cut government spending and benefits. The fear of being left out of the Eurozone's prosperity, however, motivated domestic political change, though not without creating tensions that linger today.

Since the euro was launched in 1999, member nations have faced a transformed political environment. Their ability to influence domestic economic conditions has been reduced because interest rates are now set by the ECB, not by policy makers in each country. This puts national leaders in a very awkward position: Their citizens hold them accountable for national economic conditions, but the leaders are left with few traditional economic policy tools to affect these conditions. For example, the Spanish government cannot spend its way out of a recession or print money to pay unemployment benefits, because it does not have the full fiscal autonomy it had when the peseta was its sovereign currency. Instead, it might have to lower the minimum wage or reduce welfare benefits to attract business and create jobs—policies that would be politically divisive indeed.

The euro is economic "superglue"; it binds together the nations of the Eurozone and gives them good reason to try to work out national differences as the EU expands. However, the cost is that domestic political differences and disagreements are magnified. Dealing with this issue is a significant political challenge in the current financial crisis. In order to maintain a stable euro (i.e., to avoid inflation and to achieve a stable external value), the members of the Eurozone have agreed to some basic rules for their fiscal policies in a so-called stability pact adopted in 1997. For instance, a country's annual budget deficit should not exceed 3 percent of its GDP and total government debt cannot amount to more than 60 percent of its GDP. With the current crisis, these criteria cannot be met and exceptions are necessary. Even if the euro is currently strong, the current level of government budget deficits could create considerable inflationary pressure in the near future.

## THREE CHALLENGES FOR THE EUROPEAN UNION

The current financial crisis is certainly one of the major challenges for the EU, testing its ability to coordinate an overall community response while adjusting for the different ways in which its members have been affected. The EU also faces two other important challenges. Since the enlargements of 2004 and 2007, the number of member states has risen from fifteen to twenty-seven and strained its antiquated institutions (designed in 1957 for six member states). The Treaty of Lisbon requires deep institutional reform—a process which is, as the Europeans have learned in the past, a risky one. Moreover, the EU is grappling with the question of what economic and political roles it should play in the world. Can it transform its economic power into more global political influence? Should it strive for a more independent and muscular security policy, or should it leave security issues to be coordinated with the United States through NATO?

## The Challenge of the Financial and Economic Crisis

The bankruptcy of Lehman Brothers in September 2008 was a wake-up call for the EU, a sort of financial earthquake that triggered severe financial turmoil in numerous European banks. Most European governments drafted emergency legislation to support their banks. For instance, Germany, Great Britain, and France decided in October and November 2008 to grant a total of more than 1 trillion euro (about $1.4 trillion) as guarantees for bank transactions and 185 billion euro (more than $250 billion) as state aid to failing financial institutions like France's Société Générale and Germany's Commerzbank and Hypo Real Estate.

The financial crisis quickly spread to the real economy in the fall of 2008, when European exporters—especially automotive manufacturers—suffered a severe slump in incoming orders. Many European governments responded with large economic stimulus packages in order to try to prevent the GDP from falling more than the projected 5 percent in 2009. The impact of the crisis on the labor market was considerable: From June 2008 to June 2009 the unemployment rate in the EU rose from 6.9 to 8.9 percent, and it was expected to continue to rise. Spain and the Baltic states of Latvia, Lithuania, and Estonia have been especially hard hit: their unemployment rate in June 2009 was between 15 and 18 percent.

The EU has struggled to decide on appropriate market interventions and the institutional level (national or European) at which policy decisions have to be taken. So far, economic stimulus packages are mainly a matter of domestic politics. The EU helps to coordinate such packages and to control whether state aid might distort competition among the member states of the EU. Joint action against the crisis has been difficult because of different perspectives in countries. France and Great Britain have pushed for large economic stimulus packages, whereas Germany has favored moderate action in order to avoid an excessive increase in state debt (which could create the next bubble crisis). In December 2008, the EU decided on a 200 billion euro stimulus package (about 1.5 percent of the EU GDP), but it was mostly the sum of national packages plus some funds that had been reallocated by the European Commission.

Despite agreement that stimulus packages are necessary to respond to the crisis and can be financed by allowing higher public debt, there is a severe disagreement about when the public debt needs to be reduced. The Euro Stability Pact allows all Eurozone members to have a deficit of three percent of the GDP. It also allows for exceptions in times of a severe recession. Germany is the leader of the group of countries claiming a "short" exception: Governments should come back to a balanced budget as quickly as possible, because high deficits can cause inflation and aggravate economic instabilities. On the other side, France leads the countries that claim that in a recession higher state debts can stimulate economic growth and achieve economic stability. For the French government, the current recession is an occasion to question the usefulness of the Euro Stability Pact, which it had only reluctantly agreed to in 1997.

By late 2009, Greece began to fall into a severe crisis as investors feared that the country might default on its huge public debt. Eurozone members, especially Germany and France, were forced to consider bailing Greece out while the country made deep spending cuts that were politically unpopular. Some officials and EU critics have suggested that Greece and other countries such as Ireland, Spain, Portugal, and Italy that have not been able to limit their public debt should drop out of the Eurozone.

In addition to economic stimulus packages, the EU participates together with Germany, Great Britain, France, and Italy in the meetings of the "Group of 20" to reform global financial markets regulations. Here again, national divergences are visible: Whereas the German and the French governments are promoting strong new safeguards on financial markets, Great Britain wants to avoid a too strong foreign control of the "City"—London's powerful financial marketplace.

However, in another policy field the financial crisis seems to be strengthening the EU. Until recently, the regulation and supervision of financial markets were left to individual nations. In 2009, the European Commission drafted legislation to transform three already-existing EU committees with advisory powers over banks, insurances, and securities into a European System of Financial Supervisors (ESFS). The agencies belonging to this system would coordinate national supervisors, harmonize national regulatory rules, and directly supervise some pan-European institutions such as credit rating agencies.

Overall, there are two lessons about regionalism in IPE that we can learn from the EU's reaction to the financial crisis. First, it is much easier to reduce trade barriers than to agree on common policies that involve spending substantial amounts of tax money. The right to decide about the allocation of public funds is historically perceived as a fundamental right by the national parliaments in the EU. Therefore, economic and social policies will rather remain at the national level. Second, crises can reinforce the nation-state rather than strengthen regionalism. Despite the positive commentaries of the EU Commission on its web site, the major political answers to the crisis are national answers, not European ones.

## The Challenge of the Democratic Deficit and "Finalité"

The Treaty of Lisbon implements considerable institutional reforms in the EU. However, it is questionable whether these reforms will solve the issues concerning the institutional design of the EU. Two dominant issues are discussed among Europeans: the democratic deficit and the need to decide about political "finalité."

The democratic deficit of the decision-making processes in the EU is because of a lack of transparency of EU institutions and of the distribution of responsibilities between EU and national institutions. Qualified Majority Voting (QVM) in the Council of the EU requires a majority of three-quarters of the weighted votes—a fact that encourages logrolling and the claim of compensatory payments. The search for compromises in the European Council or the Council of Ministers is done behind closed doors, hence there are few chances to understand afterward who was responsible for which decision. Frequently, national politicians claim positive decisions of the Council to be their personal achievements and blame the EU partners or the EU Commission for decisions that are perceived as negative by their electorate. As a result, it is difficult to attribute responsibility, which would be crucial for democratic control.

The EU's perceived "democratic deficit" is aggravated by the fact that the European Parliament does not work like national parliaments. First, the EP does not vote the commissioners like a national parliament votes for a government. It has only the right to approve (or to reject) the nominations made by the European

Council. Second, the EP is mainly involved in decisions like tariffs, technical standards, competition policy, and agriculture policy—topics which are important but which hardly attract popular attention. Decisions on security, economic, and social policies that dominate political debates are decided either outside the EP or at the national level. Third, in EP elections the people do not vote as Europeans. Voters mainly perceive EP elections as an opportunity to give a lesson to their national government. Therefore, the democratic deficit of the EU appears also as a deficit in terms of a European public: A democracy needs a "demos," a people, but Europeans don't perceive themselves as a European people. This is also noticeable in the turnout in EP elections, which has constantly declined from 62 percent in the first direct elections in 1979 to 43 percent in 2009.

The question of "finalité politique," as Europeans call it in French, is essentially this: What should be the final design of the EU's institutions? In other words, where should the bicycle ride end? With the Treaty of Maastricht, the door was open for establishing a closer political union. The rejection of the Constitutional Treaty in 2005 and the adoption of the Treaty of Lisbon indicate that the EU will remain a compromise between diverging interests:

- The founding members, especially France, Germany, and Italy, favor a strong political union which guarantees peace and freedom in Europe and which serves as a model of regionalism for other parts of the world.
- The southern countries Greece, Spain, and Portugal, who joined in the 1980s, receive significant financial aid from the EU to support their comparatively weak economies and to promote political stability. For them, one major task of the EU is the redistribution of wealth.
- Great Britain perceives the EU as a means to realize a free-trade area in Europe and is opposed to creation of a political union. The Scandinavian countries (Sweden, Denmark, and Finland), who joined the EU in order to benefit from the Single Market, share this perspective in many respects.
- The Eastern countries like Poland, Hungary, and the Czech Republic joined the EU to reorient themselves toward the West after 40 years of Soviet domination. They are interested in promoting the Single Market, but they fear a strong political union. Politicians of these countries like to compare Brussels (the "capital" of the EU) with a new Moscow.

Considering these very different motives for being a member of the EU, it seems probable that the EU will remain a compromise—a model of regionalism, which is neither a strong political union (a "United States of Europe") nor a mere free-trade area.

## Challenges in World Politics

Often the EU is criticized for being too slow or too weak in its reactions to new economic or security challenges that it faces in world politics. What are the main foreign policy challenges of the EU today? The dominant economic challenge is the financial crisis which by early 2010 was threatening to send Greece into default on its public debt. In addition to responding on the domestic level to this crisis, the EU is involved in a global response, especially through its involvement in the G-20. Among the objectives of the EU in the G-20 negotiations are the strengthening of the role of the IMF and the tightening of global financial markets regulations. For instance, the EU has pushed for strict regulation of hedge funds and control of offshore banking.

Growing economic competition from countries like India and China is yet another challenge to the EU. To keep its technological lead in sectors like machinery and equipment, fabricated metal products, and chemicals, the EU will need to reinforce its research and development efforts with a special emphasis on cross-border R&D cooperation.

A third economic challenge with an important political impact is energy policy. Like the United States, the EU is mainly dependent on fossil fuels. Approximately 37 percent of its energy needs are met by oil, 24 percent by gas, 18 percent by coal, 14 percent by nuclear power, and 7 percent by renewables. Most of the gas used in the EU comes from Russia (about 42 percent), and Russia has shown in recent years that it will not hesitate to use its gas exports for political pressure. Most Russian gas is transported to Europe through pipelines that pass through the Ukraine. In recent winters, Russia has repeatedly accused the Ukraine of stealing gas or not paying its debts from gas imports. To pressure the Ukraine, Russia stopped its gas exports several times—causing fallout not only in the Ukraine but also in other European countries, notably Bulgaria and Romania, where thousands of households were without heat for part of the winter. The EU has tried to diversify its gas imports by building a new gas pipeline called Nabucco, which will transport Central Asian gas through Georgia and Turkey without touching Russian soil. It has also pushed member states to reduce energy consumption by using new technologies and shifting to renewable energies.[4]

The EU is also worried about political developments in Russia. After a period of democratization in the 1990s, Russia under Presidents Putin and Medvedev has turned into an authoritarian regime. In a war with Georgia in August 2008, it ruthlessly defended its interests, considering its neighboring states as exclusive zones of interest and openly questioning their sovereignty. EU members Poland and the Baltic states, who suffered for decades under the tutelage of the Soviet Union, are eager to defend their independence from Russia in questions like the deployment of antimissile systems, which Russia considers as a potential threat.

Another major issue in security policy is the war against international terrorism. Many European member states are involved in NATO activities against terrorism in Afghanistan and the Horn of Africa. However, as in the United States, public support for troop deployment has waned as the situation in Afghanistan has deteriorated. The more general question is how independent the EU will be from the United States in its security policy.

Another major challenge for the EU is to define its relations with Islamic countries and with its own Muslim population. This is not just an issue of foreign policy: Between 5 and 10 percent of the population of countries like Germany, the Netherlands, France, and Great Britain is Muslim. Germany has many immigrants from Turkey; France has many North African immigrants; and Great Britain has large Indian and Pakistani immigrant communities. Many EU countries have had fierce debates over issues of freedom of religion and freedom of speech that involve immigrant communities, including a row in 2006 over cartoons about the Prophet Muhammad in a Danish newspaper.

Finally, the relationship between the EU and Islam has been at the core of the debate over Turkey's potential membership in the EU. Turkey has been officially recognized as a candidate for membership in the EU since 1999. In 2005, accession negotiations between Turkey and the EU started. Proponents of an accession of Turkey argue that its membership would help to build a bridge between European and Islamic countries. Critics warn that the Turkish population will surpass Germany's population in the next ten years, so that by the time of an accession, Turkey would be the largest member state. They also stress that, despite a number of political reforms in Turkey, its political and judicial system is still far from meeting European standards for rule of law and religious freedom, particularly in regard to discrimination against members of Christian churches.

## CONCLUSION

### European Regionalism in IPE Perspective

The EU likes to portray itself as a global peacemaker and as a model of regionalism for other regions in the world. The achievements of European integration after World War II are certainly impressive: Never before in history have Western Europeans experienced a comparable period of peace, freedom, and wealth. However, it would be too easy to attribute these successes to economic liberalism alone. The IPE paradigms help to paint a more complex picture of European regionalism.

In the beginning, the EU was a project of economic integration. But, as we have seen in this chapter, the purpose of economic regionalism was political: Free markets and free movement of citizens were meant to evolve into political integration. The economic-liberal creed that "trade promotes peace and democracy" is the underlying doctrine of European regionalism.

On the other hand, realism and neomercantilism have their part in explaining the European integration process. This process was made possible by the global security structure provided by NATO and the United States during the Cold War. Without the threat of Soviet aggression and the spread of communism in Western Europe, there would not have been such a willingness to cooperate. Indeed, since the end of the Cold War, political negotiations in the EU have become more complicated—not only because of the rising number of member states but also because of the rise of nationalism. For example, in the last elections for the European Parliament in June 2009, the Eurosceptic parties won 180 seats out of 736—close to one-quarter of the seats.

When considering the role of the EU in the world, we get a similarly mixed picture, combining economic liberalism and realism or neomercantilism. On the one hand, the EU is deeply enmeshed in the global trading system. It also provides political stability by acting as a negotiator in international conflicts, especially in the Balkans and in Africa. It is also a strong supporter of international institutions like the IMF in the current financial crisis. On the other hand, the EU's role in international conflicts appears often as weak. During the war between Russia and Georgia in August 2008, the EU was not able to moderate Russia; during the conflict between Russia and the Ukraine over gas prices the EU was not able to secure a continued gas supply for many of its citizens in Eastern European countries. Disagreements among the EU members and insufficient military equipment are weakening the position of the EU in many international conflicts.

On the economic level, the bright image of an EU that creates opportunities for other nations by promoting free trade also has its hypocritical, neomercantilist side. The most striking example is the CAP, which raises high barriers for the import of agricultural products from non-EU countries and which floods world markets with subsidized European products like sugar—all at the expense of farmers in Third World countries.

To explain the EU, one needs to use a combination of the IPE paradigms. The EU is neither an international organization (in terms of its cooperation between independent states) nor a federal state. Rather, it is an entity *sui generis*, a specific mix of supranational and intergovernmental elements. This is why the EU can only partly be a model for other regions in the world. It is a perfect example of regionalism, but every region needs to find its own way of regionalism.

## KEY TERMS

European Union (EU)   296
European Economic Community
   (EEC)   296
Common Market   296
European Coal and Steel
   Community (ECSC)   296
European Community (EC)   296
regionalism   296
trade blocs   297
economic integration   297
free-trade area (FTA)   297
North American Free Trade
   Agreement (NAFTA)   297
customs union   297

economic union   299
static efficiency   299
dynamic efficiency   299
trade diversion effect   300
Marshall Plan   302
Treaty of Rome   303
European Free Trade Area
   (EFTA)   305
Common Agricultural Policy
   (CAP)   306
bicycle theory   307
European Commission   307
Single European Act (SEA)   308
Treaty of Maastricht   309

Single Market   310
three pillars   310
European Council   312
President of the European
   Council   312
Council of the EU (or Council
   of Ministers)   312
European Commission   313
European Parliament (EP)   313
European Court of Justice
   (ECJ)   313
European Central Bank
   (ECB)   313
Treaty of Lisbon   296

## DISCUSSION QUESTIONS

1. What is the European Union? How has it evolved over the last 50 years? Discuss the broadening and deepening of the EU. What is its importance today?
2. The theme of this chapter is the tension between economic and political integration. Discuss ways in which economic and political integration are related.
3. Explain the difference between static efficiency and dynamic efficiency. How is each important to the integration process?
4. The widening and deepening of the EU has increased economic gains but intensified political pressures. Discuss the political problems, citing specific examples when possible.

5. What is the Common Agricultural Policy (CAP)? Explain how and why the CAP illustrates the theme of this chapter and also how it creates tensions both among EU members and between the EU and its international trading partners.
6. Discuss the political economy of the euro. What are the likely economic effects of the euro? What are its likely political effects? How is the euro supposed to solve the EU's political problems? Explain.
7. Do you think that Europe can be united? Explain what it would mean to be united and explain your position.

## SUGGESTED READINGS

Simon Hix. *What's Wrong with the European Union and How to Fix It*. London: Polity Press, 2008.
Harold James. *Europe Reborn: A History, 1914–2000*. New York: Pearson/Longman, 2003.

Neill Nugent. *The Government and Politics of the European Union*, 6th rev. ed. Basingstoke: Palgrave Macmillan, 2006.

William Wallace, Helen Wallace, and Mark A. Pollack. *Policy-Making in the European Union*, 5th ed. Oxford: Oxford University Press, 2005.

Antje Wiener and Thomas Diez. *European Integration Theory*, 2nd rev. ed. Oxford: Oxford University Press, 2009.

Steve Wood and Wolfgang Quaisser. *The New European Union: Confronting the Challenges of Integration*. Boulder, CO: Lynne Rienner Publishers, 2008.

## NOTES

1. Hendrik Hansen edited the chapter and updated several parts of it for this and the last edition of it.
2. It is important to distinguish the European Council, the Council of the EU (Council of Ministers), and the Council of Europe. The last one is not part of the EU institutions, but was founded in 1949 in the midst of the Cold War in an attempt to promote a security structure for Europe. In 2009, the Council of Europe had forty-seven members and was concerned mainly with human rights issues.
3. These are the numbers for those countries that report the composition of their currency reserves voluntarily to the International Monetary Fund; see http://www.imf.org/external/np/sta/cofer/eng/index.htm.
4. See the Internet site of the EU on energy policy: http://europa.eu/pol/ener/index_en.htm.

# Moving into Position:
# The Rising Powers[1]

The vortex of rapid growth.

Corbis 42-16335185

During his first visit to China in November 2009, U.S. President Barack Obama acknowledged the growing importance of China to the United States and the global economy. Instead of harping on Chinese protectionism and human rights violations, he emphasized—among other things—the need to gain China's cooperation in pressuring Iran and North Korea over nuclear issues, reducing climate change, and letting its currency appreciate to reduce China's massive trade surplus with the United States. Equally importantly, he wanted Chinese leaders to continue supporting the global economic recovery by stimulating their own domestic demand and financing the huge budget deficit of the United States by purchasing U.S. Treasury bills. He even announced an ambitious plan to send 100,000 American students to study in China from 2010 to 2014. His visit was a reminder that China has become a major international economic power with which the United States must coordinate its policies in order to manage some of the world's most pressing problems. China already produces more steel, coal, textiles, PCs, TVs, and cell phones than any other country. By 2010 it will overtake Japan to become the world's second largest economy. It appears that the post–Cold War era of U.S. unilateralism and hegemony is over.

The rise of China, India, and other emerging countries is rapidly changing economic and security relationships in the world. As these countries transition from state-dominated systems to market-oriented economies, they are profoundly reshaping their societies and connections to the global economy. They are affecting where goods are produced, what global poverty trends look like, and how capital flows around the world. Their insatiable demand for raw materials and consumer items is driving up global commodity prices and creating ever more strains on the environment. They are creating a more multipolar world, which some hope will usher in an age of peace and cooperation but others fear will lead to new arms races and monumental struggles over access to energy and food. Their development will determine whether hundreds of millions of people will be able to enjoy a better future and share more of the global wealth previously denied to them.

To better understand where these countries are heading and how they are changing the global political economy, we examine the process by which they have moved from one system of national political economy to another. We begin with a general overview of transition problems in formerly communist and socialist countries and the global context within which their changes occur.[2] Russia and Eastern Europe are singled out for special attention in this discussion because they represent different approaches to the problems of transition and development. We also contrast and reflect on the problems, successes, and opportunities in the two most important rising powers: India and China. Finally, we speculate about the future that awaits these nations.

Change in something as complex and important as a nation's system of political economy causes stresses and strains at all levels: individual, market, class, national, regional, and global. It is significant, therefore, that half of the world's population has been experiencing the stress of a change in their system of political economy in the last 20 years. One group of nations—the former members of the Warsaw Pact and the former states of the Soviet Union—is engulfed in the problems of the dramatic transition from communism to some form of democratic capitalism. Other nations such as China are engaged in a somewhat less extreme but perhaps even more difficult transition, from communism to market socialism.

**Market socialism** is a hybrid system that retains central power in the state but encourages private economic activities. India is in the unique position of trying to overcome grinding poverty and find a new niche in the global economy in the context of an already well-established and vibrant democratic system.

In this chapter we present a number of important theses about the rising powers. First, there is not a single path away from socialism or communism. The trajectories toward a market-oriented economy are very different, reflecting variations in countries' historical background, size, political system, and policy decisions. Second, the experiences of countries in transition lead us to question many assertions in the IPE theories we discussed in the preceding chapters. For example, China shows that economic liberals' belief that capitalism, democracy, and freedom go together may not always be true. On the other hand, some countries' phenomenal growth under market-friendly policies suggests that mercantilists overestimate the positive outcomes of state intervention in the economy. And rapid reductions in poverty in China and India belie structuralists' belief that global capitalism locks poor countries into a vicious cycle of exploitation and underdevelopment.

Third, in most countries transition has been a painful and chaotic process that has, at least in the short run, destroyed valuable social institutions and undermined social stability in pursuit of long-term economic growth and political stability. Globalization holds out the hope of a higher standard of living at the same time that it threatens institutions, cultural practices, and ways of living that many people value. For a substantial number of people in postcommunist countries, capitalism has brought sacrifice, crime, and despair. Finally, the rising powers are ineluctably forcing Europe, the United States, and Japan to change. Developed countries will have to adjust to a world of even more intense competition. This will result in the developed nations losing more of their labor-intensive manufacturing and some of their ability to dominate international institutions. Consequently, many of the "rules of the game" affecting trade, finance, and intellectual property will start reflecting the interests of emerging countries. This shift in power will create new global tensions that could just as easily lead to a more dangerous world as one based on cooperation and peaceful coexistence.

## TRANSITIONS IN THE FORMERLY SOCIALIST COUNTRIES

Although the Soviet Union came into existence in 1917, most communist or socialist regimes emerged after the end of World War II in Eastern and Central Europe, North Korea, China, Vietnam, and Cuba. For these states, political and economic power was rooted in a single party whose membership was generally limited to about 5–10 percent of the population, although a much larger percentage participated in party-led programs and movements. The official ideology of the party touted its revolutionary achievements such as eliminating inequality and promoting rapid economic development through the growth of heavy industries, infrastructure, educational and health facilities, and urbanization. Some states developed "personality cults" around political leaders like Stalin, Mao, Castro, and Kim Il-Jung, who were venerated for liberating the nation from imperialism, performing heroic deeds, and/or paving the way for rapid economic development.

Most of the means of production—factories, land, and property—were owned by the state on behalf of the people as a whole. The party-state guaranteed employment, centralized economic decision making, and eliminated most private commercial exchanges other than small-scale retailing, bartering, local agricultural trading, and black market transactions. A large state bureaucracy determined which important raw materials, goods, and services should be produced, in what amounts, at what prices, and for whose consumption. The prices of goods and services often did not reflect their true domestic or international value. Many consumer goods were of such low quality as to be virtually worthless, resulting in the waste of huge amounts of resources. Shortages of some important items were a perennial problem: Consumers struggled to find rationed supplies of bread, detergents, plumbing fixtures, and telephone hookups.

This cumbersome system of state central planning eventually resulted in a myriad of problems such as overproduction of some goods, shortages of others, and misallocation of investment. It also suffered from what János Kornai has described as "soft-budget constraints": State enterprises had little incentive to turn real profits when they could count on cheap state loans and perpetual debt forgiveness.[3]

It is important to remember that in their heydays from the 1930s to the 1970s, many socialist and communist command economies successfully generated high growth rates. The Soviets transformed their agrarian, preindustrial society into a military–industrial powerhouse in less than two generations. Their Warsaw Pact allies mostly had impressive growth rates, low unemployment, and generous social safety nets from the 1950s through 1970s. These socialist states were not democratic, consumer paradises. But they did offer development models that many developing countries and ex-colonies found compelling (see Chapter 11). They offered models based on self-sufficiency, industrialization, educational opportunity, and upward mobility for peasants and the urban poor. Their acolytes were found in Egypt, Algeria, India, and other countries that rallied to the Nonaligned Movement in the 1950s–1970s.

Contradictions in the socialist economies grew worse throughout the 1970s and 1980s. States found it increasingly difficult to deal with the effects of the misallocation of resources caused by an inefficient planning system and ignoring of fundamental market forces. Slow growth, declining productivity, and inability to match the pace of technological innovation in the West led leaders such as Soviet General Secretary Mikhail Gorbachev to seek some reform of the system starting in the mid-1980s. Gorbachev's policies of *glasnost* (openness) and *perestroika* (restructuring) were meant to reform, not eliminate, socialism. Gorbachev, along with some leaders in Eastern Europe, hoped that a limited amount of political and economic liberalization would give the populace a greater stake in the system and help reinvigorate socialism. Instead, popular political demands and divisions among party elites—and the unwillingness of key political and military elites to violently suppress widespread demonstrations and strikes—rapidly led to the unraveling and collapse of the socialist and communist regimes. By 1989, Hungary and Poland were paving the way toward democracy and capitalism, and many of their socialist neighbors soon followed. By 1991, the Soviet Union had broken up into fifteen separate countries.

Transitions from communism required reestablishing some separation between the state and the economy. Two difficult parts of this process included **marketization,** or the re-creation of market forces of supply and demand, and

**privatization,** the transfer of state-held property into private hands. In order to privatize assets like factories, shops, land, and apartments, postcommunist governments had to figure out what they were actually worth and who should get them— but the results were often unfair, undemocratic, and nontransparent.

Privatization was eventually carried out in a number of different ways, depending on the country and the kind of economic assets concerned. Some countries sold businesses directly to the employees or to the highest bidder. Other countries relied more on what is known as **voucher privatization,** under which citizens were given vouchers that they could then use to purchase shares in firms. In some countries, privatization was slow because of the fear of widespread unemployment and social unrest. Moreover, state-owned firms remain an important source of power in some postcommunist countries.

In addition to re-creating private property, states had to re-create a market in which property, labor, goods, and services could all function in a competitive environment to determine their value. Some argued that changes should be gradual to minimize social disruptions that might undermine fledgling economies and democracies. Others favored rapid market reforms that would free up prices and quickly bring an end to central planning and state subsidies for businesses virtually overnight. This policy (one particularly favored by some liberal Western advisors), which came to be known as *shock therapy*, was pioneered in Poland and later attempted in Russia.[4]

## NEW POLITICAL AND ECONOMIC LANDSCAPES

How successful have all of these reforms been? Some of the countries in Eastern Europe and the former Soviet Union ended up with relatively stable democratic political systems, while others became mired in authoritarianism or civil war. The economic record of the past 20 years is also very mixed. Almost all of the transition countries suffered severe economic decline, inflation, and political upheaval in the early 1990s. However, while some obtained relatively high rates of growth after a few years, many still suffer significant economic and institutional problems. Most countries now have market-based economies with large private sectors.

A major survey of 29,000 people in postcommunist countries conducted by the European Bank for Reconstruction and Development (EBRD) and the World Bank in 2006 provides some indication of transition results.[5] In the postcommunist countries overall, about half of the population distrusted political parties, parliaments, and the courts, indicating that even after more than 15 years of transition the rule of law was still not institutionalized in many countries. Two-thirds of people believed that corruption was as bad as or worse than in 1989. A sizable percentage of older citizens were still not convinced that a system combining democracy and capitalism is the ideal system for their country. The World Bank estimated that in 2008 at least 40 percent of people in the postcommunist states (plus Turkey) were poor or vulnerable, that is, living on less than $5 a day (see box "Waiting for Godot in Coscalia, Moldova"). Until 2005, the average real GDP of transition countries did not even recover to the 1989 level.[6] The 2008–2009 financial crisis reversed many of the recent economic gains in postcommunist countries, driving up unemployment and poverty rates.

# WAITING FOR GODOT IN COSCALIA, MOLDOVA

Although Moldova has been an independent nation-state since 1991, its citizens are still awaiting an external savior. Culturally, most of Moldova's 4.3 million residents identify with their neighbors, the Romanians. They speak the same language, seek blessings from the same Eastern Orthodox saints, and eat the same polenta and sausage dishes. However, Moldova's independence from the former Soviet Union got off to an inauspicious start, when in 1990 a province called Transnistria on the eastern side of the Dneister River broke away, taking with it much of Moldova's industrial base. From 2001 to 2009, a reconstituted Communist Party dominated the political system, undermining democratic institutions. In his 2008 bestseller *Geography of Bliss*, National Public Radio correspondent Eric Weiner deemed Moldova the "unhappiest place on earth."

The rural town of Coscalia is a case study of Moldova's problems and an example of the difficulties many rural villages throughout Eastern European have faced since the collapse of the Soviet Union. Located in a hilly region an hour southeast of the capital city of Chisinau, Coscalia has 700 homes and a registered population of 2,000. Seasonal vegetables add spice to the inhabitants' otherwise relatively dull diet of corn- and wheat-based dishes, lathered with homemade sour cream and cheese. Meals are washed down with wine that families store in large oak barrels under their houses. The most valuable assets of many families are their cows, worth $1,000 each.

It does not take long in Coscalia to realize that something seems amiss. The numerous elderly lean on their canes and walking sticks, haggling for bright yellow sunflower oil or other necessities with the proceeds of pension checks of $40 a month or less. There are few working-age men. Coscalia is a village of nurseries and nursing home. Many men and increasingly women leave when local schooling ends at age 16. Instead of scraping by on farms that generate less than the average $50 a month local salary, they try their luck in Moscow, where construction workers can earn $400 a month, or in Italy, where caring for the elderly in their homes can

pay $800 a month. Less fortunate women end up like thousands of other Moldovans as prostitutes in Italy, the Balkans, and Russia.

Even though the residents of Coscalia are hardworking and in a soil-rich valley, they struggle to survive. Few migrants become entrepreneurs at home or abroad, but their remittances keep the houses—many painted blue and white—looking idyllic from a distance. Homes in Coscalia have electricity and satellite TV, but not running water and sanitation facilities. Women rise early to haul water from wells, milk cows, feed the animals, and then prepare for work or school.

Even though over half of the residents of Coscalia are related, often by marriage, there is precious little trust among them. Pantry and cellar doors are protected with huge locks to safely store wine, congealed fat, and pickled produce for the winter. Money is often stolen from neighbors, and animals disappear. Even if the perpetrator is known, there is little the young policeman can do, and most residents simply purchase bigger padlocks.

Coscalians have found it difficult to collectively improve their lot. Cows produce more milk than can be drunk, so it is processed and consumed as cheese in the summer months; the excess goes to waste. Residents recognized the problem and agreed that the solution was a milk-receiving station that could keep milk cool until it could be sent to a nearby cheese-making plant. However, lack of trust meant that there was no way to raise the money from local residents. Eventually they found an external donor, but in the manipulations common in Eastern Europe, the grant mostly benefited one recipient rather than the larger community.

Most residents have a let's-make-do attitude which is evident in the patched together nature of shared facilities such as wells. It has not been possible to levy a small tax on the sellers at the weekly market so that they can display their goods on tables set on concrete rather than on the ground or hanging from fences. Residents still detest cooperatives because they remember that the wealthiest today are those who manipulated communist-era co-ops. However, many older residents are nostalgic for the stability of communist times. Coscalia is a sobering reminder that development is hard. Literacy, remittances, and aid have not yet made the town a beacon of hope in a troubled countryside.

Moldovans as a whole oscillate between a yearning for the dependability of communist leaders, who dictated work and put bread on the table, and a desire to enjoy the freedom of a liberated lifestyle. Theirs is not an isolated country: Moldovans every day are confronted with the economic, political, and social successes that benefited Romanians who can travel freely to EU countries. They have access to radio, TV, and articles in German, Italian, Russian, and English. However, the future of Moldova still needs trust and vision to ensure that dreams of a better life in Coscalia can turn into realities.

Table 13-1 shows per capita GDP at purchasing power parity (PPP, the equivalent in U.S. dollars in 2007), democracy scores in 2009, and growth in GDP from 1990 to 2005. It is clear that there are significant differences among postcommunist countries today. To better understand the variations in outcomes, we examine three different groups of postcommunist countries: those that have entered the EU, the former Yugoslav countries and their neighbors in the Balkans, and the former Soviet republics. There are also clear differences in the level of democracy and governance performance, as illustrated by a widely-cited set of measures called the Worldwide Governance Indicators (WGIs).[7]

The eight countries that joined the European Union in 2004—Poland, the Czech Republic, Slovakia, Hungary, Estonia, Latvia, Lithuania, and Slovenia— have embraced economic liberalism and social democracy. They now have entrenched market economies and have consolidated democratic reforms (see Table 13-1). The WGI measures for 2008 show them approaching or equaling

### TABLE 13-1

**Economic Conditions in Selected Transition Countries**

| Country | Per-Capita GDP, 2007[a] | Democracy Measure, 2009[b] | Average Annual Growth Rate of GDP (in Percent), 1990–2005[c] |
|---|---|---|---|
| Poland | $16,323 | Democracy | 2.89 |
| Hungary | $18,956 | Democracy | 1.65 |
| Estonia | $20,584 | Democracy | 5.75 |
| Czech Republic | $24,088 | Democracy | 1.26 |
| Ukraine | $6,990 | Weak Democracy | |
| Bulgaria | $11,311 | Weak Democracy | −1.4 |
| Moldova | $2,897 | Authoritarian Regime | −0.82 |
| Russia | $14,736 | Authoritarian Regime | 1.08 |
| Tajikistan | $1,843 | Authoritarian Regime | 1.26 |
| Belarus | $10,915 | Authoritarian Regime | 2.97 |
| Serbia | $10,019 | Weak Democracy | |

*Note:* GDP in the per-capita figures is measured in Purchasing Power Parity (PPP).
[a]International Monetary Fund, World Economic Outlook Database, April 2009, www.imf.org.
[b]Freedom House, *Nations in Transit 2009*, http://www.freedomhouse.eu/images/nit2009/tables.pdf.
[c]International Monetary Fund, World Economic Outlook Database, September 2006, www.imf.org.

the levels of the rest of the EU in terms of political stability, accountability, and rule of law. By the end of 2007—nearly two decades after the collapse of communism—the average GDP in these Central European and Baltic states was about 50 percent higher than in 1989, according to the EBRD. Their transitions were "successful" for a number of reasons: a precommunist history of statehood and significant economic development, historical ties to Western Europe, and rapid growth of civil society and prodemocratic political parties. The likelihood of joining the EU had a very important role in accelerating reforms. The EU offered membership, financial support, and security, which helped sustain political reform and institutional change. Foreign companies poured in large investments. By enmeshing these countries quickly in a dense set of trade, aid, political, and military relationships, the EU helped soften the economic transition and provided a clear set of regulations and benchmarks to which reformers could aspire.[8]

In contrast, the transition has not gone as well in countries in the Balkans, including Romania, Bulgaria, and the former Yugoslavia. A number of these countries suffered from ethnic fragmentation, extreme nationalism, and civil war during the 1990s. Ex-communist elites clung to power in many of these countries through newly created political parties. In the last ten years these countries have improved governance, and most of them are now considered semiconsolidated democracies (see Table 13-1). But they still face a number of problems, especially with political stability in countries like Bosnia and Herzogovenia, Serbia, and Albania. In 2006, according to the EBRD–World Bank survey, less than 55 percent of people in southeast European countries felt that their country's political or economic system was better than in 1989.

Similarly, the Commonwealth of Independent States (CIS) has had mixed transition results. CIS includes most of the ex-republics of the former Soviet Union including Russia, Belarus, Ukraine, Armenia, Azerbaijan, Kazakhstan, Kyrgyzstan, Moldova, Tajikistan, Turkmenistan, and Uzbekistan. On average, it wasn't until 2007 that the GDP in real terms recovered to 1989 levels in these countries. In 2006, only about 10 percent of households in the CIS had a bank account or a credit card. Less than 45 percent of people felt that their country's political or economic system was better in 2006 than in 1989, despite strong economic growth after 1998 in countries like Russia and the Ukraine.

In the CIS countries and the non-EU postcommunist states in Europe, unemployment fell significantly from 12.4 percent in 1999 to an estimated 8.4 percent in 2007.[9] In the same period, these countries attracted large capital inflows. But these countries were poorly integrated into the world trade system. Only recently, in 2008, Ukraine joined the WTO. Employment and growth gains began to evaporate when the full brunt of the financial crisis hit the CIS countries in 2008–2009 and a new, painful, economic recession began.

Most CIS countries (and many postcommunist countries in southeastern Europe) have been stunted by incomplete economic reforms and continued government intervention in the economy. Under these conditions the result has often been **crony capitalism,** in which some have become extremely rich, often through government connections, while many others have seen their standard of living decline.

Democracy is weakly institutionalized or absent in the CIS countries, partly because of the legacy of a long period of Soviet rule and the predominance of energy-intensive and heavy industries. In some of the countries, a new set of authoritarian leaders—often former members of the communist elite and *nomenklatura*—has consolidated power or reverted to authoritarianism. Democratic rights are restricted, and those in power have frequently enriched themselves through corrupt practices. Freedom House rates eight of the CIS countries as consolidated authoritarian regimes (see Table 13-1). The WGI measures for 2008 show that the post-Soviet countries have some of the comparatively lowest rankings in the world in measures of good governance such as political freedoms and accountability, political stability, government effectiveness, and control of corruption.

Russia exemplifies many of the problems in the CIS. Many important sectors of the Russian economy were sold in the early 1990s to a handful of local investors with ties to the government and the old *nomenklatura*. The result was the emergence of "**oligarchs**," a small number of individuals with huge influence in the economy, government, and the media. In the 1990s, Russia suffered a rapid decline in the standard of living as people found their savings wiped out and their salaries unable to keep up with rising prices. Hyperinflation was eventually brought under control, but by 1999 more than one-third of the Russian population lived in poverty. As in most post-Soviet countries, average life expectancy declined precipitously in what can be called a "mortality crisis." In 2007, average male life expectancy in Russia was only 60 years, compared to 70 years in China and 78 years in the United States.[10] Health is so bad in Russia that official statistics indicate that "at least 80 percent of all pregnant women suffer a serious pathology during pregnancy."[11]

The election of Vladimir Putin as president in 2000 brought an end to Russia's tentative experiment with democracy. Since becoming prime minister in 2008, Putin has continued to have a major political role in concert with his presidential successor, Dmitry Medvedev. Putin re-centralized political power, weakened the Duma, and cracked down on independent media and civil society. He has surrounded himself with powerful political allies called the *siloviki*—officials in the Kremlin who have backgrounds in the secret police, intelligence services, and law enforcement agencies. At the same time, he promoted a muscular form of nationalism in domestic and foreign affairs, which has manifested itself in a brutal counterinsurgency in Chechnya, invasion of Georgia, and occasional cutoffs of gas flows to Ukraine. According to political scientist M. Steven Fish, the failure of democracy in Russia is primarily due to incomplete economic reform, a weakened legislature, and the curse of natural resource wealth.[12]

Russia's economy improved by the turn of the millennium, but much of Russia's economic growth was based on oil and raw materials exports rather than the development of a diversified market economy. Although most small Russian firms are now in private hands, many of them have suffered from insolvency and interference from the state bureaucracy. Organized crime and corruption remain serious problems. President Vladimir Putin has found it difficult to eliminate a number of wasteful state subsidies. In recent years, he has gone after many of the oligarchs who benefited from privatization. The state has effectively renationalized much of the oil and gas sector, and state-owned conglomerates are also important in the automobile, aerospace, and defense industries. Oligarchs still remain important in energy, minerals, steel, and banking sectors, but many have turned to the Kremlin for help in repaying huge debts they incurred with Western creditors.

For many years to come, Russia will struggle to deal with internal economic and social problems while reasserting its role in a more multipolar world. Already it has lost a lot of potential foreign direct investment from multinational corporations fed up with the lack of rule of law and Kremlin interference in the market. For example, although Swedish retailer Ikea has spent $4 billion building 12 popular malls since 2000, it was so fed up with government corruption and fraud that it suspended all further investments in Russia in 2009. Putin's strategy of nurturing state-controlled "**national champions**" in energy and mineral sectors is a risky proposition, given the potential of world energy prices to fall and the accompanying neglect of private sector manufacturing. Because of wide-scale protectionism, Russia is the only major country that is not yet a member of the WTO.

# INDIA: THE OTHER ASIAN TIGER

While Russia is sometimes viewed as an angry bear, India has often been portrayed as a caged tiger poised to leap to unimaginable economic heights. Since its independence in 1947, it has all too often found itself in this poised stance: ready, but just not quite willing to jump. Despite progress in the recent past, India's reluctance to fully embrace economic liberalization is rooted in a variety of historical, political, and infrastructural obstacles which are self-imposed bars of its own cage. Lingering protectionist policies are compounded by a massive, inefficient, governmental bureaucracy and poor public infrastructure (water, electricity, and roads). Inadequate education and vocational training programs need to be reformed, particularly if India is to build its manufacturing sector and spread benefits to its masses. To reach its growth potential, India must also ease protectionist policies and barriers to trade, expand the export of manufactured goods, and unleash the energies of the private sector.

## Independence in 1947: Bounded Autonomy

Much can be said of India's remarkable economic growth following its famed neoliberal reforms in the early 1990s. A fundamental divergence in India's development path took place long before these reforms, however, and has its roots in the preindependence period of the late eighteenth century. India at this time was primarily an agrarian economy, although it prided itself on the lucrative exports of fine handicrafts, textiles, and spices to the markets of Asia and Europe. Britain discouraged Indian manufacturing in the early years of colonization, and instead the British East India Company made India into a subservient provider of raw materials for the manufactories of Great Britain.

The extractive nature of the Company gave way to a slightly more productive, albeit manipulative British Raj from 1858 to 1947. It was during this colonial era that Britain invested in a massive network of railways, roads, canals, bridges, and telegraph links to transport and coordinate India's vast quantities of raw goods for subsequent export, mainly to England. Additionally, intangible contributions such as the 1935 Government of India Act enfranchised a vast number of Indians who were thereby able to participate in the voting process for a newly created central government, incorporating both the British provinces and the princely states. The impact of British colonial establishments such as property rights, infrastructural development, the English language, and a broad political and legal framework aided the eventual emergence of India's democratic institutions and the fundamentals of its statehood following independence.

India's economic story after independence has demonstrated the effects of both state-led and private sector-led growth, providing a unique case study of comparative growth strategies. Following independence in 1947, India's first prime minister, Jawaharlal Nehru, promoted his vision of a self-reliant, import-substitution-led model of growth that was as independent of foreign capital as possible. This was no doubt influenced by the negative perceptions toward India's colonial experience and was driven by a fundamental mistrust of the capitalist system in the global economic regime. Nehru drew inspiration for a state-led growth model from the Soviet Union and chose a path of modernization through industrialization. Although India chose a foreign economic development model, the motives of the Indian leadership were nationalist in nature.[13] India's leaders were at the helm of the "commanding heights" of the economy, and all industries and sectors seen as essential to industrialization, such as steel, engineering, water, electricity, mining, and even finance, were dominated by public enterprises.

Unlike the Soviet Union, India retained democracy and private property. However, central planning and a massive bureaucracy stifled the private sector. Foreign investment and technology transfers were suppressed in the pursuit of protecting infant industries. The suppressive business environment characterized by protectionist policies, licenses, and regulations came to be known as the "License Raj."

Along with the protection of infant industries, India grappled with the improvement of the agricultural sector. This was because agriculture was not only an important source of revenue and food security, but overwhelmingly (and remains so today) the largest source of employment for India's population. Nehru committed to pursuing a socialist development strategy and thus established India's first Planning Commission, which devised a series of Five Year Plans focused heavily on investment in agriculture, irrigation (dams), industry, power plants, steel mills, and education in engineering and technology. Nehru's plan was not overtly based on hostility toward international capitalism but was one that would enable India to eventually become a global player and compete in a global environment once it had built up enough capital and infrastructure. Nehru and his planners distrusted world markets and the threats they presented by way of import dependency and economic imperialism.

## The Beginnings of a Mixed Economy and the Green Revolution

For a country emerging from colonial rule and adopting protectionist policies, India had a comparatively liberal regime in the sense that Nehru saw foreign investment as a stark necessity to a certain extent and he institutionalized policies that enabled foreign investment in certain industries, provided that it served the state's interests. Thus were the makings of a mixed economy. Although the state reserved the right to entry in nearly all sectors, it realized that openness to some foreign investment was necessary for an industrializing economy.[14]

No account of India's economic history and development can forsake the success of India's **Green Revolution,** however confined it was to the northern states. In the early 1960s India experienced a severe food shortage, and in the mid-1960s it started to use a new High Yield Variety (HYV) of wheat developed and funded in part by the Rockefeller Foundation. Confident of the potential to drastically increase agricultural productivity, India imported over 18,000 tons of Mexican HYV seed and distributed it across the Punjab, witnessing extremely successful results. Eventually (after a hiccup due to crop failure in the early 1970s) the country emerged out of famine and became not only an agriculturally self-sufficient nation but a surplus-exporting agrarian powerhouse. Aside from the successfully high levels of crop yields, the Green Revolution played an important part in stimulating auxiliary sectors of India's economy such as irrigation, manufacturing of fertilizers and agrochemicals and domestic transportation infrastructure. Additionally, the Green Revolution shifted India's experience with agriculture from that of subsistence to an economically viable capitalist model.

## Placing India: Recent Versus Past Growth

Critics of Nehru's state-directed policies point out that his strategies were loftily aimed at reaching a level of modernity exhibited by the Soviet Union, which was an already industrialized and militarily powerful country.[15] The persistence of state planning throughout much of India's first four decades of independence reduced incentives for private investment in industry. The inefficiency of public-sector enterprises and the overbearing restrictions imposed on private enterprises during import substitution stifled economic growth. A decline in the rate of industrial growth in the early-to-mid-1960s strained public spending. The decline was due to a variety of factors, including India's fighting two wars with its neighbors, Pakistan and China.

As India witnessed the destructive powers of a mismanaged socialist economy, the administration under Prime Minister Rajiv Gandhi (Indira Gandhi's eldest son) in the mid-1980s began to flirt with policies of liberalization. Rajiv Gandhi relaxed restrictions on large firms, eliminated price controls on cement and aluminum (which expanded construction projects across the nation), overhauled the tax system, and increased the flexibility of industrial firms which were previously licensed for specific products only.[16]

Despite large-scale capital investment during the first 30 years of independence, India averaged a modest annual economic growth rate of only 3.6 percent, and the annual GDP per capita growth rate was a mere 1.4 percent. These growth figures pale in comparison to the levels achieved following the 1991 reforms and were sarcastically dubbed "the Hindu Rate of Growth." However, the growth rates were nearly four times greater than those estimated over the 50 years preceding independence under British colonial rule.[17]

## Post-Reform Performance

During the 1980s a noticeable acceleration of growth was due in part to liberalization, a boost in public investment, and a modest engagement with the global economy. A surge in economic growth in the early 1990s proved unsustainable as India's external debt rose rapidly from $20.6 billion in 1980 to $64.4 billion in 1989. The end of the Cold War and the resulting fragmentation of the Soviet Union, India's primary trading partner, further distorted the flow of trade and aid on which India had come to depend. Additionally, the Gulf War in 1990 led to a spike in oil prices, driving India's balance of payments into a crisis in mid-1991. India's foreign debt had climbed to $72 billion, making India the world's third largest debtor at the time.

In response to the 1991 crisis, India borrowed $6 billion from the International Monetary Fund and accordingly was required to adopt a series of reforms aligned with the "Washington Consensus." India's minister of finance at the time (and current prime minister), Manmohan Singh, instituted a series of long overdue, sweeping reforms. The government's agenda included a devaluation of the rupee, a reduction in the number of industries reserved for the public sector, incentives for FDI, and allowing MNCs to have a 51 percent (majority) share holding in Indian firms. The results were almost immediately apparent.

The five years following India's 1991 liberalization registered record high annual growth rates of 6.7 percent. A vibrant world economy was eager to engage with India's economy. The services sector blossomed, accounting for nearly 70 percent of all growth during this period, overshadowing industry growth levels during this time (see box "The Case of Bangalore: Epitomizing India's Duality"). India's service sector includes India's famed software and information technology services, the export value of which rose from zero in 1991 to just shy of $40 billion in 2007–2008.[18]

Unlike many East Asian economies, India's economic performance since its 1991 reforms has been characterized by capital- and skill-intensive growth as opposed to export-led growth of labor-intensive manufactured goods. India's services sector—particularly information technology—has been a significant driver of growth.

As evidence of India's increased global presence following its reforms, over 100 of its companies have a market capitalization value of over $1 billion. Companies such as Infosys Technologies, Reliance Industries, Tata Motors, Wipro, and Jet Airways have become familiar names in the international business community. And over 125 Fortune 500 companies have research and development bases in India. Trade in goods and services as a proportion of GDP grew from 24 percent in 1995 to 49 percent in 2009, and direct foreign investment has grown from less than $100 million in 1990 to $19.5 billion in 2007. Trade with the United States, India's largest export destination of manufactured goods, has grown exponentially. By 2008, India exported $25.7 billion to the United States and imported $17.6 billion dollars worth of goods from it.

India's recent development model tenuously combines strongly protectionist state-led industrial growth with neoliberal, market-driven growth. India skipped from an agricultural economy to a service-driven economy, bypassing a labor-intensive industrial revolution. This deprives a vast majority of India's masses of employment in factories as the manufacturing sector is underdeveloped.

### Inhibitors to Growth: Labor Laws, Infrastructure, and Education

Although the preceding discussion notes India's progress in embracing economic liberalization, there is far more room for improvement. Rigid labor laws (although they affect only the 10 percent of Indians employed in the formal sector of the economy) discourage further hiring as it is very difficult, legally, to fire an employee. Poor public services, overcrowded roads, an inconsistent supply of water and electricity, and poor sewage systems all place major constraints on India's potential for further rapid industrial development and urbanization.

Another pressing issue is the substandard education system that deprives the majority of India's population of the right to proper primary schooling. Despite significant steps beginning in the late 1980s to reform education, it was only in 2002 that India legislated the right to free and compulsory education to all children aged 6–14 years. India had, around this time, become a viable investment base for MNCs in part due to the rapidly growing demand for a cheap, skilled, knowledgeable, English-speaking workforce. India has 291 universities and over 12,000 colleges, producing approximately two million degree holders per year, nearly one half of whom are engineering or technology-oriented graduates.

## THE CASE OF BANGALORE: EPITOMIZING INDIA'S DUALITY

Bangalore, located in the southern state of Karnataka, India, serves as an ideal example of both globalization's successes and challenges within the framework of India's post–1991 neoliberal reforms. The city experienced unprecedented levels of growth due, in large part, to the rapid global expansion of the Information Technology (IT) sector. At the same time, it suffered the consequences of such growth, including overpopulation, rising inequality, inadequate infrastructure, and poor governance.

Bangalore was considered a key location for software development and the outsourcing of IT-related industry for a number of reasons, including a large presence of leading universities and research institutions, an English-speaking labor pool, and an existing close-knit relationship between the government and the private sector. Bangalore is home to over 100 research universities and technical institutions, the clustering of which is replicated by that of IT firms in Special Economic Zones (SEZs) on the outskirts of the city. In 1996, when the IT revolution began to take shape, IT employees' salaries averaged six to eight times lower than that of their U.S. counterparts. Bangalore attracted the best elements of India's comparative advantage: high-skilled, English-speaking, low-wage workers.

Bangalore accounts for one-third of India's software exports and nearly one-third of total employment in Indian IT services. In 1996, Bangalore was cited as being "Asia's fastest growing city." Today, however, one sees incomplete flyover structures and buildings, overcrowding and rapid expansion of slums, traffic gridlock, and unbearable pollution. This may not seem an unusual or original story, but indeed, Bangalore epitomizes India's development character: fast-paced growth driven by the services sector, though constrained by shackling policies and a byzantine bureaucracy. Even after the reforms, the Karnataka government imposed an inhibitive entry tax of 13.5 percent on goods brought into the state.

The city, too, represents the trend of a rapidly urbanizing nation; Bangalore's population exploded from 2.9 million inhabitants in 1981 to 7.2 million in 2009. The economic repercussions of such growth are seen in skyrocketing property rates and a 25 percent increase in wage rates per year. Three new firms enter Bangalore's city limits each week. Over 900 new cars are added to Bangalore's narrow streets *every day*. One might see this as a positive change toward a developed society, but in the context of Bangalore's base for success, MNCs are increasingly discouraged by the rising costs of doing business in the city. Infrastructural development has failed to keep pace with such rapid urbanization. Bangalore was ranked last on a list of 17 Indian cities in terms of ease in starting a business, according to the World Bank's 2009 *Doing Business in India* report.

Exasperated Bangaloreans and corporations alike are flexing more political muscle to help create an easier future. Nandan Nilekani, one of India's most successful entrepreneurs, notes that the IT industry's 40 percent annual growth throughout the 1990s has created a new class of affluent, "high-impact" urban residents, and thus an increase in demand for shopping malls, better roads, more consistent water supply, and fewer power cuts.

## Outlook for the Future: The Crisis and Beyond

India's explosive annual economic growth rate peaked at 9 percent in 2007. Compared to the 6 percent growth rate during the 1980s and the 3.6 percent during India's first 30 years since independence, India's economy was hot, driven in part by a nearly $100 billion increase in foreign capital inflows over the 2003–2007 period. GDP grew at an average annual rate of more than 8 percent from 2002 to 2008.

A widely-cited comparative statistic between India and China as two emerging Asian giants is the percentage of the population in each country that is of working age. Over half of India's population is under 25, and approximately 40 percent are under the age of 18. In India, the proportion of its population of working age will continue to rise for the next few decades, whereas in China it is expected to fall. These statistics point to an emerging area of potential for India to enhance labor productivity, particularly in an expanded manufacturing sector. With over 60 percent of Indians employed in low-productivity farming, however, the need for increased employment opportunities in manufacturing and services is clear.

India has truly emerged from being relatively insulated from the global economy, as recently as twenty years ago, to becoming a significant player. India has continued to grow amid the financial crisis that swept full bloom in October of 2008. While the global financial crisis has hit India's stock market, much of India's domestic foundation remains strong. The bad-loan culture has hardly emerged within India's financial system, and Indian banking institutions are sparsely connected to overseas credit markets. The Indian government still retains majority ownership and control of its state-owned banks, which constitute approximately 70 percent of Indian banking assets.

Elements of India's early protectionist policies and the initial distrust of foreign markets expressed by Nehru have, in some sense, helped India survive the global economic slowdown. India's agricultural sector is driven by domestic consumption, and many of the government's protectionist policies apply to the agricultural sector. India's manufacturing sector has slowed down, but the repercussions are not as big as they could be, since this sector is relatively small scale. It is perhaps a consequence of the initially inhibitive policies that India is less dependent on exports and thus less susceptible to global market turmoil. India's exports amount to 22 percent of its GDP, as compared to China's 37 percent.[19]

Despite India's protectionist measures having insulated the nation from the financial crisis, infrastructure is a leading area desperate for reform in India, particularly the supply of water, electricity, and the improvement of roads across the country. India's seaports and airports are running far over capacity. Even its security systems are feeble, which was demonstrated in the security response to the three-day long terrorist attack in Mumbai in November of 2008. India currently ranks 122 out of 181 countries in the World Bank's 2009 "Doing Business" report, an unimpressive level.[20] If India is to become a global leader, there must be urgent reform in shaping the business environment to be conducive to large-scale investment and more manufacturing exports.

# CHINA IN TRANSITION: AN ANALYSIS OF PARADOXES

Though born out of the structuralist rhetoric of communist revolution, modern China in the last three decades has adopted increasingly liberal economic policies on its way to becoming a leading manufacturing power and major player in the global economy. China's strengths, however, are counterbalanced with a number of internal and external struggles associated with rapid change. Internally, the Chinese government must grapple with the growing tensions between open markets and constrained social freedoms. In its foreign policy, Beijing makes calculated realist decisions about security and economic strategy, but finds itself ever more dependent on the success and support of other nations.

This section analyzes several paradoxes that have emerged during China's development and move away from a model of classic socialism. First, Beijing has presided over a broadly mercantilist system that nevertheless is fueled by global interdependence. Second, the Chinese government has applied economic liberalism to advance its control over society. Finally, Chinese leaders have used an underlying structuralist rhetoric to foster a consumer culture. The tensions underlying these paradoxes have been thrown into relief by the recent global financial crisis which has strained China's model of social control and shaken some of its international trade relationships.

## The Roots of China's Rise: The Transition to Market Socialism

China's transition away from classic socialism began with the death of Mao Zedong in 1976. Mao had presided over nearly three decades of increasingly tenuous rule by the Communist Party. His **Great Leap Forward** (1958–1960), an attempt to organize citizens into *people's communes* of localized industrial production, undermined agriculture and led to a famine that caused the deaths of tens of millions of people. This was followed by the **Cultural Revolution (1966–1976)**, in which Mao encouraged Chinese citizens to attack the party-state itself, which he claimed had become too bureaucratic and resistant to revolutionary change. By the late 1970s, China's economy was unstable, and the legitimacy of the Communist Party was in serious jeopardy.

Mao's death instigated a power struggle that Deng Xiaoping (1904–1997) eventually won. Deng concluded that ideology alone could not sustain the party-state after the tumult of the preceding decades. He believed that major reforms to raise the standard of living for all Chinese were necessary to maintain social control. In 1978, Deng unveiled an economic reform program that he described as "socialism with Chinese characteristics" that combined elements of socialism with a greater role for markets and private property.

Two of the most important reforms that Deng initiated were in agriculture and trade. Communal farms were dissolved and farmers were granted increased autonomy in selecting which crops to plant, as well as the ability to sell excess crops in free markets. Food production soared and farmers' income increased, stimulating the growth of private rural enterprise. At the same time, Deng created what was termed "the open door." Barriers to international trade and finance were lowered, opening China to global markets, foreign investment, and technical know-how. A necessary consequence of these reforms has been a greater recognition of private property rights: Farmers gained the right to sell their land (with restrictions) in the mid-1980s, and private businesses have been gradually legalized. The role of market forces has also increased dramatically, and today, aside from major state-initiated infrastructure projects, no part of the economy is centrally planned.[21]

Unlike the transitions away from socialism in the ex-Soviet bloc, however, China has introduced these market freedoms without giving up Communist Party power. Because of the party's centrality in facilitating development, China's transition is most accurately viewed as one from classical socialism to market socialism.[22] Under this system, private enterprise and markets enjoy a more liberal macroeconomic climate but still remain what the Chinese have called "the bird in the cage"—that is, held firmly in the grasp of state control at the level of individual corporations and industry policies.[23] Many inefficient, state-run companies are kept afloat by government financial support. The government has deliberately exploited the rural population to facilitate urban development, thus widening the social and economic gaps between China's coastal areas and its interior. The Chinese state has also pursued a highly regressive taxation system in the rural areas, and as many as 40 million peasants have been deprived of their land for development since the early 1990s with little or no compensation. More than 120 million farmers have left the land to look for work in urban areas. Members of this "floating population" are in effect illegal immigrants in their own country, deprived of many of the social services available to urban dwellers and often exploited by employers without recourse.[24]

Many of these migrant workers end up in export-oriented manufacturing facilities, the backbone of China's booming economy. Guangdong province in southeastern China is the largest manufacturing region. In 2007, *The Atlantic* correspondent

James Fallows speculated that this one province in China's **Pearl River Delta** employed more factory workers than the entire U.S. manufacturing sector.[25] Guangdong produces everything from cheap children's toys to computer motherboards. At its height, the port city of Shenzhen alone shipped these goods around the world at a rate of one standard 20-foot shipping container every second, 24 hours per day. The result of China's booming export economy has been a massive current account surplus that reached $426 billion in 2008. China has used its trade surplus to accumulate massive reserves of U.S. currency and buy U.S. Treasury bills. In addition it has invested in property and stocks overseas, most recently in Africa, where it is pouring billions of dollars into new energy, minerals, and infrastructure projects. This buildup of assets has created tensions with lawmakers in the United States and other nations, which will be discussed further below.

Rapid growth has fueled tensions and distrust between the Chinese population and the Communist Party leadership. China's government has gone to great lengths to censor expressions of dissatisfaction, often with police and military force. This was demonstrated in the 1989 Tiananmen Square crackdown against prodemocracy activists and the suppression of the Falun Gong religious movement in 1999. Beyond direct repression, however, China's leaders also understand that maintaining economic growth rates and basic services are key to maintaining control.

Hu Jintao, who assumed the role of China's Paramount Leader in 2002, has pursued an agenda consistent with this belief that the party must reinforce its legitimacy by more than direct control. One of his first actions in office was the initiation of a high-profile corruption probe within the Communist Party. He has also advanced a set of policies designed to balance the imperative of rapid growth with the goals of decreasing income inequality, improving public services for the poor, and protecting the environment. Under Hu, China has also made some progress in protecting human rights. In 2005, China was estimated to carry out more than 80 percent of the world's executions, putting to death perhaps 10,000 people, many for nonviolent offenses. In late 2006, it passed legislation preventing death sentences from being imposed without the approval of the country's highest court. In October 2006, it also drafted a law designed to crack down on sweatshops and grant legal protection to workers trying to organize unions.

These expanded social services and gains in rights have helped the Communist Party bolster control domestically and gain favor internationally. However, Chinese officials have long acknowledged that the real key to the sustainability of their government is maintaining the breakneck rate of development that has been pumping wealth into the economy. Many have publicly pointed to 8 percent as a minimum annual growth rate of GDP that will forestall widespread social unrest. This minimum has been tested with the global economic downturn that began to hit China's economy in 2007 and 2008. As the effects of the U.S. real estate and financial crises spread throughout the international financial system and as U.S. consumers restricted their consumption, demand for Chinese-produced goods fell. In 2009, China's trade surplus fell by almost half compared to 2008. An estimated 20 million factory workers in Guangdong province and across the rest of the country were shut out of jobs, with little or no immediate social safety net. The government responded swiftly—both through crackdowns on protests and a massive $600 billion stimulus plan to boost domestic demand.

Economic uncertainty following the global downturn has put the paradoxes of China's development into relief. Beijing must balance its mercantilist-realist aspirations with the humbling reminder of its global economic interdependence. At the same time, it has been compelled to continue liberalizing its economy as a mechanism for maintaining its own social control. Finally, it must develop its own consumer culture and domestic spending—a task to be delicately balanced with the structuralist rhetoric and culture of saving upon which China's current export economy has been built. We will explore all of these paradoxes in the sections that follow.

## Paradox I: Mercantilism That Runs on Global Interdependence

Some Western theorists, pundits, and politicians frequently criticize the Chinese government for unfairly enabling its country's "miracle" of economic development. They have accused Beijing of keeping China's currency artificially devalued, providing unfair export subsidies, allowing inhumane working conditions, and turning a blind eye to widespread violations of intellectual property rights. Many see these policies as representing a strategic threat to the economic and security interests of the United States. They assume a mercantilist-realist agenda driving the Communist Party's efforts to turn China into a global power. China's increasing wealth has also led to its emergence as a potential counterweight to U.S. power in regional affairs. This has been a source of concern for many neoconservatives who believe the United States should use its global primacy to spread the values of freedom and democracy.

The prospect of a stronger China, with its repressive political system and human rights practices, is considered unacceptable. Under the belief that a state's internal political configuration determines its foreign policy behavior, a strong authoritarian China is by nature an aggressive China. Other fears are driven by the strategic landscape in Asia, which contains a number of dangerous flash points—including Taiwan, an independent state over which China claims sovereignty. A stronger China would have greater capacity and self-confidence to resolve such disputes militarily, which stands to damage U.S. interests in Asia, and could even precipitate war between the United States and China.

China's role in Asian economic and security affairs has mushroomed in recent years. Beijing has spearheaded regional economic integration through the East Asian Summit (which excludes the United States), and it has led talks on transforming Central Asia's Shanghai Cooperation Organization into a NATO-like military alliance. As the country with the most influence over the North Korean government, China has played a foremost role in the six-party talks aimed at convincing North Korea to abandon a nuclear weapons program. It is expanding its influence beyond Asia to include political support for some of the world's worst human rights abusers in exchange for access to much needed natural resources. At the UN Security Council, China has given diplomatic support to the government of Sudan, which is accused of contributing to genocide in Darfur, and also to Iran, which is accused of having a secret nuclear weapons program. Both countries are suppliers of energy to China. Since at least 2000, China has promised African nations billions of dollars in aid, loans, and debt cancellation in exchange for access to oil resources and Africa's markets. It has also pitched itself as a low-cost builder of roads, dams, and other infrastructure projects in Africa. It is now the second largest trading partner with the African continent after the United States.

Concerns stemming from China's actions and policies have led to noteworthy economic backlash—and not only in the United States. In 2005, the U.S. Congress blocked a bid by Chinese-backed CNOOC to acquire Unocal for $18 billion (see Chapter 3). Similar political opposition also contributed to the failure of Chinalco's June 2009 attempt to take over Australian mining company Rio Tinto for $19.5 billion. Debates around these major deals have fueled the rhetoric of apprehension in the face of China's apparent mercantilist-realist agenda.

However, the situation is more complex than the rhetoric of these fears represents. China hardly holds a blank check to leverage its economic power over other countries. China's strength as a producer is founded on an interdependence with consumers in the rest of the developed world. What's more, a strong China benefits many countries. Many economists credit China with keeping global inflation levels low by providing the world with so many cheap manufactured goods. Largely due to China's voracious demand for resources, global prices for many commodities reached all-time highs in the mid-2000s, providing a boon for countries rich in raw materials such as oil, iron ore, alumina, and copper.

China's interests are deeply interconnected with the interests of the rest of the world, to an extent that tampers its ability to exercise a realist-mercantilist agenda willy-nilly. For example, Guangdong province became the world's manufacturing center by riding the upward curve of interdependence with the global consumer economy. But when the financial crisis hit in 2008, thousands of factories closed in the Pearl River Delta. Even Dafen, a Guangdong village that produces more manufactured oil paintings than any other location in the world, has been hurt massively by the U.S. housing crisis. As Americans defaulted on mortgages and new construction ground to a halt, so too did demand for mass-produced art and knockoffs of famous pieces. The effects of the recession have been felt deeply on both sides of the Pacific.

Columnist Thomas Friedman refers to the U.S.–China relationship as a "de facto partnership between Chinese savers and producers and U.S. spenders and borrowers."[26] Historians Niall Ferguson and Moritz Schularick coined the term "**Chimerica**" to describe the phenomenon: China not only produces the affordable goods that U.S. consumers crave, but its culture of personal saving builds the credit that effectively bankrolls a culture of leveraged debt in the United States.[27] As a result of this partnership, Chinese banks hold vast reserves of foreign currency and Chinese corporations are exerting an increasing amount of influence and ownership in foreign businesses. In July of 2009, China owned nearly a quarter of all U.S. Treasury bills—worth more than $750 billion—making it the U.S. government's largest creditor. But Beijing is well aware that a quick sell-off of U.S. monetary assets, aimed at devaluing the dollar, would have unacceptably negative consequences for China's own economy and financial holdings.

Indeed, China's leaders have shown themselves to be pragmatic in foreign affairs, subordinating some interests to the imperative of preserving economic growth and securing global economic stability and cooperation. China's militarization appears designed to deter a Taiwanese declaration of independence rather than provide China with the capacity to project power beyond its immediate periphery.[28]

Even if China's motivations for militarizing are not benign—for example, allowing it to grab resources and seize disputed territory—the vitality of China's economic ties with the United States will make China exceedingly careful to not upset its relations with its key export market. The United States enjoys such a dramatic advantage in military technology that even a concerted effort by China to modernize its military would still leave the United States in a dominant position for many years.

Ultimately, the realities of global economic interdependence constrain China's ability to act rashly and malevolently in pursuit of its self-interest. While this systemic reliance doesn't reduce China's importance or power as a rising global exporter, it does create a system of conflicting incentives and pressures that complicate Beijing's choices.

## Paradox II: Liberal Economic Prosperity as a Method of Social Control

Beijing's decisions are complicated by more than economic interdependence with U.S. consumers. As the global economic downturn slowed the pace of growth in Guangdong and other provinces, the Chinese government felt increasingly at risk of popular unrest. Many believe that Beijing sees a direct relationship between economic growth and social control. China's growth rate has averaged 10 percent or more over the past three decades. As that rate fell closer to 8 percent over the course of the global economic slowdown, unrest indeed increased. China experienced tens of thousands of small protests in 2009 by laid-off workers, those whose land has been reclaimed by the government, and workers with a variety of grievances. Ethnic tensions have also erupted violently, including widespread protests by Tibetan minorities and clashes between Muslim Uighurs and Han Chinese in Western China.

Late in 2008, Beijing introduced an economic stimulus package worth more than four trillion Yuan (over U.S. $500 billion), aimed at curbing the worst of the effects of the financial crisis and taking the opportunity to build infrastructure. China has employed this strategy before: A similar government stimulus program saved both the strength of its economy and the authority of its government during the 1997 Asian financial crisis. By late 2009, the stimulus seemed to be working, with growth rebounding from a low of 6.5 percent earlier in the year.

China's efforts to quell civil unrest are hardly limited to manipulating the levers of economic prosperity. From the military actions in Tiananmen Square to strict policing of international press coverage during the 2008 Olympics, China has a notorious record of maintaining strict control over public discourse and exercising force when necessary to maintain that control. China's government widely restricts Web access, censors media, and monitors cell phones. In 2005, Yahoo (among other major U.S. Web companies) was widely criticized for not only censoring its content but also providing private user information to Chinese police. This information eventually led to the arrest and ten-year prison sentence of a Chinese journalist accused of sharing Communist Party communications with foreign news organizations.

China may be slowly realizing that such expansive and direct control over media access is increasingly unfeasible to maintain. China's Ministry of Industry and Information Technology recently backed down from a plan to mandate that strict Internet filtering software be installed on all new computers—a turn of course after a great deal of pressure from private interests both domestically and internationally. In late 2009, China's State Council announced plans to invest billions of dollars in the development of media companies—programmers of news, entertainment, and culture—that have less direct state control and more involvement from private firms. However, in early 2010 Google pulled out of China in the face of Chinese demands that it censor its Internet search engine there.

## Paradox III: Fostering a Consumer Culture with Structuralist Rhetoric

Embracing the liberal global economy has allowed China's leadership to facilitate exponential growth while maintaining social control. It has also, however, pulled the nation into a deep dependency on its export economy and a resulting massive trade surplus. As China has learned during the global economic downturn, relying on consumers outside its borders has severe risks. China's long-term challenge in maintaining a minimum level of annual economic growth is as much a matter of protecting trade as it is a task of opening market opportunities within its own economy.

Fostering such internal economic growth is in Beijing's interest for many reasons. Selling more Chinese goods inside China would provide a more reliable and stable economic model. Furthermore, many scholars maintain that bolstering its own consumer economy is one of the most important things China can do to mitigate global recession. Keeping the world economy strong (and thus the global market for its goods healthy) by fueling consumer spending inside its own borders presents a multilayered opportunity for China's leaders. There are many roadblocks on the way to boosting domestic spending. The factories of Guangdong and other producing regions are designed to make products that most Chinese are not able to afford and likely do not desire in the first place. A shift to more consumption of domestically produced goods will require significant, costly adjustments to the production and logistics infrastructure of the export economy.

Reducing the trade surplus will mean more than an infrastructure shift, however. Export-led growth has been ingrained with a host of social habits and cultural expectations—not the least of which is modest personal consumption. Even after decades of market economy growth, Chinese consumers still spend less and save far more than their Western counterparts. A recent study by private consulting firm McKinsey asserts that the average Chinese household saves 25 percent of its discretionary income, nearly five times that of the average U.S. family.[29]

Still, consumerism has been developing in China's burgeoning metropolises for several decades. In the late 1990s, there were hardly a handful of malls in the country; there are now hundreds, stocked with high-end Western brand names and tagged with equally high prices that are out of reach for most Chinese consumers. By mid-2009, there were 138 Wal-Mart Supercenters in China, a clear indication of the rising income of the growing middle class.

The consumer culture that is developing in China can in many ways be traced—ironically—to the rhetoric and policies of the Communist Party. Providing greater faith in the availability and affordability of basic social services may, in the long run, be China's ticket to instigating greater domestic consumer spending.

In this way, the command economy continues to drive the market economy—another direct challenge to the assumptions of both classic structuralism and economic liberalism. Early in 2009, China announced that along with its dramatic fiscal stimulus package, it would also accelerate plans to provide near-universal health care to its population. The plan calls for an expenditure of over $125 billion in three years to build a network of government-supported clinics and hospitals aimed at providing medical care to 90 percent of China's population.

China's mercantilist monetary policies and trade decisions are intimately tied to—and limited by—its export economy's dependence on international markets. Decades of partial economic liberalism have provided meteoric market growth, but without a great deal of political reform. In fact, China's Communist Party sees its ability to maintain economic growth rates as intimately tied to its ability to maintain its political power. These and other paradoxes pose important questions for IPE theories. Does economic liberalism depend on political liberalism and freedom of expression? Is development of a mass-consumer culture and widespread inequality compatible with the continued rule of an information-shy, power-concentrating Communist Party? Can the regime continue to engage in mercantilist behavior like currency manipulation and massive IPR violations while maintaining its pledge to abide by liberal economic norms embodied in the WTO and other international institutions? China's ongoing development trajectory will inevitably impact the way we think about the basic tenets of IPE—possibly leading to new theories and ways of understanding political, social, and economic interactions on the global stage.

# CONCLUSION

## China, India, and the Postcommunist Countries in the Global Economy

Most scholars of IPE agree that the countries we have discussed in this chapter are reshaping the global economy and will play a much more powerful role in the coming years. They often disagree, however, on what that role will be and whether it will benefit today's developed countries or lead to a more secure, prosperous, and equitable world. After briefly comparing China and India, we conclude by contrasting several points of view about what the rise of China, India, and the postcommunist states means for the global economy. Broadly speaking, some IPE theorists fear the emergence of these aspiring powers, while others see their success as vindicating globalization and laying the foundation for mutual benefit between all states.

India and China have been two of the world's fastest and largest growing economies. Both are competing for a greater global role. Due to its service-oriented growth model, India has been described as the "back-office" of the world. Because of its large FDI inflows and a relatively open trade regime, China has come to be known as the world's "workshop." While India is a liberal democracy, China has an authoritarian regime.

It was only in the late 1970s that both countries began to undertake market-oriented reforms. Both countries' per capita GDP was approximately the same in 1990, but by 2008 China's GDP per capita was twice as large as India's. There are several factors that help account for China's dramatically better performance since the 1970s. China focused more heavily on education and literacy initiatives than India. Infrastructural development was more immediate in China, and the communist government was better able to effect top-down development as compared to its democratic, pluralistic neighbor. India's probusiness reforms were not always synonymous with pro-market reforms. By contrast, China under Deng Xiaoping emphasized both rural development and openness to foreign trade and investment.

India has severely lagged behind China in development of its physical infrastructure. While China has almost 50,000 kilometers of national, divided highways, India has only 5,000 kilometers of comparable roads. Not one major city in India has a 24-hour continuous supply of water, and power outages are so frequent that major companies have to rely frequently on costly backup generators. India's rural electric supply is also sporadic and sparse.

From this comparison, it is clear that China has been the most successful in climbing the ladder of development and claiming a more powerful political and economic role in the world. Economic liberals see this in a positive light: China seems to vindicate their assertion that free markets and open trading systems lead to rapid growth and mutual interdependence. As China finds a comparative advantage in manufacturing, developed economies reap the benefit of cheaper products and rising consumption. Moreover, according to James Fallows, even as the United States loses low-profit manufacturing, its companies still reap huge profits from control of product design, branding, retailing, and after-sales servicing.[30]

China's wealth, many liberals believe, is creating unstoppable pressures for more internal democracy and forcing the country to behave more responsibly internationally, which actually strengthens institutions of global governance such as the WTO, the UN, and the G-20. In this conception, it is China that is accepting the developed world's consensus, not the developed world that is bending to China's selfish interests. As China expert Bates Gill argues, China has since the mid-1990s pursued regional and global security policies that are "practical and constructive" and broadly in line with international norms in the areas of nonproliferation, peacekeeping, and trade openness.[31] Similarly, political scientists Daniel Deudney and G. John Ikenberry argue that capitalist autocracies like China and Russia

will eventually not be able to resist pressures for political liberalization. And because they depend so heavily on foreign trade and investment, "they have a fundamental interest in maintaining an open, rule-based economic system."[32] Case in point: China has actually helped pull the world out of the global financial crisis.

Realists are less sanguine about China. They worry that its military modernization will allow it to threaten U.S. military hegemony. The "China price" for manufactured goods is weakening or destroying major industries in the developed world such as textiles, automobiles, and electronics, leading to a major loss of good jobs, and rendering developed countries more vulnerable in a potential war. The U.S. trade imbalance with China has left the United States indebted and more vulnerable should China decide to stop buying so many Treasury bills or switch to some alternative to the dollar as the global reserve currency. Realists view China as a mercantilist in disguise, unfairly violating the rules of free trade and malevolently hurting its competitors by manipulating its currency, dumping products overseas, stealing intellectual property, and subsidizing its exporters. Clyde Prestowitz sees China as a profoundly neomercantilist power that will undermine U.S. economic primacy and standards of living unless the United States responds to its unfair trade with explicit industrial policies, selective protectionism, and investments in education and R&D.[33] Derek Scissors warns that the visible hand of the state is still very important in China, as is evident in numerous price controls, state ownership or control of many large companies, and numerous regulations on foreign investments.[34]

In a related fashion, realists and structuralists fear that China's domestic policies pose a threat to its own people and the rest of the world. China's disregard for the health and safety of its own people is evident in the spread of lung diseases, poisonings, tainted products, polluted water, and workplace injuries. Its lack of quality control and regulations means that Western consumers sometimes buy dangerous products from it such as lead-tainted toys, contaminated pet food, counterfeit drugs, rotten drywall, and, yes, even honey with illegal antibiotics. Three-fourths of the world's most air-polluted cities are in China, and 70 percent of its rivers are seriously polluted. An estimated 20–30 percent of the U.S. West Coast's mercury, ozone, and air-particle pollution now comes directly from China. And China's disregard for the rights of Muslim minorities and Tibetans is mirrored overseas in its close relationship with some of the world's worst human rights violators in Sudan, Burma, and North Korea.

Most IPE scholars expect that it will take many years for India to become a global power. In the meantime, realists hope it will be a regional buffer against Islamic extremism in neighboring Afghanistan and Pakistan. Moreover, they see India as a close ally of the United States and a counterbalance to China. According to a Pew Research Center global survey in 2009, three-fourths of Indians had a positive view of the United States while less than half of Chinese and Russians did.[35] Economic liberals see in India proof that moving away from a state-dominated economy leads to rapid growth. They also are heartened that India is a model of how democracy and free markets can work even in a very poor country.

Structuralists tend to pooh-pooh the India-rising hype, noting that caste, corruption, and exploitation still leave most Indians in deep poverty. The flashy IT sector and booming services bypass most of the population. Even liberal Indian billionaire Nandan Nilekani recognizes these constraints—along with massive education, health and environmental failures. However, in a recent book he expresses confidence that India has a promising global future due to its embrace of English, **demographic dividend** (a large, young population), embedded democracy, and empowerment through technology.[36]

Scholars recognize that post-Soviet and Eastern European countries play different roles in the global economy. For economic liberals, the integration of many postcommunist states into the European Union is evidence of the triumph of the triumvirate of democracy, capitalism, and peace. By contrast, structuralists argue that many countries like Russia, Ukraine, and Moldova are worse off now than under communism because of the breakdown of the state and the unfairness that accompanied the transition to market-based economies and quasi-democratic regimes.

Realists remained concerned about the security threats from an authoritarian Russia that claims spheres of influence around its borders and eagerly uses its oil-and-gas wealth to pressure European neighbors and centralize economic power in the hands of a Kremlin-friendly elite. They find that the implosion of communism left many countries with massive economic and social problems that can affect the rest of the world in the form of organized crime, nuclear proliferation, and poor emigrants. Once a proud superpower, Russia accounts for only 1 percent of global GDP compared to the United States' 22 percent. Realists worry that as Russia becomes an ever more important energy producer, it will cooperate less with other countries. Andrew Kuchins and Anders Aslund point out that Russian leaders nurse strong grievances about Western interference in their country after the Cold War and want to reassert "hypersovereignty" and "privileged relations" with weaker neighbors.[37] Putin and Medvedev want a world in which U.S. power is diminished and a proud Russia can assert its own interests rather than simply conform to global liberal norms.

The transition away from communism is nearing the end of its second decade, and significant changes are unmistakable. State-owned enterprises have been privatized, economic liberalization has created incentives for entrepreneurialism and innovation, and foreign direct investment has accelerated. Following a steep economic decline in the 1990s, most postcommunist countries enjoyed robust economic growth from the late 1990s to 2008. For all this progress, however, many obstacles remain, and new ones have become apparent. Corruption and rent-seeking behavior stymie confidence in the economic transition and the competence of the politicians tasked with overseeing it. For many, the economic reforms proved very upsetting to established expectations and ways of life. Voters in many countries rose up in a backlash against the reformist agendas, strengthening the power of xenophobic and authoritarian elements. The global financial crisis of 2008–2009 has undone some of the economic progress in many postcommunist states.

Economist Nouriel Roubini even argues that Russia no longer should be considered one of the dynamic emerging BRIC countries—Brazil, Russia, India, and China. Despite its nuclear weapons and energy, the financial crisis has eaten up a lot of its sovereign wealth funds. He argues, "Saddled with a rustbelt infrastructure, Russia further disqualifies itself with dysfunctional and revanchist politics and a demographic trend in near-terminal decline."[38] More likely to replace Russia alongside Brazil, India, and China as first-tier economic powerhouses, Roubini suggests, are Indonesia, South Korea, or Turkey—all countries with democratic politics and competitive manufacturing and, in the case of Indonesia and Turkey, lots of raw materials and growing populations.

The transition process is extremely diverse, and the results have been dramatically different across the communist and postcommunist world. In some countries such as India and Poland, we see the institutionalization of democracy and capitalism; in others like Russia, authoritarianism and state-dominated economies remain in place. Democratic consolidation and economic growth in Eastern Europe appear to place many of these countries on a path toward becoming industrial democracies. Within much of the former Soviet Union, economic stagnation or decline, political instability, and authoritarianism are common, more closely resembling the less developed world. China remains a unique model with an enormous question mark. Its paradoxical combination of authoritarianism and consumerism, entrepreneurialism and state intervention, may unravel in coming years as China takes on more global responsibilities. And whatever the path, all these countries will continue to struggle over social demands for freedom, equality, and protection, concerns as pressing now as they were on the eve of the Russian Revolution in 1917.

## KEY TERMS

market socialism   325
*glasnost*   326
*perestroika*   326
marketization   326
privatization   327
voucher privatization   327

crony capitalism   330
oligarchs   331
*siloviki*   331
national champions   332
Green Revolution   334
Great Leap Forward   338

Cultural Revolution   339
Pearl River Delta   340
Chimerica   342
demographic dividend   347

## DISCUSSION QUESTIONS

1. How are China's reform experiences different from those of Russia and Eastern Europe? China aims to reform its market without a radical alteration in its political system. Is it possible to change the market so dramatically without changing the state? Explain.

2. Which of the three core IPE theories do you feel best explains the paradoxes apparent in China's development model? Why?

3. In many ways, China and India appear to be developing under opposite models—India focused on service industries with a robust democracy and China emphasizing export-oriented manufacturing with a strong central government. What similarities and differences exist in their models?

4. In what ways has state intervention helped and hindered the rising powers?

5. Look at the "Made in . . . ." labels on your clothes, electronics, and household possessions. What does this indicate about the role of the rising powers in global manufacturing?

## SUGGESTED READING

Anders Aslund. *How Capitalism Was Built: The Transformation of Central and Eastern Europe, Russia, and Central Asia.* Cambridge: Cambridge University Press, 2007.

Ivan Berend. *From the Soviet Bloc to the European Union.* Cambridge: Cambridge University Press, 2009.

Paul Midler. *Poorly Made in China: An Insider's Account of the Tactics Behind China's Production Game.* Hoboken, NJ: John Wiley, 2009.

Ted Fishman. *China, Inc.: How the Rise of the Next Superpower Challenges America and the World.* New York: Scribner, 2005.

Nandan Nilekani. *Imagining India: The Idea of a Renewed Nation.* New York: Penguin, 2009.

Arvind Panagariya. *India: The Emerging Giant.* Oxford: Oxford University Press, 2008.

Yuezhi Zhao. *Communication in China: Political Economy, Power, and Conflict.* Lanham, MD: Rowman & Littlefield, 2008.

## NOTES

1. Our thanks to Rahul Madhavan and Ryan Cunningham who drafted the sections in this chapter on India and China, respectively. Thanks also to Jess Martin who drafted the textbox on Coscalia, Moldova.

2. In this chapter we use the terms "communist" and "socialist" interchangeably.

3. See János Kornai, *The Socialist System: The Political Economy of Communism* (Princeton, NJ: Princeton University Press, 1992).

4. For an assessment of postcommunist transitions from the perspective of a shock therapy supporter who advised the Russian, Ukrainian, and Kyrgyz governments see Anders Aslund, *How Capitalism Was Built: The Transformation of Central and Eastern Europe, Russia, and Central Asia* (Cambridge: Cambridge University Press, 2007).

5. EBRD-World Bank, *Life in Transition: Current Attitudes*, May 2007, http://www.ebrd.com/pubs/econo/lits.pdf.

6. EBRD, *Transition Report 2008: Growth in Transition* (Foreword), November 2008, http://www.ebrd.com/pubs/econo/tr08fore.pdf.

7. The Worldwide Governance Indicators are produced and updated by staff at the World Bank and the Brookings Institution. The databases and reports on indicators can be found at http://info.worldbank.org/governance/wgi/index.asp.

8. Ivan Berend, *From the Soviet Bloc to the European Union* (Cambridge: Cambridge University Press, 2009), especially Chapter 3.

9. International Labor Organization, *Global Employment Trends-Update,* May 2009, http://www.ilo.org/wcmsp5/groups/public/—-dgreports/—-dcomm/documents/publication/wcms_106504.pdf.

10. World Health Organization, *World Health Statistics 2009,* at http://www.who.int/whosis/whostat/EN_WHS09_Table1.pdf.

11. Murray Feshbach, "The Health Crisis in Russia's Ranks," *Current History* (October 2008), p. 338.

12. M. Steven Fish, *Democracy Derailed in Russia: The Failure of Open Politics* (Cambridge: Cambridge University Press, 2005).

13. Paul Brass, *The Politics of India since Independence*, 2nd ed. (Cambridge: Cambridge University Press, 1997), p. 273.

14. For a detailed analysis of other significant events in the economic history of independent India see Arvind Panagariya, *India: The Emerging Giant* (Oxford: Oxford University Press, 2008).

15. Brass, *The Politics of India since Independence*, p. 275.

16. Panagariya, *India*, p. 83.

17. V. N. Balasubramanyam, *The Economy of India* (London: Weidenfeld and Nicolson, 1984), p. 43.

18. Reserve Bank of India, Annual Report, 2008.

19. "An Elephant, Not a Tiger," *The Economist,* December 11, 2008.

20. "Doing Business in India, 2009," *The World Bank Group.*

21. Kenneth Lieberthal, *Governing China: From Revolution through Reform* (New York: W.W. Norton, 2004), pp. 260–261.

22. Shangquan Gao, *China's Economic Reform* (New York: St. Martin's Press, 1996).

23. Barry Naughton, *Growing Out of the Plan: Chinese Economic Reform, 1978–1993* (Cambridge: Cambridge University Press, 1996), p. 120.

24. Li Zhang, *Strangers in the City: Reconfigurations of Space, Power and Social Networks within*

*China's Floating Populations* (Stanford: Stanford University Press, 2001).

25. James Fallows, "China Makes, the World Takes," *The Atlantic* (July/August 2007), pp. 48–72.

26. Thomas Friedman, "China to the Rescue? Not!" *The New York Times*, December 21, 2008, p. 10.

27. See Niall Ferguson and Moritz Schularick, "Chimerica' and the Global Asset Market Boom," *International Finance 10* (2007), pp. 215–239.

28. For an assessment of China's militarization and its implications see the *Annual Report to Congress: Military Power of the People's Republic of China 2009*, http://www.defenselink.mil/pubs/pdfs/China_Military_Power_Report_2009.pdf.

29. McKinsey Global Institute, "If You've Got It, Spend It: Unleashing the Chinese Consumer," McKinsey & Company, 2009.

30. Fallows, "China Makes, The World Takes."

31. Bates Gill, *Rising Star: China's New Security Diplomacy* (Washington, DC: Brookings Institution, 2007), p. 1.

32. Daniel Deudney and G. John Ikenberry, "The Myth of Autocratic Revival," *Foreign Affairs, 88*, no. 1 (January/February 2009), p. 90.

33. Clyde Prestowitz, *Three Billion New Capitalists: The Great Shift of Wealth and Power to the East* (New York: Basic Books, 2005).

34. Derek Scissors, "Deng Undone: The Costs of Halting Market Reform in China," *Foreign Affairs, 88*, no. 3 (May/June 2009), pp. 24–39.

35. Pew Global Attitudes Project, Key Indicators Database, http://pewglobal.org/database/.

36. Nandan Nilekani, *Imagining India: The Idea of a Renewed Nation* (New York: Penguin, 2009).

37. Andrew Kuchins and Anders Aslund, *The Russia Balance Sheet* (Washington, DC: Peterson Institute for International Economics, 2009), especially Chapter 8.

38. Nouriel Roubini, "BRICKbats for the Russian Bear," *The Globe and Mail* (Canada), October 16, 2009.

# The Middle East: The Quest for Development and Democracy

Continuity amidst change.

AP Photo, 16567191

In 1950, U.S. Secretary of State Dean Acheson forwarded to U.S. diplomats in the Arab world the following excerpt from a classified State Department newsletter:

> Anti-Americanism is resurging in the Arab world. . . . The bombings at our Legations in Beirut and Damascus; vitriolic public statements by Syria's Dawalibi, Iraq's Suwaidi and other high officials; diatribes and fantastic rumors in the vernacular press of Syria, Egypt, and Iraq; all testify to the rekindling of Arab animosity against the United States. Whether promoted by Communists or Moslem extremists, whether

encouraged by irresponsible journalists or by weak government officials who seek to divert attention from their own inadequacies, or whether attributable to a sincere objection to America's part in Palestine developments, the current emotionalism bodes no good for the interests of the United States, nor for that matter for the best interests of the Arab states themselves.[1]

In 2005, the State Department sent its new Undersecretary of State for Public Affairs, Karen Hughes, on a public relations tour of the Middle East to counter another wave of anti-Americanism that had emerged from the U.S. invasion of Iraq, the Abu Ghraib scandal, U.S. backing of Israel, and perceived hypocrisy on democracy. Hughes emphasized the importance of fighting extremism and terrorism. In 2009, President Obama himself sought to polish the American image in the Middle East, delivering an historic speech in Cairo where he stressed the U.S. commitment to fight extremism, foster Israeli–Palestinian peace, and reach common understandings with the Muslim world.

Whether at the beginning of the Cold War or during the recent "war on terror," many in the Middle East have mistrusted the world's hegemon and condemned it for caring more about its own interests than about what is good for people in the region. While the United States struggles to burnish its reputation as a promoter of democracy, women's rights, and peace, its policies on Iran, Iraq, and Israel-Palestine have fueled animosities. But many Middle East residents also have frustrations that are homegrown: poor leadership, slow economic growth, and rising social problems. How well the Middle East adapts to globalization and the financial crisis depends partly on its relationship with the United States, but also on a much larger set of internal economic, political, and social factors.

This chapter assesses the efforts of the Middle East to adapt to the global economy, provide security for its citizens, and deal with growing pressures for democracy. First, the chapter examines how the region was historically integrated into the international economy and security structure under European colonialism and during the Cold War. This is followed by a discussion of the causes of conflict and an examination of the beliefs and actions of Islamist political movements. We then assess competing claims about whether the region is "falling behind" in the global economy or successfully integrating itself into the global trade, finance, and knowledge structures. Finally, the chapter assesses why the region—with a few exceptions—has yet to succumb to the waves of democratization that have swept over other parts of the world.

The chapter lays out several broad theses regarding tensions among states, markets, and societies in the Middle East. International markets demand openness and adaptiveness, while states jealously guard sovereignty and individuals demand protection from some of the changes that globalization brings with it. With a few exceptions, the Middle East has responded to these contradictory pressures by muddling through—adopting some economic liberalism and political openness but resisting fundamental change. The weight of history is putting a damper on development. Lack of freedom is stifling innovation and accountability. Lack of economic diversification is making the region more vulnerable to economic pressures from overseas. However, oil exporters have fared well during the global financial crisis because oil prices have remained relatively high. The promises of liberalism have yet to trump the impulses of mercantilism. A shift to a new model of governance and development will, of necessity, come from bold leaders *within* the region. Outside powers will unleash more horrendous problems if they seek *military* solutions to Iraq's civil conflict, Iran's nuclear program, or Palestinian nationalism. But *negotiated* solutions to these same problems are fraught with uncertainty and risk that will not necessarily produce a better future either.

## AN OVERVIEW OF THE MIDDLE EAST

Which countries constitute the Middle East? This chapter focuses on the region that U.S. social scientists commonly refer to as the Middle East and North Africa (MENA), an area that is tied together by history, self-identification, and economic–political interactions. It includes Israel, Iran, and Turkey (all non-Arab countries) and the numerous Arab states in the *Mashriq* (Syria, Lebanon, Jordan, Iraq, and the Palestinian Territories), in the Arabian Peninsula (Saudi Arabia, Yemen, Oman, Kuwait, Bahrain, Qatar, and the United Arab Emirates), and in North Africa (Egypt, Libya, Tunisia, Algeria, and Morocco). The distance from one end of the region to the other (Rabat, Morocco, to Tehran, Iran) is nearly 3,700 miles. (See Figure 14-1.)

In addition to official languages of Arabic, Farsi, Turkish, and Hebrew, the MENA also has millions of Kurdish speakers (especially in Turkey and Iraq) and millions of Berber speakers (especially in Morocco and Algeria). Arabic is the most widely used language (even Iran, Israel, and Turkey have Arab-speaking minorities), and the majority of people are Muslims. Of a total regional population of approximately 400 million people, there are about 15 million Christians and 5.5 million Jews. Substantial minorities of Christians live in Egypt and Lebanon. Although most Israelis are Jewish, 15 percent of Israeli citizens are Muslims. Most Muslims in the MENA are Sunnis, but the majority of the population in Iran and Iraq is Shi'ite.

MENA countries share some common economic challenges but differ significantly in terms of level of development and relationship to the global economy. For example, Yemen, one of the poorest countries in the world, has a per-capita gross national income (GNI) of only $2,210, whereas Israel's per-capita GNI is $27,450—equal to that of Greece's and close to that of the most developed countries in the world.[2] Grouping countries on the basis of exports, GNI, and population yields four general categories of MENA countries (see Table 14-1). First are the big oil exporters of the Gulf Cooperation Council and Libya, with comparatively small populations and high per-capita incomes. A second group includes big oil exporters such as Iran, Iraq, and Algeria, with large populations and historically highly protectionist economies. Third are non–oil exporters such as Israel, Turkey, Jordan, Tunisia, and Lebanon, with significant agriculture, industrial exports, tourism, and openness to foreign direct investment. Fourth are the countries like Egypt, Morocco, Syria, Yemen, and the Palestinian Territories, with mostly large populations, low per-capita GNI, and high rates of rural poverty.

There is a great deal of variation in political regimes, but the Middle East as a whole lags behind every other major region of the world in terms of political freedom. Freedom House, an independent organization that annually measures

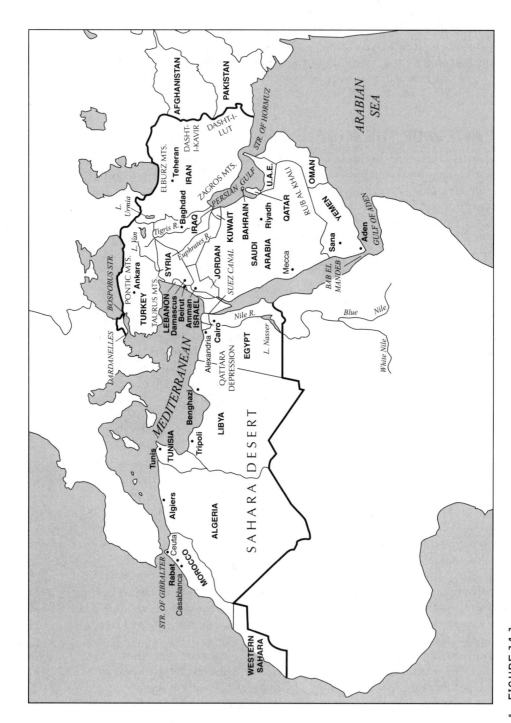

**FIGURE 14-1**
The MENA States

**TABLE 14-1**

**Economic and Demographic Differences Between MENA Countries**

| Country | Mid-2009 Population (in millions) | GNI per Capita in 2008 (in Purchasing Power Parity) |
|---|---|---|
| High-Income Oil Exporters | | |
| Saudi Arabia | 28.7 | 22,950 |
| United Arab Emirates | 5.1 | 44,600* |
| Libya | 6.3 | 15,630 |
| Oman | 3.1 | 20,650 |
| Kuwait | 3.0 | 52,610 |
| Qatar | 1.4 | 111,000* |
| Bahrain | 1.2 | 37,400* |
| Middle- to Low-Income Oil Exporters | | |
| Iran | 73.2 | 8,050 |
| Algeria | 35.4 | 7,940 |
| Iraq | 30.0 | 3,200* |
| Diversified Exporters | | |
| Turkey | 74.8 | 13,770 |
| Tunisia | 10.4 | 7,070 |
| Israel | 7.6 | 27,450 |
| Jordan | 5.9 | 5,530 |
| Lebanon | 3.9 | 10,880 |
| Low-Income, Significantly Agricultural Countries | | |
| Egypt | 78.6 | 5,460 |
| Morocco | 31.5 | 4,330 |
| Yemen | 22.9 | 2,210 |
| Syria | 21.9 | 4,350 |
| Palestinian Territories | 3.9 | 2,900* |

*GDP per capita (PPP) figures. These are from CIA, *World Factbook*, https://www.cia.gov/library/publications/the-world-factbook/index.html, accessed November 3, 2009.

*Source:* Population Reference Bureau, *2009 World Population Data Sheet*, at www.prb.org/pdf09/09wpds_eng.pdf.

countries' political rights and civil liberties, ranks only Israel (in the Middle East) as being "free."[3] Seven countries—Turkey, Lebanon, Kuwait, Bahrain, Yemen, Jordan, and Morocco—are assessed as "partly free" because they have (unfair) competitive elections and fail to ensure individual and minority rights. All eleven other countries are considered "not free." There is not a strong correlation between level of freedom and level of development in the region. And surprisingly, four of the freest countries are monarchies (Kuwait, Bahrain, Jordan, and Morocco), and two of the freest (Israel and Lebanon) make religious identity a fundamental criterion for political rights and privileges.

# THE MIDDLE EAST'S HISTORICAL LEGACY

History shapes the problems and opportunities in front of any country today. To help us understand the roots of current conflicts and the structure of current markets, we need to know something about the history of the Middle East's deep involvement in the global economy and contentious relations with the Western powers. Most of today's Middle East countries (except Iran and Morocco) were once part of the Ottoman Empire, which for hundreds of years was a commercial power in the Mediterranean and a military adversary of the European countries.

## The Ottoman Heritage

By the nineteenth century, the Ottoman Empire had turned into the "sick man of Europe." European imperial powers extended their military and economic influence, gaining commercial concessions throughout the empire. France colonized Algeria in 1832, and in the 1880s Britain and France took control of Egypt and Tunisia, respectively, on the pretext that they were no longer able to pay their debts to European creditors. The Ottomans and local rulers in the Middle East tried with very limited success to keep up with the Europeans through "**defensive modernization**"—reorganizing their governments, adopting European military technology and legal codes, and building state-owned factories.

Why was the Middle East unable to compete militarily and economically with Europe? A similar question is posed today by many in the Middle East who wonder why their countries have fallen so far behind the West in terms of technology and have been unable to challenge successfully the military "aggression" of the United States and Israel. In his influential book *What Went Wrong?*, Princeton University historian Bernard Lewis points to a lack of separation of church and state, cultural immobilism, and lack of political freedom (especially for women) as factors that hindered modernization in the Muslim Middle East.[4] Some economic historians point out that Ottoman "**capitulations**"—special economic privileges and legal rights granted to Europeans over several centuries—prevented the region from imposing high tariffs to protect infant industries. Some Muslim reformist thinkers saw decline as tied to stagnation in Islamic thought. They believed that Muslim societies could keep up with Western societies by discarding historical accretions in Islam and engaging in *ijtihad* (reinterpretation of Islamic legal sources).[5]

Alternatively, political scientist L. Carl Brown argues that the Middle East got locked into a system of international diplomacy called the Eastern Question Game, in which outside countries continuously penetrated the region and jockeyed for power. The result of this mercantilist game was that Middle Eastern political leaders tended to favor "quick grabs," eschew bargaining, and treat politics as a zero-sum game.[6] As we will see later in the chapter, the kinds of explanations we have listed here are still in vogue today as interpretations of the roadblocks for Middle Eastern countries trying to adapt to globalization.

## Twentieth-Century Colonialism and Its Aftermath

By the end of World War I, the European powers had carved up the region—excluding Turkey, Iran, and Saudi Arabia—into colonies. They drew the (often artificial) boundaries of today's Arab states and often exercised strong influence over dependent monarchical regimes in "protectorates" and "mandates." The violence that colonial powers used against inhabitants seeking independence was ferocious, sometimes setting back industrialization and state formation for decades. For example, during the "pacification" of Libya from 1911 to 1933, the Italians killed most of the country's livestock and caused the displacement, imprisonment, or death of a majority of the inhabitants.[7] During the Palestinians' Great Revolt from 1936 to 1939, Britain's counterinsurgency caused 10 percent of the entire male population to suffer imprisonment, exile, injury, or death.[8]

Soon after World War II, nationalist movements blossomed across the MENA. The Zionist dream of a Jewish state in Palestine was fulfilled in 1948 when Israel declared its independence and rebuffed an invasion by its Arab neighbors. By the late 1950s, most of the countries in the region were independent. Algerians, however, fought a brutal guerrilla war for independence from the French from 1954 to 1962, during which more than 750,000 people were killed (and many tortured by the French).

Many independent states still had to deal with a colonial legacy of exploitation and the lingering presence of European powers. In the Suez Crisis of 1956, for example, Israel, France, and Britain briefly invaded Egypt after its President Gamal Abdel Nasser nationalized the Suez Canal. The oil industries were dominated by the West's "Seven Sisters," who for decades deprived Middle Eastern countries of a "fair share" of oil revenues. Colonial powers had deliberately hampered industrialization in most Arab countries.

Ordinary citizens had little role in governance, and there was a huge economic divide between urban and rural dwellers. Poor health care and poor education were the norm, not the exception. For example, a Rockefeller Foundation–sponsored study of Egypt in the early 1950s found that about half of children died before the age of five. In a survey of five typical villages near Cairo, researchers found that nearly all inhabitants had dysentery, bilharzia, and trachoma, and two-thirds suffered from intestinal worms.[9] At the time of Algeria's independence from France in 1962, less than one-third of Muslim children were enrolled in elementary school. As late as 1970, Oman had only ten miles of paved roads and one hospital.

Arab socialists and military officers who staged a series of *coup d'états* in the 1950s and 1960s sought to break the cycle of dependency and inequality they blamed on the West and its lackeys in the region. They implemented mercantilist-style modernization programs, complete with subsidies on basic goods, state-owned industries, and high tariffs. Their success, however, was tempered by the intrusion of the Cold War into the region.

## The Cold War to the Present in the MENA

Proxy regimes relied on the superpowers for weapons and economic aid. Washington was more than happy to support authoritarian leaders like Iran's Shah as a bulwark against communism and to secure oil supplies. Moscow was eager to detach Third World countries from the Western orbit.

The Cold War had at least two lasting effects on the region. First, it pushed the oil-producing states of the Organization of the Petroleum Exporting

Countries (OPEC) to assert control over oil production and pricing. Responding to U.S. support for Israel in its 1973 struggle against Soviet allies Syria and Egypt, Arab members of OPEC nationalized oil companies and temporarily cut off oil exports to the United States. The net result in the 1970s and early 1980s was a massive transfer of wealth from industrialized nations to oil producers, whose leaders spent generously on infrastructure and education. Second, in their struggle against leftist political parties and Soviet proxies, the United States and its Middle East allies often accommodated conservative Islamist movements, even supplying massive amounts of weapons to the *mujahideen* (freedom fighters) in Afghanistan. The "blowback" from this marriage of convenience with Islamists would haunt the West in the 1990s.

At the end of the Cold War in 1990, Russia virtually disappeared from the Middle East and the United States emerged as the unrivaled external hegemon. Violent, non-state organizations such as al-Qaeda and Hizballah became the West's new bogeymen. Neoliberal economic policies spread in the face of a deep slump in oil prices that began in 1985 and mounting inefficiencies in state-dominated economies. The 1993 Oslo Accords between Israel and the Palestinians lowered the level of violence, but the Gulf states and Iran started an arms race. Military spending in the Middle East in the 1990s still averaged about 7 percent of GDP, the highest rate of any region in the world.[10] Unfortunately, a 1990s "peace dividend" never materialized. Instead, Middle Eastern countries increased military spending by 34 percent from 1999 to 2008.

Since 2001, dramatically higher oil prices have flooded the treasuries of oil exporters, allowing them to pay down foreign debt and boost government spending. The higher growth rates were welcome news for the region's people but will not end inequality. The 2008 financial crisis has crimped growth, but the region as a whole has not suffered severely. It remains to be seen if unaccountable elites will avoid the old temptation to waste new money on weapons and political patronage.

Since September 11, 2001, the geopolitical reality of the MENA states has been shaped by the crackdown on radical Islamists. The United States has been preoccupied with the war on terror and the occupation of Iraq, suffering a sharp decline in its moral authority. After a surge in American troops beginning in 2007, conditions in Iraq improved, but at a shaky equilibrium. The United States began to turn its attention to Afghanistan, withdrawing most troops from Iraq's urban areas and relying on Iraq's Shi'ite-dominated government to secure more of the country. At the same time, Israel in January 2009 launched a devastating attack on the Palestinian Islamist group Hamas in the Gaza Strip. The peace process between Israel and the Palestinian Authority came to a dangerous halt with the election of Israeli Prime Minister Benyamin Netanyahu's right-wing government in February 2009.

A new regional dynamic is the flexing of political and military muscle by the Shi'ites in Iraq, Lebanon, and Iran. In Lebanon the powerful Shi'ite Hizballah militia fought a thirty-two-day war with Israel in the summer of 2006. As Lebanon rebuilt, Hizballah flexed its muscles by briefly taking over West Beirut in May 2008. Following June 2009 parliamentary elections, it gained one-third of the cabinet seats in a unity government. Contrary to the wishes of Israel, the United States, and the European Union, Hizballah now has a powerful role in the Lebanese government and has rebuilt its weapons arsenal.

During the same period, Iran has continued to develop its nuclear enrichment capability, raising tensions with Israel, the United States, and the European Union, who have threatened the possibility of military strikes on Iran if it develops nuclear weapons. Iran's President Ahmadinejad has been defiant toward the West and has repeatedly issued vituperative statements about Israel. He won reelection in June 2009 in a presidential election that was widely viewed as rigged. His hard-line regime brutally suppressed a series of mass street demonstrations led by reformers after the election, provoking widespread international condemnation of the anti-democratic, cleric-led regime.

# THE ROOTS OF CONFLICT AND COOPERATION

This outline of Middle East history shows that there were many injustices in the past. Today there are many lingering grievances that contribute to conflict in the region. To understand why so much interstate and intrastate violence occurs, we will look primarily at political forces operating at the international and domestic levels. Of course, the MENA is not just one big zone of conflict or a vast "arc of crisis." Many forms of interstate cooperation can be identified, and with a few exceptions, countries are not on the verge of civil war. By analyzing patterns and causes of both conflict and cooperation, we can better understand the prospects for prosperity and modernization.

Tracing the roots of MENA conflict can be a difficult task, partly because the causes of violence are as much domestic as they are international and as much ideological as they are material. Conventional wisdom holds that ancient hatreds—traceable to Biblical times, the Crusades, or the Sunni–Shi'a split in early Islam—are at the heart of conflicts. This "clash of civilizations" explanation of global problems—popularized by political scientist Samuel Huntington—is tempting, especially when we look at the current war on terror. Although modern-day combatants frequently use imagery from history or holy texts to justify their struggle, we should be wary of accepting their worldviews as a basis for explaining conflict. It is more accurate to tie regional insecurity to four contemporary political factors: (1) the search by external powers for influence in the region; (2) adventurism by regional leaders; (3) oppressive regimes; and (4) the politicization of cultural and religious differences.

## Blaming the Outside World

As we have already seen, non–Middle Eastern powers have been searching for control of the MENA for centuries. Their "meddling" has often had terrible consequences. Slicing up territories or combining different ethnolinguistic and religious communities to create new states, the Great Powers often ensured future strife. During the Cold War, the Soviet Union and the United States struggled for dominance in the region by sponsoring different political forces. The superpowers' support for their proxies played a role in stoking the Arab–Israeli conflict. Staunchly anti-Israeli regimes in places such as Syria found the Soviet Union eager to sell them military equipment. On the other side, monarchs such as the King of Jordan and the Saudi royals looked to the United States for a security umbrella against pan-Arab socialist regimes seeking their overthrow. Turkey and Israel earned aid and weapons from Washington by touting their frontline role in the struggle against communism. Although Iran turned rabidly anti-American after the 1979 Islamic Revolution, Egypt under Anwar Sadat warmed up to the United States in the 1970s. Although some forms of anti-Americanism are prevalent, the majority of governments today have close military ties and/or friendly relations with the United States. Yet, Iran, Syria, Lebanon, some Palestinian groups, and some elements of the Iraqi government resist "**Pax Americana**"—a supposedly benevolent form of imperialism under which countries are expected to make peace with Israel, end terrorism, and host U.S. military bases (or at least cooperate with the United States on military and security issues).

Given the United States's deep military penetration of the MENA, most recently in Iraq, countries trying to defy the hegemon face potentially heavy costs. For example, Arab states have squandered billions of dollars in their unsuccessful wars against Israel. U.S. weapons and economic assistance to Israel for over 40 years have helped ensure that there is no fundamental change in the Arab–Israeli balance of power. In addition, the United States and its allies have imposed a variety of economic sanctions on MENA countries. These mercantilist penalties have included cutoffs of aid, freezing of assets in the United States, trade embargos, and prohibitions on Western investments.

Ostensibly designed to foster regime change or "better behavior," these sanctions have in some cases ravaged vulnerable populations without achieving their political objectives. For example, the UN's punitive (and corrupt) **Oil for Food Program** allowed Iraq to export only a certain amount of oil after 1992, and the profits were to be used to import food and medicine. This program resulted in the death of hundreds of thousands of Iraqi civilians between 1991 and 2002, and many more suffered malnutrition, disease, and declining health standards.[11] In 2006 the Palestinian population, already reeling from years of Israeli closures and trade restrictions, suffered another setback when the United States and the European Union cut off aid to the elected, Hamas-led government. Since 2006 the UN Security Council has thrice imposed moderate sanctions on Iran, including an arms export ban and financial restrictions, to try to get it to stop uranium enrichment. Only Libya caved in to international sanctions in 2003, owning up to its involvement in the 1988 airplane bombing over Lockerbie, Scotland, and agreeing to dismantle its incipient nuclear weapons program.

Three different measures provide a clear indication of how many people in the Middle East blame outsiders for regional violence. First, conservative analyst Daniel Pipes argues that for decades there has been a widespread political culture of **conspiracism** in Iran and the Arab countries, wherein the "hidden hand" of the West or Israel is seen lurking behind all the region's wars and other ills. This mindset, he asserts, encourages extremism and "engenders a suspiciousness and aggressiveness that spoil relations with the great powers."[12] Second, a discourse shared by some Muslim scholars chastises the West for its nefarious role in the region. For example, at a conference in Egypt in 2000, one prominent Muslim scholar characterized the West in these terms:

> Your globalization, oh you craven braggarts, is an arbitrary hegemony, a despotic authority, an oppressive injustice and a pitch-black darkness, because

it is a globalization without religion and without conscience. It is a globalization of violent force, heedless partisanship, double standards, pervasive materialism, widespread racism, outrageous barbarism and arrogant egoism. It is a globalization that sells illusions, leading to perdition and to burying dreams in the depth of nowhere, spreading flowers over the corpses of the hungry.[13]

Finally, public opinion polls reveal a high level of fear of the United States, *even among its Middle East allies*. A Pew Research Center survey in 2009 conducted around the world found that more than two-thirds of Egyptians, Turks, Palestinians, and Jordanians had an unfavorable view of the United States. Also, 50 percent of all respondents in Turkey, Lebanon, and Jordan were somewhat, or very, worried that the United States might pose a military threat to their country.[14]

## Blaming "Aggressive" Regional Leaders

The use of terms such as "The Butcher of Baghdad" (Saddam Hussein), "The Mad Dog of the Middle East" (Muammar Qaddafi), and the "Mad Mullahs" (Iran's Shi'ite clerics) implies that these "brutal" or "irrational" leaders are responsible for sparking conflict. Although demonizing Middle East leaders is not good social science, it is clear that **adventurism** by regional leaders since 1980 has been as important a source of insecurity as superpower meddling or transnational terrorism. Adventurism takes many forms, including territorial aggression, punitive strikes, threats of invasion, and covert operations. These acts may be designed to destabilize political rivals, expand a country's territory, or solidify control over strategic natural resources.

For example, Saddam Hussein's 1980 invasion of Iran sparked a terrible eight-year war, and his 1990 occupation of Kuwait prompted a multinational counterattack led by 500,000 U.S. troops. His actions—perhaps rooted in megalomania—can better be explained by Iraq's long-standing desire to gain ports on the Persian Gulf and dominate oil production. Morocco's 1975 takeover of the large but sparsely populated Western Sahara stemmed in part from King Hassan II's desire to boost his domestic legitimacy and control the territory's valuable phosphates and Atlantic fisheries. The post-1979 efforts of Iranian Mullahs to spread Islamic revolution throughout the Middle East contributed to instability in Lebanon, and since 2003 the United States has accused Tehran of giving assistance to Shi'ite militias in Iraq.

Israeli leaders have sanctioned the long-term occupation and settlement of Arab territories seized during wars with Palestinians and Arab armies. As a result of the 1967 Six-Day War, Israel took control of the West Bank, the Gaza Strip, the Golan Heights, and the Sinai Peninsula. A relentless program of settlement expansion has boosted the Jewish population in the Occupied West Bank and East Jerusalem to 500,000. Whatever the justifications offered by Israel, Arabs view settlement expansion as a form of colonialism that violates international law. Even the Obama administration has pressured Israel—without success—to cease building or expanding settlements, calling them an obstacle to peace. Large-scale human rights abuses have inflamed Palestinians, whose two violent *intifadas* (uprisings) in 1987 and 2000 were designed to force an Israeli withdrawal from occupied territories.

In 1982 Israel occupied southern Lebanon, and it did not fully withdraw until 2000. But in the summer of 2006 it extensively bombed Lebanese infrastructure in a month long war during which Hizballah launched hundreds of missiles into Israel. Israeli leaders have consistently justified their military engagements on the basis of their inherent right of self-defense, and they often rationalize settlement expansion as a historical right. In 2005 Israel withdrew from the Gaza Strip, but in the face of Hamas rocket attacks it invaded the Strip from December 27, 2008, to January 18, 2009. A UN fact-finding commission in September 2009 issued a report (dubbed the Goldstone Report) on the conflict, accusing Israeli forces and Hamas of committing war crimes—and possibly even crimes against humanity.[15] If nothing else, the conflict was a reminder of the terrible toll on civilians from leaders' belligerent policies in the region.

## The Oppression Factor

Regional conflicts also involve cycles of oppression–terrorism–counterinsurgency within states. Leading participants in these terrible cycles are often dominant ethno-linguistic and religious groups who subject minorities to discrimination and who try to "explain" their violence via "myths" that serve as little more than cover stories for the pursuit of self-interest. Moderate, secular Arabs claim that they are fighting retrograde Islamic fundamentalists. Islamists claim that they are fighting governing elites whose cultural beliefs reflect "**Westoxication**"—a seduction to poisonous, imported Western culture and institutions. Israel portrays its struggle as one against Palestinian terrorists. Kurds and Algerian Berbers fight perceived political and cultural oppression by Arabs. And Ahmed Hashim, a U.S. adviser to General John Abizaid in Iraq, in 2005 observed that ethnosectarian hatreds had grown in Iraq, with Sunnis viewing Shi'a as "primitive and childlike," Kurds holding contempt for non-Kurds, and Shi'a seeing Sunnis as oppressors and Kurds as "arrogant backstabbers."[16]

What these Manichean portrayals often do not explain are the politics of oppression and resistance at the heart of struggles. Although transnational terrorist groups such as al-Qaeda have caused some havoc in the region, they are far from being the central actors in MENA countries. At its base, much of the violence is a political struggle over control of the state. Kurds, Sahrawis, and Palestinians are struggling for independence and sovereignty (or at least autonomy) over a given territory in which they are currently facing political oppression. They sometimes justify violence as a legitimate tool, noting international norms of self-determination.[17]

Many Islamists seek the right to implement conservative social policies they claim are based on Islamic law. Shi'ites in Iraq and Lebanon (and to some extent in the Arabian peninsula), seeking to reverse decades of Sunni (or Maronite Christian) discrimination, are claiming political power and voice commensurate with their size of the population. And the Shi'ite movements such as Muqtada al-Sadr's Mahdi Army in Iraq claim a legitimate right to resist an occupying military power. Whether governments and occupying powers call their opponents "terrorists," or whether nationalist insurgents and *mujahideen* call their opponents "state terrorists," the fact is that all these combatants mostly injure and kill innocent civilians, not other armed fighters.

An example of the role that oppression can play in sparking conflict is provided by Lisa Hajjar, who has studied the Israeli military court system in the Palestinian Occupied Territories.[18] She finds a system of military rule and military "justice" since 1967 that regulates the movements of Palestinians and subjects inhabitants to arrest, detention, humiliation, and, sometimes, torture. Since 1967 the military courts have prosecuted more than 500,000 of the 3.5 million Palestinians in the West Bank and Gaza. The reality of constant surveillance and constant disruption of normal life has served to stiffen Palestinian resistance, some of which turns violent.

## Blaming the Islamists

Extremist Islamic movements and terrorist groups use religion as a political tool, even if reasonable people agree that these groups fundamentally misinterpret Islam. From an IPE perspective, we are particularly interested in the relationship of these movements to global and system-level processes and how these groups affect the global security structure. Some of the roots of these movements can be found in economic troubles and political repression. Rising unemployment and inequality after the 1970s pushed many poor Muslims to become foot soldiers in extremist movements. In contrast, the leaders of these radical movements often are well educated (many have science and engineering backgrounds) and from the middle class, suggesting that they feel unfairly excluded from the ruling elite.

At another level of analysis, we can see these groups as reflecting a change of ideas within the Muslim world. In the last 30 years, militant Islamist movements have spread a puritanical interpretation of Islam with emphasis on the application of Islamic law and jihadist rhetoric. Why has radicalism spread and attracted adherents to groups like al-Qaeda and Islamic Jihad in Palestine? One reason is that millions of Arabs who since the 1970s have migrated (often temporarily) to work in the conservative, oil-rich Gulf states have been exposed there to a more "fundamentalist" perspective on Islam. Second, Gulf regimes and wealthy Gulf citizens have funded *madrasas* (Muslim schools) and charities throughout the Muslim world that have sometimes taught a chauvinistic form of Islam. Iran has been a purveyor of the ideology of revolutionary Shi'ism.

Globalization empowers not just liberal, peaceful movements but their antithesis as well. Extremists are adept at using modern technology for nefarious purposes. At another level, extremists are a reaction to the perceived humiliation of Middle Eastern countries by the Americans, Europeans, and Israelis. In their writings and propaganda, extremists repeatedly invoke the presence of U.S. troops in Saudi Arabia, the Israeli occupation of Palestinian land, and the U.S. repression in Iraq as justifications for *jihad*.

## Misconceptions About Insurgency, Instability, and WMD in the Middle East

There are several common misconceptions about Middle East terrorism. First, "Islamic terrorists" are not necessarily the main groups using violence. In Iraq, for example, most of the insurgents are Sunnis and ex-Baathists who are not so much fighting for "Islam" as they are against the "injustices" of the occupying Americans and the Shi'ite-dominated government.[19] Second, the MENA is hardly the only region in the world where groups instrumentalize religion in pursuit of violent political goals. The Congo, Sudan, Colombia, and Somalia, to name just a few places, have also suffered horrible conflict by groups claiming to act in the name of their religion or ethnicity. According to the U.S. State Department's annual terrorism report, in 2008 there were more terrorist incidents *outside* the Middle East—in places such as Pakistan, Somalia, Afghanistan, and Colombia—than *inside* the region. However, in 2008 Iraq alone accounted for one-third of all of the world's deaths from terrorist incidents, according to the U.S. National Counterterrorism Center.[20]

Third, historically, violence has been used by movements seeking independence from colonial rule or liberation from oppression. For example, Hamas and Hizballah utilize violence in pursuit of explicit political goals. Interpreting them as simply using terrorism for terrorism's sake or attacking foreign occupiers because they "hate our freedoms" is a convenient way of ignoring or discounting their stated goals. As sociologist Charles Tilly has stated, "Properly understood, terror is a strategy, not a creed."[21]

Many analysts presume that the threat of weapons of mass destruction (WMD) comes almost exclusively from "rogue" regimes intent on acquiring them and/or giving them to terrorists. Saddam Hussein is exhibit number one. He used chemical weapons extensively in the 1980s against Iranian soldiers and Kurdish civilians. He also launched a serious nuclear weapons program that was dismantled under UN monitoring after 1992. Iran's development of a civilian nuclear energy program, uranium enrichment capacity, and long-range missile capacity suggests that it is putting together the pieces of a nuclear weapons program. Nevertheless, these regimes are hardly alone: Western powers and their regional allies have also been eager to acquire and use WMD or proscribed weapons.

Spain was the first country to use WMD in the region. Sebastian Balfour, a professor of contemporary Spanish studies, has carefully documented Spain's extensive use of chemical weapons—mostly mustard gas—on rebels in Morocco's northern Rif region in the 1920s.[22] France in the late 1950s and early 1960s conducted seventeen nuclear tests in Algeria's Saharan desert during Paris's development of a nuclear weapons arsenal. France also used napalm extensively against Algeria's *mujahideen* during the 1954–1962 War of Independence. Morocco used napalm against Sahrawis in the 1980s, and Algeria is suspected of using napalm against Islamist guerrillas in the 1990s. Israel is the only country in the region that is known to possess nuclear weapons—perhaps 200–300—and a capacity to deliver them against regional enemies. Even the United States has been criticized for using depleted uranium ammunition and white phosphorus incendiary devices in Iraq since 2003.

In light of Iraq's sectarian strife, battles between Israelis and Arabs, and frequent suicide bombings, many observers believe the MENA region is on the verge of political collapse. Civil wars in Lebanon (1975–1990), Algeria (1992–2000), and Iraq (since 2003) have also caused enormous damage, population displacement, and loss of life. Only a few small countries such as Tunisia and the United Arab Emirates have not participated directly in some sort of interstate conflict or been racked by domestic strife in the last thirty years.

Despite the persistence of insecurity in some parts of the region, most of the MENA's citizens do *not* face violence daily. In fact, most of the countries have low crime rates (although domestic violence against women and children remains a big problem). In the last fifteen years there has *not* been widespread political violence in the Gulf Cooperation Council, Turkey, Iran, Syria, and North Africa (except Algeria). Since 1970, only one dictator (in Iran's Shah) has been overthrown by his own people, and only one regime (in Iraq) has been overthrown by an outside power.[23] Compared to many other governments in the developing countries, Middle Eastern regimes have usually survived in the face of mounting social pressures. At the time of this writing, even Iran's clerical regime in Iran had withstood mass demonstrations in 2009—the largest protests the country has witnessed since 1979. In light of the absence of fundamental regime change in the last forty years, it is perhaps more accurate to describe the MENA as "stable" rather than "unstable."

## Cooperation at the Interstate Level

Drowned out by media coverage of regional conflicts are the many enduring forms of state-to-state cooperation in the MENA and positive relations with Western powers. Almost all the countries in the Middle East have at some time benefited from their security relationship with the United States. In 1787 Morocco and the United States signed a Treaty of Friendship and Amity that is still in force today and that constitutes the longest unbroken treaty between the United States and another country. President Woodrow Wilson supported self-determination for states after World War I, and the United States helped liberate North Africa from fascism in World War II. The United States supported Algerian independence from France, helped Israel defend itself during wars, and liberated Kuwait (with EU support) from Saddam Hussein's occupation.

Europe and Uncle Sam have extended significant security assistance to southern Mediterranean countries since the 1950s. NATO has undoubtedly secured Turkey, one of its founding members. Since the mid-1990s, the European Union has promoted formal security cooperation with southern Mediterranean countries. In the aftermath of the 2006 Israel–Hizballah War, France and Italy took the lead in contributing troops to a robust UN peacekeeping force in Lebanon.

Cooperation among Middle Eastern states is not yet well institutionalized, largely owing to historical rivalries. The Arab League, headquartered in Cairo, represents so many different countries with competing interests that it cannot easily act in concert on major issues. The Gulf Cooperation Council has probably been the most successful organization, coordinating trade and security policies. Bilateral military cooperation between Israel and Turkey and between Iran and Syria has been quite strong.

## Cooperation at the Human Level

Some of the most robust and sustained cooperation occurs within cross-national human networks. Scholars of IPE increasingly recognize that interactions between people and non-state organizations have profound effects on security and growth.

On an individual level, emigration and dual citizenship tie Europe and the United States more closely to the Middle East than many observers realize. According to Philippe Fargues, a leading French demographer, more than eight million first-generation immigrants from the Arab countries and Turkey are living in Europe, including five million North Africans and three million Turks.[24] Many came to Europe as temporary "guest workers" in the 1950s through the 1970s but stayed and raised families. For example, approximately 10 percent of the population of France is Muslim, the majority of whom are from North Africa. As is the case in the United States, many immigrants remain connected to their home countries through extended family ties and remittances (see the next section).

Many American citizens work in the Middle East, and many Middle Easterners who have become naturalized U.S. citizens retain citizenship in their country of birth. These dual citizens often vacation, work, or live in the Middle East. When war broke out between Israel and Hizballah in July 2006, there were more than 25,000 Americans living in Lebanon. American military forces evacuated 15,000 of these scared and displaced Americans, many of whom are dual citizens. European governments also rescued thousands of their own citizens from Lebanon in one of the largest international evacuations in decades. Approximately 150,000 American Jews live in Israel, most of whom have gained Israeli citizenship under the Law of Return (which grants citizenship to Jews from anywhere in the world who return to Israel). It should also be noted that tens of thousands of Americans are working and fighting "temporarily" in the region. As of September 2009, more than 124,000 U.S. troops, at least 31,000 U.S. citizens working for private contractors, and 1,000 embassy personnel were present in Iraq. (Conversely, the United States has admitted more than 35,000 Iraqi refugees into the United States since 2007). For an examination of how education ties together citizens of the West and the Middle East, see the box, "International Education and the Middle East."

## ▶INTERNATIONAL EDUCATION AND THE MIDDLE EAST

Having citizens knowledgeable about other region's languages and cultures is what political scientist Joseph Nye considers a source of a hegemon's "soft" power (see Chapter 9). For a region as important to the United States as the Middle East, it is surprising that so few Americans learn the region's primary languages—Arabic, Farsi, and Turkish—or study abroad there. In 2006, approximately 24,000 U.S. college students were taking Arabic courses—double the number since 2002—but they represented only 1.5 percent of all students taking foreign language classes.[a] The second Bush administration

significantly increased funds for training intelligence agents and military personnel in "strategic" foreign languages, but only a small percentage of those government employees who study a critical Middle East language will gain fluency or working proficiency.

Studying abroad is another way to increase cultural understanding. Although the number of U.S. students studying in the Middle East steadily increased after 9/11, the overall number of Americans choosing to learn about the region firsthand is low. In the 2007–2008 school year, only about 3,360 participated in a study-abroad program in the Middle East and North Africa—just 1.3 percent of the nearly 262,000 U.S. students who studied overseas that year, mostly in Europe and Latin America.[b]

The United States—like Europe—has for decades attracted many of the best-educated Middle Easterners to study in its universities. Many of these students stay in the United States after their undergraduate or graduate training, contributing to the U.S. economy. International political and economic trends dramatically affect which countries in the Middle East send how many students to the United States. Following the first oil boom, Iran— then a key secular ally of the United States—sent a slew of students to the United States (50,000 in 1979 alone). At the height of the second oil boom in the early 1980s, Middle East oil exporters flooded U.S. schools with students pursuing scientific and technical degrees (and English-language proficiency). By contrast, 9/11 caused a short-term decline in the number of Arabs studying in the United States, many of whom felt unwelcome or had trouble getting visas. In 2005 there were only 3,000 Saudis studying in the United States, an example of how U.S. security policies conflict with other U.S. interests. But what a difference a few years and a lot of oil revenues make: By 2009 there were nearly 12,700 Saudis studying in the United States. Turkish students are filling the void left by other Arabs: By 2009, there were 13,300

Turks studying in the United States, nearly equal to the number of Mexicans studying in U.S. universities.[c]

Many Middle Easterners return home with their U.S. or European degrees, taking up important positions in the government and the business community. Europe and the United States hope that these individuals will become surrogates for the West, spreading secular values. In addition, U.S.-style, English-language universities are popping up like mushrooms in the region. This new trend derives from the desire to modernize higher education and the need to have citizens master language and technical skills that are vital to participating in the global economy. In addition, dozens of U.S. universities in recent years have set up branch campuses in Arab countries or entered into cooperative agreements with Middle Eastern institutions of higher education. All of these educational ties have the potential to foster long-term cooperation and understanding between the West and the Middle East.

### References

[a]Modern Language Association, "Press Release," November 13, 2007, http://www.mla.org/pdf/release11207_ma_feb_update.pdf.
[b]See Institute for International Education, *Open Doors 2009* (New York: Institute for International Education, 2009).
[c]For detailed data see Institute for International Education, *Open Doors 2009*, http://opendoors.iienetwork.org.

# FACING THE GLOBAL ECONOMY: INTEGRATION OR MARGINALIZATION?

There is a significant debate among scholars about whether the MENA is "keeping up" with globalization or "falling behind" the rest of the world. It is part of a long-running discussion about the nature of "modernization" and "development." In this section we discuss two different hypotheses about economic processes in the region. The first suggests that the MENA is successfully integrating itself into the global economy and preparing for a sustainable future. The second asserts that the region is becoming increasingly uncompetitive and marginal, failing to switch to high-growth economies that can resolve sociocultural problems. As will become evident, the MENA is a very diverse region with many kinds of ties to the global economy.

## Oil, Industry, and Growth

Growth in many parts of the MENA is tied to hydrocarbons. The years 1973–1984 were a golden age for oil exporters that raised incomes dramatically and expanded infrastructure. Adjusted for inflation, oil prices from 1985 to 1999 were in a slump, lowering growth rates throughout the region. But since 2000, oil prices have recovered nicely as a result of OPEC production cuts and rising demand from China. Growth rates are healthy again. According to the World Bank, growth in the MENA (not including Turkey and Israel) averaged 5.1 percent from 2000 to 2007, one of the best spurts since the late 1970s. The World Bank predicted that the region's GDP would grow at 2.2 percent in 2009, despite the global financial crisis. The turnaround in energy prices, which could last for many years, allows Middle East oil exporters to rebuild infrastructure and boost employment. Despite a decrease in global energy demand, the oil exporters have survived the financial crisis better than most regions of the world. This was because oil prices rose to over $70 a barrel by August 2009 and these countries can draw on huge international reserves to increase government spending.

Saudi Arabia has taken advantage of its abundant hydrocarbons to expand into energy-intensive industries that benefit from subsidized domestic oil. The country has become an exporter of cement, steel, and, especially, petrochemicals that China is gobbling up. In the global petrochemicals market, Saudi Arabia is now a more important competitor with Germany, historically the world's largest petrochemical exporter. Moreover, the MENA as a whole in 2008 supplied 25 percent of U.S. crude oil needs, 50 percent of China's, and 90 percent of Japan's.

Non–oil exporters seem to be finding their own successful growth models based on a variety of paths. For example, in the space of less than twenty years, Dubai has transformed itself from a desert backwater into a transportation, financial, and tourist hub (see the box "Dubai: The Las Vegas of Arabia"). Tunisia has adopted an export-oriented strategy that looks as if it were borrowed from Asia. Like Egypt and Turkey, Tunisia has a world-class tourism sector. Non–oil exporters have fared worse since the financial crisis because of diminished exports, remittances, tourism, and FDI. However, the crisis did not result in dire consequences as these countries are not deeply integrated into global capital markets, have relatively low levels of foreign debt, were not exposed to the U.S. subprime market, and have modest levels of exports of manufactured goods.

Israel is a standout case, more developed and globalized than any other MENA country. It has transformed itself from a state-dominated economy in the 1950s that exported mostly agricultural goods and polished diamonds to a diversified industrial economy exporting mostly high-technology products. Since the U.S. technology boom in the 1990s, more than 100 Israeli companies have raised significant capital by listing on the New York Stock Exchange. Some Israel-based companies are global players, including pharmaceutical giant Teva. Israel has some of the highest numbers of engineers, scientists, and patent holders per capita of any country in the world. It has become an important exporter of information technology and advanced weaponry.

# DUBAI: THE LAS VEGAS OF ARABIA

Two generations ago, Damascus and Cairo were the "happening" places in the Middle East in terms of political ferment, economic dynamism, and cultural attraction. A generation ago, Beirut, the so-called "Paris of the Middle East," was the place to go for tourism and trade. Now the most dynamic city-state in the entire Middle East is Dubai, a small desert patch on the conservative Arabian peninsula. It is a wheeler-dealer's kind of place, open to big ambitions and grandiose schemes. How did this backwater become a fast-growing financial, trade, and tourism hub in just three decades?

Dubai is one of seven sheikdoms that make up the loosely federated United Arab Emirates (UAE). It has a coastline only 45 miles long. Before the UAE's independence in 1971, Dubai City was a sleepy town known for pearl diving that was connected to a surrounding Bedouin population. Oil was discovered in the 1960s, and the emir at the time—Sheikh Rashid bin Said al Maktoum—invested proceeds in an international airport and dredged the main harbor for international shipping.[a] He encouraged investment in high-rises and hotels and established a modern telephone system. His sons—part of the ruling Maktoum family—have invested government funds heavily in basic infrastructure. Realizing that limited oil supplies would soon diminish, they set up free-trade zones, established incentives for international container business, and made sure there were no income or corporate taxes. Theirs has been a vision of a global *entrepôt,* attracting business from any company in the world.

Openness to the world has been only part of the city-state's recipe for fast growth. Equally important has been the Maktoum family's own private investments throughout the emirates and their strong reliance on state ownership. As one author has noted, "Dubai is a leading case study in successful state capitalism. . . . [The Maktoum family's] city state has been aptly described as a family conglomerate run by Sheik Mohammed as ruler and CEO. He is the visionary behind the leading enterprises in Dubai,

including investment, media and hotel companies, as well as Emirates Air."[b]

The results on the ground stagger the imagination. The sheikhdom headquarters Al Arabiyya, a satellite TV network that is a strong rival of Al-Jazeera for the Arab news market.[c] It has two of the largest shopping malls in the world, two indoor ski slopes, and Burj Dubai, the tallest building in the world (which is twice as tall as the Empire State building). At least two large real estate developments are being built on huge artificial islands off the coast; one—called The World—consists of "several hundred man-made islands representing regions of the world in their respective continental groups. There are to be private-estate islands, resort islands, [and] community islands."[d] Despite a population of only 1.2 million people (mostly expatriates), there were more than 5 million visitors in 2005. Also under construction is a $19 billion tourist complex called Dubailand, which, when completed, will be four times larger than Manhattan and, as its promoters claim, "the biggest, most varied leisure, entertainment and tourism attraction on the planet."[e] In addition, Dubai is building the $8 billion Al Maktoum International Airport, which will supposedly become the biggest passenger and cargo airline hub in the world.

In Dubai we see the conflation of mercantilist, liberalist, and structuralist forces.[f] The state has made growth possible through its investments and policies. The international market has swarmed in to take advantage of the city-state's deregulated, Las Vegas–style economy. But the whole edifice, a structuralist would point out, rests on exploitation of hundreds of thousands of poor Asian workers and thousands of prostitutes with no unions or political rights. Like the real Las Vegas, Dubai has been hard hit by the global financial crisis since 2007. Real estate prices crashed, construction slowed or stopped on many big projects, many laborers left, tourism dropped, and the city-state was saddled with debt. Dubai's risky marriage with globalization now seems to be on the rocks.

## References

[a]Jeremy Smith, "Dubai Builds Big," *World Trade,* April 2005, p. 58.

[b]William Underhill, "The Wings of Dubai Inc.," *Newsweek,* April 17, 2006, p. 34.

[c]Lee Smith, "The Road to Tech Mecca," *Wired,* July 2004.

[d]Tosches, "Dubai's the Limit," *Vanity Fair,* June 2006.

[e]Ibid.; Seth Sherwood, "The Oz of the Middle East," *The New York Times,* May 8, 2005.

[f]For an overview of the keys to Dubai's success see Martin Hvidt, "The Dubai Model: An Outline of Key Development-Process Elements in Dubai," *International Journal of Middle East Studies* 41, no. 3 (August 2009), pp. 397–418.

## Trade and Investment with Europe and the United States

MENA countries are being integrated into the global economy through the World Trade Organization, free-trade agreements, and bilateral agreements with Europe and the United States. Since 1995, the European Union has been touting a comprehensive free-trade and cooperation agreement called the **Euro-Mediterranean Partnership (EMP)**—renamed the Union for the Mediterranean in 2008. In exchange for lowering trade barriers and reforming their economies, Arab Mediterranean countries have been receiving more aid, loans, and market access from Europe. Turkey is an EMP member but something of an exception—it has a customs union with the EU and is in accession talks. Israel is an EMP member, too, but already has a bilateral free-trade agreement with the EU. Since 1995 the EU has given the EMP members billion of dollars of aid, and the European Investment Bank has loaned at least as much. The EMP also is designed to foster security cooperation and cultural understanding. Those countries that make demonstrable progress in neoliberal reforms will gain greater aid and market access from Europe. By flexing its "soft" power, the EU is trying to accelerate growth in this part of the Middle East.

Not to be outdone by Brussels, Washington is pushing for a Middle East Free-Trade Area by 2013. In pursuit of that goal, the United States has signed bilateral free-trade agreements with five close allies, including Jordan and Morocco. The hope is that more open economies will increase trade, investment, and democracy. Since 2001 the region has become a boom market for U.S. companies. Microsoft, Cisco, Bechtel, Boeing, and General Electric—to name just a few—have garnered contracts to supply, build, and operate many new infrastructure projects. The region is a major importer of machinery, aircraft, vehicles, grain, and engineering services from the United States (and it is an even more important trade partner with the European Union and Japan).

It is also a major importer of weapons from the United States, Europe, and Russia. From 1996 to 2003, U.S. arms sales agreements with Middle Eastern countries totaled $35 billion. From 2004 to 2008, the United States supplied more than 50 percent of the conventional weapons bought by Middle East regimes. Marxist economists Jonathon Nitzan and Shimshon Bichler have argued that U.S. arms sellers (the "Arma-Core") have a common interest with U.S. oil companies (the "Petro-Core") in the periodic outbreak of wars in the Middle East, because the resulting hike in oil prices after conflicts boosts their profitability.[25] In other words, when conflicts cause oil prices to rise, Middle Eastern countries almost inevitably use the windfalls to buy more weapons. That is good for trade, but not necessarily for long-term MENA growth.

Middle East countries not only use oil revenues to import goods and services; they recycle profits back to oil-consuming countries in the form of investments in stock markets, purchases of real estate, and deposits in Western banks. This **petrodollar recycling,** first witnessed in the 1970s (see Chapter 8), jumped into high gear again after 2000, tying the economic fortunes of some MENA countries closely to the international financial system. Middle East companies and individuals looking for profitable investment opportunities abroad have bought shares in Western companies and purchased real estate. Many of the investments come from **sovereign wealth funds (SWFs),** which are large investment pools controlled by the governments of resource-rich countries like Abu Dhabi, Saudi Arabia, Kuwait, and Qatar. When the financial crisis hit in 2007, SWFs poured tens of billions of dollars into banks and companies outside the MENA, sometimes gaining equity shares and sometimes buying whole companies. The liquidity was badly needed by Western financial institutions and struggling corporations, but some U.S. and EU politicians—already concerned about dependence on OPEC oil—worried that MENA governments would use the SWFs to gain political leverage over their countries and potentially threaten national security.

There are many examples of MENA SWFs and individuals that have deep investments in the United States and Europe. As of 2006, Prince Alwaheed bin Talal, a Saudi royal family member, was the single largest foreign investor in the United States, owning significant shares in Citicorp, Apple, and Saks Fifth Avenue. Dubai Ports World, a Dubai-based company that manages port facilities around the world, is an example of the greater role of the Middle East in overseas services. The company's bid in 2006 to manage some ports in the United States provoked a mercantilist response from the U.S. Congress, whose protestations over security threats killed the deal. Since 2007, various MENA SWFs have purchased Barney's New York and bought large equity stakes in Mercedes car maker Daimler, Volkswagen, Barclays Bank, Merrill Lynch, Citigroup, and New York's Chrysler Building.

**Remittances**—money transferred by foreign workers to their home countries— also strongly integrate people in Europe and the Middle East. IPE scholars increasingly recognize that remittances from migrants can have a very positive effect on economic development. Countries in North Africa rely on billions of dollars of annual remittances from workers in Europe to help with their balance of payments and to supplement the incomes of the poor. Since the 1960s, Turkish workers in Europe have remitted an estimated $75 billion back to Turkey, providing financial security to many families. Egyptians living in Europe, the Arab countries, and North America sent more than $8 billion back to Egypt in 2008.

## Globalization in the Gulf Cooperation Council

The six countries in the **Gulf Cooperation Council (GCC)**—Saudi Arabia, the United Arab Emirates, Kuwait, Oman, Bahrain, and Qatar—are deeply integrated into the global economy not just through oil exports and SWFs but also via their labor markets. Alongside the often conservative indigenous population is a huge foreign workforce. Expatriate workers make up more than 70 percent of the entire workforce in these six countries and nearly 40 percent of all the people living there (in 2006 there were 12.5 million expatriates among 40 million people).[26]

Where do the expatriate workers come from? During the 1970s oil boom, three-fourths of immigrant workers came from fellow Arab countries. However, after the end of Operation Desert Storm in 1991, Kuwait and Saudi Arabia expelled more than 1.5 million Yemenis, Jordanians, and Palestinians as punishment for their leaders' support for Iraq's invasion of Kuwait. By 2004, one-third of foreign workers were Arabs, joined by a growing number of Indians, Pakistanis, Bangladeshis, Filipinos, and other Asians. However, the post–2000 oil boom has increased demand for more Arab workers; two million Egyptians currently work in other Arab countries.

Although the GCC has benefited enormously from the skills and low labor costs of its internationalized workforce, the region's ruling families are increasingly worried about the political and cultural dangers from heavy reliance on foreigners. Expatriate grievances have provoked some strikes and unrest. Asian women who work as nannies and domestic helpers often complain of physical and sexual abuse by employers. Gulf leaders worry that children raised by Asian nannies and taught by foreigners will lose their Arab and Islamic identity. They are also concerned about the large number of illegal aliens and "stateless" residents who are politically loyal to foreign countries.

Non–GCC countries are also turning to expatriate labor, which can usually be taken advantage of more easily than domestic workers. According to an extensive investigation by the U.S.-based National Labor Committee (NLC), tens of thousands of guest workers from Bangladesh, China, and India are working in Jordanian textile factories that export garments duty-free to the United States.[27] Many of these (often Asian-owned) companies, in which workers are frequently exploited in sweatshop conditions that the NLC asserts constitute forced labor, supply Wal-Mart, Target, L.L. Bean, and other U.S. retailers. Jordan, like its GCC neighbors, has found that importing Asian workers (especially Chinese) fuels export growth. Even Israel in the last 15 years has replaced low-wage Palestinian workers with low-wage Asians—more out of security concerns than economic ones. The presence of so many nonnational, nonunionized workers may be hampering the development of a powerful labor movement within civil society.

## The Falling-Behind Thesis

So far in this section, we have focused on evidence of the MENA's seemingly successful integration into the global economy through trade, finance, and migration. Nevertheless, there is a powerful counterargument that the Middle East is falling behind other modernizing countries and failing to move up in the global hierarchy. Many in the region itself recognize that there is little technological or industrial dynamism. Politically the region has largely been out of step with the rest of the world, ruled by monarchs and dictators that many other developing countries cast away years ago. Growth rates per capita that stagnated in the 1980s and 1990s recovered after 2000 in oil exporters, Turkey, and Israel. Many countries' economies are still dominated by inefficient state-owned enterprises and unprofitable public banks. Periodic conflict and threats of violence have stunted foreign investment. In a powerful analysis of these problems, a team of Arab social scientists published the *Arab Human Development Report 2002*, which identified the Arab MENA as suffering a gap with the rest of the world in terms of knowledge, freedom, and women's empowerment.[28]

## The Challenge of the Historical Legacy

Some of the region's inheritance from the past seems to be hampering its adaptation to globalization. As mentioned earlier, colonial powers left many unfortunate legacies. Overdependence on a single, exported commodity, such as oil, cotton, or phosphates, slowed economic diversification in some states. Colonial regulations stifled educational opportunities and growth of an indigenous private sector. Many countries did not gain full independence until the 1950s and 1960s. The loss of well-educated and entrepreneurial minorities—Greeks fleeing Turkey, Jews leaving Arab countries, French *pied noirs* abandoning Algeria—set some economies back for years. Postindependence, Arab socialist regimes expropriated foreign property and nationalized private businesses.

After independence, many countries adopted development policies that were popular and even beneficial in the short term but that eventually, by the 1980s, were burdening the economy. Agrarian reform and land redistribution lowered agricultural productivity. High tariff barriers protected inefficient domestic companies. Government subsidies, price controls, and overvalued currencies all contributed to a misallocation of resources. Nevertheless, Middle East growth rates in the 1950s and 1960s were quite remarkable in some countries such as Israel, Syria, and Iran, and most countries dramatically increased literacy and access to health care. The 1970s witnessed another growth spurt fueled by oil revenues.

Development troubles came to a head in most of the region by the early 1980s, when neoliberalism and economic reform began sweeping through many parts of the world. From 1980 to 2000, per-capita GDP in the MENA (excluding Israel and Turkey) *failed to grow at all*, while in East Asia during the same period it expanded at an annual rate of 4.1 percent.[29] Unemployment and foreign debt grew sharply. Weak or nonexistent regional stock exchanges meant that a wave of Western private investment spreading to Latin America and Asian simply bypassed the region. When was the last time you read about a U.S. company outsourcing to the Middle East? When oil prices (adjusted for inflation) began to tumble in 1983, countries began to have trouble servicing their debt. Not until 2002 did crude oil prices (adjusted for inflation) recover dramatically.

## Limits on Free Trade

Only a handful of countries in the world have yet to join the World Trade Organization, and a surprisingly large number are in the Middle East: Algeria, Iran, Iraq, Yemen, Sudan, Libya, and Lebanon. As a whole, the region also has high average tariff levels. This indicates that many regimes are reluctant to reduce protectionist barriers dramatically and adjust rapidly to international trade rules.

The MENA has not significantly diversified its exports. Eighty percent of its exports to the United States consist of oil, gas, and minerals. Although the long-term benefits of trade openness are higher growth and productivity, the short-term consequences are politically unpalatable. Many Arab businesses—especially in textiles and consumer goods—will not be able to compete with European or Asian imports, causing unemployment to rise.

Surprisingly little investment and trade occurs *between* MENA countries. Arab countries' main exports are to the industrialized countries, and the main imports they need are not produced regionally. For example, less than 4 percent of Algeria's total trade is with other Arab countries, whereas two-thirds of its trade is with the EU. Economic exchange between MENA countries will probably take off only if durable solutions to long-running conflicts are found. Until then, regional integration will remain a hostage to war and historical grievances, forcing countries to look for commercial opportunities with the West rather than in their own backyard.

Unfortunately, some MENA nations have growing *illicit* trade connections with the global economy. This often-overlooked form of integration has an important effect on security and society (see Chapter 15). If governments do not make more concerted efforts to control activities such as drug smuggling, money laundering, and corruption, social deviancy will rise and foreign investors will stay away. Morocco and Lebanon are important suppliers of marijuana to Europe, while Turkey and Iran are important countries in the transit of heroin from Afghanistan to Europe. Despite stronger border policing in Europe, illegal immigrants from North Africa and sub-Saharan Africa continue to flow across the Mediterranean to Italy and Spain. Illicit financial transactions continue in the GCC despite crackdowns on banks and unlicensed money traders since 9/11. Iran and Syria are major "covert" suppliers of weapons to Hizballah and Hamas. Corruption on international contracts—a widespread practice for decades—enriches the pockets of ruling elites.

## Societal Problems

It has become increasingly fashionable to blame sociocultural factors for the Middle East's catching-up problems. Underutilization of female human capital has been a substantial drag on MENA economies. Few countries in the world have as dismal a record of female employment as the Arab Gulf countries, where women with citizenship constitute less than 10 percent of the total workforce. Even large countries such as Algeria and Iran have comparatively low female employment rates. Education appropriate for the needs of the global market is still lacking. For example, perhaps one-third of college graduates in Saudi Arabia major in Islamic studies. Some "information-shy" regimes such as that in Iran place restrictions on access to independent newspapers, the Internet, and/or satellite dishes.

Some intrusive governments have hampered growth of dynamic private sectors. Arab elites are reluctant to break up state enterprises and downsize the public administration for fear of provoking the wrath of public-sector workers and bureaucrats. Iran is unusual in having huge conglomerates called **bonyads,** which clerics and their private business allies use to dominate the economy and siphon off public resources. It is inaccurate, however, to say that the Middle East lacks a culture of entrepreneurship. Economic dynamism in the private sector is particularly strong in Israel, Lebanon, Turkey, and Morocco. This may be due in part to the fact that large emigrant communities from these countries are present in many parts of the world, forging strong trade and investment links with partners "back home."

## The Basket Cases

The worst performers in the region are Iraq, Yemen, and the Palestinian Territories. They will be hard-pressed to recover anytime soon from the tribulations of war and endemic poverty. International economic sanctions imposed on Iraq by the United Nations in 1992 and lasting for more than a decade devastated the economy and the health of the population. Poverty and malnutrition skyrocketed, while the middle class largely collapsed. Widespread insecurity after the U.S. invasion undermined the economy even more. Billions of dollars of international aid and U.S. spending have done little to improve living conditions, mostly because the aid has been devoted to basic security operations, invested in inappropriate projects, or squandered through massive corruption. Only an end to war and growing oil exports will allow the country to recover.

Yemen has struggled for different reasons. With a large, poor rural population, its government has never had strong control over its territory. Saudi Arabia's expulsion of nearly one million Yemeni workers after the 1991 Gulf War hurt households that relied on remittances. And a majority of Yemeni males habitually chew *qat*, a mild narcotic, thereby lowering worker productivity and depleting family finances.

The Palestinian Territories for over a decade have experienced one of the worst economic declines in the world, largely as a result of deliberate Israeli policies to isolate the territories from international trade and prevent Palestinians from working in Israel. Sara Roy has meticulously analyzed the horrendous economic and social conditions for Palestinians caused by Israel's policy of imposing curfews and travel bans, expropriating land, destroying civilian infrastructure, and uprooting tens of thousands of olive and citrus trees.[30] Israel insists that its punitive actions are triggered by Palestinian terrorism and rejection of compromise leading to a peace treaty. An Israeli blockade of the Hamas-controlled Gaza Strip since 2007, coupled with the Israeli military offensive there in December 2008 and January 2009, has caused a human crisis in which two-thirds of the population live in poverty. As in Iraq, aid from outside powers (Arabs and Europeans in this case) has not proven to be a panacea. Only a final peace settlement with Israel will lay the foundation for economic recovery in an independent Palestine.

# THE CHALLENGE OF DEMOCRACY

The Middle East stands out for its apparent resistance to democracy. While a "Third Wave" of democratization swept through much of the world from the 1970s to the 1990s, Arab countries remain mired in authoritarianism. Iran's clerics have manipulated elections, limited the scope of legislative powers, and violated human rights, as demonstrated to the entire world during the brutal crackdown on reformers in the summer of 2009. As of 2009, only Israel and Turkey could be described as electoral democracies in the MENA, but even their political systems are not models of Western "liberalness." The rest of the region—despite extensive economic dependence on and pressure from the world's most powerful democracies—has yet to make a transition to constitutional, representative government.

How can we explain why most of the region's countries have not adopted democracy? Scholars have identified four main structural factors that may be to blame: the West, oil, weak civil society, and Islam. However, some optimistic scholars and policy makers dismiss the argument that these factors are unique to the Middle East and claim that there are signs that the region is ready for—and moving toward—political freedom.

## Potential Impediments to the Spread of Representative Government

Europe and the United States bear some of the blame for lingering authoritarianism. After all, it was the European powers that colonized much of the region and created many "artificial states." Rashid Khalidi, a historian at Columbia University, argues that when European powers entered the region in the late nineteenth and early twentieth centuries, they actually halted an indigenous, incipient movement toward constitutional government and rule of law. After World War II, the United States nurtured close relations with antidemocratic royal families in Iran and the Arabian Peninsula as a means of securing access to oil. In the context of the Cold War, the United States supported anticommunist leaders, going so far as to orchestrate a *coup d'etat* in Iran in 1953. Fear of Soviet expansionism led the United States to reward friendly authoritarian regimes and turn a blind eye to their human rights violations. Since the 1990s, the United States has largely tolerated regional allies' repression of Islamist parties.

Dependence on oil is another seemingly important reason for resistance to political change. Scholars use the term **rentier state** to describe a country whose economy is heavily dependent on oil and gas income and whose government derives a large percentage of its revenues from the taxation of oil exports.[31] Iran, Iraq, Libya, Algeria, and the GCC countries meet the definition of a rentier state. Because rentier states do not need to tax their citizens heavily, there are fewer demands for representation. Oil concentrates resources in the hands of a small elite, who buy political loyalty and foster political dependency. Support for this explanation also comes from the fact that the countries in the region that have no significant oil—Israel, Turkey, Morocco, Jordan, and Lebanon—are democracies or have undertaken the most political liberalization.

Weak civil society may also explain why so many MENA countries rank low on Freedom House's annual ranking of political freedoms and civil liberties in the world. Civil society is made up of autonomous social groups such as private businesses, the press, labor, and voluntary associations that historically have been forces for liberalization. These groups face significant legal restrictions in the MENA and often do not have the finances to sustain a long confrontation with the government. It could also be argued that powerful barriers to the entry of women into the workforce and lack of leadership roles for women in religious institutions have prevented a strong, representative civil society from emerging.

Religious and cultural explanations of democratic weakness in the MENA are quite prevalent, but should be viewed with much caution. Political culture in predominantly Muslim countries, to the extent that it reaffirms patriarchy, delegitimizes minority rights, and devalues secular thought, may create an inhospitable environment for freedom. Governments in the region often claim that Islamists are undemocratic forces that believe in "one man, one vote, one time." In other words, the Islamists support the idea of free elections if it will help them, but once in power they will presumably impose harsh Islamic law. Thus, authoritarian regimes argue that these allegedly undemocratic movements cannot be allowed to come to power through democratic means.

Many casual observers of the Middle East tend to believe that Islamic political parties are prone to violence and anti-Westernism. Hamas and Hizballah, some terrorist groups linked to al-Qaeda, and some militias in Iraq have engaged in numerous acts of violence that undermine the rule of law. These groups espouse a set of beliefs widely perceived as antithetical to democracy. Nevertheless, most of the large, "mainstream" Islamist movements, such as Egypt's Muslim Brotherhood and Jordan's Islamic Action Front, behave like opposition political parties everywhere in the world, seeking to build large coalitions to come to power through elections and improve their societies. Although their leaders draw upon the language of Islam, they are modern political entrepreneurs. Many of the parties are very conservative on gender issues and frustrated with U.S. and European policies, but they frequently espouse a commitment to free elections, rule of law, and social equity. Their leaders usually have the technical and organizational skills required to govern modern states. Their private welfare programs fill a large gap left by the state's breaking of its social contract since the 1980s.

Many charismatic Islamist leaders have been threatened, imprisoned, and sometimes tortured by allies of the United States. They are deeply frustrated by Israel's and the West's humiliation of their countries and the inequalities in their societies. They do not preside over monolithic movements; rather, they are all wracked by internal disagreements. Some are eager to reduce government economic regulation and wipe out corruption, which makes them much more neoliberal than revolutionary! For example, Turkey's democratically elected, Islamist-leaning governing party has worked to prepare the country for eventual membership in the European Union by passing legislation to strengthen minority rights, religious freedom, and economic reform.

Optimists dispute the assertion that nondemocratic values are pervasive in the region. Public opinion polls, including the Pew Global Attitudes surveys, indicate that people in the MENA support the idea of democracy in large numbers. Fundamental democratic values (with the exception of equal rights for women) are supported by large majorities in the Middle East, even if there are disagreements about the most appropriate democratic institutions. Economic development and social mobility may increase democratic pressures. Globalization and technological change are undermining information monopolies that governments held until quite recently.

The countries that have made the most democratic progress have for the most part not done so because of Western political or military pressure. Foreign "carrots" have induced more lasting political change than the blunt foreign "sticks" of aid cutoffs or military threats. In Turkey, for example, the European Union's offer of potential EU membership has created powerful incentives for Turkey's military and Islamist parties to adopt more democratic institutions. Royal families in Kuwait, Jordan, Bahrain, and Morocco seem to have calculated that moves toward constitutional monarchy and competitive elections will increase political stability.

## CONCLUSION

There are many contradictory trends in the MENA's political economy. Each country has its own unique set of state–society–market tensions. Some countries—like Israel and Turkey—are faring much better than the others, open to modern ideas and global interchanges. Some like Iraq are locked in the jaws of war or like Iran unable to free themselves from the specter of the past. All face some structural pressures from the international community. Forces from within society are clamoring for a role in reshaping governance, even if they disagree strongly over what an ideal nation should look like.

Each of the main IPE perspectives interprets developments in the Middle East differently, based on different assumptions about history and what motivates actors. A mercantilist would probably attribute many of the conflicts and development outcomes discussed in this chapter to the struggle by states for power and protection of national interests. Economic liberal theorists stress the inevitability of MENA change as a result of global market forces. The dynamism of Dubai and Israel, as well as the democratic advances in MENA monarchies, could be proof that free people open to the world's ideas and goods are most likely to thrive. Structuralists could point to the MENA's weak industrialization and great disparities of wealth as evidence of the exploitation inherent in global capitalism.

All of the IPE perspectives give us insights on the Middle East, but none alone can tell us how soon and how far democracy, peace, and development will spread. Our analysis of the region, nevertheless, does allow us to have some optimism. History does not have to repeat itself; the new generation in many countries is forgetting old grievances. Fears of a civilizational clash are overblown: Many Islamists are reconciled to modernity, and the ties with the West are deep. The Middle East's future will mostly depend not on the actions of foreigners but on what Middle Easterners do to, and for, themselves.

## KEY TERMS

*Mashriq*  353
defensive modernization  356
capitulations  356
*ijtihad*  356
*mujahideen*  358
Pax Americana  360
Oil for Food Program  360

conspiracism  360
adventurism  361
*intifadas*  361
Westoxication  362
Euro-Mediterranean Partnership
 (EMP)  370
petrodollar recycling  371

sovereign wealth funds
 (SWFs)  371
remittances  371
Gulf Cooperation Council
 (GCC)  371
*bonyads*  374
rentier state  376

## DISCUSSION QUESTIONS

1. Compare and contrast the economic conditions and development strategies of several MENA countries. Which countries are most prepared to face the challenges of globalization? Explain.

2. Are most of the MENA's security problems due to foreign meddling or to the bad decisions of domestic political leaders? How much should we blame "history" for today's woes?

3. What are the main impediments to democracy in the region? Will economic growth and diversification likely lead to more representative government? What are the most appropriate ways in which the Western countries could encourage democracy?

4. What are the most important "human connections" between the Middle East and the rest of the world?

Are individuals and nongovernmental organizations able to influence changes in the region?

5. How do you think that past and present human tragedies will shape the perceptions of the next generation in the MENA?

## SUGGESTED READINGS

François Burgat. *Face to Face with Political Islam.* London: I. B. Taurus, 2003.

James Gelvin. *The Israel–Palestine Conflict: One Hundred Years of War.* 2nd ed. New York: Cambridge University Press, 2007.

Clement Henry and Robert Springborg. *Globalization and the Politics of Development in the Middle East.* Cambridge: Cambridge University Press, 2001.

Rashid Khalidi. *Resurrecting Empire: Western Footprints and America's Perilous Path in the Middle East.* Boston, MA: Beacon, 2004.

Alan Richards and John Waterbury. *A Political Economy of the Middle East.* 3rd ed. Boulder, CO: Westview, 2008.

## NOTES

1. U.S. Department of State, "Circular Airgram to American Diplomatic and Consular Offices," May 1, 1950, www.gwu.edu/~nsarchiv/NSAEBB/NSAEBB78/propaganda%20003.pdf.

2. The GNI figures are calculated on the basis of purchasing power parity (PPP).

3. See Freedom House, *Freedom in the World 2009* (Lanham, MD: Rowman & Littlefield, 2009).

4. Bernard Lewis, *What Went Wrong? The Clash between Islam and Modernity in the Middle East* (Oxford: Oxford University Press, 2002).

5. See Suha Taji-Farouki and Basheer M. Nafi, eds., *Islamic Thought in the Twentieth Century* (London: I. B. Taurus, 2004).

6. L. Carl Brown, *International Politics and the Middle East: Old Rules, Dangerous Game* (Princeton, NJ: Princeton University Press, 1984), pp. 16–18.

7. For a detailed examination of Libya under the Italians see Lisa Anderson, *The State and Social Transformation in Tunisia and Libya, 1830–1980* (Princeton, NJ: Princeton University Press, 1986).

8. James Gelvin, *The Israel–Palestine Conflict: One Hundred Years of War* (New York: Cambridge University Press, 2005).

9. Cited in Manfred Halpern, *The Politics of Social Change in the Middle East and North Africa* (Princeton, NJ: Princeton University Press, 1963), p. 85.

10. Fred Halliday, *The Middle East in International Relations: Power, Politics and Ideology* (New York: Cambridge University Press, 2005), p. 153.

11. See, for example, a joint report by 13 major international NGOs titled, "Iraq Sanctions: Humanitarian Implications and Options for the Future," August 2002, http://www.globalpolicy.org/component/content/article/170/41947.html.

12. Daniel Pipes, *The Hidden Hand: Middle East Fears of Conspiracy* (New York: St. Martin's, 1996), p. 27.

13. Quoted in Fauzi Najjar, "The Arabs, Islam and Globalization," *Middle East Policy, 12* (Fall 2005), p. 95.

14. *Confidence in Obama Lifts U.S. Image around the World* (Washington, DC: The Pew Research Center, July 2009), pp. 14, 16, http://pewglobal.org/reports/pdf/264.pdf.

15. A copy of the contentious report is available at http://www2.ohchr.org/english/bodies/hrcouncil/specialsession/9/FactFindingMission.htm.

16. Ahmed S. Hashim, *Insurgency and Counter-Insurgency in Iraq* (Ithaca, NY: Cornell University Press, 2006), pp. 72–73.

17. The Sahrawi leaders of the Western Sahara, however, have never justified attacks against civilians and have not attacked the Moroccan military since 1990.

18. Lisa Hajjar, *Courting Conflict: The Israeli Military Court System in the West Bank and Gaza* (Berkeley, CA: University of California Press, 2005).

19. Hashim, *Insurgency and Counter-Insurgency in Iraq*.

20. National Counterterrorism Center, *2008 Report on Terrorism*, April 2009, pp. 10, 24, available at http://wits.nctc.gov/ReportPDF.do?f=crt2008nctcannexfinal.pdf.

21. Charles Tilly, "Terror, Terrorism, Terrorists," *Sociological Theory*, 22 (March 2004), p. 11.

22. Sebastian Balfour, *Deadly Embrace: Morocco and the Road to the Spanish Civil War* (Oxford: Oxford University Press, 2002).

23. Although Kuwait's rulers fled their country in the wake of Iraq's invasion in 1990, the United States reinstated their government at the end of the Gulf War.

24. Philippe Fargues, ed., *Mediterranean Migration: 2008–2009 Report* (European University Institute, 2009), p. 2, http://cadmus.eui.eu/dspace/bitstream/1814/11861/1/CARIM_Report_2008_09.pdf.

25. Jonathon Nitzan and Shimshon Bichler, *The Global Political Economy of Israel* (London: Pluto, 2002).

26. Andrzej Kapiszewski, "Arab Versus Asian Migrant Workers in the GCC Countries," United Nations Expert Group Meeting on International Migration and Development in the Arab Region, 2006, www.un.org/esa/population/publications/EGM_Ittmig_Arab/P02_Kapiszewski.pdf. See also Andrzej Kapiszewski, *Nationals and Expatriates: Population and Labour Dilemmas of the Gulf Cooperation Council States* (Reading, UK: Ithaca, 2001).

27. Charles Kernaghan, *U.S. Jordan Free Trade Agreement Descends into Human Trafficking and Involuntary Servitude* (New York: National Labor Committee, 2006), www.nlcnet.org/live/admin/media/document/jordan.pdf.

28. *The Arab Human Development Report 2002: Creating Opportunities for Future Generations* (New York: United Nations Development Programme, Regional Bureau for Arab States, 2002).

29. Dalia S. Hakura, "Growth in the Middle East and North Africa," *IMF Working Papers 04/56* (2004), p. 3, available at www.imf.org/external/pubs/ft/wp/2004/wp0456.pdf.

30. Sara Roy, *The Gaza Strip: The Political Economy of De-development,* 2nd ed. (Washington, DC: Institute for Palestine Studies, 2001).

31. For an overview of the "rentier state" concept, see Michael Ross, "Does Oil Hinder Democracy?" *World Politics*, 53 (April 2001), pp. 325–361.

# Transnational Problems and Dilemmas

It is increasingly clear that many problems in international political economy (IPE) are more than international: They are global in nature. That is, these problems are not just conflicts or tensions between and among nation-states. They transcend the boundaries of nation-states and have become truly global in their effects. The final part of this book looks at six aspects of these global problems. All show us the complex interactions between individuals, markets, governments, and international institutions. The global financial crisis has already begun to exacerbate some of these problems. Whether global actors will increase cooperation to tackle them or resort to ever more conflictual policies in the face of them remains to be seen.

Chapter 15 surveys illicit transactions in the global economy, emphasizing that illegal flows of goods, services, and people across borders pose important challenges to governments. IPE is about states and markets, but it is fundamentally about people, as Chapter 16 makes clear. This chapter analyzes migration, tourism, and human networks from an IPE perspective.

Chapter 17 tackles a particularly controversial aspect of North–South IPE: transnational corporations (TNCs). TNCs are seen by some as engines of growth for LDCs, and by others as tools of exploitation. Chapter 17 looks at how TNCs have in the past helped define the North–South debate and then goes beyond this framework to consider the key issues surrounding TNCs today.

Chapter 18 examines the IPE of food and hunger, with special emphasis on the roles of states and markets in contributing to food and hunger problems. Chapter 19 brings a new focus on oil and energy trends, which have become more contentious with the rise of oil prices in the last decade and the serious efforts to switch to green energy. Finally, Chapter 20 presents an analysis of the IPE of the global environment, perhaps today's most serious global issue. Global warming and the Copenhagen climate change conference of 2009 are highlighted as part of a strategic moment for environmental policies that must also grapple with deforestation and ocean nuclear waste dumping. As will become evident, the problems of food, energy, and the environment are increasingly entangled and inseparable, threatening humanity and creating new international obligations. A glossary of key IPE terms used in the text follows Chapter 20.

# The Illicit Global Economy: The Dark Side of Globalization

Violence at the heart of shadow economies.

Jacob Silberberg

*Behaving as if only the licit side of IPE exists because it is the easiest to measure and quantify is the equivalent of the drunkard saying that the reason he is stumbling around looking for his keys under the streetlight is because it is the only place where he can see. What we need are better flashlights so that we can also look for our keys down the dark alleys of the global economy.*[1]

Peter Andreas

*Dirty money kills people. How many? Since the 1950s and 1960s . . . how many people have died as a result of our failure to deal with dirty money flowing out of developing and transitional economies and into western coffers? Or, to put the question differently, how many lives could have been saved if we had put the issue on the table 40, 30, 20, or even 10 years ago?*[2]

Raymond Baker

In early 2006, U.S. immigration agents discovered a half-mile-long underground tunnel linking warehouses in Tijuana, Mexico, and Otay Mesa, California. Equipped with electricity, ventilation, a concrete floor, and water pumps, the tunnel—dubbed *El Grande*—probably took two years to build.[3] Agents suspected that it was used for drug smuggling: They found two tons of marijuana inside. They also worried that illegal aliens, terrorists, and weapons of mass destruction could have transited into the United States through this 80-foot-deep corridor. Since September 11, 2001, agents have discovered dozens of tunnels along the U.S.–Mexican border.

*El Grande* is just one link in the illicit global economy, a network of international trade relationships that brings goods, services, and people across borders every day in defiance of the laws of at least one state. Law enforcement officials occasionally give the public a glimpse of the world of illicit actors and the threats they pose. Nevertheless, illicit international exchanges usually occur in a shadowy world that most consumers never see directly.

This chapter analyzes a broad range of illicit actors and activities that pose significant challenges to governments and legitimate businesses throughout the world. The illicit global economy consists of markets that states cannot easily regulate or tax. A variety of adjectives are commonly used to describe these global markets: *illicit, illegal, informal, black, gray, shadow, extrastate, underground,* and *offshore.* The processes going on in these markets generally fall into categories such as smuggling, trafficking, money laundering, tax evasion, and counterfeiting. The actors conducting these transactions make profits by breaking laws, defying authority, ignoring borders, and often using violence to exploit other people. In previous chapters, we suggested that illegal behavior by financial elites (i.e., men and women behaving badly) was one of the causes of the global financial crisis. Ironically, the global recession is also likely to increase illicit transactions as more desperate and vulnerable people seeking money and jobs fall prey to traffickers and as struggling businesses try to cut costs by skirting the law.

Until recently, IPE scholars left the study of the illicit global economy to other social scientists. Criminologists have for years studied transnational organized crime groups. Sociologists have looked at the social effects of criminal activities such as drug trafficking and prostitution. International relations experts have been examining closely the connection between money laundering and terrorism since 9/11. Comparative politics specialists have studied the effects of corruption and clientelism on political development. Anthropologists have conducted research on informal markets in developing countries. And law professors have produced a burgeoning literature on efforts to protect intellectual rights from patent thieves and copyright infringers.

IPE scholars have increasingly recognized the theoretical and practical implications of the illicit realm. They have begun to synthesize the work of the other disciplines and branch out beyond the study of what is legal and easily measurable in the global economy. They realize that a close look at the illicit global economy helps us garner new insights about the relationships among states, markets, and societies.

Political scientist Peter Andreas notes that existing IPE perspectives help us understand some—but not all—of what we witness in the shadows.[4] Realists help us understand why security-obsessed states invest so much money and resources in international law enforcement. Liberal theorists help us understand under what conditions multilateral cooperation against crime will occur. Constructivists highlight the role that transnational nongovernmental groups play in changing the public's perception of illicit transactions. And structuralists point out that countries that rely on exports of illegal drugs and blood diamonds are stuck in a dependent, exploitative relationship with the "core" countries.

However, the illegal economy also provides a challenge to the three main IPE perspectives. Although mercantilists stress the primacy of the nation-state, the illicit global economy is full of nonstate actors that sometimes thwart the best intentions and institutions of even powerful countries. Whereas liberals focus on the market's invisible hand and individual freedom, the illicit global economy is full of powerful, manipulative criminal hands. The open commercial interchange and deregulation that liberalism promotes are supposed to lead to peace and prosperity, but in the illicit realm unfettered trade can spread horrible conflict, pervasive coercion, and social decay. Structuralists tend to portray capitalist, developed countries as exploiters of the developing countries, but in the illicit global economy, developing countries can sometimes take revenge on the rich North, as when China steals intellectual property or when **secrecy jurisdictions** (places with strong bank privacy laws) in the Caribbean attract billions of dollars from wealthy tax evaders.

In this chapter we make several arguments. Far from reducing black market activity, globalization gives criminals new ways to profit from their cross-border business. Well-intentioned attempts by governments to stop the supply of illicit products sometimes cause more harm than good. International cooperation against transnational crime is hard to sustain and often ineffective. Consumers bear as much responsibility as international suppliers for nurturing illegal commerce. The threats to national security, social well-being, and legal commerce seem to keep growing.

## THE ILLICIT ECONOMY IN HISTORICAL PERSPECTIVE

Illicit transactions did not suddenly appear a decade or so ago; there have been many illicit activities in history that have fundamentally shaped relations among states. Centuries ago European rulers and Barbary Coast potentates authorized pirates to seize other countries' ships and split the booty with them. European countries colonized many parts of the world, seizing the territory and the property of their inhabitants. Although at the time the colonial powers tried to justify colonialism as a kind of civilizing mission, their activities amounted to little more than theft.

Historians Kenneth Pomeranz and Steven Topik argue that violence used to be an important way to gain "comparative advantage" and important commercial benefits in the world. Great Britain, the United States, Spain, and other European countries moved up the rungs of the ladder of development by engaging in land grabbing, slavery, looting, and dope peddling in what we now call the less developed countries (LDCs). As both authors argue, "The bloody hands and the invisible hand often worked in concert: in fact, they were often attached to the same body."[5] They recount how Britain once forced China to buy opium; Belgium brutalized millions of Congo inhabitants and slaughtered elephants for ivory; Spain and Portugal literally plundered the Aztec and Inca civilizations; and U.S. entrepreneurs trafficked in slaves for decades.

Marxists, too, have long recognized that the development of capitalism is rooted in processes of **primitive accumulation,** whereby classes coercively or violently seize assets (such as land) from other actors. Sociologist Charles Tilly famously asserted that state-making is quite similar to organized crime.[6] Just like crime bosses, would-be leaders centuries ago used violence against their rivals and extracted "protection money" that they used to expand their territory and make war. Eventually these state-makers gained legitimacy as kings and turned extortion into legal taxation, masking their sometimes violent and thuggish beginnings.

History shows us that leaders of states have often participated in or sanctioned violent illicit activities. At the same time, these leaders have the power to define *what* is legal or illegal and *who* is a legitimate entrepreneur or an illegitimate one. We see that illicit activities can be very beneficial to some states while being simultaneously disastrous for others. Capitalism in its early stages was more like the Wild West than a contemporary, well-planned industrial park.

Illicit transactions today often mirror, replicate, or repeat these historical processes, even though we often tend to give new names to modern processes. For example, human trafficking is a modern-day form of slavery practiced around the world. Today's drug lords expropriate from peasants and addicts alike, expanding their turf and productive apparatus as would-be kings once did. Corrupt leaders in places such as Nigeria and Iraq have stolen massive amounts of public resources, just as European powers stole from the colonies that they were supposed to be helping. Some leaders in recent decades, such as Slobodan Milosevic in Serbia and Charles Taylor in Liberia, ran their states like criminal enterprises, working in cahoots with *mafiosos* to keep their kleptocracies running before they were ultimately ousted by foreign countries. Israel's seizure for decades of Palestinian real estate and farmland is little different from state-sanctioned theft by pirates and imperialists hundreds of years ago. States and entrepreneurs today still sometimes use violence and coercion to harm their competitors. Although we like to think that the excesses of the past are limited today by international law, good government, and even globalization itself, the reality is that illicit history repeats itself (albeit with new names, new faces, and new *modus operandi*).

## THE STAKES AND THE ACTORS

How big and how important is the illicit global economy? There are many disagreements about the answers to these questions, partly because extralegal transactions are so difficult to measure. Governments and multilateral institutions often engage in hyperbole, sometimes either to tout their supposed achievements against the "bad guys" or to heighten threats for political reasons. Canadian economist R. T. Naylor warns us against having too much faith in estimates of the illicit economy's size, which often are based on bad information and false assumptions. For example, he notes that a widely cited estimate of annual global sales of illegal drugs at $500 billion was concocted by a UN official giving a speech in 1989 to grab public attention.[7]

In 1996 the International Monetary Fund (IMF) estimated that criminal money laundering was worth from 2 to 5 percent of global gross domestic product (GDP). This suggests that the annual proceeds of illicit transactions may be between $600 billion and $1.5 trillion. Even this estimate is probably inflated, because it includes the amount of taxes that multinational corporations and investors evaded by shifting their money around different jurisdictions. Raymond Baker, a fellow at the Center for International Policy in Washington, DC, gives us a more reasonable calculation of "dirty money" that results from public corruption and criminal activities (other than tax evasion).[8] He estimates that annual cross-border sales of illegal drugs and counterfeit goods may amount to a minimum of $120 billion. Revenues from human trafficking could amount to $10 billion annually. International smuggling of arms, cigarettes, cars, oil, timber, and art may be worth at least $35 billion annually.

"Guesstimates" though these figures may be, they indicate that the scale of the illicit problem has important implications for development, democracy, and security. The stakes are high. Baker believes that growing illegality is a major contributor to inequality and poverty in the world: "With common techniques and use of the same structures, drug dealers, other criminals, terrorists, corrupt government officials, and corporate CEOs and managers are united in abuse of capitalism, to the detriment of the rich in western societies and billions of poor around the world."[9] Likewise, Moisés Naím, the editor of *Foreign Policy* magazine, does not believe that democracy can emerge in countries dominated by powerful criminal networks.[10] The illegal economy can also undermine fragile new democracies by putting money into the hands of rivals of the central government, corrupting institutions such as the judiciary, and decreasing government efficacy. In all democracies, it lowers social trust and the belief that one shares the same values as one's fellow citizens.

Who are the central actors in the high-stakes illegal networks? We all have a tendency to believe that the main actors are *mafia* dons, drug lords, and other organized crime figures. The ruthless criminals of Hollywood movies do exist, but full-time gangsters are only one part of a much wider puzzle. Many participants have one foot in the legal world and one in the illegal world, making it difficult to create a profile of the typical illicit actor. Participants include soldiers who loot, government officials who extort, CEOs who engage in transfer pricing, bankers who loan to Third World dictators, and consumers who buy fake Louis Vuitton handbags on eBay. Even humanitarian workers in war-torn African countries have been known to participate in diamond trafficking.

Just as law-abiding citizens sometimes dabble in the black market, well-trained, "normal" economic actors such as accountants and computer programmers sometimes lend their skills to unethical or criminal operators. For example, anthropologist Carolyn Nordstrom has pointed out that "smugglers today are more likely to be armed with a degree from a leading ICT/computer technology course than an assault rifle."[11] The work skills that the world of international trade demands are also needed in the shadow economies.

There is often no clear wall between the licit and the illicit global economy.[12] Buyers may not know (or not care to know) where their suppliers get their products. A consumer may burn CDs of illegally downloaded music at night and pay for licensed software the next day. A multinational corporation paying almost no taxes in the high-tax country where it is headquartered could be scrupulously paying corporate taxes in low-tax countries where its affiliates operate. Products that start out in some kind of shady operation often enter the "regular" market at a later point. Items produced in the legal market (such as cigarettes) may end up being smuggled across borders. Machine guns sold legally to an army in one country may end up in the arms of insurgents in a neighboring country.

# STUDYING THE ILLICIT ECONOMY: KEY FINDINGS

Studying cross-border illegal activities helps provide deeper insights into problems we see in the global economy. Consider the following questions: Why is it so hard to prevent nuclear proliferation? Why don't economic sanctions work well in changing the behavior of rogue regimes? Why aren't governments winning the war against drugs? Why did millions die from war in resource-rich Congo after 1998? In this section we examine six important analytical findings about the illicit global economy that help us answer important questions like these. These findings demonstrate the role that consumers, law enforcement, and globalization play in the growth of black markets. They also explain how illicit transactions affect war, development, and cooperation among states.

## Six Degrees of Separation

"I am bound to everyone on this planet by a trail of six people" says one of the characters in John Guare's play, *Six Degrees of Separation*.[13] In illicit markets, producers and consumers are also related to one another through a small number of people living in many parts of the world. Between a procurer and consumer are other actors, including financiers, processors, shippers, importers, distributors, and retailers. If we look at international transactions involving the movement of goods and services, we see a global chain along whose links many points of illegality can occur.

If we look at the human connection in the chain, it becomes clear that none of us is completely divorced from the illegal world. Whether at the beginning, middle, or end of a chain of market interactions, we wittingly or unwittingly are involved in a process that may have been part of the extralegal world. Sometimes we can see our part in the chain, as when, for example, American parents hire illegal aliens from Mexico to care for their children but do not pay social security tax on behalf of their employees. At other times, our part in the chain is largely invisible, as when someone buys an engagement ring for his fiancée that contains a diamond dug from a mine run by a warlord in Sierra Leone. The greater our degree of separation from the illicit part of a global commodity chain, the less we feel responsible for it.

Carolyn Nordstrom points out that ordinary consumers around the world are deeply complicit in smuggling. She found that in the African war zones where she did research, everyday, mundane commodities such as rice, cigarettes, vegetables, and antibiotics constitute a big chunk of unofficial trade.[14] One can hardly survive in some of these areas without buying smuggled, untaxed items in the informal economy. In developed countries, consumers of software, downloaded music, drugs, vehicles, art, and jeans, to name just a few products, often know that the products they are buying are knockoffs, pirated copies, untaxed items, or stolen property.

Even government officials sometimes join the illegal market, much to their embarrassment when their hypocrisy is publicly revealed. In 1998, U.S. Trade Representative Charlene Barleshefsky accompanied President Bill Clinton on a trip to China, where she urged Chinese authorities to crack down on the country's counterfeit manufacturers. While she was there, she bought some 30 fake Beanie Babies in Silk Alley, a notorious counterfeit market, and brought them back to the United States, despite a U.S. law limiting each returning family to only one Beanie Baby import (and an agreement between Ty, Inc., and China that the toys would not be sold in China).

However, a countertrend is emerging. Multinational corporations and retailers are taking into consideration that increasing numbers of consumers want to widen the degree of separation between themselves and any potential unethical or illegal practices. The fair-trade coffee movement and the antisweatshop movement have conditioned consumers to think about the ultimate effects of their domestic purchases on overseas workers. Similarly, businesses are keen not to be tainted by ties to illegal activities overseas that transnational advocacy groups are publicizing. Lowe's was one of the first home improvement retail chains to introduce a wood procurement program to help ensure that the company bought timber only from sustainable forests and not from forests that were being harvested illegally in the Third World. In the face of criticism that diamonds from some African countries were fueling wars, the De Beers company participated in a global scheme to track the origins of diamond purchases so as to weed out those coming from conflict zones. (See the box "De Beers and 'Blood Diamonds'").

## ▶ DE BEERS AND "BLOOD DIAMONDS"

Thanks to years of advertising by De Beers Consolidated Mines, the world's largest diamond multinational company, most consumers are familiar with the phrases, "A diamond is forever" and "Diamonds are a girl's best friend." In the last decade, nongovernmental organizations (NGOs) that are critical of the connection between the diamond trade and African civil wars have spread two alternative slogans: "An amputation is forever" and "Diamonds are a guerrilla's best friend." They argue that the diamond industry has helped to finance rebel groups in places such as Sierra Leone, the Congo, and Angola, where millions of people have been killed, mutilated, raped, or displaced during civil war. The recent attention to "blood diamonds" (also called "conflict diamonds") has forced the diamond industry, as well as governments of diamond-producing and diamond-receiving nations and multilateral institutions, to better regulate the international trade.

It is estimated that 500 tons of diamonds have been mined in the last 100 years, with one-third of them mined in the 1990s alone.[a] The company responsible for a large portion of diamond mining and wholesaling is De Beers, cofounded in 1880 by Cecil Rhodes, who formed a syndicate with the 10 largest diamond merchants in South Africa.

De Beers established the London-based Diamond Trading Company (DTC), which sells diamond parcels at 10 annual "sights" to approximately 125 "sightholders" who then take the diamonds to other cities, where they are repackaged for further sale to companies that then cut, polish, and resell the diamonds to independent retailers. The diamond industry operates in relative secrecy. As of 2002, De Beers reportedly controlled two-thirds of the world's annual supply of rough diamonds.[b] With De Beers' level of control of the market, close to 60 percent of the world's diamonds will go through the DTC in a given year.[c] De Beers' share in the market has declined over the decades, but the rest of the industry still relies heavily on the marketing scheme that continues to convince international consumers that diamonds are as rare as the love that inspires them to buy one.

Diamonds are perhaps the most highly concentrated form of wealth in the world. Because of the difficulty of tracing the origin of any particular diamond and the ease with which diamonds can be moved, these gems have become a key form of currency among illegitimate actors in the international market. Until the 1980s De Beers was involved directly in Sierra Leone and maintained an office in Freetown. In the 1990s it purchased diamonds in neighboring Liberia, Guinea, and Cote D'Ivoire—countries that were transit points for diamonds smuggled from war-torn Sierra Leone. Rebels in Sierra Leone also smuggled gems through Lebanese, West African, and Eastern European intermediaries. Sometimes raw diamonds were smuggled directly to the main international market in Antwerp, Belgium.

How did diamonds contribute to Sierra Leone's bloodshed? In 1991 a group of Libyan-trained rebels in Sierra Leone formed the Revolutionary United Front (RUF) and began attacking government forces. They seized some government-run diamond mines and over the next decade ran an illicit economy, smuggling diamonds to neighboring nations and trading them for weapons and drugs. The RUF also cut off the limbs of thousands of civilians. In 1999 the international community could no longer ignore the tiny West African country that was becoming one of the most dangerous locations on the globe. The civil war unleashed by the RUF had caused the death of more than 50,000 and the displacement of more than 2 million people. In January of that year the RUF attacked Freetown, Sierra Leone's capital, and conducted Operation No Living Thing—murdering, raping, and mutilating hundreds of civilians.

The United Nations helped broker a weak peace accord between the RUF and the government of Sierra Leone. The UN Security Council adopted a diamond embargo that banned the direct or indirect import of rough diamonds not sanctioned by the government of Sierra Leone through a certificate-of-origin regime. From July to October 2000 the government of Sierra Leone and the Belgium Diamond High Council created a system under which each diamond required a certificate of origin printed on security paper, registration through an electronic database, and electronic confirmation upon arrival. The RUF was quick to find a way around the new requirements, using Liberia and Guinea as cover for the export of their diamonds into the legitimate market. This prompted the Security Council to impose sanctions against Liberia in May 2001, which included a harsh ban against the export of rough diamonds.

In the face of the blood diamond problem, civil society groups such as Britain's Global Witness and Canada's Partnership Africa Canada joined diamond companies such as De Beers, the World Diamond Council, and dozens of governments to establish the Kimberly Process Certification Scheme (KPCS) in January 2003. KPCS members voluntarily cooperate and collaborate to prevent illegal diamonds from entering international trade networks and to shun countries and companies that cannot ensure that their diamonds are conflict-free. The Kimberly

Process is a significant example of a global public–private partnership to combat an illicit activity. Although it is not a panacea, KPCS has helped to foster peace in Sierra Leone and Angola, boost government revenues from legitimate exports, and make consumers more knowledgeable about where their products come from.

**References**

[a]Ingrid J. Tamm, "Diamonds in Peace and War: Severing the Conflict-Diamond Connection," *World Peace Foundation Report* (Cambridge: World Peace Foundation, 2002), p. 5.
[b]Ibid.
[c]Ibid., p. 4.

A fascinating new global trend is the rise of **socially responsible investing**. This is an effort to allow ordinary citizens to put their money in investment funds that avoid companies or countries that are perceived as being socially or environmentally unethical. Financial markets are offering new instruments for ethical investors. Related to this are a host of divestment-type movements led by some local governments, pension funds, and boardrooms to avoid investing in regimes where the capital will benefit dictators or criminals. These types of divestment strategies often indirectly target companies and countries linked to illicit activities such as land expropriation, oil corruption, and terrorist financing. Sometimes they go beyond divestment and turn into bans on doing any business or trade with certain companies and countries. Divestment strategies are basically a form of boycott that challenges economic liberal principles governing trade and capital flows.

## The Unintended Consequences of Supply-Side Policies

Another pattern is a strong tendency of governments to adopt policies designed to cut off or interdict the sources of illicit products. These policies can be described as interdiction, repression, and eradication. Political leaders like to target suppliers in foreign countries rather than demanders in their own country, even though this focus has been shown in many cases to be more expensive and less effective. For example, the United States spends enormous funds trying to stop illegal aliens from crossing the border with Mexico but significantly less money or effort punishing U.S. businesses that hire undocumented workers. Similarly, money and labor-hours expended trying to stop drug production and smuggling from Latin America far exceeds federal spending on the treatment of drug users. In the global sex industry, law enforcement has a long history of cracking down on prostitutes rather than on the "johns" who pay for their services.

The reasons states mostly go after the supply side of the problem have a lot to do with the powerful political, economic, and cultural interests in a society. Governments often feel obliged to balance entrenched special interests with the public interest. There is often a sacrifice of efficiency and social goals when powerful actors force governments to attack illicit problems in "someone else's backyard." When law enforcement tries to stop or interfere with the supply side of robust global markets, it often does not achieve the intended results. In fact, there are often perverse consequences. An illicit activity can simply be displaced from one place to another, as when a ratcheting up of policing on one part of a border causes smugglers to move to a less secure part of the border. A supply-side crackdown might drive an illegal activity further underground, making it even harder to control. And a campaign against suppliers can often increase violence and "turf wars" in a society.

Phil Williams points out that efforts to restrict activities create a **restriction-opportunity dilemma:** The more that countries try to impose arms embargoes or ban substances such as drugs or Freon, the more they "provide inroads for the creation of new criminal markets or the enlargement of existing markets."[15] Eva Bertram and her colleagues illustrate a similar unintended outcome they call the **profit paradox.**[16] When states use law enforcement to try to prohibit drugs, the reduction of supply tends to drive up prices. This bolsters the profits of those entrepreneurs willing to take the risk to keep on supplying the black market. And the higher price encourages other would-be criminals to get into the business. One result is that, after a temporary lull, supply climbs up again as criminals find more ingenious ways of getting around prohibitions—and the price goes back down. Another possible result is that the most ruthless and violent criminals gain even more dominance of the illicit market. This dilemma is evident in many areas, leading some to argue in favor of decriminalization of certain types of illicit activity.

## Globalization: The Double-Edged Sword

Liberal theory touts the positive aspects of freer international markets. In a recent book, columnist Thomas Friedman portrays a heady new stage of globalization in which changes in technology empower individuals and companies that collaborate and compete peacefully across increasingly invisible borders.[17] Like other liberal theorists, Freidman views global integration as a mostly desirable trend.

However, from studying illicit markets we learn that globalization is a double-edged sword: Open markets may increase global efficiency, but they also empower the bad guys. Although we still do not know if the ratio of illegal to legal business in the world is increasing, we can be sure that in some countries the ratio has risen. Technological change, which has become something of an object of devotion in Western societies, can also be a false idol. For each potentially desirable trend in neoliberal globalization, there is a criminal downside. This does not mean that the bad outweighs the good, rather that any compelling analysis of global change must account for negative externalities.

Naím points to the dark side of the end of the Cold War: The breakdown of the Soviet Union and the proliferation of weak, postcommunist states created new homes for illegal operations.[18] The transition to market economies gave rise to powerful *mafias*, influence peddling, and old-fashioned gangsterism. And some of the weak states that emerged from the collapse of the Soviet Union became smugglers' lairs. A case in point is **Transdniestra,** a sliver of Moldova that claimed independence in 1992 (even though no country has recognized its claim). It became a hub of weapons trafficking, contraband, and stolen cars. And at the end of the Cold War, ex–Warsaw Pact countries off-loaded many small arms into Third World markets.

Naím also identifies globalization, including deregulation and privatization, as the culprit in the rise of the illicit.[19] Deregulation of airlines and shipping industries since the 1980s has fueled arms trafficking. The rapid-fire sale of state enterprises has contributed to widescale corruption. Regional integration based on free-trade agreements weakens border control. And the opening of capital markets has facilitated the flow of "hot" money around the world (see Chapter 7). New technologies of globalization are used by shadow actors just as they are used by governments to police the bad guys. For example, global positioning system (GPS) technology helps governments track criminal activities such as illegal timber harvesting and illegal waste disposal, but it also helps drug cartels manage international logistical operations. Businesses looking for technical solutions to smuggling, such as by embedding radio frequency emitters in products, often find themselves outsmarted by criminals.

## The Problem with Coordination Between States

One of the important questions that IPE examines is why states succeed or fail in cooperating with one another. As we learned in earlier chapters, realists view states as constantly competing with one another, whereas liberals stress the ability of governments to coordinate their interactions peacefully. Another of the major findings from the study of illicit markets is that state sovereignty makes coordinated policies by states against the shadows very difficult. Why is this so?

One major reason is that states are jealous of their sovereignty. They do not like interference in their domestic affairs, and they do not want to be responsible for enforcing the laws of other states. In fact, they will sometimes take advantage of illicit activities outside their borders. Although illicit markets can threaten sovereignty, sovereignty can also shield black markets. For example, some states—such as Liberia under former President Charles Taylor—have become havens for criminal operations. They charge criminals a fee for protection behind their sovereign cocoon. In this kind of failed state, leaders can issue diplomatic passports to dubious businessmen, offer **flags of convenience** (places to register ships and airlines that actually conduct all their international business somewhere else), and allow the establishment of servers to conduct Internet gambling or pornography distribution. In exchange for a payoff, they may look the other way as criminals use their territory to smuggle goods.

These activities are part of a wider phenomenon that Ronen Palan calls the **commercialization of sovereignty**—the renting out of commercial privileges and protections to citizens and companies from other countries.[20] A state can market itself as a place to disguise the origin of dirty money. For example, dozens of mostly small countries and territories are **tax havens** (also referred to as offshore financial centers or secrecy jurisdictions), where foreigners can park their money and conduct international financial transactions with very little regulation by local officials. These places—such as the Cayman Islands—attract money launderers and tax evaders who want to stay entirely out of the reach of their home governments. These sovereign jurisdictions benefit both indirectly and directly from global crime (as well as from legitimate international business).

Pressure on pariah states is one way of trying to shut down illicit networks, but it is not necessarily the most effective. The technique often backfires. Leaders of pariah states do not always want to get rid of illicit transactions (especially if these leaders themselves are participating in illegal activities). Even if these leaders really do want to reduce corruption or shadow activities, they might not have the capacity to do so; or if they try to, they may end up being overthrown. In this latter case, punishing a government for not cooperating may have the unintended effect of weakening institution-building in poorer countries. The World Bank under Paul Wolfowitz seemed to be headed toward a punitive model of anticorruption: cutting off aid to countries that failed to stop criminal activities that siphoned off (sometimes indirectly) foreign loans and development aid. This may have deprived weak but well-intentioned leaders of the very resources and assistance they needed to fight the "bad guys" in their economy.

This raises the bigger question of under what conditions one country has the "right" to use force against another country in which illicit activities are occurring. If a government allows terrorists to launder money through its nation's banking system, does an offended country have the natural right to use force against that government? Can one country use force to prevent massive counterfeiting of its currency in another country? North Korea, for example, is a sophisticated counterfeiter of U.S. currency. If intellectual property is property and if another country allows massive piracy and counterfeiting of that property to occur, is it stealing property? Is this tantamount to grabbing another country's territory?

There are many other reasons why states do not cooperate against crime. For one thing, illicit cross-border activities often occur precisely because laws differ from one state to another. Combating this would require states to better harmonize their legal systems, which is politically unpopular. Second is a problem of defection: How to guarantee that a state will actually carry out its commitments to another? Third is a question of privacy. Effective international cooperation requires sharing information about one's citizens and companies, something states have always been reluctant to do. This is a classic mercantilist impulse. States are worried about how rival states will use this information, however well intentioned the initial cooperation.

Fourth, rival states sometimes encourage black market activities to undermine their enemies. For example, the Reagan administration sought to undermine the Soviets and leftist regimes by pouring weapons into places such as Afghanistan, Angola, and Latin America, fueling arms bazaars that remained long after covert programs ended. And R. T. Naylor reminds us that, as part of their mercantilist economic warfare hundreds of years ago, European powers tried to undermine rival states by encouraging counterfeiting, pirating, embargo busting, and the development of smuggling centers.[21]

Fifth, it is hard to obtain serious cooperation with police forces and governments that are sometimes themselves complicit in illicit activities. In many weak states, officials may protect crime syndicates, be on the payroll of syndicates, or simply look the other way in exchange for payoffs. And sometimes they are simply too afraid to take on powerful criminal organizations and drug cartels. Former Colombian drug kingpin Pablo Escobar, for example, conducted a violent campaign against the government when it came after his cocaine empire in the 1980s and early 1990s, ordering dozens of assassinations of judges, police, and reporters and bombings of public facilities.

In the absence of effective state cooperation, private companies and international civil society are stepping up to the plate to change norms and practices related to illicit activities. These voluntary efforts are not always successful, but they do put pressure on governments to do more, and they are influencing public opinion. The private sector—worried about bad press and potential legal liability—has taken the lead in establishing codes of conduct and standards of behavior for big players. For example, some of the world's largest private banks have voluntarily adopted regulations to minimize money laundering and other financial crimes. This is part of a broader, post-9/11 shift by multinational corporations to **know-thy-customer** principles, whereby multinational corporations more carefully screen their depositors, suppliers, and contractors.

**Name-and-shame campaigns** bring international attention to illegal and unethical practices. Transparency International is a prominent example of a group whose annual index of corruption—derived from surveys of businesspersons who conduct business in other countries—can pressure governments into trying to get out of the bottom of the list. Multilateral institutions can also blacklist countries that fail to adopt international financial standards. Whitelisting is another inexpensive way for civic groups and governments simply to publicize companies with clean records in hopes that the market will shift toward their products and practices.

## War and Natural Resources

It has become increasingly clear since the 1980s that black market influences on natural resources have important effects on the global security structure. Weak governments and rebel groups in developing countries need money to buy weapons, pay off supporters, and finance activities within their borders. Controlling the extraction and export of natural resources is an important way to guarantee a revenue flow. Insurgents also know that if they deprive the government of control over natural resources, they can achieve important political goals. International commodities dealers generally do not have any compunction about buying from criminal insurgents or corrupt governments.

In Sierra Leone, several factions in the civil war that devastated the country in the 1990s financed their fighting in part by illegally controlling diamond mining. (See the box "De Beers and 'Blood Diamonds'" earlier in the chapter.) Cambodia's Khmer Rouge relied on illegal timber and gem exports from the territory they controlled to fight the government in Phnom Penh in the 1980s and 1990s. Colombia's FARC rebels tax the drug trade to finance their rebellion. Rachel Stohl points out that the same networks that smuggle timber, gems, and drugs out of troubled countries also bring illicit small arms back in.[22]

In a particularly tragic case beginning in 1998, the Democratic Republic of the Congo was torn apart by militias and neighboring armies that jockeyed for control of rich mineral deposits. Armed groups with no legitimate claims to sovereignty engaged in the illegal extraction and export of minerals such as coltan, which is refined into tantalum, a high-value, strategic metal used in cell phones, computer chips, and aircraft engines. Vodafone and Motorola, manufacturers of cell phones, have pressured their suppliers to avoid purchasing coltan/tantalum from the Congo, afraid that they will be accused of being responsible for some of the slaughter.

## Corruption Is Hampering Development

Political economists have spent decades trying to explain why some countries develop and others fall behind. They have correlated many factors with develop- · ment, including the degree of trade openness, levels of political stability, and even the "squiggliness" of borders. As pointed out in Chapter 11, corruption is another key factor that is hampering poor countries. For example, former leaders of Indonesia, the Philippines, and Nigeria skimmed billions of dollars from government coffers, leaving their countries indebted and unable to attract foreign investment. Corruption in China has become an increasingly important political problem, leading to social unrest and inequality. The World Bank has launched an international campaign to promote good governance and reduce corruption.

Analysts of the illicit global economy agree that corruption is a big problem, but they argue that the cause of corruption is not simply bad leaders in developing countries. In other words, they find that corruption is a transnational process in which many legal and illegal actors are complicit. Therefore, the fight against it must focus on global actors. Economist William Easterly argues in his book, *The White Man's Burden*, that foreign aid is frequently eaten up by corrupt governments, and he calls on "utopian social planners" in wealthy countries to adopt much more humble programs to help developing countries.[23] Raymond Baker and R. T. Naylor criticize Western governments, bankers, and businesses for encouraging corruption.

# CASE STUDIES IN THE ILLICIT GLOBAL ECONOMY

Thus far we have looked at six significant analytical findings in studies of the illicit international economy. We have also estimated the stakes involved and identified some of the key players. Now we turn to some case studies—smuggling, drug trafficking, and human trafficking—to illustrate some of the general themes and to specify how and why illicit activities occur and with what consequences for societies.

## Smuggling

Smuggling is one of the oldest professions in the world. Enterprising individuals seek to profit from transporting goods across borders in defiance of the rules that political leaders have imposed on exchanges. The objects of smuggling are as numerous as the techniques to avoid getting caught. Some of the most important smuggled items are oil, tobacco, counterfeits, antiquities, animal parts, and military technology.

Cross-border transactions are illegal only if states say they are illegal. In other words, it is states that define what is smuggling and what is not, and these definitions often change over time. A product may be legal in the source country and illegal in the receiving country. Or it might be illegal in the source country and legal in the receiving country. Or it might be illegal in both countries. Which of the three cases holds will affect the scale of smuggling and the likelihood that states will cooperate to fight it.

What are the motives of those who engage in smuggling? Greed is an obvious reason. Smugglers are willing to take risks because they want to make higher profits than they could achieve through legal trade. However, keep in mind that mercantilist states also engage in smuggling for purposes of security. For example, an aspiring nuclear power such as Iran may look to the international black market to obtain uranium and nuclear technology that existing nuclear powers try to deny it. When the United States tries to restrict the sale of high technology to China, Chinese officials have an incentive to steal the technology and transfer it. Governments also feel that they have a right to defy sanctions and embargoes imposed on them by hostile powers. Despite facing strict UN sanctions, Saddam Hussein smuggled oil out of Iraq and garnered billions of dollars to keep his regime afloat in the 1990s.

How do smugglers justify their actions? Many have self-serving rationales that mask greedy impulses. Nevertheless, there are other justifications. Often smugglers simply do not recognize the legitimacy of the political authority that is regulating trade or the legitimacy of a law that makes a particular type of trade illegal. For example, importers fed up with paying bribes to customs officials may see smuggling as legitimate avoidance of a predatory government. Similarly, some smugglers feel that import taxes are too high. Some smugglers simply do not recognize borders drawn by colonial powers. Others believe that they are supplying poor people with a product at a lower price, thus offering a sort of social service. In failed states or war zones, smuggling is sometimes the only way people can get access to food, medicines, and other necessities.

Smugglers take advantage of differing laws and regulations in neighboring countries to engage in **arbitrage**—buying a product in a lower-price market and selling it in a higher-price market. This opportunity for smuggling arises from price differentials that sometimes result from cross-border variations in taxes, regulations, and availability. When governments restrict the supply of goods and services in the name of morality, public health, environmental protection, and workplace standards, they unintentionally encourage smuggling. For example, the U.S. government bans the individual reimportation of prescription drugs from Canada and Mexico, partly out of a concern for the safety of U.S. consumers and partly to protect the profits of U.S. drug companies. However, the lower prices of prescription drugs in Canada and Mexico have enticed many elderly Americans to look north and south for technically illegal sources. In a classic case, U.S. Prohibition in the 1920s spurred smuggling of alcohol from Canada. Borders in North America have always been quite porous.

Tobacco is one of the most important smuggled products in the world. The World Health Organization (WHO) estimates that about 25 percent of all exported cigarettes will enter smuggling networks, depriving governments of some $25 billion in taxes they are owed.[24] Once cigarettes are "in transit" in the global trade system, smuggling allows distributors to avoid all taxes, thus enhancing profitability. Cigarettes are often exported legally to duty-free zones outside the United States and then diverted to other countries.

The WHO has found that major U.S. and European tobacco companies are actually complicit in the smuggling, because it is a way of opening up new markets.[25] In developing countries such as Iran, cigarette manufacturing, importing, and distribution are often a state monopoly. Thus, competition from contraband cigarettes cuts into an important source of government revenue. (Developed countries often forget how much their treasuries relied on "sin" taxes on alcohol and tobacco before World War I. Today many U.S. states, for instance, continue to raise their taxes on cigarettes.)

In her study of cigarette smuggling between the United States and Canada, Margaret Beare found that traffickers included Indian tribes, diplomats, soldiers, and tourists, who took advantage of special privileges they had under the law to move tobacco products across the border.[26] Canadian consumers have been very willing participants, partly because they view high taxes on cigarettes as unfair. Since 2003, the Canadian government and the European Union have sued major U.S. and Japanese cigarette manufacturers to force them to take steps to prevent smuggling of their products. This is a move to force manufacturers to take more responsibility for knowing what wholesalers do with tobacco products and what the chain of trade is from factory to the consumer. The WHO has even proposed that every pack of cigarettes have an electronic mark on its packaging.

Another major impetus to smuggling is **differential taxation**—when taxes on the same product differ significantly from country to country. Even tax differences between states within the United States are an important cause of domestic black market operations. After 9/11, officials broke up several rings of people who were buying low-taxed cigarettes in North Carolina and Virginia, transporting the cigarettes to high-tax states such as Michigan and New York, where they were sold at a markup in the black market. U.S. federal law enforcement officials estimate that some traffickers made millions of dollars and transferred proceeds to Hizballah.[27] By 2004, U.S. authorities were investigating more than 300 cases of cigarette bootlegging.

Antiquities are also big business for smugglers. Countries as widespread as Greece, Italy, Bolivia, and Thailand have laws that severely restrict the export or sale of antiquities, which are considered part of the national patrimony. Nevertheless, the huge demand for art and antiquities in wealthy countries supports a thriving transnational trade in stolen cultural property. Simon Mackenzie points out that art dealers and collectors have a strong sense of entitlement to enjoy and preserve cultural items, and they take insufficient steps to verify the legal provenance of objects they purchase.[28]

Illegal timber trade is causing massive deforestation in places such as Indonesia, Malaysia, Burma, and South America. Timber harvested illegally on state-owned land or in defiance of national regulations finds a hungry market in Japan, China, and the United States. There is also a thriving international trade in toxic wastes. In this case, however, the smuggling route starts in developed countries and ends in poor developing countries.

Smuggling of animals and animal parts is having a devastating effect on many species around the world. One of the difficulties in stopping wildlife trade is that the more endangered the animal, the higher the price for it and the greater the incentive to poach it, which accelerates its move toward extinction. The illegal ivory trade is responsible for drastic reductions of the stock of elephants and rhinoceroses in Africa and Asia. After a multinational treaty to ban the trade of ivory came into effect in 1989, the unintended effect was an assault on hippopotamuses and walruses, whose tusks became a substitute for ivory.[29] R. T. Naylor argues that all those who consume animal products are part of the chain of responsibility for poaching and illegal trade. Blame must be pointed in the direction of the fashion and cosmetics industry, tourists who buy trinkets made from animal parts, pet owners, and zoos.[30] There are only a few degrees of separation between us and those who are destroying some animal species.

## Drug Trafficking

Drug trafficking is one of the most entrenched and lucrative illicit activities in the world. Although many drug plants, such as coca, marijuana, and poppies, are grown in developing countries and the refined drug products are mostly consumed in rich Northern countries, marijuana is one of Canada's largest cash crops, and in some states in the United States it is also a key cash crop. The United Nations Office of Drugs and Crime estimates that at least 5 percent of the world's adult population used illegal drugs at least once in 2007 (compared to 30 percent using tobacco, which helps explain why cigarette smuggling supplies a much larger market).[31] Most of the profits from the drug trade are at the retail end (in the West), where the markup on the product is the greatest.

The global fight against drugs illustrates the enormous costs and limited success of supply-side policies. Between 2000 and 2006, the United States spent $4.7 on **Plan Colombia,** an elaborate program to drastically reduce coca production in Colombia. Despite massive aerial spraying and assistance to Colombia's military, the amount of coca cultivation dropped only about 25 percent by 2007, and there was no effect on supply or prices in the United States.

Bertram et al. have attributed these disappointing outcomes to the **hydra effect,** whereby an effort to stop drug production or trade in one area simply causes it to sprout up somewhere else.[32] Whatever success there has been in breaking up big cartels in Latin America has been offset by the spawning of a larger number of smaller trafficking groups. Colombian traffickers have resorted to using makeshift submarines to transport huge cargoes of cocaine to the United States. Mexico and Puerto Rico have become drug transit centers as a result of crackdowns in South America. Mexican cartels now supply an estimated 70 percent of drugs imported by the United States, and the violent turf wars between Mexican traffickers caused more than 13,000 deaths in Mexico between 2006 and 2009.[33] The fight against the drug trade is straining the Mexican police and spreading more crime into the United States.

Drug production and trafficking have had very negative effects on society, security, and government in developing countries (and in developed countries as well). Colombian economist Francisco Thoumi has documented the pervasive effects of drugs on the economies of the Andean countries (Colombia, Bolivia, and Peru).[34] Drug revenues have funded unsustainable real estate booms and other speculative investments. There has been a sharp decline in social trust, which makes it more costly for everyone to conduct normal business. Traffickers use drug export networks simultaneously to import contraband and weapons.

Thoumi argues that programs to encourage farmers to switch to alternative, legal crops have largely failed. Returns to farmers from illegal crops usually surpass potential revenues from food crops. The United States has seen a similar problem in Afghanistan, where poppy production since the 2002 invasion has skyrocketed. The illicit industry also has profound environmental consequences. Drug production has spurred the destruction of rain forests as growers move into new territory. And in Yemen, the poorest Arab country, widespread cultivation of *qat*—a tree whose leaves are chewed for their narcotic effect—has put a strain on water resources and reduced the amount of acreage devoted to food crops.

In many parts of the world, guerrilla groups and paramilitaries have turned to drugs as an important source of revenue. Rebels in Colombia, Cambodia, and Afghanistan have all used drug revenue to buy weapons and finance their insurgencies. In Latin America as a whole, gun crime and violence tied to the drug trade have ravished major cities. A significant proportion of those who end up in prison in developed countries have some connection to drug offenses.

Can drug trafficking be stopped? Probably not. David Mares points out that Northern countries have not had much success with unilateral threats to withhold aid from countries that fail to fight drugs seriously.[35] The United States sometimes threatens to "decertify" countries that do not adhere to U.S. priorities and to cut off aid and trade privileges. Multilateral police cooperation, border controls, spraying, and anticorruption programs probably have some marginal benefits, but they rarely make a dent in overall drug flows. Even when crops are successfully sprayed and criminals jailed in supplying countries, corruption impedes criminal justice systems, a lack of resources results in poorly run prisons, and the profit motive to continue production leads to rapid relocation of destroyed crops and facilities.

Ultimately, any supply-side effort to combat elements of the drug production cycle faces these two core challenges: weak governments that struggle to implement and fulfill policies, and an end-user demand that has maintained tremendous fiscal incentives to continue producing at every level of the illicit supply chain. The European Union has focused many of its policies on the demand side, decriminalizing sales and use of marijuana. Many public policy specialists believe that demand reduction or harm reduction in consuming countries through public spending on health and education can be least costly and most effective in the long run.

## Human Trafficking

At least a half-million people are trafficked each year, mostly women and children who are forced into prostitution. According to the U.S. State Department, an estimated 20,000 people are trafficked to the United States annually. As many as 150,000 non-Japanese work in Japan's sex industry. Organized crime groups play an important role in this business. They include the Russian Mafia, the Chinese Triads, and the Japanese Yakuza. The former Soviet Union has been an important source of trafficked women since the collapse of communism sent economies in Russia, Ukraine, Moldova, and Belarus into a tailspin. Burma, Nepal, India, and Thailand are also important suppliers to the world's brothels. The trade is usually from poor countries to wealthier countries.

The roots of sex trafficking are in patriarchy and poverty. Where women and minors lack political rights, education, and legal protections, they tend to be victims of organized criminal networks. Global and national economic crises tend to disproportionately affect women and children, who are pushed into the international sex industry against their will. Child trafficking is practiced in many countries, in which poor families place children into debt bondage or indentured servitude to an employer in another country. Even governments have become direct and indirect supporters of the exploitation of women and children by sex predators. Cuba and Burma, for example, have promoted international tourism and concomitantly acquiesced in the growth of a private sex industry in order to attract foreign currency.

Illegal migration is another large and growing part of the human trafficking problem. David Kyle and John Dale point out a paradox: The more tightly a country controls its borders, the more would-be illegal aliens have to turn to traffickers to get across the border, and the higher the profits of professional smugglers.[36] Employers of illegal aliens in Europe and the United States share much of the blame for human trafficking. Powerful businesses need low-cost labor and are willing to break the law, absent credible threats of punishment. The United States and Europe are caught in a contradiction: Mercantilists and xenophobes want to restrict the flow of migrants, but liberals who want flexible labor markets and low wages favor more migrants—legal or illegal.

How can human trafficking be diminished? One way is to build fences on borders and beef up interdiction at sea. An amnesty for illegal aliens and an expansive "guest worker" program is another possibility. Advocates for prostitutes argue that if trafficked women in the sex industry were provided immunity from prosecution and protection from deportation, they would provide extensive evidence and testimony against organized crime figures. Some believe that consensual, commercial sex between adults should be decriminalized. R. T. Naylor, for example, believes that personal vice done voluntarily by adults should not be criminalized because there is no clear victim. A structuralist would argue, however, that personal choice is not really voluntary, especially in the case of poor people who are compelled to participate in illicit acts in order to obtain an income. Liberal theorists increasingly argue that labor migration is an inherent part of globalization, and states can reduce illicit flow by simply allowing more legal flows. Labor-importing countries would gain valuable, young, low-cost workers, and labor exporters would boost remittance flows to their economies.

International organizations, governments, and nongovernmental organizations (NGOs) have taken significant, albeit insufficient, steps in the last decade to tackle trafficking in persons (see the box "Child Prostitution in the International Political Economy"). In 2000 the United Nations adopted the Convention on Transnational Crime and a related Protocol to Prevent, Suppress, and Punish Trafficking in Persons, Especially Women and Children. The United States ratified the Convention and Protocol in October 2005, joining more than 150 countries that are party to the Convention. Other organizations that cooperate to combat the scourge of trafficking include the International Labour Organization (ILO) and the Organization for Security and Cooperation in Europe.

Individual states have also taken unilateral action to address the problem. In October 2000, the United States passed into law the Victims of Trafficking and Violence Protection Act, which, among other things, allows the president to impose sanctions on countries that do not meet minimum standards in fighting human trafficking. In 2009 the U.S. State Department determined that 17 countries had serious human trafficking problems and were not making significant efforts to meet minimal standards for eliminating them. Of those 17 countries, President Obama imposed full sanctions on Burma, Cuba, North Korea, Iran, and 3 other countries, but he waived sanctions on Saudi Arabia, Kuwait, Malaysia, and 5 others on national security grounds.[37] More than 30 countries—including the United States and many European countries—have extraterritorial laws that make it a crime for their citizens to engage in sex with children overseas.

NGOs have been very active against the sex trade and sex tourism industries. They publicize the poor records of governments, help women and children in danger, and lobby for better national and international legislation. The Coalition against Trafficking in Women (founded in 1988), Amnesty International, and Anti-Slavery International are important organizations with antitrafficking networks around the world. Many international charitable organizations also have programs to help the victims of trafficking.

## CHILD PROSTITUTION IN THE INTERNATIONAL POLITICAL ECONOMY: WHO'S PROTECTING THE WORLD'S CHILDREN?

Child prostitutes are perhaps the most tragic victims of the international illicit economy. The United Nations International Children Fund (UNICEF) estimates that two million children, girls and boys alike, are sexually exploited worldwide each year, particularly as part of the growing child sex tourism industry that has accompanied development. The child sex trade is part of a greater problem of indentured servitude, though prostitution is its most visible element. Children labor as indentured servants in mines and markets, in factories and fisheries worldwide. Often, children are sold to traffickers by impoverished families, who believe their children will become employed in respectable jobs where they can learn skills and earn a salary. The child then becomes indebted to the trafficker and is forced to pay back the sum for which she was purchased.

The International Labour Organization estimates that 1.2 million children are trafficked each year and that 1.8 million children labor in prostitution and pornography industries.[a] These numbers are difficult to estimate because of the clandestine nature of the trade. According to the International Bureau for Children's Rights, child trafficking generates $12 billion annually.[b]

Some structuralists argue that as a corollary to export-oriented growth, developing countries are encouraged to attract rich foreigners by strengthening their service industries, amounting to direct encouragement to the sex tourism industry. Tourist agencies in developed countries sometimes advertise the services of women and children in developing nations; in February 2004, the owners of Big Apple Oriental Tours in New York were indicted for promotion of prostitution after the nonprofit organization Equality Now pursued legal action against the company.[c] Brochures from Big Apple Oriental advertised "plenty of young women to keep you occupied for the whole trip." Aaron Sachs attributes child prostitution to the "fundamental injustice in the current materialist world order—a global willingness to sacrifice society's most vulnerable members for the sake of others' economic and sexual gratification."[d]

For instance, the "rest and relaxation" needs of U.S. soldiers during the Vietnam War were a major stimulus to sex tourism in Thailand, now one of the most notorious sites of child prostitution. In 1967, the U.S. government signed a treaty with Thailand permitting U.S. soldiers to enter Thailand for "rest and relaxation." Buttressed by Thailand's 1966 Entertainment Places Act, which legalized brothels disguised as massage parlors and other service locations, the international sex tourism industry took flight. Policies of individual nations are thus a source of the sex tourism problem.

The global AIDS pandemic is also both a fueling factor and a consequence of the child prostitution industry. Many perceive children as virginal and think they are less likely to contract HIV from children. In fact, young people are more prone to contracting HIV and then spreading the disease to other clients. Child prostitutes who have contracted AIDS may return to their rural homes if they are found to be infected, spreading the disease from urban centers to rural villages.

In 2000, the UN General Assembly adopted the Optional Protocols to the Convention on the Rights of the Child on the Sale of Children, Child Prostitution, and Child Pornography. The resolution calls for a "holistic approach, addressing the contributing factors," as well as the improvement of national policies to deal with the sexual exploitation of children.[e] Many nations have taken steps to punish offenders and reduce the sex trade in recent years. According to the *Seattle (Wash.) Times*, village surveillance committees in Africa have led to the freedom of hundreds of children from prostitution; in Ghana, the government now provides loans to mothers and has eliminated school fees in order to provide families with alternatives to selling their children.[f]

Thirty-two countries, including the United States, have enacted laws that allow citizens to be prosecuted for engaging in child sex acts abroad. Michael Clark became the first person to be charged for such activities under the U.S. PROTECT Act, enacted in 2003. Clark was arrested in Seattle, Washington, for having sex with two boys in Cambodia. He was sentenced to 97 months in jail; under the PROTECT Act, the maximum sentence is 30 years. The U.S. State Department also established the Office to Monitor and Combat Trafficking in Persons, an office that monitors countries' efforts and produces an annual report. Ultimately, children must be provided with better alternatives, such as improved access to education, and families must be lifted out of poverty. The onus of eliminating the child prostitution industry falls largely on individual nations, though nongovernmental organizations such as Equality Now play a large role in bringing offenses to the attention of the public and government agencies.

## References

[a]International Programme on the Elimination of Child Labour, *Every Child Counts: New Global Estimates on Child Labour* (Geneva: International Labour Organization, 2002).

[b]"Child Trafficking," International Bureau for Children's Rights, www.ibcr.org/PAGE_EN/E_FOCUS_3.htm.

[c]"Sex Tourism: Big Apple Oriental Tour Operators Indicted for Promoting Prostitution," *Equality Now*, www.equalitynow.org/english/actions/action_1202_en.html.

[d]Aaron Sachs, "The Last Commodity: Child Prostitution in the Developing World," *World Watch*, July 1994.

[e]"Optional Protocols to the Convention on the Rights of the Child on the Sale of Children, Child Prostitution and Child Pornography," United Nations General Assembly, May 16, 2000, available at www.unhchr.ch/html/menu2/6/crc/treaties/opsc.htm.

[f]Sharon LaFraniere, "Already Vast, Child Servitude Grows in Africa," *The Seattle Times*, October 29, 2006, p. A20.

## CONCLUSION

This chapter has examined illicit international transactions that are sometimes overlooked by IPE scholars, who have only recently begun to draw on the work of criminologists, anthropologists, and legal scholars. It has shown that many illicit activities shaped the history of the global economy. The chapter also stresses that illicit activities are sometimes an unanticipated result of global free trade, and that the well-intentioned efforts of governments to halt black markets sometimes have unintended negative consequences. Unless we recognize the terrible human exploitation that often takes place in the shadows, we cannot adequately assess the moral and ethical consequences of globalization. Furthermore, as the financial crisis throws more people into poverty, it increases the risk that they will suffer at the hands of illicit actors.

The illicit global economy has important effects on the world's security, trade, and growth. It challenges the power of sovereign states and makes global governance more difficult. It is a structure through which the world trades a wide array of products that threaten corporate bottom lines and public health. It often fuels conflict and violence, hinders development, and threatens the environment. It has the power to make the world both more equal and less fair. It shows us that globalization and technological innovation are not necessarily forces for the global good.

The illicit global economy blurs the line between the legal and illegal worlds of production, trade, and distribution. It makes it necessary for international organizations to establish and enforce new regulations and codes of conduct. It forces businesses to ask: Do I know my customers? How can I protect my property and my reputation?

It forces consumers to ask: Am I responsible for knowing where the products I buy come from? What degree of separation is there between me and others I am tied to in global commodity chains? Increasingly, international civil society is mobilizing to tackle illicit activities. NGOs realize that with pressure (and support) from the grass roots and from consumers, states and businesses can make more progress against illegal actors.

States still tend to rely on supply-side approaches to illicit problems. Their mercantilist reflex to repress and interdict clashes with the hidden hand of the market and the not-so-hidden power of transnational criminals. However, this hardly means that political authorities are helpless. Governments in Europe and North America are increasingly receptive to newer strategies such as decriminalization, harm reduction, and partnerships with civil society groups. As developing countries institutionalize democracy, increase transparency, and strengthen market regulation, they should be better able to keep illicit transactions in check.

## KEY TERMS

secrecy jurisdiction   384
primitive accumulation   385
socially responsible investing   390
restriction-opportunity
   dilemma   391
profit paradox   391

Transdniestra   391
flags of convenience   392
commercialization of
   sovereignty   392
tax havens   392
know-thy-customer   394

name-and-shame campaigns   394
arbitrage   396
differential taxation   397
Plan Colombia   398
hydra effect   398

## DISCUSSION QUESTIONS

1. List some of the reasons why people participate in illicit markets.
2. How does a focus on illicit transactions help us explain development problems in the Third World? Is illicit activity an inherent aspect of global capitalism?
3. How are licit and illicit markets tied to each other? Are all those actors who benefit directly or indirectly from illicit transactions—even if they themselves don't engage in illegal acts—to be considered "guilty?" What responsibility do consumers and legitimate businesses have for illegal transactions and illicit networks?

4. On balance, does technological progress make illicit activities easier or harder? How can governments and corporations use technology to protect themselves from shadow actors?
5. How do the major findings about the illicit global economy confirm or challenge the key tenets of mercantilism, liberalism, and structuralism?
6. What are some of the unintended consequences of efforts to regulate the illicit global economy? How can states more effectively reduce the negative consequences of black markets?

## SUGGESTED READINGS

Peter Andreas and Ethan Nadelmann. *Policing the Globe: Criminalization and Crime Control in International Relations.* New York: Oxford University Press, 2006.

Kevin Bales. *Understanding Global Slavery.* Berkeley, CA: University of California Press, 2005.

Friman, H. Richard, ed. *Crime and the Global Political Economy.* Boulder, CO: Lynne Rienner, 2009.

Glenny, Misha. *McMafia: A Journey through the Global Criminal Underworld.* New York: Alfred A. Knopf, 2008.

Moisés Naím. *Illicit: How Smugglers, Traffickers, and Copycats Are Hijacking the Global Economy.* New York: Doubleday, 2005.

R. T. Naylor. *Wages of Crime: Black Markets, Illegal Finance, and the Underworld Economy.* Ithaca, NY: Cornell University Press, 2002.

Carolyn Nordstrom. *Global Outlaws: Crime, Money, and Power in the Contemporary World.* Berkeley, CA: University of California Press, 2007.

## NOTES

1. Peter Andreas, "Illicit International Political Economy: The Clandestine Side of Globalization," *Review of International Political Economy, 11* (August 2004), pp. 651–652.

2. Raymond Baker, *Capitalism's Achilles Heel* (Hoboken, NJ: John Wiley, 2005), p. 275.

3. "Trafficking: 24 Hours on the Border" (Anderson Cooper 360 Degrees), May 19, 2006, *cnn.com*, available at http://transcripts.cnn.com/TRANSCRIPTS/0605/19/acd.01.html.

4. Andreas, "Illicit International Political Economy," p. 645.

5. Kenneth Pomeranz and Steven Topik, *The World That Trade Created*, 2nd ed. (Armonk, NY: M. E. Sharpe, 2006), p. 149.

6. Charles Tilly, "War Making and State Making as Organized Crime," in Peter B. Evans, Dietrich Rueschemeyer, and Theda Skocpol, eds., *Bringing the State Back In* (Cambridge: Cambridge University Press, 1985).

7. R. T. Naylor, *Wages of Crime: Black Markets, Illegal Finance, and the Underworld Economy* (Ithaca, NY: Cornell University Press, 2002), p. 33.

8. Baker, *Capitalism's Achilles Heel*, pp. 166–168.

9. Ibid., p. 206.

10. Moisés Naím, *Illicit: How Smugglers, Traffickers, and Copycats Are Hijacking the Global Economy* (New York: Doubleday, 2005).

11. Carolyn Nordstrom, "ICT and the World of Smuggling," in Robert Latham, ed., *Bombs and Bandwidth: The Emerging Relationship Between Information Technology and Security* (New York: The New Press, 2003).

12. Naím, *Illicit*, pp. 6–8.

13. John Guare, *Six Degrees of Separation: A Play* (New York: Vintage, 1994).

14. Carolyn Nordstrom, *Shadows of War: Violence, Power, and Profiteering in the Twenty-First Century* (Berkeley, CA: University of California Press, 2004).

15. Phil Williams, "Crime, Illicit Markets, and Money Laundering," in P. J. Simmons and C. de Jonge Oudrat, eds., *Managing Global Issues* (Washington, DC: Carnegie Endowment, 2001).

16. Eva Bertram, Morris Blachman, Kenneth Sharpe, and Peter Andreas, *Drug War Politics: The Price of Denial* (Berkeley, CA: University of California Press, 1996).

17. Thomas Friedman, *The World Is Flat: A Brief History of the Twenty-First Century* (New York: Farrar, Straus & Giroux, 2005).

18. Naím, *Illicit*, pp. 24–30.

19. Ibid., pp. 17–18.

20. Ronen Palan, "Tax Havens and the Commercialization of State Sovereignty," *International Organization, 56* (Winter 2002), pp. 151–176.

21. R. T. Naylor, *Economic Warfare: Sanctions, Embargo Busting, and Their Human Cost* (Boston, MA: Northeastern University Press, 2001).

22. Rachel Stohl, "Fighting the Illicit Trafficking of Small Arms," *SAIS Review, 25* (Winter–Spring 2005), pp. 63–64.

23. William Easterly, *The White Man's Burden: Why the West's Efforts to Aid the Rest Have Done So Much Ill and So Little Good* (New York: Penguin, 2006).

24. World Health Organization, *The Cigarette "Transit" Road to the Islamic Republic of Iran and Iraq: Illicit Tobacco Trade in the Middle East*

(WHO, 2003), available at http://www.emro.who.int/TFI/TFIiraniraq.pdf.

25. Ibid.

26. Margaret Beare, "Organized Corporate Criminality—Corporate Complicity in Tobacco Smuggling," in Margaret E. Beare, ed., *Critical Reflections on Transnational Organized Crime, Money Laundering and Corruption* (Toronto, ON: University of Toronto Press, 2003).

27. Sari Horowitz, "Cigarette Smuggling Linked to Terrorism," *The Washington Post*, June 8, 2004, p. A1.

28. Simon Mackenzie, "Dig a Bit Deeper: Law, Regulation and the Illicit Antiquities Market," *British Journal of Criminology, 45* (May 2005), pp. 249–268.

29. R. T. Naylor, "The Underworld of Ivory," *Crime, Law, and Social Change, 42,* no. 4–5 (2004), pp. 261–295.

30. Ibid.

31. United Nations Office of Drugs and Crime, *2009 World Drug Report*, 2009, p. 15. http://www.unodc.org/documents/wdr/WDR_2009/WDR2009_eng_web.pdf.

32. Bertram et al., *Drug War Politics.*

33. Carlos Bortoni, "Violence in Mexico," *Harvard Political Review,* Fall 2009, p. 13.

34. Francisco Thoumi, *Illegal Drugs, Economy, and Society in the Andes* (Baltimore, MD: The Johns Hopkins University Press, 2003).

35. David Mares, *Drug Wars and Coffeehouses: The Political Economy of the International Drug Trade* (Washington, DC: CQ Press, 2006).

36. David Kyle and John Dale, "Smuggling the State Back In: Agents of Human Smuggling Reconsidered," in Rey Koslowski and David Kyle, eds., *Global Human Smuggling: Comparative Perspectives* (Baltimore, MD: The Johns Hopkins University Press, 2001).

37. "Memorandum of Justification Consistent With the Trafficking Victims Protection Act of 2000, Regarding Determinations With Respect to 'Tier 3' Countries," September 14, 2009, at http://www.state.gov/g/tip/rls/other/2009/129593.htm.

# Migration and Tourism:
# People on the Move[1]

Tourists and immigrants inevitably cross paths.

Monica DeHart

As noted in Chapter 1, international political economy (IPE) is not just about states and markets. Movements of people are every bit as controversial and important as flows of corporate bonds, auto parts, prescription medications, or arms. Indeed, their consequences shape how states, international organizations, nongovernmental organizations (NGOs), and local communities perceive and negotiate their relationship to people inside and beyond national borders. Whether it is the global circulation of unskilled migrant laborers, technology industry professionals, political refugees, tourists, terrorists, or NGO activists, new patterns of human flows have been a central feature of IPE.

The United Nations estimates that about 191 million people, or almost 3 percent of the world's population, are migrants living away from their native country.[2] Their movement can be related to the collapse of governments; efforts to gain "guest worker" privileges in another country; the need to escape war, poverty, or natural disaster; or simply the search for freedom and prosperity. Unlike migrants, tourists travel for reasons related to leisure and recreation. To many people, travel is an escape from the routines of everyday life. However, the tourist industry now plays a central role in both the domestic economy and global standing of many nations. Taken together, migration and tourism highlight both the opportunities and inequalities that shape regional development and undergird new global connections in the current context of economic uncertainty.

These different forms of global movement raise questions about some of the basic precepts of IPE. For example, what is the impact of transnational human flows on economic development in both home and host countries? What happens when people increasingly define their identities, communities, livelihoods, politics, and leisure activities in terms other than those related to the nation-state? And what effects do these movements have on the four structures of IPE (security, production and trade, knowledge and technology, and money and finance)?

In response to these questions, this chapter examines how migration and tourism shape the behavior and outcomes of international and national actors and policies. It highlights the inequalities and contradictions that continue to structure the direction and effect of global human flows. It also examines the new strategies employed to regulate human flows and protect individual rights as people increasingly live, work, and play in places other than their nations of birth.

## ON THE GLOBAL FAST TRACK: THE IPE OF MIGRATION

We frequently hear stories about how our globalized world has allowed mobile, enterprising migrants to access resources and opportunities unimaginable in their home country. This perspective chalks up immigrant success or failure, belonging or marginalization, to individual actions and values that are sometimes extended to an entire ethnic or national group. In this section of the chapter, we question the assumptions and implications of that perception. For example, which forces govern who migrates, how, and to where? How is the immigration experience shaped by whether one is white or black, male or female, urban and educated or a rural peasant? How do certain patterns of migration reproduce inequalities between regions and groups rather than transcend them? Although increased global migration seems to point to expanding opportunities for individual autonomy and mobility, immigrants' experiences ask us to reconsider the ongoing structural inequalities that condition their movement and ultimate migration outcomes.

While human movement is a common feature of our world, the notion of migration can be something of a moving target. In its simplest sense, **migration** refers to movement from one place to another—to a nearby city, another region, or another country entirely. Migration may be temporary or permanent; there is nothing about the notion of migration itself that guarantees either the length of residence or the strength of the commitment to the migratory destination. The reasons for migration are diverse: People may not have permanent work or sufficient resources to sustain themselves in their home environment. They may wish to pursue advanced educational or professional opportunities. They may not be able to express their ideas or practice their religion in the way that they choose. They may face environmental devastation or threats to their personal safety. They may be separated from family members. Therefore, when we speak of migration, we are referring to a wide variety of circumstances, motives, and experiences, each with different implications for individuals, states, and the international community as a whole.

Migration has long been an integral force in shaping both individual nation-states and their relationships to one another within the global landscape. **Internal migration**—movement from rural to urban areas or from one area of the country to another—has been a central feature of IPE theories of development (see Chapter 11). In these theories, migration within the nation has often been seen as a crucial step toward modernization (see the box "China: Bringing Development Home" below).

Global migration rose to unprecedented numbers at the end of the nineteenth century; however, it has been in the latter part of the twenty-first century that the volume, reach, and pace of global migration have taken on their current intensity.[3] Whether we are talking about unskilled labor or highly educated professionals, **transnational migration** describes the now-frequent process by which people cross state borders in search of temporary work or for other reasons. Breakthroughs in technology and travel have allowed a broad array of people to move across borders and time zones as part of (or to ensure) their daily lives. Both men and women have blazed new migration trails and contributed to the construction of vibrant multicultural communities that extend across the globe. In 41 countries, migrants constituted as much as 20 percent of the total population![4]

The increased scale and frequency of transnational migration of the last four decades has been accompanied by new patterns of movement. Whereas previous travel routes were characterized by journeys east and west, or colonial forays south, current migration is characterized by more south–north or even south–south migration. One-third of international migrants moved from developing to developed countries (often from former colonies), while another third moved from developing to other developing countries. Nearly six of every ten international migrants now live in high-income countries that include developing countries such as Bahrain, Brunei, Kuwait, Qatar, the Republic of Korea, and Saudi Arabia.[5]

## CHINA: BRINGING DEVELOPMENT HOME

China's road to modernization can be charted through its citizens' changing migration paths over the past two decades. Domestically, the introduction of the market economy and the shift from collective to household production systems made many Chinese rural farmers "surplus" labor. In response to these changes, and the growing economic opportunities in the cities, many rural residents have taken part in a large-scale exodus from the countryside. By 2003, China's rural–urban migrants, known as the "floating population" was estimated to have reached 140 million.[a] In the cities, successful rural migrants have started informal businesses such as those found in the Beijing's growing garment industry. More commonly, they have filled the ranks of the urban workforce whose low wages underwrite the success of China's exports in the global market. Migrants' contributions to China's national development were made especially visible in the 2008 Beijing Olympics, where venues were constructed in large part by former farmers, who represent 70 percent of the construction industry.[b]

Globally, China has produced a large number of professional migrants who are contributing to national development in a very different way. In 2006, Chinese immigrants constituted 4.1 percent of immigrants to the United States. Overall, these Chinese immigrants were more likely to be working in science and engineering occupations, with one quarter of the men working in management, business, finance, or informational technology.[c] Because of their high education level, these migrants have played a central role in economic and job growth in the U.S. technology industry (Chapter 10). However, instead of constituting a drain on Chinese human resources, they have increasingly become a source of human and economic capital gain for their nation of origin as well. In a 2009 study titled "America's Loss is the World's Gain," 72 percent of the U.S.-based, professional Chinese migrants interviewed indicated that they thought professional opportunities were now better in China than in the United States.[d] In the context of the global economic recession, many Chinese professionals were thus returning home to job and capital markets that were still growing, rather than shrinking. Validating this perception, many return migrants reported faster movement up the management ladder, better compensation, and more professional recognition in China. Therefore, while the current economic downturn has been global in scope, for China's mobile professionals, migration to the United States has increasingly served as more of a career detour than a destination, with the road to prosperity leading home.

## References

[a]See People's Daily Online, "China's Floating Population Tops 140 Million," July 28, 2005, http://english.people.com.cn/200507/27/eng20050 727_198605.html; and Li Zhang, *Strangers in the City: Reconfigurations of Space, Power and Social Networks Within China's Floating Population* (Stanford, CA: Stanford University Press, 2001).

[b]Xinhuanet, "Beijing Increase Migrant Workers Salary for Construction of Olympic Venues," January 19, 2007, http://en.beijing2008.cn/ 27/97/article214009727.shtml.

[c]Terrazas, Aaron Matteo, and Vhavna Devani, "Chinese Immigrants in the United States," *Migration Information Source*, June 13, 2008, www.migrationinformation.org.

[d]Wadha, Vivek, A. Saxenian, R. Freeman, G Gereffi, and A. Salkever. "America's Loss is the World's Gain: America's New Immigrant Entrepreneurs, Part IV," March 2009, http://ssrn.com/abstract=1348616.

People were once presumed to migrate in order to take up permanent residence in their destinations; this kind of movement *into* a new country for the purpose of settling and becoming a resident of that country is called **immigration**. Contemporary migration, however, is now less unidirectional, and often more fluid in terms of its duration. **Circular migration** refers to the process by which migrants' movement shifts back and forth between home and work communities in response to different economic opportunities, employment conditions, and family responsibilities. For example, every September, thousands of young men from Mali and Niger travel to the Cote D'Ivoire and other West African countries to seek wage-labor opportunities along the coast. They remain in these jobs until the spring, when they return home to attend to their crops.[6] Similarly, women from the Philippines and mainland China migrate to Hong Kong to work as domestic labor for wealthier, professional families. When their employment contract term is up, they must return home; however, they often solicit a new contract to revisit Hong Kong for another cycle of labor.[7]

The scale and frequency of temporary labor migration is also encouraged by growing transnational networks of kin and neighbors on whom migrants can depend to find residence and work. This pattern of **chain migration,** whereby a migrant "links" up with social networks abroad, promotes the concentration of migrant communities in enclaves or gateway cities, which are oriented around immigrant culture and practical needs. In these enclaves, it is possible for a migrant to speak his or her native language, buy "home-style" food, make quick wire transfers to people back home, and practice local customs.

For example, Roger Rouse studied the large numbers of Mexicans who moved between Aguililla, Michoacan, and Redwood City, California.[8] The concentration of migrants moving between one small town in Michoacan and Redwood City had become so marked by the mid-1990s that many people began referring to parts of Redwood City itself as Aguililla. Indeed, most men in the community spent a portion of their lives moving back and forth across the border between what were, in essence, the two communities of Aguililla. Community members were able to draw on a deeply embedded transnational network to facilitate ongoing transfers of people, money, and resources.

## Migrating Toward Development

Transnational migration circuits and the social networks on which they are built are an essential part of the changing economic conditions and political relations associated with globalization. As global capitalist production becomes more mobile, migrant workers tend to move to labor markets where there is high demand and low domestic supply. For this reason, migrants often fill jobs at both ends of the labor market. Engineers and scientists take highly specialized professional positions within the technology or aerospace industries. Unskilled workers fill labor and service jobs that few native workers will do—for example, in the food service and garment industries, meatpacking, domestic labor, or agriculture. Furthermore, declining population growth in countries like Japan and in much of the European Union, including Germany, Italy, Austria, and France, has increased the need for workers in general, thus making them a prime destination for foreign labor migrants.[9] From Saudi Arabia to Spain to the United States, changing economic and demographic conditions have required most developed countries to make some accommodations for migrant labor within their borders.

The current global pattern of transnational migration has created new opportunities and challenges for individual migrants and states alike. States with high demand for foreign workers, such as Singapore, Kuwait, or Germany, have developed temporary foreign worker, or **guest worker,** programs that regulate the provisional admission, residence, and employment of a specific class of migrant labor. In many cases, these migration policies usually do not allow whole families to enter the country or provide for long-term residence. Until 2000, this was the case for Turkish migrants in Germany; however, new rules now allow German-born children of Turkish migrants to automatically receive German nationality, but by age 18, they must choose between German or Turkish citizenship. Therefore, many are now campaigning for the possibility of dual citizenship status, as is afforded to other EU residents. For the most part, guest worker programs are aimed at maximizing cheap labor and then keeping migrants moving, rather than creating new nationals.

A prime example of this kind of program was the U.S. Bracero Program. Between 1942 and 1964, the initiative permitted the entry of temporary workers from Mexico to fill U.S. wartime labor shortages in the agricultural sector. By the 1950s, however, the United States sought to deter the permanent settling of Bracero workers and the entry of new Mexican migrants, to prevent the expansion of immigrant labor into nonagricultural sectors and to curb the rising levels of unemployment among domestic laborers.

As these examples suggest, migrants are subject to different degrees of privilege or prejudice as they move between labor markets. Because of their conditional labor and residency status, guest workers can be especially vulnerable to labor rights violations, discrimination, and abuse. In a recent study of Jordanian garment factories, Bangladeshi workers who were interviewed reported that their employers had confiscated their passports, forced them to work 48-hour periods, provided insufficient sleeping accommodations, and refused to pay mandated overtime pay.[10] The situation for undocumented workers can be just as bad or worse, as these workers often have no recourse in filing complaints against employers who abuse or fail to pay them.

At the international level, migrant rights come under the purview of the Office of the United Nations High Commissioner for Human Rights. However, as people increasingly live their lives in places outside their place of birth, states and IOs alike have recognized the need for new forms of global governance that can regulate human flows and protect individual rights. International treaties like the United Nation's 1990 International Convention on the Protection of Rights of All Migrant Workers sought to clarify migrant worker categories and reiterate receiving states' responsibility to protect migrants' rights. This convention built on previous resolutions passed by the International Labor Organization that "advocate the principles of equal treatment, equality of opportunity and non-discrimination" for all workers.[11] In 2006, the United Nations sponsored a High-Level Dialogue on International and Migration, at which member states actively debated "how to maximize the development benefits of international migration and minimize its negative impacts."[12] This event spawned the formation of the Global Forum on Migration and Development as a consultative body through which states could address migration issues and develop partnerships.

Despite these developments, much of the work to protect migrant rights and resolve migration conflicts has tended to fall to bilateral and regional negotiations over residence and labor conditions in particular countries. For example, the South American Conference on Migration ("Lima Process") and the Regional Conference on Migration ("Puebla Process") are two regional groups that have worked to protect migrants and facilitate their remittances in Latin America. In

Asia, the Ministerial Consultations on Overseas Employment and Contractual Labour ("Colombo Process") has sought to promote legal migration and intergovernmental cooperation.[13] While these consortiums have created regional standards and promoted collaboration on migration, it is often still at the level of bilateral diplomacy that the concerns of specific national origin migrant groups are addressed. Therefore, when U.S. president Obama met with Mexican president Felipe Calderon and Canadian president Stephen Harper at the "three amigos" summit in Mexico in 2009, the question of how to regulate the flow of migrants, trucks, and epidemics constituted the main focus of conversation.

On the other end of the labor spectrum, educated professionals are often highly coveted by both sending and receiving states alike. Indeed, many developing nations have lamented the loss of their most talented citizens through transnational migration. **Brain drain**—a process by which educated members of a society migrate to more developed nations where there are higher salaries and more employment opportunities—has been responsible for reducing the human resources necessary for many states' own development. In response to a grave shortage of domestic nurses in 2006, U.S. lawmakers decided *not* to place limits on the number of visas allotted for foreign nurses. The move, however, frustrated residents in the Philippines and Fiji, who feared that their most valuable health care resources would be wooed away.[14] As a result of conflicts like these, some developing countries have instituted sanctions (with mixed results) to keep their professionals at home or to ensure their return from education abroad in order to guarantee the repatriation of valuable knowledge and technology.

Perhaps the biggest reason why migration can be attractive to both migrants and sending states is the opportunity for **remittances**—income earned abroad that is sent back to the home country. Global remittances have doubled over the last decade, reaching $232 billion by 2005.[15] Migrant remittances to Latin America were estimated to total $55 billion, amounting to the largest source of income for the top recipient nations, where it surpassed even foreign aid and foreign investment.[16] At the microlevel, remittances are used to supplement individual household incomes, but they are also important for offsetting the cost of education and health care. Furthermore, in some cases, hometown associations—formed by migrants from a single community—have consolidated their remittances to finance infrastructure and development projects in their home communities.[17] At the macrolevel, remittances provide an essential means of shoring up a nation's credit worthiness and providing foreign currency to prevent balance-of-payment crises. For these reasons, even IOs such as the United Nations and the World Bank have promoted "mainstreaming" migration as a central feature of global development efforts.[18]

Some states have developed diverse legal and financial incentives to keep their mobile populations invested in economic and political processes at home. Mexico and Guatemala are among a growing number of states that have instituted dual citizenship designations in order to maintain allegiance among their citizens abroad. India created a new citizenship category altogether for its emigrant citizens—Non-Resident Indian (NRI). To further encourage capital flows from residents abroad, some states have enabled foreign currency holdings and enacted "matching funds" programs that reward migrants for investing at home. The Mexican government in particular has collaborated with Wells Fargo and Bank of

America to allow its citizens to open U.S. bank accounts with a Mexican national identification card that it grants through its consular agencies in the United States. The Central Reserve Bank of El Salvador authorized Salvadoran Banks with branches in the United States to serve as remittance agencies.

In the context of the recent global economic recession, however, it is unclear how sustainable migrant remittance income may be as a source of local, national, and regional development efforts. States like Japan, South Korea, Spain, and Dubai—recipients of large migrant labor flows—have begun instituting programs that encourage guest workers to return to their home countries. In what some economists have called the "biggest turnaround in migration flows since the Great Depression," some migrants themselves are choosing to forego emigration or, if already abroad, to return home (see "China: Bringing Development Home" box).[19] Mexico, the largest source of migrants to the United States, is a case in point. Mexican census data released in 2009 documented a 25 percent decline in the number of Mexicans emigrating to the United States compared to the previous year. Furthermore, the high unemployment rates that wracked the U.S. construction industry at the end of 2007 contributed to a 3.6 percent decline in remittances to Mexico between 2007 and 2008, with a precipitous 8.7 percent decline in money transfer in the first four months of 2009.[20] Considering that remittances from the United States amount to about 3 percent of Mexico's GDP and its third largest source of income (behind tourism and oil), it is easy to see how quickly the new opportunities brought by migration can also breed new challenges for states that have grown dependent on remittance income.

Transnational migration has clearly become a defining quality of global capitalist production. The economic benefits it offers to individual migrants, sending states, and receiving nations have generated new and different patterns of human flows across the globe. Nonetheless, as described above, the global fast tracks to economic development are often built along lines of global inequality in terms of who can move, who benefits from that movement, and how sustainable those benefits might be. Therefore, it's important to explore the social and political dimensions of transnational migration to understand what other forces shape the nature and consequences of global human flows.

## Citizenship and the Politics of Belonging

Can a person be a citizen in more than one country and, if so, how does he negotiate multiple political allegiances? What role do cultural and social differences play in shaping the conditions for citizenship? A closer look at global flows forces us to question the assumption that national identity, politics, or even development is rooted within the boundaries of the nation-state. With the help of new information technologies and a highly mobile population, national identity politics may be enacted across the globe. Furthermore, transnational communities formed around beliefs, identities, or politics that are not tied to a particular state reflect new kinds of human connections that raise new challenges for both the states that contain them and the international political economy in general.

Some of the most heated debates about migration in the United States and Europe have centered on the social and political implications of migrants. Given that one of the chief functions of the modern state is to control its borders and protect its citizens' rights, some see unauthorized migrants as a threat to the political sovereignty and security of the nation. Rather than getting the necessary work permits before entering the country, **irregular migrants** enter a country without visas or stay on after their work visas have expired and thus lack the necessary documentation to remain in the country legally. Senegalese and other sub-Saharan migrants have been entering Spain in large numbers over the past few years through the Canary Islands (a Spanish territory just off West Africa) or Malta. In 2006, their large numbers caused a humanitarian crisis in the Canary Islands and also protest from native Spanish residents, who saw them as a threat to economic stability and national security. In Brunei, the high level of temporary migrant labor from India and the Philippines provoked the formation of a special task force to "apprehend" workers who had stayed in the country beyond the stipulated term of their work visa.[21] These cases point to the challenge of regulating migrant flows and control over one's borders.

The EU has grappled with this issue as it has extended membership to some post-Soviet states and now contemplates Turkey's admission. With the inclusion of poorer Eastern European members in 2004, many of the original EU members imposed migration limits to mitigate the prospective flood of migrants that they feared would move westward. Indeed, anti-immigrant campaigns invoked the "Polish plumber" as a symbol of the cheap migrant labor they claimed would take over local jobs. While studies show that Eastern European migrant numbers did increase substantially, their employment fueled growth and did not depress wages, as feared.[22] What is more, non-EU nationals outnumbered migrants from new to old EU countries. Therefore, one of the main points of opposition to Turkey's inclusion has been the ongoing fear of waves of cheap labor from Asia and the Middle East. These fears grow in part out of the fact that Turkey, like Spain, is no longer defined by outmigration of its citizens but rather by inmigration—in this case, of migrants from Afghanistan, Bangladesh, Iraq, and Iran, as well as former Soviet states. These irregular migrants often move to transit states such as Turkey, as a first step toward greater economic opportunities in more affluent countries of the EU. In the context of increasing regional migration, the migration policies of individual EU member states thus come to matter greatly.

**Citizenship** is a legal category that entitles a person to full and equal rights within a given state, perhaps most importantly including the right to vote. However, states have various means of assigning that status. Citizenship may be granted based on birth, ethnicity, or naturalization. Anyone born on U.S. soil is eligible to apply for citizenship. Furthermore, once immigrants to the United States obtain a "green card," they can eventually earn the chance to be naturalized as citizens. Because they provide immigrants the opportunity to become permanent residents, countries such as the United States or Australia are known as **settler states.** By contrast, people born on German soil do not necessarily receive citizenship. Instead, German citizenship is granted through one's parents: One must have a German mother or father, or a parent with established permanent residence, to become a German national. Restrictive migration policies in countries such as Japan and Saudi Arabia make it even harder for migrants to become citizens of those countries.

Another way that people can make a claim for permanent residence in a country that is not their own is through refugee status or asylum. Indeed, refugees currently account for 23 percent of all international migrants in the least developed countries.[23] **Refugees** are displaced people who are unable or unwilling to return to their country of origin because of fear of persecution on account of race, religion, nationality, membership in a particular social group, or political opinion. A Sudanese victim of factional violence who has moved to a temporary camp in Chad could be considered a refugee. Often the UN High Commission on Refugees may be responsible for negotiating a permanent resettlement destination—either in Chad or in another country—for this Sudanese refugee.

People who seek **asylum** are also permanently displaced people who face persecution in their home countries. These immigrants, however, often make their claims for protection to a court within the nation in which they hope to reside, usually from within that nation's territory. In the first half of 2008, Iraqis constituted the top nationality seeking asylum in the industrialized world, representing 12 percent of asylum claims submitted. Applicants from Russia, China, Somalia, and Pakistan followed to constitute the other top asylum-seeking nationalities.[24] Interestingly, by the end of 2008, four-fifths of all refugees were hosted by developing countries, with Pakistan hosting the largest number in relation to its economic capacity (USD GDP). Germany was the first developed country with the most refugees per USD GDP. South Africa was the largest recipient of individual asylum applications.[25]

Citizenship and asylum are more than just legal categories; they are also the highly politicized subject of geopolitics. A recent legal study showed that the U.S. government has granted political asylum to 80 percent of Cuban asylum applicants, but only 10 percent of Haitian applicants. This discrepancy in asylum rates reflects the U.S. government's policy of recognizing Cubans as political refugees fleeing an authoritarian, communist regime, while Haitians tend to be seen as economic migrants rather than refugees.[26]

Even when foreigners acquire legal residence or citizenship in their adopted countries, states often struggle with integrating them into the social fabric of their new homes. One reason for this struggle is that instead of following a process of **assimilation**—whereby an immigrant takes on the values and customs of the new prevailing culture—immigrants may retain a strong connection to their culture or nation of origin. **Diaspora** refers to communities that have retained a common identification with their homeland, despite being displaced and dispersed. The Jews' expulsion from Babylon in the fifth century B.C. and the transatlantic African slave trade during the sixteenth to nineteenth centuries established the Jewish and African diasporas as the original diasporic communities. In both of these cases, peoples' forcible displacement from their homeland produced transnational communities that continued to identify with a common history and identity even though they might speak different languages and be citizens of other states.

Today, the concept of diaspora has expanded to refer to a much broader array of transnational communities. We can talk of the Indian, Iranian, Filipino, Chinese, or Haitian diasporas as communities created through an intense process of migration and global dispersion. Diasporic communities may be linked to a specific nation-state—such as the case of the Irish diaspora—or may be a stateless nation—such as the Kurds. Regardless of type, diasporas are increasingly significant both for the new kinds of social, political, and economic organizations they represent and also for the effects they have had on political and economic processes in their home countries. For instance, Haitian migrants in New York see their long-term residence and labors abroad as part of a concerted campaign to improve and support their homeland, something Nina Glick-Schiller and Georges Fouron have called "long-distance nationalism." In this formulation, the Haitian community is defined not by its residence on Haitian soil but rather by its common Haitian blood and obligation to the homeland.[27]

New information technology has played an important role in supporting diasporic communities. Now, even when immigrants cannot easily or frequently travel between origin and adoptive countries, they can keep abreast of local news through online media, participate in virtual chatroom conversations with other diaspora members, and manage individual and group finances through Internet banking. Many local communities have created Web pages to keep residents living abroad informed about local needs and goings-on, as well as to stimulate outside investment and participation in local events. The global expansion of cellular phone service to rural areas, as well as Internet conferencing services, have facilitated real-time communication between immigrants and their kin in historically remote areas. All of these technologies allow people to maintain social connections across borders, preserving community language, identity, and politics at any distance.

Many receiving states have had to contend with the complex political implications of diaspora. In February 2006, when a Danish newspaper published a cartoon satirizing the Prophet Muhammad, a group of Denmark's fundamentalist Muslim clerics lobbied the embassies of 11 "mostly Muslim" countries to demand a meeting with Denmark's prime minister. The Danish prime minister's refusal provoked a boycott of Danish goods across the Middle East, as well as violent protests against European offices, media, and tourists throughout the region. This example demonstrates how a transnational community can be mobilized not simply on the basis of a common national identity but also on the basis of a common religious identity. With Islam as Europe's fastest-growing religion, the social and political implications of an increasingly active Muslim diaspora have become the source of much debate across the continent.

Even when migrants actively embrace their new host society, discrimination and inequality can deprive migrants of everyday privileges afforded to native residents. Often this marginalization coincides with perceived differences in language, customs, and cultural values. In some cases, higher population growth rates among immigrant families have meant that the immigrant population is growing faster than the native-born population, leading nativist constituencies to worry about becoming a minority in their own country. Consequently, immigrant struggles for social recognition and political inclusion have fueled some of the major social and political conflicts in recent years. The term **cultural citizenship** effectively describes immigrants' demands within these conflicts—that is, they seek a sense of social belonging that is not contingent on assimilation, but rather is built on a respect for diversity.

Two weeks of rioting by youth in Paris suburbs during 2005 illustrate this point. The clashes between youth and the French police were attributed largely to the extreme social marginalization and impoverishment experienced by North African immigrants and their descendants, despite their official French citizenship. This contradiction prompted a *New York Times* article to raise the important question, "What makes someone French?"[28] Because the French have always insisted on a secular national identity, they have glossed over racial and cultural distinctions rather than try to address their social and political effects. The French government's 2004 ban on the wearing of head scarves or other religious paraphernalia in public schools illustrates just such an attempt to suppress the visibility of cultural differences. Nonetheless, many of France's European counterparts are trying to find a way to recognize diversity, both to create a more multicultural society and also to defuse the move by disenfranchised immigrant youth toward radical or fundamentalist organizations.

As the French case makes clear, the increasingly multicultural societies created by transnational migration require new ways of thinking about what makes someone an authentic citizen of the nation and thus bring into focus contradictions in the definition of the nation itself. Porous state borders and fluid patterns of human movement challenge the assumption that the modern nation is defined not only by a sovereign state but also by a singular, common history and culture. This challenge is true in the United States, as well, although immigration is a central feature of U.S. national identity. For example, in 2006 a musical collaboration produced the first Spanish-language version of the U.S. national anthem ("The Star Spangled Banner"). "Nuestro Himno," as the track is called, emerged at a moment of intense national debate over the immigration question. It called attention to what many view as the increasingly diverse and politicized reality of U.S. national culture. However, it also perturbed many pundits who saw the song as an attack not only on the United States's primary language—English—but also on the Anglo values and identity that they claimed defined U.S. history.

Both the French and the U.S. immigration debates highlight the importance not simply of cultural values, but also of race, in defining the terms of national identity and citizenship. To explain the marginalization of immigrant groups, many scholars of U.S. immigration history have compared the experience of early twentieth-century immigrants from Europe with the experience of post-1965 immigrants from Asia and Latin America. Although earlier immigrants were originally identified as distinct races—Irish, Italian, Jewish—their "racial" difference largely disappeared as they assimilated to Anglo values and became upwardly mobile. Consequently, these European immigrants have increasingly been seen as "white." By contrast, later immigrants with darker skin or other phenotypical differences have been unable to shed their racial identities even when they assume "American" values, speak English, and acquire middle-class status.[29] In these cases it is the perceived racial difference, as much as or more than cultural difference, that explains specific groups' lack of cultural citizenship.

While new patterns of international human flows are often celebrated as evidence of the emancipatory potential of globalization, a closer look at the contours of those flows demonstrates how racial, gender, class, and national differences (among others) continue to exert a strong influence over individual and group mobility and the outcome of that movement. In other words, does the fact that Dominicans emigrate in high numbers and remit large amounts of money to the

Dominican Republic evidence growing individual freedom and a globalized form of national development or ongoing dependency and underdevelopment? Certainly many individual Dominicans and even the Dominican national economy as a whole have benefited greatly from migrant labor in the United States. Nonetheless, the lack of domestic jobs in the Dominican Republic and the nation's reliance on the United States for its development accentuate the ongoing inequalities that shape transnational migration. These are the contradictions inherent in the new forms of human movement and connections emerging through globalization.

## The IPE of Transnational Human Flows

Clearly, then, new global migration and settlement patterns present many opportunities and challenges. Politicians, policy analysts, academics, and community members often debate these trade-offs in terms that invoke IPE theories. For example, orthodox economic liberals (OELs) argue that migrant labor is a natural part of the free-market system and therefore should be allowed to flow freely. From this view, foreign labor supports economic growth in industries in which domestic labor is too expensive or unavailable. Even if immigrant labor displaces small numbers of native labor, depresses wages, or requires benefits, neoliberal perspectives highlight these facts as economic trade-offs that are outweighed by the lower prices enjoyed by consumers, the higher profits enjoyed by employers, and the generalized levels of economic growth that result from immigrant labor. Supporting this view, a recent study estimated that legalizing the more than 12 million irregular migrants in the United States would cost approximately $54 billion in benefits between 2007 and 2016; however, those costs would be offset by $66 billion of new revenue that immigrant workers would add to the Treasury through income and payroll taxes, Social Security withholding, and fines and fees required by law.[30]

Heterodox interventionist liberals (HILs) also tend to support migration on the basis of their belief in the individual's right to freedom of movement as part of a bundle of basic human rights. This view is especially prevalent in cases of migrants fleeing repression or violence in their home country because, according to liberal political philosophy, our obligations as humans extend beyond national borders. What many HILs call for, then, is simply more effective ways of regulating the flow of immigrants across borders. The work of the ILO and the UN's High-Dialogue on International Migration and Development are two examples of efforts to formulate these regulations and global standards.

Some of the most strident opposition to migration these days comes from economic national-realist types who claim that migrants pose a threat to national security in the form of lost domestic jobs and lower wages, especially for low-skilled native workers. Many critics claim that immigrants place a heavy toll on health care, schools, and other state services.[31] This perspective has fueled vigilante groups such as the Minutemen in Texas and Arizona, who claim that their efforts to patrol and actively deter immigration along the U.S.–Mexico border are born of a sense of patriotism and defense of U.S. sovereignty.[32] Similarly in Europe, conservative politicians in Italy, France, the Netherlands, and Britain have made nativist politics and opposition to immigration a central feature of recent elections.[33] This perspective is mercantilist because of its economic nationalist sentiment and use of comparative advantage to justify limits on the mobility of labor. In its current ideological manifestation, mercantilist positions also tend to equate domestic political security with economic security, worrying that migrants represent serious breaches to both.

Structuralists may also oppose some dimensions of migration, but for radically different reasons than their mercantilist counterparts. Structuralists view increasing migration as a result of the underdevelopment produced by global inequality. From this standpoint, the global division of labor is responsible for creating impoverished nations whose citizens have no choice but to migrate in order to support their families. Free-trade zones flood local markets with foreign goods, destroying local production and local enterprises so that workers must migrate to find new labor opportunities. Furthermore, structuralists often criticize the exploitation of these unskilled migrants within the richer countries as further evidence of the need to restructure the terms of global capitalist production and trade (see Chapters 4 and 6).

Constructivist theory (see Chapter 5) would also point to multiculturalism and citizenship as elements in the political and economic debates on immigration. North American society has struggled to assimilate its large numbers of Latino and Asian immigrants—a task that some claim has been made easier by the shared faith between immigrants and natives, as well as the active role that churches play in integrating new arrivals. In Europe, large numbers of Muslim immigrants from Northern Africa and the Middle East have made cultural assimilation more difficult and, in a post-9/11 world, the stakes higher. In both places, states and citizens are grappling with how to reconcile democracy's values with changing demographics and cultural politics.[34]

In today's highly mobile landscape, global migration is clearly an important subject for IPE. As the above debates evidence, the question is rarely whether or not global migration should happen, but under what conditions and with what ends. Both individuals and states can benefit from transnational human flows, but they raise the questions such as: Does transnational movement represent growing freedom or ominious challenges to security? Who bears responsibility for migrants: the sending or receiving states? What new forms of global governance would be effective in regulating migrant movement and rights? Resolving the cultural politics that emerge from the increasingly diverse constituencies that transnational flows produce and the economic challenges that arise from economic downturn highlight the double-edged sword of these human dimensions of globalization.

# GOING MOBILE: THE POLITICAL ECONOMY OF INTERNATIONAL TOURISM

Like migration, tourism refers to the movement of individuals from one location to another. However, unlike temporary and permanent migrants, tourists travel for reasons related to leisure and recreation. Voluntary travel across international borders produces the single largest transnational flow of human beings in the world. According to the World Tourism Organization (UNWTO), international tourist arrivals grew from 25 million in 1950 to 922 million in 2008.[35] Despite the down-turn in the global economy that began in 2008, the UNWTO estimates that tourist arrivals will reach 1 billion by 2010 and over 1.5 billion by 2020.

The growing transnational flow of people, embodied by the international travel and tourism industry, stems from the same technologies and institutional arrangements associated with the global flow of goods, ideas, and money. To a large degree, discrepancies in wealth and power between individuals and countries, and interactions between states and markets, determine the distribution of benefits and costs of tourism, not to mention the distribution of actual tourists. Further, many economic liberals portray tourism as a path to development, political legitimacy, and peace, while structuralists see tourism as a destructive force. Mercantilists meanwhile eschew the moral debate and instead focus on how to promote national security while at the same time attracting more tourists and tourism revenues than other states. As political economists like to point out, tourism involves unavoidable trade-offs that benefit some while hurting others. Tourism generates revenues, but comes with a price. When faced with the choice of whether or not to participate in tourism, the majority of individuals, and all but the most isolationist states in the world, accept certain trade-offs as a worthy price to pay. Despite the recent slowdown in the growth of international tourism caused by the current global economic recession, the flow of tourists crisscrossing the globe is in the long term almost certain to continue.

## Engine of Economic Growth or Tool of Exploitation?

In the decades following World War II, the reconstruction of war-torn Europe, the growing prosperity of the North American and Western European middle class, and the implementation of policies aimed at encouraging economic growth led to the rapid expansion of international tourism. Reflecting an economic liberal perspective, tourism advocates argued that countries should use their comparative advantage in cultural traditions, historical sites, or attractive natural landscapes in order to attract tourists and the money that they bring. In these early days of the modern tourism boom, few questions were asked about the potential harmful consequences of tourism, particularly because the economic benefits of tourism promotion seemed so significant and lasting.

There is no doubt that tourism produces tangible economic benefits. The most obvious and attractive to governments around the world is the creation of direct revenues that flow from tourist spending both before and during their trip, as well as from tourist payments of taxes while traveling in the host country. International tourism receipts, defined by the World Trade Organization as all payments made by international tourists for goods and services (such as food, drink, accommodation, airfares, souvenirs, and entertainment), stood at $944 billion worldwide in 2008.[36] As direct revenues circulate and are re-spent in the local and national economy, backward linkages to other sectors of the economy, such as transportation, construction, and agriculture, also take place as tourists stimulate demand for certain goods and services. The direct revenue created by the initial spending of tourists therefore multiplies as it percolates throughout the economy and creates linkages to industries not directly related to travel and tourism.

Tourism is an important source of revenue for governments of tourist-receiving countries. Its importance is further illustrated when examining tourism's relative contribution to the GDPs of popular tourist destinations. It is commonly accepted in the field of tourism studies that when tourism contributes 5 percent or more to a national economy, it is considered a highly significant component of the economy.[37] Out of 172 countries or dependencies for which such statistics are available, over one-third (61) feature economies in which tourism contributes 5 percent or more of the total value of the economy.[38] For the world economy as a whole, the travel and tourism industry generates roughly 3 percent of total GDP. When tourism's indirect impact on economic activities is included, this figure rises to 9 percent.[39]

Many less developed countries that depend on just one or two primary commodities for the bulk of their export earnings turn to tourism as another source of national income, thereby diversifying the economy. Moreover, for economies heavily burdened by external debt, tourism provides a valuable source of foreign exchange by producing direct revenues for businesses and various levels of government. The United Nations Conference on Trade and Development points out that tourism ranks as a top three export for 19 LDCs and is the single largest source of foreign exchange earnings in seven LDCs.[40] Further, the combined tourism export earnings of all LDCs account for over 15 percent of all non-oil export receipts. Overall, tourism accounts for over one-third of all export earnings in 28 countries or dependencies, most (but not all) of which are LDCs.

The creation of employment is another economic benefit of tourism that attracts the attention of governments hoping to create sources of income for its citizens. It is estimated that roughly 77 million people work in the travel and tourism industry around the world.[41] The travel and tourism industry accounts for roughly 3 percent of total world employment. Although most employment in the travel and tourism industry is concentrated in hotels, tour operators, airlines, and travel agencies, tourists also stimulate indirect employment in other sectors that meet the needs of tourists, but that are not dependent on tourism alone. For instance, since hotels require many goods and services, including marketing, security, and catering, companies that offer these services are induced to hire workers, thereby creating more employment.

As a result of both its association with fun and pleasure and its association with the benefits discussed above, tourism is seen by the vast majority of governments, organizations, and tourists themselves as an economic panacea and "smokeless industry," providing income and employment without requiring the construction of polluting factories. This represents the liberal view of tourism as a progressive force; communities and countries take advantage of their natural or cultural comparative advantage and contribute to a positive-sum game whereby tourism provides benefits for tourists and hosts alike. The OEL perspective asserts that states should take a laissez-faire approach to tourism and allow the travel and tourism industry to develop naturally since doing so will most likely maximize the inevitable economic benefits produced by participation in international tourism. In many ways, this approach to tourism reflects the wider economic liberal assertion that globalization offers enhanced financial opportunities for poor individuals and countries.

Popular especially in the 1950s and 1960s, the economic liberal view on tourism is today still common in the marketing activities of travel and tourism businesses and government "tourist boards," as well as in promotional organizations such at the UNWTO and World Travel and Tourism Council (WTTC). Those who espouse an OEL perspective also support the General Agreement of Trade in Services, a WTO agreement that establishes rules governing trade in services, including the "Tourism and Travel-Related Services" cluster. GATS requires that members of the WTO grant foreign-owned companies free access to domestic markets in services and avoid giving preferential treatment to domestic companies over foreign-owned services firms.

In the late 1960s and early 1970s, the economic liberal approach to tourism faced serious questioning from those who challenged the wisdom of unfettered markets. At this time, critics began depicting tourism as a destructive force that promises many benefits, but in practice creates more problems than it solves. While some proponents of the critical perspective on tourism are HILs wishing to use government intervention to minimize some of the costs created by natural market activities in tourism, most are structuralists who believe that the exploitation and inequality inherent to capitalism and global economic relations poison tourism, particularly for developing countries.

Structuralists point out that the direct revenue so touted by boosters of tourism growth is offset not only by direct expenditures such as advertising but also by **revenue leakages** which result in tourism receipts being leaked out of an economy as repatriated profits to foreign-owned multinational tourism corporations. Revenue leakages are also caused by payments for imported goods and services required by the tourism industry (such as bathroom fixtures in hotels) or tourists themselves (such as luxury food items not grown locally). Most estimates of revenue leakages suggest that over half of all tourist-related spending leaks out of, or never even makes it to, destinations in the developing world.[42] Further, the majority of economic benefits associated with tourism are concentrated in the hands of the economic and political elites who have the capital and political connections to utilize the opportunities afforded by investment by tourism multinationals.

It is true that tourism creates employment, structuralists argue, but the jobs made available by tourism are low skilled, are often dangerous, and feature little room for advancement because of poor pay and few benefits. Tourism is also a notoriously fickle industry. Small changes in tourist tastes, or more significant events within the destination itself such as political instability or natural disasters, can severely damage a country's tourism industry. Coupled with the seasonal, casual, and part-time nature of much tourism in most destinations, the vulnerability of tourism to changes in demand often weakens the potential of tourism as a development strategy.

Structuralists also liken modern international tourism to neocolonialism, whereby formally independent states still suffer from unfair relationships associated with colonialism. Dependency theory links the development of the industrial, wealthy core countries of the world to the exploitation and underdevelopment of the poor, weak, and dependent former colonies in the periphery of the world system (see Chapter 4). Based on a dependency approach, structuralists point out that tourist destinations in the developing world serve as the **pleasure periphery** for core countries. For North American tourists looking for a cheap sunshine holiday, the islands of the Caribbean region serve the role of a pleasure periphery. Similarly,

Southeast Asia and the Mediterranean basin (southern Europe and North Africa) provide pleasure peripheries for Japan/Australia and Northern Europe, respectively.

Economic liberals argue that travel is directly linked to economic prosperity. In particular, affluence leads to higher levels of discretionary household income (money that is not spent on basic needs such as food, housing, clothing, etc.). As the number of individuals with discretionary income grows, demand for travel services also grows. A clear indication of the connection between economic prosperity and travel is the recent explosion in domestic and international tourism in and from China. China's rapid economic growth since the 1980s has resulted in a dramatic growth in domestic tourism, as well as a surge in outbound tourism. By 2020, China is projected to be the fourth largest source of international tourists in the world.[43] Improved infrastructure, government policies that encourage openness to the outside world, and economic growth in neighboring countries have also made China a major tourism destination. In 2007, China was the fourth most popular tourism destination in the world (55 million international arrivals), surpassed only by France (82 million), Spain (59 million), and the United States (56 million).[44] China is set to become the world's number-one tourism destination in terms of arrivals by 2020.

The global economic recession that began in 2008 threatens to curb the virtually uninterrupted growth in international travel and tourism that the world has seen since the 1950s. Just as travel always increases as societies grow more productive and wealthy, people always cut down on travel in difficult or uncertain economic times; this is especially true with long-haul international travel. As a result of the recession facing most industrialized countries, the WTO estimated in mid-2008 that international tourism would decline by 2–3 percent in 2009.[45] The impact of the financial crisis on international tourism would seem to cast doubt on the idea that tourism will inevitably continue its postwar expansion. Indeed, many destinations around the world have seen a dramatic decline in international tourism demand because of the erosion of consumer confidence. However, the consequence of the global recession on tourism illustrates not just the vulnerability of tourism to global economic and political forces but also the resiliency of tourism in the face of barriers to its growth. In particular, although discretionary, luxury items such as vacations are usually the first things to be cut by consumers in an economic downturn, international tourist arrivals nevertheless increased by 2 percent in 2008.[46] At a broader level, the questioning of market fundamentalism that the financial crisis has prompted has been largely absent in discussions of tourism: States affected by a reduction in tourism continue to hold a free-market perspective on tourism and show no signs of challenging the "more-is-better" philosophy underpinning state tourism policies.

## State Management and Promotion of Tourism

States figure prominently in the supply of tourism. The supply side of tourism includes factors that pull, or attract, tourists to a destination. In contrast to destination-based circumstances that shape supply, the demand side of tourism relates to forces generated within tourist-producing countries that push tourists to take vacations. While states in destination countries certainly strive to influence tourist demand, they are usually powerless to affect push factors in tourist-generating countries such as technological innovation, rising life expectancy, urbanization, and rising discretionary income.[47] For this reason, virtually all states, regardless of their level of wealth or dominant political system, attempt to influence the supply-side factors driving tourism. Public administration becomes crucial in this regard, because the drafting and implementation of government policies regarding tourism greatly affects the ability of a country to attract and service international tourists, as well as to curtail the negative consequences of tourism.

Though popular tourist destinations are usually positioned naturally to attract visitors because of unusual geographical landscapes or exotic cultural attributes, tourism destinations are in fact created, not born. In other words, it takes both states and markets—and specifically states acting to influence market forces—in order for a location to become attractive and accessible, let alone even known in the first place, to international tourists. One such case is Cancun, the famous sunspot destination located on the northeast coast of the Yucatan Peninsula in Mexico. In 1967, the Mexican government identified Cancun as a **growth pole,** a deliberately chosen location meant to serve as an engine of economic growth in the surrounding region. This growth pole strategy quickly transformed Cancun from a sparsely populated coconut plantation and site of small Mayan ruins into a globally renowned beach resort destination with almost half a million permanent residents, hundreds of hotels, and four million international tourist arrivals per year.

With few exceptions, governments around the world prefer policies that promote tourism growth, placing top priority on maximizing tourist arrivals and expenditures, despite the negative costs associated with hasty tourism development. States, therefore, often intervene directly in the economy to create financial, regulatory, and social environments conducive to rapid tourism growth. The exception to this growth-at-all-costs pattern is the Himalayan mountain kingdom of Bhutan, which unlike the overwhelming majority of other states, particularly those in the developing world, heavily restricts the growth of tourism through policies that exclude all but the wealthiest tourists. The Bhutanese government demands that every tourist pay daily tariffs, surcharges, and expenditures totaling a minimum of $250 per night, and issues visas only to those on expensive organized group tours. By tailoring tourism toward a wealthier clientele, Bhutanese tourism authorities are able to generate greater per-tourist revenues while at the same time limiting the social, cultural, and environmental impact of tourism in Bhutan.

For states that promote tourism, there is a risk of becoming too popular as a destination. Without state management and regulation of tourism growth, destinations tend to become loved to death by eager tourists. The very natural attractions that draw tourists in the first place often become threatened as visitors quickly exceed the destination's carrying capacity. During the 1980s, governments, tourists, and tourism businesses responded to concerns about the negative tourism impacts by shifting toward **alternative tourism,** a form of tourism that provides alternatives to mass tourism experiences based on the standard "sun, sea, and sand" formula. The most popular example of alternative tourism is **ecotourism,** defined by the International Ecotourism Society as "responsible travel to natural areas that conserves the environment and improves the well-being of local people."[48] In addition to drafting appropriate laws, and enforcing existing ones, in order to minimize the environment impact of tourism, states can promote ecotourism by restricting the number of tourists in sensitive areas. States can also create national parks and wildlife reserves that provide the locations for many ecotourism activities. Unfortunately, with rare exceptions, governments having to choose between rising tourist arrivals, and therefore profits, and environmental protection almost always pick the former.

The mercantilist approach to tourism is important when one considers other ways states limit access to travel within their borders. States determine which nationals are allowed entry and under which conditions (permissible length of stay, for example). Countries that enjoy a close relationship, usually reflected in high cross-border traffic among its citizens, allow each other's visitors to enter easily. Until 2009, Canadians wishing to visit the United States required only a valid driver's license. On the other hand, some states forbid or heavily restrict the entry of the nationals of particular countries. Several countries—including Afghanistan, Algeria, Comoros, Indonesia, Iran, Libya, Pakistan, Somalia, Saudi Arabia, and Tunisia, among others—refuse to recognize passports from Israel, thereby precluding travel to those countries by Israeli citizens. On the whole, tourist access to other countries varies widely. Citizens of Denmark, Finland, Ireland, and Portugal can enter 156 countries and territories without needing a visa, but tourists from Afghanistan, Iran, Iraq, Pakistan, and Somalia enjoy this privilege in only 25 or so countries.[49]

Perhaps the most important role played by states insofar as tourism is concerned is the management of a country's international image. Changing tastes and preferences among international tourists makes it difficult for tourism planners to predict whether a destination will remain popular in the future. Tourist demand depends heavily on prevailing perceptions of a destination. Thus, anything that alters perceptions in a negative manner carries enormous implications for the travel and tourism industry in host societies. Natural disasters, political stability, and terrorism are all examples of forces that can dramatically shift demand away from a destination. States therefore often focus a great deal of energy and resources on countering the negative impacts of such events.

Natural disasters make popular headlines in newspapers and television news reports. Despite how limited the impact may be, especially in geographical terms, the average person with no detailed knowledge of (or specialized interest in) the affected country naturally forms a negative mental association with that country and becomes much less inclined to travel there. The damage unleashed by the natural disaster is then compounded by the loss of income created by a drop in tourist demand. The Indian Ocean tsunami in December 2004 that killed over 200,000 people resulted in extensive damage to the infrastructure of several tourist-dependent economies, including the Maldives, Sri Lanka, southern Thailand, and India's Andaman and Nicobar Islands. Further, much of the tsunami footage transmitted nonstop on television screens around the world featured shots of floating tourist corpses and waves crashing into tourist hotels. The immediate drop in tourism to these regions only made things worse, as tourism revenues rendered even more necessary by the tsunami dried up overnight.

Aside from damaging media coverage of natural disasters, reports of political instability also strike fear in the hearts of potential tourists, as the cases of Kenya,

Israel, and South Africa illustrate. Of course, states that help foster political stability assist their tourism promotion efforts. However, promoting stability at the expense of human rights can also backfire, as the example of Burma (Myanmar) illustrates.

## BURMA TOURISM BOYCOTT: SHOULD YOU STAY OR SHOULD YOU GO?

To most people, travel and tourism are usually innocent affairs, devoid of any political significance. However, a vacation can be a matter of life or death to others. A prime example of the political significance of tourism and the high personal stakes involved in a person's decision to travel is provided by the case of international travel to Burma.[a] In 1988, demonstrations against the military regime of Burma ended with the massacre of thousands of students, monks, workers, and farmers. In 1990, Burma's ruling council, known as the State Law and Order Restoration Council (SLORC),[b] allowed elections in which the National League for Democracy (NLD), led by Aung San Suu Kyi, won over 80 percent of parliamentary seats. However, the military rulers of Burma prevented the NLD from assuming power. Despite being given the opportunity to leave the country at any time, Aung San Suu Kyi has instead chosen to stay in Burma to fight for democracy. As a result, the military rulers of Burma have kept her under house arrest for all but 6 years in the 20 period between 1989 and 2009.

In 1995, several British nongovernment organizations (NGOs), most notably the Burma Campaign UK and Tourism Concern, launched a campaign against tourism to Burma, arguing that guidebook publishers, tour operators, and tourists should avoid promoting tourism to, operating in, or traveling to Burma due to ongoing human rights abuses. Reports from human rights organizations confirm Burma's terrible human rights record. Amnesty International and Human Rights Watch, for example, report the use of forced labor, torture, extrajudicial execution, child labor, child soldiers, forced relocation of villages, and rape against dissidents, particularly non-Burman ethnic minorities such as the Karen.

Supporters of the Burma tourism boycott campaign give many reasons to avoid travel to Burma. First, Aung San Suu Kyi supports the boycott and has repeatedly asked tourists not to visit Burma until its political situation has improved. Second, even for those using privately owned accommodation and transportation, it is difficult to travel to Burma without providing income for the military regime. Tourist spending and investment related to tourism infrastructure, such as roads, railways, airports, and hotels, contribute directly to sustaining a military junta that threatens and uses force to suppress its own people. Third, undemocratic governments facing a question of legitimacy at home can turn to participation in the international tourism industry as a means of bolstering their legitimacy and credibility. A visit to Burma, according to critics, serves as a stamp of approval of the political status quo. Fourth, evidence from several sources, including NGOs, journalists, and the U.S. State Department, indicates that human rights abuses in Burma are directly related to official efforts to attract or service international tourists. Whether forcing residents from their homes in order to build golf courses and hotels, or using forced labor to prepare ancient temple ruins for tourist arrivals, the Burmese government frequently violates human rights in the name of tourism development. Fifth, the number of ordinary Burmese who benefit from tourism, and who are potentially harmed by a tourism boycott, is small compared to the number of people who suffer because of the continuing rule of military elites, most of whom are sustained partly by tourism revenues.

In 2000, the Burma Campaign UK and Tourism Concern called for a boycott of Lonely Planet, the largest independent guidebook publisher in the world, for its continued publication of a Burma guidebook. In spite of the bad publicity generated by the boycott of its products, Lonely Planet continues to publish its Burma guidebook. By providing a detailed discussion of both reasons to go *and* reasons to stay, the company argues that it "aims to provide independent travellers with balanced information so that they are able to reach their own informed conclusions."[c] Lonely Planet points out that tourism is among the few economic opportunities available to poor Burmese. Further, a careful traveler is able to divert spending into privately owned businesses not connected to the government. Most importantly, Lonely Planet believes that economic and political isolation only serve to bolster, rather than diminish, the power and authority of autocratic regimes.

Whether the choice is made to stay or to go, one cannot escape the political implications of the seemingly innocent act of choosing a holiday destination.

### References

[a]Burma was renamed *Myanmar* by the country's military rulers in 1989. Several countries, including Australia, Canada, the United Kingdom, and the United States, continue to use the name *Burma* in defiance of the current military regime.
[b]SLORC was renamed as the State Peace and Development Council (SPDC) in 1997.
[c]See http://www.lonelyplanet.com/help/faq_myanmar.htm.

The means by which tourists are able to travel from one country to another are also employed by individuals intending to commit acts of terrorism. In addition to combating terrorist organizations that target their citizens, states also attempt to counter the damage done by terrorism to their tourism industries. Terrorists favor tourists as targets for several reasons: some tourists travel to remote, dangerous locations that serve as the base of terrorist groups; tourists are much "softer" targets than heavily defended military or political sites; the killing of tourists generates extensive international media coverage; and terrorism disrupts economies dependent on tourism revenues, thereby helping to cripple unpopular regimes.[50] Since the late 1990s, tourists have become especially popular targets for terrorist organizations. In 1997, terrorists killed close to 60 foreign tourists at Luxor in Egypt. In 1999, 17 tourists visiting Uganda's Bwindi's National park were kidnapped (and eight later killed) by Hutu extremists from Rwanda. In 2001, Abu Sayyaf, a militant Islamic group, took 20 local and foreign tourists hostage on the island of Palawan in the Philippines. It is significant that the first people to die in the September 11, 2001, attacks on the World Trade Centers in New York and the Pentagon in Washington, DC were travelers aboard aircraft, and that jet airplanes, the most important technological innovation leading to the growth of travel and tourism, were used by the hijackers as weapons. Since September 11, 2001, terrorists have continued to carry out attacks against tourists in many countries, including Chad, Egypt, India, Indonesia, Kenya, Mali, Mauritania, Pakistan, and the Philippines.

States that experience terrorism within their borders usually react immediately to restore their international image in order to lure back tourists. The United States after September 11, 2001, stands as an exception. Because the majority of the 19 hijackers that carried out the attacks entered the United States on tourist visas, concerns were raised that freedoms given to tourists to visit the country were being abused by individuals who intended to participate in terrorist acts against Americans. As a result of domestic political pressure, the U.S. government implemented several measures aimed at better screening and monitoring of visitors to the United States: This includes, since 2004, the requirement that all visitors with a visa entering the United States at air and sea ports have fingerprints and photographs taken. Due to deteriorating global perceptions of the United States, and the more stringent entry requirements imposed by the U.S. government on visitors, the number of international tourists visiting the United States fell by 20 percent between 2000 and 2003; it took six full years after the attacks of September 11, 2001, for the number of international tourists visiting the United States to reach pre-9/11 levels.[51]

Economic liberals are quick to point out that quick action on the parts of business and government can reverse the initial losses associated with tragic events, such as natural disasters, outbreaks of disease, and acts of terrorism; the evidence seems to confirm this view. Despite suffering a 23 percent drop in tourist arrivals in the year following a devastating terrorist attack that left 161 foreign tourists dead in 2002, the island of Bali in Indonesia quickly returned to pre-bombing levels and by 2004, exceeded the number of international tourists in 2002 by 13 percent.[52] Further, following a subsequent (but far less deadly) terrorist attack in 2005, tourist arrivals in Bali initially dropped, but by 2008, arrivals had exceeded 2005 levels by 42 percent.[53] The persistent growth in global tourism praised by economic liberals is so assured, it seems, that even fear of death at the hands of terrorists is not enough to thwart our desire to travel.

## Social and Cultural Dimensions of Travel and Tourism

The structuralist and constructivist perspectives on tourism that emerged in the 1960s and 1970s called attention to the harmful consequences of tourism. Though many of these criticisms challenged the existing euphoria prevalent in studies of tourism's economic impacts, it was the social, cultural, and environmental side effects of rapid incorporation into global tourism networks that generated the most concern. Social status has long underpinned motivations for travel, from the 1840s, when Thomas Cook first took English industrial workers to seaside resort towns, to contemporary travelers who seek out locations off the beaten track as markers of superior taste and style. Social class also determines who can afford to travel in the first place.

Culture is also a crucial component of travel to many destinations for two reasons. First, throughout history, tourists have been motivated to visit cultures perceived to be exotic and unfamiliar. A desire for cultural authenticity has long characterized tourism, and some scholars have even argued that modern tourism is premised on the search for authenticity. As the global proliferation of Western material goods seemingly erases cultural differences, tourists strive to experience a level of cultural authenticity that lies beyond the superficial, and supposedly inauthentic, "front stage" where hosts perform mostly for tourist consumption. Second, despite the role played by cultural "otherness" in luring foreign tourists, the majority of international tourists visit countries with similar cultural traits, particularly in language or religion. Cultural affinity is the reason that the British are the second largest inbound tourist market in Australia, and why U.S. residents made over 13 million trips to Canada in 2007.[54] Every year, millions of people travel on religious pilgrimages, the most sizeable consisting of Muslims fulfilling their obligation to make the *hajj*, the pilgrimage to Mecca in Saudi Arabia.

Tourist demand stimulates both the rejuvenation of cultural traditions and the rehabilitation of historical architectural monuments. Funds that are collected as entry fees and donations at historical sites can be put to use on the site itself, but more importantly, the interest shown in historical sites by tourists motivates governments to allocate resources to the rehabilitation and maintenance of such sites. Without the incentives created by tourism revenues, historical sites such as Angkor Wat in Cambodia, Machu Picchu in Peru, and the ancient city of Timbuktu in Mali would likely have remained crumbling ruins, or at least would have received far less attention and funding. In many cases, governments wishing to restore an historical site for tourism or other purposes succeed in acquiring funds from the United Nations Educational, Scientific, and Cultural Organization (UNESCO), which maintains a World Heritage list of cultural and natural properties deemed essential components of global heritage.

Critics of the unregulated nature of global tourism argue that the presence of highly conspicuous tourists in local communities has two negative social and cultural costs. First, tourism is accused by critics of increasing criminal activity, especially in destinations whose residents are much poorer than the tourists visiting them. Several factors make tourists good targets of criminal activity: they are likely to mistakenly stray into unsafe areas or become lost; tourists are more likely than locals to be taken advantage of due to their lack of familiarity with local norms or procedures; a holiday mentality makes tourists more trustful and less alert; and tourists are apt to display objects of value such as money, jewelry, and cameras openly and without caution.

The second cost associated with the interaction of rich tourists and poor locals is the way in which tourism tends to have a **demonstration effect,** whereby some locals, especially youth, come to desire the material objects—and emulate the values, lifestyles, and behavior—of wealthier foreign tourists. As youth who interact with tourists adopt foreign, usually more modern, cultural values, social tension can occur between older members of the community who worry about the loss of traditional values and those who interact directly with tourists and wish to reject or modify traditional cultural practices. Aside from possibly fostering a sense of inferiority due to creating a desire for, but inability to purchase, expensive material objects possessed by tourists, the demonstration effect is especially a concern when locals interact with tourists who exhibit sexual promiscuity or the open use of drugs and alcohol.

Tourist demand for cultural artifacts and traditions perceived to be exotic transforms certain aspects of host cultures into commodities to be bought and sold. The **commodification** of culture initiated by tourism ultimately strips the original meaning and purpose from cultural objects, customs, and festivals as locals respond to commercial pressures and incentives. Critics of tourism-induced cultural commodification decry the production of "airport art," bastardized versions of traditional arts and crafts sold as cheap tourist trinkets in airports and shopping malls. Rather than being allowed to evolve naturally, according to indigenous needs, cultural performances change in substance, timing, or length in response to the entertainment demands and short attention spans of most package tourists.

Most structuralists disagree with the rosy view that tourism promotes peace, security, and tolerance. The reason is that the vast majority of tourists receive information from enormous multinational tourism companies that are concerned more with profit than accurate or balanced representations of host cultures. Though states can change perceptions abroad through their actions, governments are limited in their ability to change tourists' deep-seated cultural preconceptions because stereotypes are created or at least maintained by tour operators and travel agents that reduce complex cultures to a few recognizable, palatable nuggets for tourist consumption.

Economic liberals often argue that, yes, tourists may have inaccurate or simplistic ideas about the cultures of their hosts, but don't the interactions between tourist and host that travel permits help to foster better cross-cultural understanding? Again, structuralists would suggest that this may be possible under the right circumstances, but in practice, tourists and their hosts are positioned unequally in wealth and power, especially when tourists from wealthy countries visit destinations in developing countries. Tourism is a service industry and thus demands a certain level of servility. Since tourism centers on pleasure and recreation, there is even greater pressure for employees to ensure that the customer is satisfied. Moreover, tourists tend to travel in an "environmental bubble" where encounters with locals outside the tourism industry are rare, fleeting, and predictable. Instead of challenging servile and demeaning views of their people, states and local tour operators often perpetuate the problem by reassuring tourists in brochures and other advertisements that locals will cater to their every whim.

The most visible social cost of tourism in many destinations is prostitution. Several factors help to explain the connection between tourism and prostitution. People on vacation tend to spend money much less cautiously than when at home. A holiday frame of mind, characterized by inversions of normal routines and patterns of behavior, also encourages some tourists to engage in activities, such as paying for sex, that are normally avoided at home. Irregular patterns of spending and behavior, combined with the spatial concentration of tourists in conspicuous locations of consumption and hedonism, create a market for local sexual services. It is therefore no surprise that in virtually all popular destinations, especially in poor countries, sex is easily available for purchase by tourists. Even in strictly controlled societies such as Cuba, the sex trade is supported partly by certain segments of tourists.

The most insidious side of the tourism-prostitution relationship is the sexual exploitation of children by tourists. Though some tourists who purchase the sexual services of locals may be unaware of the young age of the sex worker, most tourists who engage in such activities with minors are fully aware of what they are doing. A lack of alternative means of survival, sexual abuse, and the collusion of corrupt government officials and police officers help to sustain this trade. In response to the moral condemnation generated by images of tall male Western foreigners walking hand in hand with young Cambodian, Costa Rican, or South African girls (or boys), countries such as the United States, Australia, and New Zealand have passed laws that allow them to prosecute citizens who travel abroad to purchase sex from minors. Though progress is slow, governments of sex tourism destinations are also starting to take greater action, the most notable example being the 2005 arrest and imprisonment in Vietnam of British rock star Gary Glitter on charges of committing obscene acts with children.

In sum, to those who are fortunate enough to afford it, travel is an escape from the routines of everyday life, but tourism should, in addition to providing pleasure, receive serious academic and policy consideration due to its widespread and growing global significance. Tourism is fundamentally an IPE issue, with political, economic, social, cultural, and environmental implications. Patterns and trends in the global travel and tourism industry closely mirror, and in some cases magnify, such features of the world system as global integration, inequality, and the clash between traditional and modern culture. In short, tourism is the perfect embodiment of the interconnections, tensions, and benefits associated with globalization.

## CONCLUSION

Migration and tourism represent two of the most significant forms of contemporary human flows, each with important consequences for IPE. These forms of movement are shaped by different motives, ranging from the migrant's drive for economic gain, the refugee's flight from persecution, and the tourist's desire for recreation and exploration. Each also denotes different temporalities, such that while a tourist's travels are temporary, a migrant's sojourns may extend out for several years or even a lifetime. For all their differences, however, the two phenomena are related. It is no coincidence that poor laborers often leave the very places that wealthy Northern tourists seek out as exotic tourist escapes, while the migrants seek jobs in the industrialized countries that wealthy tourists flee in search of recreation. Therefore, global flows crystallize many of the inequalities inherent in globalization. Both forms of movement are structured by national security considerations, global markets, emerging technologies, and capital flows. Consequently, they draw our attention to the changing sources of labor and resources in a shifting landscape of production

and distribution. Both have the potential to serve as powerful sources of economic development, yet they also demand new strategies for governance that can facilitate economic flows and protect vulnerable constituencies across borders. Taken together, both provide us with a clear sense of how human flows intersect with IPE structures to create new opportunities and challenges for a variety of international actors.

IPE theories are useful for making sense of the stakes of these global human flows. Economic liberals might see merit in the unfettered movement of both migrants and tourists across the globe because of the important roles that they play in the global marketplace and for the freedoms that their movement embodies. Structuralists, on the other hand, often criticize both of these forms of human movement because of the way they reflect and reproduce global economic inequalities. Mercantilists would evaluate the impact of migration and tourism in relation to the state's political economic interests. In either case, highlighting the interaction between human flows and political economic forces allows us to discern how the same global connections that bring economic prosperity can also be tenuous and potentially unsustainable forces for long-term economic development. More importantly still, they allow us to appreciate the implications of these flows not just for states and international institutions, but for the very people who are on the move in this age of uncertainty.

## KEY TERMS

migration   407
internal migration   408
transnational migration   408
immigration   409
circular migration   409
chain migration   410
guest worker   410
brain drain   412

remittances   412
irregular migrants   414
citizenship   414
settler states   414
refugees   415
asylum   415
assimilation   415
diaspora   415

cultural citizenship   416
revenue leakages   422
pleasure periphery   422
growth pole   424
alternative tourism   424
ecotourism   424
demonstration effect   429
commodification   429

## DISCUSSION QUESTIONS

1. What is the difference between a migrant and an immigrant? Under what circumstances is that distinction useful?
2. What trade-offs are involved in "mainstreaming migration" as a national development strategy? Explore the different stakes of such a strategy for countries such as the Philippines, Senegal, India, or El Salvador.
3. Compare a female Cambodian refugee living in Wisconsin with a male irregular migrant from the Dominican Republic living in New York City. What similarities and differences might characterize their (a) reasons for coming to the United States, (b) their

economic opportunities within the United States, and (c) their experience of cultural citizenship within the United States?
4. What makes tourism an attractive option for the state? How does tourism create risks for the state? Why is it necessary for destination states to be concerned about making tourism environmentally sustainable?
5. What are the rewards and risks of tourism according to liberals, mercantilists, and structuralists?
6. What are the political, economic, and social trade-offs associated with tourism?

## SUGGESTED READINGS

### Migration

David Fitzgerald. *A Nation of Emigrants: How Mexico Manages its Migration.* Berkeley and London: University of California Press, 2009.

Ruben Martinez. *The New Americans: Seven Families Journey to Another Country.* New York: The New Press, 2004.

Caroline Brettell and James Hollifield, eds. *Migration Theory: Talking Across the Disciplines.* New York: Routledge, 2000.

Stephen Castles and Alistair Davidson. *Citizenship and Migration: Globalization and the Politics of Belonging.* New York: Routledge, 2000.

Monica DeHart. *Ethnic Entrepreneurs: Identity and Development Politics in Latin America.* Stanford, CA: Stanford University Press, 2010.

### Tourism

Sharon Gmelch. *Tourists and Tourism: A Reader.* Long Grove, IL: Waveland Press, 2004.

Alister Mathieson and Geoffrey Wall. *Tourism: Change, Impacts, and Opportunities.* Harlow, England: Pearson Prentice Hall, 2006.

Martin Mowforth and Ian Munt. *Tourism and Sustainability: Development and New Tourism in the Third World,* 3rd ed. London: Routledge, 2009.

Richard Sharpley. *Tourism, Tourists and Society,* 4th ed. Huntingdon, UK: ELM Publications, 2008.

David Weaver and Laura Lawton. *Tourism Management,* 3rd ed. Milton, Australia: John Wiley, 2006.

# NOTES

1. Nick Kontogeorgopoulos and Monica DeHart are the authors of this chapter.

2. United Nations, *International Migration and Development: Report by the Secretary General* (New York: United Nations, 2006), p. 12.

3. Giovanni Gozzini, "The Global System of International Migrations 1900 and 2000: A Comparative Approach," *Journal of Global History, 1*, no. 3, pp. 321–341.

4. United Nations, *International Migration and Development.*

5. Ibid.

6. T. Painter, S. Dusseini, S. Kaapo, and C. McKaig, "Seasonal Migration and the Spread of AIDS in Mali and Niger," International AIDS Conference, Amsterdam, 1992, 8:D425, www.aegis.com/conferences/iac/1992/PoD5228.html.

7. Nicole Constable, *Maid in Hong Kong* (Ithaca, NY: Cornell University Press, 1997). Also see Sze Lai-Shan, "New Immigrant Labor from Mainland China in Hong Kong," *Asian Labor Update*, no. 53 (October–December 2004), http://www.amrc.org.hk/alu_article/discrimination_at_work/new_immigrant_labour_from_mainland_china_in_hong_kong.

8. Roger Rouse, "Mexican Migration and the Space of Postmodernism," *Diaspora, 1* (1991), pp. 8–23.

9. Jeffrey Fleischman, "Europe in Immigration Quandry," *The Seattle Times*, June 7, 2006, p. A3. Also see Edward Alden, Daniel Dombey, Chris Giles, and Sarah Laitner, "The Price of Prosperity: Why Fortress Europe Needs to Lower the Drawbridge," *Financial Times*, May 18, 2006, p. 13.

10. Steven Greenhouse and Michael Barbaro, "The Ugly Side of Free Trade," *The New York Times*, May 3, 2006, p. C1.

11. See the standards set forth by the ILO's International Migration Programme at http://www.ilo.org/public/english/protection/migrant/areas/standards.htm.

12. United Nations General Assembly (2008), "International Migration and Development: Report of the Secretary General," Sixty-third session. At http://www.unhcr.org/refworld/docid/48e0deca2.html.

13. Ibid., p.17.

14. Celia Dugger, "U.S. Plan to Lure Nurses May Hurt Poor Nations," *The New York Times*, May 24, 2006, p. A1.

15. United Nations, *International Migration and Development*, p. 54.

16. See Ernesto Lopez-Cordova and Alexandra Olmedo, "International Remittances and Development: Existing Evidence, Policies and Recommendations," Paper prepared for the G-20 Workshop on Demographic Challenges and Migration, August 27–28, 2005, in Sydney, Australia, available online at http://www.iabd.org.

17. Manuel Orozco, "Mexican Hometown Associations and Development Opportunities," *Journal of International Affairs, 57* (Spring 2004), pp. 33–34.

18. H. E. Sheikha Haya Rashed Khalifa, "Closing Statement by the President of the 61st Session of the General Assembly," High-Level Dialogue on Migration and Development, United Nations, September 14–15, 2006, at http://www.un.org/migration/gapres-speech.html.

19. Barta, Patrick and Joel Millman, "The Great U-Turn," *The Wall Street Journal* (Eastern Edition) New York, June 6, 2009, p. A-1.

20. Bank of Mexico (2009), "Las remesas familiares en 2008," http://www.banxico.org.mx/AplBusquedasBM2/busqwww2.jsp?_action=search.

21. M. K. Anwar, "Brunei Immigration Enforcers Launch 'Ops Berkas,'" *Borneo Bulletin, Financial Times* Information Limited—Asia Intelligence Wire, January 6, 2006. At http://www.brudirect.com/DailyInfo/News/Archive/Jan06/060106/nite05.htm.

22. "EU Thumbs-Up for Polish Plumber." BBC World News. Tuesday, November 28, 2008. At http://news.bbc.co.uk/2/hi/uk_news/7735603.stm.

23. United Nations, *International Migration and Development*, p. 42.

24. United Nations Refugee Agency (UNHCR) (2008) "First Half Asylum Statistics for Industrialized Countries," at http://www.unhcr.org/cgi-bin/texis/vtx/search?page=search&docid=48f742792&query=First%20Half%20Asylum%20Statistics%20for%20Industrialized%20Countries.

25. United Nations Refugee Agency. "2008 Global Trends: Refugees, Asylum-seekers, Returnees, Internally Displaced and Stateless Persons." Country Data Sheets. June 16, 2009. At http://www.unhcr.org/4a375c426.html.

26. Rachel Swarns, "Study Finds Disparities in Judges' Asylum Rulings," *The New York Times*, July 31, 2006, p. A15.

27. Glick-Schiller, Nina and Georges Fouron, *Georges Woke Up Laughing* (Durham, NC: Duke University Press, 2001).

28. Craig Smith, "France Faces a Colonial Legacy: What Makes Someone French," *The New York Times,* November 11, 2005, p. A1.

29. See Aihwa Ong, *Buddha is Hiding: Refugees, Citizenship, and the New America* (Berkeley: University of California Press, 2003). Also see Karen Sacks, "How Did Jews Become White Folks?" in Steven Gregory and Roger Sanjek, eds., *Race* (New Brunsick, NJ: Rutgers University Press, 1994), pp.78–102.

30. June Kronholtz, "Politics & Economics: Immigration Costs Move to the Fore; Differing Estimates Open New Battleground Over Senate Bill," *The Wall Street Journal,* May 24, 2006, p. A4. See also Edurdo Porter, "Illegal Immigrants Are Bolstering Social Security with Billions," *The New York Times,* April 5, 2005, p. A1.

31. Ibid.

32. Diego Cevallos, "U.S.-Mexico: 'We'll Do it Ourselves' Say Immigration Vigilantes," Inter Press Service, June 14, 2006.

33. See, for example, Mark Rice-Oxley and James Brandon, in "Britain, Far-Right Push Threatens Tony Blair," *The Christian Science Monitor,* May 6, 2004, p. 1; "World Briefing Europe: The Netherlands: Government Resigns," *The New York Times,* July 1, 2006, p. A6; Peter Keifer and Elisabetta Povoledo, "Illegal Immigrants Become the Focus of Election Campaign in Italy," *The New York Times,* March 28, 2005, p. A8.

34. Alden et al., "The Price of Prosperity."

35. UNWTO, *UNWTO World Tourism Barometer,* June 2009, p.3. At http://www.unwto.org/facts/eng/pdf/barometer/UNWTO_Barom09_2_en_excerpt.pdf.

36. Ibid.

37. David Weaver and Laura Lawton, *Tourism Management,* 2nd ed. (Milton, Australia: John Wiley, 2002), p. 245.

38. Ibid., pp. 417–425. Dependencies are territories that lack formal independence, but which in some cases enjoy limited sovereignty (for example, the British "overseas territories" of Bermuda and British Virgin Islands, or the French "overseas departments" of Martinique and Réunion).

39. World Travel and Tourism Council (WTTC), *Executive Summary: Travel and Tourism Economic Impact—Executive Summary* (London, WTTC, 2009), pp. 3–4. At http://www.wttc.org/bin/pdf/original_pdf_file/exec_summary_2009.pdf.

40. United Nations Conference of Trade and Development (UNCTAD), *Information Economy Report 2005* (Geneva: United Nations, 2005), pp. 161 and 182. The seven LDCs in which tourism is the largest source of foreign exchange earnings are Comoros, Gambia, Maldives, Samoa, Tuvalu, Tanzania, and Vanuatu.

41. WTTC, *Executive Summary,* p. 4.

42. Martin Mowforth and Ian Munt, *Tourism and Sustainability: Development and New Tourism in the Third World,* 3rd ed. (London: Routledge, 2009), p. 186.

43. Weaver and Lawton, *Tourism Management,* p. 90.

44. UNWTO, *Tourism Highlights 2008* (Madrid: UNWTO, 2009), p. 5. At http://www.unwto.org/facts/menu.html.

45. UNWTO, "World Tourism in the Face of the Global Economic Crisis," Press Release, 5/12/09. http://www.unwto.org/media/news/en/press_det.php?id=4181&idioma=E.

46. UNWTO, *UNWTO World Tourism Barometer,* p. 3.

47. See Weaver and Lawton, *Tourism Management,* pp. 70–82.

48. The International Ecotourism Society, "What is Ecotourism," At http://www.ecotourism.org/site/c.orLQKXPCLmF/b.4835303/k.BEB9/What_is_Ecotourism__The_International_Ecotourism_Society.htm.

49. Henley and Partners (an international consulting firm) has complied a Visa Restriction Index, which ranks countries according to the freedom of international travel that their citizens enjoy. See http://www.henleyglobal.com/visa_restrictions.htm.

50. Weaver and Lawton, *Tourism Management,* p. 104.

51. U.S. Department of Commerce, International Trade Administration, "International Visitation to the United States: A Statistical Summary of U.S. Arrivals (2008)." At http://tinet.ita.doc.gov/outreachpages/download_data_table/2008_Visitation_Report.pdf.

52. Bali Tourism Authority, *Direct Foreign Tourist Arrivals to Bali by Nationality by Month in 2005*. At http://bali-tourism-board.com/files/By-nationality-2001-2005.pdf.

53. Bali Tourism Authority, *Direct Foreign Tourist Arrivals to Bali by Nationality in 2004–2008*. At http://baliprov.go.id/assets/statistikpariwisata/statistik5.pdf.

54. Canadian Tourism Commission, "2007 Facts & Figures Year Review." At http://www.corporate.canada.travel/docs/research_and_statistics/stats_and_figures/snapshot_YearInReview_2007_eng.pdf.

# Transnational Corporations: The Governance of Foreign Investment[1]

Workshop of the World.

Jacob Silberberg

One of the distinctive features of the twenty-first century is the central role played by transnational corporations (TNCs) in IPE. The international production and trade, monetary and finance, security, and knowledge and technology structures are all greatly affected by TNCs. TNCs compete in regional and global markets and engage in foreign direct investment (FDI), which is much sought after by national governments seeking jobs, technology, and the resources for economic growth. TNCs have always been controversial because of the power they seem to possess and because their "global reach" makes them difficult for nation-states to regulate or control. Perceptions of TNCs have evolved as IPE has changed over the past sixty years. TNCs have been perceived as agents of capitalist imperialism, tools of U.S. hegemony, and state-level actors engaged in "triangular diplomacy" with states and other TNCs. With the rise of China, India, and Brazil as important economic powers and homes of fast-growing TNCs, new perceptions of TNCs may emerge. While the importance of TNCs to IPE analysis remains clear, much about their future nature and impact is still uncertain.

This chapter looks at the contemporary pattern of TNC investment and answers a number of important questions: What exactly are TNCs? Where do they operate and why? How much power do they have? And to what extent can their activities and interactions with nation-states and workers be regulated by formal global regimes? Finally, we also consider how increased global competition and the recent severe economic crisis that began in late 2007 might impact the **foreign direct investment (FDI)**, TNC operations, and the globalization juggernaut.

The main points this chapter makes are as follows: First, TNCs are critical actors in the international political economy because they operate in markets that span national borders and often transfer badly needed resources and know-how to countries pursuing economic growth and development. Second, these corporations engage in FDI for a variety of reasons: to exploit a competitive advantage they may have; to gain access to cheaper labor or to natural resources; to circumvent trade barriers or currency instability; to be close to their customers; and to respond to the strategic moves of other TNCs. Third, FDI has grown dramatically over the last sixty years, fueled by technological changes facilitating international transportation and communication and the spread of economic liberalism across the globe.

Fourth, for much of the post–World War II period, the great bulk of FDI was done by rich, northern countries in other rich, northern countries. Today things are changing, as what are known as the BRIC countries (Brazil, Russia, India, and China) have become significant homes and hosts of FDI. Many are concerned about the impact TNCs from BRIC and other developing countries may have on economic competition and political relations among states. Fifth, many TNCs are powerful enough to engage in negotiations with states and can from time to time win such favorable concessions that from a structuralist perspective they can be seen as neo-imperialist exploiters. Finally, there are signs that a new kind of TNC is emerging, one that is more networked and globally integrated with complex supply chains.

## WHAT ARE TNCs?

Before we begin, however, we must deal briefly with terminology. Businesses that compete in global markets have been given different names at different times and in different fields of study. Once they were called simply *international businesses*, to distinguish them from firms that operated in local or national markets. For many years the term **multinational corporation (MNC)** was applied to indicate that the firm operated in several different national markets. As global markets and production structures have emerged, the accepted term has become **transnational corporation (TNC)**. The prefix *trans* means *to go beyond*, and the markets where these businesses compete are regional, as in NAFTA or the European Union, or global and clearly go beyond or transcend national markets.

You might not have encountered the term *transnational corporation* before, but you certainly are familiar with the businesses that wear that label, the items they produce and sell, and the markets where they live. It is estimated that there are about 79,000 TNCs in the world today with 790,000 foreign affiliates. Together they employ about 82 million workers. Table 17-1 displays a list of the 20 largest nonfinancial TNCs in 2006, as compiled by the United Nations Conference on Trade and Development (UNCTAD), ranked according to foreign assets owned. (Rankings of TNCs vary according to year and whether the list is based on assets, revenues, or profits. The seating order varies, but the names for the most part remain the same, though notice that General Motors, number 4 in the previous edition, is no longer on the list.)

## TABLE 17-1

### Twenty Largest Nonfinancial Transnational Corporations in 2006, Ranked by Foreign Assets

| Rank | TNC | Headquarters Country | Market |
|------|-----|----------------------|--------|
| 1. | General Electric | United States | Electrical and electronic equipment |
| 2. | British Petroleum | United Kingdom | Petroleum |
| 3. | Toyota Motor Corporation | Japan | Motor vehicles |
| 4. | Royal Dutch/Shell Group | United Kingdom/Netherlands | Petroleum |
| 5. | ExxonMobil Corporation | United States | Petroleum |
| 6. | Ford Motor Company | United States | Motor vehicles |
| 7. | Vodafone Group | United Kingdom | Telecommunications |
| 8. | Total | France | Petroleum |
| 9. | Electricite De France | France | Electricity, gas, water |
| 10. | WalMart Stores | United States | Retail |
| 11. | Telefonica SA | Spain | Telecommunications |
| 12. | E.ON | Germany | Electricity, gas, water |
| 13. | Deutsche Telekom A.G. | Germany | Telecommunications |
| 14. | Volkswagen Group | Germany | Motor vehicles |
| 15. | France Telecom | France | Telecommunications |
| 16. | ConocoPhillips | United States | Petroleum |
| 17. | Chevron Corporation | United States | Petroleum |
| 18. | Honda Motor Co Ltd. | Japan | Motor vehicles |
| 19. | Suez | France | Electricity, gas, water |
| 20. | Siemens AG | Germany | Electrical & electronic equipment |

*Source:* United National Conference on Trade and Development (UNCTAD), *World Investment Report 2008.*

# TRANSNATIONAL CORPORATIONS IN PERSPECTIVE

TNCs are constantly in the news, but they are anything but new themselves. TNCs have existed for hundreds of years; some of the earliest TNCs were state-chartered organizations such as the East India Company, which was granted a monopoly of trade with the East Indies by Queen Elizabeth I in 1600. These firms neatly combined visions of a business empire with the imperial territorial ambitions of the home states.

(TNCs today are private business firms that compete in transnational, regional, and global markets) They are distinguished by the FDI that they undertake as part and parcel of their operations. TNCs operate in markets that span national borders and so necessarily make investments in production, research, distribution, and marketing facilities abroad, often transferring technology abroad in the process. FDI is extremely important to countries seeking resources for economic growth, which amounts basically to all countries. The fact that TNCs are the institutions that allocate FDI resources makes them critical actors in IPE.

It is tempting but dangerous to generalize about what the 79,000 TNCs are and how they behave, beyond saying, as we have here, that they are creatures of transnational markets that have command of valuable FDI resources. A certain stereotyped image of TNCs has been formed in the press and elsewhere, however, and it is important to take a close look at it. Stereotypes are usually distortions based on a few exceptional cases, and this is true of TNCs as well. Here are some "facts" commonly associated with TNCs. They are as follows:

- gigantic business organizations that dominate production, investment, and employment worldwide. They control global markets.
- invest in less developed countries to exploit their cheap labor and natural resources. TNCs gain and the countries of the South lose as natural resources and cheap labor-intensive commodities are traded for manufactured goods produced in the North.
- are so large that they dwarf all but a few states. They are the most powerful actors in the world today.

Let us look at these stereotypes to see how well they explain the actual pattern of TNC activities today.

## How Large are TNCs?

Some TNCs are *very* large, but in general, TNCs come in different sizes and compete in markets of different scales. For example, the U.S.-based company General Electric, the largest TNC in the UNCTAD ratings for 2006, owned $442 billion in foreign assets. By comparison, the firm ranked 25th, Proctor & Gamble of the United States, had foreign assets of just $64 billion. Statoil Asa of Norway, the 100th ranked TNC, had foreign assets of $18 billion. If we were to continue down the list through the nearly 79,000 other TNCs, we would come to some very small firms indeed. These businesses might be TNCs, and they might even be quite large compared to the typical firm competing in a local market, but they are of an altogether different scale from the "giants."

When we talk about giant TNCs, then, we are really talking about the largest 100 or 200 firms, not about TNCs generally. These business organizations are very large, as has been said before, because the markets they compete in are very large and often require huge investments—markets such as electronics and electrical equipment (including computers), oil and gas, telecommunications, motor vehicles and parts, food and beverages, and pharmaceuticals.

There are several ways to measure the relative size of TNCs, and it is useful to look at several of them to get a better perspective on the competitive landscape. UNCTAD lists TNCs according to the value of their foreign assets, a good approach because it stresses the effect of FDI. Large firms that do not invest abroad and therefore do not own foreign assets would not appear on this list at all. The *Financial Times*, the distinctive pink-toned British newspaper, publishes a Global 500 listing based on the total value of company shares on world stock markets. Firms need not be TNCs to appear on this list, since rankings are based on share value, not FDI, but in practice many of them are. Table 17-2 lists the top fifteen firms from the *Financial Times* list. As you might imagine, the financial crisis caused a 42 percent drop in the market value of these 500 companies from 2008 to 2009. Oil producers overtook banks to become the top two companies. In 2003 there were no Chinese companies in the *Financial Times'* top fifteen, but by 2009 there were four (including Hong Kong), a clear indication of China's rising power and ability to weather the financial crisis relatively well.

Microsoft, the sixth most valuable firm in the *Financial Times* Global 500, competes in a global market and is a technology leader, but it does not in fact engage in a great deal of foreign investment, so it does not even appear among the top 100 firms in the UNCTAD rankings. Microsoft does not invest abroad so much as it forms partnerships and alliances with foreign firms. This is a fundamentally different strategy from FDI.

Wal-Mart Stores is a big firm (by market value) and also a major foreign investor (number 10 on the UNCTAD list), but it is perhaps most noteworthy because of its large global workforce, estimated at about 2.1 million workers in 2009. Many TNCs, however, do not employ as many workers as one might suppose given their economic scale. They are more important for the technology they can supply (Microsoft) or the FDI they can provide (Exxon Mobil) than for the absolute number of jobs they can create.

In conclusion, the largest TNCs are very large indeed, but not all TNCs are huge business operations. Many of the world's largest businesses do not engage in substantial amounts of FDI and do not, therefore, rank among the leading TNCs. The key aspect of TNCs to keep in mind is not their size, which varies, but their ability to provide FDI.

## The Recent Rise of TNCs

If you imagine that TNCs have become more pervasive in recent years, you are correct. According to UNCTAD, the total amount of inward FDI flows increased dramatically from an average of about $225 billion worldwide in the period 1990–1995 to nearly $1.8 trillion in 2007 (FDI decreased after 2001,

## TABLE 17-2

**Largest Global Companies by Market Value, 2009**

| Company/Market | Country | Market Value ($ Billion) | Employment Total |
|---|---|---|---|
| 1. Exxon Mobil: oil and gas | United States | 337 | 79,900 |
| 2. PetroChina: oil and gas | China | 287 | 477,800 |
| 3. Wal-Mart Stores: general retailers | United States | 204 | 2,100,000 |
| 4. Industrial and Commercial Bank of China: banking | China | 188 | 385,600 |
| 5. China Mobile: telecommunications | | 175 | 138,400 |
| 6. Microsoft: software and computer services | United States | 163 | 91,000 |
| 7. AT&T: telecommunications | United States | 149 | 302,700 |
| 8. Johnson & Johnson: pharmaceuticals | United States | 145 | 118,700 |
| 9. Royal Dutch Shell: oil and gas | United Kingdom | 139 | 102,000 |
| 10. Procter & Gamble: household goods | United States | 138 | 138,000 |
| 11. Chevron: oil and gas | United States | 135 | 67,700 |
| 12. Berkshire Hathaway: nonlife insurance | United States | 134 | 246,000 |
| 13. China Construction Bank: banking | China | 133 | 298,600 |
| 14. IBM: software and computer services | United States | 130 | 398,500 |
| 15. Nestlé | Switzerland | 130 | 283,000 |

*Source: Financial Times*, Global 500 2009, May 29, 2009.

however, falling to $648 billion in 2003 due to a number of factors including economic recession and falling stock markets). This rise in TNC investment reflects the growth of transnational markets, both regional, as in the EU and NAFTA, and global. UNCTAD identifies three forces driving this transnational market growth: policy liberalization, technological change, and increasing competition.

More and more countries have sought to attract FDI inflows to create jobs and encourage economic development. Since the early 1980s many LDC governments have adopted the "Washington Consensus" policies, for example, which facilitate open trade and free capital mobility. These policies create an environment more conducive to TNC investment. Countries that enter the main regional economic groups—NAFTA and the EU—adopt especially liberal trade and investment rules. China's entry into the World Trade Organization accelerated inward FDI flow. Countries such as India and Japan that have been slow to abandon mercantilist policies are disadvantaged in the competition for FDI resources, though that seems to be changing with India. FDI is still controversial, but virtually all nations now actively seek FDI resources to advance their economic agendas.

Technological change has also encouraged FDI by reducing transportation and communication costs. Taken together, technological change and policy liberalization have expanded the domain of transnational markets relative to markets that are mainly domestic. This means that firms in these markets face greater competition than ever before. Competition for new markets, to gain technological advantages, or to find cheaper production processes, further accelerates the FDI process. Unlike the first TNCs, which benefited from monopoly power, most TNCs today are driven to invest abroad by the competitive environment found in transnational markets, the policy liberalization that encourages that competition, and the technological changes that make foreign investment more efficient.

## The Pattern of TNC Operations

Many people imagine that most TNCs are North-based businesses that have shifted production to the less developed South to take advantage of cheap labor or natural resources, but the facts do not support this conclusion. Most TNC investment is in fact North–North rather than North–South, and there is even an emerging pattern of some South–North TNC activity as firms from developing countries enter global markets and acquire foreign business assets. Four TNCs on UNCTAD's top 100 list are headquartered in newly industrialized countries: Hutchinson Whampoa (diversified businesses, Hong Kong), Petronas (oil and gas, Malaysia), Singtel Ltd. (telecommunications, Singapore), and Samsung Electronics (electronics, South Korea).

If we look at where FDI originates (by headquarters countries of TNCs), we find that the industrialized North dominates, as expected. Over 85 percent of global FDI flowed out of the developed countries, according to UNCTAD, with the member states of the EU (combined total of nearly 68 percent), the United States (19 percent), Japan (4 percent), and Switzerland (4 percent) at the head of the table. No surprises here!

But whereas many people imagine that TNCs mainly invest in low-wage developing countries, in fact the majority of FDI flows goes into the high-wage North because this is where the transnational markets are and because North countries have advanced technology and skilled workers whose high wages are matched by their high productivity. Of a total of $1.8 trillion of FDI inflows in 2007, for example, $1.2 trillion (about 68 percent) went to countries of the industrial North, led by the member states of the EU ($804 billion or 43 percent of total FDI inflows). Of the remainder, $237 billion (almost 13 percent) was invested in the United States by non–U.S. TNCs.

A great deal of FDI is regionally based, flowing out of countries in the EU into other EU countries and out of countries in NAFTA and into other NAFTA countries. This makes sense because TNCs tend to evolve and expand to compete in particular markets. While markets for some commodities are truly global, especially petroleum and some primary products, much recent market growth has been regional, driven by the EU and NAFTA expansion. The EU and NAFTA combined accounted for over 63 percent of all inward FDI in 2007.

About $500 billion (about 27 percent) of FDI went to a group of countries that UNCTAD calls "developing countries," which excludes oil exporting countries and the "least developed countries." Asian countries received almost $250 billion c FDI in 2007, with China ($84 billion) and Hong Kong ($60 billion), also now pa of China, getting the lion's share. Two giant Asian economies, which until recently had domestic regulatory regimes that were perceived to be biased against foreign investment, were now seeing rapid growth in inward FDI, with India and Japan each receiving $23 billion.

Latin America and the Caribbean received $126 billion of FDI in 2007, with Brazil ($35 billion) and Mexico ($25 billion) at the head of the pack. African nations tend to attract very little FDI, a total of just $53 billion in 2007, with few nations attracting FDI of more than a few hundred million dollars. For the most part Africa is essentially ignored by TNCs because these countries do not have large markets, because they lack skilled labor, or because political or social instability makes them an undesirable investment target.

Most "global" businesses are not really global at all, it seems, but instead channel investment to particular regional markets, leaving out large parts of the world's population, especially in Africa. But perhaps in a sign that the North–North pattern may be changing, a survey of 3,000 TNCs by UNCTAD in 2008 found that China, India, United States, Russia, Brazil, and Vietnam, in that order, were seen as the most attractive locations for future FDI.

## What Determines Where TNCs Invest?

The stereotype that TNCs only invest where labor and natural resources are cheap is clearly not a good general explanation of TNC behavior, although it does apply to some specific situations. A great deal of FDI goes from rich, high-wage countries such as Germany to other rich, high-wage countries such as the United States. And, in any case, the theory that TNCs go where labor is cheap is at best an incomplete theory since labor is cheap in many parts of the world—so why do TNCs invest here (China) instead of there (Kenya) since wages are low in both places? The question of why TNCs invest where they do is thus a very interesting one. Since there are thousands of TNCs in the world, it is unlikely that a single theory can explain all of their behavior. Here are several explanations that attempt to account for different aspects of TNC behavior.

## Product Cycle Theory

Why do TNCs invest abroad, especially in other high-wage countries, when they face so many obvious disadvantages in doing so? A U.S. company setting up operations in France, for example, must deal with different laws and regulations, different labor practices and union restrictions, a different language and culture, and a variety of other difficulties. It would seem that a French firm that is already equipped with this "local knowledge" would have a distinct competitive advantage. Why not simply reach an agreement to have the French firm produce and sell the product under license?

TNCs do not make much sense in highly competitive markets with standardized products and technology, where everyone has equal access to resources and decisions are made on the basis of cost or price alone. In markets like these, the disadvantages of operating abroad would doom any foreign firm. TNCs make sense, however, if they possess some particular knowledge or advantage that compensates for other disadvantages. Raymond Vernon's ***product cycle theory*** provides one explanation for TNC investment behavior.

Vernon was particularly interested in TNCs that produced technologically sophisticated products, where a firm might possess a technological advantage over competitors, and in the surprisingly common phenomenon of trade reversals, where the country that invents a product sometimes finds itself a few years later importing that same item from abroad. His three-stage product cycle theory explains how this can happen and how TNCs are created in the process.

In the first stage of the product cycle, a firm in a high-income country identifies a need that can be satisfied with a technologically sophisticated product. For example, the modern mobile phone satisfies the needs of people who want to remain in communication in many locations. Countries like the United States, Japan, and the EU have the technology resources to address this sort of need and the income to pay for the products, which are often very expensive in the early stages. In the first stage, therefore, companies like Motorola (United States) or Nokia (Finland) invest millions of dollars in product development and production to develop products to satisfy a home-country need.

Once the product has been developed and a market created at home, it is possible to export to other countries where consumers or businesses may have similar incomes and living standards. In the second stage, therefore, mobile phones may be exported to other high-income areas of Asia, Europe, and North America. The firms become multinational or transnational in this stage, according to Vernon's theory, as they establish sales offices and some production or distribution facilities abroad. Some of the North–North FDI that was discussed earlier occurs in stage 2. Finally, the technology has become standardized to the point where the product may be produced more efficiently in a newly industrialized country such as Mexico or Malaysia. At this point production moves abroad and the TNC makes another foreign investment.

Note that technology and market factors are important elements of the product cycle explanation of TNC behavior. Products are invented and developed where technology is abundant and incomes are high. The market expands to other high-income countries once the product has been developed, and FDI follows as firms rush to compete in the bigger market. Finally, when the technology matures, production becomes transnational via FDI flows.

## Appropriability Theory

Developed by Richard Caves and others, **appropriability theory** helps explain why Vernon's product cycle firms invest abroad rather than licensing production to a local firm or taking on a local partner. The appropriability theory argues that some firms become TNCs because they have too much to lose if they enter into partnerships or licensing agreements with foreign firms, which might in fact appear more profitable in terms of a simple dollars-and-cents calculation. This is especially true if the firm has some specific "intangible asset" such as a valuable trademark or copyright, or has invested in new technology, a proprietary process (such as Coca-Cola's secret formula for its products), or efficient management techniques found in some Japanese firms.

The fear is that these advantages or technological innovations will be stolen, copied, or otherwise "appropriated" by the competition if the firm does not retain full control over them. If the firm gives up control of foreign production, distribution, or sales, it risks losing control of its key competitive advantage. The foreign partner or licensee might copy the product and sell pirated versions, for example, or learn how to manufacture the product itself and go into competition with the originating firm.

The only way to be sure that the key competitive factors are protected (and not appropriated by foreign firms) is to keep full control of the process. This means FDI when entering foreign markets, creating wholly owned subsidiaries. Rather than licensing agreements, TNCs engage in FDI, according to this theory, as a defensive measure.

## TNCs AND UNDERDEVELOPMENT

Stephen Hymer, a path-breaking radical (Marxist-structuralist) political economist, was among the first to see that TNCs sometimes exist to protect and exploit unique advantages—factors such as those just discussed that might give them monopoly power and the ability to earn excess profits. Hymer argued that the desire to retain monopoly power and also to exploit foreign markets caused TNCs to engage in patterns of FDI that do not foster economic development, but rather lead to the "development of underdevelopment" (see Chapter 4).

If corporate headquarters executives fear that their competitive assets will be appropriated or diluted, they will tend to keep control of them at home and be sure that strategic decisions are made by home-country, not host-country, executives. This creates what is called the **branch factory syndrome**, whereby critical technology and the most productive assets remain securely at headquarters while inferior technology and less productive assets are transferred abroad, to the branch factory. FDI that builds branch factories may transfer technology and create jobs, in this theory, but the technology will always be inferior and the jobs will never be as good as in the headquarters firm.

Hymer's theory, like the appropriability theory, views FDI as essentially a defensive mechanism that seeks to keep inside the TNC the key advantages it possesses. Hymer goes further, however. In linking TNC strategy to an international division of labor that privileges the industrial core and systematically prevents periphery countries from catching up, he adopts a structuralist perspective on TNCs and FDI, conceptualizing the international economy as an arena of conflicting interests between actors with unequal power.

### Politics and Protectionist Barriers

Political factors can also be important in TNC strategy. TNCs depend on open international markets. They need to be able to invest abroad, of course, but they also depend on the ability to import and export. Trade barriers make their internal operations less efficient and disadvantage them compared with the domestic protected firm. This explains in part why so much FDI is regionally based, such as FDI within the EU or within NAFTA. The lower trade and investment barriers within the regional blocs encourage intra-bloc FDI compared with other patterns of FDI.

Interestingly, however, trade barriers can also encourage certain types of TNC behavior. Some FDI is an unintentional result of mercantilist policies designed to keep out foreign products. A foreign firm can get around a tariff barrier by establishing a domestic factory and, in a sense, becoming a domestic firm. In the early 1980s, for example, the United States negotiated a voluntary export agreement with Japan that was intended to protect U.S. auto firms while they developed more fuel-efficient models. The agreement put numerical limits on car exports from Japan to the United States. The limits did not apply, however, to autos produced in the United States and sold by Japanese firms, so long as most of the parts and assembly took place in the United States or Canada. Honda, Toyota, and Nissan all began to invest in production facilities in North America so that they could retain or even expand their market despite the trade barriers.

In the U.S.–Japan auto agreement case, a policy that was intended to keep out foreign cars instead attracted foreign FDI and probably strengthened the Japanese firms. Such "defensive" FDI is not always possible or profitable, of course, but where it is, it helps us understand why firms invest abroad.

Politics can affect FDI patterns in other ways as well. The Boeing Company, for example, markets its commercial aircraft to many airlines that are owned by governments or whose decisions are strongly influenced by government policy makers. Boeing often finds that, to get a large order for its aircraft, it must accept "offsets," which are agreements that certain components will be produced in the country buying the airplanes. Investment resources and technological know-how are sometimes exchanged for purchase orders. In situations like these, as Susan Strange pointed out, TNCs may become so involved in international politics that their negotiations, with host states and home states as well as with other TNCs, are more like diplomacy than simply business.

## Currency Instability

TNCs are especially susceptible to the effects of unstable foreign exchange (FX) rates because they often have costs that are denominated in one group of currencies and earn revenues in other currencies. An unexpected shift in exchange rates can raise effective costs and reduce the value of revenues. Some international businesses have seen profits collapse into loss and foreign markets disappear due to exchange rate swings. In 2003, the world's largest food company, Nestlé, announced that profits had fallen by half despite a higher quantity of goods sold, due to the unexpected appreciation of the Swiss franc. What Nestlé gained through its increased sales, it lost many times over in the FX markets.

There are many ways to reduce this exchange rate risk, including the use of complex financial instruments. One very direct way is to establish production facilities in each major market so that costs and revenues largely accrue in the same currency. The problem of currency instability is a factor that drives TNCs to behave more like national firms than like global giants.

The combination of trade barriers and exchange rate factors encourages firms to produce goods in the countries where they are sold rather than simply exporting from a central location. The globalization of markets, therefore, is sometimes associated with what might be called "multi-local" production and a corresponding pattern of TNC investment. That is, the corporation is regional or global, but each country's operations are configured along more national or local lines in order to minimize or avoid trade barriers and currency problems.

Another pattern of FDI occurs when FX rates are misaligned, either undervalued or overvalued, as explained in Chapter 7. When a currency is overvalued, for example, imported products are systematically less expensive than domestic goods. This can be a strong incentive for firms to invest in foreign production facilities. The foreign factories may be more or less efficient, but they benefit from advantageous FX rates.

The U.S. dollar was considerably overvalued during the early 1980s, for example—a fact that encouraged U.S. firms to set up offshore production facilities. The effect of the overvalued Japanese yen was so significant in the late 1980s that a Japanese term, *endaka*, was coined to describe its effect. The *endaka* effect was to force Japanese firms to set up production networks throughout East Asia and Southeast Asia and to ruthlessly cut costs at factories in Japan. *Endaka* was very stressful to Japanese businesses, but it forced them to evolve into superefficient TNCs. More recently, the weak dollar (it depreciated by 33 percent against the Euro between 2000 and 2007) has driven many European companies to set up operations in the United States.

## Location-Specific Advantages

Some FDI, as we have seen, is driven by the desire to protect firm-specific advantages, such as proprietary processes or trademarks. At other times, however, FDI may be influenced by location-specific advantages. Some of these advantages are obvious, such as access to natural resources that are available only in specific locations. At other times, the advantages are more complicated. For example, if you want to compete in the computer software market, you'd need to set up shop where the best people are. This means that you would invest where many other firms have also located, so that you can benefit from the pool of highly trained individuals in that area and the intense competition and constant innovation that is built into this environment. You would channel FDI to Redmond, Washington (Microsoft's home), the Silicon Valley of California, and probably to Bangalore, India. These and just a few other places in the world have the right technological and human environment to make your firm very competitive.

In the same way, if you wanted to compete in the world market for eyeware, such as designer sunglasses, you would probably open a facility near Belluno, Italy. As Michael Porter explains in his book *The Competitive Advantage of Nations*, this region of northern Italy is where the world's top eyeglass design and manufacturing facilities are found and where the world's pickiest eyeglass customers live, too. It is impossible to compete successfully in the global market without being exposed to the intense and innovative competition in this local market. Most of the quality ~eware in the world is manufactured by companies that have at least some of their ~cilities in Belluno.

### Competition

Finally, it is important to remember that TNCs are transnational because the markets where they compete are transnational. In some cases, a firm may be driven to invest abroad because of simple competitive pressures: If one firm does not contest this market, other firms will, and they may gain an advantage from doing so. In this regard, firms may act a bit less like coolly rational profit maximizing enterprises and a bit more like mercantilist states, which see an opponent's gain as their own potential loss.

To summarize, some TNC investments are driven by the desire to exploit low wages or cheap natural resources but, given the types of products that TNCs produce and their actual pattern of FDI, other factors are much more important. TNCs invest abroad to protect a competitive advantage, to exploit a monopoly position, to get around trade barriers, to avoid currency problems, to take advantage of special production environments—and because they are driven to do so by their competition with other TNCs.

## HOW POWERFUL ARE TNCs?

Many people assume that TNCs are very powerful because they are such large organizations and because, through their FDI flows, they influence the global distribution of investment and technology. Some people go so far as to assert that TNCs are as powerful as states—or more powerful than states.

One commonly cited "fact" is that fifty-one of the top 100 "economic entities" are corporations—and the other forty-nine are countries. This statistic is based on tables that compare the gross domestic products of countries with the total revenues of corporations. The sales of the top 200 corporations are calculated to have combined sales that are greater than those of all of the countries of the world combined, minus the ten largest countries. The message of such data is obvious: TNCs are bigger than all but the biggest nation-states and must, therefore, have tremendous power. This message is also, of course, nonsense. To make this comparison is to misunderstand what a TNC is and also to misunderstand what a state is.

From a technical standpoint, comparing countries and TNCs this way is comparing apples with oranges. The gross domestic product of a country is not equivalent to the total revenues of a corporation. Wal-Mart has high revenues, to be sure, but why are its revenues the correct measure of Wal-Mart's power and not its wage bill, its net profit, its employment total, its FDI resources, or the technology that it can potentially offer a host country? One suspects that total revenues are selected simply because they are large and therefore make Wal-Mart appear large relative to states. TNCs do have tremendous influence over economic resources, but not so much as this biased methodology suggests.

The second problem is that this analysis compares TNCs and nation-states in strictly monetary terms, ignoring many factors that really matter a great deal more.

This focus on one factor, money, is ironic because many critics of TNCs criticize corporations for ignoring important nonmonetary factors, such as security or the environment. States possess territory and make laws; they have sovereignty, citizens, and they have armies and navies. They have legitimacy, too, which means that the international community accepts their right to make important social decisions. TNCs have none of these things, unless you think that employees or customers are the same as national citizens. Even the giant Wal-Mart Stores, which have over two million employees, have fewer workers than most countries have citizens, if we want to use this as our measure. States are fundamentally different from TNCs, and attempts to compare their power and influence based on simple numerical indicators must inevitably distort reality. Both states and TNCs have power, and so sometimes they must negotiate and engage in diplomacy; but their powers differ and so their relationship is complex and evolving.

# CHANGING REACTIONS TO TRANSNATIONAL CORPORATIONS

Apart from business leaders and economists, who tend to view the growth of TNCs as the natural consequence of emerging regional and global market structures, most authors interpret the expansion of TNCs as a decisive shift in the balance of power in IPE. They speculate about who will benefit from this shift and argue about how. Several quite distinctive viewpoints have emerged that we will discuss in this section: TNCs as a form of capitalist imperialism, TNCs as a tool of U.S. hegemony, and TNCs as state-level actors in IPE.

## TNCs and Capitalist Imperialism

TNCs and FDI were distinctive elements of the first modern era of globalization, which reached its zenith about a hundred years ago and ended with the opening shots of World War I. V. I. Lenin famously characterized this era in a book title as *Imperialism: the Highest Form of Capitalism*. Lenin focused on "finance capitalism," not TNCs *per se*, but his approach and many of his conclusions are easily applied to TNCs. Lenin argued that colonial imperialism had been replaced by economic imperialism. Foreign armies and occupying forces were no longer necessary because the same result (exploitation by and dependency on the capitalist core) could now be accomplished by foreign investors and business corporations.

If you read Lenin's famous little book on imperialism, you will quickly appreciate that it is very much a creature of a particular time and place, full of references to long-forgotten people and events. It was not a book written for the ages but rather an argument written in the present tense. His indictment of international investment as a form of imperialism, however, does live on through books such as William Greider's *One World, Ready or Not: The Manic Logic of Global Capitalism*.[2]

Stephen Hymer is responsible for the direct link between TNCs and imperialism today, as was discussed earlier in this chapter. Hymer's path-breaking theory of TNC behavior suggested that many TNCs engage in FDI because they wish to exploit a monopoly position while protecting a key asset, such as a trademark or a patented process. Their profit-maximizing strategy is to exploit the foreign market in favor of higher profits at home. In terms of financial strategy, terms of trade, and technology transfer, Hymer's analysis predicts that TNCs will engage in a pattern of behavior that is imperialism in everything but name.

## TNCs as Tools of U.S. Hegemony

TNCs came to be viewed by many as tools of U.S. hegemony during the Cold War era. There were several reasons for this association. First, U.S. TNCs were especially active and focused on foreign expansion in the immediate post–World War II years. U.S. foreign policy seemed to be directed in part to creating opportunities for U.S. firms to expand abroad. And once FDI had taken place, U.S. investments abroad created economic interests favorable to U.S. policies. So it seemed as though the U.S. promoted its TNCs and they in turn supported U.S. policies.

IPE scholar Robert Gilpin, writing in his 1975 book *U.S. Power and the Multinational Corporation*, argued that American-based TNCs were a tool of U.S. hegemony. Citing a famous international economist, he asserted that

> As Jacob Viner has pointed out, from the initial movement of American capital and corporations abroad the State Department and the White House have sought to channel American investment in a direction that would enhance the foreign policy objectives of the United States. With respect to the foreign expansion of the multinational corporation, these objectives have been seen as maintaining America's share of world markets, securing a strong position in foreign economies, spreading American economic and political values, and controlling access to vital raw materials, especially petroleum.[3]

One example of Gilpin's thesis is found in the role that the Boeing company played in U.S. relations with China over the last forty years.

President Richard Nixon went to China in 1972 in a move to solidify U.S. hegemony relative to the USSR (an event so dramatic that it is even cited in *Star Trek VI: The Undiscovered Country*: "There is an old Vulcan proverb: Only Nixon could go to China."). He also went to sell airplanes, specifically Boeing 707s like Air Force One, his official airplane. Although American and Chinese officials made endless toasts, it was the aircraft sale that sealed the deal by providing meaningful economic benefits to both countries. Chinese purchases of Boeing aircraft later in the 1970s were symbolic of Chinese commitment to modernization and U.S. government commitment to closer diplomatic relations with China. President Deng's tour of Boeing assembly facilities near Seattle to mark U.S. diplomatic recognition is but one example.

By the mid-1970s, when Gilpin's book appeared, U.S. hegemony was apparently in decline. U.S. wealth and power had not declined in *absolute* terms, but Europe and Japan had closed the gap, resulting in a *relative* decline in U.S. influence. Ironically, Gilpin viewed this as a consequence of the strategic use of U.S. FDI.

From a political perspective, the inherent contradiction of capitalism is that it develops rather than that it exploits the world. A capitalist international economy plants the seeds of its own destruction in that it diffuses economic growth, industry, and technology and thereby undermines the distribution of power upon which that liberal interdependent economy was rested.[4]

Gilpin was concerned that the relative decline of U.S. hegemony would bring an end to the international political environment that had made the expansion of U.S. TNCs and the development of Europe and Japan possible. He feared a return of protectionism as had occurred when British hegemony declined at the end of the nineteenth century.

Thirty years after Gilpin's book, the viewpoint that American TNCs are tools of U.S. hegemonic strategy no longer dominates the debate, but it has not entirely disappeared. The global influence of U.S. media TNCs has been frequently cited in this regard. U.S. films and television broadcasts are seen around the world, and the Internet is dominated by U.S.-based content providers. To the extent that these media outlets present world events and daily life in ways that emphasize U.S. values and interests or that view U.S. policies favorably, these TNCs are a source of what Joseph Nye calls "soft power."[5] Some have argued that this soft power advantage is even more important to U.S. foreign policy in the long run than is its clear military dominance.

## TNCs as State-Level Actors

The decline of U.S. hegemony did not end the era of TNC expansion, as Robert Gilpin suspected, but it did change its pattern. Protectionism did increase, both in the United States and elsewhere, but trade barriers can actually encourage FDI, as was noted earlier in this chapter. The most important change, however, was probably the rise of non-U.S. TNCs, especially firms based in Japan. TNCs based in the "triad" of Japan, the EU, and the United States intensified their foreign investment activities. The United States, which had become accustomed to its position as a "home country" for U.S.-based TNCs, found itself also a "host country" to major TNCs based in Japan and Europe. The previously accepted distinction between home and host countries was starting to disappear, replaced with the realization that we are all host countries now.

The list of potential host countries expanded dramatically with the collapse of communism in 1989. Many countries, including even Russia, opened their doors to FDI and the resources and technology that it promised. Other events brought even more countries into the world economy. The end of apartheid in South Africa, for example, also attracted inward FDI and allowed South African firms an opportunity to expand abroad (SABMiller, formerly South African Breweries, is the world's second largest beer producer today, for example, with production facilities in more than forty countries). And perhaps most consequential of all, economic policy liberalization in China and India opened the two largest countries in the world to flows of inward and outward FDI.

In their 1991 book *Rival States, Rival Firms*, John Stopford and Susan Strange coined the term "triangular" diplomacy to describe the pattern of state–TNC relations that they saw emerging. In the past, they wrote, firms had competed with other firms and states had engaged in diplomacy with other states.[6] Now, they said, the largest TNCs had more power relative to states and relative to competitive markets, too. Diplomacy, where actors bargain with each other, was a more accurate description of where the world was heading. States still bargained with other states, they said. And, although businesses were still in competition with each other, the largest TNCs often bargained with each other much as states did. More and more often TNCs would form alliances or other working arrangements to help them develop technologies and spread the risk of new investments.

An example of firm-to-firm diplomacy was New United Motor Manufacturing, Inc. (NUMMI), a joint venture between fierce competitors Toyota and General Motors (GM). NUMMI was established in 1984 when Toyota agreed to take over operations in GM's least efficient factory, located in Fremont, California. Using Japanese management techniques, Toyota soon had the NUMMI factory running at world-class quality and efficiency, churning out cars for both Toyota and GM. The NUMMI alliance, just one of many among automotive companies, allowed GM and Toyota to share risk, share markets, and combine strengths even as they competed for the same customers.

State–TNC bargaining is the third side of the diplomacy triangle. Both states and TNCs control valuable resources and they need each other. States would like access to the investment resources and technology that TNCs can offer. TNCs, for their part, desire access to the natural resources and skilled labor that states control and, of course, they also seek access to national markets for the goods and services that they produce. (A state that ignores education and training for much of its population and thus offers mainly unskilled labor has little to bargain with and can expect to attract low-productivity sweatshop-type FDI.) Since each side has much to offer and much to gain, it would seem that mutually advantageous agreements should be easy to achieve. But it is not as simple as that because both states and TNCs face competition.

Because TNCs are generally in competition with other big businesses for transnational markets, they have a strong incentive to attempt to negotiate the most favorable terms possible for their FDI projects. TNCs typically seek favorable tax treatment, state-funded infrastructure, and perhaps even weakened enforcement of some government regulations. A weak state, or one with few productive resources and a weak market system, may be at a fundamental disadvantage in such negotiations. Competition from other states may force it to grant many concessions to attract FDI. This is true both in LDCs and in advanced industrial economies.

In the early 1990s, for example, the German automaker Mercedes Benz (MB), now DaimlerChrysler, announced that it would build a factory in the United States to produce a Mercedes sports-utility vehicle (SUV). MB had much to offer in this FDI project, although perhaps its most valuable bargaining chip was its reputation for quality. If a state or locality could satisfy MB, it would be a sign that it could meet high quality standards. More FDI would be likely to follow. The stakes, therefore, were very high in bargaining over this investment.

MB increased its bargaining power by creating competition for its FDI. MB published its requirements for the FDI project and invited a large number of state and local governments to make bids for the factory. By 1993 the list was narrowed to three options: potential factory sites in South Carolina, North Carolina, and

Alabama. All three states had right-to-work laws that limited union power. North Carolina offered $108 million worth of investment incentives. South Carolina offered a package similar to the one that had previously attracted a BMW factory; the total value was about $130 million. Alabama won the bidding, however, with a package worth $253 million. The value of Mercedes' end of the FDI package itself was $300 million.

The story of how Alabama, a state with a reputation as a backward place holding few attractions for MNCs, won the investment highlights the bargaining power TNCs often have in negotiations with states. Alabama's incentive package included $92 million to purchase and develop the site; $77 million for improvements to highways, utilities, and other infrastructure; tax abatement on machinery and equipment; and $60 million on education and training. The University of Alabama chipped in and agreed to run a special "Saturday School" to help the children of German Mercedes managers keep up with the higher standards in science and math back home in Germany. All this would be paid for by the taxpayers of Alabama. The governor of North Carolina was particularly upset by a tax break the Alabama legislature passed (labeled by some the "Benz Bill"), which allowed Mercedes to withhold 5 percent of employees' wages to pay off Mercedes debts.

The wooing of Mercedes went beyond financial incentives. It included an offer to name a section of an interstate highway "the Mercedes-Benz autobahn," airplane and helicopter tours, visits by the governor of Alabama and other state officials to Mercedes headquarters in Germany, a billboard in German near the site welcoming Mercedes, and the governor driving a Mercedes as the official state car. It is not surprising to read that a Mercedes executive claimed it was "Alabama's zeal" that was the deciding factor. In return, 1,500 workers got good-paying jobs, with the likelihood that several more thousand jobs would be created in supplier firms, restaurants, and the like.[7]

The lesson seems clear: When a TNC has unique resources to offer while the state has few and faces stiff competition from other states, the TNC has a tremendous advantage and the diplomacy can be very one-sided. This need not always be the case, however; if states make their own investments in education, resources, infrastructure, and so forth, then they can have the upper hand. The competition that TNCs face from each other can press them to make concessions, too.

It is controversial to say so, but the conventional wisdom until just a few years ago was that TNCs generally come out ahead in TNC–state negotiations. Not in every case, of course, since TNCs are so many and so diverse and states are a mixed bag as well, but perhaps more often than not. TNCs are "footloose" and have many possible investment options, whereas states are rooted, like trees, in the territory they control. TNCs ought to be able to play one state against another to get the best terms, as in the case of the MB factory in Alabama. A shadow of doubt has fallen over this viewpoint in recent years, however, as the level of competition among TNCs has heated up.

Several European countries held auctions for third-generation (3G) wireless telecommunications rights beginning in 2000, for example. At stake were a limited number of slots in the part of the electromagnetic spectrum reserved for cutting-edge wireless communications networks. The bidding among telecom TNCs for these licenses was intense, and the sums that were paid to the European governments were astronomical—about $108 billion just for the right to set up the networks. Vodafone, a British mobile phone company, ranked high on the FDI list shown in Table 17-1 because of its huge investment in these networks in Europe.

It is clear today that the telecom TNCs overbid for the 3G rights; the payments are much higher than justified by potential revenues. Did the states "win" the diplomacy? In a dollars-and-cents view, yes it appears they did. They received very large payments that allowed them to balance shaky budgets. In the long run, however, the outcome is less clear because the states do need the TNCs (and their resources) as much as the TNCs need the states (and their resources). When competition drives a bargain too far on either side, it puts the other party at risk and suddenly the whole enterprise is in jeopardy.

This is what bothered Raymond Vernon when he wrote his 1998 book *In the Hurricane's Eye: The Troubled Prospects of Multinational Enterprises*. Vernon was very concerned that competition among TNCs was forcing them to squeeze states for more and more concessions. Although we say that the states are squeezed, it is of course the citizens of the states who feel the pressure. They are squeezed in terms of higher taxes or reduced government services, lower labor standards, lax environmental enforcement, and in other ways. How would they react? One possibility is that they would react politically, putting pressure on their governments to protect them and to adopt protectionist measures generally. This was Vernon's fear. Although Vernon wrote prior to the protests at the 1999 WTO meetings in Seattle, the chaos of those protests is very much the eye of the hurricane he was describing.

TNCs thrive in a liberal global political and economic climate. Ironically, just as many observers were predicting the endless expansion of TNCs, creating *The Borderless World* (the title of a book by Kenichi Ohmae[8]) and David Korten's *When Corporations Rule the World*.[9] Vernon saw the potential for a great collapse. *The Hurricane's Eye* concludes with this warning:

> The great sweep of technological change continues to link nations and their economies in a process that seems inexorable and irreversible. . . . Yet the basic adjustments demanded by the globalization trend cannot take place without political struggle. Too many interests in the nation-states see the economic risks and costs of the adjustments involved, even if justified in the longer terms, as unfairly distributed and deeply threatening. . . . But a prolonged struggle between nations and enterprises runs the risk of reducing the effectiveness of both, leaving them distracted and bruised as they grope towards a new equilibrium. To shorten that struggle and reduce its costs will demand an extraordinary measure of imagination and restraint from leaders on both sides of the business-government divide.[10]

## A GLOBAL FDI REGIME?

The logical place for leaders of "imagination and restraint" from both business and government to negotiate would have been the Multilateral Agreement on Investment (MAI) talks, which were sponsored by the Organization for Economic Cooperation and Development in the mid-1990s. The intent was to create a regime to provide governance for FDI in the same way that the WTO provides governance for international trade. What kind of governance? The goal of the MAI talks was to set norms and standards for states–TNCs negotiations.

Both sides of the table have something to gain from an international investment agreement. TNCs, for example, would like to be assured of "national treatment." Under the WTO, nations can impose certain trade restrictions at the border, but once a product is inside the border it cannot be discriminated against in favor of domestic products. National treatment of international trade prevents domestic discrimination against foreign products.

National treatment for FDI would mean that, while a state has the right to regulate inward investment at the border, once that investment has been made it must treat the local subsidiary of the foreign TNC the same as it treats similar domestic firms. There must be no domestic discrimination against TNC affiliates, even if this means giving them tax preferences or subsidies intended for domestic firms only. This is one of several items on the TNC agenda that would make FDI more efficient and less vulnerable to political forces.

Although it might be too much to expect from an international agreement, TNCs would benefit if the nation-states were to coordinate or harmonize their regulation of big businesses. Increasingly, as we have noted, TNCs are driven to form alliances and to merge operations in order to be competitive with other TNCs. But because of their broad reach, TNCs often find themselves subject to antitrust or competition regulation in several different jurisdictions. If these regulatory regimes had similar policies and standards, this would cause little bother, but rarely is this the case.

The United States and the EU in particular have adopted different norms for business mergers, and when TNCs wish to join operations, they frequently confront the need to gain approval in both places. This problem appeared dramatically in 1996, when the EU competition regulators initially opposed approval of a merger between two U.S.-based aircraft firms, Boeing and McDonnell Douglas, which had been given a green light by U.S. authorities. It was suddenly very clear that an agreement between two U.S.-based firms could be vetoed by another government, if both firms had important operations there. Subsequently the EU did veto a merger between General Electric and Westinghouse, both U.S.-based TNCs, despite prior U.S. government approval. Both firms suffered significant reversals when their merger plans were called off.

Although TNCs cannot escape government controls such as antitrust approval for mergers and acquisitions, it would clearly be in their benefit if they were subject to one set of rules, not many contradictory ones. For their part, states have a number of important interests that could be served by a multilateral agreement. These might include a set of standards for TNC behavior (to prevent labor rights abuses, for example) and rules on transfer pricing. When a TNC transfers resources (say, auto parts) from one subsidiary to another, it has to set an internal price, called the *transfer price,* which is used to calculate the profits and therefore establish the tax liability of operations in each country. It is well known that transfer prices can be manipulated to create artificially low taxable profits in jurisdictions where tax rates are high and artificially high taxable income for operations located in countries where tax rates are low. Transfer price manipulation is essentially a way for TNCs to escape taxation to a certain degree, making it difficult for a state to enforce its own tax law. An investment agreement could prevent this.

A multilateral agreement would also be useful if it set rules to prevent states from getting caught up in bidding wars for TNC projects such as the MB factory in Alabama. If states would agree to abide by rules about what incentives they could provide, all might benefit in the long run. Some studies suggest that state incentives and giveaways are ultimately not very important in the pattern of FDI location, except perhaps on the margin. Typically, market factors tend to be more important in the decision to invest abroad at a particular location than all the goodies that states put in the packages they use to entice foreign firms. In the end, FDI largely goes where it would have gone, but with the bonus payments thrown in. The only way to stop this, however, is for all the states involved to agree to tie their own hands, and that is what international treaties and agreements are supposed to do.

The OECD's attempt to negotiate an MAI failed, perhaps predictably. Instead of binding rules, all that could be agreed on was a set of voluntary guidelines, which hint at what might have been accomplished but was not. Why did the MAI negotiations fail? The short answer is that states were unwilling to give up the right to pursue their national self-interest. States were unwilling to sign away the right to discriminate in favor of domestic firms when this seemed prudent and to bid lavishly for foreign factories when the opportunity was presented.

Other factors also prevented agreement. LDCs, most of which are not members of the OECD, feared that the rules would be biased against them and would only serve to encourage FDI-based imperialism. Some richer countries, including Canada and France, were unwilling to give up the right to discriminate against foreign media firms. They feared that their distinctive national cultures would be washed away in a flood of U.S. music, film, and television programming. The United States, for its part, wanted to preserve the right of its states to regulate such factors as foreign ownership of farmland.

Finally, it must be said that the OECD was probably the wrong organization to negotiate an international agreement of this importance. Often called "the rich man's club" of nations, the Paris-based OECD evolved out of an international organization originally set up to administer postwar Marshall Plan funds. Its 30 members are advanced industrial countries. Although OECD nations account for the bulk of FDI, and so have a strong interest in an FDI agreement, both outflows and inflows, it is difficult to conceive how nonmember states such as India and China could ever accept a set of rules they had no direct voice in writing. Recently a movement has appeared to resume talks on a global FDI agreement within the broader framework offered by the WTO. The WTO membership includes many more countries that belong to coalitions such as the G-20 that are making their voices clear that they are a force to be reckoned with in this debate.

The WTO may be a better forum to discuss FDI issues, but agreement may not be any easier to reach. Although all nations have an interest in reaching an agreement regulating TNC and state policies regarding FDI, their interests are not all the same, and conflict is inevitable on almost every issue. It is ironic that negotiations to regulate foreign investment are as much about tensions between states with different interests as they are about tensions between states and market forces. In the absence of international agreements to regulate TNC behavior, NGOs have stepped into the breach and mounted campaigns to pressure TNCs to behave in socially responsible ways toward their foreign workers.

# TNCs, GLOBAL COMMODITY CHAINS, AND THE ISSUE OF ACCOUNTABILITY

Traditionally, many transnational corporations had one of two types of organizational structure. They are either vertically integrated firms or horizontally integrated firms. More recently, as we discuss later in the chapter, a new TNC structure has appeared: the globally integrated enterprise based on a **global commodity chain**, whereby the TNC does not in fact own most of the elements of its foreign operations. With improved information technology, some TNCs, like Boeing or IBM, find that they can "outsource" vital functions to foreign-owned firms. The TNC builds a transnational network of contacts and contracts that it coordinates to create a regional or global business presence.

Nike, for example, is a high-profile TNC, but you will not find it ranked near the top of the FDI rankings of firms. Nike owns very few production assets either outside or inside the United States. Most Nike products (its line of baseball caps is a notable exception) are manufactured and distributed by foreign-owned firms under contract to Nike. Both the vertical elements of Nike's production (from design to raw materials to finished shoes and apparel) and the horizontal elements of its distribution are chains of contracts and business relations that are coordinated (or "linked," since this is a chain) by Nike but owned by other firms. The one asset that Nike absolutely controls and guards jealously is its brand name, its image, and the famous "swoosh" trademark.

Global commodity chains raise all sorts of interesting questions in IPE. An important and controversial question concerns accountability. TNCs are often called to account for the activities of their foreign subsidiaries. But is a TNC accountable for what is done in its name by subcontracting firms? When Nike was criticized for labor conditions in factories in its chain, it did eventually respond to change them. A TNC might not be legally accountable, but in competitive market environments it sometimes must establish accountability for actions of other firms in order to have credibility in the marketplace and legitimacy in its negotiations with states, other

TNCs, and nongovernmental organizations that are concerned about corporate social conduct.

The issue of sweatshop conditions in some apparel global commodity chains illustrates this point. Although they do not directly own the factories where their products are made, apparel TNCs are increasingly being pressed to take responsibility for the working conditions there. Some of the NGOs that have targeted sweatshops and focused on improving working conditions in them are Global Exchange, Clean Clothes Campaign of Europe, Co-op America, Sweatshop Watch, and the United Students Against Sweatshops, which was set up in 1998 at Duke University. Other university groups are part of a large network of more than 110 academic institutions focused on generating a code that permits only "sweat-free" clothes. In September of 2002, some twenty-six apparel companies signed an agreement to establish a monitoring system that would oversee working conditions in their subsidiaries in developing countries. Some 250 U.S. companies have created codes of conduct for their subcontractors.[a]

Many TNCs, especially those concerned about their reputation and the image of their brands, have taken the issue of accountability very seriously. The NGO Business for Social Responsibility (BSR) defines its goal as "achieving commercial success in ways that honor ethical values and respect people, communities, and the natural environment." BSR argues that **corporate social responsibility (CSR)** can have a positive effect on business performance. Among other things, it can improve financial performance, reduce operating costs, enhance brand image and reputation, increase sales and company loyalty, increase productivity and quality, and help retain employees. BSR also claims that "mainstream investors increasingly view CSR as a strategic business issue."[b] Companies that have been recognized for their commitment to CSR are the Co-operative Bank, Starbucks Corporation, B&Q, and Novo Nordisk.

It remains to be seen, however, whether the CSR movement will create widespread change in TNC behavior. Some scholars have questioned the effectiveness of CSR, seeing it as window dressing by a few high-profile TNCs concerned about corporate image and therefore likely to result only in short-lived and marginal changes in business conduct.[c] Robert Reich, for example, argues that "companies are neither moral nor immoral" and that what drives the behavior of TNCs and other companies are deeper structural forces and not the ethics of their top executives. Reich and others advocate multinational and national regulations or enforceable rules of conduct that would apply to all corporations. As global commodity chains become more important in transnational production, the question of their accountability and how to respond to them will continue to be a central issue on the public policy agenda.

### References

[a]See Robert Collier, "For Anti-Sweatshop Activists, Recent Settlement Is Only Tip of Iceberg," *San Francisco Chronicle*, September 29, 2002. See also John Miller, "Why Economists Are Wrong About Sweatshops and the Antisweatshop Movement? *Challenge* 46 (January–February 2003), pp. 93–112.

[b]See Business for Social Responsibility, "Overview of Corporate Social Responsibility," www.bsr.org/BSResources/IssueBriefDetail.cfm, 2003.

[c]See David Vogel, *The Market for Virtue: The Potential and Limits of Corporate Social Responsibility* (Washington, DC: Bookings Institutions Press, 2005); and Robert Reich, *Supercapitalism: The Transformation of Business, Democracy, and Everyday Life* (New York: Alfred A. Knopf, 2007). For a critical view on Nike's claim that it has complied with its agreement to monitor its facilities, see Richard Read, "Nike's Focus on Keeping Costs Low Causes Poor Working Conditions, Critics Say," *The Oregonian*, August 5, 2008.

## CONCLUSION

### Transnational Corporations Today

Change and uncertainty are the hall marks of this period in IPE and because we are right in the middle of what could be a major transition, the future seems open and somewhat unclear. What we can identify are some current, powerful developments that are likely to affect the pattern of FDI flows and the identities and perhaps the behavior of TNCs. The developments we discuss below raise many crucial questions, making this an exciting time for students of IPE and TNCs.

A potentially game-changing development, as we have alluded to already, is the spectacular economic growth of countries like China and India. Just as the rise of Japan and the newly industrialized countries spawned successful competitors to Western TNCs in previous years, we are now seeing enterprises from countries like Brazil, Russia, China, and India, known collectively as BRICs, challenge the dominance of Western TNCs. Companies like InBev, a Belgian-Brazilian conglomerate, is now the largest brewer in the world after buying Budweiser, and Lenovo, a Chinese computer maker, bought IBM's personal computer business and is now challenging Hewlett-Packard and Dell all over the world. As more countries make the shift from the periphery to the semi-periphery or even to the core of the world system, new TNCs enter the global marketplace and competition intensifies. A recent book by members of the Boston Consulting Group argues that the process of globalization has advanced so far that we are now in a condition they call "globality." Whereas global business used to be a "one-way street" benefitting TNCs from the North, it was now a two-way process, with TNCs from the North and the BRICs "competing with everyone from everywhere for everything."[11]

One casualty of this battle has been what we might call the home-country preference. In the past many TNCs did treat home-country operations differently from foreign ones, sacrificing some profit if necessary to maintain ties with home-based stakeholders. Many TNCs find that they can no longer afford to give home-country preference in an environment of increasing competition. TNCs look to their own interests now, not the interests of the home country or any other country. As far as states are concerned, the uncertain recent economic climate makes attracting FDI even more important. FDI means jobs, technology, and economic growth, which is what everyone wants in a stagnant or slow-growing economy.

Partly in response to this intensified competition and partly in response to the new possibilities created by technological changes in communication and transportation, we are beginning to see the arrival of the truly global corporation; what Samuel Palmisano, the CEO of IBM, calls the **"globally integrated enterprise."**[12] Such corporations become adept at integration—at linking together multiple partners and suppliers from around the world to collaborate and share in the finance, design, and production of new products rather than at conducting all phases of their business in-house. In contrast to the pressures to internalize activities implied by the appropriability theory and the branch factory syndrome we discussed earlier, TNCs' mode of operation now shifts toward externalizing some of the activities they used to conduct in-house. They do this both to reduce their vulnerability by spreading the risks of operating in a more competitive and uncertain environment and to take advantage of the opportunities globalization presents to tap into pools of talented labor across the globe. The box below focuses on the production of Boeing's new airplane, the 787, and provides a striking example of this.

## OUTSOURCING AND THE GLOBALLY INTEGRATED ENTERPRISE: BOEING'S 787 AIRPLANE

Boeing, one of the two leading producers of airplanes, launched the development of its new airplane, the 787 "dreamliner," with a revolutionary new business strategy. The plane would not only be made of composite material rather than metal, but 70 percent of it would be produced by suppliers and subcontractors located all over the United States and the world (among the countries involved are Japan, China, South Korea, Australia, Russia, Canada, England, France, Sweden, and Italy). What is notable about its new strategy is that certain key partners, known as "tier one suppliers," are responsible for all the design, engineering, manufacturing, and assembly of various sections of the airplane. So, for example, the wings, at one time considered by Boeing to be key sources of its competitive advantage, are now being produced by Japanese firms with help from Boeing. Below these firms are hundreds of "tier two suppliers" and their subcontractors who feed smaller parts up the line of a long and complex global supply chain. Boeing now sees system integration and final assembly as the source of its competitive advantage.

The outsourcing, according to Leslie Wayne, "is so extensive that Boeing . . . has no idea how many people around the world are working on the 787 project."[a] Not to be outdone, Boeing's rival, Airbus, itself the creation of four European countries, plans to outsource 60–70 percent of the value of the new planes it produces, with much of this work, and therefore many jobs, going to non-European countries. The advantages to such a business strategy are clear for Boeing, Airbus, and other TNCs. They can gain access to large pools of skilled and talented employees around the world, sometimes at lower cost as with Boeing's use of Russian engineers in Moscow. They can sweeten their relations with foreign governments by building up the technological and managerial expertise of their suppliers, thereby facilitating better state–TNC interactions and in Boeing's case bigger sales of its airplanes. And they can reduce their financial risk of embarking on expensive new products and projects by sharing the cost with partners around the world (some 40 percent of Boeing's $8-billion development cost is apparently being borne by partners).

But the consequences for the home country are less clear. Boeing workers are especially worried about what this extensive outsourcing means for their jobs. A recent study of Boeing workers, for example, found that some two-thirds of engineers thought that outsourcing threatened their future job security. Interviews with Boeing workers revealed deep anxiety about what this new business strategy meant for the future of the company and the availability of good jobs for Americans. Employees talked about "giving away the farm" or losing "hard-learned and expensive know-how" and worried about how such outsourcing might damage Boeing's long-term viability as well shrinking the middle class and the "national tax base."[b]

The emergence of such globally integrated corporations raises several questions for students of IPE. Will the interests of TNCs and home countries become even more complex and decoupled than they already are? Will such cross-national business partnerships and collaboration in production and finance help form a fledgling "global governing class" that shares interests and power but is increasingly deaf to the needs of the citizens of their putative home countries, as Jeff Faux argues in *The Global Class War*?[c] Will the fact that offshore outsourcing increasingly threatens the jobs of service workers and skilled professionals, such as accountants, computer programmers, and engineers, and not just blue-collar workers and the unskilled, create sufficient political heat that politicians will respond with measures to slow the process or assist the vulnerable? And will the spread or export of "good" jobs across the world by these global corporations help raise the living standards of developing countries or will they exacerbate class inequalities?

### References

[a]Leslie Wayne, "Boeing Bets the House" *The New York Times*, May 7, 2006, p. BU7.

[b]Edward Greenberg, Leon Grunberg, Sarah Moore, and Pat Sikora, *Turbulence: Boeing and the State of American Workers and Managers* (New Haven, CT: Yale University Press, 2010).

[c]Jeff Faux, *The Global Class War* (Hoboken, NJ: Wiley and Sons, 2006).

If some political, economic, and technological developments are pushing TNCs to delink their interests from those of their home countries, others are raising concerns about a stealth return of mercantilism into the global economy. **Sovereign Wealth Funds (SWFs)** are state- or government-owned rather than privately held assets originating mostly from commodity-rich countries like Russia, Abu Dhabi, and Norway, as well as from countries with large export surpluses like China. Their size and rapid growth (from $500 million in 1990 to $5 trillion in 2008); their secrecy and lack of accountability to shareholders, regulators, or voters (many come from nondemocratic countries); and their potential investment in strategically important Western enterprises worry many commentators.[13] Larry Summers, a Professor of Economics at Harvard and Director of the National Economic Council in the Obama administration, sees a potential threat to the liberal global system from mercantilist actions by foreign governments which, as he puts it, might ask an "airline to fly to their country, want a bank to do business in their country, or want a rival to their country's champion disabled."[14] Defenders of SWFs point out that they have been operating for some time with no evidence that they're pursuing anything other than healthy financial returns. As these funds continue to grow, with some estimating that their value will top $10 trillion by 2013, we can expect the debate and calls for their regulation to heat up.

Does the emergence of the BRICs countries and SWFs as important sources of FDI change the role of TNCs in the global economy? Will the executives running these funds and the new TNCs from emerging countries be as footloose and disconnected from the interests of their home communities as CEOs from developed countries or will they act mainly to further the interests of their home counties, as some commentators fear? Can FDI originating from China, a country still ruled by the communist party, still be characterized as a form of imperialism? Will these new TNCs act with greater concern for labor and environmental rights than long-established TNCs or will they be compelled to behave like all the others by the pressures of global competition? Whether SWFs and TNCs from emerging countries end up rewriting the rules of the liberal global system or not, there is little doubt that they symbolize a rebalancing of power relations in that system.

Finally, we have to ask what kind of impact the severe economic recession that began at the end of 2007, the worst since the 1930s, is likely to have on FDI and TNCs. Flows of FDI tend to follow global economic conditions. They expand in good economic times and contract during recessions. So, for example, FDI surged in 1999 and 2000, plummeted in the wake of the September 11, 2001, terrorist attacks, and then resumed its upward trend, reaching a new historic high in 2007. The recent recession is likely to slow or even reverse this growth as TNCs have both less cash on hand and less access to credit to fuel their international expansion. But the severity of this recession raises a more fundamental question for students of IPE and TNCs. Have the dislocations and shocks to the financial system so shaken confidence and support for globalization among elites and citizens around the world that we might be in for a period of retrenchment, with less open borders, less international trade, and less FDI? Will TNCs retreat to the relative safety of their home countries, thereby derailing the globalization juggernaut?

Although the United Nations body that tracks world investment trends (UNCTAD) sees no signs of a major transformation in the global economy at this time, it is making its best judgment based on current conditions. As the global economy recovers, we can expect the underlying economic and technological forces integrating the world economy to continue to drive the expansion of FDI and TNCs, but perhaps now with less enthusiasm for free-market nostrums and greater domestic and international regulation of economic activity. But if the crisis is prolonged or deepens, with many millions more suffering the effects of unemployment and lower income, the likely political fallout becomes more uncertain. History reminds us that in response to severe economic crises, political forces can reshape the international order, as they did for example in the 1930s. Prognostication is therefore a dangerous game.

## KEY TERMS

multinational corporation (MNC)  438
transnational corporation (TNC)  438
foreign direct investment (FDI)  437

product cycle theory  444
appropriability theory  444
branch factory syndrome  445
transfer pricing  455
global commodity chain  457

corporate social responsibility  457
globally integrated enterprise  459
sovereign wealth funds  460

## DISCUSSION QUESTIONS

1. What are transnational corporations and how are they different from other business firms?
2. Why do TNCs engage in foreign direct investment when there are good reasons why they might be less efficient than foreign firms? What is right and

what is wrong with the following statement: "Most TNCs invest in less developed countries because of the low wages that they can pay there."

3. How have reactions to TNCs changed in the last half century? Why? Explain briefly.

4. How would an international agreement on governance of FDI benefit TNCs? How would such an agreement benefit states? What prevents such an agreement from being realized? Explain.

5. Explain the changes currently underway in the pattern of FDI and in the organization of TNCs? What are some of the implications for IPE of these changes?

6. Considering the severity of the financial crisis that began in late 2007, what do you think might be some of the consequences for FDI and TNCs over the next 10 years? Will liberal economic policies and open borders beat a retreat or does the crisis mean just a temporary setback for the forces of globalization? Explain.

## SUGGESTED READINGS

Robert Gilpin. *The Challenge of Global Capitalism: The World Economy in the 21st Century*. Princeton, NJ: Princeton University Press, 2000.

William Greider. *One World, Ready or Not: The Manic Logic of Global Capitalism*. New York: Simon & Schuster, 1997.

Stephen H. Hymer. *The International Operations of National Firms: A Study of Direct Foreign Investment*. Cambridge, MA: MIT Press, 1976.

David C. Korten. *When Corporations Rule the World*. West Hartford, CT: Kumarian Press, 1996.

Raymond Vernon. *In the Hurricane's Eye: The Troubled Prospects of Multinational Enterprises*. Cambridge, MA: Harvard University Press, 1998.

## NOTES

1. Leon Grunberg revised this edition of the TNC chapter.
2. See William Greider, *One World, Ready or Not: The Manic Logic of Global Capitalism* (New York: Simon & Schuster, 1997).
3. See Robert Gilpin, *U.S. Power and the Multinational Corporation: The Political Economy of Foreign Direct Investment* (New York: Basic Books, 1975), p. 147.
4. Ibid., p. 260.
5. See Joseph Nye, *Soft Power: The Means of Success in World Politics* (Cambridge, MA: Perseus Books Group, 2004).
6. See John Stopford and Susan Strange, *Rival States, Rival Firms: Competition for World Market Shares* (Cambridge, England: Cambridge University Press, 1991).
7. David N. Balaam and Michael Veseth, *Introduction to International Political Economy*, 2nd ed. (Upper Saddle River, NJ: Prentice Hall, 2001), p. 361.
8. See Ken Ohmae, *The Borderless World* (New York: Harper & Row, 1990).
9. David C. Korten, *When Corporations Rule the World* (West Hartford, CT: Kumarian Press, 1996).
10. Raymond Vernon, *In the Hurricane's Eye: The Troubled Prospects of Multinational Enterprises* (Cambridge, MA: Harvard University Press, 1998).
11. Samuel Palmisano, "The Globally Integrated Enterprise," *Foreign Affairs*, May–June 2006.
12. *The Economist*, "Special Report on Globalization," September 20, 2008.
13. Harold Sirkin, James Hemerling, and Arindam Bhattacharya, *Globality: Competing with Everyone from Everywhere for Everything* (New York: Business Plus, 2008).
14. Tim Weber, "Who's Afraid of Sovereign Wealth Funds?" *BBC News*, January 24, 2008.

# Food and Hunger: Market Failure and Injustice

Every last grain counts.

Jacob Silberberg

After World War II there were periods of massive hunger, primarily in developing nations. For the last half century, however, the world food problem has been viewed primarily as one of *excess supply* and *weak demand* for agricultural commodities and foodstuffs. Once again in the summer of 2008, the international community was caught off-guard by a combination of low levels of commodity reserves and high food prices.

Beginning in late 2005, food prices steadily increased, benefiting many farmers but also increasing the number of poor and hungry. The United Nations Food and Agricultural Organization (FAO) reported that world food reserve stock levels reached a record low of a 55-day supply. Before long, protests and riots over high food and gasoline prices broke out in many countries, including Mexico, Indonesia, and Ivory Coast. In Haiti, the prime minister was driven from office. In some countries, hoarding and panic buying resulted. Major food outlets in the United States limited rice purchases. To encourage production, some states responded to the crisis with new farm subsidies. At least forty-seven nations, including Russia, China, and India, either imposed bans on agricultural exports or dropped trade tariffs to encourage imports to help protect their consumers from hunger.

This new world food crisis generated intense debate over its causes and effects. State officials, international organizations (IOs), media outlets, and academics offered many explanations for the crisis including: (1) a weak U.S. dollar that helped draw down commodity reserve levels; (2) environmental events that placed a natural limit on commodity production, particularly in developing nations; (3) income and population growth in the newly industrialized countries (NICs), which sparked renewed fears of famine and starvation throughout the world; (4) new U.S. and EU requirements for biofuel production that reduced the amount of commodities available for food consumption; (5) investment speculation on agriculture commodities; and (6) the persistence of war, disease, and government mismanagement. The world food crisis also incited debate over possible solutions, which included new **genetically modified organisms (GMOs)** and production techniques; a new Green Revolution; United Nations **World Food Program (WFP)** efforts to increase food aid to the neediest nations; the reduction of trade barriers; and measures to improve food distribution while overcoming conflict and war in many poorer countries.

This chapter attempts to answer several overarching questions about the "perfect storm" that resulted in a new world food crisis in the spring of 2008. First, what explains the dramatic, sudden changes in global supply and demand conditions between 2005 and 2008? Second, when too much food and the *lack of demand* for it were viewed as major policy issues before 2005, why weren't the excess supplies of food fed to those who needed them the most? Third, why were food and hunger problems not dealt with more effectively, causing hunger and starvation to remain predominant features of the international political economy? Finding answers to these questions will help clarify the roots of the recent food crisis, which we argue are part of a perpetual feature in the global food production and distribution system.

After stating our theses in this chapter, we outline some of the political, economic, and social structural elements of the global food production and distribution system. In a brief history section we then discuss some of the important recent developments in food and hunger conditions and policies. We then use the three dominant IPE perspectives (see Chapter 1) to explain the primary factors that experts and policy officials suggest contributed to the latest world food crisis. The chapter ends with a short overview of popular proposals to solve the crisis and a discussion of some of the implications of our work for management of global food and hunger problems.

We present three main theses in this chapter. First, despite arguments to the contrary, it is clear that the current world food crisis is *not* primarily a product of lower commodity supplies accompanied by a dramatic rise in both income and population. Rather, the imbalance between supply and demand merely begs the question of why prices increased so much over roughly a three-year period before the crisis was acknowledged and why commodities ended up in short supply so suddenly. We argue that the seeds of the global food and hunger problem remain rooted in poverty and a mismanaged food distribution system.

Second, despite different macroeconomic conditions, hunger and starvation are *permanent structural* features of the global political economy. The recent world food crisis only magnifies the extent to which political, economic, and social structures of power reign over the market. Poor people still *consistently* lack access to adequate food supplies, while most people in developed countries have access to relatively inexpensive agricultural commodities and food products.

Third and finally, we contend that management of the food production and distribution system suffers from the conflicting *interests and values* of different food actors, including states, international organizations, multinational corporations, and subnational groups. These actors form networks that are not insulated from complicated economic development, energy and environmental issues, or security problems, making it nearly impossible to create an effective global food policy to overcome hunger.

## AN IPE OF FOOD AND HUNGER

An IPE of hunger helps explain how a combination of political, economic, and social factors affects national and international food and hunger issues. Realists view the world as a self-help system in which nation-states must compete for power and wealth to improve their relative security. States regulate both national and international markets to serve state interests. Nations with the capacity to produce large agricultural surpluses, including the United States, Canada, France, Australia, Brazil, and Argentina, often benefit from the dependency of other nations on their food exports. Surplus commodity producers also employ *export subsidies* and other trade-enhancing measures to clear **local markets,** generate new markets, and earn foreign currency.

On the other hand, major commodity *importers* sometimes adopt production-enhancing and trade protectionist measures to enhance their own food security. These measures often complicate international trade negotiations such as those in the current Doha round of the WTO (see Chapter 6). Many states are concerned about being dependent on agricultural exporters during a time of crisis or war, when cutting off food supplies may weaken their nation's security. For many nations in Asia or Africa, accessibility to limited amounts of exported rice can mean the difference between maintaining a healthy diet and slipping into a state of malnutrition and hunger.

Many experts agree that **transnational agribusiness corporations (TNACs)** such as Archer Daniels Midland, Conagra, and Monsanto can both help and hinder food systems. Most industrialized countries have chosen not to seriously restrict agribusiness practices. Regional organizations such as the EU protect farmers with production enhancements, tariffs, and subsidies that distort global supply and demand, possibly contributing to world hunger. IOs such as the UN's FAO and the WFP are often accused of not doing enough to resolve hunger. However, many nongovernmental organizations (NGOs) such as Bread for the World and *Médecins Sans Frontières* (Doctors Without Borders) work effectively to combat hunger throughout the world. Finally, subnational groups like

**Community Supported Agriculture (CSA)** play key roles in food production and distribution at the local level in some countries.

Economic liberals stress that farmers, special interest groups, and agribusinesses in the major grain-producing countries often "capture" the policy-making process in order to enhance farm income through subsidies, trade tariffs, and/or exports subsidies. U.S. and EU politicians often justify these support measures on the basis that they also keep food prices lower than they would be under "free market" conditions. However, farm supports artificially inflate commodity prices and often lead to excess production, distorting the market's automatic supply–demand adjustment mechanism.

From the late 1970s to the crisis of 2008, many orthodox economic liberals (OELs) viewed the world food and hunger problem as a failure of market forces to balance supply with demand. *If* markets were depoliticized—the state's role was limited and the market decided policy outcomes—enough food would be produced to feed everyone in the world and would be distributed through trade to those who needed it. For heterodox interventionist liberals (HILs), the picture is more complicated. They are skeptical that states can resolve the myriad conflicting domestic and international interests that give agricultural trade its quasi-protectionist flavor. Fair trade practices and agreements are preferred over free trade, partially to account for the impact of trade policies on society and food security.

Finally, structuralists tend to view the current world food crisis as an extension of a food quandary dating from the 1950s: Low income and poverty have been the major causes of hunger, not overpopulation or lack of production. They charge that the cheap food policies of major producers have benefited the rich to the detriment of the working class and poor. In many countries, officials promote the production of some commodities based on factors such as producer ethnicity, religion, class, history, and other political interests. In Ethiopia, Somalia, the Darfur region of Sudan, Congo, Kenya, and Zimbabwe, social and political factors have resulted in groups of people intentionally being underfed or even starved to death. However, some structuralists would *support* "multifunctional" protectionist trade policies to help promote local producers of indigenous crops and enhance state independence while insulating local production from the vagaries of the international political economy.

## A BRIEF HISTORY OF GLOBAL FOOD AND HUNGER ISSUES

In the twentieth century, most industrial nations saw production subsidies and new agricultural production technologies increase commodity surpluses while demand stayed weak. Farmers in the major grain-growing nations, including the United States, Canada, the European Community (now the EU), and Australia, often complained about low food prices and low farm incomes. They pressured their legislatures for subsidies and protectionist trade measures in order to bring farm incomes up to the level of nonfarm workers. Depending on the country, farm programs included support for wheat, corn, soybeans, sugar, cotton, feed grains, and other specialty crops. Many farmers benefited from a combination of deficiency payments or direct income, conservation policies, and national commodity storage programs that removed commodities from the market.

A farm-food policy network composed of farm groups, agribusinesses, legislators, and executive agencies such as the U.S. Department of Agriculture had a vested interest in sustaining farm incomes above what they would have been under free market conditions. But taxpayer-funded policies were expensive and economically inefficient. As oversupply continuously drove down farm prices, the pressure on states to sustain farm incomes only intensified. Legislators in the world's leading democracies felt compelled to help their farm constituents, even if it meant employing inefficient protectionist measures. Production surpluses helped accomplish a variety of political, economic, and social objectives. For example, in the 1960s and 1970s, surplus corn, butter, cheese, and other commodities played a major part in subsidized U.S. school lunch programs. Domestically, "cheap food" policies increased consumption of especially wheat, corn, and feed grains and were politically popular with wealthy farmers and low income groups.

Food was also an important element of state power. Food-importing states were vulnerable to food-exporting states. The United States routinely used food as a tool to achieve a variety of foreign policy objectives. Aid efforts helped the United States unload its commodity surpluses overseas. U.S. Public Law (PL) 480 and the "Food for Peace" program made food aid easily available to states that were anti-communist and whose economies were potential markets for future sales of U.S. commodities and commercial products.

Throughout the second half of the twentieth century, the United Nations estimated that an average of 800 million people, primarily in the least developed nations, did not receive the required amounts of protein and calories to fight off diseases such as kwashiorkor and marasmus associated with malnutrition. Hunger came to be viewed as the result of inadequate food production coupled with over-population, a problem that seemed endemic to developing nations. The solution seemed fairly simple: Help LDCs produce more food while encouraging them to lower their population growth rates. Yet many officials (especially from states with large commodity surpluses) suggested that foreign aid would help governments overcome production shortfalls and infrastructure problems, making it easier for them to invest in modernization programs of their own.

Many government officials and academic experts predicted that LDCs would eventually overcome their hunger problems as their economies modernized. The World Bank and other financial institutions funded development projects that promoted industrialization modeled on Western nations. In the 1960s, the Ford and Rockefeller Foundations supported **Green Revolution** research to help LDCs increase production and develop new varieties of wheat in Mexico and rice in the Philippines. Many experts to this day claim that the Green Revolution helped millions of people in developing nations avoid hunger.

Yet none of these measures could overcome the malnutrition and starvation that routinely occurred in India, parts of Southeast and East Asia, and Africa. In addition, overpopulation and rising birth rates were predicted to wreak havoc on countries like India and China. In his work entitled "Lifeboat Ethics," biology professor Dr. Garrett Hardin suggested that the industrialized nations were not likely to transfer a sufficient amount of resources to poorer-overpopulated developing nations to stave off their hunger.[1] Hardin proposed that if the industrialized nations (who were in the lifeboat) did not want to be swamped by the growing masses in developing nations, they were ethically obligated to cut off food aid and other assistance to save themselves. Food aid was an *unethical* disservice to those whose lives would end when it was discontinued.

Many critics argued that Hardin's analogies were flawed. Even if the world did have a finite amount of resources, the earth had not reached the point where there were just enough resources available for a certain number of people to live comfortably while others perished. Critics asked: Must those in the industrialized nations live as lavishly as they do compared with people in developing nations? Might the "haves" share with the "have-nots"? How can the major commodity producers such as Canada, the United States, and the EU justify their huge surpluses while so many people in the developing regions of the world are malnourished or starving?

## A World Food Crisis and a Paradigm Shift

During the 1972–1973 world food crisis, another explanation of hunger and food insecurity emerged. In 1972 the FAO announced that supplies of world grain reserves had reached record low levels and surpluses usually available to food-import-dependent nations were no longer available. For the next two years, hunger increased in some of the poorest regions of the world. The crisis began when, following a shortfall in Soviet wheat production, the United States subsidized sales of wheat and other grain to the Soviet Union as part of an effort to improve U.S.–Soviet relations, driving up prices and drawing down U.S. wheat stocks.

In 1973 the United States devalued its dollar, which made U.S. grain exports more attractive to nations that wanted to upgrade their diets to include more wheat. Many major grain corporations stood to gain from the shipment of these grains to commercial buyers. Just when poorer countries found themselves most dependent on commodity exports, wheat and feed grains were rerouted to industrialized nations that could more easily afford them. The nations that had relied on food imports to meet basic needs were no longer able to afford the higher prices.

Concurrently, the OPEC oil cartel embargoed shipments of oil to the United States and dramatically raised the price of oil (see Chapter 19). Many non-oil-exporting LDCs reluctantly adopted food self-sufficiency policies and limited food imports to pay their higher oil bills. Some food dependent poorer nations were also crippled by routinely occurring monsoons in Asia and drought in the Sahel region of Africa where almost a million people starved to death when food relief efforts were intentionally blocked.

In the mid-1970s Francis Moore Lappé, Joseph Collins, Susan George, Colin Tudge, and others challenged Hardin's assumption that overpopulation was the root of the hunger problem. What became known as the "**Food First**" argument claimed that hunger resulted more from poverty and income distribution than from reduced production and overpopulation.[2] **Food Firsters** cited demographers who maintained that population growth rates decreased in developed nations when their economies transformed from an agricultural to an industrial base. According to the **demographic transition theory**, as people lived longer and per capita income increased, population growth rates naturally slowed. With development and higher personal income, financial security would take away the incentive of poorer people to have more children.

These Food Firsters also pointed out that people in LDCs often adopted measures to control population growth during times of drought or severe food shortages. With the possible exception of China, massive social intervention programs to control population growth did not work. Moreover, in India and elsewhere, these programs were viewed as another example of Western imperialism because they blamed developing nations for overpopulation instead of focusing on income distribution or Western (over)consumption habits. Furthermore, limiting population growth would *not* necessarily guarantee that food would be available to poorer members of society, as the number of hungry in developed societies demonstrates. Estimates showed that enough food was produced in the world to feed each person more than 2,700 calories a day. What developing societies lacked were distribution channels necessary to ensure that all individuals received the daily minimum requirements of nutrients and calories, and the financial resources to either produce or purchase what they needed.

The Food First people also drew attention to hunger and food security from an increasingly global IPE perspective. They outlined some of the political, economic, and social factors that have made it difficult to solve the poverty and food distribution problems that create global hunger. Food Firsters and other structuralist critics also tended to share a structuralist belief about the necessity food security arguing that hunger was *not endemic* to LDCs but rather a byproduct of their political and economic relationship to the industrialized nations, shaped by *asymmetrical international interdependence*. In fact, before colonization, developing regions of the world were relatively food self-sufficient. Colonization and interaction with the industrialized nations via trade, aid, and investment had "immiserized" their local economies. The developing nations such as South Korea and Taiwan that overcame poverty and hunger were the exception to the rule, given huge amounts of aid they received due to their strategic relationships with Western powers.

## Hunger amidst Plenty

After the food crisis of the 1970s ended, food security conditions did not improve for people living in LDCs. Instances of mass starvation mounted during Bangladesh's civil war. Food was intentionally used as a weapon in other wars, including Ethiopia and the "killing fields" of Cambodia. Throughout most of the 1980s, the Sahel region of Africa experienced several more rounds of mass starvation and hunger. Yet producers continued to reduce food aid and shift it into concessional (trade) channels.

Efforts by international food relief organizations such as the FAO and Office of the UN High Commissioner for Refugees (UNHCR) resulted in few victories when it came to dealing with hunger in the most ravaged nations. In 1992, the United States set a new precedent by sending its forces (backed by a UN resolution) into Somalia to feed millions of starving people besieged by civil war. But following an ambush that killed seventeen U.S. soldiers, the multilateral force withdrew from Somalia. Today, Somalia has become a prime example of a "failed state" known for not only hunger and famine but also instability and war.

During the rest of the 1990s and into the early 2000s, civil war contributed to the deaths of millions by starvation in Rwanda, Sudan, Angola, Ethiopia, Sierra Leone, and Liberia. Meanwhile, Tanzania, Namibia, Botswana, Malawi,

Mozambique, Lesotho, Swaziland, Zambia, and Zimbabwe regularly face hunger due to drought. Many of these states also must overcome high incidences of HIV infection, which has worsened their hunger problems. Private organizations, including World Vision, *Médecins Sans Frontières*, and Oxfam, have been unable to do much to halt the spread of hunger and starvation on the continent. In 1996, the FAO sponsored a world food conference in Rome, where 187 states pledged to halve the number of hungry people in the world within twenty years, to approximately 400 million, Realistically, little progress toward these objectives has been made, and little is expected given that the global financial crisis that started in 2008 has led to cutbacks in promised of food aid.

## AN IPE OF THE GLOBAL FOOD CRISIS OF 2008

In the spring of 2008, a "perfect storm" of factors resulted in the most recent global food crisis, unexpectedly producing shortages and abnormally high prices for agricultural commodities and food products worldwide. The following is a list of the six factors most often cited as causing the crisis:

- An *undervalued U.S. dollar* that led to a severe drawdown in U.S. commodity stocks.
- Natural *resource limits* including drought, lack of water, and climate change that contributed to commodity production shortfalls throughout the world.
- Unusually high levels of *speculation* (investments) in agricultural production that helped drive up commodity and food prices.
- The increased use of new technologies such as *biofuel* production in the United States and the EU that diverted food away from developing regions.
- The *overreliance* of many developing nations on *cheap food policies, inappropriate development strategies, and inappropriate technologies* to relieve hunger.
- The continued presence of *war, disease, corruption* and other unfavorable political and economic conditions that severely weaken food production and distribution systems.

In this section, we employ the three IPE perspectives to explain how each of these factors contributed to the supposed crisis, as well as some possible solutions proposed by a variety of experts, organizations, and agencies.

### An Undervalued U.S. Dollar

An undervalued dollar was not the main cause of the World Food Crisis of 2008 but an intervening variable that exacerbated it. A weak U.S. dollar made U.S. grain more affordable, causing other nations to import more of the commodity. As U.S. supply levels dropped to record lows, food prices rose, driving speculation and increasing the probability of an investment bubble in agricultural commodities.

And yet this hardship for both consumers and the world's hungry was viewed as a blessing by many U.S. farmers who had faced low commodity prices for decades. Farmers in grain producing nations expected to be able to increase production to meet both the future demand related to rising populations and higher incomes in countries like China and India and the increased demand for biofuels. An increase in commodity exports would also improve the U.S. balance of trade. Former USDA official Robert Lewis called for quadrupled world grain production to feed the world's growing population *at the level of U.S. average consumption.*[3] Lewis recommended that U.S. and EU farmers continue to receive production subsidies because they are caught on "an economic treadmill" and deserve higher wheat prices to cover fixed production costs for land, diesel, fertilizers, and other inputs associated with skyrocketing oil prices in the spring of 2008.

## Natural Limits, Population Growth, and the Return of Malthusian Nightmares

Against this background many experts also blamed recent production shortfalls on some combination of droughts, lack of water, and global warming in different grain growing regions of the world. Some identified increased demand for more expensive food products in "newly emerging" nations such as China and India. Some of them theorized that global climate change and the earth's rising temperature led to declines in yields of wheat, rice, and corn. In 2005, the UN's FAO warned that global warming was likely to increase drought and desertification in Africa, decreasing farmland by 1.1 billion hectares (2.6 billion acres) by 2080.[4] Lester Brown, head of the Earth Policy Institute in Washington, DC, reports that water shortages are a major cause of the world food crisis. Beginning in 2005, droughts and unexpected bad weather in the United States, the EU, Russia, Ukraine, and Argentina contributed to record low commodity stockpile levels. Over the last decade Australia has been hit by intense droughts that have made it difficult to generate its usual commodity surpluses of wheat. Shrinking ground water levels occurred in both China and in India's Punjab state. Aquifers in the Sahara and in the southwest of the United States were also at record low levels.[5]

Brown expects that by 2050 the planet will have 3 billion more people—totaling at least 9 billion. Although he acknowledges that population growth rates have *slowed* from 2 percent in 1970 to 1.2 percent in 2005, he predicts that global population will soon outrun global commodity supplies. Many of the poorer countries of Asia, Latin America, and Africa (especially the Democratic Republic of the Congo, Rwanda, and Tanzania) are expected to grow their populations by an estimated 74 million (the size of two Canadas) per year. This combination of production shortfalls and population growth raises the possibility of another "Malthusian nightmare" of too many mouths to feed.

As noted above most structuralists disagree that the world does not have enough food to feed everyone. The Food Firsters Lappe, Collins, and Rosset argue that while there could be 74 million more mouths to feed every year, more people are buying more meat and more food is going into biofuel production. Hunger remains primarily a byproduct of inequality and exploitation rather than lack of production or overpopulation. Similar arguments are made by some HILs and neomercantilists, who argue that as China and India have rapidly developed their industrial sectors, they have *deliberately* slowed grain production, becoming more dependent on commodity imports in order to meet a dramatic increase in the demand for soybeans, feed grains, meat, and non-traditional commodities and food. Many HILs would argue that this was a rational economic strategy on the part of Chinese and Indian officials. Other experts are certain that market forces accompanied a second Green Revolution-fueled by new production technologies-will help food production keep pace with population growth and higher incomes.

To most experts, these interrelated issues require a complex solution beyond simply increasing production to keep up with demand, which has often justified state intervention in the economy.

## The Role of Speculation

When investors purchase stock in agricultural commodities, they often bid up its value, which translates into higher commodity and food prices. For three years before the world food crisis, huge investment firms began pouring billions into booming markets for corn, wheat, and soybeans. Many TNACs invested in grain elevators, ethanol plants, fertilizers, and farmland in the United States, Brazil, sub-Saharan Africa, Argentina, and even England.[6] This development was part of a global tendency toward investment in other nonagricultural commodities including oil but also natural gas, gold, copper, aluminum, zinc, and other resources. Driving market prices higher was the industrialization of China and India but also Saudi Arabia and Russia.[7] Finally, another interesting development has been the purchase of land and investment in commodity production by Saudi Arabia, China, South Korea, Kuwait and others in Sudan, Pakistan, Cambodia, Ethiopia, and the Democratic Republic of Congo to export back to the home country.[8] Many structuralist critics have noted the extent to which these foreign operations contribute to socio-political tensions in countries whose resources are being used to feed people in other states while locals are driven out of agriculture or remain hungry.

OELs argue that speculation in agricultural commodity production played only a *small* role in driving up food prices. They claim markets markets were merely responding to record population and income growth rates in China, India, and Saudi Arabia, where higher income also generated demand for more expensive and higher protein content foods. Speculation helps agribusinesses and other TNCs earn income for the country in which they originate, which may in turn help feed and provide people with jobs. Speculation can also be a *good* thing because it locks in higher food prices and provides farmers with incentives to increase production in places such as Russia, Ukraine, Kazakhstan, and Brazil. In both the United States and the EU many farmers even asked to roll back conservation programs that limited commodity production.

Yet many HILs remain skeptical of speculation. It helped generate another economic bubble, similar to the industrial bubble in Southeast Asia during the later 1990s, the hi-tech bubble in the United States in the late 1990s, and the recent housing bubble in the United States. The poor have always been hurt the most by "artificial price increases," which undermine the positive effects of speculation. Still another concern was that, given state and local distribution policies, the benefits of speculation were not guaranteed to help the hungry. Finally, if demands for energy and oil continued to grow in China, India, Russia, and Mexico, food prices could be expected to rise to the point of ultimately producing a global fight between food and energy.

Most structuralists condemn speculative investment derivatives in agricultural production for pushing food prices beyond the impact of normal supply–demand conditions and increasing the chances of hunger in developing nations. Two recent studies of the impact of speculation on agricultural commodities show that "increases in futures-trading volume drove cash-price volatility up" which had "causal effects on inflation."[9] Speculation then, helped to lessen the possibility of achieving the UN's Millenium Development Goal of halving hunger by 2015.

## Biofuels

**Biofuels,** initially derived from plants high in sugar or vegetable oils, at first thrilled government officials, agribusinesses, and farmers. Many politicians hoped they would reduce dependency on oil imports. As the market grew, state officials hoped biofuels would eat up their surplus agricultural commodities, provide farmers with an opportunity to maintain production and price levels for their agricultural commodities, and weaken farm pressure on governments to maintain expensive domestic subsidies and agricultural trade protection.

As commodity prices increased steadily between 2005 and 2008, the United States, the EU, and Brazil (who together produce 90 percent of the world's biofuels) assertively promoted biofuel production. During those three years, Brazil increased its biofuel production by 200 percent, and sugar cane production became one of the pillars of its economic development strategy. In 2007, the U.S. Department of Energy spent $1 billion to help develop the next generation of biofuels. The U.S. Congress imposed a 35 percent biofuel supply requirement by 2020, while the EU required that 5.75 percent of its member states' fuel supply must be composed of them by 2010.

However, a year before the food crisis of 2008, biofuels were a heavily politicized issue. Critics charged that they could, in effect, "be the single most destructive set of policy mistakes made in a generation."[10] New studies raised questions about the efficiency of biofuels and their connection to rising food prices. Once the crisis began it was harder *not* to connect biofuels to declining levels of commodity reserves and record food prices. Two World Bank officials argued that biofuels were the biggest single contributor to the overall rise in grain prices, while an agency report claimed they contributed to a 75-percent rise in food prices.[11] Even the USDA's ex-chief economist Keith Collins suggested that ethanol was a "foot on the accelerator" of corn demand, leading to higher commodity prices by an estimated 50 percent between 2000 and 2006.[12]

**The Mixed Views of Economic Liberals**   Many economic liberals remain undecided about biofuels and their connection to hunger. When the food crisis began, gas, oil, and other energy costs were at record highs. At the Rome Food Summit in June of

2008, the USDA Secretary Edward Shafer contradicted his predecessor when he admitted that biofuels raise global food prices, but only by 2–3 percent.[13] However, Shafer also claimed that biofuels helped lower oil and petroleum costs and protected the environment. Many HILs believe biofuels warrant tax incentives, preferential government purchases, and state sponsored research grants. In cases such as Brazil's Petrobras, public–private business relationships have generated preferential purchases of biodiesel feed-stock from small farmers.

More than a few experts (including the economically conservative CATO institute in Washington, DC) questioned the greenhouse emissions associated with biofuels. Two academic experts argued that it takes seven gallons of oil to produce eight of ethanol. Furthermore, growing, soybeans, and other plants and converting them into biofuels can use more energy than the bio-ethanol or bio-diesel generates.[14] Finally, biofuels may contribute to water shortages in the Rio Grande, China's Yellow River, and India's Punjab state.

By the winter of 2008, after a good deal of critical press coverage, many HILs admitted that biofuels were not as energy efficient as they had hoped and might play a bigger role in the food crisis than previously realized. Suzanne Hunter of Sterling Biofuel International Limited argues that still not enough is known at this time about the efficiency, effects, and costs of biofuels.[15] She anticipates the development of a second generation of advanced biofuels, such as biobutanol and synthetic diesel, to be derived from switchgrass, garbage, and algae, rather than agricultural commodities. Biofuel supporters hope these nonagricultural sources will produce more efficient fuels, but contend that biofuels presently serve useful purposes. In regions in which the poor are vulnerable to hostile climates, an alternative energy source can help improve lives. And in nations such as India and China, where sustained economic development is emphasized, biofuels could result in a net reduction of greenhouse gas emissions.

**Mercantilists Cross Paths with Economic Liberals** Mercantilists tend to either support or reject biofuels based on their impact on national political and economic interests. In the United States for instance, ethanol accounted for only 6 percent of U.S. corn production in 2008, but is expected to absorb as much as one-quarter of the crop for bio-ethanol production in the next five years. (Soybeans now make up 40 percent of U.S. acreage). This shift in production decreased the volume of wheat being produced, contributing to higher international wheat prices. And because the United States supplies a quarter of the world's wheat, U.S. food donations to the WFP and other aid organizations decreased.[16]

In response to these conditions, many countries, including Ukraine, Argentina, Kazakstan, and Vietnam, embargoed commodity exports in order to meet local demand. China had been the world's largest soybean exporter but, to meet rising demand, became a major importer of soy to feed its pigs and cattle. Likewise, in reponse to the growing international ethanol market, China also limited its own exports of corn and as noted above, invested heavily in agricultural commodity production in many African nations. For many mercantilist-realist state officials, these policy moves raised concern about the impact of decreased Chinese soy exports on other states importing from China including a number of poorer developing ("failed") states, many of whom have direct ties to terrorist groups.

In order to produce more political and economic stability in biofuel markets, some mercantilists favor establishing governance and sustainability standards with other nations. The EU attempted to coordinate state efforts in the community to produce sustainability criteria for land-use requirements for biofuels, and the G8 has created a Global Bioenergy Partnership (GBEP) to facilitate international collaboration on bioenergy and energy security, food security, and environment sustainability. An international Biofuels Forum includes producers and consumers from Brazil, China, India, South Africa, the United States, and EU. At the 2008 Rome Food Summit, the Organization for Economic Cooperation and Development (OECD) argued for fewer protectionist trade policies so that farmers could benefit from higher food prices, while calling on all states to phase out mandates for biofuels. The Food Summit Report itself called for making food security, protecting poor farmers, promoting broad-based rural development, and ensuring environmental sustainability the primary goals of state biofuel policies.[17] Yet an international multilateral agreement on biofuels would be difficult to negotiate, primarily due to the number of complicated factors involved.

The lack of agreement on a new international set of biofuel standards is rooted in a variety of conflicting national domestic interests and pressures. Many states argue that regulation measures are resticted by national farm support measures. Just before the food crisis, most farmers in surplus producing states were pleased with higher prices linked to the strong demand for the corn and soy used to produce biofuels. During the food crisis, however, consumer groups became more critical of declining reserve supply levels and food price hikes. President Bush and Congress continued to set even tougher standards for future biofuel production and fuel mixture levels. Different U.S. states pursued different policies. California governor Schwarzenegger's executive order established a Low Carbon Fuel Standard (LCFS) or goal of 10 percent decrease in carbon-intensity biofuels by 2020, then drop. The Bush administration opposed the measure, but the Environmental Protection Agency under the new Obama administration accepted it.

Some mercantilist concerns about biofuels overlap with those of structuralists, who worry that increasing support for biofuels will eventually concentrate land ownership and corn production on industrial farms while emptying the breadbaskets of the United States and other countries.[18] The development of biofuels could weaken national economies by decreasing domestic production and weaken food security by increasing dependence on agricultural imports.

**Structuralists**   Most structuralists are even more skeptical of biofuels than HILs or mercantilists. They argue that the market will not solve the hunger problem with biofuels or other technology. Instead, biofuel production often negatively impacts food policy. Increasing biofuels shifts fields from wheat and soy to corn, driving up food prices and decreasing food quality. The amount of land necessary for production squeezes out small farmers while using excessive amounts of water, pesticides, and chemicals. And although a shift to biofuels is meant to decrease vulnerability to Middle Eastern whims, nations will be vulnerable to drought and other weather-related phenomena. Finally, as dependence on corn increases, input costs will also increase, creating new investment bubbles in areas such as fertilizer and land.

Many structuralists share the mercantilist concern that industrial agriculture decreases the number of small farmers, weakening both individual and national self-sufficiency. A classic example is the development strategy of Brazil, where increased soybean production is meant to help feed the urban poor, increase exports, and contribute toward alternative energy.[19] However, President Lula's farm policy involves transferring peasants to remote areas and applying industrial agricultural production techniques to large plantations. These plantations encroach further and further into the Amazon rainforest, damaging its ecological system, polluting ground and river water, and threatening indigenous tribes.

Structuralists are critical of those who support the green revolution or biotechnology in developing nations and overlook the fact that many LDCs continue to grow cash crops for export instead of producing food for domestic needs. This contributes to centralizing smaller farms into larger enterprises in many countries such as China, Argentina, and Brazil.[20] Many structuralists worry that attempts to diffuse biofuel (and thus GMO) production throughout the developing world will increase environmental damage and widen income gaps, both within developing nations and between the rich North and poor South. To structuralists such as Raj Patel, these trends ultimately enhance the economic power of agribusinesses and their influence in developing nations.[21]

It is unclear how much biofuels alone were responsible for food crisis of 2008. Like speculation, biofuel production increased pressure on the market, this time by shifting agricultural commodities away from food production. Although there was not a commodity shortage, the amount of commodities devoted to food production increased, spiking the cost of food and the number of hungry. When food prices fell, the controversy diminished. Many supporters *and* detractors of biofuels wait for the development of new technology that converts biofuel from nonagricultural biomass material. Meanwhile, given the conflicting state and nonstate actor interests at stake, states have not been anxious to either regulate biofuel production or agree to international standards.

## LDC Overreliance on the Industrial Agricultural and Development Models

The primary reason that many LDCs have relied upon industrial and agricultural development models can be explained by the different perspectives held by experts, and the way that governments and IOs responded to their arguments. For mercantilists, the issue of income inequality and poverty in the international system is important only because of its effects on security interests. On the other hand, structuralists have been the most vocal that the cause of the 2008 world food crisis was not a supply–demand problem, but the *consequence* of failed efforts to apply the industrial model of development to problems related to food and hunger in most developing nations. Furthermore, the roots of high food prices during the recent crisis are an extension of a long-term food crisis associated with the institutions and workings of capitalism and the state system that supports and protects it. Yet the most popular model of development, economic liberalism, has overlooked income distribution and poverty as the primary causes of underdevelopment and hunger.

**OELs: Production Efficiency and Open Markets**  Since the end of World War II, many Western development experts have argued that economic growth and coordination between industry and agriculture would gradually transform the food system and solve hunger problems. Many OELs today would argue that the recent food crisis demonstrates that LDCs have *not* pursued the standard Western agro-industrial development strategy far enough. They focus on theories of trade developed by the economist David Ricardo (see Chapter 6), arguing that LDCs should specialize in producing bananas, coffee, sugar, tea, and other commodities specific to their geography. These exports earn foreign exchange and allow food-deficit nations to import the corn, wheat, rice, and other commodities other nations produce more efficiently. The large plantations devoted to soybean production in Brazil and the increase in industrial chicken farms in the Philippines are examples of how the application of modern technology enhances production, earns foreign exchange, and increases food security.[22]

Two ardent supporters of a popular model associated with agro-industrialization are Alex and Dennis Avery. They and other economic liberals propagate the idea that, due to difficult growing conditions, the only way to produce enough food for a growing population is to allow TNAC's to industrialize agriculture.[23] According to this model agro-industrial production methods help save on fertilizer production, transportation, and production marketing. TNAC contracts with local farmers are a "form of risk aversion between farmers and companies" like Cargill and Conagra, helping smaller farmers earn more income than they would otherwise. One of the other reasons that GMOs receive such strong support is the modernization factor. GMO crops require capital-intensive, rather than labor-intensive, agricultural systems, which reduce inefficiencies and lead to wider profit margins. Finally, laborers are also then freed to move into other employment opportunities, often created by TNAC foreign investment.

One of the most controversial elements of the agro-industrial model is its emphasis on the use of GMOs. Two FAO economists, Terri Raney and Pirabhu Pingali, argue that first Green Revolution in the 1960s produced enormous benefits in Asia, Latin America, and parts of Africa.[24] Now consumers are to benefit from a second "gene revolution" that spread transgenic organisms from North America into many developing countries. Currently, GMO foods are produced in eighteen countries and included in 70 percent of processed food in the United States. Many support GMOs, citing increased effeciency and nutritional value along with a decrease in environmental impact. GMO crops include plants engineered to be drought-resistant, allowing them to grow in arid areas such as sub-Saharan Africa. In nations such as Uganda, where growing conditions are poor, GMO crops like disease-resistant maize are viewed as necessary to feed the large number of hungry Ugandans.[25] Other crops are fortified to protect against pests and plant diseases, decreasing farmers' dependency on pesticides, fertilizers, and toxic herbicides which often deplete the land and pollute water sources. Despite reports to the contrary, scientist William Atkinson argues that there have been no documented adverse effects of GMO food on humans.[26]

During the 1980s and into the 1990s, OELs also supported the neoliberal structural adjustment policies (SAPs) of the WTO, the IMF, and the World Bank (see Chapters 6, 7, 8, and 11) because they emphasized industrial productivity and economic growth while downplaying agricultural self-sufficiency.[27] OELs routinely argued that these policies helped bring millions of people out of poverty and increased food security.[28] Food aid should be used only in short-term emergencies and as part of humanitarian relief efforts, as aid can easily distort local and global markets. However, many OELs also viewed dependency on long-term aid, and food aid in particular, as likely to contribute to corruption and be a disincentive to both local food production and distribution, especially in developing nations.

**HILs Shift the Food and Hunger Agenda**   In the last decade HILs have become more critical than OELs of the supposed benefits of the agro-industrial development model. While still supportive of a role for markets in food production and distribution, their criticisms of TNACs can be reduced to five interrelated issues: trade policy, production efficiency, corporate monopolistic tactics, the impact of agro-industrial polices on the environment, and food and safety issues including the role of GMOs.

Most HILs would agree with the primary assertions included in a recent UN report by the International Assessment of Agricultural Science and Technology for Development (**IAASTD**) which suggest that industrial agricultural systems are contributing to the destruction of ecosystems, exacerbating global warming, are too dependent on fossil fuels, and are likely to widen the gap between rich and poor.[29] The IAASTD rejects the agro-industrial model of commodity production, pointing out that the emphasis on large-scale Brazilian soybean production and cattle grazing accelerates the destruction of rainforests, diminishes the quality of soil, and irrevocably alters a unique ecosystem.

Yet when it comes to GMOs, HILs have mixed views. Some view them as necessary to provide enough consumable commodities. For example, Paul Collier claims that the ban on GMOs has slowed down the application of technolgy to agriculture, leading to lower yields and higher food prices. For Collier, there is no better alternative in the face of overpopulation and environmental change.[30] Yet it appears that this argument—that GMOs produce more food than their traditional counterparts—may have been made in haste. In a series of studies carried out over the past three years, researchers at the University of Kansas found that "GM soya produces 10 per cent *less* food than its conventional equivalent, contradicting assertions by advocates of the technology that it increases yields."[31]

This is one of the many reasons HILs are not sanguine about a second Green Revolution, believing the solution to hunger lies not in science alone but in altering food distribution channels and addressing social inequalities, although little research has been done toward this goal.[32] They reference studies which state that modified crops decrease ecological diversity, contribute to an increased reliance on industrial methods, and actually increase poverty. Many of the modified crops have not been subjected to comprehensive tests enough to determine their safety on either the environment or humans. In fact, plants that have been genetically engineered to be resistant to herbicides have a negative impact on the environment, as farmers are more likely to spray indiscriminately across their fields, creating a greater likelihood of pollution in both the soil and water runoff.

Unlike traditional agriculture, GMOs are a business controlled by large agricultural corporations. The crops are patented as intellectual property, leading to high costs in initial investment as well as fixed costs for specialized inputs purchased from the manufacturer. Scientists have been concerned that intellectual property rights (IPRs) would limit seed conservation, sales, and access to patented material needed by researchers. However, the firm Syngenta did manage to obtain free licenses from thirty-two corporations and academic institutions to develop locally adopted varieties of grain in Bangladesh, China, India, Indonesia, the Philippines, South Africa, and Vietnam. Seeds from these plants were to be distributed free to those earning less than $10,000 a year.

As more and more TNACs encourage the governments of less developed nations to plant GMOs, more small and family farms disappear. Plots of land that previously featured crops such as sorghum, pearl millet, and chickpeas are now devoted to wheat, rice, and soybeans, decreasing ecological diversity and increasing the risk of crop failure. In addition, the excess from these plantations is funneled into the trade markets rather than being sold at low prices to those most in need.

Many HILs support free trade, but more in theory than in practice. For example, Joseph Stiglitz, a supporter of economic liberal ideas and globalization, raises many doubts about the trade and development strategies of the IMF, the World Bank, and other IOs. Often these organizations view problems through only an economic lens and thus create policies that benefit elites and people in urban areas but that inevitably hurt the world's poorest. True food security requires the reform of "free trade" policies and the adoption of fair trade policies so that globalization benefits a greater number of people, especially the poor.[33] Fair trade policy is usually quasi-protectionist and multifunctional in terms of its goals, creating policies that take into account economics, development issues, sociological concerns, and politics.

Many HILs agree with OELs about the detrimental effects of long-term aid on local food production and distribution in developing nations. However, in the late 1990s, in recognition of the limited success of the globalization campaign to help developing nations, many HILs renewed their faith in foreign and food aid policies and in the ability of IO agencies and NGOs to deal with an assortment of hunger issues. Foreign aid discussions were more comprehensive, with food and hunger issues playing only one (important) part in a range of efforts to improve global health. Increasing foreign aid and reducing world hunger by 50 percent became major goals of the Millennium Development Goals (MDGs) (see Chapters 8 and 11). Interestingly, while many states and aid agencies promised to double aid to Africa by 2010, aid for agriculture was actually cut.

According to Jeffrey Sachs, the Columbia University development expert, some forty-fifty countries are in desperate need. In the summer of 2007, the UN WFP reported that it fed some seventy-three million people annually in seventy-eight countries, yet reached only 10 percent of the world's hungry, while 25,000 people a day died of hunger.[34] Africa alone needs $8 billion per year in donor financing to finance improved seeds, fertilizer, irrigation systems, and extension training directed at sustainable food production. In response to the current financial crisis, Sachs has recommended the establishment of a single international account called the Financial Coordination Mechanism (FCM) that targets money from G8 states specifically at small-scale farmers.

**Structuralists**   Many structuralists agree that, as discussed above, the food crisis of 2008 brought short-term production loss, a devalued dollar, investment speculation, and the diversion of food surplus into biofuels. However, these factors were *not* the *root* causes of the crisis. They mask a long-term problem that has barely changed since the 1960s, when the major grain producing nations began accumulating surpluses: Instead, hunger is the result of the inefficient use of food resources rather than the lack of sufficient commodities.[35]

Many structuralists trace hunger in developing nations back to the colonial policies of the developed nations. Today's rich core states have dominated trade networks since the sixteenth century, colonizing and exploiting peripheral regions of the world for their resources and labor. Dependency theorists (see Chapters 4 and 6) have argued that increased connections to the West in the 1950s and 1960s focused on support for the urban-industrial sector of the economy, while the poorer enclaves, including agriculture, became *more* impoverished and *less* likely to have adequate food supplies.

After World War II, the free-trade policies of the rich states made poor countries more dependent on developed nations for many goods and services. Industrialized states continued to pressure many developing nations to include industrial agriculture in their larger model of development. Many economic liberal development experts assumed that if the overall economy grew, agriculture would follow, but the agriculture sectors of many of these economies often deteriorated. Now many of the urban poor, as well as laborers on large farms and plantations, go without enough to eat because they lack the economic resources to pay for enough food. Agricultural surpluses were still not being used to fight hunger. Instead, since the mid-1960s the major commodity exporting nations have disposed of their huge commodity surpluses as part of their trade and aid programs. As Walden Bello aptly states, this model is not only inappropriate for most developing nations but actually helped "manufacture" the current food crisis.[36]

Structuralists challenge the OEL argument that some nations have a comparative advantage in producing grain efficiently, and those states should distribute surplus grain to others. They believe that these policies reflect the influence of the wealthy, whether they be nations, corporations, or individuals. In the mid-1970s, developing nations were encouraged to borrow money to finance their industrial development programs. When development did not occur as anticipated, borrowers were pressured into rescheduling their debt and submitting to the IMF and World Bank's SAPs that favored investment in high value crops, including soy beans in Brazil, vegetables in Mexico, beef in Costa Rica, chickens in the Philippines, and peanuts in Senegal. Money earned from these crops was meant to service the mounting debt of these countries. Yet, as exports increased, so did interest payments as a percentage of expenditures, and investment in agriculture plummeted. Many states that had been food exporters were forced to rely on imports to feed their people. Cheap imports also undercut the price of domestic commodities, helped drive smaller farmers out of business, and increased dependence on food imports.

Many structuralists note that economic liberal policies had the same effect on trade. When Mexico joined NAFTA in 1994, and the Philippines joined the WTO the next year, both nations were swamped with cheap corn and rice imports.

"De-peasantisation" occurred when massive numbers of people were forced to abandon their agrarian heritage for urban slums. Brazil lost five million farmers over the last decade while the Philippines lost half of its grain farmers.[37] In many cases the dislocated headed north to the United States and Canada in search of unskilled jobs (see Chapter 16), weakening local food production systems. This left many debtor states vulnerable to TNACs seeking investment opportunities, allowing officials the opportunity to modernize their agricultural sectors. Paradoxically, incidences of hunger actually *increased* and poorer states found themselves more food insecure and dependent on imported commodities.

Today many African agricultural systems are going through the same transformational process that occurred in Asia and Latin America. Productivity has increased in Niger, Tanzania, and Rwanda, yet the number of hungry has risen commensurate with food price hikes. According to many structuralists, hunger in these situations is not the result of any specific food crisis. Before and during the recent crisis, local agro-industrial producers contracting to companies such as Cargill, Archer Daniels Midland, Tesco, and Carrefour recorded huge profits.[38] While these companies focused on the export markets, local people subsisted on substandard diets and the remainder of local staple crops.[39] The market-based agro-industrial model also led to many cases of fiscal mismanagement, corruption, income disparities, a collapsed currency, and the loss of personal savings.[40]

Many structuralists are more suspicious of foreign aid than HILs, as it can lead to increased dependency on major grain exporters and food aid donors, even when there is no hunger emergency. Exempting short-term humanitarian crises, all forms of aid are regarded as another means of domination by developed over developing countries. During the Cold War, U.S. PL 480 food aid was a way to establish new markets for U.S. commodities after recipients "graduated" from the program. This goal continues to be part of an explicit TNAC effort to shift LDC consumer tastes away from locally-grown crops, toward wheat, corn, and soy, the seeds of which are owned, cultivated, and marketed by selective producers who practice industrial agricultural production techniques.

Structuralist criticisms of globalization and economic liberal policies increased in the late 1990s, with experts arguing that state and IO officials did not focus enough on the relationship of aid to poverty, its impact on small farmers, and on the factors that deterred local food production and left states reliant upon importing food or receiving it as aid. Yet, due to the lack of state funding, many IOs, NGOs, and private foundations have sought to help LDCs modernize their agricultural sectors while fighting hunger. The Gates Foundation has been cooperating with the FAO and WFP to generate a second green revolution in Africa. Along with these efforts the Millennium Goals are primarily aimed at developing local markets by promoting technological and market-based solutions. On the other hand Robin Broad and John Cavanaugh believe that the solutions of these organizations are nothing revolutionary because they continue to rely upon economic development as a cure for poverty rather than accepting that development can contribute to it.[41] According to Vandana Shiva, Gates is the "greatest threat to farmers in the developing world" because these programs stand to greatly benefit major firms like Monsanto and Syngenta.[42]

These and other structuralists have focused on shifting the global food agenda away from agro-industrialization to promoting self-suffiency and self-reliance at the local level. While there are many issues for developing nations to overcome, the ideas have caught on in many parts of the world, as discussed in the box below.

## GETTING BACK TO LOCAL MARKETS[a]

The financial crisis of 2007 has acted as a wrench thrown into the entire food debate. The global impact of a few nations' economic troubles has led a growing number of leaders worldwide to question conventional wisdom of economic liberal policies, international free trade, and more specifically the impact of industrialized food production on the global food production and consumption system. These officials point to fluctuating currency values and the experience of debtor nations within the developing world that have driven up food prices in spastic fits, increasing political instability along with chronic hunger. Many leaders are asking why they should rely on corporate commodity chains when they can improve food security in their own local backyards and garden plots, in the hands of their own people, rather than those in corporate boardrooms.

An unlikely alliance is forming between some economic liberals and structuralists in favor of reform. The motivations of structuralists have remained the same—to promote self-sufficiency and better tasting and more nutritious food. But some economic liberals are beginning to accuse government-backed international corporations of undermining free enterprise, which is in theory based on individual and family entrepreneurship as opposed to massive, publicly traded, politically powerful corporate entities. Instead, momentum is growing behind the idea that returning control of food production to small time farmers will not only enhance food security, but may improve the economies of developed and developing nations alike.

Supporting a more sustainable food system and promoting greater food security often take place locally and not just in the meeting rooms of the WTO or USDA. Participating in growing one's own food in a home garden or community garden, donating or sharing excess within the community, asking for local and organic produce at the grocer, shopping at farmer's markets, eating in season, and joining a Community Supported Agriculture (CSA) farm are just some of the ways consumers are joining with producers within their local communities to build the foundation of political reform.[b] Cities from Chicago to New York and from Shanghai to Mexico City host a proliferation of programs designed to bring the bounty of urban agriculture to the hands of the people, while innovative development programs are returning traditional forms of agriculture and varieties of crops to regions previously dominated by industrial monocropping.[c]

At this point political will and social recognition of this movement are being challenged by powerful lobbies of consolidated agriculture. Without political and economic pressure from the world's consumers in support of fair, natural, and sustainable food, the movement may stagnate, or reform may be weak and ineffective. While Generation X traditionally has a reputation for social and political apathy, a change is slowly taking place in today's youth, who are beginning to test their social power and trying to inspire multiple generations around them. Rather than being dazzled by technological change and corporate power, some young citizens today are promoting change and directing their own role in history.

### References
[a]Kendle Bjelland and Brendan Hammond researched and drafted this material.
[b]See for example, Brian Halweil, "The Case for Local Food," *World Watch Magazine*, May/June 2003.
[c]See Lester R. Brown, "*Feeding Eight Billion People Well*" in his *Plan 4.0: Mobilizing to Save Civilization* (New York: W. W. Norton & Co., 2009).

**Mercantilists**  Mercantilists view the agro-industrial model and its component parts of trade, aid, and use of GMOs as being both helpful and damaging to domestic and international objectives. After World War II, many realist-oriented foreign policy officials viewed hunger problems in relation to the needs of war victims. Officials supported the Stages of Growth model of development (see Chapter 11) because its goals dovetailed nicely with support for the IMF, the World Bank, and the GATT, containment of communism (see Chapter 9), opening up markets for Western FDI, and promoting capitalism in LDCs. As LDC economies grew, industry was to help support commodity production, which would feed their growing populations. Yet, as we have discussed above, the attempt to employ the industrial agriculture model to developing nations has proven *not* to be the successful case many had hoped it would be.

Mercantilists are divided about the utility of food aid and its connection to hunger. Some supported efforts to use food aid to help contain communism during the Cold War. In the early 1980s, President Reagan cut grain sales to the Soviet Union when it invaded Afghanistan. Food aid and selective trade measures were used as instruments to pressure Asian nations, including Japan, South Korea, and Bangladesh, into cooperating with the United States and its allies. Aid also served as a disposal mechanism for commodity surpluses, benefiting wealthier farmers and agribusinesses.

By the late 1980s, the U.S. State and Commerce Departments and USAID officials were actively promoting the agro-industrial model as a method of integrating poorer economies into the global political economy. Support for foreign aid declined and emphasis was put on "trade instead of aid." LDCs were encouraged to grow their economies by promoting industrial goods for export while importing cheap food from developed nations. After the fall of the Soviet Union in 1990, realists emphasized the links between the agro-industrial model and national interests, including open-market policies, globalization, and the promotion of democracy in states that were susceptible to authoritarian regimes.

After 9/11, realists were more willing to use food aid as a counterterrorism tool. Food served a number of security objectives in Sudan, Somalia, North Korea, Iraq, and Iran. Other realists question the ability of food aid to achieve those objectives. In many cases aid supplies are often targeted at groups who support government policies, to the detriment of the poor and hungry. In Ethiopia and Sudan, it is hard to target and coordinate food aid with security operations. As aid is considered a strategic resource for combatants, it is often stolen or captured by insurgents and sold to businesses or officials in other states. Finally, often food aid shipments are redirected to other national ports during shipment, especially during emergency periods when food prices are higher.[43]

In 2008, President Bush promised that the United States would spend almost $50 million to fight hunger in Africa with emergency food aid.[44] He noted that the United States intended to spend almost 25 percent of this assistance to help farmers in developing nations "build up local production." Many would argue that the president's remarks promoting food self-sufficiency appeared to contradict his efforts to support biofuel and GMO production. While it appears that the United States is shifting its policies to put more emphasis on helping local farmers, it is not clear that global food security will take precedence over domestic priorities.

Many mercantilist-realists have mixed views of development efforts by IOs and civil society to resolve issues of poverty and hunger through economic development. Some suggest that it might be in the interest of the industrialized nations to increase food aid and agricultural assistance to states like Pakistan and Afghanistan, where poverty and hunger undermine social stability and strengthen terrorist groups. Meanwhile socialist leaders in Venezuela, Bolivia, and Ecuador, for example, suggest that the promotion of agro-industrial and economic liberal policies and aid continue to contribute to widespread poverty and hunger.

## War, Disease, Corruption, and Government Mismanagement

Many experts and officials point to these four interrelated factors that in some cases exacerbated, if not caused, hunger during the world food crisis of 2008. All four usually appear together, especially in the poorest countries, most of which are in Africa.

OELs usually focus on corruption and government mismanagement more than the other two conditions. William Easterly for one, focuses on both foreign aid and national officials in poorer countries who are in league with corrupt businessmen or investors.[45] Often large bureaucracies provide jobs to people who fail to accomplish the simplest of tasks. These positions also offer opportunities for nepotism and siphoning off funds to those they are supposed to regulate. One example is the ministries of agriculture at the federal state and local levels in Nigeria that drain off public funds to elites and their friends when it comes to lucrative programs for fertilizer imports, subsidization, and food distribution.[46] Officials and their associates often meet in expensive hotels and dine on expensive foods imported from Europe and the United States.

For Easterly, corruption and poor management are significant barriers to economic development. He and other neoliberal-oriented experts assume that economic development of these states would significantly relieve hunger. However, in a fascinating account of an IO contractor titled *The Economist's Tale*, Peter Griffiths would largely agree with Easterly about the impact of corruption and poor management on hunger. And yet he arrives at the opposite conclusion.[47]

In one instance Griffiths conducted a study in Sierra Leone to determine if people would be able to feed themselves during another bad harvest season. He soon discovered that it was hard to figure out the price of rice in the country, let alone how much of it was stored where. Much of it that was imported was often reshipped to other countries in the region to earn more for either the state or their business partners. At the time, Senegal had both an agricultural commodities board and a separate rice board that determined rice prices and reserve levels. Different parts of the country grew different types of rice alongside other indigenous crops that made it hard for IOs and NGOs to determine the severity of supply and demand. In many cases, past IO and NGO projects had failed miserably, only to be replaced by other well-intended efforts to deal with hunger.

Often these projects were not directed at hunger alone but at education and health care.

Griffiths and many structuralists agree with HILs and mercantilists that corruption usually benefits not only local elites but international corporations and shipping companies. More importantly, though, it was the ideological environment of neoliberal ideas at the time during the Reagan administration that promoted economic growth and deregulation of the domestic and international economy that spurred on a good deal of corruption and mismanagement. Walden Bello supports this same argument about the role of ideology. He suggests that when states practice neoliberal policies, the result is often that private companies crowd out competition from other companies when the state is withdrawn.[48]

Some neomercantilists such as Ha-Joon Chang suggest that in certain cases corruption can actually help developing countries in any number of ways that include the delivery of services to service clients and moving around bureaucratic barriers.[49] Of course, it is usually difficult to know precisely when a bit of corruption is warranted over improving bureaucratic efficiencies.

When it comes to diseases and wars, most scholars agree that they are directly responsible for hunger, if not starvation. As noted above in the history part of the chapter, food is routinely used as a strategic weapon. *The Economist* reports that in the Horn of Africa region that includes Somalia, Ethiopia, and Kenya, 17.5 million people are starving because of a combination of long-term drought and civil and ethnic conflict.[50] While the WFP has been trying to feed people, fighting in Ethiopia's Ogaden region makes it hard to help. Food prices are high, in part because food convoys are highjacked.

War is also a notable feature of Central Africa where Tutsi forces in Congo who escaped Rwanda in 1994 have fought government forces over control of minerals and other natural resources, leaving scores of people hungry and seeking shelter in refugee camps. Civil wars and local violence have also occurred in Kenya, Somalia, and Sudan. One of the most notorious cases has been the Darfur region of Sudan where over 300,000 people have died in the past eight years. The connection of war to hunger and other systemic diseases such as AIDs is obvious. People who are hungry are least likely to respond to medication, if they can afford it. Most experts also point out that when these societies and their governments collapse, civil strife, violence, hunger, and other calamities are most likely to result.

## CONCLUSION

The IPE of hunger and food issues touches on at least seven of the main themes of the text (see Chapter 1). After World War II the issue was framed primarily as one of whether supply would be able to keep up with increasing demand. Issues of production outweighed those of distribution until the 1970s, when Food Firsters focused on political and economic factors that determined who would eat, how much, and at what price.

From the early 1980s until now, officials have emphasized economic liberal market solutions to hunger. Food itself has often been used to achieve a variety of state political and economic objectives. As the number of hungry people in the world remained relatively constant, the role of IOs in helping to feed more people was relatively weak and ineffective because states were not willing to give IOs much authority.

The 1990s saw more criticism of globalization and economic liberal policies along with a broader agenda of food and hunger issues related to food sustainability, the viability of the industrial food model, and issues of equality and social justice. Many structuralists raised questions about the extent to which market-oriented food policies served the interests of those who were most hungry. Recently, more experts have accepted the idea that markets alone are not likely to solve the problem of hunger.

Bigger than normal food shortages between 2005 and 2008 that supposedly contributed to a world food crisis helped clarify a few issues related to food and hunger policy. The dramatic spike in prices was not related to real production shortages as much as it was to a perfect storm of factors including speculative investment, increased pressure on production due water shortages, income growth in many of the emerging economies, biofuel production, and the persistence of war, famine, and disease.

Since then the connection of food and hunger to an assortment of energy and environmental issues has become clearer. A new food agenda appears to be emerging in different nations and regions with more emphasis on production self-sufficiency and sustainability at the local level. Whether or not this outlook will actually help feed more of the world's poorest remains to be seen, but many are willing to try another approach that centers on sustainable local food systems.

Meanwhile it remains hard to separate solutions to hunger from state interests and food security from economic growth. Food is recognized as a right in words only. In the short run the influence of politics on market forces is not only acceptable, but necessary, as the many causes of hunger make it exceedingly difficult to find a single solution that includes overcoming poverty and the impact of distribution. Policy issues to be addressed include: decisions about the impact of biofuels made from agricultural commodities; the cost and benefits of state support for food production; the use of GMOs blended with more traditional crops and methods to maintain soil fertility and drought relief that come with modern approaches to crop science; and the role of trade in development policies. Perhaps due to the food and global financial crises have generated interest in and reasons why it is, necessary to look for ways to reembed the market back into society at the local level and do more to proactively solve food and hunger problems, for everyone's sake.

## KEY TERMS

transnational agribusiness
corporations (TNACs)  465
Food Firsters  468
demographic
transition  468

Green Revolution  467
Biofuels  473
GMOs  464
Community Supported
Agriculture (CSA)  466

local markets  465
World Food Program (WFP)  464
IAASTD  478

## DISCUSSION QUESTIONS

1. Do you agree with the Food Firsters that population and lack of production are as important as poverty and political issues when it comes to the causes of world hunger? Explain.
2. Explain in some detail why OELs in particular looked at food and hunger problems in the 1990s the way they did? Do you agree with the authors that those ideas and policies have not been all that successful when it comes to dealing with hunger? Explain.
3. Discuss at least three connections between the world food crisis and the current global financial crisis, if any.
4. Discuss at least three connections between hunger, energy, and environmental issues—depending on whether or not you have read either of the next two chapters.
5. Are you optimistic or pessimistic about efforts to promote self-sufficiency through local markets to deal with hunger issues? Why or why not?

# SUGGESTED READINGS

Milan Brahmbhatt and Luc Christiansen. "The Run on Rice," *World Policy Journal*, XV (Summer 2008).

Angel Gurria. "And Prosperity for All: A View from the OECD," *World Policy Journal*, XXV (Summer 2008).

Frances Moore Lappe, Joseph Collins, and Peter Rosset. *World Hunger: Twelve Myths*. New York: Grove Press, 1988.

Peter Griffiths. *The Economists Tale: A Consultant Encounters Hunger and the World Bank.* New York: Zed Books, 2003.

Raj Patel, *Stuffed and Starved; The Hidden Battle for the World Food System*. New York: Melville House Publishing, 2008.

# NOTES

1. Garrett Hardin, "Lifeboat Ethics: The Case Against Helping the Poor," *Psychology Today*, September 1974, pp. 38–43 and 124–126.

2. France Moore Lappe, Joseph Collins, and Peter Rosset, *Food First: Twelve Myths About World Hunger* (New York: Grove Press, 1988).

3. Robert G. Lewis, "What World Food Crisis," *World Policy Journal*, 25 XXIV (Spring 2008) 34.

4. See Shaena Montanari, "Global Climate Change Linked to Increasing World Hunger," *World Watch*, Washington, DC (September/October 2005), 18.

5. See Lester Brown, "Voices of Concern," interview on Nova, PBS at http://www.pbs.org/wgbh/nova/worldbalance/voic-brow.html; www.pbs.org/wgbh/nova/worldbalance/voic-brow.html.

6. Diana B. Henriques, "Food is Gold, and Investors Pour Billions Into Farming," *The New York Times*, June 5, 2008.

7. See Clifford Krauss, "Commodities' Relentless Surge," *The New York Times,* January 15, 2008.

8. Thalif Green, "Land Grabs for Food Production under Fire," October 23, 2009, at http//ipsnews.net/news.asp?idnews=48979.

9. See Noemi Pace, Andrew Seal and Anthony Costello, "Has Financial Speculation in Food Commodity Markets Increased Food Prices," *The Lancet*, No. 371 (May 17, 2008) p. 1650.

10. See Peter Brabeck-letmathe, "Biofuels Are Indefensible in Our Hungry World," *The Wall Street Journal*, June, 13, 2009.

11. Milan Brahmbhatt and Luc Christiansen, "The Run on Rice," *World Policy Journal*, XXV (Summer 2008), pp. 29–37.

12. See Andrew Martin, "Food Report Criticizes Biofuel Policies," *The New York Times*, May, 30, 2008.

13. Ibid.

14. See Susan S. Lang, "Cornell Ecologist's Study Finds that Producing Biofuels and Ethanol from Corn and Other Crops Is Not Worth the Energy," Cornell University News Service, July 5, 2005.

15. See Suzanne Hunter, "Biofuels, Neither Savior nor Scam: The Case for a Selective Strategy," *World Policy Journal*, XXIV (Spring 2008), pp. 9–17.

16. For a brief overview of this issue see Andrew Martin and Elisabeth Rosenthal, "U.N. Says Food Plan Could Cost $30 Billion a Year." *The New York Times*, June 4, 2008.

17. See Elisabeth Rosenthal, "U.N. Says Biofuel Subsidies Raise Food Bill and Hunger," *New York Times*, October 8, 2008.

18. See for example, Dan Morgan, "Emptying the Breadbasket," *The Washington Post*, April 29, 2008.

19. Clemens Hoges, "A 'Green Tsunami' in Brazil: The High Price of Clean, Cheap Ethanol," *Der Spiegel*, January 24, 2009.

20. See Richard McGregor, "China's Farmers Change the Way They Work," *Financial Times*, May 8, 2008.

21. See Raj Patel, *Stuffed and Starved; The Hidden Battle for the World Food System* (New York: Melville House Publishing, 2008).

22. See Byeong-Seon Yoon, "Who is Threatening Our Dinner Table? The Power of Transnational Agribusiness," *Monthly Review, 58*, no. 7 (2006).

23. Alex Avery and Dennis Avery, "The Local Organic Food Paradigm," *Georgetown Journal of International Affairs*, IX (Winter–Spring 2008), pp. 33–40.

24. See Terri Raney and Pirabhu Pingali, "Sowing a Green Revolution," *Scientific American*, September 2007, pp. 104–111.

25. See Jeremy Cooke, "Could GM Crops Help Feed Africa?," May 30, 2008, http://news.bbc.co.uk/1/hi/world/africa/7428789.stm.

26. See William Atkinson, "The High Tech Menu," in Andrew Heintzman and Evan Solomon, eds., *Feeding the Future* (Toronto, ON: House of Anasi Press), 2006.

27. See for example, Avery and Avery, "The Local Organic Food Paradigm," and Louise Blouin MacBain, "Doha's Good Deeds," *World Policy Journal*, 26 (Summer 2008), pp. 39–44.

28. See for example David Dollar and Aart Kraay, "Spreading the Wealth," *Foreign Affairs*, *81* (January/February, 2002), pp. 120–33.

29. See the International Assessment of Agricultural Knowledge, Science and Technology for Development (IAASTD) 2008 report for a detailed discussion of hunger, agriculture, global warming, and the agro-industrial model at http://www .agassessment.org/.

30. Paul Collier, "The Politics of Hunger," *Foreign Affairs, 87* (November–December, 2008).

31. See Geoffrey Lean, "Exposed: The Great GM Myth," *The Independent UK*, April 20, 2008.

32. See for example, Miguel Altieri, *Genetic Engineering in Agriculture*, 2nd ed. (Oakland, CA: Food First, 2004).

33. See Joseph Stiglitz and Andrew Charlton, *Fair Trade For All: How Trade Can Promote Development* (Oxford: Oxford University Press, 2005).

34. See Jeffrey D. Sachs, "A Breakthrough Against Hunger," at http://www.guatemala-times.com.

35. See Lappé, Collins, and Rosset, *Twelve Myths about World Hunger.*

36. See Walden Bello, "Manufacturing a Food Crisis," *The Nation*, June 2, 2008.

37. See Marco Visscher, "Fatal Harvest," *Ode Magazine*, http://www.odemagazine.com/doc/4/fatal_harvest/.

38. See David Kesmodel, Lauren Etter, Aaron O. Patrick, "Grain Companies' Profits Soar As Global Food Crisis Mounts, *Wall Street Journal*, April 30, 2008. See also Grain, "Making a Killing From Hunger, April 2008, http://www.grain.org/articles/?id=39.

39. See Byeong-Seon Yoon, "Who is Threatening our Dinner Table? The Power of Transnational Agribusiness," *Monthly Review, 58,* no. 7, (2006).

40. See Sara Miller Llana, "Gap between Rich and Poor Widens in Argentina," *The Christian Science Monitor*, January 27, 2008.

41. See Robin Broad and John Cavanaugh, "The Hijacking of the Development Debate: How Friedman and Sachs Got It Wrong," *World Policy Journal, XXIII* (Summer 2006), pp. 21–30.

42. Vandana Shiva's comment was made at a talk in San Francisco, California in February, 2009. See http://www.thebreakthrough.org/blog/2009/02/is_bill_gates_a_menace_to_poor.shtml For a discussion the issue of the relationship of hunger to the issue of the Gates Foundation support for a second Green Revolution see Eric Holt-Gimenez, Miguel A Altieri, and Peter Rosset, "Ten Reasons Why the Rockefeller and Bill and Melinda Gates Foundations' Alliance for Another Green Revolution Will Not Solve the Problems of Poverty and Hunger in Sub-Saharan Africa," Food First Policy Brief No. 12, October 2006.

43. See for example Laura Blue, "On the Front Lines of Hunger," *Time International*, June 30–July 7, 2008.

44. See "Bush Asks Congress for $770 million in Emergency Food Aid," May 2, 2008, at http://www.sundancechannel.com/sunfiltered/tag/global-food-security/.

45. William Easterly, *The White Man's Burden: Why the West's Efforts to Aid the Rest Have Done So Much Ill and So Little Good* (Cambridge: Cambridge University Press, 2006).

46. See "Nigeria: Let Us Close Down Agriculture Ministry," http://allafrica.com/stories.

47. See Peter Griffiths, *The Economist's Tale: A Consultant Encounters Hunger and the World Bank* (New York: Zed Books, 2003).

48. See Walden Bello, "Destroying Africa Agriculture," *Foreign Policy in Focus*, June 3, 2008.

49. See Ha-Joon Chang, *Bad Samaritans: The Myth of Free Trade and the Secret History of Capitalism* (New York: Bloomsbury Press, 2008), especially pp. 160–181.

50. "The Tragedy of the Decade?" *The Economist*, October 30, 2008.

# Oil and Energy: Dependency and Resource Curses[1]

How many more shipments will there be?

Jacob Silberberg

The year 1973 was a turning point for the international political economy. The international balance of wealth and power shifted away from the United States to its European allies, Japan, and a number of militarily weak, oil-producing nations. When the United States supported Israel in its 1973 war with Egypt and Syria, Arab members of the **Organization of Petroleum Exporting Countries (OPEC)** oil **cartel** a group of business firms or nations that try to control the supply and price of a certain commodity or product banned exports of petroleum to the United States and other allies of Israel. For a short period of time, because of its control over oil resources and its ability to generate price increases for those resources, OPEC seemed to hold nation-states hostage. World oil prices skyrocketed, and gasoline at the pump had to be rationed in many industrialized nations. Vast sums of money were suddenly tranferred to oil-producing states in the Middle East. Because petroleum had become so vital to every aspect of an industrial society, the lives of most people in the world were disrupted.

By the time the dust settled a year later, the world oil market was dominated by OPEC. Oil prices continued to rise, and individuals, industries, and nations felt the sting of burdensome oil payments. The OPEC oil embargo of 1973–1974 was like an earthquake that rocked the international political economy—with short, sharp jolts that shook international institutions and changed the global political and economic landscape for years to come.

In the subsequent thirty-five years the global political economy would be rocked several times again—by the collapse of the Soviet Union in 1990, the 9/11 attacks in 2001, and now the global financial crisis. As we discuss in the next chapter on the environment, a global summit in Copenhagen in early December of 2009 wrestled with the issue of global warming that many would suggest has put the earth on the edge of yet another major crisis. Many argue that global warming and other issues related to the type and amounts of energy consumed in industrialized nations and fast-growing emerging economies are pushing the limits of the earth's capacity to withstand increasing temperatures associated with the use of what has until recently been viewed as relatively "cheap oil." Since 1973 states have adjusted to often wide swings in market prices for oil and other resources. Sustaining access to and control over oil has produced many security issues, especially for the major powers (see Chapter 9). Other states that discovered large deposits of oil, copper, and other minerals often incurred more of a curse than a blessing when it came to the did not encounter a blessing so much as a "curse" when the resources caused destabilizing corruption, violence, and even war that resulted from the discovery.

This chapter looks at the recent history of oil and the role of OPEC in its production and pricing. We discuss some of the political and economic tensions that have arisen due to the interdependence between oil-producing and oil-consuming nations. These stresses include security issues, oil as a resource curse, the issue of peak oil, and efforts to produce new energy sources.

There are several interrelated theses in this chapter. First, problems surrounding oil have become increasingly *global* in nature. Second, because oil production and distribution are associated with wealth and power, they create added tensions associated with risk and uncertainty in the international political economy. Third, the IPE of oil and energy reflects a delicate *balancing* act between states, markets, IOs, and major oil companies. Fourth, markets tend to work when there is plenty of the resource, but not when resources are critically scarce. Scarcity imposes heavy costs on those without major energy resources, making them vulnerable to others, which often destabilizes their society. Fifth, oil can be a curse instead of a blessing to producing states, exacting inequality between the haves and have-nots of society. Sixth and finally, efforts to deal with the scarcity of oil are directly connected to the issue of global warming, whose solution requires developing alternative sources of energy.

# OPEC AND THE IPE OF OIL

As a cartel, OPEC in the early 1970s attempted to control oil production in ways that increased commodity prices and profits for its thirteen members.[2] Collectively, cartel member agreed to an output quota less than the amount that would be produced under competitive market conditions. Collectively, they were able to employ production quotas to limit production and impose an export embargo, which quickly raised the price of oil. Although profit is generally the main purpose of cartels, some believe that OPEC was also quietly seeking retribution for colonialism and western domination of the international political economy. Given that OPEC is composed of sovereign nation-states and not ordinary business firms, its actions were also conditioned by each member's desire for wealth, political power, and national security.

OPEC was formed in 1960 when many of the major oil-exporting nations—most of which are Middle Eastern—sought to gain more control over and profit from the oil located under their national territory. Up until then, the production, processing, marketing, and pricing of oil had been dominated by seven major multinational oil corporations—the "seven sisters"—five American, one British, and one Anglo-Dutch company.[3] Host nations often felt exploited and dominated by the oil companies, and eventually formed OPEC to advance their common interests.

OPEC's power derived from the developed world's economic reliance on petroleum imports. Before World War II the United States had been the world's largest oil producer and exporter. After World War II, developed countries became more dependent on foreign oil as recovery progressed and the demand for petroleum accelerated. In the early 1960s, coal still accounted for roughly 41 percent of the world's *total* energy consumption, compared to 29 percent for oil. By 1973, increasing reliance on oil as a primary source of the world's energy, coupled with increasing demand for Middle East oil as the biggest, cheapest surplus pool of petroleum available, made countries more vulnerable to the growing assertiveness of Middle Eastern suppliers.

Western corporate control over oil gradually weakened in the face of a variety of political and economic conditions. The precedent for a new relationship between host governments, the oil companies, and the industrialized nations was established in 1969 when Libya pressured Occidental Petroleum, a small U.S. company dependent on Libyan supplies, into granting new price concessions to Libya. Host countries were able to gradually wrangle bigger concessions from the oil companies. Libya had demonstrated that revenue for host countries could be raised by increasing oil prices. OPEC as a whole, then, soon became more aggressive on questions of production, price levels, and taxes.

# THE OIL CRISES OF THE 1970s AND EARLY 1980s

The first OPEC oil shock occurred in late 1973 when Arab states within OPEC imposed a successful oil embargo on the United States and the Netherlands for supporting Israel in the October 1973 war. Almost overnight, OPEC's "oil weapon" increased the price of a barrel of oil in the international marketplace from $2.90 to $11.65—a jump of over 400 percent. In reaction to OPEC's bold move, in early 1974 the United States tried unsuccessfully to form an oil consumers' "countercartel". France and other West European countries along with Japan counted on bilateral agreements with single OPEC producers to solve their oil import problems. The oil companies themselves went along with OPEC price hikes because they could easily pass higher gas prices on to consumers.

By the mid-1970s, OPEC "unilaterally" (by itself) had gained control over oil prices. Saudi Arabia, the largest oil producer and exporter, influenced OPEC's policies the most. With its huge reserves, vast financial reserves, and relatively small population, the Saudis could play the role of OPEC's swing producer—adjusting production levels to maintain price targets. In other words, the Saudis played a key role in raising the price of Middle Eastern oil, but they were also willing to make up for production cuts during times of recession or to cut production enough to keep prices stable. Other OPEC members, including Iran and Iraq, often favored production cuts to drive up oil prices above the rate of inflation in the West.

In the wake of the 1973 crisis conservation efforts and economic recession in the West led to a slackening of demand in world oil markets. In a famous speech on American energy policy given in April of 1977, President Carter labeled conservation efforts in the United States "the moral equivalent of war." The U.S. Congress offered a series of tax incentives to those who reduced energy consumption by insulating their homes, and the highway speed limit was reduced to 55 miles per hour. Newly discovered supplies of petroleum in the North Sea, Alaska, and Mexico also started to come on line. The United States also created a Strategic Petroleum Reserve that would release oil to the market in the case of another crisis.

A second global oil shock occurred near the end of the decade when Iranian fundamentalists finally succeeded in toppling the U.S.-backed Shah of Iran in 1979. The ensuing panic in world oil markets—followed by the onset of the Iran–Iraq War in 1980—pushed the price of a 42-gallon barrel of crude from $13 to $34 by the early 1980s. In less than a decade, then, the oil-dependent economies of the world saw their import bills for petroleum leap by almost 1,200 percent.

How was it that a full five years after the Arab embargo of 1973, Iran—accounting for less than 20 percent of all OPEC exports—could once again throw the international economy into disarray? Oil producers sell their product to the world by way of two different (but related) markets. A long-term contract market accounted for most sales in the late 1970s: the contract between oil company and producer, reflected in the price set by OPEC. Oil not sold on this market was traded on the international **spot market price,** which reacted swiftly to the withdrawal of Iranian oil in late 1978. As spot market prices shot up, the gap between these prices and long-term market prices widened. The primary beneficiary of such a gap was the oil companies, whose long-term contracts gave them a supply of oil at a relatively cheap, stable price, which they could then sell at prices reflecting the spot market frenzy. OPEC states began to place their own surcharges on top of prices previously determined by OPEC. However, some OPEC members began to break long-term contracts in order to sell their oil on the more lucrative spot market. The Saudis tried to keep the others in line, but the momentum was inexorable. The outbreak of the Iran–Iraq War again destabilized oil markets. World production decreased by roughly 10 percent, driving up the spot market price of oil to $42 a barrel.

The two OPEC oil crises changed the views of officials, experts, and the public about national security in several ways. The crises helped shift attention away from the East–West conflict to growing tensions between industrialized Northern countries and Southern developing nations. Whereas LDCs had been important to the United States as allies in the battle to contain international communism, now they were important for resources related to security. The crises also made it more difficult for oil-importing states to insulate themselves from the international political economy. The oil crises also made states more aware that their military power was dependent on access to natural resources and raw materials to feed the economy's industrial base. In 1980 President Carter announced his "Carter Doctrine," proclaiming that the United States would "use any means necessary including military force" to protect its interests in the Middle East.

Another result of the changing IPE of OPEC and oil in the 1970s was a dramatic shift in the patterns of world finance (see Chapter 7 for a broader discussion of this development). Suddenly in 1973–1974 a massive flow of funds was redirected first to the Middle East oil exporters, then to world financial markets, and then, ultimately, to the rich and poor oil-importing countries. **Petrodollar recycling** accounts for the need of oil-rich countries and their banks to lend money to their oil-poor customers. This re-circulation of money can also be thought of as one of the seeds of the debt crises many developing nations would suffer in the 1980s and 1990s (see Chapter 8). Finally, the oil crises helped propel the world toward the globalization of financial markets as we know them today.

# OIL AND OPEC IN THE 1980s AND THE 1991 GULF WAR

OPEC's problems in the 1980s were based on the success it had in raising oil prices in the 1970s. A decrease in the demand for oil atrributed in part to the recession caused by OPEC, along with an increase in non-OPEC production, helped transform the world, resulting in long-term surpluses and downward pressure on prices. Even when the Iran–Iraq War moved into the Gulf itself in the mid-1980s, and tankers and production and shipping platforms became the objects of attacks, no further run-up in oil prices occurred. Soon OPEC's ability to control world energy prices and markets all but collapsed. In fact, in 1983, for the first time in the organization's history, OPEC actually *reduced* the price of its "benchmark crude," which contributed to its erosion as an effective, cooperative price-setting cartel.

By the end of the Iran–Iraq War in 1988, oil prices in "real terms" were below their 1974 level. High oil prices in the 1970s had provided all the incentives necessary for Mexico, Norway, Britain, and the United States to develop new oil fields. Although finding and producing oil in the stormy North Sea and the frozen Alaskan North Slope were technically and physically challenging and enormously expensive, the high price and uncertain supply of oil made these expenditures politically and economically attractive at the time.

OPEC fell into a **prisoner's dilemma** that in theory characterizes all cartels. While it is in the cartel members' *collective* interest to cut production to push up prices, once prices have increased it is in *each individual member*'s interest to expand output to raise more revenue, which in turn drives down the price of oil. This conflict between the group's interests and each member's interests became a major issue for OPEC. OPEC hung together rather tightly as long as oil prices were rising, and in spite of the incentive each nation had to "defect" by increasing output beyond the production quota. But when prices began to fall and non-OPEC members received the benefits of the cartel's self-restraint, it was too much for many OPEC members to bear.

Fed up with other OPEC members, Saudi Arabia continued production over quotas, flooded oil markets in 1985, and drove crude oil prices down to $10 a barrel. Oil prices would stay low through the rest of the 1980s, causing economic problems in highly-indebted oil producers such as Nigeria and Algeria. Lower prices in the mid-1980s would also punish nations like Mexico that had invested in high-cost oil production based on the assumption that high prices were here to stay. This rapid, dramatic price drop was a boon to oil consumers, of course.

In sum, the decade of the 1970s showed how much economic *and* political power a small group of nations could have when they were able to exercise control over a scarce resource. On the other hand, the 1980s saw increasingly complex interdependence among nation-states and markets making it difficult for *any* nation (even powerful Saudi Arabia) to completely control world oil prices. The unified efforts of OPEC in the 1970s gave way to a more chaotic oil regime in the 1980s, and falling oil prices were its hallmark.

It was déjà vu all over again when oil prices shot up in August 1990 due to military conflict in the Middle East. The conflict this time was between two Arab nations, Iraq and Kuwait. This time, oil was both a tool in the conflict and the source of the conflict itself. The feud between Iraq and Kuwait had a long political history. Iraqi president Saddam Hussein was particularly incensed by what he took to be Kuwaiti cheating on its oil production quotas set by OPEC. Any such cheating, of course, would only further depress the price of petroleum, and Baghdad figured that Kuwaiti deceit had, by 1990, cost the Iraqi state treasury billions in lost oil revenues. Kuwait was also accused of duplicitously taking more than its share of oil from the neutral zone between the two countries and of pushing too hard for repayment of loans made to Iraq during the Iran–Iraq War.

Iraq's occupation of Kuwait City was reminiscent of 1980 when Iraqi troops pushed toward the Iranian oil fields in the early days of that war. Had Iraq gained control of either Iran's or Kuwait's oil fields, its influence as a regional—and global power might have grown immensely. The addition of either neighbor's oil reserves to Iraq's own would have made it a strong second to Saudi Arabia as the world's premier oil producer. Iraq's occupation of Kuwait was also a threat to which consumer states, having grown used to a world of diminished oil prices and "oil power" in the 1980s, quickly responded. Leading a UN-sanctioned coalition, the United States moved with military force in "Operation Desert Storm" to liberate Kuwait.[4]

The economic impact of the Gulf War on oil prices was short-lived. Oil prices doubled in the wake of the Iraqi invasion but dropped back to their previous low level after Iraq was routed in February 1991. Saudi Arabia remained the linchpin in OPEC and a primary security interest of the United States. With the collapse of the Soviet Union in 1990 and the Gulf War victory, the United States had a free hand to influence developments in the Middle East oil-producing countries.

## THE 1990s AND BEYOND

For most of the 1990s a relative calm characterized the IPE of oil and OPEC. Demand for petroleum increased commensurate with the demand for energy in general. Globalization was in full swing. Under the Clinton Administration (1993–2001), deregulation and the opening of markets led to increased economic growth in the United States and the rest of the world. Low oil prices allowed U.S. industries to prosper economically but also to increase their dependence on oil. Low oil prices were passed onto consumers in the form of cheaper energy prices, gasoline, and manufactured goods.

The International Energy Agency (IEA) reported that in 2000 world demand for oil was 75 million barrels per day and was forecast to rise 2.4 percent per year from then on. The Middle East had 63 percent of the world's oil reserves, 25 percent of which was in Saudi Arabia, 11 percent in Iraq, and 9 percent in both Iran and the United Arab Emirates. Oil remained the biggest source of the world's energy, even though between 1973 and 1996 it *dropped* from 45 to 35 percent of the world's total energy consumption as new sources of energy such as nuclear power were developed. During much of the 1990s, oil prices remained relatively low—roughly $10 a barrel less than they were in the 1980s—despite some price spikes in short periods of time. OPEC nations were greatly concerned and adopted a number of strategies to stabilize oil prices and maintain their profits. One strategy was to ask non-OPEC oil-producing countries such as Russia, Mexico, and Norway to help push prices back up by limiting their oil production.

In 1998, in the middle of the Asian financial crisis, the price of oil dropped to $9.64 a barrel. OPEC finally responded by dramatically cutting back production quotas to push the price of a barrel of oil back up to $26. Saudi Arabia wanted to keep prices high, but not so high as to stifle demand or encourage competition from other sources. Its objective was to keep oil prices within a margin of $22 to $28 a barrel. And of course this required it to keep nonmembers from producing too much. If it were to have used its surplus capacity, it could have once again driven *down* oil prices.

The terrorist attacks of September 11, 2001 raised fears of a new energy crisis. Oil prices increased, but only very gradually. The unexpected development that helped keep oil prices in check was the emergence of Russia as a key player in the oil regime. Edward Morse and James Richard argue that there was a struggle between Russia and Saudi Arabia—the world's two largest oil producers—for dominance of the global oil regime. Russia had been quietly increasing its output of oil and was able to outproduce Saudi Arabia by about one-third.[5]

Saudi Arabia was very aware that Russia and other former Soviet states had the ability to increase output for years to come, potentially hurting Saudi Arabia, Kuwait, and other OPEC members that had state monopolies disallowing foreign investment in oil. Meanwhile, Russia attempted to reform its economy by encouraging more investment in oil production. Because demand from the United States and Southeast Asia was expected to increase dramatically, Russian leaders attempted to portray its firms as reliable suppliers poised to displace OPEC as the key energy supplier to the West if OPEC once again tried to impose an embargo.

However, Shibley Telhami et al. argue that Russia does not have enough oil reserves—only 5 percent of the world's total production—to play a hegemonic role in the global oil regime.[6] And Russia depends on oil exports for almost half of its hard-currency export earnings. The United States gets only 3 percent of its oil from Russia. Meanwhile, China had been importing more oil from the Middle East—60 percent of its oil imports.

## Oil and Operation Iraqi Freedom

In 2001 a report by the National Energy Policy Group projected that the United States would continue to depend on Persian Gulf oil from Saudi Arabia, Iran, Iraq, Kuwait, and the United Arab Emirates, who together controlled 63 percent of known reserves at the time. U.S., Russian, and Mexican reserves together were much bigger than those of the Gulf region, but the ability to boost production capacity was limited.

The War in Afghanistan and the 2003 American-led invasion of Iraq predictably raised several energy resource issues. The Bush administration explicitly denied any connection between U.S. oil interests and the war in Iraq, except insofar as oil would be key source of income for Iraq in the reconstruction process following the war. Critics claimed the United States wanted to establish a "footprint" in the region to influence developments in the Caspian basin region where new fields and pipelines connected Central Asia to Europe. Directly related to this concern was the growing influence of President Putin, who sought to revitalize Russia's influence as a great power in the region. Michael T. Klare makes the case that all of these motives required the establishment of U.S. military bases in the region. Given Saudi intransigence to allow U.S. bases on Saudi soil, the United States positioned bases in Turkey, Kyrgyzstan, Uzbekistan, Afghanistan, and Pakistan, along with those in Kuwait, Oman, and Qatar.[7]

While there may never be a clear answer about the role that oil played in the United States's decision to invade Iraq, the price of oil dramatically increased beginning with the start of the Iraq war in 2003. By July 2008, oil prices peaked at $147 per barrel and were nearly six times what they were at the beginning of the war. The dramatic decrease in Iraqi oil supplies combined with significant increases in oil consumption by China partially explain the dramatic increase in oil prices. Generally these increases also corresponded to speculation in oil and increases in stock values.[8]

The war in Iraq also raised the age-old security question about U.S. dependence on foreign oil. Barack Obama campaigned on promises to help the United States achieve energy independence. He claimed that oil "bankrolls dictators, pays for nuclear proliferation and funds both sides of our struggle against terrorism."[9]

## OIL RICH . . . OR POOR?: THE RESOURCE CURSE[a]

The geopolitical shifts and volatile oil prices we have discussed thus for are not the only problems that oil exporters face. In addition, When countries rich in natural resources nevertheless remain relatively undeveloped because of government mismanagement and corruption, the phenomenon is referred to as a **resource curse**. Instead of "black gold," oil in some countries has become what a Venezuelan who helped found OPEC called the "devil's excrement." Countries in Africa that have oil, such as Nigeria, Angola, Equatorial Guinea, and Chad, have been particularly vulnerable to this curse. Equatorial Guinea has come under the attention of several organizations for its high poverty rate despite surging government revenues from oil that reached $4.8 billion in 2007.[b]

U.S. companies have also been charged with corrupt behavior in resource-rich countries. In 2009 Royal Dutch Shell appeared before a U.S. court to respond to allegations of crimes against humanity in connection with the 1995 hanging of Ken Saro-Wiwa, a prominent Nigerian environmentalist who spoke out about oil production in the Niger Delta. In Kazakhstan a U.S. businessman was charged with bribing the president with $78 million to secure oil field contracts for Western oil companies.

Even without corruption, resource-rich countries often do not receive the full benefit of these resources. With oil, poorer countries need significant foreign investments in order to drill and develop their energy sectors. Ghana, for example, a country president Obama lauded for its strong democracy, has recently opened up oil fields to foreign companies. However, current contracts only entitle the government to 10 percent of the profit.[c] The energy minister of Ghana, Mike Oquaye, has acknowledged that this percentage is quite low, but says that it was necessary to entice oil companies. This

has also been the case in Iraq. It was only after making several concessions that the Iraqi government was successful in making its first contracts with China's National Petroleum Company and others.[d]

One reason international oil companies demand such high compensation, aside from the costly investments in capital, is the risk that comes from operating within a country that is unstable. In Iraq, the government has opened up bidding on oil fields in Kirkuk, a region whose sovereignty is constitutionally in dispute. This increases tensions and violence between the Turkmen, Kurds, and Arabs who inhabit the region. In Nigeria, civil war has raged for decades in part over territory disputes in oil-rich regions. In Sudan, a 2005 settlement that divided up oil revenues between the North and South and ended two decades of fighting, is re-sparking violence. In Uganda, a 2009 announcement of the discovery of 800 million barrels of oil has sparked conflicts between the Congolese and Ugandans. Oil companies that choose to operate under such circumstances often become targets of protest and violence. In Iraq, Chinese workers at the Ahdab oil field hardly leave their compound for fear of being kidnapped. In Nigeria, militants regularly attack oil facilities and tankers, often taking workers captive in the process.

### References

[a]Georgina Allen researched and wrote the material for this box.

[b]Jad Mouawad, "Oil Corruption in Equatorial Guinea," *The New York Times*, July 9, 2009.

[c]Jeffrey Marlow, "Ghana Girds for Vagaries of Oil Production," *The New York Times*, August 19, 2009.

[d]Rod Nordland and Jad Mouawad, "Iraq Considers Giving Foreign Oil Investors Better Terms," *The New York Times*, March 18, 2009.

## The Double Whammy: Volatile Oil Markets and Prices

Many view oil as one of the contributing factors to the 2007 financial crisis (see Chapter 8). Dramatic increases in the price of oil are thought to be "the straw that broke the camel's back." For those who believe that the war in Iraq was a war for oil, the accumulation of U.S. debt from the war has also slowly reduced confidence in the U.S. economy. Even so, the war is certainly not the only reason for the upward trend in oil prices that occurred during the Bush presidency. Over the last decade, dramatic growth in world consumption—driven largely by the China—has increased demand for oil. During this period, China's oil consumption alone has more than doubled to eight million barrels a day. Typically, oil supplies decrease during times of political instability in oil-producing countries, as has been the case in Iran and Nigeria, and of course Iraq.

Perhaps the most controversial issue surrounding the spike in oil prices in July 2008 was the role of investment speculation in oil. Some maintain that soaring prices were in response to intentional restrictions on supply by the oil-producing countries. Others, however, asserted that a weakened U.S. dollar drove many financial investors to invest in natural resources like oil, driving up its price. High oil prices, especially in 2007 and early 2008, were felt around the world. Balances of trade shifted strongly in favor of oil-exporting countries as oil importers had to spend increasingly more. In the United States, higher oil prices meant more debt, both public and private. U.S. automakers were forced to file for bankruptcy with fewer and fewer Americans willing to purchase vehicles that were not highly fuel efficient. Airlines suffered from rapidly increasing oil prices, as fuel generally makes up as much as a third of their budget. Gas ate up more and more discretionary income as it cost more than $4 a gallon in the United States. The increased costs of transporting goods were passed onto consumers, even for the most basic of items such as groceries.

The recent spike in oil prices was partly responsible for another crisis of sorts. As discussed in Chapter 18, the cost of fuel dramatically increased the price of transporting goods, which translated into higher prices for many agricultural commodities. High fuel prices spurred investment in alternative fuel sources, the most popular being biofuels, which diverted American corn from international markets. In many poorer countries, imported staples doubled in price, sparking civil unrest and destabilizing many already fragile governments.

As we stressed in Chapter 8, large flows of investment into the United States from Asia and oil-producing countries made it possible to keep U.S. interest rates low, which also helped generate a real-estate bubble that was responsible for so many bad loans and the eventual collapse of Wall Street. By the time the financial crisis came to its head in the fall of 2008, oil prices had already started dropping. OPEC responded with surprising solidarity by immediately restricting output, but could not respond quickly enough to offset the effects of Wall Street and rapid decreases in demand. Oil prices bottomed out at $33 per barrel in December 2008.

A year later, OPEC had managed to stabilize the price of oil at their "Goldilocks" price of $70 per barrel. In other words, prices were sufficiently high for oil-producing countries to reap the benefits and continue oil exploration, but not so high as to cripple the world economy any more. Paul Krugman argues that the price of oil continues to reflect speculation. Oil inventories have become so high that they are even being held in offshore tankers (sometimes called oil sharks) in addition to conventional storage facilities. Thus, many oil-producing nations and investors are concerned that potential damage from *plunging* oil prices in 2008 will continue in the future.

Initially, Russia was quite cooperative with OPEC. It sent delegates to OPEC meetings to discuss possible coordination of production limits, and OPEC reiterated its desire to have Russia join forces. By late 2009, however, Russia had broken with OPEC and increased production, much to its own benefit. The governments of both Venezuela and Russia decided to open up oil fields and renegotiate current contracts with foreign oil companies in hopes of increasing revenues. During this time of increased production, Russia surpassed Saudi Arabia as the largest exporter and one of the biggest benefactors of oil. Meanwhile, OPEC countries have had to suffer through decreases in government budgets. The rebellious actions of Russia and Venezuela should come as no surprise. Both of these countries are considered petrostates—oil-producing countries with somewhat authoritarian regimes that try to use their oil as a political weapon. Most recently, in January of 2009, Russia cut off a Ukrainian gas line serving many parts of Europe.

Table 19-1 highlights the amount of oil, coal, and natural gas produced in the world in 2008. It is important to note that a report released by the Cambridge Energy Research Associates in March 2009 predicted that in 2014 the world would be producing 101.4 million barrels a day instead of 109 million barrels a day as predicted before the drop in prices. If so, this could lay the groundwork for yet another steep rise in oil prices if and when demand rebounds from the current global crisis. It could also be more evidence of "peak oil" discussed below.

## OPEC: A CARTEL IN DECLINE?

Under these volatile conditions it is difficult to predict OPEC's power and influence in the future. Generally speaking, many scholars believe that as alternative

### TABLE 19-1

**Largest Producers of Coal, Oil, and Natural Gas, 2008 Values**

| Largest Producers of Coal | | Largest Producers of Oil | | Largest Producers of Natural Gas | |
|---|---|---|---|---|---|
| Country | Mil. Tonnes | Country | Thousands of Barrels Daily | Country | Bil. Cubic Meters |
| China | 2,782.0 | Saudi Arabia | 10,846 | Russian Federation | 601.7 |
| United States | 1,062.8 | Russian Federation | 9,886 | United States | 582.2 |
| India | 512.3 | United States | 6,736 | Canada | 175.2 |
| Australia | 401.5 | Iran | 4,325 | Iran | 116.3 |
| Russian Federation | 326.5 | China | 3,795 | Norway | 99.2 |
| South Africa | 250.4 | Canada | 3,238 | Algeria | 86.5 |
| Indonesia | 229.5 | Mexico | 3,157 | Saudi Arabia | 78.1 |
| Germany | 192.4 | United Arab | | Qatar | 76.6 |
| Poland | 143.9 | Emirates | 2,980 | China | 76.1 |
| Kazakhstan | 114.7 | Kuwait | 2,784 | United Kingdom | 69.6 |
| | | Venezuela | 2,566 | | |

*Source:* Statistical Review of World Energy 2009, bp.com.

sources of energy become more affordable, oil will gradually become less desirable. As oil consumption around the world declines, so will OPEC's influence on the price of oil and the global political economy. Certainly, as new oil-producing nations come on line, the influence of OPEC depends on its relationship to these countries. The case of Russia's shifting relationship to them from time to time is a good example. There are also a myriad of good political, economic, and social reasons for wanting to keep the price of oil within a range set by OPEC that allows Russia and other petroleum-exporting nations to participate in the oil system.

Depending on political circumstances, it cannot be ruled out that as oil prices decline, OPEC and Saudi Arabia, especially, could try to push prices back up. Many experts suggest that any transformation away from oil is likely to take at least twenty years.[10] Between now and then the Saudi royal family could fall or Iran could replace Saudi Arabia as the swing nation in OPEC. Russia could gain control over oil production in the Caspian region—or any number of political events could still easily effect OPEC's influence over the global oil system. Of course, any attempt by OPEC to raise world market prices today would be terribly costly (and therefore politically difficult for the cartel) because OPEC members would need to cut production to make up for the rising production of non-member countries.

Still another problem for OPEC is the "defection" of many of its members who have a history of cheating on their production pledges (based on the economic payoffs for defection). The Gulf War reduced OPEC solidarity by driving a wedge between Saudi Arabia and Iraq. Many oil companies have invested heavily in the development of new oil reserves in non-OPEC nations. These huge investments have begun to generate increased oil supplies that dramatically affect OPEC's price-setting ability. Non-OPEC production (not counting oil from Russia and the United States) rose from 9 million barrels per day in 1976 to 26 million bpd in 1995.

Many reject the idea of peak oil (see box "Peaked Out" below) or believe that new technology will help overcome the problem of oil scarcity. In the past the search for oil and development of oil assets was full of expensive risks that limited the ability of new firms and new nations to enter oil markets. Recent technological changes have reduced both risks and costs. Computer technology has made the search for oil more scientific and reliable. New drilling techniques have reduced the investment needed to exploit oil reserves once they are located. As a result, many

## ▶ PEAKED OUT[a]

The idea that every natural resource including oil, natural gas, and coal is finite is not that difficult to grasp. What is more challenging is to realize and accept the impact that the end of cheap oil could have on our lives.

Production rates after discovery of oil and other resources grow exponentially until reaching a tipping point or peak, after which they decline, usually rapidly, until the resource is completely depleted. In 1956

geophysicist M. King Hubbert, working at the Shell Oil Company, first proposed the controversial idea that the world would run out of oil at some point.[b] Many of the predictions based on what is now referred to as the Hubbert Curve have come true. Hubbert accurately predicted a peak in U.S. oil production between 1965 and 1970. After 1970, U.S. oil production declined until a small uptick occurred when oil was discovered in Alaska. Many countries have already passed their oil peak: Argentina, Australia, Colombia, Cuba, Egypt, Iran, Libya, Russia, South Africa, the United States, and Yemen. The majority of current predictions for world **peak oil** fall between 2010 and 2015.

However, the exact date of peak oil is not so important. It is not the last drop that matters, but the "tipping point," because from that point onward there will be less and less oil available and its cost could become higher and higher if sufficient alternative sources of energy are unavailable. As many economists note, supply should dictate demand instead of the other way around. And life as we know it will necessarily change. For the industrial world, it will be the end of the Age of Cheap Oil. The latest sources of oil that generate excitement are much more difficult and expensive to extract, such as the tar sands in Canada, which require water and natural gas to produce the steam needed to separate the oil from the sands.

What are some of the political and social consequences of peak oil? Long before the last drop of oil is extracted, its price is likely to become prohibitive for most of its current applications. Some applications are obvious: gasoline for your car, jet fuel for your airplane trip to Mexico at spring break, diesel for heating your home, and anything made of plastic. Almost anything processed or manufactured or that needs to be shipped around the world to get to a store near you also depends on oil. Modern society as we know it has been utterly dependent on cheap oil.

Responses to peak oil vary by state and the groups within them. Cuba, for example, after losing oil imports from the former Soviet Union, has been forced to realize a post-peak oil society in the past 15 years.[c] The island nation now utilizes less oil-based transportation, has moved populations to more rural areas, and has created many small organic farms without petroleum-based artificial fertilizers or fuel for large farm machinery. Other groups that have responded to the problem of peak oil vary from "head for the hills" survivalists to those who believe it is another reason to deal with climate change by switching to alternative energy sources. Some people are enthusiastic about a transition to a post-peak oil future where societies must relocalize, cooperate, and live a slower-paced life.[d]

### References

[a] Kristi Hendrickson (Phd in Physics) researched and wrote the material for this box.

[b] "The Hubbert Curve: Its Strengths and Weaknesses," by J. H. Laherrère, version proposed to *Oil and Gas Journal* on February 18, 2000. For film of Hubbert, see the video *A Crude Awakening: The Oil Crash*, Docurama Films, 2006.

[c] *The Power of Community: How Cuba Survived Peak Oil*, Arthur Morgan Institute for Community Solutions, 2006 (DVD).

[d] Rob Hopkins, *The Transition Handbook: From Oil Dependency to Local Resilience*, (White River Junction, VT: Chelsea Green Publishing, 2008).

economic liberal critics claim that oil supplies are both greater and more flexible than in the past. Under this scenario, OPEC's market power is likely to wane.

Many realists and structuralists are not as sanguine as their economic liberal counterparts. With peak oil upon the world now, finding more oil will only become harder and more expensive in relation to the amount found and processed. This could generate more domestic conflict and exacerbate security concerns and global inequality. Above all, as world leaders become increasingly convinced of the need to reduce carbon emissions and agree to do so (see Chapter 20), demand for oil is likely to drop, something most officials in developed nations have been looking forward to. If the oil-producing nations have any chance at maintaining their powerful positions as energy exporters, it is no wonder many of them have been recycling their petrodollars into greener technology (discussed below).

In the long run, given the unstable sociopolitical systems of many oil-rich OPEC members and the fact that oil is a nonrenewable source of energy, the cartel's influence is likely to decline as oil runs out and/or alternative energy resources are developed. For now, even if they do not get much press, OPEC ministers routinely set production quotas aimed at finding a price within targeted profit margins that reflects member and non-member interests alike. Even if OPEC's power is not what it once was, certainly because of the size of its reserves and the politics that go into its decisions, it will remain a major player in the oil regime. Finally, many realists would argue that for a variety of political, economic, and even social reasons related to the United States' relationship with Saudi Arabia, it is in the interest of both countries to have the Saudis maintain a dominant role in OPEC.

## THE CHANGING CONTEXT OF OIL AND ENERGY

For developed nations, the 2012 expiration date of the world's most comprehensive treaty on the environment, the Kyoto Protocol, has brought a new sense of urgency to the goal of collectively addressing climate change. Many oil-producing countries are justifiably fearful that a new agreement that severely restricts emissions could weaken their economies and governments. This is because the burning of fossil fuels is one of the largest contributors to greenhouse gas accumulation. Global warming was the main issue at stake in the Copenhagen meeting in December 2009.

Saudi Arabia has dealt with this situation in two ways. First, it has been the most vocal in demanding that if the world agrees to limit their greenhouse emissions, oil-producing countries should be the first to be compensated. Indeed, the International Energy Agency has predicted that if the world comes to an agreement on cutting emissions, OPEC would suffer a 16-percent decrease in revenue from 2008 to 2030.[11] However, many developed nations have protested against assistance, arguing that aid ought to be allocated to those countries most in need. Given the wealth accumulated by many oil-producing nations, many would not qualify for such assistance under conditions likely to be agreed to in any aid package.

There is much evidence to suggest that Saudi Arabia and other states see the handwriting on the wall. Table 19-2 highlights the top 10 energy consuming nations in the world. Many oil-dependent states are spending more to develop alternative energy resources that will decrease their dependency on imported oil. Ironically, the Saudis and other oil producers are currently investing in renewable energy technologies themselves, without any assistance. In fact, the Gulf region is quickly becoming a hot spot for green technology on several fronts, hoping to preserve its role as a leading energy exporter.[12] According to *The New York Times*, the Crown Prince of Abu Dhabi announced that he would invest $15 billion in renewable energy.[13] This is an enormous sum, especially when one considers that President Obama has proposed investing a similar amount for new energy development in the entire United States. Part of the Prince's investment will go toward the creation of a model city, Masdar, that will generate no carbon emissions. According to one company involved in the Masdar project, the astonishing size of these investments will have a "**forcing effect**" by both inventing green technologies and using them on a large enough scale to make them affordable. One university in Saudi Arabia has awarded a Stanford scientist $25 million to research ways to make solar power competitive with coal. In November of 2008, Qatar announced that it would give more than $220 million to a British investment fund managed by the non-profit Carbon Trust to develop low carbon technologies.

## TABLE 19-2

### Top Ten Energy Consumers

| Primary Energy Consumption | | Nuclear Energy Consumption | | Hydroelectricity Consumption | |
|---|---|---|---|---|---|
| Country | Mil. Tonnes Oil Equivalent | Country | Terawatt-Hours | Country | Terawatt-Hours |
| United States | 2,299.0 | United States | 848.6 | China | 585.2 |
| China | 2,002.5 | France | 440.3 | Canada | 369.5 |
| Russian Federation | 684.6 | Japan | 251.7 | Brazil | 363.8 |
| Japan | 507.5 | Russian Federation | 163.0 | United States | 250.6 |
| India | 433.3 | Germany | 148.8 | Russian Federation | 167.0 |
| Canada | 329.8 | Canada | 93.3 | Netherlands | 140.5 |
| Germany | 311.1 | Ukraine | 89.8 | Norway | 140.5 |
| France | 257.9 | Sweden | 64.3 | India | 115.6 |
| South Korea | 240.1 | Spain | 59.0 | Venezuela | 86.8 |
| Brazil | 228.1 | United Kingdom | 52.5 | Japan | 69.2 |

*Source:* Statistical Review of World Energy 2009, bp.com.

Green energy development has made advances in other places in the world as well, albeit much more modestly. As of 2006, the world's sources of renewable energy are mainly biomass, hydro, solar, wind, geothermal, hydrogen fuel cells, and biofuels. World investment in renewable energy more than quadrupled between 2004 and 2007, with solar, wind, and biofuels receiving 82 percent of this money in 2007.[14] Nuclear energy is not considered renewable, but it does not emit carbon and currently produces more energy than any other renewable resource. While statistics have been fairly encouraging, the financial crisis and subsequent credit crunch have taken a serious toll on renewable energy investment, which has leveled off considerably since 2007.

The Chinese government has played such an active role in their renewable energy sector that it is being accused of "green protectionism." It has invested heavily in alternative energy sources such as wind, solar panels, and nuclear power, while seriously considering refitting coal-producing plants with sequestration technology that buries $CO_2$ emissions underground.[15] China argues that it makes more sense, considering the scope of measures adequate enough to stave off detrimental climate change in a country its size, to develop and manufacture solar panels and wind turbines domestically.

However, others have argued that China has taken protectionism to such an extreme in its industrial policies that it is causing discontent amongst manufacturers in the renewable energy sector, particularly wind and solar. Competitors have accused the Chinese government of giving preferential treatment to local companies. The Chinese government has put off signing the WTO side agreement that would prohibit it from establishing rules that require multinationals to buy only

Chinese goods.[16] Likewise, these rules provide incentives for Chinese energy companies to purchase cheaper quality materials at home. Many international manufacturers of renewable energy equipment have found it very difficult to access China's large energy market. These measures give Chinese manufacturers economies of scale, which is likely to make it highly competitive on the international market.

Because renewable energy start-up investments are so costly, they often require some government financial support and collaboration. For example, the U.S. electric grid system is not currently well-equipped to handle intermittent sources of energy such as wind and solar energy. Part of the Obama administration's stimulus package includes money to update this system. According to some sources, there is also a shortage of experts in renewable energy. Electrician training requires five to six years, and at current rates the United States is only training enough to replace those who are retiring.

Many U.S. investors are waiting until 2010 to see if the United States adopts emissions limits that will make carbon-intensive energy sources more expensive and thus less attractive in comparison. As demand for energy in general decreases, banks have also become increasingly hesitant to make loans to renewable energy entrepreneurs. The stimulus packages of governments like China, Germany, Spain, India, Italy, and Abu Dhabi have attempted to bypass this obstacle by providing a variety of tax incentives for companies looking to invest in renewable energy.

The United States has arguably not done enough to support the development of alternative energy. One notable critic is Thomas Friedman, who since 2006 has made dependency on foreign oil and a new green economy the focus of a new book and many op-ed pieces in *The New York Times*. For Friedman and scores of others, the United States should be leading in efforts to promote the development of alternative energy.[17] Of course, many experts argue that nuclear energy ought to be viewed more positively as a solution to energy scarcity, primarily because other technologies have either proved to be unworkable or will not produce enough to meet demand.

Finally, with the onset of the global financial crisis, more experts are pointing out that without a profound shift in values at this critical point in time, the consequences of not promoting new energy sources could be disastrous—a topic we take up related to global warming in the last chapter of the book. Interestingly, a number of writings on the subject point to a speech President Jimmy Carter delivered on July 15, 1979, entitled "Energy and the National Goals—A Crisis of Confidence." Recall that the president gave this speech at a time when the United States made it a policy to be less dependent on oil imports. Carter said,

> In a nation that was proud of hard work, strong families, close-knit communities, and our faith in God, too many of us now tend to worship self-indulgence and consumption. Human identity is no longer defined by what one does, but by what one owns. But we've discovered that owning things and consuming things does not satisfy our longing for meaning. We've learned that piling up material goods cannot fill the emptiness of lives which have no confidence or purpose.

One of the points the president was making is that the goal of creating new energy alternatives is something states, businesses, and other actors can *choose* to accomplish.

# CONCLUSION

The IPE of oil and energy demonstrates a number of the major themes of the text discussed in Chapter 1. One dominant theme is that for most of the state actors involved, domestic interests have taken precedence over global obligations. OPEC members found it in their interest to cooperate with one another, given that once OPEC states gained control over their oil, withholding it from the industrialized states so quickly and dramatically drove up its price. Oil is a case of where state collective actions affect market outcomes and in turn, changing market outcomes condition state behavior.

The two oil crises of the 1970s helped position Saudi Arabia as a powerful swing state that could control prices by offsetting production levels of other states. Saudi Arabia's hegemonic position married nicely with U.S. economic and military security interests. In the 1980s and 1990s OPEC gradually lost its tight grip on oil prices due to the development of oil in other countries, which led to oil surpluses and lower prices. Since 1998 prices have risen—partly due to OPEC production cuts and Chinese demand. China's economic success has also provided it with the income to spend for development of oil in other countries, but also for the development of alternative energy resources at home.

The line between political and economic security has become even more blurred since the 1990s. OPEC's leverage against the world oil market is much reduced by the growth of production in other countries. It would seem less likely all the time that OPEC or another resource-based cartel could emerge to impact the global economy the way that OPEC did in the 1970s. The latest financial crisis demonstrated the solidarity of OPEC members, but even this was not enough to ensure that oil prices rebounded after their dramatic fall in July 2008. The unpredictability of oil prices has also meant financial troubles and political instability for the governments of oil-producing nations.

Record oil and fuel price hikes in 2008 worried many officials in both oil-exporting and oil-importing nations. Investments in alternative energy sources have increased in some countries as part of their recovery efforts. The exclusive club of oil companies has been replaced by a hypercompetitive market that relies on the free flow of information and high technology to remain viable. In this market no single petrostate or even small group of states alone has the power to control the prices or distribution of scarce commodities and resources. Global warming is likely to shape developments related to oil and energy.

# KEY TERMS

Organization of Petroleum
  Exporting Countries
  (OPEC)  489
cartel  489

spot market  492
petrodollar recycling  493
Prisoner's Dilemma  494
resource curse  497

Oil Sharks  498
petrostates  499
peak oil  501
forcing effect  502

# DISCUSSION QUESTIONS

1. One weakness of a cartel such as OPEC is that it is subject to the prisoner's dilemma problem. State the prisoner's dilemma problem in general and explain how it applies to the specific case of OPEC.
2. How are the oil crises of the past different from the spike in oil prices in 2008? What were the major causes and effects of increases in oil prices in each case?
3. What is the biggest threat posed by U.S. dependence on oil? Security? Economic stability? The environment? Explain with examples from the reading. Finally, discuss how these policy issues are related to energy but also to one another.

4. Define "peak oil"? Do you believe in this theory? If so, what will be the impact on both oil producers and consumers?

5. Discuss the future of renewable sources of energy. Will the oil-producing states maintain their role as the leading exporters of energy or will big energy consumers step up their domestic energy production? What country or group of countries, do you feel will have the most control over energy supplies and prices in the future? Why

## SUGGESTED READINGS

Al Gore. *Our Choice: How We Can Solve the Climate Crisis* Emmaus, PA: Melcher Media and Rodale Press, 2009.

Daniel Yergin. *The Prize: The Epic Quest for Oil, Money and Power.* New York: Free Press, 1992.

Michael T. Klare. *Blood and Oil: The Dangers and Consequences of America's Growing Dependency on Imported Petroleum.* New York: Henry Holt & Co., 2004.

Marshall I. Goldman. *Petrostate: Putin, Power, and the New Russia.* New York: Oxford University Press, 2008.

Peter Maas. *Crude World: The Violent Twilight of Oil.* New York: Alfred A. Knopf, 2009.

William R. Clark. *Petrodollar Warfare: Oil, Iraq and the Future of the Dollar.* Gabriola Island: New Society Publishers, 2005.

## NOTES

1. Georgina Allen helped research and update this chapter based on coverage in the third edition of the text.

2. The members of OPEC in 1973 were Iran, Iraq, Kuwait, Saudi Arabia, Venezuela, Abu Dhabi, Algeria, Libya, Qatar, the United Arab Emirates, Nigeria, Ecuador, Indonesia, and Gabon. Ecuador and Gabon left OPEC in the 1990s, and Indonesia suspended membership in 2009. Angola joined in 2007. Not all oil-exporting countries are members of OPEC. Russia and Mexico, for example, are non-OPEC oil exporters, and the United States, although not a net exporter of oil, is currently the largest oil-producing nation in the Western hemisphere.

3. For a detailed account of the role of the oil companies in the Middle East, see Daniel Yergin, *The Prize: The Epic Quest for Oil, Money, and Power* (New York: Simon & Schuster, 1991).

4. For a detailed account of Operation Desert Storm, see Kendall W. Stiles, *Case Histories in International Politics*, 3rd ed. (New York: Pearson Longman, 2004), pp. 133–152.

5. Edward Morse and James Richard, "The Battle for Energy Dominance," *Foreign Affairs, 81* (March/April 2002), pp. 16–31.

6. Shibley Telhani, Fiona Hill, Addullatif A. Al-Othman, and Cyrus Tahmassebi, "America's Vital Stakes in Saudi Arabia," *Foreign Affairs, 81* (November/December 2002), pp. 167–179.

7. See Michael T. Klare, *Blood and Oil: The Dangers and Consequences of America's Growing Dependence on Oil* (New York: Metropolitan Books, 2004), pp. 152–175.

8. A chart mapping oil prices against the stock prices of major oil companies in 2006–2008 is available at http://static.seekingalpha.com/uploads/2008/9/8/saupload_2008_08_07normalstockpriceslarge.jpg.

9. "Obama Announces Plans to Achieve Energy Independence," *The Washington Post*, January 29, 2009.

10. See Michael Klare, "The Era of Xtreme Energy: Life After the Age of Oil," *TomDispatch.com*, September 22, 2009.

11. Jad Mouawad and Andrew Revkin, "Saudis Seek Payments for Any Drop in Oil Revenues," *The New York Times*, October 13, 2009.

12. Elisabeth Rosenthal, "Gulf Oil States Seeking a Lead in Clean Energy," *The New York Times*, January 12, 2009.

13. Ibid.

14. UNEP, "Global Trends in Sustainable Energy Investment 2009," http://www.unep.org/pdf/Global_trends_report_2009.pdf.

15. For a more detailed discussion of carbon sequestration, see Matthew Wald, "Refitted to Bury Emissions, Plant Draws Attention," *The New York Times*, September 22, 2009.

16. Keith Bradsher, "China Builds High Wall to Guard Energy Industry," *The New York Times*, July 9, 2009.

17. See, for example, Thomas Friedman, "Have a Nice Day," *The New York Times*, September 9, 2009.

# The Environment: Steering Away from Global Disaster[1]

Interrelated issues of pollution, waste, development, and the environment.

Jacob Silberberg

Today's ecological and environmental problems are increasingly *global* in nature. In the first decade of the 2000s, aside from the usual stories about the effects of global warming, the international media covered melting glaciers, the threatened extinction of polar bears, the sheen of plastic junk covering wide swaths of the Pacific Ocean, and the impact environmental problems are having on developing nations. Popular documentaries included Al Gore's *An Inconvenient Truth*. In a controversial report, former World Bank economist Nicholas Stern warned that global warming could have a disastrous effect on the world's economy. In another report, the International Panel on Climate Change (IPCC) stated categorically that global warming is real and has the potential to do unlimited damage to different societies and political-economic systems.

These developments have compelled scientists and other experts from different parts of the world to suggest that we are on the precipice of yet another global disaster—one from which there may be no recovery—threatening quite possibly the existence of mankind. They have also been front and center in shaping the current international debate on environmental policy. At the center of that debate has been the issue of global warming. In talks to deal with the problem that concluded in Copenhagen in December of 2009, a weak interim agreement was reached that produced a glass half empty–half full scenario. Countries could not agree on how much they should be required to reduce their greenhouse emissions. On the other hand, the United States and China (the world's two biggest emitters of greenhouse gases), Brazil, India, and South Africa put measurable reduction targets on the negotiating table and established a process for achieving a binding accord in future negotiations.

Conflicting state and regional interests—along with stubbornness—have foiled efforts to deal with global warming and other significant environmental problems. Two dilemmas exist. In order to overcome their recessions at home, most states are trying to increase economic growth, which in turn contributes to global warming. At the same time, states are trying to create or sustain wealth for today's generation, but without leaving a despoiled and depleted environment for future generations. For now it is clear that the international global political economy has not seen much progress in resolving these fundamental dilemmas.

In this chapter we discuss some political, social, and economic aspects of global environmental problems. A brief history documents the broadening scope of those problems for states, international organizations (IOs), many nongovernmental organizations (NGOs), epistemic communities, and even some influential "personalities." Since the end of the Cold War, increasing interdependence and globalization have made it difficult for any single nation to solve the problems.

Throughout this chapter we focus most on the issue of global warming because it has dominated debate about the environment for the past decade. We discuss some of the evidence for and against the idea that global warming is harmful and why it and other related problems have been difficult to manage. Finally, we explore a variety of proposed global solutions to environmental problems, focusing on the roles that states, markets, technology, and even ethical values play in reform efforts.

We present three significant theses. First, in the case of the environment a constructivist paradigm shift (see Chapter 5) in thinking about the relationship of people to the environment has been going on at the global level since the early 1990s. The result is the emergence of an alternative set of ideas about how to wed modern industrial society with preservation of the global environment and national and subnational cultures. Second, because of the environment's impact on national economies and security, states are facing unprecedented global political-economic pressure to grapple with these problems. Third and finally, market-based or one-size-fits-all solutions alone will not effectively resolve most environmental issues, especially those associated with global warming.

# THE WIDENING SCOPE OF ENVIRONMENTAL PROBLEMS: A BRIEF HISTORY

Beginning in the eighteenth century during the industrial revolution, science and technology were harnessed to produce new labor-saving devices, industrial machines, and goods for mass consumption. Karl Marx and many of his contemporaries in the mid-nineteenth century complained of the damaging effects that "satanic mills" had on labor but also on the physical presence of England's bigger cities (see Chapter 4). Manufacturing industries in Europe were fueled by great quantities of inexpensive natural resources and raw materials. On the European continent air, water, and soil pollution spread beyond local areas. The development of the gasoline-powered engine at the end of the nineteenth century shifted demand away from coal and steam to oil and petroleum-based energy resources. Resources remained plentiful in supply and relatively inexpensive in cost—transportation being the biggest expense.

As industrialization spread throughout Western Europe and the United States, industrial pollution gradually became a bigger international problem—that is, it covered several or more nation-states. For instance, in the 1920s, the United States and Canada argued about the residue of lead and zinc smelting in British Columbia that was carried down the Columbia River into the United States. For the most part, however, environmental issues in the industrialized world were viewed as state-based problems.

The global magnitude of environmental problems was not fully realized until the 1960s. In the United States, global resource depletion became one of the issues of the student movement and the environmental movement that developed at the same time. As the absolute amount of pollution discharged worldwide grew, so did scientific knowledge and public awareness.[2] In 1972 the Club of Rome issued a shocking study, *The Limits to Growth*, arguing that if post–World War II levels of economic activity and environmental abuse continued, it would be the *environment*, not land, food, or other factors, that would limit global progress.[3] The OPEC oil embargo of 1973 and resulting high oil prices also pushed the issue of energy resource scarcity onto the agenda of many nation-states (see Chapter 19). Many developed and developing nations became aware of their dependence on oil to sustain industrialization and economic growth.

Meanwhile, the United Nations made its debut as an important actor in the debate on the environment in 1972, hosting the Conference on the Human Environment in Stockholm, Sweden. The conference announced an Action Plan for the Human Environment with 109 recommendations for governmental and international action on a wide variety of environmental issues. More importantly, it created an organization called the **United Nations Environment Program (UNEP)** to draft treaties, provide a forum for cooperation, and create databases for scientific assessments of the environment. The first UN agency to be headquartered in a Third World capital—Nairobi, Kenya—UNEP has over the years built an extensive network of smaller organizations around itself while coordinating action within the United Nation on environmental problems. It works on joint ventures with other agencies and organizations, including NGOs. UNEP has always had a funding problem, receiving significantly less than other UN agencies. With a staff of only 300, it cannot muster the authority to coordinate larger agencies. It also has to rely on national governments to implement its policies—actors that may see UNEP as merely another voice for frustrated ex-colonies.

From the 1980s onward, environmental problems continued to gain political recognition. In 1980, President Jimmy Carter commissioned *The Global 2000 Report to the President*, which predicted continued population growth, depletion of natural resources, deforestation, air and water pollution, and species extinction.[4] Even British Prime Minister Margaret Thatcher and Soviet Foreign Minister Eduard Shevardnadze gave speeches connecting the environment to global security. According to Shevardnadze, the environment is a "second front" that is "gaining urgency equal to that of the nuclear-and-space threat."[5] National and international attention to environmental issues reached new heights in response to notorious ecological (mis)management such as oil spills, acid rain, nuclear reactor incidents, droughts, deforestation, and oil, chemical, and toxic waste spills.

In the United States, however, environmentalism met some increased resistance. Oil supplies gradually became more plentiful and their price declined or held steady, weakening interest in resource scarcity and environmental problems. In a rebuke to the 1980 report commissioned by president Carter, Julian Simon and Herman Kahn wrote *The Resourceful Earth: A Response to Global 2000*.[6] Kahn went on to refer to the fatalistic outlook of the ecopessimists as "globaloney." Reagan and Bush senior aligned themselves with optimists who downplayed threats to the environment, arguing that more studies needed to be done. Furthermore, they claimed that many of the measures proposed to protect the environment were too costly and unfairly penalized businesses. Many U.S. officials adopted a neoliberal position that technology and markets could better solve these problems than coordinated efforts by nation-states in international forums.[7]

Despite the broad range of perspectives at the time, the UN made its way to the forefront of the debate in the late 1980s by publishing a report entitled *Our Common Future* that shifted attention to the connection between the environment and the survival of developing nations. Sometimes referred to as the Bruntland Report because the chair of the UN commission was Gro Harlem Bruntland (who later became the prime minister of Norway), the report linked hunger, debt, economic growth, and other issues to environmental problems. In 1987 diplomats signed the UN-sponsored Montreal Protocol to Control Substances that deplete the ozone layer, which required states to reduce chlorofluorocarbon (CFC) production by one-half by the year 2000. This treaty was in response to the 1985 discovery of a hole in the stratospheric ozone layer over Antarctica in 1985.

CFCs, which are used in many industrial products and processes, were targeted as the largest source contributing to **ozone depletion**. CFCs were long used in refrigerants, aerosol propellants, cleaning solvents, and blowing agents for foam production, but the chlorine atoms in these compounds destroy ozone. The effects of a depleted ozone layer around the earth are global in scope, including a dramatic increase in the incidence of melanoma skin cancer and cataracts, as well as damage to crops and ocean phytoplankton. Scientists estimate that even if CFCs were completely banned, the ozone-layer problem would last at least another 100 years given the present level of atmospheric CFC concentration. The Montreal Protocol was later amended to call for a complete halt to CFC production. To this day, the treaty is considered one of the most successful treaties on the environment, as all 192 UN member states have ratified it.

# THE PROLIFERATION OF ACTORS AND IPE PERSPECTIVES

In the last 300 years, as environmental problems have gone from being local and often temporary to being global and possibly permanent, the actors associated with managing them have also increased in number along with, in some cases, the scope of their interests, jurisdiction, and constituencies. However, more actors and more interconnections among them have also complicated the management of many environmental problems. Generally though, the different actors can be described or categorized as states, NGOs, IOs, or businesses.

Many nation-states deal with environmental problems in ways reflecting different political, social, and economic systems. State environmental regulations are prevalent in many Western European nations. In some EU nations, "green" and other political parties influence state environmental policy in this direction. However, in many less developed countries (LDCs) environmental issues often produce tension between supporters of economic development and those who favor some combination of income redistribution, conservation, and sustainable development. One group of experts reports that by the mid-1980s, 110 LDCs and thirty developed nations had created environmental ministries or agencies.[8] However, there is much evidence that these agencies often do not comply with regulations or are simply ineffective.

One theory forwarded by Detlef Sprintz and Tapani Vaahtoranta is that many states tend to be "pushers" of environmental policies or "draggers" to the extent that they outright support or oppose them or fail to implement them fully.[9] When it comes to more controversial issues where the potential consequences are certain or measurable, states are more likely to act as draggers. As demonstrated later on in the chapter, when it comes to addressing the issue of global warming, for many years the United States has been a dragger.

NGOs are also influential environmental actors. Some have annual budgets far exceeding GDPs of many nations. The largest NGOs work in international humanitarian aid, many of which address environmental issues. Other well-known NGOs working strictly on environmental issues are the World Wildlife Fund, Greenpeace International, the National Geographic Society, Friends of the Earth, the National Audubon Society, and the Sierra Club. Some of these groups focus strictly on fundraising and organizing environmentally related projects or awareness campaigns, while others such as Greenpeace aim to influence national and international environmental legislation. The size, cohesiveness, and effectiveness of all these groups vary in different nations, depending on the extent to which environmental causes permeate not only politics but also popular culture, music, and even religion. For many environmentalists in developed countries, the environmental cause has become another basis on which to attack the alienated individualism of a consumption-oriented capitalist society.

IOs have helped states to overcome the free-rider problem (see Chapter 2) to the extent that, by promoting cooperation and assigning costs to organization members, problems can be worked on in a collective fashion. When the environmental movement was first taking off in the late 1960s, Garrett Hardin in his article the "Tragedy of the Commons"[10] described the challenges of protecting **collective goods** that are shared by everyone and owned by no one, in particular the environment. As the tragedy of the commons explains, many resources are prone to abuse because property rights and freedom rationally compel but also allow us to (over)produce as much as we can. This analogy of why the earth's resources are overused and fouled typifies the debate over global warming and resource abuse as harm to the atmosphere is shared by all the inhabitants of earth.

Given that one of its objectives is development, the UN has been more active than any other IO in dealing with environmental problems and policies. Aside from UNEP, the United Nations has several other agencies whose work either directly or indirectly influences the environment. A few of these bodies are the Food and Agriculture Organization (FAO), which monitors global hunger and but poverty in LDCs; the UN Population Fund, which supports population-control programs in South Korea, China, Sri Lanka, and Cuba; and UN regional and global population conferences.

The environment's connection to investment and trade policies has been a topic of negotiations in the General Agreement on Tariffs and Trade (GATT) and World Trade Organization (WTO) rounds.[11] The WTO implemented a series of provisions referred to as Multilateral Environmental Agreements (MEAs) that were to accommodate the use of trade-related measures and the environment. In some cases, LDCs were exempted from GATT articles and WTO agreements so they could place national environmental goals ahead of their obligation not to use protectionist measures. Lower environmental standards often translate into lower production costs, thus giving these LDCs an advantage on the world market.

The World Bank established a General Environment Fund (GEF) to help developing nations bring proposed projects into line with international environmental standards and goals. However, it has been criticized for its lack of aid and for support of Structural Adjustment Policies (SAPs) which stress economic growth over the environment.

Businesses have also played an unexpected role in environmental activism. Large international conferences on the environment have attracted large companies looking to contribute their knowledge on the topic, bridging an unlikely partnership between entrepreneurs and policy officials. Until recently, their attitude has been that environmental rules and regulations are annoying and lead to inefficiencies, to say the least. However, as environmental problems have become more pronounced, the definition of efficiency has come under attack for not including the cost of environmental damage. Many corporations such as British Petroleum (BP) make protection of the environment part of their marketing strategy.

## THE SCIENCE AND DISPUTED FACTS OF GLOBAL WARMING

The issue of **global warming** and greenhouse gas emissions has gradually become the most important issue framing international debate on the environment. For decades scientists have been researching the ability of greenhouse gases to trap heat in the earth's atmosphere, but it has only recently become widely accepted that the earth's temperatures are in fact increasing over time as a result of increases in the earth's greenhouse gases. Many of these gases, which include carbon dioxide, nitrous oxide, methane, CFCs, ozone, and other infrared-absorbing gases, naturally occur in the atmosphere. Many scientists believe that *human* sources of greenhouse gases, such as carbon dioxide produced by the burning of fossil fuels (coal, oil, and natural gas) and the burning and clearing of land for agricultural purposes, make up the largest concentration of the greenhouse gases, and are thus the main causes of global warming. The Mauna Loa laboratory, whose estimates are regarded as some of the most accurate, puts carbon dioxide levels in the atmosphere at 387 parts per million, up 40 percent since the industrial revolution, and the highest level seen in the last 650,000 years.[12]

Global warming has also come to the forefront of the debate on the environment because of its relationship to a number of other issues. A 2009 report by the Global Humanitarian Forum concludes that global warming is causing more than 300,000 deaths and $125 billion in losses each year.[13] The report also asserts that another 325 million people, mostly in the developing world, are being seriously impacted by the effects of global warming. Sir Nicolas Stern's report accepts the conclusion that global warming is a crisis and estimates that it could cost the world 5–20 percent of its economic output "forever," but that trying to forestall the crisis would cost only 1 percent of the world's GDP.[14] These numbers are a reflection of changes in weather patterns that have resulted in extreme conditions for people across the world in the form of heat waves, unpredictable precipitation, and hurricanes.

Extreme weather conditions have the potential to impact society in a number of ways. Decreased rainfall and droughts threaten U.S. agricultural production in the Western states and Great Plains region, as well as growing conditions in Europe and many developing nations, all the while impinging on international food security. In particular, Australia has suffered from several years of back-to-back droughts. Recent heat waves and wildfires have taken lives around the world, most notably in the summer of 2003, when temperatures reached record highs of 104 degrees Fahrenheit in Europe, killing upwards of 30,000 people. Average world temperatures are projected to increase between 1.8 and 4.0 degrees Celsius by the end of the twenty-first century, melting glaciers and producing a rise in sea level on all coasts, damaging groundwater supplies, covering many island nations, and producing large numbers of refugees from coastal regions in Bangladesh, China, Egypt, and island nations in the Pacific. Flooding and warmer temperatures are also known to increase the occurrence of food-borne illness and infectious diseases transmitted by mosquitoes. The IPPC concludes that humans are likely contributing to the growing number and intensity of tropical storms in the North Atlantic.

One of the biggest names in the global warming debate is Al Gore. After serving as Vice-President under the Clinton administration, Gore became very active in raising public awareness of environmental problems. In 2006, he was featured in a film that documented his activism, outlined evidence of global warming, and warned of its potential catastrophic risks. *An Inconvenient Truth* went on to win an Academy Award, and in 2007 Gore shared a Nobel Peace Prize with the IPCC.

Another recent activist on the environmental scene is Thomas Friedman, the *New York Times* op-ed writer known for his books that explore globalization. In his latest book, *Hot, Flat and Crowded*, he argues that the United States has surprisingly not fulfilled the role that it should as a world energy leader.[15] Globalization, Hurricane Katrina, and 9/11 brought the issues of environmentalism and energy to mainstream America but. The United States has not done enough to promote a green technological revolution that is necessary to combat global warming.

## Climate Change Skeptics

Some experts remain skeptical about the extent of global warming and climate change. For example, Richard Lindzen, Professor of Atmospheric Science at MIT, suggests that although levels of carbon dioxide in the atmosphere have increased by 30 percent since the turn of the last century, these claims "neither constitute support for alarm nor establish man's responsibility for the small amount of warming that has occurred."[16] Recent weather patterns simply reflect natural variability. Unusually high volcanic activity between 1940 and 1975 may help explain the release of abnormal amounts of sulfate particles. Others argue that carbon dioxide is less potent than other greenhouse gases because half of it is absorbed by oceans, green plants, and forests (so-called "**carbon sinks**").

On a side note, carbon sinks are really part of a broader debate on two other major environmental issues: oceans and forests. Deforestation means less vegetation to help absorb carbon dioxide. Scientists are also studying how forests' ability to absorb carbon dioxide is affected by temperatures. Deforestation is predominantly occurring in emerging economies where LDCs are heavily dependent on income from the timber it generates and crops grown on deforested land. Tropical rain forests now represent roughly 5 percent of the land surface of the earth, half of what they did fifty years ago. Some 30 million acres of forest are cut down each year. By one estimate, it would take 320 million acres (roughly twice the size of Texas) to begin to replace the rain forests that play such an important role in absorbing carbon dioxide.[17] Aside from its impact on the atmosphere, deforestation harms biodiversity of both plants and animals, and thus the development of future pharmaceuticals. It leads to increased watershed runoff, which has been known to desertify countries such as Somalia and Sudan. Land that has been desertified is also likely to exaggerate the effects of flooding by reducing the earth's ability to absorb water and by causing landslides.

Scientists have also recently concluded that warming ocean temperatures are decreasing the ocean's ability to absorb carbon dioxide. If temperatures continue to increase, so will the inability of oceans to absorb greenhouse gases, only exacerbating the current situation. However, even if the oceans were not losing their ability to absorb greenhouse gases, increasing levels of carbon dioxide in the ocean have led to ocean acidification, which threatens coral reefs and many delicate ecosystems and food sources around the world. Acidification inhibits the ability of many sea creatures to properly form their shells. In the event that these creatures become unable to survive, there would be a massive disruption to the ocean food chain. Coral reefs are also thought to protect the land from storm surges and hurricanes.

Some skeptics argue that temperature readings supporting the theory of global warming have been distorted by their proximity to urban areas, which have a tendency to be warmer. Even if this were not the case, computer models cannot accurately account for complex interactions of oceans with atmosphere, cloud behavior, and the role of water vapor. These critics sometimes point to the occasional decrease in average world temperatures on an annual basis, as well as recent events like snow in Baghdad. Still other skeptics believe in global warming but argue that there may be possible benefits to warmer climates such as increased farming capacities in cooler areas. Some even go so far as to argue that the existence of greenhouse gases in the atmosphere will stave off the next ice age!

# GLOBAL MANAGAGEMENT OF CLIMATE CHANGE

Despite some continued skepticism in the scientific community to this day, international efforts to deal with global warming have been around for some time. The first multilateral negotiations occurred at the 1992 "**Earth Summit**" in Rio de Janeiro. Officially titled the UN Conference on the Environment and Development (UNCED), 178 national delegates, 115 heads of state, and more than 15,000 environmental NGO representatives focused their attention primarily on **sustainable development,** or ways to accomplish what seems like contradictory objectives: generating wealth and development while preserving the environment. The Earth Summit resulted in the creation of several documents including the Rio Declaration on the Environment and Development, but also the Convention on Biological Diversity, and most importantly, the **Framework Convention on Climate Change (FCCC),** which later served as the basis of the Kyoto Protocol.

## The Kyoto Protocol

In December 1997, a third Conference of the Parties (COP), or meeting for the signatories of the Earth Summit's FCCC treaty, was held in Kyoto, Japan, where 2,000 representatives from 159 countries met to strengthen the treaty.[18] This meeting resulted in the creation of the **Kyoto Protocol,** which required industrialized countries to reduce their greenhouse gas emissions by more than a third by 2012, or 5.2 percent below the 1990 level of emissions. A key proposal of the Kyoto Protocol was the use of **emission credits** as part of a **cap and trade** system (discussed below), whereby countries could buy and sell or swap emission production quotas with one another. The Kyoto Protocol was designed to become valid once fifty-five countries—who together were responsible for at least 55 percent of all 1990 carbon dioxide emissions levels—ratified the treaty. Finally, it is important to note that as part of an agreement to give the nonindustrialized nations more time to develop and adjust to emissions targets, they were not given any targets in the Kyoto accords but only encouraged to adopt target levels of their own.

One of the most serious challenges immediately encountered by the Kyoto Protocol was that many of the details of the treaty were initially left undefined. Every year thereafter, a COP was held in a different city to further discuss the details of the protocol. An option discussed in these meetings was for the United States to either cap its production of emissions or buy its way into compliance with the Kyoto Protocol by paying Russia and other countries to cut their emissions more than the treaty required. The United States, the EU, Canada, Russia, and Australia, among others, also wrangled over such issues as the use of carbon sinks that allowed countries such as the United States and others to escape real reductions in the use of fossil fuels.

After five COPs and much debate over many interrelated issues, in 2002 moderate concessions were eventually made that resulted in more countries ratifying the treaty, bringing the total number to ninety-eight, nearly double what it was a year earlier. These countries included more than half of the world's twenty-five most populated countries, and all fifteen EU members at that time. However, without ratification from key players like Russia and the United States, the 55 percent condition of global emissions remained unfulfilled, keeping the protocol from officially going into effect.

In January 2005 the EU bloc implemented the first phase of its own "emission trading scheme." Shortly thereafter Russia finally ratified the Kyoto Protocol. Because the accord became binding at this point, 180 countries met in Montreal to discuss how to implement the goals that had been established in Kyoto eight years previously. By then some nations such as Canada were "backsliding" on their willingness or ability to comply with the protocol and rejected its original Kyoto emission targets. Australia finally ratified the Kyoto Protocol in late 2007, leaving the United States as the only major industrialized developed nation to withhold participation. However, Australia has since failed to enact meaningful legislation to curb greenhouse gas emissions, which means that they remain one of the highest per capita polluters in the world. These sorts of behaviors on the part of the major industrialized nations have left many other nations unwilling to meet their emissions goals.

The United States, represented by the Clinton administration, originally signed the Kyoto Protocol in November 1998. However, the U.S. Senate passed a resolution 95–0 informing then President Clinton that it would *not* ratify the treaty unless the same limitations put on the United States and other industrialized nations applied to developing countries, or the developing nations committed themselves to a complex scheme for trading emission permits and credits. In the spring of 2001 the new George W. Bush administration suddenly withdrew entirely from the Kyoto Treaty. It claimed that the new treaty would cost the United States $400 billion and 4.9 million jobs. U.S. officials went on to cite natural gas and fossil fuel shortages as reasons to *expand* U.S. energy supplies. The Bush administration also remained skeptical that there was enough evidence that power plant emissions contributed to global warming or that global warming itself was a serious problem.

The Bush administration's response to global warming mirrored its reaction to many security issues, which was to "go it alone" mixed with suspicion of IOs and charges that international agreements such as the Kyoto accords limited state sovereignty. The administration went on to announce its own plan for an 18 percent cut in greenhouse gases by providing businesses with incentives to invest in cleaner technology. The administration also promoted voluntary compliance with a variety of efficiency-enhancing measures that would purportedly take 70 million cars off the road or remove 500 million metric tons of greenhouse gases from the atmosphere. Meanwhile, the development of hybrid cars, biodiesel fuel, and alternative energy sources was quietly and quickly emerging in reaction to consumer demand for cleaner and more sustainable sources of energy.

# THE RUN-UP TO COPENHAGEN

In the Meetings of the Parties (MOPs) following Montreal, the focus was on a successor to the Kyoto accords, which are slated to expire in 2012. Several meetings took place to discuss the topic, and aside from agreeing to meet in Copenhagen, Denmark, in December of 2009, progress in outlining any concrete agreement was very slow. Media coverage of the run-up to the Copenhagen meeting was overshadowed by events surrounding the global financial crisis, which left many states unclear as to how the crisis would impact their environment policies. Since then many businesses and governments have been forced to reevaluate their budgets, priorities, and risk-taking in consideration of the financial crisis. The Obama administration has taken some steps to promote a green U.S. economy, but under the umbrella of its economic stimulus package, only 10 percent of which has gone toward the financing of green projects. Some have also been concerned that the financial crisis will affect developed nations' willingness to aid LDCs in green energy development.

Before the Copenhagen meeting, there seemed to be widespread agreement amongst world leaders who supported the Kyoto agreement that in order to stave off serious climate change, a 50 percent reduction in world emissions (from the 1990 baseline) was necessary by 2050. However, this would not be possible without an agreement that included the United States, China, and other major emissions producers (see Table 20-1 below) to adhere to emission targets. In the new agreement, developing nations would also need to set limits to their emissions and be bound to an international carbon control regime. Furthermore, developed nations

| **TABLE 20-1** | |
|---|---|
| **Biggest Contributors to Carbon Dioxide Emissions, 2008 Values** | |
| Country | Carbon Dioxide (mil. Tonnes) |
| China | 6,896.5 |
| United States | 6,371.4 |
| Russian Federation | 1,690.3 |
| India | 1,419.4 |
| Japan | 1,390.6 |
| Germany | 857.9 |
| South Korea | 663.6 |
| Canada | 656.2 |
| United Kingdom | 580.9 |
| Iran | 510.0 |

*Source:* Statistical Review of World Energy 2009, bp.com.

must be willing to provide assistance to developing nations to shift away from emission-producing industries and deforestation in their development strategies.

Before the meeting, China was not receptive to establishing verifiable emission limits. From 2000 to 2008, its greenhouse gas emissions increased by nearly 120 percent compared with the United States, whose emissions grew by 16 percent in the same period, making China the largest net emitter of greenhouse gases in the world.[19] China had taken some initiatives on its own, setting strict fuel-economy standards and energy-efficient building codes and developing wind energy and other alternative energy sources. India had already implemented measures that are expected to reduce its carbon intensity by 25 percent.[20] India's proposal was more modest than China's because its emissions and GDP are about 30 percent of China's. Yet, National Geographic's *State of the Earth 2010* edition predicts that 583 million Indians will join the middle class by 2025, which is significantly more than the entire population of the United States. Finally, India also strongly supported efforts to stave off significant emission increases, but only if it were to receive major financial assistance from the developed world.

As in the case of the WTO negotiations, before Copehagen coalitions of nations formed on the basis of similar political, economic, and social values. In response to mounting pressure from the developed world to cut emissions, China, India, South Africa, and Brazil formed the "Basic Group" to represent their collective interests. They pointed out that most of the greenhouse gases in the atmosphere today are the result of cumulative damage over the years from the developed world. The Basic Group also argued that, while collectively their greenhouse gas emissions are significant, their per capita emission output still falls far behind that of the United States and other developed nations, which in the case of the United States is nearly four times that of China's. Thus, the Basic Group rejected the possibility of a binding agreement, at least in the near future. Above all, they protested the fairness of limiting carbon emissions for them when developed nations had ample time to grow their economies without environmental restraints.

Brazil and Indonesia, the fourth and fifth most populated countries and large greenhouse gas emitters, are unlike China and India in that their carbon dioxide emissions come mostly from nonindustrial sources such as deforestation. These countries were willing to cooperate but would require aid from developed countries to help phase out the practice.

By 2050, LDCs are expected to account for most of the long-term buildup of gases, yet the Kyoto Protocol exempted them from cuts required by the treaty. For this reason, developing nations as a whole generated serious attention during climate talks. Nearly all of the countries in the Southern hemisphere are parties to the Kyoto Protocol. Opposition voices from LDCs echoed many of the same sentiments of the Basic Group who formed an alliance with the Group of 77 (G-77). Many African and Latin American countries were supportive of a treaty that limits their emissions, but wanted guarantees they would get their share of aid from the developed nations to help them cut emissions. Some developed nations such as the United States argued in favor of LDC participation as a condition of its own participation in the negotiations. Yet developed countries resisted transferring any more financial resources to developing nations as a condition for their support for an agreement.

Amongst the developed nations, two different coalitions emerged: the EU and the "Umbrella Group." Although there is no official list for the Umbrella Group, it included the United States, Canada, Australia, Great Britain, and Japan. Even Japan, who had difficulty meeting its Kyoto targets, finally met its reduction targets for the first time in 2009.[21] The Umbrella Group was comparatively less willing to adopt measures that the rest of the world considered acceptable. Just before the meeting the Australian government defeated legislation to implement a cap and trade system which would result in a 5 percent reduction for this same time period. Japan offered to cut their emissions by 25 percent of their 1990 levels by 2020, but conditioned on the participation of countries like China. Realistically, the offers made by developed nations did not meet what is generally accepted as sufficient to stave off serious climate change, nor did it meet the conditions set forth by China and India.[22]

In an effort to maintain confidence in the carbon market of their cap-and-trade scheme the EU had already promised to set emissions targets at 20 percent below their 2005 levels by 2020. The EU also pledged to pay $10.5 billion to help developing countries over the next three years. The greenhouse gas emissions of Eastern European ex-Soviet bloc countries have been increasing slowly, but greenhouse gas levels there remained at least 25 percent below their 1990 baseline levels.[23]

## Copenhagen and Beyond

After an intense two week of negotiations on climate talks at Copenhagen, 193 countries produced what most experts view as a rather weak accord that in principle only *begins* the process of reaching a number of binding agreements on greenhouse emissions, deforestation, verification, and shielding poor countries from the impact of climate change. The main points of agreement in the Copenhagen accord—that are not legally binding—are as follows:[24]

- Developed countries will reduce emission levels individually or jointly based on pledges made before the conference.
- Developing countries are to monitor emissions and compile data "with provisions for international consultations and analysis."
- Developed countries will raise $100 billion a year by 2020 to help poor countries fight climate change.
- New funds will be provided to help pay countries to preserve forests.
- The increase in global temperature should be below 2 degrees Celsius.

Most criticisms of the agreement came from the EU members and poorer nations that felt left out of the negotiations. Small island nations complained that the 2 degree-Celsius target is still too high and that soon many of them will be completely wiped out. Jeff Sachs labeled the two-and-one-half-page agreement a sham. Others suggest that the whole effort helped to further divide the northern rich states from the poorer developing nations.

Supporters of the agreement included the Basic states who managed to keep the accord nonbinding. Some NGOs like the Sierra Club praised it for taking a first step on the issue of global warming. Finally, many pointed to President Obama's efforts to negotiate directly with the leaders of Basic states as a breakthrough that brought both China and the United States to the negotiating table. At one point the president and Secretary of State Hillary Clinton "crashed" a meeting of the other delegates and joined in the discussion, demonstrating what some claim to be needed leadership on these sorts of issues.

The debate over methods for limiting emissions is expected to be a big issue on the agenda of the next climate-change meeting in Mexico City in 2010. For now the most popular policy proposal has been the cap and trade system whereby limits on greenhouse gas emissions have been designated on a per country basis, with the exception of the EU bloc. Participating developed nations have been given targets as a ratio of their 1990 emissions levels, which ultimately translates into limits on emissions. The Kyoto Protocol established operational rules for carbon trading, accounting methods, and carbon offsets—projects such as reforestation that can be substituted for the purchasing of carbon credits. Rules regarding the distribution of emission allowances within a country were left up to the individual countries to decide. The governments of most signatories to Kyoto decided to auction off their allowances in the form of "permits" to energy-intensive businesses. Once the governments of participating countries have distributed these permits, businesses could buy and sell them on the international market as they please. Advocates maintain that this system addresses the key problems underlying climate change by establishing overall limits on greenhouse gases and forcing those who are producing/consuming to pay for negative externalities, while simultaneously permitting the flexibility of the market to set prices on greenhouse gas emissions.

Another proposal is a simple carbon tax that supporters like Al Gore believe would be simpler to implement and enforce. They argue that a cap and trade system is in practice no different than a carbon tax system whereby the cost of greenhouse gas emissions is ultimately passed on to the consumer in the form of higher prices. Gore advocates "tax what you burn, not what you earn," but also acknowledges that a cap and trade system in the United States would be easier to coordinate with the policies of other countries.[25] It is unclear if U.S. voters would countenance a carbon tax. Critics of cap and trade regimes also point out that in Europe heavily lobbied governments ultimately gave away many permits, passing up potentially significant sums of money. For now it remains to be seen what the next climate-change meeting in Mexico City in 2010 will bring.

## SOLUTIONS: A GREEN IPE?

Many debate whether in a political-economic environment in which pressure on the earth's resources is likely to grow, especially in the face of the current global crisis, nation-states and international businesses will be willing to commit themselves to objectives that do not require excessive amounts of natural resource consumption. Will new technologies help solve environmental problems or simply make them worse? This raises an even more fundamental question: How do actors reconcile social values that emphasize economic growth and consumption with values that are more environmentally friendly? We will try to answer these questions briefly, focusing on the most popular solutions to environmental problems and on the role the international political economy plays in them:

- Limit population growth
- Develop and rely on new technologies
- Let markets solve environmental problems
- Create a new world order

## Limit Population Growth

Many studies demonstrate that (over)population can play a role in damaging a local environment.[26] However, there is still no conclusive evidence that overpopulation itself is a problem of *global* proportions at this point (see Chapter 18).[27] The world population has indeed grown significantly since World War II and is expected to level off in 2050, but the unknown relationship of population and GDP Purchasing Power Parity makes it equally difficult to understand the implications of limiting population as environmental policy. China provides an interesting case study of this relationship because of their domestic policies on reproduction. While China's population has grown by approximately 4 percent since 2000, as cited earlier, their greenhouse gas emissions have grown by about 120 percent in this same time period. This indicates that income may have a much stronger relationship to environmental degradation than population. Studies that purport to show that income levels for all people in LDCs have risen since the early 1990s include India and China in their calculations. Thus, when it comes to demographics it is these two countries that worry officials the most.[28]

Even without policies that limit population growth, the **demographic transition**, which accounts for population growth rates, could slow down naturally as people's income and standard of living increase. Assuming this is true, the global population problem is actually more a problem of unequal distribution of wealth between the have and have-not nations and of unequal distribution of income within developing societies. This explanation strongly echoes the sentiments of many structuralists. In other words, places with relatively low population growth rates have relatively high consumption rates, and thus have a more profound impact on the environment. The reverse would also be true of places like developing countries with relatively high population growth rates.

Does that mean that nothing should be done about current overpopulation problems in some nations? In the short term, many nations *should* make efforts and receive help to slow their population growth rate because of the economic burden more mouths place on their societies. Most have done this through education and by providing people with a means of birth control. For many humanists and culture experts, the empowerment of women and society's guarantee of political rights based on democratic principles are the best solutions to poverty and overpopulation problems. In all cases, better distribution of income is likely to slow population growth rates naturally. However, the point is that if slowing population growth rates are accompanied by an increase in income, population control alone will not solve most environmental problems and may even exacerbate them. For most experts, then, other policies and measures regulating patterns of consumption are needed to promote environmental sustainability.

## New Technology

New technology has offered some hope for significant changes in the way people consume. Since global warming has become the number one threat to the environment, renewable energy has become a trendy area of technological innovation. "Super grids," or high tech networks that can transmit electricity in high volumes across long distances, are likely to replace outdated electrical grid systems in countries like the United States, allowing for more efficient transmission, distribution, and storage of energy. This system is much better suited for the prevailing renewable energy sources like wind and solar power, encouraging further investment in renewable energy. Several different auto makers have released hybrid vehicles that get as many as 48 miles per gallon. The use of biofuels as an efficient and viable source of energy is also being heavily explored, making use of anything from corn to algae as an input. Roughly 20 percent of U.S. landfills are now collecting the methane produced by waste to generate electricity.[29]

To name a few other projects that are currently in the works, the University of Minnesota is developing two cohabitating organisms, one which converts carbon dioxide into sugars and another that transforms sugars into diesel. MIT is in the process of developing a liquid battery that will smooth out intermittent flows of energy from sources like solar and wind power. United Technologies is looking at ways to use low energy sources like enzymes to absorb carbon dioxide emissions from power plant stacks.[30] The U.S. Department of Energy has also recently pledged $27.6 million dollars in grant money to research **carbon sequestration,** or methods of storing carbon deep underground. This technology could be particularly helpful to coal-fired power plants, especially considering that coal remains a major portion of U.S. energy.

A nation's access to modern technology affects more than just its carbon output. Technology is not politically or socially neutral. It often involves the use of dangerous chemicals and potentially damaging processes, but it has also helped cut down on pollution and solve a number of other, related problems. With the development of biofuels, for example, critics have also questioned the morality of using edible products in the production of energy when so many people in the world go hungry (see Chapter 18). Economic liberals in particular like to focus on technology as a factor that can do more good than harm when it comes to the environment, yet many businesses refrain from investing in technology until the government has first provided substantial grants and subsidies for research. As with anything, public support for government involvement can sometimes be difficult to gain. Even with government aid, many new technologies are unaffordable, especially in relation to older, more readily available technologies. Globalization and technology sharing have helped to overcome this problem, but many believe that globalization was also the mechanism by which world consumption was able to increase so dramatically, testing the earth's environmental limits.

Appropriateness is also an issue. Many poorer countries do not need or want more sophisticated technologies until they are better equipped to use them. In many cases, what markets produce in new technologies are not yet appropriate for many of the poorer LDCs. Many NGOs like World Vision, KickStart, and MicroEnergy Credits have made appropriate technology a primary objective of their development strategies. Access to (appropriate) technology in LDCs has seen recent improvements in part as a response to the explosion of microcredit as a development tool. Many microfinance banks are now partnering with organizations like MicroEnergy Credits and KickStart to create green microfranchises for loan clients. KickStart, for example, requires that its products be highly profitable, affordable, portable, storable, easy to use, durable, made from common materials, culturally appropriate, and environmentally sustainable.[31] Their people are "in the field" and can assess what works best for people in different cultural and political settings.

## ◥ A HYBRID SOLUTION: MICROENERGY CREDITS[a]

As the number of actors involved in international environmental issues increases, the traditional categories describing the *types* of actors involved have in some instances become less relevant. MicroEnergy Credits (MEC), a Seattle-based "social enterprise," is an excellent example of this trend. They address a number of issues confronting LDCs by facilitating partnerships between businesses and NGOs, while capitalizing on agreements negotiated by IOs and states.

As described in the chapter, when Kyoto took effect in 2005, all the developed countries that participated became subject to limits on carbon emissions. Many businesses in these countries were subsequently faced with the decision to either limit their emissions or buy credits on the international market. MEC was established to help LDCs profit from the developed world's sudden demand for these carbon credits. By promoting clean technology, MEC has been able to reduce carbon outputs in LDCs and then sell these energy savings as carbon credits on the international market.

While the concept of using technology to free up credits is fairly common, the methods by which MEC has accomplished this are quite innovative. The first step in their unique system is forging a partnership with a microfinance institution, or an organization specializing in the banking needs of the poor. These banks are most well known for microcredit programs in LDCs, whereby entrepreneurs can obtain loans for as little as $25 in some places. MEC enters into a contract with the bank, helping them to develop and market green technologies for microloan clients. The client is then able to purchase a piece of equipment that permits them to conduct business in a more

energy efficient way and/or allows the client to sell clean energy to others in the vicinity.

Once the bank has finalized information on the number of clients using this technology, MEC conducts an audit to determine the resulting reduction in carbon emissions. MEC purchases these carbon credits from the bank, aggregating and packaging them from their various bank partnerships so that they may be sold on the international market. In order to actually sell these credits, MEC has partnered with EcoSecurities, a larger company that specializes in the buying and selling of credits from developing countries. EcoSecurities then purchases these credits from MEC and securitizes them for the carbon market.

Such a system would not be possible without collaboration from many different actors. In this example, the details of the Kyoto Protocol were worked out through an IO, UNEP. Credit allowances were divided up on a per state basis (with the exception of the EU). Both MEC and EcoSecurities are technically for-profit businesses, taking a percentage of profits from each sale. However, many microfinance banks still rely heavily on donations to cover the high overhead costs involved in doing business in the developing world. Thanks to this system, MEC's partner banks now have an additional source of income. The combined efforts of these actors have not only resulted in the reduction of LDCs' carbon footprint, but have also directly impacted the lives of many impoverished individuals by providing them with access to energy, income, and even improvements in health.

[a] Georgina Allen researched and drafted the material in this box using information from MicroenergyCredits.com

Some of the least technical solutions to global warming are actually considered to have some of the largest potential. Given that carbon sinks absorb roughly 60 percent of carbon emissions, their preservation seems an important factor in staving off major carbon accumulation in the atmosphere.[32] With the creation of a cap and trade system, companies selling carbon offsets in the form of reforestation have generated steam. These companies are also being hired to offset the carbon emissions of things that are not regulated by cap and trade. For example, some vacation companies are now offering zero carbon footprint trips. Additionally, depending on the location and the chosen method of reforestation, there are likely to be long-term financial benefits of reforesting.

## Markets for the Environment

Despite the popularity of economic liberal ideas and globalization, the increasing severity of energy and environmental problems has raised many questions about the ability of markets to solve these problems. Kyoto ultimately resulted in the creation of a market-based system. Given the limited debate on the effectiveness of cap and trade, it seems likely that any successor to this treaty will continue to employ this system. The privatization of environmental problems has helped to reduce greenhouse gas emissions while generating significant amounts of wealth. As of 2008, the World Bank estimates the world carbon market at $126 billion, nearly double its 2007 value. The explosion of green, organic, and local products is readily apparent, with many big vendors now offering eco-friendly products. The entrance of green products into both household and financial markets is certainly a step in the right direction.

Even so, free markets are not an end-all solution to environmental problems for a number of reasons. Economic costs of pollution are often hard to calculate. Some authority like the state has to impose sanctions on violators or assign property rights. Commodifying environmental problems makes them subject to the whims of the economy. As we saw in the last chapter, the financial crisis has slowed investment in renewable energy. Furthermore, the cap and trade system has made permits subject to speculation, which as we also know from the financial crisis can have serious consequences.

More businesses are taking into account objectives other than purely economic ones such as the "public interest" in supporting the environment. "Green products" and "fair trade" items have in fact become big business. Likewise, enterprises that specialize in the production of environmentally-friendly items have become big investment opportunities. In an article titled "Will Big Business Save the Earth?" Jared Diamond describes the ways that three big American businesses are making a difference. Wal-Mart has dramatically reduced the fuel consumption of its truck fleets, eliminated packing waste, and phased out products like wild fish that are unsustainable. Coca-Cola is cutting back on water usage and using organic materials instead of petroleum to make bottles. Chevron is using cleaner practices as a way of avoiding future potential expenses in the form of oil spill cleanups, lawsuits, and retrofitting.[33]

The emergence of businesses as actors on the environment is consistent with the economic liberal IPE perspective that markets will ultimately provide the best solution to environmental problems. Some HILs believe that environmentally-unfriendly products will eventually become undesirable, either because their true cost will be reflected in the price or because the preferences of consumers will change in favor of new green products. Mercantilists tend to believe that the state must play a more aggressive role in addressing environmental problems by outlawing environmentally damaging activities and taxing goods that are known to cause harm to the environment. Structuralists view environmental degradation in terms of elite control over scarce resources.

Meanwhile, fluctuating demand and prices for oil have made some businesses hesitant to make new investments in the sustainable energy sector. In fact, the International Energy Agency (IEA) predicts that between 2008 and 2030, oil consumption in the OECD countries will decline by 0.3 percent annually.[34] In 2009 the UNEP reported in *Global Trends in Sustainable Energy Investment* that investment, stock prices, and company startups in sustainable energy struggled starting in the second half of 2008.[35] These trends challenge the economic liberal perspective that markets are best suited to solve environmental problems.

## A New World Order

Given the hypercapitalistic nature of the world economy today, it is no surprise that the Kyoto treaty produced a market-based solution. Critics have always been cynical about capitalism and its effects on the environment. Although no comprehensive, postcapitalist system has been developed, the idea of sustainable development is beginning to take root among officials dealing with the interrelated issues of development, food and hunger, energy, and the environment.

Despite broad agreement about the worthiness of sustainable development, actually achieving it is another matter. The failure thus far to develop a global political economic system that encourages environmentalism, or even to negotiate a realistic successor to Kyoto, cannot be taken as evidence of ultimate failure. States have found it in their interest at times to work with IOs and NGOs, often times relying on markets, but also at times looking elsewhere for solution. We detect only a trend in this direction and not as yet a complete transformation. This is not to say that IOs are no longer at the mercy of nation-states.[36] Whether states will endow them with more authority to act over the heads of their creators, however, is yet to be seen.

Even so, the lack so far of an adequate solution to global warming has left many pessimistic about the potential of IOs to solve these problems, especially given the competitive nature of states and markets in the global political economy. UNEP did get remarkable participation with the Kyoto treaty, as nearly every UN member eventually ratified the treaty. But with more being asked of countries of varied developmental stages, creating an all-encompassing successor to the Kyoto treaty has become a very complex task. Many were hoping to have concrete details of Kyoto's successor finalized by the end of 2009, but as large countries like the United States and China continue to debate the details, optimism is waning. Even if the politics of a global treaty on global warming are eventually worked out, many are skeptical that IOs like UNEP really have the power to monitor and enforce such an agreement, especially when considering that some aspects may directly conflict with the rules of the WTO.

The environment is one issue where grassroots campaigns have gained significant strength, as buying local is considered by many to be an important component of green living. As shown in the box above on MicroEnergy Credits, "social enterprises" are challenging the idea that the objectives of businesses in the developed world are inherently at odds with the objectives of environmentalists and developing countries. One of the most inspiring examples of micro-solutions being used to address macro-problems has occurred within the United States, where twenty-two U.S. states have pushed utility companies to generate energy from renewable resources by 2020.[37] Eleven states have set goals to reduce greenhouse emissions by as much as 33 percent below 1990 levels by 2050. Some U.S. cities have adopted measures to cut their use of greenhouse emissions far below the standards of the Kyoto Protocol. In essence, elements of civil society are going around the U.S. government to deal more assertively with the problem of global warming. Because states and cities are also much closer to the interests of their constituents than is the federal government, these efforts reflect an increasing amount of citizen support for policy change.

One other positive development is related to the world economic downturn, which may actually help world reductions in greenhouse gas emissions. The obvious explanation is greenhouse gas emissions' close relationship with GDP. Theoretically, the financial crisis has required many governments to play a more active role in their country's economy. The larger role of the public sector is generally thought to have been the push behind more investment in areas that are not purely driven by prospects for financial gain. According to Professor Ross Garnaut, in addition to this, temporary reductions in energy consumption in response to this economic downturn have given countries some "breathing space."[38] The combination of a more *active* government role and a short-term slowdown in energy consumption has bought many countries the necessary influence and time to restructure their economies in ways that will have long-term impacts on their carbon footprint. If this indeed turns out to be the case, this lends credibility to the mercantilist outlook that the state must play an active role in protecting us from the potential consequences of climate change. Whatever the case may be, there is no debating the fact that the domestic situation of countries impacts their willingness to deal with managing environmental issues on a global level.

Bjørn Lomborg, a widely acknowledged but highly controversial figure in the environmental debate who has spoken out on behalf of LDCs interests, has argued that the money that would be required to solve this problem might be better spent on other problems in developing nations, such as access to safe drinking water, assistance in overcoming HIV/AIDs, and efforts to continue economic development. Therefore, the industrialized states should prioritize their goals and spend more wisely for those things that will reduce emissions, but not to the point of overlooking measures that will help developing countries tackle their immediate problems.[39] Lomborg's arguments correspond to those of other development experts. Solving environmental problems must be subordinated to more immediate development objectives such as recovery from the global financial crisis. For many LDCs, dealing with global warming would mean conserving energy resources, which translates into slowing down economic development and industrial activity. Furthermore, it is still the case that the industrialized states have generated the most pollution and caused the most damage to the earth's resources.

## CONCLUSION

Since World War II environmental issues have shifted from issues dealt with mainly by intermittently cooperating nation-states. With accelerated industrialization and globalization in the 1980s, environmental problems became more global and interconnected with development, energy, and security. Until recently, cooperative efforts to solve international environmental problems have ended up on the rocks of history either due to the unwillingness of states to sacrifice domestic interests for the sake of international cooperation or because of the confrontational political-economic relationship of the North to the South.

In the 1990s the magnitude of scientific data and stories of remarkable weather changes pointed to global warming as a scientific fact. Meanwhile, globalization increased industrial production and world consumption, releasing unprecedented levels of emissions into the atmosphere. These developments fostered a sense of urgency around the issue of global warming and developing alternative energy sources to oil, helping spread awareness of global warming and raising public support for action. The ongoing threat of terrorism in the world has also made dependence on nonrenewable sources of energy from the Middle East and elsewhere increasingly undesirable. Many suggest that with the onset of these events, a perfect storm has formed that threatens the planet and humankind.

The onset of a financial crisis in 2007 also made addressing environmental issues all the more financially difficult and hard to adjust to socially. At the same time, the crisis may have bought many governments the necessary time to implement green programs. Technological advancements continue to excel at exponential rates, many as part of state stimulus plans for economic recovery. Certainly globalization has also helped to accelerate the rate of technological innovation.

Many nation-states have difficulty reconciling their domestic needs and interests with pressures to cooperate with other states, IOs, and NGOs, to solve environmental problems. This has been demonstrated by the incredible difficulty the world has had in negotiating a successor to the Kyoto accords. Even so, in some cases it would appear that in response to threats to all nations and the planet, many states may be on the cusp of making some dramatic policy changes.

In this situation the question of *cui bono?* is still on the mind of policy makers, businesses, and the public alike. Agreement at Copenhagen assumes that these actors still have choices to make about how to solve this problem. While IOs can help coordinate policy, their overall effectiveness may be limited. They must not be viewed as the only vehicles of change, as communities, states, NGOs, and businesses can all influence the choices of governments and individuals. Solutions to pressing environmental issues require something more dynamic and complicated than open markets alone. We do not know how much time the world has left to establish a new global order.

## KEY TERMS

UNEP  509
ozone depletion  510
collective goods  512
global warming  512
carbon sinks  514

Earth Summit  515
sustainable development  515
Framework Convention on
  Climate Change  515
Kyoto Protocol  515

emissions credits  515
cap and trade  515
demographic transition  521
carbon sequestration  522

## DISCUSSION QUESTIONS

1. Discuss the Tragedy of the Commons. In what ways does this concept contribute to our understanding of environmental problems?

2. The authors assert that environmental problems have become increasingly global in scope. What factors—political, economic, and social—contributed most to this trend? Explain. (*Note:* The category *economic* includes such items as trade and finance and also the role of knowledge and technology.)

3. Do you believe that climate change poses a serious threat to the planet? Discuss the roles that the financial crisis, rapid technological innovation, dramatic increases in world consumption, and international security play in solving global warming. How is each of these things beneficial and detrimental to environmentalism? Explain.

4. In considering the outcome of the Copenhagen talks on climate change, do you think nation-states are capable of solving global environmental problems, or should we look to IOs such as the United Nations to play a larger role in dealing with environmental problems? What conditions or barriers limit the effectiveness of states, IOs, and NGOs when it comes to dealing with these issues?

5. What responsibility, if any, do developing nations have in solving global environmental problems? Do you believe that their participation inevitably means sacrificing economic growth, or environmental catastrophe? Ditto the developed states.

## SUGGESTED READINGS

Lester R. Brown. *Plan B 4.0: Mobilizing to Save Civilization.* New York: W. W. Norton, 2006.

Jeffrey A. Frankel. "The Environment and Economic Globalization," in Michael M. Weinstein, eds., *Globalization: What's New?* New York: Columbia University Press, 2005.

Thomas Friedman. *Hot, Flat, and Crowded: Why We Need a Green Revolution and How it Can Renew America.* New York: Picador, 2009.

Thomas Homer-Dixon. "On the Threshold: Environmental Changes as Causes of Acute Conflict," *International Security* 16 (Fall 1991), pp. 76–116.

Bjørn Lomborg. *The Skeptical Environmentalist: Measuring the Real State of the World.* New York: Cambridge University Press, 2001.

Detlef Sprinz and Tapani Vaahtoranta. "International Environmental Policy," *International Organizations* 48 (Winter 1994), pp. 77–106.

Al Gore. *Our Choice.* Emmaus, PA: Rodale, 2009.

Mayer Hillman, Tina Fawcett, and Sudhir Chella Rajan. *How We Can Save the Planet.* New York: St. Martin's Griffin, 2008.

## NOTES

1. Georgina Allen did research and helped draft this edition of this chapter.

2. See, for example, Rachael Carson, *Silent Spring* (Boston, MA: Houghton Mifflin, 1962).

3. Donella H. Meadows, Dennis L. Meadows, Jorgen Randers, and William W. Brehens III, *The Limits to Growth: A Report for the Club of Rome Project on the Predicament of Mankind* (New York: Universe Books, 1974).

4. See the Council on Environment Quality and Department of State, *The Global 2000 Report to the President: Entering the Twenty-First Century* (New York: Penguin Books, 1982).

5. Cited in Jessica Tuchman Matthews, "Environmental Policy," in Robert J. Art and Seyom Brown, eds., *United States Foreign Policy: The Search for a New Role* (New York: Macmillan, 1993), p. 234.

6. Julian Simon and Herman Kahn, eds., *The Resourceful Earth: A Response to Global 2000* (Oxford: Basic Blackwell, 1982).

7. See World Resources Institute, "Climate Change: A Global Concern," *World Resources 1990–1991* (Washington, DC: World Resources Institute, 1990) p. 15, Table 2.2.

8. See Matthews, "Environmental Policy," p. 239.

9. See Detlef Sprinz and Tapani Vaahtoranta, "International Environmental Policy," *International Organization,* 48 (Winter 1994), pp. 77–106.

10. See Garret Hardin, "The Tragedy of the Commons," *Science,* 162 (December 1968), pp. 1243–1248.

11. See the World Trade Organization website at www.wto.org for a detailed description of WTO activities that deal with the environment.

12. David Adam, "World Carbon Dioxide Levels Highest for 650,000 Years, says US Report," *The Guardian*, May 13, 2008.

13. Global Humanitarian Forum, "Human Impact Report: Climate Change," available online at http://ghfgeneva.org/Portals/0/pdfs/human_impact_report.pdf.

14. See "U.N. Climate Talks Make Progress on Kyoto Overhaul," *Reuters*, http://today.reuters.co.uk/misc, accessed November 24, 2006.

15. Thomas Friedman, *Hot, Flat, and Crowded: Why We Need A Green Revolution* (New York: Farrar, Straus, and Giroux, 2008).

16. Richard Lindzen, "Climate of Fear," *The Wall Street Journal*, April 12, 2006, p. 1.

17. For a more detailed discussion, see "A Forest Absorbs More Carbon Dioxide Than Was Predicted," *The New York Times*, June 8, 1993.

18. For a detailed description of the Kyoto Protocol, see Kyoto Protocol to the United Nations Convention on Climate Change, http://unfcc.int/ resource/docs/convkp/kpeng.html.

19. CIBC World Markets Inc, "StrategEcon—March 27, 2008," March 27, 2008, available online at http://research.cibcwm.com/economic_public/download/smar08.pdf.

20. "What India has to Offer in Copenhagen," *The Economist*, December 3, 2009.

21. "Update 1—Japan Greenhouse Gas Emissions Fell 6.2% Last Year," *Reuters*, October 30, 2009, at www.reuters.com/article/idUST29883120091111.

22. For a more detailed discussion see Michael A. Levi, "Copenhagen's Inconvenient Truth: How to Salvage the Climate Conference," *Foreign Affairs, 88* (September/October 2009), pp. 92–104.

23. Paul Voosen, "Creative Accounting Will Help E.U. Meet Kyoto Climate Targets," *The New York Times*, November 13, 2009.

24. See John M. Broder, "5 Nations Forge Pact on Climate; Goals Go Unmet," *The New York Times*, December, 19, 2009.

25. John Broder, "From a Theory to a Consensus on Emissions," *The New York Times*, May 16, 2009.

26. See for example, Thomas Homer-Dixon, "On the Threshold: Environmental Changes as Causes of Acute Conflict," *International Security, 16* (Fall 1991), pp. 76–116.

27. See Phillip Longman, "The Global Baby Bust," *Foreign Affairs, 83* (May/June 2004), pp. 64–72.

28. See for example, David Dollar, "Globalization, Poverty, and Inequality," in Michael Weinstein, ed., *Globalization: What's New?* (New York: Columbia University Press, 2005), pp. 96–128.

29. Al Gore, *Our Choice: How We Can Solve the Climate Crisis* (Emnaus, PA: Melcher Media and Rodale, 2009).

30. Matthew Wald, "Energy Department Aid for Scientists on the Edge," *The New York Times*, October 25, 2009.

31. See KickStart's website for a description of their products, http://www.kickstart.org/products/.

32. John Timmer, "Have We Started to Fill Our Carbon Sinks?" *ARS Technica*, November 18, 2009, http://arstechnica.com/news/2009/11/have-we-started-to-fill-our-carbon-sinks.ars.

33. See Jared Diamond, "Will Big Business Save the Earth?" *The New York Times*, December 5, 2009.

34. Phil Hart, "International Energy Agency calls 'Peak' on OECD Oil Demand," November 30, 2009, available online at http://anz.theoildrum.com/node/5990.

35. UNEP, "Global Trends in Sustainable Energy Investment 2009," available online at http://www.unep.org/pdf/Global_trends_report_2009.pdf.

36. See Jeffrey A. Frankel, "The Environment and Economic Globalization," in Weinstein, *Globalization: What's New?* pp. 129–169.

37. See Juliet Eilperin, "Cities, States Aren't Waiting for US Action on Climate," *The Washington Post*, November 8, 2006.

38. "Crisis Buys Two Years of Breathing Space," *Perth Now*, March 03, 2009.

39. See Carl Pope and Bjørn Lomborg, "The State of Nature," *Foreign Policy, 149* (July/August 2005), pp. 66–74.

# GLOSSARY

**Adventurism** Invading or taking over the territory of other states, initiating punitive strikes, threatening to intervene, using covert operations, or otherwise destabilizing other states. An example is Saddam Hussein's (Iraq) attack on Kuwait in 1990.

**Agribusiness** Another term for **Transnational agribusiness corporations**. See TNACs. Agribusinesses operate the world over in a variety of commodity and food production, processing, and marketing activities. They are often accused of exploiting labor and unduly influencing political-economic conditions in countries they invest in.

**Agro-industrial agriculture** The approach to agricultural production that has been most popular in the industrialized nations. As such it emphasizes production efficiency gained by the application of new (high) technology and fertilizers, and farming on bigger parcels of land to increase commodity production. Controversy surrounds its usefulness and impact on developing nations. See de-peasantisation.

**Alternative tourism** An alternative to mass tourism experiences of the standard "sun, sea, and sand" formula. Ecotourism is an example of alternative tourism meant to promote responsible travel to natural areas that conserve the environment and improve the well-being of local people.

**Anti-Ballistic Missile (ABM) Treaty** A 1972 agreement between the United States and the Soviet Union not to deploy more than one defensive missile system each. The rationale behind the agreement was that it enhanced strategic deterrence and mutual assured destruction. See MAD.

**Appreciate** A term used in foreign exchange markets to describe the rise in value of one currency relative to another. Currencies tend to appreciate when the demand for them increases. This can hurt trade, though, if the currency value appreciates too much. See *Depreciate*.

**Appropriability theory** A theory that transnational corporations engage in foreign direct investment in order to keep firm-specific advantages from being appropriated or acquired by competitors.

**Arbitrage** Buying a product in a lower price market in order to sell it in a higher price market. Price differences between markets are often the result of differing laws, taxes, and regulations. When legislative action increases the price of a good that is available in neighboring jurisdictions at a cheaper price, smuggling is encouraged, which fuels a black market for the good.

**Assimilation** A process by which one adopts the customs and values of another culture. Relative to migration, assimilation implies that a person's original culture is replaced by the prevailing culture in the destination country.

**Asylum** Refuge for a displaced person who cannot return to his or her country of origin because of fear of persecution on account of race, religion, nationality, membership in a particular social group, or political opinion. An asylum seeker solicits permanent residence in another country through application to that country's courts, often from within that state's territory.

**Asymmetric information** A problem that exists especially in rural credit markets, in that the lender does not know what borrowers all know, which is who is trustworthy and who is not. This lack of information forces lenders to charge high interest rates, which discourages borrowing in general.

**Balance of payments (BoP)** A financial tabulation of all international economic transactions involving a nation in a given year. How much money or wealth a state earns or spends annually impacts the value of its currency, interest rates, and trade policy, among other things. Ideally, states would earn as much as they spend. One of the main roles of the IMF until the 1980s was to manage the international balance of payments.

**Balance of power** A popular and controversial realist theory that ascribes to states a certain amount of power based on a variety of tangential and intangential factors. In theory, states cluster (or ally with one another) depending on shared national interests—in opposition to states with conflicting interests. Peace among nations is usually associated with an *approximate equilibrium* in the distribution of power between nations in this system. This distribution of power results in a bipolar (2), tripolar (3), or multipolar (3+) structure. Others argue that peace is achieved when a hegemon, or dominant power, orders the security structure—referred to as unipolarity or hegemony. See *Bipolarity and Hegemony*.

**Benign mercantilism**   A defensive strategy that seeks to protect the domestic economy against damaging international political and economic forces. In contrast to malevolent mercantilism, it seeks to expand a nation's political and economic influence *intentionally* and at the expense of other nations, beyond what is needed for protection. However, what one nation intends as benign can be interpreted by another as malevolent (hostile).

**Bicycle theory**   A theory stating that as a bicycle must keep moving to maintain its balance, the European Union must constantly move forward (in terms of regional integration) in order to maintain political unity. The term is also applied to trade policies in the context of continuing to bring down tariff barriers for fear of protectionism setting back in (the bicycle falling over).

**Biofuels**   Alternatives to petroleum derived from oil, biofuels are made from plants high in sugar or vegetable oils. Many politicians hoped to reduce dependency on oil imports by absorbing surplus agricultural commodities and providing farmers with an opportunity to maintain production and price levels for their agricultural commodities. Experts disagree about how efficient biofuel production is.

**Biological and Toxic Weapons Convention (BTWC)**   An arms control convention endorsed by more than 100 nations in 1972. The signers included the United States and the Soviet Union, both of whom recognized the lethality of biological weapons and feared their ability to control them during a war. The BTWC restricts research on biological weapons to defensive measures, but makes no provisions for inspection because biological weapons are easy to hide. Iran, Syria, Russia, and at least sixteen other countries have been suspected of either producing biological weapons or conducting research in this area.

**Bipolarity**   An international security structure with two centers of power that manage the security structure. Theoretically, each dominant state or "pole" and those states in its "sphere of influence" compete with others to keep the distribution of power relatively equal between them. During the Cold War the international security structure tended to be bipolar with the preponderance of hegemonic military power distributed between the United States and the Soviet Union.

**Bonyads**   Quasi-independent conglomerates and charitable organizations in Iran dominated by clerics and private business allies that siphon off public resources and dominate some sectors of the economy.

**Bourgeoisie**   In Marxian analysis, the bourgeoisie is the capitalist class, made up of those who own the means of production. In everyday language, this term often refers to the wealthy and cultural elites of society who have the preponderance of political power. See *Proletariat*.

**Brain drain**   The exodus of highly-educated, professional migrants out of their country of origin toward economic or social opportunities in another country. This phenomenon is especially significant for Third World countries, whose most skilled residents often move to the First World.

**Branch factory syndrome**   A syndrome where the headquarters of many major transnational corporations fear losing information to a rival firm if it is transferred to subsidiaries of the corporation in other countries. Therefore, what information that is transferred tends to be less important.

**Bretton Woods system and conference**   Bretton Woods, New Hampshire, was the site of a series of meetings that took place in July 1944 among representatives of the Allied Powers of World War II (including the United States, Britain, France, Canada, the Soviet Union, and many smaller states). The Bretton Woods agreements sought to create a post–World War II international liberal economic order managed by the International Monetary Fund, the World Bank and (later) the General Agreement on Tariffs and Trade.

**Bubble**   A financial market condition in which expectations of higher prices drive market prices higher, often to unsustainable levels. Bubbles usually implode when investors stop financing certain projects or industries and can result in economic recession and high levels of unemployment.

**Cap and trade**   A controversial policy proposal put forward by some states in the Kyoto accord and at the 2009 Copenhagen meeting that allows countries to buy and sell or swap emission production quotas with one another in the international market. States would not be allowed to go over their emission target limits without purchasing (or trading for) a portion of another state's emission limits. Some view cap and trade as a market solution to an environmental problem.

**Capital controls** Government rules and regulations that seek to limit or control inflows and outflows of money or international investment funds in one or more nations. The goal of capital controls is to maintain orderly international capital movements and prevent financial and foreign exchange instability.

**Capital flight** The process whereby investors transfer their investment money out of a country that is suffering or can be expected to suffer a financial crisis. Often associated with TNC investment, currency speculation, risky portfolio capital ventures, and issues of state regulation of the economy.

**Capitalism** A political ideology identified with capitalists or the owners of capital and society's wealth. Today, however, it usually refers to a market-dominated system of economic organization based on private property and free markets.

**Capitulations** Special economic privileges and legal rights granted to Europeans by the Ottoman Empire, which prevented the Ottomans from imposing tariffs to protect their infant industries. The enforcement of capitulations is offered as one explanation for the failure of the Ottoman Empire to catch up with Europe's growing power during the nineteenth century.

**Carbon sequestration** A method of storing carbon underground, which if perfected could be particularly helpful in reducing the amount of carbon produced by coal energy sources.

**Carbon sinks** Typically, forests and large bodies of water that absorb considerable amounts of carbon dioxide from the atmosphere. Planting forests became an acceptable method of offsetting carbon emissions for countries who are party to the Kyoto Protocol.

**Cartel** A group or bloc of firms or nations that cooperate with one another to control the production and price of a commodity or a particular product. The Organization of Petroleum Export Countries (OPEC) is an example of an oil cartel that in 1973 drove up the price of oil to punish states who supported Israel in the Six-Day War with Arab states.

**Central bank** The chief monetary institution of a nation. Central banks regulate domestic financial institutions and influence domestic interest and foreign exchange rates. The central bank of Great Britain is the Bank of England, which issues British currency.

**Chain migration** A situation in which migrants move to "link up" with previous family members or social networks in their new community or society.

**Cheap food** Two of its characteristics are that food is mass produced by conventional (agro-industrial) means of production. It is also often subsidized by the central government of a state, which helps lower its market price.

**Chemical Weapons Convention (CWC)** An arms control agreement which went into effect in 1997 to eliminate all chemical weapons by 2007. As of May 2009, it had been signed by 188 countries.

**Chimerica** Niall Ferguson's term that accounts for the growing interdependence between China and the United States. China has made a good deal of money based on exports to the United States, which in turn needs China's investments in U.S. businesses and U.S. Treasury securities to offset growing debt. Meanwhile, China is also under pressure to invest more in its own economy so as to overcome many of its own socio-economic problems.

**Circular migration** Back-and-forth migration between two or more locations; part of an ongoing pattern of temporary migration and return to the country of origin.

**Citizenship** A legal term related to one who owes allegiance to a particular nation or government. Recent controversy surrounds the issue of citizenship requirements for immigrants, asylum seekers, and other groups of people who seek to live and work in another country.

**Classical mercantilism** Historically, state policies that focused on intentionally gaining national wealth and power at the expense of other states. These measures included export subsidies, import barriers, and other efforts to generate trade surpluses and to protect domestic producers.

**Claw back** An EU effort to reclaim as registered geographical indications certain generic names and icons associated with distinguished or recognizable goods such as "champagne" in France.

**CNN effect** The pressure put on nation-states or the United Nations to "do something" when the news media generates a good deal of interest in situations such as massive starvation in Somalia (1992), fleeing refugees in Rwanda (1994), or the earthquake in Haiti (2010).

**Cold War** A phrase first used by Bernard Baruch in 1948 to describe the military and political confrontation between the United States and the Soviet Union and their respective allies that did not turn into a (hot) military conflict, many theorists argue, because of the devastation associated with the use of nuclear weapons. Nonetheless a period of great tensions and *threats* to use military force.

**Collective goods** Tangible or intangible goods that, available to all members of society or consumers of the good, can be denied to no one. The issue of collective goods raises questions about who should pay for these goods when they are provided to the entire group, regardless of who pays for them. No single person or entity has an incentive to pay for it and thus enjoys a "free ride" when others do help pay. Often applied to such issues as air, land, and water pollution.

**Colonialism** The practice of the major European powers (and later the United States, Germany, and Japan) of taking over or controlling other weaker states or regions.

**Commercialization of sovereignty** The process of one state renting out commercial privileges and protections to citizens and companies from another state. Examples of this trend include offering flags of convenience and serving as tax havens. In this way, one state's sovereign privilege is used to undermine the sovereign power of another state to regulate their citizens' and companies' behavior.

**Commodification** The process whereby a price is established for a commodity or item that can be bought and sold. Karl Polanyi and others argue that commodification of land, labor, and capital was necessary in England in the seventeenth and eighteenth centuries to make capitalism work. In the context of tourism today, commodification refers to the transformation of cultural objects and values into commodities in response to tourist preferences and demands.

**Common Agricultural Policy (CAP)** The system of controversial agricultural subsidies employed by the European Union that protects EU farmers through export subsidies, tariffs, and income-support measures. While many big farmers and agribusinesses support these measures, consumer groups and their representatives oppose them for claiming a large part of the EU budget, driving small farmers out of the market, and producing unhealthy food.

**Common market** A term usually used to refer to the level of economic integration process of the members of the European community (now the EU) whereby members go beyond a customs union. See *customs union*. A common market goes the next step and promotes the freedom of movement of capital, labor, goods, and services. Until the 1990s, the common market was also the popular name of what was essentially the European community.

**Community Supported Agriculture (CSA)** Small local food producers, marketers, or collectives who distribute produce to their customers on a weekly or biweekly basis. Part of an effort to encourage local food production, sustainability, and the enhancement of local markets.

**Comparative advantage** See *Law of comparative advantage*.

**Comprehensive Test Ban Treaty (CTBT)** A controversial effort initiated by the Carter administration in the late 1970s to stop the testing of all nuclear weapons. The motives behind the measure included increasing the chances that weapons would *not* work, if they were not tested. This would make states less willing to use them. The measure has never been ratified by the United States.

**Compulsory license** A license that a government grants to a local private company or state agency, with or without the consent of the rights holder, to produce and sell a good under patent.

**Conditionality** A controversial policy of the International Monetary Fund that ties short-term loans to certain conditions designed to improve *current account* balances. In general, the making of loans subject to domestic economic and political reforms that also promote economic liberal policies and values. See *Structural Adjustment Policies*.

**Conspiracism** A political culture widespread in Iran and Arab countries that blames covert Western and Israeli manipulation for regional or national problems. Some scholars worry that this mind-set encourages extremism by engendering a mind-set of permanent suspicion toward the West and Israel.

**Constructivism** A school of thought in international political economy that argues that international structures and institutions have no intrinsic causal power distinct from the values, beliefs, and interests that underlie them. States are not only political actors, but also social actors insofar as they adhere to rules, norms, and institutional constructs that reflect society's values and beliefs. These values are not static but are the result of ongoing social construction.

**Contagion** A financial crisis that spreads to other national economies through international linkages such as capital, currency, money, and commodity markets, trade interdependence effects, and shifting market psychology. This phenomenon was observed during the East Asian financial crisis of 1997–2000, which despite starting in Thailand quickly spread to almost all parts of Southeast Asia. The recent global financial crisis began in the United States in 2007 and by the end of 2008 had spread throughout the world.

**Copyrights** Government-granted rights to artists and creators to prevent others from reproducing, publishing, or selling their work without permission. This legal protection is granted to the producers of original works, including literary, artistic, and scientific works, but also books, movies, television programs, music, magazines, photographs, software, and databases.

**Core** A term used in Modern World System analysis in reference to the interaction between the *core* or more developed capitalist part of the economic system, and the *periphery*, or less developed part of the system. These terms can refer to international geographic regions (e.g., *North–South*) or to sectors within a particular economy. See *Modern World System*.

**Corn Laws** Protectionist trade barriers that reflected the interests of the land-owning farmers from 1815 to 1846 and that restricted agricultural imports into Great Britain. When the interests of manufacturers gained control of the Parliament the Corns Laws were repealed, signifying the emergence of economic liberal ideas about free trade.

**Corporate social responsibility** A term used to describe the efforts of the TNCs (and domestic businesses as well) to behave in ways that demonstrate respect for people, communities, and nature. Corporations such as Nike often adopt these practices because they generate business for the corporation.

**Council of the European Union** A main lawmaking body of the EU, composed of a single representative from each member nation. Ministers from different states specialize in a variety of issues. The main functions of the Council are to decide European legislation that often requires cooperation with the Commission and the Parliament. The Council's most important areas of decision-making powers are in foreign policy, fiscal policies, and economic policies.

**Creative industries** Competitive knowledge-based industries in design, arts and entertainment, biotechnology, health-care technology, and defense.

**Credit default swaps** Schemes in the United States whereby investors could, in effect, buy insurance that big banks and the American Insurance Group would default on repaying their loans. Many investors covered themselves by betting that the banks would both fail and not fail. When subprime defaults and bankruptcies rose, the banks and AIG did not have the money to pay claims on CDSs, which helped precipitate the U.S. financial crisis.

**Crony capitalism** A derogatory term applied to close business–government relations in Asian and other countries, especially when these links foster corruption. Often offered as an explanation for financial crises or as a reason for failure to achieve development.

***Cui bono*? (kwee bo no)** A term that literally means "who benefits?" Susan Strange advised using the term as a place to start when analyzing any IPE issue. As benefits drive actions, so we should "follow the money" to discover in whose interest are the actions and institutional processes under study.

**Cultural citizenship** An understanding of citizenship that refers not simply to legal rights but also to a sense of belonging and entitlement that is achieved through cultural difference rather than assimilation.

**Cultural Revolution** A movement led by Mao Zedong in China from 1966–1976 to purge the Communist Party of "bourgeois" influences and mobilize urban youth in the Red Guards. Caused massive social disruption, a decline in industrial production, and persecution of intellectuals.

**Currency crisis** A condition that occurs when a nation's currency suffers a substantial short-term drop in its foreign exchange value as a result of a financial bubble, a speculative attack, or another international financial situation. Some economic historians argue that currency crises are endemic to capitalism.

**Currency exchange rates** The amount of money or goods a currency of one country will buy when converted to the currency (money) of another country. Exchange rates continuously change as a result of the supply and demand for money, which in turn helps establish the price of goods and services in each country.

**Customs union** A group of nations that agrees to eliminate trade barriers among themselves and adopt a unified system of external trade barriers. The Treaty of Rome created a customs union in the form of the European Economic Community.

**Defensive modernization**   Efforts to catch up with other states by reorganizing the government, military, economy, legal system, or other institutions. During the nineteenth century, the Ottoman Empire pursued defensive modernization in order to rival Europe's growing imperial power but met with limited success. The inability of the Middle East to modernize is variously blamed on a lack of separation of church and state, cultural immobilism, and lack of political freedom.

**Demographic dividend**   Nandan Nilekani's argument that India's growing population can actually be an asset to its future growth.

**Demographic transition**   The point at which population growth rates decrease as death rates decrease and per-capita income levels rise. The argument often made by those who reject the idea that limiting population growth alone will lead to economic development or will solve global hunger.

**Demonstration effect**   A sense of inferiority related to the desire for, but inability to purchase, expensive material objects possessed by tourists. This happens usually in the case of tourism where locals, especially youth, come to desire the material objects—and emulate the values, lifestyles, and behavior—of wealthier foreign tourists.

**De-peasantisation**   When peasants or small farmers are driven off the land by government policies or agribusiness practices that lead to low income for producers. A variety of trade practices are often cited for having the same effect on peasants.

**Dependency theory**   A theory of the relationship between industrialized (*core*) nations and less developed (*periphery*) nations that stresses the many linkages that exist between them to make less developed countries dependent on richer nations. These linkages include trade, finance, and technology.

**Depreciate**   A term used in foreign exchange markets when one currency falls in value relative to another currency. See *Appreciate and Devaluation*. Currency depreciation can be both a benefit and cost to nations.

**Devaluation**   Also termed currency depreciation. A situation in which the value of the domestic currency is reduced relative to foreign currencies. Devaluation increases the prices of imported goods, while making exports relatively less costly to foreign buyers.

**Developmental capitalism**   A term used to describe the system of political economy of postwar Japan where state policies encouraged industrial growth, especially through export expansion. Japan's policies became a model for other developing nations, especially in Southeast Asia.

**Dialectical process**   A way of thinking in Eastern and Western philosophy whereby contradictions between two conditions or opposing forces result in something new. A thesis, countered by its antithesis, produces a synthesis of the two or something new. This idea was made popular by Karl Marx and many of his followers and policy makers who subscribed to his philosophy and ideals.

**Diaspora**   Transnational communities that identify with a common homeland, history, and ethnic identity despite their citizenship in other countries. Diasporas may be tied to a particular nation-state or simply reflect a particular national identity.

**Differential taxation**   A major incentive for smuggling. When taxes on the same product differ significantly between countries, a black market opportunity is created to buy the product in the low-tax jurisdiction to resell it in the high-tax jurisdiction after a substantial price markup.

**Discourse analysis**   A tool often used by constructivists who trace changes in language and rhetoric in the speeches and works of important officials or actors on the state or international level. Of interest are officials who talk their state's interests into existence, sometimes by adopting a discourse that resonates with an important lobbying group or sector of public opinion.

**Dispute Settlement Panel (DSP)**   A panel of the World Trade Organization composed of impartial trade experts who rule on trade disputes. The panel can impose trade sanctions on member states that violate trade agreements.

**Dynamic efficiency**   An idea that a larger and more competitive market is likely to be more innovative and cost-effective. In the case of the European Union, when internal trade barriers are removed, previously protected firms are forced to compete with one another, forcing firms become more efficient and "nimble."

**Earth Summit**   The 1992 meeting in Rio de Janeiro—officially titled the UN Conference on the Environment and Development—that focused on ways to sustain economic development while preserving the environment. The meeting produced a Biological Diversity Treaty and set in motion an agreement on greenhouse emission cuts that resulted in the Kyoto Protocol in 1996.

**Eastern question game**   Countries outside of the Middle East jockey to penetrate or otherwise control Middle Eastern states in the zero-sum style of power politics. Middle Eastern leaders responded to the opportunity for "quick grabs" at the expense of long-term development.

**Economic integration**   The process by which a group of nation-states agrees to reduce protectionist measures, thereby exposing their industries to more competitive producers, for the sake of creating a larger and more tightly connected system of markets.

**Economic liberalism**   The ideology and IPE perspective that holds that nations are best off when the role of the state in the economy is minimized. See *Laissez-faire*. Economic liberalism derives in part from fear of state abuse of power and in part from the philosophy of individualism and liberty of the eighteenth-century Enlightenment. Economic liberal ideas have been popular since the late 1970s and served as the foundation for the political-economic objectives associated with globalization.

**Economic nationalism**   A variation of mercantilist ideas. Economic nationalism holds that states have to intervene in the market for the sake of their wealth and power. Alexander Hamilton and Friedrich List are two famous proponents of economic nationalism.

**Economic union**   A degree of economic integration that goes beyond that found in a customs union. An economic union eliminates both tariff and nontariff barriers to trade and finance among a group of countries. It also relegates a good deal of political and economic authority to a central political agency or group of institutions. See the *European Union (EU)*.

**Ecotourism**   Responsible travel to natural areas that conserves the environment and improves the well-being of local people. Ecotourism has become a profitable business venture in different parts of the world.

**Embedded liberalism**   Under the Bretton Woods economic system, states were to be responsible for management of the domestic economy but within an economic liberal international system that brought down trade barriers and opened up states to the freer movement of finance and capital. As states gradually pursued these policies, this compromise would become *implanted* in the minds of actors, institutional procedures, and society. See Keynesian compromise.

**Emerging economies**   Nations making a transition from state-controlled systems of political economy to more market-oriented policies. Includes China, India, Indonesia, Malaysia, the Philippines, South Korea, Thailand, Argentina, Brazil, and the Russian Federation. By the late 2000s, many of these nations played an increasingly large role in different international institutions and agencies. See *G-20*.

**Emission credits**   An implementation mechanism for the Kyoto Protocol, which allows countries to buy and sell carbon dioxide production quotas from one another. See *Kyoto Protocol*. Many experts support the idea because it establishes a market for these credits, and makes markets part of the solution to climate change.

**Epistemic communities**   Networks of experts working on a particular international problem who often frame the issue for policy makers and the public, and offer solutions. For example, an epistemic community has mobilized around the issue of global climate change, with many scientists, nongovernmental organizations, and the media bringing attention to the threat and advocating solutions.

**Euro-Mediterranean Partnership**   A free-trade and cooperation agreement between the EU and a number of MENA (Middle Eastern and North African) states in effect since 1995. In exchange for lowering trade barriers and initiating economic reform, the Arab Mediterranean countries can expect greater market access into Europe, as well as more European aid, loans, and investment. Renamed the Union for the Mediterranean in 2008.

**European Central Bank (ECB)**   Established in 1998, the ECB administers the European System of Central Banks. The ECB works with national banks to define and implement the single monetary policy of the European Monetary Union. It conducts foreign-exchange operations and manages foreign reserves with an objectives of promoting financial stability.

**European Coal and Steel Community (ECSC)**   An organization established in 1952 to integrate the coal and steel resources of six European nations. Eventually evolved into the European Economic Community.

**European Commission**   An unelected body created in 1967 whose commissioners are appointed by members states but who are not responsible to them—to implement the treaties agreed to by member states. Commissioners propose new laws and run the day to day operations of Community affairs.

**European Community (EC)**   In 1967 the EEC merged with the European Coal and Steel Community and the European Atomic Energy Commission to become the EC. As a group the EC grew in number of member nations from 6 to 12 nations engaged in economic (and to a lesser extent, political) integration. Taken together, the EC member states formed the largest single market in the world. After the Maastricht Treaty was signed in 1992 the EC moved beyond economic integration to merging national societies and different political functions and institutions. See *EEC and EU.*

**European Council**   A body made up of the heads of state and government of EU members that makes strategic political decisions regarding foreign relations, dispute resolution, and amendments to the EU treaties.

**European Court of Justice (ECJ)**   The highest court in the European Union, made up of one representative from each member state for a six-year term. The ECJ's official function is to ensure that European Union law is applied uniformly in each member state.

**European Economic Community (EEC)**   The original European "Common Market" of six countries created by the Treaty of Rome in 1957—France, (West) Germany, Italy, Belgium, the Netherland, and Luxembourg—who reduced trade barriers amongst one another and established a common tariff around the community to protect its producers. In 1967, the EEC merged with the European Coal and Steel Community and the European Atomic Energy Commission to become the EC. See *EC.*

**European Free Trade Area (EFTA)**   Promoted by Great Britain in 1960, it was comprised of states that did not belong to the European Economic Community. Its members removed trade barriers among themselves, but maintained the right to levy tariffs on third countries.

**European Monetary Union (EMU)**   The agreement of many European countries to adopt a common currency—the euro—which was introduced in 2002. At the time of this printing, there are now 16 members of the Euro-zone. The global economic crisis has generated some reconsideration by a number of states as to whether they can comply with conditions established to stay in the EMU.

**European Parliament (EP)**   An institution unlike a traditional parliament. Its elected representatives from European Union member states sit with their peers from the same party in other states, rather than with their national colleagues. Socialists from all EU nations act together, for example, as do conservatives, Christian Democrats, Greens, and other party groups. The EP's main political functions are, first, to participate in drafting policy programs and European legislation; second, to cooperate with the Council of Ministers in European legislation; third, to vote on the EU budget, which is negotiated by the Council; and fourth, to approve and control the European Commission.

**European Union (EU)**   Successor organization to the European Community as defined by the 1992 Maastricht Treaty. Note that the EU is not yet a union in the formal sense. For now it preserves some member states' rights. At the same time in some policy areas true supra-national institutions with authority independent of states do exist.

**Exchange rate**   The ratio of exchange between currencies of different countries (e.g., between the dollar and the yen). Changes in the exchange rate affect the prices of goods in international trade and therefore have important internal effects in nations. The international system of exchange rates was based on fixed (pegged) exchange rates during the Bretton Woods period (1946–1973) and earlier in the period of the gold standard in the late nineteenth century. After 1973, the exchange rate system was based on flexible (floating) exchange rates. Theoretically, fixed exchange rates are determined by international agreements among states; flexible exchange rates are supposedly determined by market forces. See *Currency exchange rates.*

**Export subsidies**   Protectionist measures that effectively reduce the price of an exported product, making it more attractive to potential foreign buyers.

**Export-oriented growth**   A tactic for economic growth that focuses on exports and integration into global markets. Popular amongst many emerging market economies such as China. Contrast this policy with *Import-substituting industrialization.*

**Fair trade**   Often presented as an alternative to free trade, fair trade mixes protectionism and free trade to "level the playing field" for domestic producers. The fair trade movement is also defined as an initiative spearheaded by international nongovernmental organizations to provide higher prices for certified goods such as coffee, timber, and a host of other products in developing countries.

**False consciousness**   A belief of the workers in the legitimacy of capitalism. The superior financial resources of the capitalists typically means that the procapitalist messages—the benefits of free trade, the need for low taxes on the rich, the problems with unions, and so on—will be stronger than those favored by workers. According to Marxists, capitalists not only exploit workers but manipulate the beliefs of workers so that they are ignorant of, or apathetic about, their own exploitation.

**Feminism**   An alternative analytical perspective that applies the lens of gender to problems in the international political economy. Feminism seeks to describe and explain many of the hidden assumptions about gender in mercantilism and realism, liberalism, and structuralism.

**Flags of convenience**   Legal businesses and criminals are permitted to register their airplanes and ships in a country even though they will conduct most of their business (licit or illicit) elsewhere. In exchange, host countries typically receive lucrative registration fees, payoffs, or "protection money."

**Food First**   A thesis introduced in the 1970s by Frances Moore Lappé that hunger is actually caused by deficiencies in income and land distribution, rather than lack of food production or overpopulation. According to the proponents of this theory, hunger is *not endemic* to less developed countries, but is a *byproduct* of their political and economic relationship with the industrialized nations.

**Food security**   An element of national security that expresses concerns about the security of a nation's food supply. To account for the distribution of food, the term also applies to individuals as opposed to a whole nation or geographic region.

**Forcing effect**   A situation where a market for a product will be created when demand for it is high enough. Growing demand for large, environmentally-friendly building projects has been solely responsible for the creation of certain green building supplies.

**Foreign direct investment (FDI)**   Investments made by a company (often a transnational corporation) in production, distribution, or sales facilities in another country. The term *direct* implies a measure of control exercised by the parent company (U.S.–based IBM, for example) on resources in a host nation such as Mexico.

**Framework Convention on Climate Change (FCCC)**   This environmental treaty was produced at the Earth Summit and later modified, resulting in the Kyoto Protocol.

**Framing**   A term that constructivists use to describe the process by which global actors define the essence of a particular global problem—what is causing it,

who is involved, its consequences, and how to resolve it for the purpose of promoting a particular explanation or outlook about this problem.

**Free trade**   One of the most popular policies advocated by economic liberals. In keeping with the *laissez-faire* notion that government intervention in the economy undermines efficiency and overall wealth, free trade removes protectionist measures (tariffs, quotas, etc.) that are designed to insulate domestic producers from international competition. See *Comparative advantage*. Free trade has been a major goal of most international trade institutions since 1947.

**Free-trade area (FTA)**   A group of nations that agrees to eliminate tariff barriers for trade among themselves, but that retains the right of individual nations to set their own tariffs for trade with nonmember nations.

**General Agreement on Tariffs and Trade (GATT)**   An international agreement in 1947 that became the basis of international trade negotiations to reduce trade barriers among its many member nations. GATT negotiations took place over a period of years and were termed "rounds," as in the Kennedy round and the Tokyo round, which reduced trade barriers for manufactured goods, and the Uruguay round, which aimed to create freer trade in services and agricultural goods. GATT was incorporated into the World Trade Organization in 1995.

**Genetically modified organisms (GMOs)**   Living organisms that have had their genetic code altered for commercial or scientific gain. For example, a crop might be genetically modified to enhance desirable nutritional qualities. Critics of GMOs worry about the loss of native biodiversity, the accompanying shift to monoculture farming techniques, and a greater reliance on herbicides.

**Geographical indicators (GIs)**   A term used for products that comes from specific locales with some characteristics attributable to those locales. Examples are French cognac, champagne, and scotch.

***Glasnost***   Russian term for the policy initiated by Soviet Premier Mikhail Gorbachev in the late 1980s that involved opening up the Soviet state to political reform. It was meant to complement economic reform, or *Perestroika*.

**Global bioenery partnership (GBEP)**   Promoted by the FAO, the GBEP is a partnership between public, private, and civil society groups committed to promoting bioenergy for sustainable development in developing nations.

**Global civil society**   Another term for nongovernmental organizations and nonprofit organizations whose focus is usually the improvement of political, economic, and social conditions in developing nations.

**Global commodity chains**   Networks of firms created for the production, distribution, and marketing of various products.

**Global governance**   The rules, institutions, and processes that affect international cooperation in a specific issue area and management of transnational problems like climate change, environmental damage, and organized crime. The concept emphasizes that mechanisms affecting cooperation involve many state and private actors and many levels of governance at the international, regional, and local levels.

**Global value chains**   An update on product cycle theory that accounts for "the full range of activities that firms and workers do to bring a product from its conception to its end use and beyond." Different firms in different countries are linked in a set of relationships (or a division of labor) that leads to the delivery of goods and services. Many Western firms' part in these chains deal with finance, basic research, design, product-branding, and marketing. LDCs want to move up the value chain from low-wage manufacturing and subcontracting to more profitable activities.

**Global warming**   An increase in the temperature of the earth's atmosphere that results from the greenhouse effect. A hotly debated topic at the December 2009 meeting in Copenhagen as to how much climate change is caused by human-made and natural forces.

**Globalism**   The ideology underlying economic *globalization*. Based on economic liberal principles and ideas, globalism holds that the internationalization and integration of markets will provide a vehicle for enhancing global economic well-being. A popular ideology among supporters of both economic liberalism and globalization.

**Globalization**   The process by which the pursuit of economic liberal ideas and policies have led to increased economic growth throughout the world. Globalization also connotes increasing economic interdependence as well as the spread of Western (U.S.) cultural influence all over the world.

**Globally integrated enterprise**   Increasingly, TNCs do not in fact own most of the elements of their foreign operations. With improved information technology, some TNCs such as Boeing or IBM can easily "outsource" vital functions to foreign-owned firms. Many TNCs build their own transnational network of contacts and attempt to create a regional or global business presence.

**Grameen Bank**   An important microcredit bank founded in Bangladesh by Mohammad Yunus in 1976. These kinds of banks are an increasingly popular method of helping usually poor women in poor countries create small business enterprises.

**Great Leap Forward**   A 1958 economic and social development program in China that organized a half-billion peasants into 24,000 "people's communes."

**Green Revolution**   An effort in the 1960s composed of various scientific, technological, and economic programs that attempted to increase food production in India, the Philippines, and other developing countries by introducing fertilizers, hybrid plant and seed strains, and modern farming techniques. While commodity production did increase, many local people remained poor because they could not afford these commodities.

**Growth pole**   A strategically-selected location meant to serve as the center of economic growth for surrounding areas. Through investments in infrastructure and incentives meant to attract capital and labor, governments stimulate economic development by concentrating resources on the growth pole.

**Guest worker**   A nonresident foreign worker. Guest workers engage in temporary employment within a foreign state, but both the length of their residence and the conditions of labor are stipulated by that state, which also prohibits the possibility of their permanent residence or citizenship.

**Gulf Cooperation Council (GCC)**   A grouping composed of Saudi Arabia, the United Arab Emirates, Kuwait, Oman, Bahrain, and Qatar. These six countries share a heavy reliance on foreign workers, which make up a significant proportion of their combined workforce.

**Hard currency**   A currency of known value that can readily be exchanged on foreign exchange markets and is therefore generally accepted in international transactions. Examples of hard currencies today include the U.S. dollar, the Japanese yen, the euro, and the Swiss franc. See *Soft currency*.

**Hard power**   Military, and in some cases, economic power. Hard power refers to state tools to influence, persuade, or coerce through the direct application of power and wealth. See *Soft power*.

**Heavily indebted poor countries (HIPCs)**   A designation for forty-one of the world's poorest countries, mostly in Africa. These countries suffer from high poverty and high incidences of HIV/AIDS.

**Hedge funds**   Investment funds that seek to profit from small differences in asset prices that are likely to converge. In general, hedge funds "bet" that asset prices will move in certain predictable ways. Hedge funds play an important role in *speculative attacks*.

**Hegemonic stability theory**   A theory that posits that one country that is unusually rich and powerful dominates other states or the entire international system for a length of time, during which it establishes and enforces a set of rules that regulate various elements of the international political economy.

**Hegemony**   Dominance or leadership, especially by one nation over other nations. The theory of hegemonic stability holds that the international system achieves growth and stability only when one state acts as the hegemon, dominating the others but also paying the costs associated with counteracting problems in the international system.

**Heterodox Interventionist Liberals (HILs)**   Those who support more than a minimum amount of state intervention in the economy—so as to preserve the market and make it work more efficiently and effectively for the majority of people in society.

**HIPC Initiative**   An effort beginning in the late 1990s to cancel the debt of the indebted poor countries.

**Historical materialism**   The idea, central to Marx, that social and political institutions are built on a physical foundation of the economy, not ideas alone.

**Hot money**   Highly interest-sensitive short-term international capital movements that can both help and hurt different states. Many developing nations seek out this source of finance to support their new and fledgling industries. Likewise, many developed states have an interest in not regulating financial flows across borders for the sake of economic growth. Finally, many experts would like to see states put restrictions on hot money for the sake of limiting its negative effects on local economies and societies.

**Hydra effect**   Efforts to reduce the supply of an illegal commodity (e.g., drugs) are often counterproductive because a crackdown in one area triggers movement of illicit goods to a different area. U.S. antidrug efforts in Latin America have spawned new organizations in Mexico and Puerto Rico.

*Ijtihad*   In Islamic law, an independent interpretation of a contemporary problem not identified precisely in traditional Islamic texts. Also shorthand for "independent thinking."

**Immigration**   Movement into another country with the intention of becoming a permanent resident in the destination country.

**Imperialism**   An idea associated with the works of J. A. Hobson, V. I. Lenin, and R. Luxemburg. A superior–inferior relationship in which people have been subordinated to the will or interests of a foreign state. Classical imperialism is often associated with historical periods that correspond to conquest and colonization of developing territories by developed "modern" industrialized nations. Neoimperialism today often reflects control over people as a result of trade or foreign direct investment in another country.

**Import quotas**   Limits on the quantity of an item that can be imported into a nation. By limiting the quantity of imports, the quota tends to drive up the price of a good while at the same time restricting competition.

**Import-substituting industrialization (ISI)**   An economic development tactic that attempts to encourage domestic industrialization by restricting imports of industrial products. Contrast this strategy with *Export-oriented growth*.

**Industrial policy**   Economic policies designed to guide or direct business investment and development. Such policies often include support for businesses and trade protection.

**Infant industries**   New industries in any nation that are disadvantaged by older and more efficient industries. Most mercantilists and economic liberals suggest that in the case of immature industries, trade and other protective measures are justified until the newer industries have time to compete fairly with more mature industries.

**Informal economy**   The part of an economy that is unregulated and usually does not pay taxes. In a less developed country, most street vendors, for example, would be classified as "informal."

**Integration**   In IPE, integration occurs when nation-states agree to unify or coordinate some political and economic activities. Economic liberals tend to support integration because it enhances efficiency and productivity.

**Intellectual hegemony**   Antonio Gramsci's theory that the dominant class maintains its position through the creation of an ideology or worldview that is accepted by society and thereby controls its actions. In Gramsci's view, social control is achieved by both coercion (police and military action) and consent (through intellectual hegemony).

**Intellectual property rights (IPRs)**  Patents, copyrights, trademarks, and other rights to ownership or control of creations and expressed ideas. Major controversy surrounds the issue of an unfair advantage the rich industrialized states have over developing nations when it comes to protecting IPRs. Many structuralists argue that IPRs should be outlawed, if not weakened significantly, so as to enable developing nations to acquire necessary technology and low-priced goods.

**Interdependence**  Usually thought of as interconnectedness between nations and other actors in the international political economy conditioned by trade, aid, finance, and investment. Reactions to interdependence include the need to cooperate but also negative reactions related to the vulnerability and sensitivity it engenders.

**Internal migration**  Migration of an individual or group within a single nation-state, often from one region to another or from the rural to urban locations.

**International Assessment on Agricultural Science Technology and Development (IAASTD)**  A critical 2008 Intergovernmental Report that suggests that industrial agricultural systems contribute to the destruction of rainforests, soil, and ecosystems, and also help widen the gap between rich and poor.

**International Criminal Court (ICC)**  Since the 1990s a number of international courts have been established to adjudicate the behavior of states and especially individuals when it comes to violating human rights during war and conflict. The ICC meets in the Hague in the Netherlands and has prosecuted cases related to violations in, among other places, the Balkans, Rwanda, and Liberia.

**International knowledge and technology structure**  One of Susan Strange's four dominant global structures. The set of institutions and practices that condition the production, exchange, and distribution of knowledge and technological goods and services.

**International Monetary Fund (IMF)**  Created as part of the *Bretton Woods* system, the IMF is an organization of over 150 member states charged with stabilizing the international monetary system. The IMF makes loans to member states when they experience severe *current account deficits*. These loans are made subject to enactment of economic reforms, a practice called *conditionality*.

**International political economy (IPE)**  The interdisciplinary social science that examines the dynamic interactions between markets, states, and societies, and how the tensions and conflicts between these arenas both affect and reflect conditions outside the nation-state and society. The term "political economy" has other meanings. In economics, for example, political economy is the name sometimes applied to Marxist analysis and sometimes to scientific economic tools used to analyze political behavior.

***Intifada***  Literally means the "uprising" of the Palestinians against Israeli occupation of the West Bank and the Gaza Strip. There have been two intifadas—the first beginning in 1987 and the second starting in 2000.

**Intraregional trade bloc**  A trade agreement where nation-states in a particular region remove barriers to trade with the other members of the region. The Asian Pacific Economic Cooperation Forum (APEC) is an example of an intraregional trade bloc that aims to integrate eighteen Asian and Pacific nations into a nonbinding arrangement that would gradually remove trade barriers among members by 2020.

**IPE structures**  Susan Strange's categories of networks of actors, institutions, and processes that manage the affairs and problems in each of four distinct foundations of the global political economy: production and trade, knowledge and technology, money and finance, and security.

**Irregular migrants**  Migrants who reside and work in a foreign country without the appropriate legal documents. These workers may have entered the country without permission or entered with a visa but then stayed on past the limits of that permission.

**Keynesian compromise**  An aspect of the *Bretton Woods* system. Nations retain the ability to intervene in their domestic economies but are limited in this by their agreement to limit interference in international economic markets.

**Keynesian theory (Keynesianism)**  To be Keynesian is to be in agreement with the general thrust of the political economy of John Maynard Keynes. A general definition is to believe that there is a positive role for the state to play in domestic affairs (fighting unemployment and poverty, for example) and in international affairs (the kind of role conceived for the International Monetary Fund and the World Bank). Keynes's views were influenced by the catastrophe of World War I and the Great Depression of the interwar period. His ideas were reflected in the Bretton Woods institutions and policies and have gained renewed attention related to the global economic crisis.

**Know-thy-customer** A principle of due diligence in banking whereby providers of financial services are expected to verify the identity and check the background of potential clients to determine if they are involved in money laundering or other criminal or risky activities.

**Kyoto Protocol** A protocol (or set of informal procedures and norms, but not a formal treaty) agreed to in Kyoto, Japan, in 1997 that established carbon emission standard goals and procedures for all states. In order to deal with the problem of global warming, states agreed to achieve these goals within a set period of time. While many states signed the agreement and implemented the protocol, many of the industrialized states were either reluctant to or did not (e.g., the U.S.). China, India, and other emerging economies were not required to adhere to the agreement but encouraged to do so, which created a good deal of controversy. The protocol came into effect in 2005.

**Law of comparative advantage** According to David Ricardo, the theory of comparative advantage holds that nations should produce and export those goods they can produce at a lower cost than other nations and import those items that other nations can produce at lower cost. Often cited as the foundation of free trade policy.

**Levels of analysis** The four levels of analysis are the individual, state/societal, interstate, and global levels. The levels-of-analysis approach was originally developed by political scientist Kenneth Waltz to help understand different explanations and sources of international conflict and war.

**Life cycle of ideas** As part of the constructivist approach to IPE, the aim is to determine where ideas and norms originate, spread, the other ideas they conflict with, and how they become "naturalized," that is, accepted by states and IOs as the self-evident justification of policies. Researchers often go back in history to examine individuals or movements that promoted what at the time seemed like important

ideas. Due to the global economic crisis a number of experts have explored the origins and development of economic liberal ideas and policies.

**Malevolent mercantilism** Intentionally harmful policies that aim to defeat an enemy or potential enemy. Associated with Germany and Japan before World War II.

**Managed trade system** Strong political and social interests often call for trade protection that often creates a political climate incompatible with completely free trade. A managed trade system often reflects a political compromise or mixture of economic liberal and mercantilist trade policies most states and even the World Trade Organization can adhere to.

***Maquiladoras*** Assembly plants in Mexico that use foreign parts and semifinished products to produce final goods for export. Structuralists are critical of maquiladoras for their use of exploited labor, hazardous working conditions, and environmental damage.

**Marketization** Part of the process of economic transition from classical socialism to capitalism. When a particular commodity has been marketized, its exchange becomes governed by supply and demand rather than according to central planning.

**Market socialism** A popular term in the 1990s that accounts for the effort by former Soviet bloc countries to combine their socialist economies with features of market economies. Some of the more successful have been Hungary, Poland, and the Czech Republic. Many former and even still communist developing economies (e.g., China) have been or are pursuing the same objective.

**Marshall Plan** An assistance program that provided $12 billion in aid to European countries. Named for U.S. secretary of state George C. Marshall who proposed the program in 1947. The program is also called the European Recovery Program.

**Marxism** An ideology that originated in the works of the German sociologist Karl Marx (1818–1883). Many strains of Marxism have evolved from Marx's works. Generally, Marxism is a critique of *capitalism* (as distinct from *economic liberalism*). Marxism holds that capitalism is subject to several distinctive flaws. Marxism tends to view economic relations from a power perspective (capital versus labor) as opposed to the cooperative relationship implicit in economic liberalism. See *Structuralism*.

**Mashriq** The region of Arab-speaking countries to the east of Egypt, including Syria, Lebanon, Jordan, Iraq, and the Palestinian Territories.

**Mercantilism** A seventeenth-century ideology that made accumulation of national treasure the main goal of government officials and society. Today, it is an economic philosophy and practice of government regulation of a nation's economy in ways that increase state power and security. Policies of import restriction and export promotion (to accumulate treasure at the expense of other countries) follow from this goal. See *Economic nationalism*.

**Microcredit** The practice of providing very small loans to groups of people (usually women) in less developed countries who share the risk of repaying the loans. Muhammad Yunus is credited as the founder of the movement and the Grameen Bank in Bangladesh, which disperses microcredit loans. Microcredit has been heralded for its promise to directly overcome poverty by putting money into the hands of those who actually need it, thus encouraging sustainable private-sector development. It has also served as a model in some industrialized countries.

**Migration** Movement of an individual or group from one place to another, often in pursuit of political or religious freedom, economic opportunity, reunification with family, or access to specific resources.

**Millennium Development Goals (MDGs)** United Nations–sponsored initiatives to work on a local level to achieve the eradication of extreme hunger and poverty, universal primary education, gender equality and the empowerment of women, reduction in child mortality, improvement of maternal health, as well as efforts to combat HIV/AIDs, malaria, and other diseases, ensure environmental sustainability, and develop a global partnership for development.

**Modern world system (MWS)** A theory of economic development based in part on Marxist-Leninist ideologies. The MWS views economic development as conditioned by the relationship between the capitalist *core* and the less developed *periphery* nations. The historic mission of the core is to develop the periphery (often through the *semiperiphery*), but this development is exploitive in nature.

**Monetary and finance structure** One of Susan Strange's four dominant global economic orders. The international network of institutions, practices, and arrangements that condition the use and exchange of financial resources such as capital and currency. The international finance and monetary system includes institutions that condition the distribution and payment of international debts.

**Most favored nation (MFN)** A trade principle under the World Trade Organization, whereby imports from a nation are granted the same degree of preference as those from the most preferred nations.

*Mujahideen* A term meaning Islamic freedom fighters. It often refers to the warlord leaders of local tribes, who in the 1980s became famous for their resistance to the Soviet Union in Afghanistan, with the help of American weapons and training. This support has been blamed as a source of blowback, whereby America's former surrogates have formed terrorist organizations targeting the United States.

**Multilateral approach** A term that accounts for the way states and their leaders view the world. The George W. Bush administration looked at the world from a unilateral perspective that emphasized the dominant role of the United States in the global political economy. The new Obama administration has supposedly shifted its focus to a more multilateral outlook which sees the United States as one among many other major powers. This distinction has consequences for how cooperative states are amongst one another and how common issues are dealt with.

**Multinational corporation (MNC)** An international business firm that engages in production, distribution, and marketing activities that cross national boundaries (see *Foreign direct investment*). The critical factor is that the firm has a tangible productive presence in several countries. This factor distinguishes an MNC from an international firm, which produces in one country and exports to other countries. See *Transnational corporation (TNC)*.

**Multipolarity** A security structure with more than two centers of power. Contrast with *bipolarity*.

**Mundell trilemma** Named for Nobel laureate Robert Mundell. A property of different national monetary systems where it is impossible to achieve three objectives at once: foreign exchange stability, capital mobility, and national economic independence. Two of these goals always complement one another while contradicting the third objective. Each state decides which two objectives to pursue based on its history, national interests, and international political-economic conditions.

**Mutual assured destruction (MAD)** The Cold War strategy of the United States and the Soviet Union under which each had sufficient military power to destroy the other even if in doing so it destroyed itself. This supposedly ensuring that neither nation could realistically "win" a nuclear war.

**Name-and-shame campaigns** Ways of pressuring companies and countries to change practices that are illegal or perceived to be unethical by bringing international attention to them.

**Nation-state** Synonymous with the term "country," since the seventeenth century the nation-state has been the major political (sovereign) unit of the international system. The nation-state joins the nation—a group of people with a shared sense of cultural identity and territoriality—with the state—a legal concept describing a social group that occupies a territory and is organized under common political institutions and an effective government. As sovereign entities, nation-states have the right to determine their own national objectives and to decide how they will achieve them.

**National champions** Key domestic companies or industries that a government deliberately nurtures for long-term development through subsidies, trade protection, and other forms of support. Although some national champions become globally competitive, they tend to reduce competition in their home economy.

**National Missile Defense (NMD)** A type of missile defense states (in particular the United States and Russia) deploy so as to be able to knock down incoming ballistic missiles. This was outlawed, with the exception of one site in each nation in 1972. The idea was reinvigorated under the Reagan administration who proposed to modernize the U.S. system by deploying a number of space-based defenses. NMD remains controversial related to the cost of the program and how much it may incite other states to deploy such systems. See *ABM Treaty*.

**Neoconservatives (neocons)** The term applies to those today who have a conservative economic outlook. However, the term "neocons" is also associated with officials in the George W. Bush administration who held a unilateralist outlook that included the use of force whenever the United States felt it necessary or justified. Other elements of the outlook included the idea that the United States would promote and maintain an empire so as to be able to impose peace on the world on its own terms.

**Neoimperialism** An element of the structuralist interpretation of capitalism. *Core* nations exploit the periphery and create dependency on it through financial, production, and trade structures throughout the world. While classical imperialism employs force to achieve its ends, neoimperialism emphasizes the use of others nonmilitary tools to subjugate and dominate weaker states. See *Imperialism*.

**Neoliberalism** A viewpoint that in the early 1970s favored a return to the economic policies advocated by classical liberals such as Adam Smith and David Ricardo. Neoliberalism emphasizes market deregulation, privatization of government enterprises, minimal government intervention, and open international markets. Unlike classical liberalism, neoliberalism is primarily an agenda of economic policies rather than a political economy perspective. See *Market fundamentalism* and *Neoconservatism*.

**Neomercantilism** A version of mercantilism that evolved in the post–World War II period. Rather than focusing on surplus producing trade policies, neomercantilism today includes a wide variety of protectionist trade, finance, and development policies to generate wealth and enhance national security.

**NINJAs** Stands for "no income, no jobs, and no assets." In the run-up to the current global economic crisis, loan officials purposefully targeted these people because the officials would not have to be responsible for the loans, which had been packaged and sold off to investors all over the world. These sorts of schemes directly contributed to the global economic crisis.

**Nondiscrimination** A principle of the World Trade Organization system whereby products of different nations are treated equally (and equally with domestic products once imported). The products of a specific nation cannot be discriminated against under this rule. See *Most favored nation*.

**Nongovernmental organizations (NGOs)** National and international voluntary organizations that have played an increasingly bigger role in the global political economy since the end of the Cold War. Some suggest that they fill in where states have failed to act; likewise many NGOs can provide services states cannot. Examples of NGOs include Greenpeace, the Red Cross, and Doctors Without Borders. See *Global civil society*.

**Nontariff barriers (NTBs)** Alternative ways of limiting imports, including government health and safety standards, domestic content legislation, licensing requirements, and labeling requirements. Such measures make it difficult for imported goods to be marketed or significantly raise the price of imported goods.

**North American Free Trade Agreement (NAFTA)** A free-trade area among the United States, Canada, and Mexico, fully implemented in 2005. The NAFTA treaty was signed in 1992 and took effect in 1994. The treaty remains controversial to the extent that there is no agreement about how much it has bene-fited its members.

**North–South**   The relationship between developed, industrialized countries (the North) and less developed countries (the South). This concept is often associated with core–periphery analysis but can also be simply a descriptive device.

**Nuclear taboo**   A widely shared reluctance by states since World War II to use nuclear weapons, significantly due to the moral restraint of public opinion and the efforts of a worldwide antinuclear weapons movement.

**Odius debt**   Foreign liabilities incurred by a former corrupt regime that leaves the new government owing tremendous sums of money to banks and investors. The burden of servicing this debt often stifles devel-opment efforts. Many experts argue that these debts should be forgiven for the poorest of nations to better their chances of development.

**Oil-for-Food Program**   A UN program applied to Iraq after the Persian Gulf War (1990–1991) that allowed Iraq to sell some of its oil in international markets in exchange for income to buy food and emergency aid supplies. It was a controversial program to the extent that many Iraqi and some UN officials were accused of corruption related to implementing the program.

**Oil sharks**   Tankers that sit offshore oil-consuming countries during times of intense speculation on oil. Oil is held in these tankers until prices shoot up, at which it is brought ashore and sold.

**Oligarchs**   A term that usually connotes a small group of people who attempt to control a government for their own benefit. In Russia, for example, wealthy media heads and oil company owners in the 1990s challenged state officials over a variety of issues.

**Organic intellectuals**   In Antonio Gramsci's theory of *intellectual hegemony*, these are intellectuals who are raised within the prevailing system and whose ideas therefore reinforce that system.

**Organization of Petroleum Exporting Countries (OPEC)**   An organization of nations formed in 1960 to advance the interests of Third World oil exporters. In 1973 OPEC embargoed oil exports to the United States and the Netherlands, setting off a flurry of price hikes and notice of OPEC's new found political-economic power.

**Orthodox Economic Liberals (OELs)**   A group of people who strictly adhere to a more rigid interpretation of economic liberal ideas, values, and policy prescriptions. Most agree that instead of the state, "open" or "free"

markets should be allowed to determine socio-political outcomes whenever possible.

**Outsourcing**   When a firm transfers part (or all) of the production process for a good or service to another country. Many economic liberals consider outsourcing to be part of the process of the globalization of international production and trade. These movements of jobs overseas involves displace-ment of a number of people.

**Ozone depletion**   In 1985, a hole in the ozone layer was discovered over Antarctica. It was blamed on the use of chlorofluorocarbons, a particular type of greenhouse gas used in many household products, which were later banned by the UN Montreal Protocol of 1987.

**Paradox of globalization**   While globalization has bene-fited many people because it has generated a good deal of wealth, at the same time it creates conditions that undermine support for it. The increased gap between the rich and poor is an example of this paradox.

**Paradox of thrift**   If one individual saves much more income, rationally speaking,  that individual may be more secure economically. If everyone does this, how-ever, the combined actions can cause a recession and everyone is less secure economically. The paradox of thrift then is an example of the potential problems of an unregulated economy. Keynes supported an active role for the state in the economy to help overcome this problem.

**Parallel imports**   Refers to imports of patented, trade-marked, or copyrighted goods into a specific market without the permission of the intellectual property rights owners who want to sell the good at different prices in different countries.

**Partnership for Peace (PfP)**   A North Atlantic Treaty Organization program in the 1990s created to promote cooperation between former Soviet bloc countries and NATO.

**Patents**   A term used to refer to the exclusive rights that a government issues and confers to make, use, or sell an invention for a period usually of twenty years (counted from date of filing). These rights are also given to encourage research and innovation. Many companies argue that without them they would be unable to capture all of the benefits of their R&D expenditures. Criteria for gaining a patent varies from one country to another.

**Pax Americana**   The period of U.S. hegemony follow-ing World War II. "Pax" means "imposed peace," which implies that the period of peace after the war was imposed by the United States similar to the Pax Britannica of Great Britain during the eighteenth and nineteenth centuries. Some critics use the phrase to equate U.S. power with neoimperialism today.

**UN Peacekeeping Operations (PKOs)** United Nations–sponsored troops from different nations assigned to deal with conflicts in different countries. Peacekeeping was adopted in the early 1950s as an alternative to intervention by the major powers in conflicts that could involve them in war. PKO missions are located in developing regions of the world, especially in the Middle East, Africa, and parts of Asia.

**Peak oil** The controversial idea that the world's production of oil will reach a maximum point, after which it will gradually run out. Experts disagree when that will be, if it hasn't already occurred. Many also disagree about the consequences of peak oil in terms of the price of oil and its impact on society when global production starts to go down.

**Pearl River Delta** In 2007, *The Atlantic* correspondent James Fallows speculated that one province in China's Pearl River Delta employed more factory workers than the entire U.S. manufacturing sector. These workers are the backbone of China's export-led growth that has led to China's trade surplus and massive reserves of U.S. currency, which in turn the Chinese have used to buy U.S. Treasury bills. See *Chimerica.*

**Perestroika** Russian term for restructuring or economic reform, especially economic programs implemented in the Soviet Union in the mid-1980s. See *Glasnost.*

**Periphery** The nonindustrialized countries of the modern world system that produce agricultural goods and natural resources. See *Core* and *Modern world system.* The Modern world system theory hypothesizes that peripheral states (e.g., developing countries) are usually made worse off as a result of interaction with core states.

**Petrodollar recycling** Since 1973, the system whereby oil exporters recirculate payments for imported oil through the global financial system to provide loans to oil purchasers, fund imports by oil producers, and purchase foreign assets.

**Petrostates** Oil-producing countries with governments that are not hesitant to use their oil as a political weapon. Russia and Venezuela are often referred to as petrostates.

**Plan Colombia** A recent program of U.S. aid to Colombia to reduce coca production (and as a result, cocaine imports to the United States) by, among other things, spraying defoliants. Despite the $4.7 billion price tag between 2000 and 2006, coca cultivation has not dropped. This illustrates the difficulty of supply-side policies in the global fight against drugs.

**Plaza Accord** An agreement in 1985 between the G-5 states (Great Britain, West Germany, France, Japan, and the United States) in New York City to intervene in currency markets to cause the depreciation of the U.S. dollar. An example of how pressure by the U.S.' allies took precedence over the Reagan administration's preference for non intervention in the economy.

**Pleasure periphery** Regions in the periphery of the world system that serve as recipients of pleasure-seeking tourists from core nations in the industrialized world. Examples vary from hiking in the rainforests in Columbia to sexual encounters in Thailand.

**Positive-sum game** Any interaction between actors that makes all participants simultaneously better off. See *Zero-sum game.*

**President of the European Council** The Head of the European Council of the European Union is elected every two and a half years. Heading the Council provides a distinct advantage to the representative's state given that he or she sets the Council agenda.

**Primitive accumulation** A Marxist concept that is hypothesized to be at the root of capitalism's initial development. The process is one of coercive or violent seizure of assets (particularly land).

**Prisoner's dilemma** A term coined by Princeton mathematics professor A. W. Tucker to describe a situation in which the best interests of persons in society taken individually are opposite from those of the same individuals taken as a group. A group may benefit the most if everyone cooperates on an issue, for example, however each individual often faces an incentive to "defect" and eschew cooperation for the sake of making the most of the situation for himself or herself.

**Privatization** Part of the process of economic transition from classical socialism to capitalism in which state-held property and assets are transferred into private hands. See *Market socialism.*

**Problematization** An important domestic and international process by which states and Transnational Advocacy Networks construct a problem that requires some kind of coordinated, international response. Some problems are simply talked into existence. What people care about in the world is a reflection of our social environment, culture, and beliefs we share with others in our society. Some problems are "constructed" by political elites, powerful lobbying organizations, and social groups.

**Process innovation**   Inventions and improvements for producing existing goods, services, and techniques that do not result in new items. See *Product innovation*.

**Product cycle theory (or Product life-cycle theory)**
Terms coined by Harvard political economist Raymond Vernon to describe production and trade patterns stemming from product innovation and technological diffusion.

**Product innovation**   Pattern of inventions that focuses on creation of new goods and services, not refinements of existing items. See *Process innovation*.

**Production and trade structure**   The institutions and practices that condition the production, exchange, and distribution of goods and services in the international political economy. International trade is a key component of the production structure. Essentially, the factors that determine what is produced, where, how, by whom, for whom, and on what terms. See *International division of labor*.

**Profit paradox**   When law enforcement tries to ban an item for which there is high demand (e.g., drugs), the reduction in supply drives up prices in the short term, but this bolsters profits for those willing to illegally supply the item, thus encouraging others to enter the illegal business. Thus, the temporary reduction in supply is reversed as criminals find ways around the ban.

**Proletariat**   In Marxian analysis, the class of workers who do not own capital and who are exploited by the bourgeoisie.

**Protectionism**   Policies that either restrict or promote trade such as import tariffs or export subsidies that benefit domestic producers. Protection also signifies an attitude whereby states feel compelled to use a variety of measures to defend what they feel are attempts by others to weaken it.

**Public goods**   Goods or services that, once provided, cannot be denied to one person and at the same time benefit everybody simultaneously. A lighthouse or national security is a classic example of a public good.

**Publicity rights**   The names, images, or identifying characteristics of famous people. Some countries allow celebrities to control use of them (with exceptions for news reporting). These rights can be inherited or sold

to third parties who want to use them for marketing purposes.

**Reaganomics**   President Reagan helped make popular economic liberal ideas in the 1980s. Aside from free trade and limited state intervention in the economy, he promoted the idea that public debt would be overcome by "supply-side economics" or the idea of growing the economy by decreasing taxes.

**Realism**   A theory of state behavior that focuses on the acquistion of power to enhance state security. The national interest is a determinant of state behavior. In the view of realists, states, like individuals, tend to act in their own self-interest.

**Reciprocity**   A principle of the World Trade Organization system whereby trading partners simultaneously reduce trade barriers, providing each greater access to foreign markets.

**Refugee**   A displaced person who cannot return to his or her country of origin because of fear of persecution or due to destruction caused by war or natural disaster. Refugees are often assisted and relocated by an international body such as the United Nations Office of the High Commissioner for Refugees.

**Regime**   The idea that when it comes to a particular problem or issue in the global political economy, various rules, norms, institutions, and decision-making procedures condition actor expectations and behavior regarding that problem. The oil regime, for example, includes the nation-states, international organizations, private-sector firms, markets, agreements, and so on, that condition policy expectations and procedures when it comes to oil production, exchange, distribution, and related activities.

**Regionalism**   A movement toward "clubs" or associations of nation-states in a geographic area that cooperate to achieve goals that may be specific such as trade policy or general such as political stability.

**Regional trade agreements (RTAs)**   Agreements between different states in a geographic area to reduce trade barriers between them. RTAs are often easier to form than global trade agreements because there are fewer interests to reconcile. Some economic liberals oppose RTAs out of fear that they deter *global* free trade.

**Remittances**   Payments made by a migrant to family or friends in the country of origin. The global economic crisis has severely decreased the amount of money migrant workers have been able to send back to their families in their mother countries.

**Rentier state** A country that earns a large proportion of its government revenue from taxes on oil and gas exports. In the cases of Iran, Iraq, Libya, Algeria, and other Gulf Cooperation Council states, the wealth generated from this income is usually concentrated in the hands of a few people.

**Rent seeking** Efforts to achieve personal gain by creating an artificial scarcity rather than through efficient production. Many corrupt activities can be viewed as examples of rent-seeking.

**Research and development (R&D)** An activity undertaken in states to develop new technologies and advance creation of new products and innovative processes. This activity occurs in government-funded research institutions and within private companies and is important for scientific advancement.

**Reserve currency** A currency that is held by a nation's central bank in its foreign exchange reserves. The U.S. dollar is the world's most common reserve currency, and many international transactions and commodities are priced in U.S. dollars.

**Resource curse** This phenomenon describes how many countries that are relatively wealthy in natural resources remain underdeveloped because of government mismanagement and corruption. Optimism based on high demand for local oil—for example, in the case of Nigeria—can easily cause misery for many people.

**Restriction-opportunity dilemma** A situation in which efforts to ban a material in high demand (e.g., drugs and guns) are often counterproductive because they make the black markets provision of the material more profitable.

**Revenue leakages** In tourism, the loss of revenue resulting from imports of goods and services required by tourists and tourism businesses, including food, hotel fixtures, advertising costs, repatriated profits, and airport equipment.

**Rogue states** States that are regarded as hostile or that refuse to cooperate with other states. Iran, Syria, and North Korea are often cited as examples. These states are also cited as potential sources of terrorism.

**Secrecy jurisdictions** Countries with strong banking privacy laws such as Switzerland or the Bahamas. Tax evaders and money launderers exploit these privacy guarantees to hide billions of dollars from their governments.

**Security community** Many constructivists (and realists as well) have found that sometimes seemingly hostile rivals cooperate with one another because they have a shared understanding that they are part of a "security community"—a group of people with a sense of a shared moral purpose and a certain level of mutual trust. A good example is the Organization for Security and Cooperation in Europe (OSCE), which was set up in the mid-1970s as a process by which the Cold War antagonists could cooperate on security matters in Europe, eventually changing the nature of their relationship to one another.

**Security dilemma** A situation in realist-mercantilist thought that when one state does something to protect itself or to enhance its defensive capabilities, another state views the behavior as threatening. This is because it interprets the first state's behavior as raising the possibility of war or conflict because it has strengthened its capabilities.

**Security structure** The sets of institutions, practices, and beliefs that condition international behavior as it relates to national security issues. The Cold War international security structure is often cited as an example of routine behavior by the United States and Soviet Union related to an agreed upon framework of rules and practices.

**Semiperiphery** An intermediate zone between the *core* and *periphery*. South Korea and Taiwan might be considered part of the semiperiphery today in the *modern world system* theory. See *Core*.

**Settler states** Countries such as the United States and Australia which allow immigrants the opportunity to become permanent residents and/or naturalized citizens.

**Siloviki** The powerful political allies of former Russian president Putin—called the *siloviki*—who have backgrounds in the secret police, intelligence services, and law enforcement agencies. These friends and allies have helped Putin recentralize political power, weaken the Duma, and crack down on independent media and civil society.

**Single European Act (SEA)** The 1992 agreement on the part of European Union members to advance to the next stage of integration: a union. In policy terms, this meant extensive coordination on monetary policy and investment regulations, services, migration, labor, and foreign policy, to name only a few items. The measure was approved by all member states by referendum in each state.

**Single Market** In 1992 the members of the European Community passed the Single European Act that created a single market with a customs union and freedom of movement of labor and capital. This act led to passage of the Treaty of Maastricht in 1993 and creation of the European Union (EU), along with other steps to further integrate the members of the European community. See *Treaty of Maastricht*.

**Social learning**   A process that occurs when international regimes regulate a problem such as climate change after epistemic communities (experts) teach policy elites and international institutions about the problem. Epistemic communities provide political negotiators with "usable knowledge" that is credible, legitimate, and salient—to persuade them to adopt treaties even though the negotiators may have been politically reluctant to do so initially.

**Socially responsible investing**   A trend whereby investors avoid certain types of companies and countries that they perceive to be socially or environmentally unethical, such as those involved in land expropriation, oil corruption, terrorist financing, human rights abuses, or unsustainable environmental practices. These investment strategies challenge economic liberal principles by subordinating market efficiency to concerns of justice.

**Soft currency**   A currency of uncertain value (due, perhaps, to high inflation rates) that is not generally accepted in international transactions. Soft currency can usually be spent only within the nation that issues it, whereas a *hard currency* can be exchanged and spent in most nations. Some soft currencies, such as the ruble in the former Soviet Union, are called "inconvertible currencies" because it is illegal to convert them into hard currencies.

**Soft power**   The power to influence the environment of international affairs through such intangible factors as culture, values, and ideals. Soft power is less direct than *hard power* but sometimes more effective.

**Sovereign wealth funds (SWFs)**   Large amounts of capital that have accumulated in the hands of states with large balance-of-payments surpluses. Many OELs have argued that those states should have invested a good deal of their SWFs in U.S. investments, which would have helped offset U.S. debt and prevented the global economic crisis.

**Sovereignty**   The seventeenth century idea related to the ability to make the final decision in any society. For realist-mercantilists sovereignty also refers to independence from control by an outside power.

**Specialization**   Part of the economic liberal argument—an economic motive—for free trade. Adam Smith, Ricardo, and others advocated that trading nations should concentrate their production in sectors where they possess a comparative advantage. In an age of competitive globalization, different states and regions of the world are driven to specialize in particular parts of the production process. Quite often this specialization does not reflect a natural advantage but one that is intentionally fostered by different state policies, resulting in tensions over the motives behind different trade policies.

**Speculation**   To make an investment in a foreign currency based on the belief that the currency will increase in value, allowing the speculator to earn a return when the currency is sold. See *Speculative attack*.

**Speculative attack**   A situation where the demand for a currency quickly deteriorates causing speculators to sell off large quantities of a currency in the hope that they will be able to buy it back later at a lower price. This often results in a dramatic devaluation of the currency, which weakens the purchasing power of those left holding the devalued currency.

**Spot markets**   Markets where oil is sold on the market outside OPEC's established pricing structure. When OPEC member states decided not to cooperate with the cartel's oil production goals, they sold oil to anyone who would buy it from them (on the spot!).

**Stag hunt**   Jean Jacques Rousseau's analogy of five hunters trying to catch a stag (deer) by cooperating with one another. The analogy forces us to consider whether it is rational to cooperate to solve problems with one another, or not to—given that someone else may choose not to cooperate and ruin things for everyone. The analogy is often applied to security situations that require cooperation to move forward on a problem like arms control.

**State**   A legal concept describing a social group that occupies a defined territory and is organized under the political authority of leaders and institutions Theoretically, a state has some degree of independence and autonomy. According to realist thought, states are the primary units of the international political and legal community. As sovereign entities, they have the right to determine their own national objectives and the strategies (including the use of force) to achieve those goals.

**Static efficiency**   An efficient use of current resources, especially specialization according to the comparative advantage. See *Dynamic efficiency*.

**Strategic resources**   Resources such as oil and rubber whose supply and demand have important consequences for the national security of a nation.

Most nations fear become overly dependent on others for the resources they lack.

**Strategic trade policies**   Efforts on the part of the state to purposefully create comparative advantages in trade by methods such as subsidizing research and development of a product or subsidizing an industry to increase production to the point at which it can move up the "learning curve" to achieve greater production efficiency than foreign competitors. Strategic trade practices are often associated with state industrial policies—that is, intervention in the economy to promote specific patterns of industrial development.

**Structural Adjustment Programs (SAPs)**   Economic policies that seek to reduce state power and introduce free market reforms to less developed countries to help them establish a foundation for economic growth. The International Monetary Fund often makes the adoption of SAPs a condition for financial assistance.

**Structuralism**   An IPE perspective that accounts for the political–economic interconnectedness (structural relationship) between any number of entities: the *bourgeoisie* and *proletariat*, the *core* and *periphery*, and the *North* and *South*. A number of ties bind these entities to one another, including trade, foreign aid, and direct investment. Much debate exists as to whether and how structural conditions can be changed or reformed. See *Marxism*.

**Subprime mortgage loans**   Home loans made by banks in the United States to customers who did not have to meet the higher standards for loans as they did before the mid-1990s. Easier terms such as little evidence of the ability to pay or lower credit scores greatly increased the number of people who "qualified" for home loans. For many experts, subprime mortgages directly contributed to the global economic crisis and manifest some of the worst traits of the U.S. style of capitalism today.

**Super 301**   An aggressive U.S. trade policy created in the 1970s and designed to open foreign markets to U.S. exports.

**Sustainable development**   A pattern of economic development that is consistent with the goal of nondegradation of the environment. A popular idea accepted by many. Controversy surrounds the many problems of implementing the objective as it requires tradeoffs and choices many find unacceptable.

**Tax havens**   A name for mostly small countries and territories that have protective banking privacy laws.

These sovereign jurisdictions attract tax evaders and money launderers who wish to hide their earnings from their home government so as to avoid paying taxes on the money or provoking inquiries into the (often illicit) sources of the income.

**Top currency**   A currency in great demand because of its central role in international trade and financial transactions. The U.S. dollar has played the role of top currency since World War II.

***Torschlusspanik***   The point in a financial crisis where investors realize they are about to lose on the investments and try to "disinvest" or get out of the market. In so doing they help generate a feeling of panic whereby other investors quickly abandon their investments before they become worthless.

**Toxic securities**   Packages of investments such as risky subprime mortagages that were "bundled" and sold to investors all over the world. Eventually many banks could not cover their "toxic securities," which led to the implosion of the real estate market and global financial crisis in July 2008. Congress hastily passed a "rescue plan" to try to assure investors that these securities would be covered. *See TARP.*

**Trade bloc**   A group of nation-states united by what for the most part are regional trade agreements. See the *European Union* and the *North American Free Trade Area.*

**Trade diversion effect**   The impact of a trade bloc. Although trade is often enhanced amongst members of a trade bloc because of lower internal barriers, this comes partly at the expense of trade diverted from more efficient non–bloc countries that are still subject to trade barriers.

**Trademarks**   Signs or symbols (including logos and names) registered by a manufacturer or merchant to identify goods and services. Protection for trademarks is usually granted for ten years and is renewable. Examples of trademarks include the Nike swoosh, the brand name Kleenex, and MGM's lion's roar.

**Trade-Related Aspects of Intellectual Property Rights (TRIPs)**   An international agreement that is part of the WTO and that requires minimal standards of protection of copyrights, patents, trademarks, and other forms of intellectual property.

**Traditional Knowledge**   The accumulated knowledge and practices of indigenous or local communities as they relate to such things as plants, plant uses, agriculture, land use, folklore, and spiritual matters.

Indigenous peoples and local communities preserved and developed a wide variety of plant diversity through harvesting and breeding practices, and in fact many of the major food crops in North American and Europe originally came from these local communities.

**Tragedy of the commons** Term coined by Garrett Hardin to describe situations in which human nature, rationality, and political freedoms drive individuals to overuse communal resources. Hardin recommends strong government action to limit population growth to save the earth's resources.

**Transdniestra** A part of Moldova that declared independence in 1992, though this claim has not been recognized by any other country. Ambiguity about its status and a lack of strong government have transformed the region into a hub of illegal activities, especially for trafficking in weapons, stolen cars, and other contraband.

**Transfer pricing** An attempt on the part of transnational corporations to shift their accounting measures between subsidiaries in other countries so as to avoid taxes. One of the advantages transnational corporations have when investing in other countries, but that critics charge make it difficult to develop local economies.

**Transit states** States that serve as halfway points for transnational migrants en route to another destination country.

**Transnational advocacy networks (TANs)** International networks of activists who attempt to influence states regarding various political and social issues, including migration and refugee policy, for example.

**Transnational agribusiness corporations (TNACs)** See *Agribusiness*.

**Transnational corporation (TNC)** A term to describe large businesses that compete in regional or global markets and whose business environment therefore extends beyond any given nation-state. The key characteristic of a TNC is a high level of foreign direct investment. Also called multinational corporations.

**Transnational migration** The movement of an individual or group across national borders.

**Transparency** The public's ability to see how decisions are made. In the case of global financial institutions such as the International Monetary Fund, some argue that greater transparency would improve investors' decision making and prevent financial crises from developing.

**Treaty of Maastricht** This treaty creating the *European Union* was ratified by members of the European Community in 1993. It signified agreement to a more advanced stage of integration in the economy, but also social and political institutions and policies.

**Treaty of Rome** A 1957 treaty among France, Great Britain, West Germany, Belgium, Italy, Luxembourg, and the Netherlands that established the European Economic Community.

**Troubled Asset Relief Program (TARP)** The $700 billion recovery effort initiated by the George W. Bush administration and approved by Congress to deal with the financial crisis in October of 2008. The Obama administration has continued to implement the plan, which essentially put $250 billion into U.S. big banks in the hopes of getting them to loan more to one another and to Main Street banks and financial institutions.

**United Nations Conference on Trade and Development (UNCTAD).** Created in 1964, UNCTAD was a UN institution for developing nations. Meeting every two years, it was designed to check the influence of the Organization of Economic Cooperation and Development (OECD), which reflected the political and economic interests of the developed nations.

**United Nations Environment Program (UNEP)** This UN agency was created to aid in the drafting of treaties, provide a forum for cooperation, and create databases and references for scientific assessments of the environment. UNEP helped create the Intergovernmental Panel on Climate Change, and the organization has made recommendations for treaties such as the Kyoto Protocol.

**Uruguay round** Set of negotiations among the members of the General Agreement on Tariffs and Trade (1986–1994) that focused on reducing trade barriers, especially regarding services and agricultural goods.

**Voluntary export restraint (VER)** or **Voluntary export agreement (VEA)** An agreement that limits the quantity of an item a nation can export. Importers ask exporters to "voluntarily" set limits on the numbers of exports, backed by an implied threat of economic sanctions or some form of retaliation if the exporter does not comply with the importer's request.

**Voucher privatization** A method of privatization used by some transitional economies in which citizens are given vouchers that can be used to bid for shares in state-owned firms. In contrast to privatization through direct sale to an outside investor, voucher privatization is less able to bring new capital and expertise into the economy.

**Washington Consensus**   The viewpoint, often evidenced in the policy proposals of the U.S. Treasury Department, the World Bank, the International Monetary Fund, and the World Trade Organization, that less developed countries should adopt policies to reduce inflation and fiscal deficits, privatize, deregulate, and create open markets. See *SAPs.*

**Weapons of mass destruction (WMD)**   Technologically sophisticated weapons that have the potential to kill large numbers of people, such as nuclear, chemical, and biological weapons.

**Westoxication**   The idea prevalent in the Middle East of seduction to imported Western cultural ideas and institutions. Anti-Western leaders and some terrorists often cite it as a motive for their opposition to the United States and other industrialized states' values and institutions.

**World Bank**   Officially called the International Bank for Reconstruction and Development (IBRD), the World Bank is an international agency with over 150 members. Created by the Bretton Woods agreements in 1944, it originally worked on the reconstruction of Europe after World War II. Today, the World Bank makes low-interest loans and grants to less developed countries to stimulate economic development.

**World Food Program (WFP)**   The UN agency designated to distribute food aid to the neediest of nations. Often viewed as a frontline agency for relief efforts in humanitarian emergencies but also in civil conflicts.

**World Trade Organization (WTO)**   Successor organization to the *General Agreement on Tariffs and Trade.* Recently the WTO has been criticized for failing to complete the Doha round of trade negotiations. Increasingly, many developing nations have been unwilling to promote these talks with the developed nations.

**Zero-sum game**   An activity whereby gains by one party create equal losses for others. The concept plays a major role in the realist-mercantilist perspective.

# GLOSSARY OF ACRONYMS

| | |
|---|---|
| **APEC** | Asia-Pacific Economic Cooperation |
| **BoP** | Balance of payments |
| **CAP** | Common Agricultural Policy |
| **CSA** | Community Supported Agriculture |
| **EEC** | European Economic Community |
| **EFTA** | European Free Trade Area |
| **EMU** | European Monetary Union |
| **EU** | European Union |
| **FDI** | Foreign direct investment |
| **GATT** | General Agreement on Tariffs and Trade |
| **GBEP** | Global Bioenergy Partnership |
| **GDP** | Gross domestic product |
| **GMO** | Genetically modified organism |
| **GNP** | Gross national product |
| **GSP** | Generalized System of Preferences |
| **HIPCs** | Heavily indebted poor countries |
| **IAARD** | International Assessment of Agricultural Science and Technology for Development |
| **IBRD** | International Bank for Reconstruction and Development (also World Bank) |
| **IMF** | International Monetary Fund |
| **IOs** | International organizations |
| **IPE** | International political economy |
| **IPRs** | Intellectual property rights |
| **ITO** | International Trade Organization |
| **LCFS** | Low Carbon Fuel Standard |
| **LDC** | Less developed country |
| **MAD** | Mutually assured destruction |
| **MDGs** | Millennium Development Goals |
| **MENA** | Middle East and North Africa |
| **METI** | Ministry of Economy, Trade, and Industry |
| **MFN** | Most favored nation |
| **MNC** | Multinational corporation |
| **NAFTA** | North American Free Trade Agreement |
| **NATO** | North Atlantic Treaty Organization |
| **NGO** | Nongovernmental organization |
| **NIC** | Newly industrialized country |
| **NIEO** | New International Economic Order |
| **NTB** | Nontariff barrier |
| **OECD** | Organization for Economic Cooperation and Development |
| **OPEC** | Organization of Petroleum Exporting Countries |
| **PPP** | Purchasing power parity |
| **SALT** | Strategic Arms Limitation Treaty |
| **SAP** | Structural Adjustment Program |
| **TNAC** | Transnational agribusiness corporation |
| **TNC** | Transnational corporation |
| **TRIPs** | Trade-Related Intellectual Property Rights |
| **UNCTAD** | United Nations Conference on Trade and Development |
| **USTR** | U.S. Trade Representative |
| **VER** | Voluntary export restraint |
| **WFP** | World Food Program |
| **WIPO** | World Intellectual Property Organization |
| **WTO** | World Trade Organization |

# INDEX

9/11
    antiglobalization and, 18
    attack on travelers after, 427–428
    Bush administration, second term,
        15, 98, 214
    cigarette bootlegging investigations,
        after, 397
    cultural assimilation, Muslims, 419
    environmental issues, 514
    food aid after, 483
    global fear and, 3
    globalization and, 19, 211
    illicit transactions, MENA
        countries, 374
    international tourists, (U.S.), 428
    "Islamo-fascism", 98
    multilateral trade negotiations
        (Doha), 144
    political economy after, 490
    security structure after, 15

Abizaid, John, 362
Accountability, TNCs, 457–458
Accumulation of capital. See Law of
    concentration
Acheson, Dean, 351
Adenauer, Konrad, 302
Adler, Emanuel, 109
Adventurism, 359, 361
    defined, 530
Afro-Asian Bandung Conference
    (Indonesia), 269
Agribusinesses
    defined, 530
    liberal view, 465
    mercantilist view, 465, 476
    structuralist perspective, 473, 476
Agricultural commodities
    biofuels and, 473–474, 531
    export revenues for LDCs, 273–274
    food prices 2008, 470, 476, 498
    global food crisis, 465
    investors and, 472
    OELs and, 472
    overseas market for U.S., 142
    Senegal's policy on, 484
    speculation impact on, 472–473

weak U.S. dollar and, 470
after World War II, 463
Agro-industrial agriculture, 530
AIDS epidemic, 254, 289, 292
Alex, Avery, 477
Algeria, 355, 357
    sovereign wealth funds, 169
Allen, Georgina, 183, 497, 523
Al Maktoum, Sheikh Rashid bin
    Said, 369
Almond, Gabriel, 202
Al-Qaeda, 214, 217, 220, 229, 231,
    358, 362–363, 377. See also 9/11;
    Terrorism
Alternative tourism, 424
    defined, 530
Altman, Roger C., 221
American Federation of Labor
    and Congress of Industrial
    Organizations (AFL-CIO), 146
American International Group (AIG),
    4, 196
Andreas, Peter, 115, 382, 384
Animal smuggling, 397
An Inconvenient Truth (Gore Al),
    507, 513
Annan, Kofi, 228
Anthropology, 7
Anti-Ballistic Missile (ABM)
    Treaty, 217
    defined, 530
Anti-Counterfeiting Trade Agreement
    (ACTA), 251, 253
Antipersonnel landmines (APLs),
    117–118
Antiquities, 395, 397
Apartheid, 151, 451
Appreciation, 160
    defined, 550
Appropriability theory, 444–445, 459
    defined, 530
Arbitrage, 396
    defined, 530
Argentina
    current account balance, 169
    Development Agenda for WIPO, 253
    external debts of, 201

foreign exchange rates, 159
sovereign wealth funds, 169
Argentine financial crisis, 174–175
"Arma-Core," 370
ARMs (adjustable rate mortgages), 4
Asian financial crisis. See also
    Financial crisis
    defined, 188–190
    effects of, 190
    IMF and, 187
    low price of oil after, 495
    World Bank and, 284–285
Asian Tigers, 19, 67, 148, 273–274,
    277, 281, 283. See also Specific
    countries
    India, 332–338
Asia-Pacific Economic Cooperation
    (APEC), 145–146
Aslund, Anders, 347
Assimilation, 415–416, 419
    defined, 530
Association of Southeast Asian
    Nations (ASEAN), 146
    in Clinton administration, 44
Asylum, 415
    defined, 530
    in practice, 415
Asymmetrical international
    interdependence, 469
Asymmetric information, 288
    defined, 530
Atkinson, William, 477
Australia
    coal producer, 499
    current account balance, 169
    extreme weather conditions in, 513
    global emissions, 516
    Kyoto Protocol and, 516
    polluter, 516
    sovereign wealth funds, 169
Avery, Dennis, 477

Bagehot, Walter, 206
Baker, James, 185
Baker Plan, 185
Baker, Raymond, 383, 386, 395
Balaam, David N., 227